THE CAMBRIDGE SOCIAL HISTORY
OF BRITAIN 1750–1950

VOLUME 1
Regions and communities

THE CAMBRIDGE SOCIAL HISTORY OF BRITAIN 1750–1950

VOLUME 1

Regions and communities

Edited by

F. M. L. THOMPSON

Director of the Institute of Historical Research
and Professor of History, University of London

CAMBRIDGE UNIVERSITY PRESS

Published by the Press Syndicate of the University of Cambridge
The Pitt Building, Trumpington Street, Cambridge CB2 1RP
40 West 20th Street, New York, NY 10011–4211, USA
10 Stamford Road, Oakleigh, Victoria 3166, Australia

First published 1990
First paperback edition 1993

Printed in Great Britain by The Bath Press, Avon

British Library cataloguing in publication data

The Cambridge social history of Britain 1750–1950.
Vol. 1: Regions and communities.
1. Great Britain. Social conditions, 1714–
I. Thompson, F. M. L. (Francis Michael Longstreth)
941.07

Library of Congress cataloguing in publication data

The Cambridge social history of Britain 1750–1950.
Includes bibliographies and indexes.
Contents: v. 1. Regions and communities –
v. 2. People and their environment – v. 3. Social
agencies and institutions.
1. Great Britain – Social conditions. 2. Social
structure – Great Britain – History. 3. Social
institutions – Great Britain – History. I. Thompson,
F. M. L. (Francis Michael Longstreth).
HN385.C14   1990   306′.0941   89–9840
ISBN 0 521 25788 3 (v. 1)
ISBN 0 521 25789 1 (v. 2)
ISBN 0 521 25790 5 (v. 3)

ISBN 0 521 25788 3 hardback
ISBN 0 521 43816 0 paperback

Contents

Tables

Contributors

W. A. ARMSTRONG is Professor of Economic and Social History at the University of Kent at Canterbury. He has worked extensively in the field of nineteenth-century historical demography, and recently published *Farmworkers: a Social and Economic History, 1770–1980* (1988).

C. BABER is Senior Lecturer in Economic History at the University of Wales College of Cardiff. He has written mainly on the industrial history of South Wales, and is the joint editor of *Modern South Wales: Essays in Economic History* (1986).

P. L. GARSIDE is Senior Lecturer in Environmental Health and Housing at the University of Salford. She has worked extensively on the housing and planning history of London, particularly in the twentieth century, and is co-author of *Metropolitan London: Politics and Urban Change, 1837–1981* (1982).

D. W. HOWELL is Senior Lecturer in History at the University College of Swansea. His work has concentrated on the history of rural society in Wales, and his books include *Land and People in Nineteenth-Century Wales* (1978) and *Patriarchs and Parasites: The Gentry of South-West Wales in the Eighteenth Century* (1986).

ROSALIND MITCHISON is Emeritus Professor of Social History at the University of Edinburgh. Her work has covered a wide range of Scottish agricultural, demographic, and social history, and her books include *Lordship to Patronage: Scotland, 1603–1745* (1983).

D. J. ROWE is Senior Lecturer in Economic History at the University of Newcastle upon Tyne. He has written many articles on the society and economy of the north-east in the eighteenth and nineteenth centuries.

T. C. SMOUT is Professor of Scottish History at the University of

St Andrews. He has worked extensively in modern Scottish economic history, and his books include *A History of the Scottish People* (1969).

F. M. L. THOMPSON is Director of the Institute of Historical Research and Professor of History at the University of London. His books include *English Landed Society in the Nineteenth Century* (1963) and *The Rise of Respectable Society* (1988).

J. K. WALTON is Senior Lecturer in History at the University of Lancaster. A historian of leisure as well as of the north-west, his books include *The Blackpool Landlady: A Social History* (1978) and *The English Seaside Resort: A Social History, 1750–1914* (1983).

Editorial preface

The historian's job is to find out about the past and make it intelligible and accessible to the present. Such an apparently straightforward task is by no means as simple as it may sound. Finding out what happened and interpreting it in patterns and designs which make sense of the past are complicated and demanding processes, requiring scholarship and expertise of a high order, but their value remains limited unless the results are communicated in a language and form which reach beyond the restricted circle of fellow-specialists. Communication is particularly important for social history, a field whose contours and boundaries have altered out of all recognition in the last generation, a subject which is bubbling with the vitality of an outpouring of monographs and journal articles, and a young discipline which lacks the settled framework of a conventional orthodoxy or a received interpretation within which or against which new departures or open rebellions can be placed or assessed. The old stand-bys – constitutional history, political history, diplomatic history, ecclesiastical history, for example – all have these established frameworks which define their subject matters and enshrine explanations of the course of history. These are widely familiar, although often misleading or mistaken; this means that the terms of debate are well understood, that revisions are easily recognised as revisions, and that the iconoclasm of overturning entrenched views does not go unnoticed. Economic history, while much younger than these other subjects, has nevertheless established its rules of enquiry, its methodologies, and its canons of debate, even if it has never succeeded in staking out a territory with sharply defined and stable boundaries. Some might say that it has dug a groove for itself which succeeds in shutting out adequate consideration of factors of central importance, for example the nature and operation of demand and of consumption, in which social history can be illuminating and supportive.

Social history derives its appeal and fascination in no small measure from its open-endedness, its freedom from the constraints of a formal tradition, its eclectic habits, and stands in no need of being rendered into an authorised version. This is just as well, for orthodoxies are not created by editorial decree and if perchance they are fashioned by bands of disciples then the three volumes of this series are in little danger of becoming a Cambridge gospel, for the authors do not belong to any one single camp and do not have a common axe to grind. That is not to say that they are a particularly disputatious or dogmatic bunch, but simply that they are a team of individualists each of whom has been invited to bring their own scholarly judgment to bear on the task in hand. That task is to communicate the fruits of recent writing and the most recent research in social history to the wider audience of students who are curious to know what the specialists have been doing and how their work fits into a general picture of the whole process of social change and development. There are two ways of producing a synthesis: single-handed combat, in which one author takes on the whole field and produces a digest and interpretation of a large slice of history; or a team effort, in which the field is sliced up among contributors according to their expertise and the overview is a co-ordinated package of separate authoritative elements. As with individual sports and team games, tennis and cricket or golf and football, each approach has its own attractions and disadvantages, for players and spectators alike, and each has its partisans. There are several examples of solo syntheses on offer in the field of modern social history, notably from Penguin, Fontana–Collins, and Hutchinson. As the author of one of these it is not my purpose to decry their merits. No doubt their main strength comes from the coherence and unity which a picture of an entire landscape may have when seen through one pair of eyes and painted by one hand, and their main weakness from the inability of a single pair of eyes to see everything or to be well educated and well informed about the structure and meaning of all the features in that landscape.

Such virtues and vices are neatly balanced by the collaborative synthesis, in which each major feature is given critical appraisal by a leading specialist, while the landscape as a whole is left to look after itself in the expectation that an impression will form in the mind of the beholder. It would be unwise to try to compensate for this by raising an overarching superstructure over the individual contributions in these volumes, for that would come close to courting a disaster akin to those which customarily visit university buildings designed in committee. The design of this, the first enterprise to marshal the resources of the multi-author technique to view the entire sweep of modern British social history, does, however, call for explanatory comment and description.

In the last generation or so social historians have been casting their nets wider and wider, into waters previously unnoticed and unexplored by historians as well as into those formerly fished with the conventional equipment of the political, administrative, or trade-union historian. So far has this gone that it is sometimes said that all history which is not concerned with the technicalities of high politics, diplomacy, or econometrics has become a kind of social history. This social history has moved a long way, in its intellectual approach as well as in its subject matter, from the 'history with the politics left out' which still served as a definition of social history in the 1940s. There may not be a 'new' social history in the same way that there is a 'new' economic history as a school of thought applying econometrics and models drawn from economic theory to the understanding of historical economic phenomena; but social historians draw widely on concepts from historical demography, social anthropology, sociology, social geography, and political science, as well as from economics, and are well aware of the importance of quantification. Social historians operating in this conceptually eclectic and experimental fashion do not have the methodological certainty, unity, or rigidity of 'new' economic history, and deal in conclusions which are probable and plausible rather than directly verifiable.

This social history has generated many vigorous controversies and debates on topics within the period covered by this series: on the standard of living, class formation, the labour aristocracy, or social control, for example, and more recently on gender roles and women's emancipation. These issues have not been picked out for separate treatment in these volumes. The debates are best followed in the original exchanges, or in the several admirable surveys which are available, and references can be found in the bibliographies here. The issues, moreover, are best understood when placed within the framework of the conditions, customs, and institutions that shaped the way in which the people lived. Hence questions of class, social relationships, gender differences and roles, and social conflict are discussed in the context of a series of particular themes which constitute the main elements in that framework. The thematic structure means that much matter of interest is left out, because it chances to fall into one of the oubliettes between themes; but while there is no attempt at a literally complete coverage, taken together the chapters add up to a comprehensive and balanced account of the complexity, and diversity, of the interactions between continuity and change which have determined the development of British society in the two centuries since 1750.

The series, indeed, provides three social histories of these two centuries, each one complete in itself at a level of partial coverage. That is to say, the volumes themselves are not divided chronologically, but into three broad thematic clusters: regional communities; social environment; and social institutions. Much of the recent pioneering work in social history has advanced through intensive study of particular localities and communities, and Volume 1, *Regions and Communities*, draws on this approach by presenting a series of chapters on the social histories of distinctive regions. This is not an attempt to parcel up the whole of Britain into a number of regions, which could run the risk of reducing social history to a sub-branch of local history. It is, rather, a collection of studies of regions – if Scotland and Wales can forgive the label – whose separate identity is clearly established by their distinctive national, institutional, legal, and administrative histories, and of those of undisputed significance as examples of immense social and economic change (the north-west), concentration of power and wealth (the metropolis), and violent changes in fortune (the north-east). The obvious geographical gaps in this disposition are bridged by two chapters, on the countryside and on the city, whose 'regions' are not localities with fixed boundaries but shifting social territories defined by environmental, occupational, and cultural criteria. Regional communities, their social cohesion, disintegration, and reformation, are strongly influenced by regional economies, and this volume, therefore, is more directly concerned than the following two with the links between economic history and social history, and with explicit confrontation of the interaction of economy and society.

Where questions of social structure and class relations are raised in the setting of specific localities in Volume 1, in Volume 2, *People and their Environment*, they are approached, using national data and national patterns, through a collection of studies of the living and working environment. The family and household, the social implications of demographic change, domesticity and the separation of home and workplace, housing and the changing meaning of the home, the working environment and employer–worker relationships, nutrition and patterns of food and drink consumption, and leisure and popular culture are the themes of this volume. Together they show how the social order was shaped, reproduced, and changed through the processes of getting, spending, and staying alive, through family, marriage, home, work, consumption, and leisure. These agencies both generated and mediated social tensions, but the more explicit, institutionalised, efforts to protect the social order, to control or suppress conflicts, to influence attitudes and behaviour, and to manipulate social conditions are reserved for Volume 3, *Social Agencies and Institutions*. Much of the running was made by those in power and authority, and the chapters on government and society which explain the changing impact of government on people's lives and the changes in popular expectations of what government could and should provide, as well as the chapter on crime and policing, are central to this theme. Most socialisation, however, took place through voluntary and non-official institutions that were largely generated from within a social group and not imposed upon it. These are the subject of chapters on philanthropy and voluntary associations; while education, religion, and health were in a half-way position, partly the province of official and often coercive action, partly a sphere of voluntaryism, self-help, and self-determination.

Each volume is self-contained, with its own set of bibliographies, and with each chapter carrying its own chronology of the 200 years. Together the three volumes, with their three different and complementary angles of approach, are designed to offer an integrated and well-rounded social history that is exciting and challenging, as well as being as up-to-date as the contributors, who have written at different times within the last five years, can make it.

F. M. L. THOMPSON

CHAPTER 1

Town and city

F. M. L. THOMPSON

A regional approach to social history obviously works primarily within geographical boundaries, and it is the long accumulation of the effects of topography and its influence on patterns of settlement and administrative and economic structures which is at the root of those regional identities that can be observed through the many superimposed layers of national and international forces, religious and class divisions, and inward and outward migration. A simplified picture suggests that by the early seventeenth century Britain possessed a reasonably unified and integrated ruling class, predominantly landed, following on the union of the crowns and the Tudor development of central power. Although the eighteenth century was to be half over before many of the Scottish elements slotted firmly into place in this class, it was one which was broadly homogeneous in culture, in life style and aspirations; its members spoke the same language, if not always the same dialect until the second half of the nineteenth century, they intermarried freely, and any surviving regional differences between them were romantic displays of custom rather than matters of serious social or political consequence. By the mid-eighteenth century the professional, financial, and mercantile middle class were similarly broadly unified, with value systems and social customs which transcended regional boundaries, although the marked differences between the legal systems of England and Scotland meant that professionally the British legal world has never become fully integrated. It is true that manufacturers and industrialists, who in any case were only beginning to rise above provincial obscurity in the early nineteenth century, stood apart from this bourgeois circle, and to some extent continued to do so into the twentieth century. It is also true that among the farmers were to be found many families of authentically middle-class wealth and status who nevertheless remained prov-

1

incial and distinctively regional in their social horizons and behaviour. All the same it can be argued that by the later eighteenth century regional differences of any significance, in speech, dress, diet, housing, work practices, employment customs, sports, entertainments, and to some extent in religious practices and other rituals, had become the preserve of the working classes, among whom farm workers and country craftsmen were the chief transmitters of tradition and custom although they were closely supported in this by many more urban trades at least into the later nineteenth century.

This class-chronological perspective on the regional dimensions in British social history, which is implicit in the other chapters in this volume, needs to be complemented by a parallel approach to different kinds of social region, which are also spatial but whose defining characteristics are environmental rather than geographical. Town and country, urban and rural are distinct, mutually exclusive, categories part of everyday terminology for describing places and expressing perceptions, labels used in drawing administrative, fiscal, and legal distinctions between places and between the inhabitants of those places, but they are attached to areas which expand and contract through changes in use and settlement, and are not territorially predetermined in the fashion of traditional provinces and regions. The task of this chapter is to enquire in what ways, and for how long, urban environments shaped, or contained, a distinctive social experience, perhaps cutting across class differences and regional differences, which contrasted with the life and manners of the countryside. The chronology is that of the move from a minority urban culture to an urban domination so complete that urban ways and urban values have taken over the whole of society. Urbanisation has been so throughgoing in the two centuries since 1750 that is has in effect liquidated what was a social region, by turning it into the nation.

I

The town and country dichotomy is a useful analytical device, but its drawbacks and limitations in describing economic and social realties, or indeed political and administrative facts, need to be understood from the outset. Rural society was proclaimed by the census authorities to have become a minority of the nation in 1851: 50.1 per cent of the population of England and Wales, and 51.8 per cent of the population of Scotland, were reported to be living in urban areas.[1] The census authorities, however, had only imperfect means for classifying areas as either urban or rural, not simply because the legal and local government arrangements prevailing in 1851 were inadequate for drawing a sharp line between town and country, but more importantly because the organisation and structure of the economy, and the patterns of settlement and of social relations, meant that no such sharp line existed in reality. In defining the town population, legal status was indeed of considerable help; the inhabitants of municipal boroughs and of places administered under a specific Town Improvement Act were obviously townspeople. But in addition the census counted as urban all who lived in 'towns of some 2,000 or more inhabitants, without any organisation other than the parish vestry', provided, that is, there were 2,000 or more people in a single enumeration district, which was normally a complete parish or township. A town can, naturally, be defined in a number of different ways, taking account of size, function, occupational structure, housing density, and legal status; but on any definition it is apparent that the 1851 classification is likely to have overstated the degree of urbanisation by including many parishes that were in reality large agricultural villages firmly anchored in rural society. The prevalence of very small burghs in Scotland, which were municipal in form, coupled with the circumstance that several Scottish 'towns' with less than 2,000 inhabitants were classed as urban in 1851, accounts for the rather unexpected, and as it turns out misleading, impression that Scotland was slightly more urbanised than England and Wales, with its implied corollary that Scottish urban growth had been faster in the previous hundred years or so.[2]

These criteria continued to be used for enumerating the urban population until the 1881 census, by which time the recently established urban sanitary districts, created by the public health legislation of 1872 and 1875, were available as conveniently appropriate units. From

[1] *1851 Census of Great Britain*, I, Table VII (England and Wales), pp. cciv–ccvii, Table XIV (Scotland), pp. ccxviii–ccix. A. F. Weber, *The Growth of Cities in the Nineteenth Century* (1899; reprinted 1967), pp. 46, 58. Later recalculations give the urban population of England and Wales as 54 per cent in 1851: C .M. Law, 'The Growth of Urban Population in England and Wales, 1801–1911', *Transactions of the Institute of British Geographers*, 41 (1967), pp. 125–43.

[2] *1871 Census of England and Wales*, IV, Introd., p. xxxii. In 1851 thirteen burghs in Scotland and eight boroughs in Wales had less than 1,000 inhabitants: *1851 Census of Great Britain*, I, Tables VII and XIV.

1901 onwards the urban district councils, established by the 1894 Local Government Act in the wake of the creation of county councils in 1888, were used in censuses, along with county boroughs and municipal boroughs, to distinguish urban areas and urban population from the rural residue. For the 1851–71 period, therefore, the census 'town' was a place, whether parish or township, which had 2,000 or more inhabitants; most historians have taken this to mean, plausibly but not strictly accurately, that the census 'town' had a minimum population of 2,500.[3] From 1901 the census 'town' was, at the least, an area administered by an urban district council; although no minimum population was prescribed for qualifying for this form of local government, it has been widely assumed, because it is convenient to believe that census returns are a reliable source of a long run of comparable figures, that urban district councils also had a minimum population of 2,500.[4] In practice urban district councils could well owe their existence to history, tradition and local politics, rather than to size or the possession of recognisably urban physical or economic features. Thus in 1901, 15 per cent of the urban district councils in England and Wales, 170 of them, had populations of less than 2,500. The smallest, Childwall in Lancashire, on the fringes of Liverpool, had no more than 219 people; in all there were 28 districts with less than 1,000 inhabitants. Moreover, the 170 tiny towns or pseudo-towns included 22 municipal boroughs, hangovers from the days of medieval charters, into an age in which local government experts thought that a borough needed 10,000 people at the very least.[5]

Two conclusions can be drawn from this. First, at the end of the nineteenth century after upwards of a couple of centuries of rapid urban growth there were still many places that were indubitably 'towns' which were exceedingly small. For example, Aldeburgh (Suffolk), Appleby (Westmorland), Bromyard (Hereford), Church Stretton (Salop), Fishguard (Pembroke), Lampeter (Cardigan), Lyme Regis (Dorset), Montgomery, Padstow (Cornwall), Rothbury (Northumberland), Seaton (Devon), Stow-on-the-Wold (Gloucester), Walton-on-the-Naze (Essex), or Woodstock (Oxford), all looked and

---

[3] B. T. Robson, *Urban Growth: An Approach* (1973), pp. 46–60, discusses the efforts, particularly by C. M. Law, to recalculate census returns from 1801 to 1911 taking a 2,500 town population threshold.

[4] P. J. Waller, *Town, City and Nation: England, 1850–1914* (Oxford, 1983), pp. 2–8, gives urban population figures for 1851 to 1911 using the 2,500 population threshold.

[5] *1911 Census of England and Wales*, PP1912/13, CXI, Table 8, pp.10–40. In Scotland forty-three burghs had less than 2,000 inhabitants, eighteen of them less than 1,000: *1911 Census of Scotland*, I, p. xvii.

behaved like towns. They had inns, hotels, boarding houses, banks, a variety of shops, professional services, markets, and well-established hinterlands; they were something different from either overgrown villages or merely residential clusters. Several of them were ancient boroughs; all of them in 1901 had less than 2,500, many of them less than 2,000, inhabitants. Second, there were also many administrative areas with small populations which were classified as urban that had a few genuinely 'urban' characteristics. For example, the Lincolnshire villages of Roxby (population in 1901, 389) and Ruskington (population 1,196) had the status of urban districts , but were in fact far more rural and agricultural than the market town of Spilsby, which administratively was simply part of a large rural district.[6] These two factors pulled the urban–rural calculations in opposite directions, but it cannot be assumed that they neatly cancelled each other out. It was indeed argued by C. M. Law that the administrative definitions, and subjective judgments of individual enumerators, in the 1851 and 1861 censuses caused a marked understatement of the urban population, through the exclusion of many suburbs, which lay beyond the administrative boundaries of their parent towns, and the exclusion of many mushrooming industrial, mining, or dormitory villages which particular enumerators happened not to think of as 'towns' although their populations exceeded the notional 2,000 threshold that was supposed to have been uniformly applied. Law then recalculated the urban population in all the pre-1914 censuses using his own threshold of a minimum population of 2,500 in a parish or township, with a minimum density of one person per acre, showing for example that on these definitions 54 per cent of the people of England and Wales were urban in 1851, rather than the 50.1 per cent stated in the census itself.[7]

The important point is not whether the urban population was 50 per cent or 54 per cent of the whole in 1851, but that there is no simple, straightforward, objective, and generally applicable definition of a town, and hence there are no clear-cut boundaries of urban society. Arbitrary decisions are inescapable in any system of classification. Law defended his choice of a population threshold of 2,500 partly on the grounds that in practice it excluded the smaller market towns whose activities were closely connected with the rural way of life. It is reasonable to want to exclude smaller market towns from the

---

[6] R. J. Olney, *Rural Society and County Government in Nineteenth-Century Lincolnshire* (Lincoln, 1979), p.141.
[7] Law, 'Growth of Urban Population', pp. 125–43.

urban family when interest is concentrated on the distance separating a town's economy from agriculture. Yet for other purposes the exclusion must seem arbitrary and subjective, for as the 1851 census Report itself observed the interdependence of town and country, of agriculture and trade and industry, was in many respects increasing rather than diminishing with the growth of the urban element.[8] The exclusion of places which were almost wholly devoted to servicing agriculture might result, in extreme cases, in refusal to accept that Chicago or Winnipeg, or nearer home Grantham or Luton, were towns at all until they cut loose from directly agriculturally dependent industries and businesses at a late stage in their development. Law concluded that by 1841, 48.3 per cent of the population of England and Wales was urban. By adding back the smaller market towns to his figure it might well be argued that the half-way mark in urbanisation had already passed in 1841. Such an adjustment is unimportant except as an indication that the economic relationship between town and country ranged all the way from complete dependence on the farming of the immediate region to complete isolation from the immediate region and dependence on the operations of international markets, and that perhaps the only economic characteristic which all towns had in common was that a majority of their economically active population was not engaged in tilling the fields.

The spatial relationship between town and country, or more accurately the spatial configuration of towns, adds a further complication to the delineation of urban and rural populations. In the mid-nineteenth century the administratively urban areas, particularly of the largest and most rapidly growing towns, understated the size of urban populations because suburbs and satellites lay beyond city limits, far more than they overstated the size because they embraced thinly populated rural fringes. By the end of the century the boot was on the other foot, after half a century of municipal imperialism had succeeded in annexing considerable rural territories through boundary extensions intended to safeguard lines of future expansion and appropriate their rateable values for the mother-city. The statistical effect was more to exaggerate the physical area occupied by towns than to inflate their total populations, since these open spaces and farmland fringes remained lightly peopled, but the population effect was not negligible. It was not until 1951 that the census tried to tackle this

[8]   *1851 Census of Great Britain*, I, Report, p. lxxxiv.

problem. The Report then acknowledged that 'for some time it has been felt that the customary analysis of the population by types of Administrative Area may not give an accurate picture of urban development', because the area of borough and urban district councils often contained 'tracts of land that cannot fairly be called urban in character' while rural district councils contained some land that ought to be called urban. The 1951 data were, therefore, analysed on new definitions which classified every whole ward or parish as either 'built-up land' if it had a population density of more than ten people to the acre, or rural land. The result showed that more than 12 per cent of the people living in urban administrative areas should more properly be termed rural, while 7 per cent of those in rural administrative areas were in fact urbanised. The most dramatic distortions in the conventional measures which were revealed were that well over one third of the 'true' rural population were to be found in urban administrative districts; that Wales taken on its own was evenly balanced, half urban and half rural, rather than being 70 per cent urban; and that no more than 72 per cent of the population of England and Wales were urbanised, against the 81 per cent of the conventional calculation.[9] There is no way of projecting these corrections backwards to pre-1951 censuses with any degree of reliability; but the fact that the 1951 urban proportion, 72 per cent, had already been surpassed in 1891 in both the official contemporary census classification and in Law's revised estimates, must give pause for thought about the scale, timing, and pace of the whole process of urban growth.

All this amounts to saying that all measures of towns and of their place in the nation which rely upon criteria of population size, population density, and administrative treatment are inherently uncertain and imprecise at the margin between town and country. Yet there are no other criteria which offer at least this degree of approximate precision and this possibility of reasonably comparable measurements over a long period of time. If this is true of the period since 1801, with the decennial censuses supplying increasingly reliable and sophisticated figures, it is even more true of the pre-census age. A goodly number of local head counts, however, were made in the course of the eighteenth century, either by town governments or by private individuals curious about the population and resources of their locality. The historian of eighteenth-century towns, P. J. Corfield,

[9] *1951 Census of England and Wales*, General Report (1958), pp. 60, 83, and General Tables (1956), Table 3.

Table 1.1 *Percentage of the population of England and Wales living in towns, 1700–1951*

	Towns 2,500–10,000	Towns 10,000–100,000	Towns over 100,000	All towns
1700	5	2	11	18
1750	6	6	11	23
1801	10	13	11	34
1851	10	19	25	54
1901	9	25	44	78
1951	1	16	55	72
[1951			54	81]

Sources: 1700: Corfield, *Impact of Towns*, Table II; 1750: *ibid.*; 1801: Law, 'Growth of Urban Population', Table XI; 1851: *ibid.*; 1901: *ibid.*; 1951: 1951 census, new definitions; [1951]: 1951 census, old definitions.

has examined more than 125 such listings, and from their evidence and the nonquantitative evidence of topographical and literary sources has provided informed estimates of eighteenth-century urban population. Absence of evidence prevents her estimates from incorporating the fine adjustments of the census-based calculations, and in particular the difficulty of identifying and quantifying the smaller and more obscure places among the 500 market centres of 1700 which might have passed the 2,500 population threshold she adopts, may have led to some undercounting, but they provide a firm foundation for depicting the broad outlines of long-run urban growth.[10]

These outlines are summarised in Table 1.1, and both the immense impact of urban growth and the long-drawn-out nature of the transformation of a predominantly rural society into a predominantly urban society are readily apparent. The full power of the urbanising impulse can be better appreciated if growth rates are considered alongside the static proportions of Table 1.1. In each fifty-year period until 1901 the urban population increased at more than twice the rate of the population as a whole, with especially strong spurts in the first half of the eighteenth century and the first half of the nineteenth century. The scale of urban expansion between 1700 and 1750 was, of course, tiny by later standards: the urban population increased from 970,000 to 1,380,900 while in 1901 it numbered 25.3 million, and in 1951 between 31.5 and 35.3 million according to which definition is used.

[10]   P. J. Corfield, *The Impact of English Towns, 1700–1800* (Oxford, 1982), Tables I and II, pp. 6–9. See also C. W. Chalklin, *The Provincial Towns of Georgian England* (1974), pp. 3–54.

But it took place in a period of only modest increase in the population as a whole, roughly from 5 million to 6 million, being quite largely sustained by immigration from the country districts; and it happened before any of the great technical and organisational changes in manufacturing industry, although there were important developments in trade and finance, and to some extent in inland transport, in the first half of the eighteenth century. This is not to suggest that there were no economic causes and effects of the expansion of towns. But it does show both the importance of 'pre-industrial urbanism', which had been gathering pace from the later seventeenth century, and the clear conceptual as well as chronological distinction between urbanisation and industrialisation.[11]

That distinction inevitably becomes blurred after 1750, since the growth of industry and the growth of the urban population so clearly coincided, and since so many of the rising giants among cities – Glasgow, Birmingham, Manchester, Leeds and Sheffield, for example – were closely associated with manufacturing. Even though the most rapidly growing towns included ports and resorts which had comparatively minor industrial sectors, if any – Liverpool, Bristol, Newcastle, Hull, Bath, or Brighton – it can be argued that they owed their livelihoods to industrial wealth and to the commerce generated by industry. While London, far and away the largest town of all, was also far and away the largest manufacturing town in the country, although not the seat of large-scale or heavy industry. Nevertheless, the oscillations in the intensity of urban growth over long periods suggest that if it was not autonomous, then it was dependent on industrial development, and economic growth more generally, only in indirect and complicated ways. Thus, the early years of the industrial revolution and the significant increase in the rate of economic growth in the second half of the eighteenth century rather surprisingly produced a deceleration in urban expansion: total urban population indeed doubled between 1750 and 1801, but while this was twice the rate of growth of the population as a whole, in the previous half-century towns had grown two and a half times as fast as the whole population. Between 1801 and 1851, which may be pictured as the half-century in which the key industries of early industrialisation, cotton, iron, and coal, consolidated their position in the economy, urban growth again accelerated to two and a half times the pace of the increase in population

---

[11] Corfield, *Impact of Towns*, pp. 7–15; Chalklin, *Provincial Towns*, pp. 17–20.

as a whole. This familiar picture of the most rapid urban growth going hand in hand with the most rapid industrial expansion did not, however, persist into the second half of the nineteenth century. It is now fashionable to see the seeds of industrial decline germinating in this half century, and it is true that in terms of international comparisons Britain was losing its position as leading industrial nation by the last quarter of the century. Still, the years between 1851 and 1901 were the years when industrialisation really took hold, the years when steam power and machine methods broadened out from their previously narrow base and took over the whole general range of manufactures, the years when the railways produced their full impact on the economy, and the years in which total industrial production increased more than in any other fifty-year period in the last two and a half centuries.[12] Urban expansion of course remained vigorous; but it fell back to no more than double the rate of general population growth, thus leaving the first half of the nineteenth century as the period of the most intense relative growth of town populations in British history, even though it was the second half of the century which saw by far the greatest addition to the absolute numbers of towndwellers ever experienced.

The different, and at times contrasting, dimensions of the scale, and of the process, of urbanisation are quantified in Table 1.2. Perhaps the most striking feature is the great change which has come over the scene since the beginning of the twentieth century. It certainly cannot be argued that the first half of the twentieth century was a period of spectacular, let alone uninterrupted, economic growth, with the disruption of two world wars and the troubles of the interwar economy. Nonetheless, the years between 1901 and 1951 saw the arrival of motor vehicles, the spread of electricity, and the development of many new industries, and it was mainly because of these that total industrial production in fact increased nearly as much in these fifty years as it had done between 1851 and 1901. Urbanisation, however, showed no response to this industrial growth. On any definition of 'urban' the process of urban growth slowed to a snail's pace after 1901; on the new, more sophisticated, definitions produced in the 1951 census it even seemed that a reverse flow had developed,

[12]   Industrial production and broad rates of increase in it, taken from P. Deane and W. A. Cole, *British Economic Growth 1688–1959*, 2nd edn (Cambridge, 1967), Table 37, p. 166, and C. H. Feinstein, *Statistical Tables of National Income, Expenditure, and Output of the U.K. 1855–1965* (Cambridge, 1976), Table 51, T111–13.

Table 1.2 *Relative and absolute growth of the urban population of England and Wales, 1700–1951*

	Total urban population (000s)	Increase in urban population (000s)	Increase in urban population as multiple of total population increase
1700	970	—	—
1700–50	—	411	2.47
1750	1,381	—	—
1750–1801	—	1,344	2.15
1801	3,009	—	—
1801–51	—	6,679	2.52
1851	9,688	—	—
1851–1901	—	15,684	2.0
1901	25,372	—	—
1901–51	—	10,277	1.14
1951	35,336	—	—
1901–51	—	6,147	0.71
1951	31,519	—	—

Sources: 1700–50: Corfield, *Impact of Towns*, Table I; 1750–1801: *ibid.*; 1801–51: Law, 'Growth of Urban Population', Table XI; 1851–1901: *ibid.*; 1901–51: 1951 census, old definitions (first set of figures); 1901–51: 1951 census, new definitions (second set of figures).

possibly from as early as the 1920s, with rural population increasing slightly faster than the urban for the first time since the seventeenth century.

A large part of this twentieth-century halt in urban growth was simply the necessary demographic effect of the previous urban expansion. Once the urban population had become the decisively predominant part of total population, then the major part of any further increases in total population was bound to be generated by the urban population itself, so that the growth rates of the two were likely to converge. This is broadly what has happened since 1901. The twentieth-century demonstration that urbanisation has reached saturation point when somewhere between three-quarters and four-fifths of the population live in towns nevertheless remains important. The year 1901 marked the end of a process of urban expansion which had started in the seventeenth century, and the appearance of a mature, fully urbanised society. It would be grossly misleading, however, to leave any impression that the mature urban society of the twentieth century has been in any way static. For one thing the urban population has continued to increase, and between 1901 and 1951 at least 6 million people were added to the towns. But above all internal shifts within the urban structure and between different levels of the hierarchy of towns, which had been happening throughout the centuries of urban growth, continued and were intensified in the twentieth century.

The rise of the large towns with populations over 100,000 can be seen in Table 1.1. Throughout the eighteenth century London was the sole town of this size, and with its population rising from just over half a million to just under one million in the course of the century it was in a class of its own, as it has remained. By the 1820s London had been joined in the 100,000-town league by Liverpool, Manchester, and Birmingham. By 1851 four more towns Bradford, Bristol, Leeds, and Sheffield had passed this mark; in 1901 there were twenty-eight towns, outside London, with more than 100,000 people, and forty six in 1951 (one, Halifax, entered the league briefly in 1901 and 1911, and then fell back below the threshold). Outside London, a quarter of the urban population lived in these towns in 1851, two-fifths in 1901, and more than two-thirds in 1951. To put it in another way, if the 'typical' town is pictured as the kind of place in which more than half of the urban population lives, then leaving London aside again, for most of the eighteenth century this was a town with less than 10,000 inhabitants; by the beginning of the nineteenth century this had become a town with under 20,000 people, and by mid-century one with under 50,000. By 1901 more than half the urban population outside London lived in towns with more than 50,000 people, but it was only after 1931 that the large towns with more than 100,000 inhabitants became typical in this sense. Moreover, it was the twentieth century which coined the term 'conurbation' to describe the super-large urban concentrations that are agglomerations of once-separate towns, and for a brief spell between 1974 and 1986 gave the concept administrative expression in the six Metropolitan Counties of Greater London, south-east Lancashire, the West Midlands, West Yorkshire, Merseyside, and Tyneside. The conurbation of Greater London, as a practically continuous built-up area much larger than the administrative areas of the Cities of London and Westminster, had existed as a physical, economic and social fact at least since the sixteenth century, and had been recognised by the census from the start, long before the inner core of greater London was officially delineated by the Metropolitan Board of Works in 1856 and the London County Council in 1888. The provincial conurbations were taking shape in the last quarter of the nineteenth century, although some well-known examples of physical union despite civic separation, such as Manchester and Salford or Newcastle and Gateshead, had occurred earlier. The terminology to describe them was no doubt invented, by Patrick Geddes in 1915, because the phenomenon already existed on the ground. But it was the interwar developments of housing estates and bus routes which finally knitted these conurbations together as physical entities, and the census authorities were not moving far behind the times when they first recognised the six conurbations as distinctive areas in 1951; 40 per cent of the total population and nearly 50 per cent of the urban population were then living in them, and 37 per cent of the non-London urban population. Arguably, the representative townsman had become a resident in a million-strong sprawl (though one of the six conurbations, Tyneside, remained just below the million mark).[13]

This survey of a few of the more prominent features in the history of urban population and town sizes since the eighteenth century is most notable for the uncertain and even contradictory nature of the pointers it provides for the arrangement and periodisation of any treatment of the urban process. From a distance 1851 stands out as the great landmark, the watershed between predominantly rural premodern Britain and predominantly urban modern Britain; but on a closer approach its significance dissolves as doubts over the meaning of 'urban' reduce it to a mere statistical abstraction. If we follow Waller in agreeing that a 'proper' town, of a size, appearance, and presence to mark it off clearly from being a village, was a place with over 10,000 people, then this landmark should be moved forwards to 1871.[14] This is a tenable position; but scarcely more tenable than a proposition that the essential difference between pre-modern and modern, in

---

[13] It is interesting to note that Scotland showed a greater degree of urbanisation, and of concentration in a single town, than England and Wales, but a less pronounced general development of large towns, apart from Edinburgh and Glasgow, there being only a further two with more than 100,000 people: Aberdeen (from 1881) and Dundee (from 1871).

	Urban pop. as percentage of total pop.	Increase in urban pop. as multiple of total pop. increase	Pop. of Glasgow as percentage of total pop.	Pop. of towns over 100,000 as percentage of total pop.
1801	30	–	4.7	0
1851	52	2.65	12.5	19.5
1901	74	2.2	20.1	36.0
1951	83	1.93	21.3	37.6

[14] Waller, *Town, City and Nation*, p. 6.

urban terms, lies not in the presence of undifferentiated towns but in the presence of 'large' towns. 'Large' towns, in turn, may be defined as those with more than 50,000 people, in which case the landmark shifts to 1901; or those with over 100,000 when it becomes 1931. Again, a qualitative rather than quantitative judgment could select 1811 as one turning point, when the first towns outside London passed the 100,000 threshold (Liverpool, Edinburgh and Glasgow, in size order), and 1911 as a second, when Glasgow became the first city outside London to exceed the 1 million mark, to be followed in 1931 by Birmingham. In their way these are all useful milestones, marking significant and interesting points along the path of urbanisation, and others can be readily devised to record key changes in urban perceptions, environments, or institutions. The truth is, however, that the concept of urban society as a homogeneous and autonomous sector of society is too much of an abstraction for it to be sensible to attempt to construct an urban chronological framework which is independent of the conventional periodisation employed in discussing the broader context of economic, political, technological, and demographic changes and developments within which urban society was shaped. Which means in practice that the two centuries after 1750 are most conveniently sliced at 1815 and 1914, even if this makes the historian's knife cut through many important urban threads.

II

In the eighteenth century anyone who said 'town' was likely to mean London. London was unique in Britain, well over ten times larger than the second city (Norwich in 1700, Bristol by 1750), and without equal in Europe. The trappings of big city life, the grandeur and the squalor, the wealth and the misery, the elegance and the filth, the perpetual bustling activity, the power, the pleasure, and the pain, were to be found in London alone. To be sure, Norwich had wealth, Bristol had bustle, and Bath had grace; but in comparison with London anywhere else seemed small, sleepy, and of little account. Echoes of London's dominance of the language of towns can of course still be heard. The 'town' in the distinction between town and country membership, subscriptions, or clothes, of many clubs, associations, or fashion guides refers only to London. 'Going up to town' is a phrase understood not merely in the south-east but throughout educated England, for going to London, and until the 1960s at railway stations 'up' platforms and 'down' platforms were universally intelligible as serving trains going to, and coming from, London. It was this equation of 'town' with London which gave eighteenth-century views on the merits and demerits of urban life most of their sharp flavour, for it was the virtues and vices of London in particular which were at issue.

The debate on the threat to morality and public order posed by the giant city was already old when the eighteenth century started. Arguments were reiterated rather than refined or developed; the sink of iniquity, the bottomless pit of corruption, the unruly mass of ungovernable people, remained opposed by the counter-images of the bastion of civilisation against barbarism, the cradle of enlightenment, refinement, and taste, and the heart and brain of the whole kingdom, in the days of Cobbett and Wordsworth – who denounced the 'infernal wen' and the 'dissolute city' – at the end of the century, just as they had been a hundred years earlier. The eighteenth century adds two names to those who have shown appreciation of London's charms in memorable phrases, Alexander Pope and Samuel Johnson; but it did not add any new ideas.[15] Contemporaries were understandably fascinated, even mesmerised, by the enormous size and complexity of London and its apparent power to direct and control the life of the entire nation, not only through the instruments of government, but through the channels of trade, credit, investment, opinion, fashion and taste. It was not until the 1830s and 1840s that perceptions of town life ceased to be monopolised by London as sole exemplar, and were generalised to register feelings about large towns in general. Although the town–country debate continued in educated opinion and in literature, and indeed was sharpened under the influence of Ruskin and William Morris, the 'country party' increasingly focussed their polemic on the ugliness, filth, and squalor of the great industrial cities which housed the smokestack industries.[16] What was left from the earlier tradition was a feeling of envy and resentment of London's dominance, of political power, of wealth, of intellectual and cultural life, a feeling shared by and perhaps nurtured in the great provincial cities. The town–country dichotomy had become overlaid by the capital–provinces split, and from the 1870s the majority of the provincial population was itself urban.

[15] Alexander Pope: 'this dear, damn'd distracting town' ('Farewell to London'). Samuel Johnson: 'When a man is tired of London he is tired of life' (Boswell's *Life of Johnson*, 20 Sept. 1777).

[16] F. M. L. Thompson, 'Towns, Industry, and the Victorian Landscape', in S. R. J. Woodell, ed., *The English Landscape* (Oxford, 1985), pp. 168–72.

It is understandable that many people thought of eighteenth-century London as some strange and unfamiliar monster, and it is true that it contained many mysterious and dangerous courts and warrens, and whole districts, which were seldom penetrated by outsiders. Yet one socially important part of London life was simply an annual migration from the countryside. The roots of the London season go back to the movements of the Court and the meetings of Parliament, just as the town houses of the nobility and gentry can be traced back to the inns and palaces kept by medieval bishops and magnates, mainly along the strand connecting the City and Westminster. The establishment of the regular, and lengthy, winter and spring season, however, was an eighteenth-century development, strongly influenced by the regularity of parliamentary sessions that followed the Glorious Revolution and the aristocratic dominance which it, and its sequel of the Hanoverian succession, entrenched. The social life of the season, with plays, operas, concerts, masked balls, soirées, salons, and firework displays, became increasingly elaborate, and required an increasing supply of imposing residences, as well as specialised public buildings, to support it. Many of the wealthiest and most powerful aristocrats built and re-built their London hotels in the Italianate or Palladian mode on the grand scale; Devonshire, Chesterfield, Burlington, and Spencer Houses during the reign of George II, for example, and Lansdowne, Chandos, Derby, and Carlton Houses in the 1770s and 1780s; Buckingham House, built by John Sheffield, Duke of Buckingham, in the early eighteenth century and subsequently purchased by George III, was a redbrick member of this group. Most of the nobility and the county families who came to London for Parliament and the season were content with more modest, though still substantial, houses in the fashionable West End squares; the main thrust behind the development of elegant Georgian London, indeed, came from their demand.[17]

The season was an annual gathering of the country's elite for purposes of political, social, sexual, and commercial intercourse. It was a time for business and for pleasure, for politicking, matchmaking, horse-trading, seeing bankers, raising loans, consulting family lawyers, gambling, dancing, and intriguing. It was a time when architects and artists, actors and musicians, medical men and ambitious preachers found patrons and audiences and secured employment,

[17]   John Summerson, *Georgian London* (1945) remains the standard work on the architectural history of 'polite' eighteenth-century London.

while wits and courtesans made their reputations. Its start brought an annual flurry of orders and activity to an array of luxury trades, in dressmaking, millinery, tailoring, and hatmaking, in jewellery and clockmaking, in cabinetmaking and coachbuilding; and its end brought a slack summer and unemployment. The ripple effects of the season extended more widely than this, into the food and drink, and service, trades and occupations; and the participants in the social life of high society were not limited to aristocracy and gentry, the financial and mercantile elite of the City becoming more nearly on terms of social equality in the course of the century.[18] The important point, however, is that the elite which went in and out of London like the tide was the country elite, the landed elite of landed magnates, county families, and knights of the shires. Eighteenth-century England is often depicted as being governed by a network of country houses; for nearly half of every year this network moved to London and became a network of town houses. The elitist experience of London and the elitist view of urban society, was distinctly limited and calculated to avoid unpleasantness. But it is important that the most powerful, influential and wealthy layer of society was at home in both rural and urban worlds, even if screened from the poorest and most distressing parts of either. They displayed in their own persons and life style the interdependence of town and country, and their outlook was unlikely to encourage the development of any strong or powerful anti-urban or anti-London feelings.

At the beginning of the eighteenth century it is quite probable that those persons of quality who had any experience of town life at all were more familiar with London, and accumulated a more prolonged acquaintance with it, than with their own local town. It is true that the functional links between the local gentry and market and county towns, in matters of trade and justice, were of long-standing, and became stronger as the administrative role of the justices of the peace, meeting in quarter sessions in the county town, increased. Social links, however, did not begin to develop strongly until the later seventeenth century; by the mid-eighteenth century most county towns had become important social centres for the gentry, and many had developed regular social seasons, providing for those who could not afford the visit to London an attenuated version of its round of cultured pleasure and entertainment. In the eighteenth century many of the

[18] N. Rogers, 'Money, Land and Lineage: The Big Bourgeoisie of Hanoverian London', *Social History*, 4 (1979), pp. 437–54.

county gentry and some of the lesser nobility cultivated the habit of residing in their county town for part of the year, and acquired town houses, to which the surviving Georgian parts of many provincial towns still bear some witness. The more attractive and impressive cathedral cities, where dignified cathedral closes populated with congenial social brethren in the shape of the gentry-clergy of dean and chapter were at hand, where perhaps the preferred sites for this form of aristocratic urbanisation: the building of such town houses in York, Chester, Lincoln, Norwich, Salisbury, and Winchester is particularly notable. Non-cathedral towns, however, were also the subject of contemporary comment on the number and style of their resident gentry: Preston, Derby, Shrewsbury, Stamford and Bury St Edmunds would figure in any list.[19]

The gentry who owned town houses were greatly outnumbered by the gentry who came as visitors for the major social events, as to race week at York from the 1730s, or simply for the evening, as to the annual 'stuff ball' in Lincoln from the 1780s.[20] Social life required special cultural buildings, and the central features of the gentrification of the towns were the theatre and the assembly room, meeting the demand of the country gentry and the cultured town elite for entertainment, dancing, music, cards, and gossip. Purpose-built theatres, replacing earlier makeshift and temporary rooms in inns and barns used by travelling companies, began to appear in the largest provincial towns in the 1740s and 1750s. It is indicative of the general, and not exclusively aristocratic-gentry, complexion of this new stage in urban culture that the earliest provincial theatres were built in 'non-gentry' towns like Birmingham, Liverpool and Plymouth, as well as in Norwich, which although a county town of gentry resort was also the largest manufacturing town in the country until the 1780s. In the later eighteenth century theatre-building became widespread, and by 1815 there were well over 100 provincial theatres: they were part of the urban furniture of every self-respecting town with cultural aspirations. It is not surprising that the larger towns with a prosperous resident commercial and professional middle class could support

[19]   Peter Clark, 'Introduction', in Peter Clark, ed., *The Transformation of English Provincial Towns, 1600–1800* (1984), pp. 27–9. 48. J. V. Beckett, *The Aristocracy in England, 1660–1914* (Oxford, 1986), p. 368.

[20]   Peter Borsay, '"All the Town's a Stage": Urban Ritual and Ceremony, 1660–1800', in Clark, ed., *Transformation* p. 233. Olney, *Nineteenth-Century Lincolnshire*, p. 14: the stuff ball was so-named because each year the patroness of the ball chose the colour of the year, and the purchase of woollen ball dresses was meant to encourage the local cloth industry.

theatres. The immediate point is that so also could the smaller county towns and lesser places, drawing in their gentry patronage: places such as Colchester, Stamford, Salisbury, Chichester, Winchester, Devizes, Maidstone and Newbury.[21]

So also, at a rather more rarified level, with assembly rooms, which drew for their model not on London, whose polite society was far too large and complex to fit into a single multi-purpose social building, but on the spas, especially Bath whose first assembly room was built in 1708. Major regional centres like York, Lincoln, Canterbury, and Norwich had acquired assembly rooms by the 1750s and smaller centres such as Beverley or Newark followed suit later in the century. As with theatres, assembly rooms were not an exclusive gentry preserve, and the rising industrial and port towns equipped themselves with them in the second half of the eighteenth century. In the long-established and much slower growing provincial towns, which in 1815 still contained perhaps half of the country's urban population outside London, the theatre and the assembly room, along with the elegant town houses, were the architectural evidence of the entry of the aristocracy and gentry into urban society in the course of the eighteenth century. Their simultaneous appearance in Birmingham and Liverpool, Manchester and Newcastle, Leeds and Plymouth, signified that there was something of a common urban culture, in artefacts perhaps more than in their manner of use, at a time when urban economies and social structures were rapidly diverging onto increasingly separate paths.

The main growth path between 1750 and 1815, as it was to continue to be thereafter, lay with industrial and commercial towns which had no direct links with or dependence on the countryside or agriculture and its fortunes, and whose social structures had at their apex a bourgeois elite. The older regional centres, the county towns, the towns with a gentry presence and a distinct reliance on the prosperity of their agricultural hinterlands, were on a path of slow growth; the smallest market towns, with little or no gentry patronage, were already on a stagnant or declining path as better road, and above all canal, transport rendered them redundant. There was one group of rapidly growing towns, however, in which the landed aristocracy supplied the engine of growth: the spas and resorts. The fashion for taking

---

[21] C. W. Chalklin, 'Capital Expenditure on Building for Cultural Purposes in Provincial England, 1730–1830', *Business History*, 22 (1980), pp. 51–70. The resident populations of Stamford, Chichester, and Devizes, for example, were under 4,000 in 1801.

the waters spread rapidly from the chronic invalids seeking cures to the leisured classes seeking pleasure in Restoration England, and for a time in the late seventeenth century wealthy Londoners made the wells and springs of Hampstead, Epsom, and Dulwich into the focus of lively little resorts for modish day-trippers.

It was the hugely successful exploitation of the rediscovery of the thermal baths at Bath, however, and the invention of an attractive and highly mannered social ritual of amusements, distractions, and indulgences to surround the sulphurous business of bathing and purging, which launched the first free-standing spa town on its eighteenth-century career as the resort at which the aristocracy and the fashionable had to be seen. Next to the London season a stay in Bath became almost obligatory for the social elite, and in the permanently leisured atmosphere and close quarters of a holiday town Bath may even, for a while, have superseded London as the aristocracy's most effective marriage market. In the 1660s Bath had a population of scarcely more than 1,000; by 1750 it was in the region of 7,000 and by 1801 was only just short of 35,000 – growth rates which more than matched those of most of the 'new' industrial towns, and an absolute size which put it on a par with Newcastle and Portsmouth, and well ahead of Bradford, Halifax, or Hull, at the beginning of the nineteenth century. These figures are for the resident population, which by the mid-eighteenth century included numbers of retired, or permanently invalid, gentry and rich bourgeois, although by far the greater part of the population was employed in the services which sustained the resort's amenities, not least in the building trades which were engaged in making Bath into England's eighteenth-century architectural showpiece.

The number of visitors to Bath, many of whom spent a whole summer season there, is not recorded. They were numerous enough to support a third set of assembly rooms, launched in 1769, as well as an unrivalled concentration of valetudinarian and social facilities in the baths, pump rooms, several theatres, promenades, bowling green, and public gardens; and they were largely aristocratic, or members of fashionable London society. Bath had imitators but no serious rivals, before 1815, as a resort town. Tunbridge Wells was readily accessible from London, and attracted some royal, and aristocratic, attention; it copied many of Bath's arrangements, from quite early in the eighteenth century, both for amenities and for a carefully managed social calendar, but it never achieved the same kind of fashionable glamour.

Towards the end of the century it was becoming more of an upper-class retirement town and less of a smart resort. With rather under 5,000 inhabitants in 1801 it was modestly thriving, but somewhat less so than its northern equivalent, Scarborough, which developed initially as a spa more than as a seaside town, and which attracted many of the northern nobility and gentry to its summer seasons around mid-century. Among the inland spas only Cheltenham had begun to grow rapidly before 1815 (its population increased fourfold between 1801 and 1821), but it was still a very small place at the end of the eighteenth century even though well enough known as a sedate alternative to Bath for George III to have made a visit in 1788. Its day lay ahead in the nineteenth century, as did that of Leamington, Harrogate, or Buxton, in times when the patronage of the ever-expanding numbers of leisured wealthy, rather than the custom of the limited and almost finite ranks of the landed classes, became the key to success.

In the longer run Bath, the high society resort, was overshadowed by the expansion of the affluent middle classes and the diffusion of the holiday habit, outnumbered by the new resorts which catered for this market, and forsaken by the fashionable set who sought novel and more exclusive watering holes on the Continent. In the short run the challenge, in the closing years of the eighteenth century, arose from the sea, bathing in which had been growing in popularity since the 1740s. Scarborough was obviously well placed to make the switch from spa to sea-bathing town, and did so. But by general consent the seaside phenomenon of the age was Brighton. It already had sea water baths and assembly rooms by the 1770s; but its dizzy rise as a fashionable, racy, but aristocratic, resort dated from the arrival of the Prince of Wales (Prince Regent, later George IV) and his entourage in 1783, and his building of the Royal Pavilion, at once exotic, myster-ious, *risqué*, and royal. Between 1783 and 1801 Brighton's population doubled, to reach 7,000; it doubled again between 1811 and 1821, to 24,000 and in the following decade grew by another 70 per cent, showing the highest growth rates of any town in Britain. Already by the early 1820s Cobbett was remarking disapprovingly and incre-duously on the stock-jobbers who 'skip backward and forward on the coaches, and actually carry on stock-jobbing in Change Alley, though they reside at Brighton'.[22] No doubt extremely few stock-jobbers, or anyone else, attempted regular commuting before the

[22] Quoted by J. H. Clapham, *An Economic History of Modern Britain: The Early Railway Age, 1820–50* (Cambridge, 1950 edn), p. 9.

railway, though it is just conceivable that the odd one may have kept a weekend house in Brighton; but the more general implication is quite true, that the majority of Brighton's well-to-do residents, and of her visitors, were not gentry at all. Many of the Prince Regent's cronies, after all, were more than a shade vulgar, although others of them were aristocratic Whigs. Nevertheless, Brighton was much frequented by the less unbending aristocracy and gentry in its early days; and it continued to have a formal Master of Ceremonies on the Bath model, orchestrating the major social events, until 1855, while a decidedly aristocratic autumn and pre-Christmas season lingered on until about 1870.[23] If 'old ocean's bauble' was the gayest and most fashionable place in Regency England, Weymouth was the premier resort of the older and more elderly aristocracy who had got used to its quieter and more decorous ways while accompanying George III on his annual seaside trips from 1789 onwards. Weymouth was small and it did not experience any period of hectic growth; yet in 1801 it was as much as half the size of Brighton, while before 1851 it had shrunk, relatively, to one eighth of Brighton's population.

Apart from these three, Brighton, Scarborough, and Weymouth, the only seaside resort of note in the first decade of the nineteenth century, and in the same population league as them, was Margate. In the early, exploratory, days of sea-bathing Margate had attracted some aristocratic visitors, but by the 1790s this phase was past. In 1800 it was estimated that the Kent hoys, which were barges taking Thanet grain to London, brought back a return cargo, ballast as it were, of 18,000 visitors to Margate. This made it too populous a resort for high society, though not exactly a plebeian one; the crowds were well-dressed Londoners, 'decent tradesmen' and the like, and Margate was a long way yet from becoming Whitechapel by the sea. For traditional high society of aristocracy, gentry, and court to have scored three resorts out of four was impressive, but less significant than its contribution to the totality of the aristocratic participation in, and familiarity with, a large slice of eighteenth-century urban life, in London, county towns, spas, and seaside resorts. They did not dominate such towns, by and large they were not permanent residents in them, and only in smaller resorts could it be argued that their custom was the basis of any town's economy. The point is, however, that the landed classes far from being alienated or distanced from towns

[23] Waller, *Town, City and Nation*, p. 143. J. A. R. Pimlott, *The Englishman's Holiday* (Hassocks, Sussex, 1976 edn), p. 122.

became more closely involved with them in the course of the eigh-teenth-century, and got into the way of thinking of towns as pleasant places arranged for their comfort, convenience, pleasure, and amuse-ment. Viewed from the top, while there were physical differences, in the main agreeable, between town and country, there were no tensions or conflicts between rural society and urban society; they were simply seasonally complementary parts of society.

Unpleasant towns were those outside the aristocratic orbit; although occasionally visited out of curiosity by explorers, they remained largely unknown territory not on any social route, where new forms of urban society developed with minimal links with agriculture or rural society. Individuals naturally might have strong preferences and prejudices, and not all aristocrats liked or admired the 'pleasant' towns. When one of the old school, Lord Torrington, commented in 1788 that 'Brighton appear'd in a fashionable, unhappy, bustle, with such a harpy set of painted harlots, as to appear to me as bad as Bond St. in the spring', he might almost have been anticipating the disdain of Cobbett, the agrarian radical.[24] Torrington's view of Manchester in 1790, however, would have been shared by man of fashion and old-fashioned dyspeptic nobleman alike: 'this great, nasty, manufac-turing town; looking exactly like Spitalfields, and those environs ... who but a merchant cou'd live in such a hole; where the slave working and drinking a short life out, is eternally realing [sic] before you from fatigue, or drunkenness.'[25] Cobbett, on the other hand, since his chief ground for condemning Brighton was that it was a parasite, an excres-cence, which produced nothing – 'a place of no trade; of no commerce at all; it has no harbour; it is no place of deposit or of transit for corn or for goods or for cattle' – would have been logically obliged to have approved of Manchester, perhaps only grudgingly because the agricultural produce which it processed was of foreign origin.[26] Attempts to sort towns into sheep and goats on some criterion of utility, classing as worthy those which made useful things or handled useful commodities, and the others as frivolous and harmful, appealed to neo-physiocrats and Manchester men, who divided mankind into the industrious and the idle, but were inherently flawed. Cobbett himself, for example, did not reckon tea was a useful article at all,

[24] C. Bruyn Andrews, ed., (a selection from) *The Torrington Diaries* (1954 edn), 'A Tour into Sussex, 1788', p. 127.
[25] *Ibid.*, ' A Tour in the Midlands, 1790', pp. 258–9.
[26] Quote by Pimlott, *Englishman's Holiday*, p. 10.

regarding it as debilitating and degrading. Social and moral judgments of towns did indeed relate to their functions, but reflected notions of acceptability and familiarity which in turn depended on the standpoint of the observer and whether there was anything to do or see in this town or that.

'Unpleasant' towns, in the eighteenth century, were on the whole not especially grubby or squalid; they were merely unfamiliar to polite society. They were of two main kinds: ports (with which dockyard towns can be bracketed, slightly artificially, since these were distinctively royal naval creations) and manufacturing towns. The ports were one of the striking urban growth points of the eighteenth century. London, naturally, was the country's unrivalled premier port which handled three-quarters of England's entire overseas trade at the beginning of the century. Not only did the volume of overseas trade increase dramatically during the century, perhaps sixfold, but with London's share of the increased total falling to perhaps 60 per cent by 1800 and continuing to decline until it stabilised at around one third from 1850 onwards, the outports flourished mightily. This redistribution of trade channels stemmed from the nature of the goods being handled, their origins and destinations whether for processing, consumption, or export, and the means and capacity of inland transport; it did not cut London out from trading in sugar, tea, coffee, tobacco, cotton, or grain, or from exporting woollens, cottons, hardware, or pottery, but it gave openings for some outports to rival or surpass London in particular lines. The effects were to be seen clearly in the growth of Bristol from a population of about 22,000 in 1700 to 50,000 by 1750 and 61,000 in 1801; and most clearly of all in the rise of Liverpool, its great rival in the Atlantic trade, which had perhaps 5,000 or 6,000 people in 1700, 22,000 in 1750 and 83,000 in 1801. The third port of this size and importance, Newcastle upon Tyne, which with Gateshead had a population of about 29,000 in 1750 and 42,000 in 1801, prospered as a result of London's growth not as a reflection of London's relative decline in overseas trade, and was engaged in the coastal trade in coal far more than in exports, although it was far from being merely a coal port. These three were joined before 1801, as ports with over 20,000 people, by Hull and Sunderland, and by 1811 Yarmouth had just slipped into the same company. The dockyard towns, by contrast, did not grow out of trade flows but out of strategic and administrative naval decisions. Chatham was the earliest, much favoured in the later seventeenth century while the Dutch were the chief naval enemies, and by 1700 it had at least 5,000 people. In the eighteenth century the Admiralty's attention turned to France and the Channel, and the Chatham dockyards ceased to be the main point of expansion. Along with the other Medway towns Rochester and Gillingham, Chatham formed part of an expanding Victorian urban area which was to reach a combined population of over 100,000 by 1901, but its economic drive came much more from cement and agricultural machinery than from naval work. The favoured dockyards of the eighteenth century were Portsmouth and Plymouth, and much Admiralty investment was concentrated there; at Plymouth, indeed, the Admiralty founded a new town, Dock, for the shipyard workers in 1689, while Portsmouth properly denoted the dockyard area with the majority of the inhabitants living in Portsea which originated as a suburb in the 1730s. By mid-century both had populations of over 10,000 and by 1801 Plymouth had 40,000 and Portsmouth 33,000.[27]

The ports belonged to a very old and traditional type of town with a well-established social structure headed by dynasties of greater merchants, filled in the middling ranks with those involved in the fitting out and provisioning of ships and sailors, and largely supplied with shipyard and boatyard workers, seamen and their hangers-on, and dockers, in the lower levels. They had corporations of long-standing, and if these were of varying degrees of competence and corruption they were at least a recognised form of established municipal authority. The fast-growing ports certainly faced social stresses as well as economic opportunities during the eighteenth century; they were digesting a great increase and diversification in the numbers and types of 'quayside' industries and their workers, at the same time as housing and services came under pressure from straightforward trade and port expansion. Expansion, however, was within the framework of an essentially stable and orderly society; if the dockyard towns could not draw on the same tradition of social order as the ports, they could substitute the disciplines of naval control. There was here not so much a new form of urban society as an old one writ large.

The new form of society was in the manufacturing towns, itself a novel term in the early eighteenth century, although many instances

---

[27] Population figures from Corfield, *Impact of Towns*, pp. 15, 44; Chalklin, *Provincial Towns* pp. 13, 20, 23–4, 44, 48–51. Southampton did not top the 20,000 mark until the 1830s; its great growth period, as an Atlantic terminal, came in the second half of the nineteenth century.

could have been cited before 1700 of concentrations of textile manufacture in old towns: Norwich, the largest of them all, but among the second-rank regional centres Canterbury, Colchester, Coventry, or Exeter would certainly have been numbered among the textile towns. Defoe, one of the first to speak of 'manufacturing towns', captured their novelty in the 1720s:

> Let the Curious examine the great Towns of Manchester, Warrington, Macclesfield, Hallifax, Leeds, Wakefield, Sheffield, Birmingham, Froom, Taunton, Tiverton, and many Others. Some of these are meer Villages; the highest Magistrate in them is a Constable, and few or no Families of Gentry among them; yet they are full of Wealth and full of People, and daily encreasing in both; all of which is occasion'd be the meer Strength of Trade, and the growing Manufactures establish'd in them.[28]

Defoe's glimpse into the future was inspired if not 100 per cent accurate; he could be awarded eight out of ten (literally, out of eleven) for spotting industrial winners, four which were destined to lead the first division and four to become solid members of the second eleven. His forecasting mistakes are at least as interesting as his emphasis on the absence of gentry patronage or traditions of corporate government, and its customary accompaniment of craft organisations, as common ingredients in commercial success. Frome, Taunton, and Tiverton certainly do not appear on anyone's list of the great industrial towns of the nineteenth century. Yet in the 1720s Tiverton was the chief manufacturing centre of serges, in the sergemaking district, which included Taunton, that was centred commercially on the Exeter market and whose trade, mainly in exports, was orchestrated by Exeter merchants. With a population of around 9,000 Tiverton was a more considerable manufacturing town than Birmingham, Manchester, or Leeds at this time. In the event it stagnated in the eighteenth century, with a collapse in the demand for serges which had already begun when Defoe was writing, and actually lost population. Frome, the centre of Somerset's fine cloth industry, went through a similar cycle of prosperity and decline, with a fifty-year lag.[29]

These three textile towns which fell by the wayside in the course of the eighteenth or early nineteenth centuries, however, were at the

---

[28] Quoted by Corfield, *Impact of Towns*, p. 23.
[29] C. Wilson, *England's Apprenticeship, 1603–1763* (1965), pp. 189, 290. Clark, 'Introduction', in Clark, ed., *Transformation*, p. 26. Chalklin, *Provincial Towns*, p. 33. Clapham, *Early Railway Age*, p. 46.

time of Defoe's writing using precisely the same spinning and weaving technology, and precisely the same mercantile organisation, as those with whom the future lay. Of Defoe's 'winners' only two, Birmingham and Sheffield, were non-textile towns. The expansion and prosperity of the rest depended, at least until the 1780s, on hand spinning and handloom weaving and on the enterprise of merchant-manufacturers who organised and financed increasingly elaborate and extensive put-ting-out systems. Manchester passed the 20,000 population mark in the 1750s and Leeds in the 1780s, and probably both had equalled or surpassed Norwich, also reliant on traditional methods and organi-sation in its cloth manufacturing, before the factory and mechanised production made much impact.The urbanisation of industry, in other words, preceded 'modern industrialisation' of factories and machines, chiefly because urban locations offered advantages in access to markets, merchants, services, and labour supplies, particularly of skilled labour, which outweighed the cheaper labour of cottage and village industry. The new machines of the industrial revolution, par-ticularly the spinning machines, were in any case water powered, and perhaps a majority of the great new spinning mills of the 1770s and 1780s, employing their hundreds of women and children, were to be found in isolated rural or small village locations rather than in the major towns. At the same time urban water-power sources were developed with considerable engineering ingenuity, for example in the small towns of the Gloucestershire cloth district in and around Stroud, but above all in the ring of satellite cotton towns round Man-chester that were growing very fast in the closing decades of the cen-tury, and in the second tier of West Riding woollen and worsted towns.

It was in 1781 that the Manchester manufacturers went, 'Steam Mill Mad', as Boulton reported to Watt on the effects of the introduc-tion of the rotative steam engine which could be applied to driving spinning machinery.[30] Before then there had been scarcely a handful of mills actually in Manchester, which acted rather as the commercial centre of the cotton industry and the place where the specialised finish-ing processes were carried out, than as the location of the primary spinning and weaving. Thereafter mill-building went on apace; by 1802 Manchester and Salford had more than fifty spinning mills, and

---

[30] Quoted by A. E. Musson, 'Industrial Motive Power in the United Kingdom, 1800–70', *Economic History Review*, 2nd ser., 29 (1976) p. 429.

by 1815 half as many again, virtually all steam-driven, by this time including the first few mills housing powerlooms. The mill chimney had become the characteristic, dominant, feature of the skyline; but it was still much less dominant in the secondary cotton towns like Bury or Oldham, which used a high proportion of water power, or in the other textile towns such as those of the West Riding woollens and worsteds, Nottingham with its lace, or Coventry with its ribbons, where the adoption of the mill or factory form of organisation as well as the adoption of steam power were much more gradual.[31]

As late as 1850 well over half the steam power used in manufacturing – that is, excluding mining, which geology made into a largely non-urban industry – was in the textile industries, and a third or more was in the cotton mills alone.[32] Before 1815 the concentration of the early steam engines in cotton spinning mills, and of course in copper mines and collieries, was much more marked.[33] This might prompt the conclusion that factory chimneys, smoke, and grime were becoming part of the urban scene in the very late eighteenth century, and before 1815, only in a few, exceptional, cotton towns. This would certainly be true of the chimneys, but not of the smoke. It was Sheffield which struck Lord Torrington in 1789 as 'a great black manufacturing town', and Sheffield had no factories, no steam engines; it was a town of small workshops, and its cutlery, files, and chisels were made with hand tools and water-driven tilt-hammers and grinding wheels. It was black, as Torrington observed from one of the surrounding hills, because there were 'in the valley beneath, the furnaces vomiting forth their amazing fires, which make this country in an eternal smoke'.[34] It was, indeed, the industries which used coal as a fuel which were creating dark and dirty towns, not those which were adopting powered machinery. Birmingham, with its metal-working workshops, its buttons, and its screws, was one such, but the real dirt was in the smaller satellite towns where the heavy forge work

---

[31] Ibid., pp. 417, 431.

[32] Ibid., p. 435. The precise figures, but not the general proportions of industrial distribution, are modified by J. W. Kanefsky, 'Motive Power in British Industry and the Accuracy of the 1870 Factory Return', Economic History Review, 2nd ser., 32 (1979), pp. 360–75.

[33] For the industrial distribution of the early steam engines, see J. R. Harris, 'The Employment of Steam Power in the Eighteenth Century', History, 52 (1967).

[34] Andrews, ed., Torrington Diaries, 'A Tour in the Midlands, 1789', p. 170. Wolverhampton, in 1792, was termed 'a large black ill-paved town' by Torrington, and Wednesbury 'another overgrown village, blacken'd with its trees and hedges by the forge fires', pp. 449–50.

was done and where there were collieries and iron works: Wolverhampton, Walsall, Willenhall,Wednesbury, Darlaston, Dudley, and the rest which were already getting known as the Black Country. Merthyr Tydfil was another, the classic one-industry iron town, growing from nothing in 1750 to be the second largest town in Wales by 1801 and the largest by 1821, all blast furnaces and rolling mills and 17,000 people entirely dependent on them. The Potteries, notoriously five towns as well as Stoke and never happily united into a single city even in the twentieth century, made a fourth grimy district, an embryonic conurbation which housed more than 20,000 people by 1801 and in 1811 was larger than Bolton or Bradford, Huddersfield or Oldham. There were some engine houses and chimneys in the Potteries by the late eighteenth century, but they were used in preparatory processes for driving clay and flint mills and colour grinding pans, while the main production processes remained practically untouched by mechanisation until the 1840s; the dominant feature of the industrial landscape before then was the coal-fired bottle oven.

Manufacturing towns before 1815 were thus not, in essence, factory towns; and only the minority among them whose industries centred round furnaces, forges, and ovens were becoming visually unattractive and physically repellent through their smoke and grime. Even this factor can be exaggerated, since in all the larger towns domestic fires were the main smoke producers, and the household market probably accounted for more than half of total British coal consumption at the beginning of the nineteenth century. The distinction is useful, however, for it indicates that this initial phase of urban growth, by and large before factories and before steam-powered machinery, produced only a handful of towns which were strange, alien, and potentially alarming. Thus of the seventeen largest provincial towns which had populations of over 20,000 in 1811, eight were ports or dockyard towns, among which only Sunderland, wholly devoted to the coal trade and coal shipping, was perhaps entirely alien to traditional elites. The other nine were manufacturing towns, and they are harder to categorise; but only two, Sheffield and Stoke, were definitely, and a further two, Birmingham and Manchester, possibly, seriously soot blackened; six of the nine, including Birmingham, Manchester and Sheffield, had theatres and assembly rooms as early as the 1770s, and merchant-gentry elites that were cultured and had some contacts with neighbouring gentry society; only three, the cotton towns of Stockport and Bolton, and Stoke, may have been alien in the way that Sunderland was alien.[35] It may indeed be more useful to visualise the groups of secondary manufacturing towns, of which only Bolton and Stockport had as yet passed the 20,000 population mark, as the radically new feature of the period before 1815, phenomena remote from previous urban experience, raw in their stark structure of industrial workers and employers unrelieved by any considerable commercial or professional elements, visually and architecturally mean and monotonous, committed to unremitting work and devoid of cultural trappings. These were the cotton towns of south-east Lancashire, outside Manchester; the towns of the Black Country, outside Birmingham; and in lesser degree, because many of them had ancient urban traditions and were not mushroom growths, the West Riding cloth towns, outside Leeds. They did not cause much of a stir, simply because they were not as yet very large and hence were fairly unobtrusive; but they contained the essence of industrial-urban society.

The new-style manufacturing towns of the front rank which were emerging in the second half of the eighteenth century were obviously different in economic functions and occupational structures from the larger seaports, which they were beginning to equal in size. But while contemporaries were correct to stress the essential distinction that the former were peopled almost entirely by tradesmen and manufacturers, while the latter had more variety and colour in their social structures, the broad similarities should not be overlooked. To start with, none of them were narrowly based economically on a single industry or branch of an industry: their directly manufacturing activities were diverse, tending to a concentration on the more skilled and specialised finishing and assembling processes, and in addition they were all important regional centres with the variety and range of trades that implied. Manchester, for example, although in many ways the leading exemplar of a 'new town' of this sort, was already a considerable enough town in 1653 to have been made a parliamentary borough, short-lived, in the Protectorate.[36] To be sure, in the second-rank manufacturing towns it may also have been literally true that the industrial workers did not form a majority of the working population; but in their case the supporting and economically dependent role of the

---

[35]   Torrington visited the new theatre in Sheffield (built in 1773 to replace the original 1763 building) in 1789 and approved of it warmly: *ibid.*, 'A Tour in the Midlands, 1789', p. 171. For the merchant-gentry of Leeds see R. G. Wilson, *Gentlemen Merchants: The Merchant Community in Leeds, 1700–1830* (Manchester, 1971).

[36]   The Instrument of Government, 1653, cl. X, S. R. Gardiner, *The Constitutional Documents of the Puritan Revolution, 1625-60* (Oxford, 1947 edn), p. 408.

non-manufacturing labourers and tradesmen was obvious. Of greater significance, the manufacturer, as an entrepreneur and employer, was typically a merchant-manufacturer. The modern industrialist, as owner of the means of production and direct employer and manager of the production workers, was of course beginning to appear: this is what Richard Arkwright, Robert Peel, Samuel Oldknow, Benjamin Gott, James Marshall, Josiah Wedgwood, Matthew Boulton, and the others in the well-known gallery of the early captains of industry were all about. They were the harbingers of the future, but down to 1815, and indeed for many further decades, the great bulk of industrial production was organised and managed on more traditional lines, while the early industrialists themselves were successful precisely because they were good at trading and marketing. The largest industrial employers in 1815 were the manufacturers who had thousands of outworkers, handloom weavers, on their books, perhaps combining this with the more direct employment of a few hundred spinners in spinning mills which they owned.

The implications of this were twofold. First, the merchant-manufacturers in the ordinary running of their businesses had to maintain extensive and regular contacts not merely with a multitude of outworkers both in town and in the surrounding country villages, but also with the rest of the country, particularly with London, where they found their markets. Especially if these markets included exports they moved in the same orbit as the great overseas merchants who formed the mercantile aristocracy of the seaports. It would be unduly mechanistic to claim that the whole aura of sophisticated and refined mercantile culture, itself enmeshed with aristocratic taste and influences in fashion, manners, and fine arts, automatically rubbed off on everyone in the provinces who became a merchant on a large scale; but clearly the channels were open for this cultural flow. Second, since factory or mill workers still formed such a small element of the industrial workforce, the great majority of workers in the manufacturing towns, despite the obvious occupational differences between those in cotton, wool, metals, and pots, lived in broadly similar conditions with similar social and industrial relations. These in turn did not differ greatly from conditions in the great seaports. This was very evident in housing, where there was a simultaneous development in the last quarter of the century of building on a large scale specifically for working-class occupation, as distinct from earlier improvisations and tenementing of once-grander houses. Courtyard tenements, cramming the maximum number of dwellings on to narrow plots with tunnel access to a street, and back-to-backs, placing the largest amount of housing on rather larger plots, made their appearance at this time in Liverpool, Manchester, Leeds, Hull, Birmingham, and Nottingham, for example.[37]

There were differences within the family of large towns. Liverpool, for instance, already went in for cellar dwellings on a scale of insalubrity unknown elsewhere; and there appears to have been a north-south division, if Birmingham is temporarily made an honorary member of the north, in the sense that the back-to-back never became common in London, Bristol, Portsmouth, or Plymouth, where terraced cottages for the workers were the norm. There were also great differences in working conditions and in the pattern of employment. There were many more openings for women to have jobs in the textile towns than in the metal towns – though in the Black Country they worked in the nailmaking forges – or in the seaports, where the gainfully employed were thought to be all domestic servants or prostitutes. Work on the quays, and later docks, was more intermittent and casual than in any other occupation. At the other extreme skilled artisans in the metal trades or in the dockyards could expect to be in regular work; while domestic outworkers who owned their own equipment were more independent than those who did not, but hired loom and frame from an employer. Differences and distinctions in grades and conditions, such as these, meant that there was nothing like a uniform or coherent urban working class, even if the difficulties of communicating between the separate towns had not been so great. On the whole, at the lower level, each town was its own society, with links to the surrounding country from which so many of the town's inhabitants had migrated and with which there were many working connections, rather than links with other towns; except that in some of the traditional crafts, especially in the skilled building trades, men tramped from town to town on recognised job-finding routes. And on the whole that society was small scale and cellular, revolving round family, neighbourhood, pub, and small workshop, loom-shed, or workroom, in a manner which for those who did not have the historian's advantage of knowing what was to come after exhibited much stronger

[37]   S. D. Chapman, 'Working-Class Housing in Nottingham', and M. W. Beresford, 'The Back-to-Back House in Leeds, 1787–1937', both in S. D. Chapman, ed., *The History of Working-Class Housing* (Newton Abbot, 1971). Chalklin, *Provincial Towns*, pp. 196–220.

signs of continuity with traditional forms than marks of revolutionary changes. In a somewhat paradoxical way the period when urban expansion first became marked, but when urban society still remained in a minority position which might have been expected to highlight its peculiarities, was in fact a period when it seemed familiar, comfortable, and unthreatening, in a remarkable number of different ways, to aristocracy, gentry, bourgeoisie, and working people.

III

Urban society became more complicated, more stratified and more regulated in the course of the nineteenth century. It became more settled and accepted, in the sense that by 1900 the great majority of its members were town-born and the days when first-generation towndwellers who had moved in from the country, or from Ireland, formed from half to nearly three-quarters of the adult populations of almost all the larger towns, were half a century away.[38] Whether it had grown to maturity may be doubted, if the concept of maturity implies stability, for that had not been attained. What cannot be doubted is that at some point in the nineteenth century, closer to 1881 than 1851, urban society became the normal setting of more than half of the British people, and that by 1914 it so dominated the nation that in figures, if not in sentiment, it was the nation. Yet one of the paradoxes of the century was that as urban living became normal and typical, rather than unusual and unrepresentative, towns became less familiar, less understood, and less acceptable to the educated and propertied classes. More precisely, the triumph of urbanisation proved to be a socially divisive more than a socially unifying process, and the divisions within Victorian urban society, between the agreeable and the disagreeable, the comfortable and the bleak, the amusing and the shocking, the pleasing and the menacing, were sharper than any eighteenth-century divisions between town and country.

The social divisions and tensions within the nation – never so simple as the conventional three-class wisdom suggests – had many roots: the ownership and organisation of industry and business, the distribution of wealth and property, the distribution of incomes, education, occupation, and religion are the chief elements. The specifically urban element in the development of social structure and in the expression

---

[38] Michael Anderson, *Family Structure in Nineteenth-Century Lancashire* (Cambridge, 1971), p. 73.

of social conflict lay in the physical environment of the towns, which was the most typical setting within which the primary factors operated; in the residential social segregation, which came to characterise all the larger towns, and which emphasised the separate identities of different social groups even if it did not necessarily stir up conflict between them; and in the physical proximity of groups at the margin, which nurtured the passion for fine distinctions and subtle nuances of differentiation of status which marked all levels of Victorian society, and were only slightly less cherished by the working classes than by the middle classes. Towering over all these urban features was the growth in the sheer size of the largest towns and the second-rank industrial and commercial towns, which so far outdistanced the country towns that remained simple market centres as to leave them in a different, traditional, 'Barchester' world – more part of rural or ecclesiastical society than of Victorian urban society.

The increase in scale lay at the root of a profound change in the urban consciousness of the intellectual and political classes, which surfaced in public discourse and policy proposals in the 1830s and 1840s not only directly concerning health and housing in towns, but also relating to education, religion, and policing, which all came to be seen as primarily urban problems; only the poor law, anachronistically, was still treated as essentially a rural matter.[39] There were many reasons for this concern with the towns, and motives of self-interest and self-preservation may well have outweighed the stirrings of social conscience or the promptings of brotherly love: fear of the disorderly, subversive, and perhaps insurrectionary potential of unregulated and masterless urban masses, and dread of the uncontrollable spread of disease from the great unwashed to polite society, were powerful reasons for concern. But at the same time as the rulers, the policy-makers, the critics, and those involved in forming what they convinced one another was 'informed public opinion' were paying increasing attention to the towns – by which were meant the somewhat loosely defined 'large' towns – they, and their social groups, were becoming increasingly distanced from, and detached from, large districts in the towns and large areas of urban life, which they thereupon perceived as 'problems'. The other prime effect of the increase in scale, besides serving to focus attention on towns, was to divide and atomise urban society into separate social parts, so that in many locations

[39] For fuller treatment of these topics, see Volumes 2 and 3.

and in many respects urban society ceased to exist as a coherent structure and became more of a collection of distinct communities or social structures sharing a common infrastructure of buildings and services, cohabiting in an atmosphere of mutual ignorance and suspicion.

Disengagement and retreat into select segregation was most obvious among aristocratic and gentry circles. By the 1850s the habit of keeping town houses had all but vanished, except in London and, for a remnant of non-metropolitian lairds, in Edinburgh. In Edinburgh, indeed, it is more accurate to say that the grandest and most elegant of the town houses in the New Town were taken over by a professional and ecclesiastical elite, for it remained a capital city for advocates and ministers of the Church of Scotland though not one for aristocratic high society or for politicians. Elsewhere some towns became so altered in character that the gentry were driven away by the dirt and smoke: thus the charms of Preston as a market town, port, and social centre were obliterated by the rise of the mill chimneys which had made it into a large cotton spinning town by mid-century. In most cases, however, the gentry opted out of continuing to keep houses in the provincial towns, and were not squeezed out by the growth of manufacturing or any other economic change that might render a town disagreeable. They opted out of the likes of York and Stamford, Shrewsbury and Carmarthen, if anything because such towns remained too quiet, dull, old-fashioned, and unexciting, not because they became too populous or plebeian.[40] County families continued to patronise race meetings, assemblies, annual balls, and other social events with a county town setting, but they came as visitors and no longer as seasonal residents. Improvements in communications, oiling the wheels of fashion, concentrated the seasons of town residence more and more exclusively on London and on the more agreeable resorts, at home or on the Continent, where the gentry and aristocracy could congregate together.

In London the aristocratic presence was highly visible, highly compact, and increasingly divorced from the rest of the city. The 1820s were a time of growing rivalry in pomp and display among the town mansions or aristocratic hotels, the response of the private sector to the schemes of Nash and George IV for giving the imperial capital a suitably royal and monumented facelift. The extravagance and

---

[40]   David W. Howell, *Patriarchs and Parasites: The Gentry of South-West Wales in the Eighteenth Century* (Cardiff, 1986), p. 190, noting the town houses of the gentry in Carmarthen.

splendour of the conversion of Holdernesse House into Londonderry House, Park Lane, by the third Marquess, and the refacing and extension of Apsley House for the Duke of Wellington, were but leading examples of a general process of enlarging and embellishing the leading town houses to cater for high society's competitive drive for private ballrooms or private art galleries. Building, or extensive rebuilding, continued, as with Hertford House off Park Lane which the Marquess of Hertford built in the 1850s largely to house his art collection, and which he left to his illegitimate son Sir Richard Wallace, whose widow in turn left the collection to the nation. A few of the great houses vanished, as when the magnificent sixteenth-century Northumberland House was demolished in 1874 to make way for Northumberland Avenue, and the Duke was forced back on Syon House as his nearest approach to a town residence. On the whole, the great aristocratic town mansions survived in full residential and social working order until 1914. They had to share their space in Piccadilly and Mayfair with clubs, which in some respects were the poorer gentry's substitute for a private residence, with hotels – the Ritz appeared in 1906 – and with the wealthiest, most socially acceptable, or most determinedly aspiring members of the non-landed monied and propertied classes. Denied continued exclusive possession of their eighteenth-century territory, by commercial pressures and rising property values, the aristocratic and fashionable world rapidly settled Belgravia as it developed from the late 1820s through to the 1850s, a district of elegant squares and frontages, not of individual palaces, but emphatically an aristocratic district.

The ruling class did not make as emphatic and imposing an architectural statement in their capital city as did, for example, the Habsburg nobility in nineteenth-century Vienna.[41] One reason was that the ruling class in Britain was less a matter of status and precedence, which required outward show, than of influence and connections, which required indoor splendour and facilities; another was that the English (and the Scottish and Welsh) lavished their main architectural attentions on their country houses, which were their power bases. Even so, Victorian London had a well defined, and opulent, aristocratic quarter; and its demands for service, food and drink, fashionable clothes, luxuries of many kinds, and entertainment, while seasonal, were of decisive importance to the economy of the entire West End.

---

[41]   Donald J. Olsen, *The City as a Work of Art: London, Paris, Vienna* (1986), pp. 13–15.

In that part of the year which was not appropriated by the winter and spring season in London, or by residence on their country estates for shooting and hunting, the nomadic gentry came to concentrate their periods of recuperation and refreshment on a relatively small selection of resorts which were able to maintain the right tone of seclusion and enjoyability. Bath was largely abandoned, having become too common; even Cheltenham, growing fast in the 1820s as a more sedate and less crowded version of Bath, attracted retired people of means, military and naval officers, and Indian and colonial servants, rather than the aristocracy. Alone among the inland spas in the late nineteenth century, Harrogate enjoyed a reputation for attracting aristocratic society, England's answer to Wiesbaden, Marienbad, or Karlsbad, which were the most stylish and cosmopolitian curing-grounds for the nobility of Europe from the 1860s.[42] At the seaside, also, the aristocracy and gentry ceased to visit the widely scattered small resorts, in family groups, as they had done in the late eighteenth century; withdrew from Brighton and Weymouth by the 1840s, with the demise of royal patronage; and abandoned the great majority of the resorts to the middle classes and the superior working classes. By 1871 probably only Hastings and Torquay, out of the forty-eight seaside resorts listed in the census, enjoyed aristocratic favour; Hastings because it was quiet, dignified, and at the same time sufficiently inexpensive to appeal to impoverished gentry, and Torquay because it offered a winter season for those who could not afford London.[43]

From the 1830s onwards the aristocracy might be wintering in Cannes or Nice, and thirty years later could be heading for Deauville or Biarritz or any one of a dozen French and Italian resorts. Rail travel and Channel steamers had opened out, and virtually created out of former tiny fishing villages, a whole new array of eminently agreeable towns which greatly expanded the horizons of aristocratic urban experience, although introducing little greater variety into its quality. The effect within Britain, however, was to narrow down and restrict the range of towns of which aristocracy and gentry had the direct experience of residence and of forming, for considerable parts of the year, part of an urban community. This contraction of the aristocratic element in urban society, and its near total concentration on the capital

---

[42] Waller, *Town, City and Nation*, p. 134; E. J. Hobsbawm, *The Age of Capital, 1848–75* (1975), pp. 204–5.
[43] Pimlott, *Englishman's Holiday*, pp. 114, 269.

and just one or two other towns, in some ways left the stage clear for the non-traditional, non-landed, upper middle class to supply the dominant urban elites. But it was also offset, in some degree, by the role of some landowners, as individual estate owners rather than as members of a social group, as urban landlords.

This was a role which expanded almost automatically with the growth and physical expansion of towns, but fortuitously in its particular locations since it depended very largely on the lucky accidents of long-owned and inherited fields and farms chancing to lie in the path of urban development. Thus, Sir John Ramsden owned the major part of Huddersfield in the 1880s not because he had created the town but because the Ramsden family estate already controlled most of the land in the direction of Huddersfield's rapid expansion after the 1830s; although being a shrewd businessman Sir John did take the precaution of acquiring one or two small adjoining estates in order to protect his land monopoly.[44] Much the same can be said of the many other landowners who were turned into very large, often locally dominant, urban landlords by the process of urban growth. A questionnaire addressed to 261 provincial towns in England and Wales in 1886 revealed that at least 109 of them had 'large areas' owned by individual ground landlords, most of whom were also large landowners of the landed classes. On the other hand, no less than 134 towns replied that they did not have any large ground landlords at all; Halifax, for example, close to Huddersfield geographically and industrially, and in size and rate of growth, claimed to have no large or particularly noticeable ground owners.[45]

It was thus largely a matter of chance whether any particular town had any strategically placed large landowners, made wealthy and influential by the course of nineteenth-century expansion, just as it was a matter of chance whether any particular large landowner found himself enriched by crops of houses on his estate. The one area in which landowners perhaps created their own urban wealth by their own initiatives, as distinct from receiving it as a present from market forces which they did not control, was in the creation of some of

---

[44] Richard Dennis, *English Industrial Cities of the Nineteenth Century* (Cambridge, 1984), pp. 148–9, 157.

[45] *SC on Town Holdings*, PP 1887, XIII, questionnaire circulated by Charles Harrison, solicitor, pp. 677–812. Many of the large landowners who were significant urban landlords are listed by D. Spring, 'English Landowners and Nineteenth-Century Industrialism', in J. T. Ward and R. G. Wilson, eds., *Land and Industry* (Newton Abbot, 1971), pp. 39–40, 42–3.

the new resorts which grew on virgin sites. Classic examples were Eastbourne, conjured by the Duke of Devonshire out of virtually nothing but fields and cliffs in the thirty years after 1849; Skegness, raised by the Earl of Scarborough on some unpromising Lincolnshire sand dunes from the 1870s; and Bexhill, propelled into unlikely but successful high-class rivalry with neighbouring Eastbourne and Hastings by the efforts of Earl de la Warr in the 1880s and 1890s. There were many more landowner promotions among the nineteenth-century resorts, some successful, some not. There were also many new, or rapidly expanding, resorts which were not the creatures of landowner initiatives: Brighton, Blackpool, Clacton, or Southend, to cite examples across the spectrum of social reputations.[46]

There has been much discussion among urban and social historians of the effects of the structure of landownership on the physical and social character of urban developments. The picture is a complicated one, but it is clear that unified ownership of a sizeable tract of potential building land did not necessarily and uniformly lead to the development of high-class residential districts or towns of a superior and elegant style even amongst the new resorts; in the working towns, where industry, trade, commerce, and the professions were carried on, the connection between unified ownership and fashionable, or comfortable middle-class, districts was even less certain. Local topography, accessibility, proximity of industries, especially the obnoxious ones, and the character of adjoining areas were among the determinants of the social configuration of new urban developments which frequently cut across or negated the influence of patterns of land-ownership.[47] It is also clear that in many towns those who became large urban landlords also became powerful and influential figures in the political and social life of the town, and this happened whether or not the landowner attempted to, or succeeded in, peopling his urban property with a superior class of residents. The Duke of Devonshire and his agent dominated the life of Eastbourne until the 1890s, and in the 1890s the Earl de la Warr was personally the leader of Bexhill society: these were instances where the towns were indeed successfully moulded in the image of their aristocratic owners. The Earl of Scarborough and his agent, however, were similarly honoured

[46] David Cannadine, *Lords and Landlords: The Aristocracy and the Towns,1774–1967* (Leicester, 1980), pp. 62–6, 408–12. John K. Walton, *The English Seaside Resort: A Social History, 1750–1914* (Leicester, 1983), chap. 5.

[47] Cannadine, *Lords and Landlords*, pp. 391–416, summarises this discussion and examines its historiography.

and treated with deference by Skegness, although the town was deliberately developed for lower-class trippers and had no pretensions to a high tone.

Moreover, individual aristocrats were the uncrowned kings of several of the largest towns, and whether their urban properties housed the wealthiest and smartest quarter in town or the industrial and working-class areas, they were treated as grandees. In Cardiff, virtually the creation of the second Marquess of Bute who built the first coal docks in the 1830s and owned much of the land on which the expanding town was built, the Bute interest was dominant until the 1870s, while the Earls of Derby were continuously influential in Liverpool society and politics even though their party allegiances veered back and forth between Whig and Tory. These two families had dignified seats in or close to their towns, Cardiff Castle and Knowsley, just as the Devonshires and de la Warrs had residences in Eastbourne and Bexhill, and this real presence no doubt helped the aristocratic influence. The Dukes of Norfolk, however, were rarely seen in Sheffield, where they owned a large industrial and working-class district, but non-residence did not curtail their influence in the town. The reverse could equally well be true: Lord Calthorpe and his agents carefully nursed the transformation of his Edgbaston estate into the home of Birmingham's elite, but the Calthorpes, although they temporarily reverted from being absentee landowners living in Hampshire to residing in reach of Birmingham at Perry Hall in the middle years of the century, never established themselves as the leaders of that elite.[48]

The social significance of the rise of the aristocracy as large urban landowners thus varied widely from place to place. In essence there were three groups of towns: those which had no outstanding landowners, were built on land in fragmented ownership, and were predominantly freehold towns; those which did have large tracts of building land in single, often aristocratic, ownership, were leasehold towns, but had no dominant and influential aristocratic interest; and finally those where dominant estates and dominant influence went hand in hand. Manchester, Leeds, Newcastle, and Bristol were leading members of the first group, to which Brighton and Blackpool also

---

[48]   M. J. Daunton, *Coal Metropolis: Cardiff, 1870–1914* (Leicester, 1977), pp. 167–9. P. J. Waller, *Democracy and Sectarianism: A Political and Social History of Liverpool, 1868–1939* (Liverpool, 1981), pp. 71–4, 179–80. Cannadine, *Lords and Landlords*, pp. 41–5, 155.

belonged; Birmingham, Bradford (Earl of Rosse), Stockport (Lord Egerton of Tatton), and Sunderland (Bishop of Durham, Sir Hedworth Williamsom of Whitburn) may be placed in the second category; while Barrow-in-Furness (Duke of Devonshire), Preston (Earl of Derby), Southport (the Scarisbricks), or Whitehaven (Earl of Lonsdale) can readily be added to Cardiff, Huddersfield, Liverpool, Sheffield, Bexhill, and Eastbourne in the final group without in any way completing the roll-call.[49]

Where an aristocratic presence on the ground was translated into effective social and political leadership it seems to have been the result of a combination of factors: the absolute size and wealth of the particular urban estate, and its relative size in relation to that of the town and the town's business and cultural areas; residence and personal appearances that were not too infrequent; and personal commitment, or at least involvement of a local estate office and a team of local estate officials, in the cultivation of an interest. Three stages have been discerned in the Victorian life-cycle of these 'aristocratic' towns. A phase of rapid expansion and building on the estate lasting, in most cases, until the 1860s or 1870s, during which paternalist direction and control were as evident in local government as in the provision of basic utilities and amenities, and the landowner acted as the focus both for deferential and obsequious adherents seeking advancement and power, and for radical opponents of privilege and dependence also seeking advancement and power. The second phase, in the 1870s and 1880s, saw the triumph of the municipal critics of aristocratic domination, the flowering of civic independence, and the relegation of the landowners to a lower profile in social and political affairs. Finally, from 1890 to 1914, the liberated and self-confident cities turned to their erstwhile aristocratic patrons as decorative and ornamental figureheads, and made them lord mayors and mayors, dignified ceremonial figures whose rank rubbed off on the municipalities but who had become harmless and powerless. The third Marquess of Bute, becoming mayor of Cardiff in 1891, was 'the first peer to hold the highest municipal office in any English or Welsh borough for several generations – certainly since the Reform Act', and he was followed in the next twenty years by a parade of the major local landowners

---

[49] The listing is illustrative, not comprehensive. Complete analysis would require, in particular, detailed local knowledge of the society and politics of the 109 towns which were stated, in 1886, to have one or more very considerable groundowners.

into the mayoralties of Belfast, Dudley, Longton, Liverpool, Preston, and Sheffield.[50]

In theory a marked distinction might have been expected between the urban elites of the first two groups of towns, able to produce their own leaders, their own ethos, and their own culture without aristocratic interference and free from any taint of toadying to aristocratic whims or values; and those of the third group, whose separate and independent social development might have been stunted and distorted by deference and paternalism. In practice no such clear differentiation between the upper middle classes of the major Victorian towns is readily apparent, although the striking impression made by Manchester, Birmingham, and Leeds, at rather different times and in different ways, in national political life, in forming public opinion, and in intellectual and cultural life, in contrast to the more muted and conformist showing of Liverpool or Sheffield, may owe something to these influences. Neither was any differentiation more discernible in the tier of rather smaller towns where direct contact between leading business and professional men and the local landowner and his agents was more feasible as an instrument of social control. The upper middle class of Cardiff, the leading coal shippers and shipowners, was no more deferential or subservient than that of Newcastle, indeed was possibly less so since a higher proportion of Newcastle's leading citizens had family or property links with Northumbrian county society, and Cardiff's merchants were, at least by the 1880s, defiantly independent of the Bute interest.[51] Moreover, while it is true that the top layer of society in landowner-created resorts was very different from that in the great manufacturing and port towns, there was not a great deal of difference between Eastbourne, where Devonshire was an active influence, and Bournemouth, where the two or three considerable landowners chose to remain passive and unobtrusive.[52] Differences in the top level of urban society were primarily functional. Resort-town elites, heavily weighted with retired people and rentiers, were more socially conservative, more preoccupied with the conventions of gentility and respectability, and more derivative and imitative in their opinions, than the elites of the great industrial and commercial towns with their business and professional leaders. The presence or

[50]   Cannadine, Lords and Landlords, pp. 46–52.
[51]   Daunton, Coal Metropolis, pp. 155–9.
[52]   Richard Roberts, 'The Corporation as Impresario: The Municipal Provision of Entertainment in Victorian and Edwardian Bournemouth', in John K. Walton and James Walvin, eds., Leisure in Britain, 1780–1939 (Manchester, 1983), pp. 140–2

absence of an active and interventionist urban aristocrat was of marginal importance.

The limited range of landowner influence was a function of town size. In a very small town it remained possible for the whole community to feel very conscious that it lived in the shadow of the castle, and in Arundel or Petworth, Alnwick or Stamford, the small middle class of lawyers, other professional men, and larger merchants were as deferential towards the Duke of Norfolk, Lord Leconfield, the Duke of Northumberland, or the Marquess of Exeter as were the humbler townsfolk, down to 1914 and beyond. The very large towns were simply too big and too complicated in their business and social arrangements for this type of personal attachment to function, so that the aristocratic element, where it existed at all, was no more than a minor thread in the fabric of the urban middle classes, whose pattern was determined by more weighty, and more uniform, considerations of income, wealth, religion, education, and political party. The aristocratic influence, at least as a matter of sentiment and prejudice, may indeed have worked more strongly on the lower middle class and the deferential working classes, especially where they saw their prosperity, and their town's prosperity, as being closely identified with a single, preferably titled, landowner.

Ownership was, therefore, more important as a bond joining certain aristocrats and members of the gentry to the urban scene and linking their fortune to the health of certain towns, than as a factor in moulding the texture of urban society. The idea and practice of the aristocratic life was, however, a countervailing force which exerted a substantial influence on Victorian urban society, both in furnishing some of its values and attitudes, and in inducing some of its wealthier members into partially or completely deserting the city. The gentrification of the bourgeoisie in manners, behaviour, family life, and social conventions, frequently remarked and most marked among the upper middle class of the leading businessmen, industrialists, and members of the older professions, was clearly something which happened in towns.[53] It is not so clear that it was an urban phenomenon, in the sense of a socialising process deriving from the specifically urban character of the conditions in which these middle classes had their being. Acceptance of the model of gentility, and of its rules of social conduct, evolved by the aristocracy and gentry came, it can be argued, because

[53] Lawrence Stone and Jeanne C. Fawtier Stone, *An Open Elite? England, 1540–1880* (Oxford, 1984), pp. 409, 411.

that aristocratic elite was so dominant in the political and social life of the nation and because its domination was not so rigidly exclusive as to render unattainable hopes of some degree of social acceptance and assimilation, through emulation on the part of the wealthy middle classes.[54] Such acceptance did not come automatically nor was it unchallenged within the bourgeoisie. Otherwise there would have been no call for Matthew Arnold's contemptuous dismissal of the crass materialism and naked money-worship of the middle class in *Culture and Anarchy* (1868); neither would it have been possible to claim to identify an independent, non-deferential and non-aristocratic, middle-class culture in mid-Victorian cities.[55]

The city provided a home for both types, and may be considered a more or less neutral environment. The sturdily independent middle-class culture was perhaps more characteristic of the major provincial towns than of London; and, among them, more characteristic of the great industrial towns than of the great ports, such as Liverpool and Bristol which were socially more in the hands of traditional mercantile elites with their leanings towards gentry values. The independence was expressed in proud self-reliance, disdain of aristocratic patronage, repudiation of idleness, luxury, and conspicuous display, belief in the career open to talent rather than to breeding and rewards for individual effort and merit rather than for good connections, and fervent commitment to the virtues of work, earnestness, sobriety, and strict sexual morality. The work ethic is the shorthand phrase customarily used to describe these qualities. They have also been enlisted as the core of the entrepreneurial ideal which defined middle-class values; but they are perhaps best understood as constituting the secular arm of the evangelical movement that was probably the single most powerful force in British society in the first half of the nineteenth century.[56] The trouble with evangelicalism is that it cut across the classes. It may indeed have achieved a solid and widespread middle-class base by the early Victorian years, even though it had originated

[54] Leonore Davidoff, *The Best Circles: Society, Etiquette and the Season* (1973), pp. 21–2.
[55] An independent middle-class culture, with strong sectarian and evangelical roots, is identified in Leonore Davidoff and Catherine Hall, *Family Fortunes: Men and Women of the English Middle Class, 1780–1850* (1987); and, with intellectual roots, in R. J. Morris, 'Middle-Class Culture, 1700–1914', in Derek Fraser, ed., *A History of Modern Leeds* (Manchester, 1980), esp. pp. 212–14. In a different way, uneasily linked to the emergence of an English national consciousness, it is the central theme of Gerald Newman, *The Rise of English Nationalism, 1740–1830* (1987).
[56] The 'entrepreneurial ideal' is defined and discussed by H. J. Perkin, *The Origins of Modern English Society, 1780–1880* (1969), esp. pp. 221–30, 276–81.

among members of the gentry and the gentry fringe; but evangelicalism certainly appealed to , and influenced, a section of the aristocracy, who turned from frivolity and indolence to serious business
and good works, and its influence in spreading notions of self-respect
and respectability to sections of the working classes was immense.
The pan-class appeal of evangelicalism was a source of strength in
the rise of Victorianism and the Victorian family ideal, but its very
diffusion, as well as its sectarian aspects, made it a weak vehicle for
defining a distinctive urban middle-class culture, capable of making
a sustained and independent contribution to the development of the
nation.

A second, and eventually more serious, source of weakness in the
cohesion of the urban middle class was that fractions of the class
never accepted the evangelical canons of behaviour, seeing comfort,
pleasure, and display as proper rewards and necessary confirmations
of their worldly success, and came to have reservations about living
in the city at all. Adultery, indeed, may never have become acceptable,
or at least tolerated, in the families of the Victorian civic patriciate;
otherwise there was little difference between lives in their houses, with
droves of servants, teams of gardeners, coach-houses, conservatories,
music rooms, billiard rooms, and ballrooms, and country-house living.
To be sure, many grandees continued to build their grand mansions
in the city or in the near outskirts. Thus, the blanket manufacturer
Benjamin Gott and the flax spinner John Marshall built themselves
large mansions on the hills above the Aire, allegedly to dominate
the workers in their factories down below in Leeds; Titus Salt's son
built a 'Wagnerian retreat' in the woods above his father's mill complex of Saltaire, Bradford; the carpet manufacturing Crossleys built
imposing houses on the edge of Halifax, close to their mills, and
Edward Akroyd, worsted manufacturer, placed his great house across
the street from his mill and model factory village of Akroydon, Halifax;
John Fielden, cotton manufacturer, built Dobroyd Castle, towering
over the family town of Todmorden; and leading Birmingham families,
the Chamberlains and the Cadburys, lived in enormous houses set
in private parks complete with private golf courses, towards the southern edge of the city.[57] Very many more of the upper middle class,

---

[57]   Morris, 'Middle-Class Culture', p. 208. C. Treen, 'The Process of Suburban Development in North Leeds, 1870–1914', in F. M. L. Thompson, ed., *The Rise of Suburbia*
(Leicester, 1982), p. 182. M. Girouard, *The Victorian Country House* (1979), pp. 10,
207–10, 404, 414.

affluent but less wealthy than the notabilities, lived in slightly more modest grandeur in the grand villas of Edgbaston, Victoria Park in Manchester, Sefton Park in Liverpool, Headingley in Leeds, Kelvinside in Glasgow, Broomhall in Sheffield, The Park in Nottingham, and their equivalents in other large towns.[58] A further fraction, however, took to living outside the city altogether, and thus established a detached or semi-detached relationship with their source of income and place of business.

Both Engels and Faucher, from very different ideological standpoints, observed of Manchester in the 1840s that the great mill owners and other leading citizens deserted the town every evening, retiring to their houses in the country at some distance from the centre.[59] This kind of wealthy commuting was not new to the nineteenth century; for centuries some of the wealthiest London merchants had lived in country houses, or country villages, a dozen or more miles from the City, either year-round or during the heat and stench of summer. What was perhaps new was the adoption of the habit in the provinces and by the prosperous middle class below the top level of wealth. The very wealthiest, who acquired country houses and landed estates, can be divided into two groups: those who continued in business, often financial but in several instances industrial, and became commuting amphibians, equally at home in the world of the hunting field and the world of counting house; and those who transformed themselves and their heirs into landed gentry. The numbers in the two groups taken together were small, a matter of no more than 200 or 300 individuals over the century; but possibly as much as 80 per cent of the very wealthiest members of the upper middle class, who left personal fortunes at death of £½ million or more, belonged to one or other group.[60] This movement was the continuation of a long tradition, magnified in scale by the nineteenth-century expansion in the overall numbers of the very wealthy.[61] More novel was the settlement

58   Glasgow, Nottingham, and Sheffield are discussed in M. A. Simpson and T. H. Lloyd, eds., *Middle-Class Housing in Britain* (Newton Abbot, 1977). See also Cannadine, *Lords and Landlords* pp. 124, 402; and Donald J. Olsen, 'House upon House', in H. J. Dyos and Michael Wolff, eds., *The Victorian City*, vol. 1: *Images and Realities* (1978 edn), pp. 341–5.

59   F. Engels, *The Condition of the Working Class in England* (Panther edn, 1969), pp. 79–80. L. Faucher, *Manchester in 1844* (1844), p. 26.

60   F. M. L. Thompson, 'Life after Death: How Successful Nineteenth-Century Businessmen Disposed of their Fortunes', *Economic History Review* (forthcoming).

61   W. D. Rubinstein, *Men of Property: The Very Wealthy in Britain since the Industrial Revolution* (1981), esp. chap. 2.

of the 'stockbroker belt' of Surrey and Berkshire from the 1850s onwards by business and professional men who did 'something in the City' and were well-heeled without being super-wealthy.[62] This was a leap out of and beyond suburbia, over intervening countryside to desirable residences in Leatherhead or Woking, Sunningdale or Wokingham, and was only made possible by the development of train services. A generation later the development of similar dormitory satellites, as distinct from the earlier suburbs, could be seen round the great conurbations of Merseyside and Manchester, the West Riding towns and Birmingham, and Clydeside.

These movements may or may not have produced a haemorrhage of wealth and talent from the city, business, and industry, flowing to waste in the countryside: it is always possible to argue that stockbrokers do better business on golf courses. It is clear, however, that these developments weakened, diluted, or destroyed any psychological, social, or political identification with the city in which business life was carried on, on the part of a significant section of the upper middle class, and weakened it more seriously among the pseudo-gentry countrydwellers than among those who merely lived in leafy suburbs. Inevitably affinities with the place where home was, where the family lived, and where weekends were spent, perhaps formerly a small country town or overgrown village, were likely to be stronger than those with the place where the working days were spent. Leadership of the work-town passed by default to those who lived there all the time: the local builders, traders, shopkeepers, perhaps the resident doctors and solicitors, even the teachers, all of whom were in the middling to lower end of the middle class. Fractured in these several ways the upper middle class was not in a strong position to nourish a vigorous or coherent urban culture, or to form a powerful independent force in politics or government. The fragments of the bourgeois elites which did identify closely with their cities, for relatively short periods and against these other trends, left their mark on the city centres with the imposing, self-confident, and didactic mid-Victorian town halls, libraries, and museums that were planted by short bursts of civic pride and free spending in Manchester and Leeds, Birmingham and Sheffield, and many other towns. They are a small taste of what might have been achieved by prolonged and consistent civic leadership and willingness to spend money on public projects,

[62] M. H. Ferguson, 'Land-Use, Settlement, and Society in the Bagshot Sands Region, 1840–1940' (unpublished PhD thesis, University of Reading, 1980), pp. 199–213.

to counteract the prevailing impression of muddle, meanness, and materialism in Victorian cities. The patchwork nature of the urban environment, islands of dignity and grandeur in a great dreary sea of the nondescript, the monotonous, the dingy, and the squalid, was symptomatic of the fragmented nature of urban society and its failure to develop a structure and a style clearly differentiated from rural society, or from society at large. The failure was less a product of social tensions and conflicts within the urban environment than a product of that environment itself which impelled those who could escape it to quit, and a product of the wider social and property arrangements of the country, which permitted those who wanted to quit to make good their escape.

Urban society, in the large towns, was continually losing people from the top; at the bottom it was continually recruiting, in far greater numbers, from the surrounding countryside, from the smaller towns, from Ireland, and in the 1880s from Eastern Europe. The immigrants were a mixed bunch, far from uniform in class, education, or skills. Some used the large towns, especially London and Liverpool, as staging posts for eventual long-distance migration to North America or Australasia, and were only transient members of British urban society. The country girls who were the favoured domestic servants of the comfortable middle classes went to live in respectable districts and amply-provided households, even though their own living and working conditions may have been deplorable, and a few of them remained in service for the rest of their lives. After a spell of several years spent in propping up the urban middle-class life style they might marry into the urban lower middle class or respectable working class, or they might withdraw from urban society altogether and return to the country. Some immigrants were already established in middle-class careers, and moved directly into new houses in the newest suburbs of the edges of the large towns: it is a mistake to suppose that new suburbs were entirely populated by townsfolk moving out from increasingly unattractive inner city areas.[63] Others, with skilled trades, moved into quarters already appropriated by their brethren. Urban growth was a very complicated process, physically and demographically, not a simple matter of incoming hordes of the penniless making for the centre and displacing established residents in ripple

[63]   J. M. Rawcliffe, 'Bromley: Kentish Market Town to London Suburb 1841–81', in Thompson, ed., *Rise of Suburbia*, pp. 27–91.

motions towards the outer rings; there was also a bee-swarming effect, with the latest arrivals clinging to the edge of the urban swarm.

Nevertheless, an inward movement of the poor migrants and an outward movement of the better-off and more respectable were the rhythms of the urban process most visible to contemporaries, and those most likely to appal or terrify them with the prospect of a runaway growth and explosion of inner areas bursting with over-crowding, destitution, dirt, disease, and discontent. The fastest grow-ing towns in the first sixty or seventy years of the century were by definition towns drawing in a great and continuous influx of people. Levels of urban mortality, becoming accurately established in the 1830s and 1840s, were such that no urban population was capable of repro-ducing itself let alone furnishing any natural increase. It was only in 1840 that William Farr, in the recently established Registrar General's Office, expressed what at the time seemed the very optimis-tic view that 'there is reason to believe that the aggregation of mankind in towns is not inevitably disastrous' provided some tolerable stan-dards of sanitation and limits on overcrowding could be achieved.[64] Previously, all large towns had been regarded as graveyards; figures made famous by Edwin Chadwick when he quoted them in his 1842 *Report on the Sanitary Condition of the Labouring Population* showed that the average age at death of workers in Manchester was less than half that of rural labourers in Rutland; and constant replenishment was the sole means of sustaining urban populations.[65] The general perception of observers, who were mostly clergymen and medical men, was that the replenishments were young, inexperienced, and unfamiliar with the techniques and conventions of living in towns, which was true; and that they huddled together in urban pockets which they swiftly made into slums, awash with all manner of filth, ordure, irreligion, immorality, ignorance, and lawlessness, which was a melodramatic distortion of the truth.

Irish immigrants stuck out like sore thumbs from their host popula-tions, being different in dress, speech, and above all in religion, and were readily identified as distinct, sub-standard, communities. Because they came from a very different cultural background, as well as from a rural life, it was easily assumed that they brought with

[64] *Second Annual Report of the Registrar-General*, PP 1840, XVII, William Farr, Appendix, p. xi.
[65] Edwin Chadwick, *Report on the Sanitary Condition of the Labouring Population of Great Britain* (1842), pp. 155–60.

them a set of habits which were wildly inappropriate to urban living, and indeed were calculated to foul the urban nest. Perhaps the most remarkable expression of the conventional wisdom about the frightfulness of the Irish and their urban squalor came from Engels, supposedly the humane, rational, labourer's friend, but no more immune to racial prejudice than the most bigoted capitalist. The most horrible district which he knew in the Manchester of the 1840s was called Little Ireland, a group of a few hundred mean cottages set in 'masses of refuse, offal, and sickening filth', inhabited by 'a horde of ragged women and children swarm[ing] about here, as filthy as the swine that thrive upon the garbage heaps and in the puddles'. 'The race that lives in these ruinous cottages,' he concluded, 'behind broken windows, mended with oilskins, sprung doors, and rotten doorposts, or in dark, wet, cellars, in measureless filth and stench, in this atmosphere penned in as if with a purpose, this race must really have reached the lowest stage of humanity.' That race, he argued, was disposed by nature and environment to careless and feckless behaviour, and had brought its dirty habits with it into the hearts of the great English and Scottish towns. 'Filth and drunkenness, too, they have brought with them', importing a mud-cabin level of existence into Britain and degrading and corrupting the English workers through their presence and their competition in the labour market. The Irishman, he claimed,

deposits all garbage and filth before his house door here, as he was accustomed to do at home, and so accumulates the pools and dirt-heaps which disfigure the working-people's quarters and poison the air. He builds a pig-sty against the house wall as he did at home, and if he is prevented from doing this, he lets the pig sleep in the room with himself. This new and unnatural method of cattle-raising in cities is wholly of Irish origin ... he eats and sleeps with it [his pig], his children play with it, ride upon it, roll in the dirt with it, as anyone may see a thousand times repeated in all the great towns of England ... The Irishman is unaccustomed to the presence of furniture; a heap of straw, a few rags, utterly beyond use as clothing, suffice for his nightly couch. A piece of wood, a broken chair, an old chest for a table, more he needs not ... when he is in want of fuel, everything combustible within reach, chairs, doorposts, mouldings, flooring, finds its way up the chimney ... At home in his mud-cabin there was only one room for all domestic purposes; more than one room his family does not need in England. So the custom of crowding many persons into a single room, now so universal, has been chiefly implanted by the Irish immigration.[66]

It is all too easy, when strong emotions are involved, to mistake the effects of poverty and ignorance for the effects of racial

[66] Engels, *Condition of the Working Class*, pp. 93, 123–5.

characteristics, and Engels had many successors, as well as predecessors, who attributed incorrigible wickedness to race. His pig-effect
differed from the common interwar coals-in-the-bath syndrome only
in that the latter was a class, rather than a racial, prejudice, holding
that the British working class was congenitally of too low intelligence
to grasp the proper use of baths. The physical conditions of Little
Ireland undoubtedly existed as Engels described them; what he saw were
the living conditions of the poorest and most destitute families cata-
pulted from a rural midden-heap which they had left under the pressure of extreme want and the hope of finding more to eat in the
towns, struggling to survive in an urban midden-heap. They chanced,
in this case, to have come from Ireland, and Irish immigrants with
their lack of skills and lack of useful contacts in British towns were
easily pushed to the bottom of the heap in the British labour market.
By no means all Irish immigrants, however, lived in such sub-human
conditions. Disregarding the very small numbers who were already
in middle-class professions before they migrated, and the somewhat
larger numbers who were in skilled trades, many immigrants found
reasonably regular employment, especially in the building, construction, clothing, and textile industries, even if it tended to be in the
lower-paid ends of those occupations, and lived above the midden-
heap level. The Irish navvies, building many of the railways in the
1840s and later, although nomadic and at most only temporarily urban,
were highly paid and lived boisterously and extravagantly. Neither,
on the other hand, were all the inhabitants of the notorious human
cesspits of the large towns Irish. Keeping pigs in the backyard or
in the house was held by many besides Engels to be an Irish badge.
But in the 'Potteries' of North Kensington, a festering spot only
slightly less notorious than the rookeries of St Giles, Holborn, there
were three times as many keepers of pigs as there were Irish-born
heads of families in 1851; and in towns such as Ipswich, West Hartlepool, Stratford-upon-Avon, or Stirling, which had no Irish colonies,
pig-keeping was a rampant nuisance until late in the century, strongly
defended by the poor as a cheap and efficient addition to their diets.[67]

It is less surprising that incoming waves of country bumpkins, innocent of previous urban experience, brought their country habits and
practices to town, than that it took municipal authorities a generation

---

[67] Lynn Holles Lees, *Exiles of Erin: Irish Migrants in Victorian London* (Manchester, 1979),
pp. 93–115, 119–21. Anthony S. Wohl, *Endangered Lives: Public Health in Victorian
Britain* (1983), pp. 82–3.

or so to grasp that the threat to public health was serious and that something had to be done about it. Open midden-heaps began to be tackled by bye-laws and inspectors of nuisances from the 1840s, but in some places it was not until the 1870s that the pigs came in for official attention. The Irish spread out over most of urban Britain, but most towns they were thin on the ground: only in London, Liverpool, Manchester, and Glasgow were there large Irish colonies in 1851 of more than 50,000 apiece, although there were also several rather smaller towns, such as Newcastle, Bradford, or Stockport, where the Irish-born formed around 10 per cent of the total population and definitely made their presence felt.[68] Every large town, however, had its blackspots, its sinks of misery and degradation, its slums, Leeds, Sheffield, or Birmingham with around 4 per cent of their populations Irish-born just as much as Liverpool or Manchester. The very poorest, the friendless, the unemployable and the casually employed gravitated to these areas, exciting pity, philanthropy, evangelising missions, and soup kitchens, when they did not inspire fear and disgust. Victorians often pictured these enclaves as nests of the criminal class; they may well have contained some professional thieves and fences, for Fagin was not an entirely imaginary character, even if the criminal class itself was no more than an irrational fantasy. The inhabitants are better thought of as an urban under-class, eking out an existence in the towns but barely part of urban society. They were so little attached to the mainstream of society that the favoured solution of social reformers at the end of the century to the problem of this residuum, both of Booth of the Salvation Army and Booth of *Life and Labour of the People in London*, was to detach them altogether and banish them to isolated labour colonies. There they might be reformed physically and morally, but the labour market would at least be insulated from their baleful influences.[69]

This under-class contained some of the new migrants as well as some of the longer-settled urban population, but it lacked the inner cohesion or stability of other classes in society. Its members were constantly on the move, most often in a ceaseless recycling process as they flitted from slum to slum to escape the rent collector or the bailiff, but occasionally moving upwards into greater security of job

[68] Dennis, *English Industrial Cities*, pp. 36–7, Table 2.3, gives figures of the Irish-born for 1851 and 1901 for a selection of thirty English and Welsh towns.

[69] J. Brown, 'Charles Booth and Labour Colonies, 1889–1905,' *Economic History Review*, 2nd ser., 21 (1968). The Salvation Army also bought some farms to turn into labour colonies.

and home; they could hardly sink any lower, except into the grave, for theirs was the basement level for the downwardly socially mobile.[70] They possessed a sub-culture, dominated by the tricks and dodges of keeping alive on no resources, the art of 'shooting the moon' as moonlight flitting was termed, and especially later in the century by practised cunning in exploiting to maximum advantage the multiplicity of charities bent on alleviating distress. Impermanence of residence, which frequently changed every few months, inhibited the growth of community feeling and solidarity, and not surprisingly this group was not easily politicised and was more notable for its consistent apathy than for any threat to rise up and terrorise and ransack the respectable, despite bourgeois apprehensions and, as in the rampage down Pall Mall in 1886, one or two genuine alarms.[71] This group was the most deprived, the most downtrodden, and the most degenerate in society, but also perhaps the least dangerous because it was so atomised and demoralised.

The herd instinct of huddling together for mutual support, comfort, and self-preservation in a strange and possibly unfriendly surrounding world was much in evidence in the channelling of the great migration flows into the cities; and operated in only a rather more stately and measured fashion in guiding the movements of more settled towndwellers towards socially homogeneous and segregated residential districts. It was plain for all to see that all the major urban reception camps had distinctive Irish quarters in which new arrivals could expect a welcome and help from compatriots who were frequently from the same county or village back home; and that they tended to stay there, for the sake of companionship, from the similarity of jobs, and above all to sustain their religion, not offend their priest, and – at least by the 1870s – conserve access to their Catholic schools. The more the Irish preserved their individuality the more they were likely to be derided or disliked by their Scottish or English fellow-workers, the harder it became to melt away into the general structure of urban society and the more their separation was perpetuated. Some melting away, or assimilation, and intermarriage did occur, as also did geographical dispersal within the city without loss of Irishness; for in an urban way of life in which social networks and contacts could

---

[70] David Englander, *Landlord and Tenant in Urban Britain, 1838–1918* (Oxford, 1983), pp. 9–10, 34–5.

[71] G. Stedman Jones, *Outcast London: A Study in the Relationship between Classes in Victorian Society* (Oxford, 1971), pp. 291–2.

increasingly be maintained through associations which were not necessarily rooted in tightly-knit residential communities, spatially compact Irish quarters lost some of their rationale. The size and scale of the Irish quarters is difficult to establish. The Irish probably colonised discrete blocks of housing, enclaves of courtyard dwellings, or streets, rather than entire neighbourhoods like town wards or parishes, so that at the level of census enumerators' districts, even in 1851 which reflected a preceding period of peak immigration, the Irish-born show up as a large minority in their places of concentration not as denizens of completely Irish ghettoes. The flow of fresh immigrants fell away in the second half of the century, particularly as the Irish outflow was increasingly directed across the Atlantic, and this explains the decline in the proportion of Liverpool's population which was Irish-born from 22 per cent in 1851 to under 7 per cent in 1901, or in Bradford's which fell from 9 to 1.5 per cent. The Irish, however, did not dwindle as an element in the urban scene at quite the pace which these figures suggest. The census only recorded birthplaces, not religion, nationality or ethnicity, and undoubtedly a high proportion of the second and third generation descendants of immigrants regarded themselves as Irish. It was probably particularly the case in the major centres that the London-Irish, the Glasgow-Irish, or the Liverpool-Irish, who carried Irish cultural and social traditions into the twentieth century, were far more numerous than merely the Irish-born who lived in those cities: it could be plausibly asserted in the early twentieth century that Liverpool was a quarter or a third 'Irish'.[72]

The Irish tended to remain together and apart from the rest of the urban community for decades and generations after the initial transitions to the town. During the second half of the century their settlements tended to become more dispersed, in a larger number of smaller clusters, and to look more like other working-class districts than the pig-sties which had so shocked Engels, differentiated maybe only by their church, their school, and pubs monopolised by Irish labourers. The Jews, arriving in large numbers from Eastern Europe and Russia in the 1880s and 1890s, formed the second wave of foreign immigration, and very much followed the Irish model as they settled in distinct quarters in Spitalfields and Whitechapel, Leeds and Manchester, and established their dominance of the clothing trades. English migrants, on the other hand, and in a slightly more ambivalent way

---

[72]   Lees, *Exiles of Erin*, pp. 46–8, and chap. 3

the Welsh migrants who moved in considerable numbers to Liverpool and London as well as to the towns of the South Wales coalfield, pursued a strategy of clustering settlement which saw them through the first shock of urbanisation and then rather rapidly became absorbed and assimilated into the different occupational and social strata of urban life.

The capacity of urban society to absorb and assimilate incomers did not only depend on the ability to furnish jobs and housing, although that was obviously very important, and the fact that the expansion of jobs and house-room not infrequently got out of phase with the inflow of people was a serious cause of hardship and social friction. It also depended, critically, on the migrants' habit of making for the same town, and the same street within it, as forerunners from their family or village had done. It has long been known that a marked feature of townward migration was the prominence of short-distance movements from villages and lesser towns in the immediate hinterland of the larger, reception, towns, with the longer distance movements of the Irish from across the sea standing out as exceptional, and this pattern has been confirmed in many studies.[73] This in itself created a possibility that a newcomer would not be a lonely and isolated individual adrift in a strange and intimidating town, but would have the opportunity of settling with, or near, relatives or friends. Detailed confirmation that this opportunity was grasped comes from the study of mid-nineteenth-century Preston, which shows that it was quite common for extended families of grandparents, uncles, aunts and cousins to assemble themselves around the parent–child nuclear family as the product of stages of migration, not indeed always under one roof or in a single household, but sometimes in a number of adjoining and neighbouring houses.[74] This arrangement provided a life support system in which the mutual, and perhaps carefully reciprocated, aid of kin could help with such crises and catastrophes as sickness, childbirth, job-finding, unemployment, baby-minding, widowhood and old age. It is possible that the need to construct such

[73] A. Redford, *Labour Migration in England, 1800–50*, 2nd edn (Manchester, 1964). Dennis, *English Industrial Cities*, pp. 33–4, and J. R. Kellett, *The Impact of Railways on Victorian Cities* (1969), pp. 406–8, give summaries of several of the post-Radford studies. The continuing dominance of comparatively short-distance migration post 1945 is shown by M. C. Carr, 'The Development and Character of a Metropolitan Suburb: Bexley, Kent', in Thompson, ed., *Rise of Suburbia*, Table 19, p. 241. Among some categories of skilled workers, and the professions, longer distance migration was always present.

[74] Anderson, *Family Structure*, esp. pp. 56–67, 136–61, 170–9.

kinship networks as a form of basic social security, in the fast-growing towns where external agencies like the poor law, dispensaries, hospitals, almshouses, or labour exchanges were unreliable, inadequate, hostile, or not yet invented, was the compelling reason for reconstituting the extended family in an urban setting. For in the rural society from which most migrants came the extended family was completely unknown as a kinship group living in a single household; and although it undoubtedly existed as a social construct for occasions of conviviality and sociability, it was either unnecessary or impossible as a social security network, depending on the effectiveness of the rural paternalism of squire and parson or the depths of rural poverty which might put aiding a relative in distress beyond contemplation.

These urban extended families were characteristic of mid-century Oldham as well as Preston.[75] It is possible that the form was more extensive in cotton towns than in others, perhaps because greater openings for the employment of women and children, and the generally higher level of family earnings, made aid more affordable and more certain of being reciprocated. But unless the entire arrangement is thought to have been a product of rational and financial calculation, with little place for sentiment, affection, and uncosted neighbourliness, it is reasonable to suppose that it was to be found throughout the Victorian urban scene as a significant form of social organisation. It may well have been a transient form, lasting for a generation in individual migrant families and dwindling in general importance as most towns became demographically self-sustaining and hence less reliant on in-migration, in the later nineteenth century. The constant moving about of working-class households, with no more than one fifth remaining in the same house from one census to the next and about a quarter staying at the same address for less than a year as the typical pattern of mobility in the middle of the century, would in any case seem likely to have made it difficult to maintain family contacts, or indeed the cohesion of street-neighbourhood groups based on propinquity rather than, or as well as, kinship.[76] It could be argued with some plausibility that the vigorous family networks and the tightly-knit neighbourhood communities were likely to be confined to the minority of long stayers who put down roots, the one fifth who stayed put for at least ten years or the one third or so who lasted for at least five years; the majority who were footloose

---

[75]   John Foster, *Class Struggle and the Industrial Revolution* (1974), pp. 96–7.
[76]   Dennis, *English Industrial Cities*, Table 8.1, pp. 256–7.

may have been so, at least in part, precisely because they lacked the attachment to particular houses and streets which was created by these arrangements.

Future research may clarify these problems of typicality. Meantime, the persistence of extended family networks, as centres of family (frequently grandmotherly) moral authority as well as of crisis management, and of neighbourhood social cells, albeit selective in their membership on internal criteria of respectability and roughness, are well attested in the classic slum in Salford in the 1900s, recollected by Robert Roberts, in the post-1945 Bethnal Green studied by Young and Willmott, and in several other studies.[77] There is a strong suggestion in this evidence of a highly durable social formation; originating in the huddling together of migrant kin for mutual comfort and support in a strange environment, it was perpetuated in the customs of settled and townbred families, and became grafted on to, or shaded away into, the non-kinship groupings of friends and neighbours. These networks, which by the early twentieth century had come to be thought of as traditional, began to be seriously eroded in the interwar years by slum clearance schemes and rehousing in council housing estates, which split up wider family groupings into nuclear cells and atomised and scattered street communities. After 1950 they virtually collapsed, in the tower block and new towns phase of massive decanting of population from the old inner city areas, aided and abetted by many other factors among which the role of the welfare state as a substitute for families and neighbours must be recognised.

In their prime these networks were the main sinews giving the social fabric of the towns some stability, cohesion, and orderliness. They were the main reasons why the anomie, anarchy, and collapse of social order, so much feared by early Victorian observers of the large towns, never materialised. Investigators and reporters from the middle classes – medical men, clergymen, social reformers – were shocked and horrified by many things which they saw and smelt in the poor quarters of the major towns: overcrowding, malnutrition, raggedness, ignorance, ill-health, the stench of the great unwashed and of sewage suppurating in the courtyards and running in the streets, all these things were evident and were described and

---

[77] Robert Roberts, *The Classic Slum* (Manchester, 1971), esp. chap. 3. Michael Young and Peter Willmott, *Family and Kinship in East London* (1957), pp. 104–16. See also Standish Meacham, *A Life Apart: The English Working Class, 1890–1914* (1977), pp. 45–59.

measured. But what alarmed them most about what they saw was the structural and moral collapse of society in the great cities. They saw the comfortable and educated classes withdrawing to their own elegant and salubrious preserves, abdicating their responsibilities for the working classes and leaving them to their own devices; and they thought they saw the working classes as merely teeming masses of individuals promiscuously thrown together, scurrying about between work, pub, and lodgings in random and rudderless throngs, an inchoate horde portending the breakdown of society and a return to something like the law of the jungle. An obscure cleric, giving evidence to a select Committee, may stand for the conventional mid-century view when he drew attention to

the gradual separation of the classes which takes place in towns ... whereas formerly rich and poor live in proximity and the superior classes exercised that species of silent but very efficient control over their neighbours ... In small towns there must be a sort of natural police ... operating upon the conduct of each individual who lives ... under the public eye; but in a large town he lives, if he chooses, in absolute obscurity.[78]

The remedies proposed were such things as sewers and piped water, street paving and housing bye-laws, for the physical conditions; and police, schools, teachers, churches, and ministers for the social and moral conditions. Providing these was what Victorian social policy, voluntary as well as governmental, was all about. Increasing supplies, mainly from the 1830s and 1840s onwards, but in the case of some sewering and some schooling from the earlier decades of the century, definitely made towns healthier and people better educated by the early 1900s; less decisively, they contributed to making towns more orderly and disciplined places where popular behaviour, at least in public, could for the most part be relied upon not to offend the middle classes. Such agencies, however, played no more than a minor part in vanquishing anomie or urban alienation, since those were imagined rather than real dragons. The family and street networks were affairs of relationships, not of visible objects and conditions, and it is understandable that they remained unseen and unremarked by observers preoccupied with the physical, social, and moral defects of urban living conditions. The informal network communities were indeed supplemented by, and in time to a significant extent replaced by, more formal and selective associations that were easily visible to outsiders.

[78] SC on Criminal and Destitute Juveniles, PP 1852, XXIII evidence of M. D. Hill, q. 386.

Most of these were generated from within the working classes, and frequently rested on workplace contacts. Friendly societies and trade unions were of this kind; savings groups like holiday clubs, clothing clubs, and the early 'terminating' building societies of the 1830s and 1840s, and mutual interest groups of the pigeon-fancying, dog-breeding, or dart-playing variety, might stem from either workplace or pub. Other associations, notably the workingmen's clubs of the 1860s, were initiated by middle-class reformers but quickly appropriated by self-governing workingmen; while church or chapel drew in a section of the working classes, and although church remained firmly in the control of the superior classes some chapels at least were in effect run by and for the working classes. All the associations, societies, clubs, and congregations of these types served – alongside their primary purposes – to reinforce the identification of their individual members with a social group, and thus strengthened the fabric of urban society as a cohesive social structure and not a mere aggregation of rootless and shiftless individuals.

The overwhelming majority of these associations were male preserves – working women, for example in the cotton mills, perhaps finding a place in the mill holiday club but in nothing else – and, within that gender restriction, were largely confined to the skilled and more highly paid men. Their effects in welding individuals into groups, although marked, were therefore limited. The informal networks, by contrast, by definition involved the active participation of women, who often controlled the complicated apparatus of family customs, rituals, and obligations, and who managed the friendships and animosities of the street. Moreover, these networks seem to have been spread widely amongst all levels of the working classes, and may well have been most important for survival in times of hardship, and for companionship, and have been most persistent, in the poorest sections. Apart from the nuclear family itself they were the most widespread form of social institution in the great manufacturing and commercial towns of Victorian Britain, and arguably they were the most purely urban element in urban society. That is, the extended family, even as a set of regular contacts between members who lived in independent households, apparently did not exist or was uncommon in pre-industrial Britain, except in higher social reaches such as the aristocracy, whose kin kept in touch for financial, social or political advantage, or the cousinhoods of Quakers, Unitarians, and other sects, which underpinned very successful banking and trading

services; while the street-neighbourhood was a product of the environment of single-class streets, itself a product of the large towns.[79]

Residential social segregation may not have been entirely a nineteenth-century invention, but if it existed before it was mainly at a
house-by-house level, and in small-scale towns individual streets and
districts were commonly socially mixed in character. Eighteenth-
century London pointed the way to the future, for the great West
End developments were unmistakably designed for predominantly
single-class occupations, although in making provision for the service
needs and convenience of the wealthy residents the developments
also ensured some degree of discreetly hidden social mixture. Social
segregation came to all the great nineteenth-century towns, and it
struck early Victorians as a recent development. It was fundamentally
a product of the press of numbers, the resulting congestion, dirt,
and stench of the older central districts, and of the English preference
for low-rise family housing. High-rise apartment or tenement blocks
offered a solution to problems of dirt, noise, and smell by rising above
them, and could produce a form of vertical social stratification operating through differential rent levels, as happened in Paris; tenements
in Glasgow, however, were broadly one-class habitations, although
accommodating different layers of status and income within the working classes. Two- or three-storeyed housing, on the other hand, necessarily led to lateral or spatial segregation if there was to be any
segregation at all. The process of segregation had generally been seen
as a move by those who could afford it to escape from insalubrious
and unpleasant areas, and to cluster in groups in more attractive districts according to house values and individual tastes, leaving the
great residue of the working classes to make do with whatever housing
was left unclaimed. The clustering of groups with similar standards,
aspirations, and income levels was also stimulated, if not dictated,
from the supply side by the tendency of builders and developers to
construct blocks or small neighbourhoods of a uniform housing type
for reasons of construction economies and profit maximisation, and
sometimes because ground landlords stipulated that they should do
so.

The working classes were not relegated to vast undifferentiated
ghettoes, as the development of the street-neighbourhoods showed
in social and cultural terms. Physically there were differences in the

[79]   Davidoff and Hall, *Family Fortunes*, pp. 86–7, 99–103, 321–2, discuss middle-class,
mainly Quaker, extended family networks.

size and quality of the working-class housing stock between two-, four-, and six-roomed houses, between pre- and post-bye-law housing, and between all these and 'made down' middle-class family housing which was tenemented often in one-room units for working-class use. All these grades and qualities were marked by different rents, and were tenanted by families with different earnings and at different stages of their life-cycles. Thus there was residential segregation within the working classes, with strong occupational lines of demarcation, so that railwaymen's quarters, bus and tram worker's quarters, and docker's districts could be readily distinguished as well as the more obviously superior districts favoured by skilled craftsmen; while slums which appeared indistinguishably awful to the fashionable visitors of the 1880s were unerringly sorted out into the deserving and the disreputable by their residents. The working classes also remained much more intermixed with other classes than was suggested by the clearcut separation and segregation which Engels claimed to see in Manchester of the 1840s and other great industrial towns.[80] This was partly an effect of the desire of the superior classes to have their supporting services and their lowly providers close at hand, but was chiefly the effect of the slow pace of development on any particular tract of land, and of the fragmented and poorly targeted nature of building operations. Towns as entities grew and expanded their housing stocks at a spanking pace; but so many separate building estates were likely to be active simultaneously that every sizeable one of say 50 acres or more was liable to be fifty years in the building from the first houses to the completely built-up state.[81] The result was that consumer fashions and tastes changed during the prolonged development period, builders came and went with different ideas and resources, and it was unlikely that a large tract could sustain a uniform social character or avoid having desirable and less desirable sections. Moreover, the fragmented building industry, operating in thousands of small businesses, tended to behave like a flock of sheep, all surging together into an upswing in the building cycle and all stopping together when the market became over supplied, and all trying to build houses of the highest value and highest class which an optimist might think suitable for their plots and locations. The result of this was a continual tendency to overstock the market with higher class houses, and to force the least well capitalised builders

[80]   Engels, *Condition of the Working Class*, p. 79.
[81]   Thompson, ed., *Rise of Suburbia*, p. 22.

to let the working classes into houses, or districts, which had initially been intended for higher class occupation, in order to get quick returns on their outlays.

The end product of these factors, despite the undoubtedly strong herd instinct impelling like to seek to live with like for a whole complex of cultural, financial, moral, sanitary, and aesthetic reasons, was that the actual social geography of Victorian towns was more of a mosaic of small pieces of class presence than a bold pattern of broad sweeps of class separation such as segregation theory might imply.[82] Within this structure it was the upper middle class of the most successful professional and business families which was able to lay claim to undisputed possession of the largest continuous slices of urban territory and preserve them from unwelcome intruders, because they were the group best able to afford defences – sometimes physical barriers, like gated roads – against invasion or social deterioration of their neighbourhoods, best able to afford to move to the most up-to-date houses and the latest in fashionable districts, and best able to afford large houses, large gardens, and low densities which necessarily made their urban quarters much larger in extent, per household, than those of any other class. Beneath this summit of exclusiveness, however, segregation was a matter of a street or small group of streets, rather than a question of entire parishes, wards, or even census enumerators' districts (which typically had a population of 200 to 300 households) having a single-class character. The socially mixed nature of most urban precincts made it difficult for loyalties to the city, to political causes, or to religious or cultural activities to grow out of strictly localised territorial roots. Socially homogeneous or like-minded elements required to be brought together and mobilised through workplace, pub, church, chapel, friendly society, trade union, club, and association; it could not be assumed that they would be in touch through living cheek by jowl. Whether the proximity and intermixture of the classes fostered social harmony and tolerance through familiarity and mutual understanding, or emphasised class feelings and tensions through the constant reminders of differences, is another question.[83]

The residential pattern which matured in the second half of the century contained hundreds of internal frontiers between class and

---

[82] Dennis, *English Industrial Cities*, pp. 211–21. Booth's 'Descriptive Maps of London Poverty', 1889, in Charles Booth, ed., *Life and Labour of the People in London*, 1st ser., *Poverty*, 4 vols. (1889–91) and the later 'Descriptive Maps' of 1897–8 in 3rd ser., *Religious Influences*, 7 volumes (1902–3), show the mosaic effect in colour.

[83] Waller, *Town, City and Nation*, p. 115.

class, sometimes clearly marked by a physical feature like a railway track, but as often an invisible line between the right side and the wrong side of a street that was very apparent to the residents who defended it. The most jealously guarded frontier was the line between classes with marginal differences in incomes or wealth, the lower middle class and the upper working class. The lower middle class of shopkeepers, small businessmen and clerks rarely had incomes any higher than those of skilled workers, and family earnings may well have been lower since it was not done for wives to go out to work. Nevertheless, the lower middle classes considered themselves socially superior, in education, respectability, refinement, and life style. Lower middle-class housing and the better kind of artisan housing were very similar. Both classes lived in terrace houses with front parlours dignified with separate entrances leading off diminutive front passages, or halls; both would have back extensions housing a scullery with an extra bedroom on top; and both would have to put up with outside privies, at least until the 1890s. The lower middle classes might well look for more bay windows and a more prominent display of fancy brickwork or stonework for lintels and other embellishments, and might exhibit a greater expanse of lace curtains, than their working-class rivals. Inside, the working-class terraces probably housed a higher proportion of lodgers, since middle-class values did not permit open acknowledgment of reliance on this source of subsidiary income as a means of affording the rent, although the paying-guest euphemism helped to get round this obstacle. This difference between the two classes, however, was not readily visible to the public eye.[84]

Lacking emphatic architectural statements of their superiority, and being unable to afford, in the lower rungs of clerkdom, the easily recognisable middle-class badge of servant-keeping, the lower middle class developed the cult of the genteel as their distinguishing mark. This had many elements, of thrift, sobriety, abstemiousness, disapproval of frivolity, abhorrence of debt, suppression of sexuality, careful parading of attendance at church or chapel, and emphasis on keeping up appearances, which could be found in other social groups as well. The distinctive feature was the merging of these values into a culture of self-consciously virtuous small-mindedness whose purity was protected from contamination by elevating the practices of privacy and

[84]   The refinements, subtleties, and contortions in the architectural expression of class and sub-class distinctions are graphically discussed by Stefan Muthesius, *The English Terraced House* (1982), esp. pp. 236–56.

of keeping oneself to oneself to the level of a doctrine. This creed prevented strangers prying into the reality behind the façade, a reality where material possessions or moral conduct might differ from the claims of outward appearance. Away from the home base young clerks on holiday in Margate or Southend, or on a Saturday night out at the music hall, might be as lecherous, vulgar, or drunken as anyone else; but the prim and prudish respectability of the home, hypocritical or not, was the necessary guarantee of their status. Carefully isolating themselves from the groups below, the lower middle class made themselves into the most solitary, least neighbourly, and least gregarious class in Victorian society. They could not join in the pub culture, or join friendly societies or gardening clubs, because of their working-class associations; they could scarcely bring themselves to use publicly subsidised or publicly provided services like voluntary schools, Board schools, the hospitals which grew out of poor law provisions from the 1860s onwards, sometimes even the public libraries, because these compromised self-reliance; and, except towards the upper end of the class among the richer shopkeepers and the very highest paid superior clerks, they could not join the secure middle-class world of lit. and phil. societies, subscription libraries, local athenaeums, chambers of commerce, and, of lower esteem and at the end of the century, rotary clubs.

Church or chapel were the only communities to which the lower middle class could belong without running any risk of tainting their social standing or ruining their pockets. This might seem to define the class in religious rather than in social or occupational terms. Yet despite the prominence of religion in family life and in the upbringing of their children, and despite the close links between church or chapel membership and respectability, white-collar workers were by no means conspicuous for regular church attendance.[85] Thus, although a religious basis for their values was vital, assiduous participation in organised religion does not seem to have been essential. Hence the lower middle class did not balance their deliberate rejection of tightly-knit street or neighbourhood communities, which were working class, by identification with cohesive religious communities, and could not aspire to integrate with the mutual interest clubs and associations of the established middle class. This left them as fundamentally a class without cohesion, isolated in their family units where

[85]   Hugh McLeod, 'White Collar Values and the Role of Religion', in Geoffrey Crossick, ed., *The Lower Middle Class in Britain, 1870–1914* (1977), esp. pp. 61–8, 86–8.

households uncluttered with either servants or resident kin gave the purest Victorian performance of the nuclear family turned in on itself and surviving on its own material, moral and intellectual resources. This strongly individualistic existence had a tough fibre of self-discipline and self-improving motivation, and the urge to distance themselves from the working classes was complemented by an almost obsequious deference to their social superiors and desire to emulate their manners, speech, dress, and presumed opinions. The atomisation and fragmentation of the lower middle class did not, therefore, threaten social order in any way with a rising tide of rootless, unattached, undirected, individuals. Nevertheless, it represented the closest approach to the generation of an amorphous anomie in Victorian urban society; and it was essentially a product of the growth of large towns, for without them white-collar occupations hardly existed at all or at most in such small numbers in the lesser country towns that no distinct group could emerge.[86]

The lower middle class, the most amorphous and most cellular, the least cohesive and least assertive, group in society, were understandably not remarkable for their cultural or intellectual achievements or independence. Successful men of talent from this social background were, by definition, propelled upwards by their success into the middle or upper middle class, as H. G. Wells was propelled from his draper's assistant beginnings into fashionable literary society. The domestic problems, social life, and daily little crises and anxieties of the class were indeed preserved for all time in *The Diary of a Nobody* (1892), which made Mr Pooter into the stock figure of high Victorian petty gentility; but that did nothing to raise the standing of the class. The great petty bourgeois colony of south London was described by Walter Besant in 1899 as

a city without a municipality, without a centre, without a civic history; it has no newspapers, magazines or journals; it has no university, it has no colleges, apart from the medical; it has no intellectual, artistic, scientific, musical, literary centre ... its residents have no local patriotism or enthusiasm ... it has no theatres except of a very popular or humble kind; it has no clubs, it has no public buildings.[87]

They may have created a cultural desert and attracted the nearly

---

[86] Geoffrey Crossick, 'The Emergence of the Lower Middle Class in Britain: A Discussion', in Crossick, ed., *Lower Middle Class*, pp. 11–60; see also Geoffrey Crossick, 'Urban Society and the Petty Bourgeoisie in Nineteenth-Century Britain', in Derek Fraser and Anthony Sutcliffe, eds., *The Pursuit of Urban History* (1983), pp. 306–25.

[87] Walter Besant, *South London* (1899), quoted by Waller, *Town, City and Nation*, p.41.

universal contempt of the intellectual and literary classes, but the small shopkeepers, tradesmen, and businessmen, abetted by the growing numbers of white-collar workers, virtually took control of the cities in the course of the fifty years before 1914.

They did this in a three-pronged infiltration of urban affairs, as ratepayers, as councillors, and as the heart of the new local government bureaucracy. The first two roles fell to them largely through the voluntary withdrawal and retreat of the more substantial middle classes, and the third as a result of the expansion of municipal responsibilities of which they, as ratepayers, generally disapproved on grounds of expense and ideology. Municipal greatness, therefore, was thrust upon the lower middle class, in measure against its will if it had been capable of having a will, not achieved by a collective struggle or as the fulfilment of cherished class aspirations. Lower middle-class householders did not pay large amounts of rates as individuals, compared with those higher up the scale who occupied large villas and mansions, but collectively they were a considerable force with a considerable potential for feeling aggrieved. Small traders and businessmen were oppressed by the burden of rates on their businesses as well as their homes, and reckoned this became a triple imposition when they were also small property owners with their savings invested in a row of cottages of the kind normally let to working-class tenants who did not pay rates separately but compounded for them as an element in the weekly rent, leaving the housing landlord to pay the rate to the council. Little wonder that ratepayers' associations were endemic in the municipal life of Victorian towns, mainly drawn from the petty bourgeoisie, mainly short-lived, and mainly concerned with organising resistance to some particular piece of proposed municipal expenditure. The reputation of these associations, not undeservedly, was for being small-minded and shortsighted, dedicated to keeping rates down at the cost of being the mainstay of the 'dirty party' which regarded sewers and sanitation as unnecessary, and the stand-by of the 'economisers' who rejected any rate-provided civic improvements or amenities.[88]

Nevertheless, Victorian towns were swept into the era of sanitary improvements, sewage schemes, paved streets, new town halls, public parks, public libraries, public washhouses and baths, rate-supported schools, and increasingly in the last quarter of the century

[88]   Avner Offer, *Property and Politics 1870–1914: Landownership, Law, Ideology and Urban Development in England* (Cambridge, 1981), pp. 297–301.

municipally owned waterworks, gasworks, tramways, and electricity undertakings. Sometimes they were swept kicking and screaming into the nineteenth century, prodded and pushed by central government and statute; but just as often they made their own way under local leaders with larger views of the physical necessity, humanitarian desirability, and longer term commercial benefits of civic improvements. Sometimes these local leaders were members of the urban elite, prominent business and professional men securely located in the upper middle class. Joseph Chamberlain, mayor of Birmingham between 1873 and 1876 and the driving force of a civic gospel of dynamic improvements and betterment, is most commonly cited as the paradigm of this type. He is in danger of being the sole example. The attempt to elevate Samuel Smith, one of Bradford's leading manufacturers, mayor from 1851 to 1854, and moving spirit in the building of St George's Hall for public concerts, to the Chamberlain level has not been notably successful.[89] There were indeed other wealthy businessmen who became civic benefactors and dignitaries – Sir Peter Fairbairn, brother of the better known engineer, William, who was knighted because he happened to be mayor of Leeds when Victoria opened the magnificent new town hall in 1858, or Sir W. H. Wills, tobacco millionaire and Bristol town councillor in the 1870s and 1880s, are cases in point – but they tend to be remembered for their benefactions rather than for their municipal achievements.[90] It is even possible that the time was never ripe for the urban middle class to play the decisive leading role in civic affairs: until the 1870s they were overshadowed by the landed patricians, and were in general reluctant to devote time to public life; after the 1870s they increasingly withdrew into the country and did not involve themselves in the everyday running of their cities.[91]

Sometimes, however, the local leaders of municipal expansiveness came from below the elite level, and this may have been the more typical situation. The largest merchants and manufacturers had industry-wide regional, national, and world interests and markets, and their fortunes were not closely dependent on the condition or standing of any particular municipality, unless it happened to wield direct control over such essentials as their transport services. There was,

[89] Asa Briggs, *Victorian Cities* (1963), p. 155.
[90] H. E. Mellor, *Leisure and the Changing City, 1870–1914* (1976), pp. 89–93, 104–5.
[91] David Cannadine, 'Introduction', in David Cannadine, ed., *Patricians, Power, and Politics in Nineteenth-Century Towns* (Leicester, 1982), pp. 8–11. Mellor, *Changing City*, p. 93.

therefore, no strong economic motive for involving themselves in municipal government, and when they did do so it was likely to be for reasons of political ambition, religious duty, humanitarian impulse, or social conscience. The lives and livelihoods of lesser men, by contrast, were centred on and largely circumscribed by the one particular town in which they lived and carried on their businesses, and their fortunes were bound up with the good order, health, amenities, and reputation of that town. In addition to any calls of local patriotism or civic duty such men could have strong, but not necessarily narrow or venal, self-interested motives for entering municipal government, motives which could lead to support for civic improvements as being good business almost as easily as they could lead to cheese-paring inaction as being good for keeping the rates down. Local solicitors, doctors, estate agents, and other professional men, from the middling part of the middle class, were frequently to be found among the improvers, and were perhaps the most disinterested parties. But there were also members of the petty bourgeoisie, shopkeepers, traders, builders, and the like whose enlightened self-interest led them to support, and pay for, not merely the utilitarian sanitary improvement, of their town but also its embellishment with amenities.[92]

Moreover, the tensions and oscillations between economy and improvement were not the only, or necessarily the most important, issues affecting participation in municipal government. Routine administration of building bye-laws, housing regulations, street cleansing, lighting, fire brigades, and other features of municipal housekeeping appeared humdrum and boring to the professional and business elites, and made council work seem petty, unattractive, and unrewarding. But these things affected the business prospects, trading conditions and property-owning interests of the petty bourgeoisie very directly, and quite apart from any suspicion of self-seeking such as local builders were prone to attract, they could legitimately find the detail of council work important and rewarding. Their commitment to the town and identification with its interests was mirrored by the migration of the wealthy to leafy outer suburbs which might not be administratively within the core borough at all, or to small country towns swelling into satellites under railway stimulation by the closing decades of the century, which were definitely in a separate municipal sphere. The political traditions and complexions of both

[92]   Daunton, *Coal Metropolis*, pp. 149–63.

large and middle-rank towns were very varied, and so too was the
social composition of their councils. It would be wrong to suppose
that there was a uniform trend towards domination by publicans,
high-street traders, and local builders; indeed, the study of Birmingham and Leeds suggests that a lower middle-class grip was
broken by the entry, or re-entry, of big business into the council
chamber in force in the 1870s in the first city and the 1890s in the
second.[93] That may well have been an effect of swings in local party
politics more than of changes in the attitudes of either the business
elite or the borough voters. In any case, it is well established that
small traders and businessmen formed a significant element on town
councils at least from the 1835 Municipal Reform Act onwards, and
that by the early 1900s they, plus the local professional men who
were generally middling middle class rather than upper middle class
in income, status, and outlook, together normally furnished the clear
majority of town councillors.[94]

The majority, reckoned in terms of social and occupational backgrounds, did not necessarily command power and influence in the
boroughs. That depended on political alignments, for it is a carefully
cultivated conservative myth that local government was in some way
apolitical and non-party until the rude intrusion of Labour into a previously unsullied field. Party spirit and organisation, not always coin-
cident with national or parliamentary parties, was vigorously and
often viciously present throughout the Victorian period.[95] It depended
on leadership, often provided by individuals from minority, elitist,
social groups. Moreover, effective power was tending, from around
the 1880s onwards, to slip away from elected councillors into the hands
of the permanent officials: town clerks, commonly solicitors, had long
been important; they were joined by engineers, surveyors, architects,
and career administrators, who had great empires of gasworks,

[93] E. P. Hennock, 'The Social Composition of Borough Councils in Two Large Cities,
     1835–1914', in H. J. Dyos, ed., *The Study of Urban History* (1968); E. P. Hennock,
     Fit and Proper Persons: Ideal and Reality in Nineteenth-Century Urban Government (1973),
     part II, chap. 5.
[94] Daunton, *Coal Metropolis*, pp. 152–3; Mellor, *Changing City*, p. 87; Waller, *Democracy
     and Sectarianism*, pp. 151–2; Waller, *Town, City and Nation*, p. 291; Richard Roberts,
     'Leasehold Estates and Municipal Enterprise: Landowners, Local Government, and
     the Development of Bournemouth, *c.* 1850 to 1914', in Cannadine, ed., *Patricians,
     Power, and Politics*, p. 198; R. Newton, 'Society and Politics in Exeter, 1837–1914',
     in Dyos, ed., *Study of Urban History*, p. 313; Derek Fraser, *Urban Politics in Victorian
     England* (Leicester, 1976), pp. 130–3.
[95] Fraser, *Urban Politics*, pp. 13, 92–3; Derek Fraser, *Power and Authority in the Victorian
     City* (1979), pp. 148–55.

waterworks, sewage systems, power stations, tramways, schools, libraries, parks, and from the 1890s, in a small way, housing projects, to design, construct, and operate. Municipal bureaucracy and its servants were a large, expensive, and in their 'municipal trading' or 'municipal socialist' hats, very controversial sector of late Victorian and Edwardian urban life.[96] Chief officers' jobs were important openings for the new professions; although their salaried nature posed problems for the consultant-client version of the professional ethic, the salaries themselves were handsome enough in the largest cities, at around £1,000 a year towards the end of the century, to place some borough engineers or medical officers of health safely in the upper middle class.[97] Many of the municipal servants, particularly where a borough employed direct labour on construction works, were part of the working classes, normally with the privileged status of secure and regular employment. In between there came a large slice of middle- to lower middle-class jobs: the chief officers of the lesser or more parsimonious boroughs, the subordinate professional staff, the clerical workers, and, after 1902, the main mass of schoolteachers, who had previously been employees of the School Boards. The business of town government, as it moved from the minimal functions of the 1830s to the wide array of activities of the 1900s, became an important engine of middle- and lower middle-class growth, and made the genteel, respectable, unadventurous, conventional middle-brow tone of urban society self-perpetuating.

As the process of urbanisation peaked and levelled out in the years just before 1914 it was apparent that it had spawned an urban environment with considerable areas of squalor, nastiness, and drabness, which posed unresolved problems that increasingly clamoured for attention. Urban society, on the other hand, had developed a reasonably stable structure: there were conflicts, complaints, and discontents, but these operated within a social order which, although its legitimacy might not be universally accepted by all classes, was not likely to collapse into anarchy or social revolution, nor yet the aimless incoherence which had been the nightmare of some intelligent early Victorians. That social order had outgrown its earlier aristocratic and patrician cocoon, of which the only significant traces left were in London high society and in the ornamental and ceremonial appearances of individual aristocrats in what had once been 'their' towns. It had

[96]   Offer, *Property and Politics*, pp. 221–2, 302–8.
[97]   Wohl, *Endangered Lives*, pp. 186–7.

also largely shed the urban aristocracy, which may be variously termed the aristocratic bourgeoisie, the business and professional elite, or the upper middle class. This class, insofar as it had not withdrawn entirely into the country, might retain very large economic interests which were located in towns, but was extensively gentrified in manners, education, values, and residential style; it was no more than semi-urban, and its members did not readily identify with the fortunes and aspirations of any one particular town. The most purely urban elements in urban society, substantially created by urbanisation, were the working class and the lower middle class. Neither in fact was a class with any readily perceptible cohesion, consciousness, or culture. The working class of manual workers was a bundle of classes defined by earnings, skill, occupation, regularity of employment, unionisation, or religion: distinctions which existed within urban settings but did not derive from them. The urban response of the working classes, the neighbourhood community, tended to promote an inward-looking cellular structure, not class solidarity. Even more, the lower middle class was a social analyst's convenience, as a category of discourse, rather than a social reality; its members were so permeated with the introversion of family privacy and independence that they had difficulty in relating at all closely even to neighbours in the same occupational and cultural fraction of this much fragmented class. The economic, social, and political dynamics of urbanisation, however, had projected the lower middle class into a prominence which far exceeded its expectations and its capacity to develop constructive, rather than merely negative, ideas on how to use this position.

The working classes were the first to move, seeking unity through political and industrial organisation, and in the twenty years before 1914 beginning to break into urban local government on a much wider front than they were achieving nationally at the parliamentary level. After 1918 their power in the towns, and national policies intended either to propitiate the working class or improve its welfare, initiated a destruction of the social texture and culture of the Victorian town that was more widespread than the concomitant demolition of parts of its physical fabric. The lower middle class moved late, often seemed to be defeated, even annihilated, in detail, and never capitalised on its urban potential within strictly urban limits. But when it found its votes, and its voice, it entered into its national inheritance in 1979, with far more devastating effects.

IV

In the nineteenth century the towns rose to numerical dominance without gravely embarrassing the old order save in the few years before 1832 when the unrepresented towns seemed to pose a real threat to the unreformed parliamentary system. In 1885 the ancient distinction between county and borough seats in Parliament vanished without causing a tremor, except among the political parties jockeying for position, and the country settled almost without noticing into a political system in which the typical constituencies were, and are, centred on towns or are sub-divisions of the larger towns. Not the least of the reasons for this barely resisted or regretted abandonment of tradition was that at the political level the towns had turned out to house both parties, Liberals and Conservatives, and to offer prospects and pickings for both, and had not developed as the exclusive electoral property of one side. Moreover, at the ideological and social level it had turned out that the towns had not developed a strong, independent, and separate identity or culture of a kind which could rival and overwhelm the country-based forces of the traditional ruling class. Urban elites, indeed, had shown considerable propensity to merge with the aristocratic-gentry upper class, so that in many vital respects urban society was a structure without a top storey.

This does not mean that some general process of gentrification and infiltration of gentry values precipitated British economic decline by sapping the spirit of enterprise and overthrowing the work ethic.[98] Far from it. Businessmen continued to work in towns, some very successfully, some less so, and almost all industrial firms and their works were located in towns: that was where the wealth came from. Many businessmen, however, and in the course of the twentieth century most, detached themselves for all other purposes – residence, social life, education, recreation, involvement in public life – from their workplace. The loss of interest in municipal government by the city fathers, already evident in the late nineteenth century, became almost total after the First World War.[99] It is symptomatic that whereas Victorian millionaires were likely to give art galleries, public parks, or colleges to their native towns, twentieth-century tycoons are much more likely to endow Oxbridge colleges or set up national charitable

---

[98]   The argument of Martin J. Wiener, *English Culture and the Decline of the Industrial Spirit, 1850-1980* (Cambridge, 1981).

[99]   B. T. Robson. 'Coming Full Circle: London versus the Rest, 1890–1980', in George Gordon, ed., *Regional Cities in the U.K. 1890–1980* (1986), pp. 227–8.

or educational foundations; even when an art collection is given to a city, as the Burrell collection to Glasgow, it is outhoused in a park where, in considerable architectural presence, it appears to belong to the public at large more than to the citizens of Glasgow. But if one twentieth-century development has been the erosion of the particularity of individual towns and the disappearance of loyalties focussed on them, except for popular attachments to city football teams which can be savagely violent in their partisanship, another has been the completion of the almost total urbanisation of British society and its culture.

This happened in spite of, and indeed to a considerable extent because of, the flight from the city of the better-off commuters, the rentiers, and the retired, who between them comprised a large slice of the upper and middling middle class. Much of this dispersal peopled the outer suburbs whose interwar sprawling was the chief instrument of the physical spread of the great conurbations, but much of it also leapt beyond them into what appeared to geographers and statisticians to be the countryside. This last process certainly had its mid-Victorian origins in the appearance of the 'stockbroker belt' phenomenon from the 1860s onwards, and its antecedents in the move of some of the very rich into 'houses in the country'; but it moved into a different gear with the availability of motor vehicles. Nineteenth-century dispersal was dependent on railways, and the horse and carriage for reaching the station from any distance, and this limited settlement in the country by townsfolk to the wealthy and the very rich; nevertheless, railways were already creating country-village satellites, like Radlett in Hertfordshire, by the 1880s.[100] Already before 1914 the motor cars of the very rich were opening up parts of the countryside hitherto considered too remote for convenient access to town: the new country house of Ewelme Down in the Thames valley near Wallingford was described as an example of this in 1912.[101] This effect moved down the social scale into the middle classes in the 1920s and 1930s as motor transport spread. Motor buses became the key to outer suburbia, which was admittedly a form of low-density urban environment usually lacking any town-like features beyond the bare essentials of shops and a cinema. Motor cars opened up new possibilities for the evolution of new breeds of middle-class amphibians who lived

[100] J. T. Coppock, 'Dormitory Settlements around London', in J. T. Coppock and H. C. Prince, eds., *Greater London* (1964), pp. 279–84.
[101] *Country Life*, 31 (1912), p. 430.

in the country and worked in the town; their appetite for ribbon development, particularly along arterial roads in the south-east, was so voracious that within little more than a decade a new term had been added to the language, the process itself had been subjected to some attempt at official control in 1933, and much professional planning opinion held that it was fast becoming impossible to tell where town ended and country began.[102]

Fanning out into the countryside had not progressed very far before it was halted by the Second World War. It was resumed with increasing intensity in the 1950s and 1960s as car ownership spread widely and two-car households became common in the middle class, but it resumed under a powerful planning regime with strictly enforced green belt policies, which at least made it plain physically and visually where the large towns ended and the country began, even if it could not oblige country dwellers to abjure urban habits. Villages and small towns in and beyond the green belts were colonised and taken over by the middle classes whose livelihoods were earned in the nearest larger towns or conurbations, and new settlements were carved out beyond the green belt fringe. The woodland inhabitants of Tewin Wood in Hertfordshire, with their large detached houses in individual clearings in the wood, commuting to work in nearby Welwyn Garden City or going up to London, enjoying their rural environment and their detachment from any rural labours, became the sociologist's paradigm of the urban-rural middle class of the 1960s.[103] These movements contributed to producing the statistical effect of a sharp slowing down of the process of urbanisation after the 1890s, and its arrest or even slight reversal from the 1920s, when that process is considered simply as a geographical question of changes in the distribution of people between urban and rural settlements.[104] The movements also suggest, however, that urbanisation as a social and cultural process continued unabated, its influence penetrating deep into the countryside on the wheels of the new transport technology without making the physical environment decisively and brutally non-rural. The new urban-rural middle classes, moreover, were part of a generalised and

---

[102]   The Ribbon Development Restrictions Act, 1933, was ineffective. In practice ribbon development was ended by the Second World War, and was not resumed after it, at least in such a crude manner. A. A. Jackson, *Semi-Detached London: Suburban Development, Life and Transport, 1900–39* (1973), p. 321; Gerald Dix, 'Patrick Abercrombie', in Gordon Cherry, ed., *Pioneers in British Planning* (1981), p. 113.

[103]   R. E. Pahl, *Urbs in Rure* (1965), esp. pp. 43–62.

[104]   See above, pp. 10–11, pp. 10–11.

unspecific urban society, not members of the society of some particular and identifiable city. A major component of their urban nature was displayed in their homes and their contents, and the remainder was expressed in a number of links and attachments to what could be a whole range of different towns which provided jobs, shops, services, entertainment, and what are termed 'high order' cultural and commercial facilities of a kind only available in a metropolis. The society to which they belonged was emphatically urban, yet it could not meaningfully be labelled with a place-name. It was the quintessential twentieth-century phenomenon, the signal that the nation had become one great extended town.

The urban–rural divide has become increasingly blurred and indistinct in the twentieth century in another way. The plateau of urbanisation left somewhere between a fifth and a quarter of the total population officially classified as non-urban at every census since 1891, but the proportion of this rather stable non-urban section which was directly involved in farming declined all the time, steadily and fairly gradually until 1945, thereafter steeply. Agriculture itself, taking farmers and labourers together, still employed nearly 10 per cent of the British male labour force before 1914. If it is assumed, for want of any direct statistics, that as many again of the population living in the country were employed in servicing agriculture or processing its products, than a clear majority of the pre-1914 'rural' population was still closely connected with the land. By 1951 agriculture employed less than 6 per cent of the labour force, and since industrialised methods of servicing farming had largely replaced rural craftsmen it may be doubted whether as much as half the 'rural' population any longer had economic ties with the countryside in which it lived. The trend was under way which by the 1970s, with a further much-slimmed farm labour force, would reduce farming to a minor, though heavily subsidised, occupation in the countryside, while elevating the great majority of the 'rural' population, perhaps as much as 75 per cent of it, into one form or another of urban expatriate. These were retired people, remittance men living on incomes drawn from investments in remote industries and places, and people working in the industries which electrification and road transport brought back into the countryside, as well as commuters. Their existence showed that many people found the countryside a pleasant and attractive place to live, so long as they did not have to work on the land. They often literally changed places with farm workers heading for the city lights and the higher living standards of industrial and urban jobs, who deserted the low wages and limited amenities of farm work just as much as they were driven away by mechanisation: the improvement and gentrification of farm labourers' cottages, some as desirable middle-class residences and some as holiday houses, according to location, began in a select way in the 1930s and blossomed into a speculator's and estate agent's paradise in the 1950s. By the 1970s deserted barns suitable, with some imagination, for conversion into comfortable centrally-heated properties had become prizes for the urban-rural middle class.

The great class switch, which in global terms ensured that rural depopulation was roughly balanced by rural repopulation – although at the regional level the net effect was a decline in population in the upland areas and a shift towards the south-east – demonstrated that many of those who could afford it preferred to live in the country, and rejected some uncongenial aspects of the quality of life in the towns. It also demonstrated that many of those who did not live well in the country found its charms resistible, and voted with their feet for the superior attractions of the quality of life in the towns. The first group brought their urban values with them into the country and, since they were never 'ruralised', became one of the principal agencies, alongside such economic and technological factors as radio, cinema, and advertising, of the diffusion of a standardised urban-based culture. The second group, like their Victorian predecessors, may have brought country-bred habits with them as individuals into the towns, but they rapidly became thoroughly urbanised, merging into the urban social structure rather than modifying or adding to it. Unlike the nineteenth century, however, the urban structure in the interwar period was changing in ways that encouraged the atomisation of society into a collection of individuals, rather than fostering the growth of tight-knit local communities. The anomie anticipated and feared by the early Victorians had at length arrived. In the short run, certainly until 1939 and perhaps until the 1960s, the effect was to strengthen class consciousness and class antagonism by weakening the power of alternative foci of group loyalties, so that what came to be seen as the traditional class structure of British society was more a result of the decay of Victorian urban society than an intrinsic part of that society's make-up. In the longer run, from the booming Britain of the 1960s onwards, the effect was more to blur the distinctions between classes, encourage the development of an almost classless low-brow version of standardised urban culture, coupled with the segregation of a de-classed and re-styled residuum in the crumbling inner cities.

Paradoxically the quality of life in the large towns was by and large improving markedly, in material terms, at the very moment when larger numbers of the middle classes than ever before decided to quit. The improvement was most visible in housing, but was also noticeable in other areas like health care, nutrition, schooling, and social security. From the standpoint of the 1980s conditions in the late 1930s were appalling, or on a charitable view primitive, as those were reflected in standard measures of mortality, life expectancy, infant mortality, school leaving age, or average level of educational attainment. There were indeed many trenchant critics of the state of society in the 1930s, who revealed the gross inequalities in the incidence of infant mortality, major diseases like tuberculosis, and in the quality and availability of education, between different social classes; and who were pioneering the thinking which became embodied in wartime nutritional measures and the post-1945 welfare state. Nevertheless, shocking as the infant mortality rate of 53 per thousand live births in 1938 may now appear, it was a great deal less shocking than the 1910 rate of 109, and the decline is a fair indication of the general improvement in health in the interwar years. Similarly, the state of education obviously left much to be desired in 1939, when the great majority of children left school at fourteen and untold amounts of potential talent were allowed to go undiscovered and undeveloped: but a near doubling in the amount of public money, central and local, spent on education between 1920 and 1939, and an increase of two and a half times in the number of pupils in secondary schools between 1914 and 1938, spoke of considerable changes. All these, since the overwhelming majority of the population was urban, were things which mainly happened in towns.[105]

Other great changes in the quality of life, and possibly those which made most impact on most people like the spread of cinemas or the rise of greyhound tracks in the 1930s, were the work of private enterprise; a few, of less popular appeal, like the Carnegie grants to the less flourishing public libraries, were the work of philanthropy. Most of the improvements in health and welfare, however, were connected with the work of local government, backed by some central

---

[105] B. R. Mitchell and P. Deane, *Abstract of British Historical Statistics* (Cambridge, 1962), pp. 37, 398–9, 418.

government finance – itself less apparent to many boroughs than stringent and unfeeling financial control by the Treasury which was an interwar anticipation of the more refined rate-capping of the 1980s.[106] Above all local government – and this meant primarily boroughs and urban districts – acquired an altogether new role from 1919 onwards as providers and controllers of working-class housing. All this meant that local government was of increasingly direct importance to the lives of ordinary people. Central government also loomed much larger after the First World War, especially in providing, financing, and policing the several systems of unemployment relief, but also in providing pensions, a large part of the finance for the public education system, and the framework of the 'panel' system of national health insurance doctors; in addition there was a growing public perception that the government was responsible for the general state of the economy, if only because it had enacted, under wartime pressures, the measures that had disrupted the allegedly self-regulating pre-1914 economy. Nevertheless, the interwar years were the heyday of local government, in the range and content of its services if not in the quality of its administration. After 1939 central government stepped in, from 1945 permanently (insofar as forty years amount to 'permanence'), as the all-important provider and controller of unemployment relief, health, education, housing, and social security, using local government as its agent in administering these policies only where specialised and centrally controlled agencies did not appear more convenient.

One general result was that it mattered who was in the town hall. More precisely, in the nineteenth century control of the town hall had mattered to ratepayers, who sought local power either to cut municipal spending or to see that it was efficiently managed, and to minority groups like sanitary improvers or reformers of public morals. In the twentieth century it mattered to the impoverished and the deprived, and to the working classes in general, and it became worthwhile for the representatives of the working classes to seek power. The politicisation of local government was a direct consequence of making its functions a prize worth fighting for, and of making a large proportion of rate-financed expenditure into a form of income and welfare redistribution. The effects were seen in the widespread entry of Labour into the council chambers, broadening out in the 1920s from the narrow bridgeheads established before 1914

---

[106]   Pat Thane, *Foundations of the Welfare State* (1982), pp. 185–9; John Stevenson, *British Society, 1914–45* (1984), pp. 318, 398–9.

in the most thoroughly working-class wards of the largest cities. Labour took temporary control of a few boroughs in 1920 and in 1929 established a firmer grip on a score or so; a great triumph came in the local elections of 1933 and 1934 when, with the parliamentary party still shattered after the 1931 split, Labour won control of Leeds, some forty other boroughs, and the greatest prize of all, the London County Council. After 1945 Labour entered into its urban inheritance, becoming the normal ruling party in all the northern and Midland towns, and London, and elsewhere in the south at least the alternative ruling party.

Whether Labour control made much difference to what actually happened in the towns has been questioned.[107] That is important in assessing the record of local government or political parties, but is neither here nor there beside the key point that in organising support at the ward level the Labour party was the agent of class formation, and indeed, through equal but opposite stimulation of its rivals, the catalyst for a general class polarisation in the towns. To be sure, the rise of the Labour party had many facets and the movement had many sources of nourishment, notably the trade unions and the brotherly idealism of the left stiffened by the comradely discipline of 1917. The peculiarly urban element, however, stemmed from the structure of municipal government and the urge to fight local elections, which called forth a political organisation that welded together groups and individuals from a broad band of roughly similar economic and social conditions who had previously lacked either the means or the need for aspiring to the cohesion of class. It did not greatly signify that the level of turnout at local elections was low, with 30 or 40 per cent polls being usual, although this did suggest that political and class consciousness had its limits. Of greater importance, local elections were annual, except in London where they were triennial, and called for more continuous political activity and organisation than the much more widely spaced parliamentary elections. The fundamental fact of social importance, however, was that the form of political organisation was widely perceived, by working men and women and by anti-socialists alike, as being shaped on class lines. The politics were essentially national politics, although there were usually particular burning local issues as well, and the general object was to gain control of

---

[107] For example by A. J. P. Taylor, *English History, 1914–1945* (Oxford, 1965), p. 367, for the 1930s, or Anthony Sutcliffe, 'The "Midland Metropolis": Birmingham, 1890–1980', in Gordon, ed., *Regional Cities*, p. 32, for the 1950s and 1960s.

central government; but it was in the urban setting that an identity was forged for the working class, and by reaction for the lower middle class. Urban society moved a long way in the interwar years from being a cellular society to being a class society.

That process, nurtured in the womb of municipal government, quickened under the influence of changes in the fabric of the urban environment which were largely shaped by municipal government itself even though it was largely central government which called the tune and paid the bills. It is no accident that most accounts of towns and municipal corporations in the interwar period concentrate on housing, and more specifically on council housing in the 1920s, private sector housing in the 1930s, and thereafter council housing again from 1945 into the 1950s.[108] Publicly subsidised housing was the one great new departure of the projected post-1918 reconstruction which produced a major and lasting impression on British society. It had some impact on the countryside, where many farm workers were rehoused in starkly sanitary cottages, but the main thrust was in the larger towns. The initial phase, in the 1920s, was intended to bring the countrified ideal of the garden city and garden suburb to the worker, suitably filtered through the Tudor Walters rules on minimum standards for room sizes and numbers, and adjusted to the finances available.[109] The result was an economy version, or perhaps more accurately a proletarianised version, of the ideal, in which council housing estates concentrated on providing the greatest number of dwellings and eliminated most of the community-building features and amenities that had been integral to the original garden city blueprints. The individual houses, built to Tudor Walters specifications, low-rise, grouped in pairs or small blocks, set in gardens, and equipped with indoor water closets, baths and bathrooms, and arranged in curves, contours, and corners rather than gridiron street layouts, were a great advance on most pre-1914 working-class housing; only the improvement over the

---

[108]   See, for example, Waller, *Democracy and Sectarianism*, pp. 287–90, for Liverpool in the 1920s: Michael Meadowcraft, 'The Years of Political Transition, 1914–39', in Fraser, ed., *Modern Leeds*, pp. 416–22; Gordon, ed., *Regional Cities*, for chapters on Birmingham, Manchester, Liverpool, Glasgow, Leeds, Newcastle, Edinburgh, Cardiff, and Belfast.

[109]   The Tudor Walters Report, 1918, was the report of a departmental committee on 'the provision of dwellings for the working classes of England and Wales, and Scotland', and amongst other things made the first official recommendation that working-class houses ought to have bathrooms: Mark Swenarton, *Homes Fit for Heroes: The Politics and Architecture of Early State Housing in Britain* (1981), esp. chap. 5.

best of prewar terraced parlour houses could be considered aesthetic more than material. The earliest cottage estates of 1919-22, such as Roehampton and a small part of Becontree (Dagenham) for the LCC and Tang Hall in York, were architecturally reasonably satisfying.[110] With the reduced subsidies and cost-cutting later in the 1920s the cottage estates en masse, as in the bulk of the Dagenham estate or in the vast out-city Huyton estate built by Liverpool Corporation, became monotonous, architecturally unadventurous, a great deal less bosky, and featureless and characterless. By the 1930s, 30,000 people were living in Huyton without a single community centre having been built. Here was the framework for urban or semi-urban anomie, erected by authority.

The cottage estates, although subsidised, still had rents beyond the reach of the poorest. Moreover, council housing managers, after an initial period of giving a preference to ex-servicemen, tended to select as tenants those of good character and a clean record who could convincingly claim ability to pay rent regularly, thus at a stroke eliminating most of those with the most pressing need for housing and sheltering behind the convenient theory that the poorest and most deprived would benefit by 'filtering up' into the accommodation left vacant by the better-paid who had moved out. Thus, although the cottage estates normally contained a mixture of two-, three-, and four-bedroomed houses which could cater for families of different incomes and different life-cycle stages they became single-class settlements of regularly employed and moderately well-paid workers to the exclusion of both the best-paid who were quite comfortable where they were already, and the worst-paid. This carried residential social segregation to a more refined and higher pitch than it had attained in the free-market conditions of the nineteenth century. And, because the transplanting was of individual families and not of existing neighbourhoods or networks, moving into what were often housing deserts devoid of oases of community or cultural refreshment, the estates weakened or destroyed ties of kinship or occupation and encouraged a social response which was either inward-turning to resignation and apathy, or outward-looking to a class consciousness which ran in national and not particularly urban, or individual city, grooves.

Council housing efforts in the 1930s, steered by government policy, changed direction and broadly were directly engaged in tackling the

---

[110]   Swenarton, *Homes*, pp. 166–86.

needs of the poorest, in central-district slum clearance and rehousing schemes. These had analogous social effects to the cottage estates, while affecting a different layer of the working classes. In central districts land was too valuable to indulge in the luxuries of low-density redevelopment with two-storey housing, and large blocks of council flats became the typical instruments of these schemes. Flat-living or tenement-dwelling was unfamiliar in the English working-class tradition, unlike the Scottish, and in itself tended to induce discontent and alienation, quite apart from the disturbance and breaking up of established local communities usually inseparable from slum clearances. The height of 1930s high-rise for the workers (although not for some of the fashionable occupants of luxury flats) was almost insignificant if set alongside the system-built tower blocks which were to rise in the 1960s and become a byword for dilapidation and despair in the 1970s. But they were high enough, cell-like enough, and bleak enough in their common stairways and facilities, not to be loved and cherished and to play their part in breeding social dislocation and its harvest of either heightened class feeling or a sub-culture that repudiated normal standards of behaviour.

The private sector consistently out-built the local authorities in numbers of houses completed per year in every year from 1924 onwards, and came into its own in the 1930s, with annual numbers far surpassing the highest pre-1914 years and consistently ranging between twice and six times as many as the public sector.[111] These were the houses of the new waves of owner-occupiers in the middle and lower middle classes, spread out in the outer suburbs spawned by all the larger towns, in what may be termed the speculative builders' semi-detached version of the garden city dream. By 1938 about 35 per cent of all the houses in Britain were owner-occupied, and although this average conceals a large spread from 14 per cent in Nottingham to 68 per cent in Plymouth the concentration of the high ratings in the boom towns of the period like Coventry, Oxford, and Bristol, and the low ratings of the old industrial towns such as Manchester, Hull, Sheffield, Merthyr, Birmingham, Wolverhampton, or Stoke, let alone the evidence of the ring of outer suburbs and satellites which sprouted round London from Potters Bar, Rickmansworth, and Ruislip, to Surbiton, Sanderstead, Orpington, and Bexley,

---

[111]   B. R. Mitchell and H. G. Jones, *Second Abstract of British Historical Statistics* (Cambridge, 1971), p. 117. After 1945 the private sector did not overtake the local authorities in annual numbers of houses built until 1958.

suggests the strongly middle-class character of the surge in owner-occupation.[112] This Tudorised, electrified, and motorised (at least in bus services) rendering of the garden city vision might be held to have paid slightly more attention to community needs, in a basic com-mercial-philistine way, than the council cottage estates, in the lavish provision of shopping parades and super-Tudorised roadhouses; and the actual semi-detached houses, energetically plugged as 'ideal homes' in high-pressure salesmanship, were undoubtedly superior. It can also be argued that these mass-produced estates, run up at incredible speed by newly emerging large-scale building firms which became household names – Costain, Ideal Homestead, Laing, Taylor-Woodrow, and Wimpey, for example – provided for the first time a semi-urban environment which exactly suited the tastes and the pent-up latent demand of the middle and lower middle classes for comfort, refinement, privacy, and detachment from the unpleasant social and industrial features of urban living.

These housing estates ate into the countryside at a rate which deeply alarmed the proto-environmentalists of the time. Their alarm, coupled with concern at the unfortunate regional distribution or maldistribu-tion of free-market industrial and office development in the interwar years, lay at the root of the town planning legislation of 1947 and the planning system which controlled the main lines of physical urban development into the 1980s.[113] The system altered the contours and the detailed local geography of new development, but did not seri-ously affect, or curtail the continued growth of, the commuting habits on which these dispersed settlements ultimately depended. For there was no doubt that these housing estates were pleasant places to live for families whose chief ambition was to keep themselves to them-selves, to avoid any pressures for an undue show of neighbourliness, and to conduct their social lives away from home territory, anony-mously, and among networks which were not necessarily based on residential propinquity. The conflicting desires to express individu-ality and yet to seek safety in conformity were reflected in the specula-tive builders' gimcrack differentiation of near-identical houses by

[112] Mark Swenarton and Sandra Taylor, 'The Scale and Nature of the Growth of Owner-Occupation in Britain between the Wars', *Economic History Review*, 2nd ser., 38 (1985), p. 377 and Table 4, p. 387. No pre-1914 figure can be given: the notion that there were 10 per cent of owner-occupiers before 1914 is a myth or a guess, there being no reliable data or estimates.

[113] For an informative, critical, assessment of the post-1947 period see Alison Ravetz, *The Government of Space* (1986).

arbitrary variations in the shape or amount of Jacobethan or Gothic features pinned to their fabrics, and by adjoining owners' careful choice of clashing colours for their paintwork. Privacy was safe-guarded more by garden fences than by the lace curtains that had been the mark of Victorian respectability in houses which had fronted directly on to the street. Finally, respectability no longer demanded regular Sunday parades to church or chapel, which had been the chief vehicle for forming communities in middle- and lower middle-class Victorian suburbs. Where a church or chapel or probably several of them, had been essential to the tone and prospects of any substantial nineteenth-century suburban development of character, new churches were so thin on the ground in interwar estates as to be virtually invisible. The secular alternatives, like the cinema, were places for individuals or couples to retreat into romantic fantasy, not centres of community life; and the fraternisation of the golf club did not begin to percolate below the level of the affluent middle-class elite before the 1960s.

For non-working wives in particular – and they were the great major-ity of wives – these acres of semis created a cultural desert and a life of extreme monotony, somewhat relieved by the rapid spread of radio into the home in the later 1920s and the 1930s, which itself was a foretaste of the standardisation and nationalisation of culture, centrally produced by professionals and individually absorbed inside the home, that was to sweep all before it in the post-1950 triumph of television. In only lesser degree for the men also, and for the unmar-ried women who in the main did go out to work, these estates embo-died a way of life which was atomised and individualised, that lacked social cohesion except of a passive, flock-of-sheep, variety, and which generated no networks of associations or communities to stand between individuals, or families, and the state. These suburbanites, although living in greater material comfort, were fundamentally no less isolated, no less detached from their previous social, and urban, moorings, than the working classes in the council estates over which they were so keen to proclaim their superiority. Only their politicisa-tion, their development of anything approaching a class identity and class consciousness, was more hesitant and muted, and much slower in becoming assertive. To be sure, 'villa Toryism', the propensity of the suburbs to vote Conservative, had been apparent since the 1880s, and was practically axiomatic in the new suburbs of the 1930s, one of the necessary conventions as it were of respectability. This suburban

Conservatism, however, was not much more than that, a reflex action by mute followers content to act as reliable ballot-box fodder while leaving power in the hands of a gentry, professional, and business elite. It was the shock and horror of the Labour victory in 1945, and the response to it, which made it thinkable to challenge and eventually supplant the power and authority within the party of the old guard. It was a long, slow, business, working through permeation of constituency associations and penetration of adoption committees, and on to the enthronement of lower middle-class values – though now held by key individuals who had risen personally above lower middle-class levels of education or income – in the 1980s. It is fair to say that by the 1960s the suburban masses had matured from being a simple collection of politically passive individuals into a coherent national entity: they cohered in the context of Parliament, central government, and a national power struggle, not in the context of an urban environment.

The new kinds of interwar housing – the council cottage estates, the council flats, and the outer suburbs of semi-detacheds for owner-occupiers – had a great impact on society, for by 1939 they were providing over one third of the total housing stock in Britain. When building was resumed after the war the impact was intensified, with some largely superficial changes: striped trousers and bowler hats faded from the scene and commuter trains were packed with a higher proportion than before of secretaries, typists, and other female office-workers. In 1950 major changes still lay in the future: large-scale immigration, the decay of inner cities, the rise and fall of tower blocks, and the gentrification, or re-gentrification, of run-down but formerly elegant parts of the old central and inner districts.These further modified and transformed the urban setting. It was already abundantly clear by 1950, however, that 'urban society' had become little more than a loosely defined descriptive term for the location and type of physical environment in which people, groups, and classes lived, and had ceased to be a term denoting a specific kind of social structure that differed from some other kinds of social structure elsewhere in Britain.[114]

It can reasonably be doubted whether there ever was a period within the two centuries ending in the 1950s when British towns collectively sustained a complete social structure, with interrelated and

---

[114] Although it remained meaningful to call British society as a whole an 'urban society' in contrast to 'peasant societies' or 'rural societies' in other parts of the world.

cohering classes and social circles and its own interlocking elites, of the kind that constituted a distinctive and independent urban society. In the eighteenth century, and well into the nineteenth century, much of the top layer was aristocratic, with roots in the countryside and a primary role in rural society, while much of the lower layers consisted of recent, and sometimes transient, transplants from rural life. In the nineteenth century much of the top layer which had been generated from within the city removed itself from the scene, by gentrification or by high-class suburbanisation, and left the urban social structure incomplete. It was in the twentieth century that the urban social structure became not so much more incomplete as more diffused and more indistinguishable from simply the social structure of Britain at large. Plenty of urban problems remained, and intensified: poor housing and health, inner city decay, crime and violence, high unemployment, educational neglect, squalor, traffic congestion, and a long list of deprivations. Urban regions remained, as units for bureaucrats and planners to mark out and examine. Urban society, however, had merged into the nation.[115]

[115]   Andrew Lees, *Cities Perceived: Urban Society in European and American Thought, 1820–1940* (Manchester, 1985), pp. 258–68, examines the question why 'the British evinced relatively low levels of interest in and concern about the specifically urban aspects of their society' in the 1920s and 1930s.

CHAPTER 2

The countryside

W. A. ARMSTRONG

I

'England was early in the field with a productive, expansible agriculture.'[1] Among specialists in agrarian history there are diverse opinions concerning the extent of changes in farming practices and the rate at which increases in output were achieved before and during the eighteenth century, but no one disputes that England stood in the vanguard of agrarian progress. Moreover it is generally agreed that the agrarian sector was commercialised to an extent unmatched elsewhere, except in Holland. These advances had been accompanied and no doubt in some respects facilitated by changes in the composition of rural society. From the vantage point of the later eighteenth century a marked contrast with the position in contemporary Europe was discernible. English rural society in no way resembled that of territories east of the Elbe, characterised by enormous estates worked by hordes of unemancipated serfs; nor did it exhibit the pattern common to much of Western Europe, where much land continued to be held in relatively tiny units farmed by peasants. In England, through a lengthy process of evolution there had emerged a tripartite system, featuring landlords who were essentially rent receivers but who bore certain responsibilities for the provision of fixed capital; substantial tenant farmers, directly responsible for the working of the land through the application of their entrepreneurial energies and working capital; and landless or virtually landless wage earners whose contribution derived from their application of strength and skill and who were surprisingly numerous even in the sixteenth century.[2]

Implicit in the commercialisation of agriculture was a powerful

---

[1] E. L. Jones, *Agriculture and Economic Growth in England, 1650–1850* (1967), p. 47.
[2] A. M. Everitt, 'Farm Labourers', in J. Thirsk, ed., *The Agrarian History of England and Wales*, vol. 4: *1500–1640* (Cambridge, 1967), p. 462.

tendency for the sweeping away of men who did not fit neatly into these categories. These included small owner-occupiers ('yeomen'), lesser tenants and cottagers occupying a position intermediate between the wage earner and the small farmer. Small occupiers were especially vulnerable to market forces, and it is now apparent that the era of low prices, 1650–1750, had seen a tendency for land to accumulate in the hands of larger proprietors.[3] Such commercial influences were probably more effective than the Georgian enclosure acts in reducing the number of petty farmers. In the case of the small owners, it is accepted that the costs of enclosure must always have been disproportionately heavy, yet they were also variable, as was the capacity to bear them. At all events the aggregate number of individual holdings appears to have held up after 1780 in a climate of rising prices, as studies based on the land tax suggest.[4] As for small tenancies, enclosure afforded good opportunities for landlords to embark upon consolidation, but such steps were not unknown in unenclosed villages and indeed other considerations might weigh with landlords, such as the fact that occupants often had votes and paid a higher rent per acre. Today, few historians consider that enclosure invariably spelt catastrophe for the small occupier. Even among those who regard enclosure as socially regressive, the talk is of the 'likely existence of a filter down the agricultural ladder producing some degree of landlessness'.[5] The position is least clear with respect to cottagers, thought especially vulnerable because of their dependence on common land for grazing and fuel. Since there is no quantifiable source which bears directly on this problem, historians have to judge between contemporary charges and counter-charges. However, it is generally agreed that for many individuals, losses may have been serious. Not for nothing did an experienced enclosure commissioner come to lament that he had been an accessory to injuring at least 2,000 poor persons at the rate of twenty families per parish, and this and similar evidence eventually led Arthur Young to the conclusion that, in many cases, 'the poor had unquestionably been injured': however, he continued, 'these injuries ... are not mentioned to show that such enclosures should not have taken place; nor to assert that an increase in regular employment ... might not more than make amends for them, which

[3] G. E. Mingay, *Enclosure and the Small Farmer in the Age of the Industrial Revolution* (1968), pp. 26–30.
[4] See J. A. Yelling, *Common Field and Enclosure in England, 1450–1850* (1977), pp. 103–9.
[5] M. E. Turner, in *Agricultural History*, papers presented to the Economic History Conference (Canterbury, 1983), p. 50.

is another question'.[6] The suggestion that enclosure, especially where it entailed the cultivation of former wastelands (which accounted for some 28 per cent of land enclosed before 1793 and more thereafter[7]), lifted the aggregate level of wage paid employment forms a major plank in the arguments which several modern historians have opposed to earlier cataclysmic views. The well-known seasonal imbalances in the labour requirement for arable cultivation should, however, be borne in mind.[8] Thus, the impact of enclosure was far from simple and in view of the unevenness of change, the tripartite scheme must be treated with circumspection. It has value as a model, summarising some essential features of English agrarian relationships, towards which the currents of change were running. It does not offer a comprehensive description of agrarian society at any particular point in time. Even at the close of the eighteenth century, there remained twelve counties in which small farms of 100 acres or less actually predominated and they were common in six more, while farms of over 300 acres were very unusual in many parts of the country.[9] In another respect, overemphasis on tripartism can mislead. Essentially, it presents a set of functional economic categories, each peopled by individuals of very varying rank or status.

At the peak of the land-owning pyramid stood a nobility which in England was tightly defined to include no more than about 170 individuals, at least before the peerage came to be extended with new creations by the younger Pitt. Modern estimates would suggest that their average annual incomes were about £5,000 to £6,000 in the 1690s and perhaps double that a century later, although in cases such as the Dukes of Bedford, Devonshire, and Northumberland, they might reach £40,000 or £50,000.[10] The exclusivity of their marriage alliances is legendary. Strict settlements were used to advance the long-run interests of these families and jointures and portions for wives and children on reaching majority were carefully specified. Less

---

[6] A. Young, *General Report on Enclosures, 1808* (reprint, New York, 1971), pp. 12, 13, 158.
[7] M. E. Turner, *English Parliamentary Enclosure* (Folkestone, 1980), p. 71.
[8] E.g. J. D. Chambers and G. F. Mingay, *The Agricultural Revolution, 1750–1880* (1966), pp. 98–9; see also K. D. M. Snell, 'Agricultural Seasonal Employment, the Standard of Living, and Women's Work in the South and East, 1690–1860', *Economic History Review*, 2nd ser., 34 (1981), or his *Annals of the Labouring Poor: Social Change and Agrarian England, 1660–1900* (Cambridge, 1985), chap. 1.
[9] G. E. Mingay, 'The Size of Farms in the Eighteenth Century', *Economic History Review*, 2nd ser., 14 (1962), p. 469.
[10] G. E. Mingay, *English Landed Society in the Eighteenth Century* (1963), p. 21.

discrimination was practised by the gentry who were technically com-
moners, yet they included some of the greatest landowners, including
T. W. Coke the famous agricultural improver of Holkham in Norfolk.
Their ranks were repeatedly infused with new elements which in Lincolnshire included bankers and merchants such as the Ellisons from
Hull, the Becketts and Dennisons of Leeds, and the Abel Smiths and
Wrights from Nottingham; but they also encompassed numerous
minor squires in Cumberland, Westmorland, and Wales who, though
relatively impoverished, maintained a considerable pride in their
order. The lower boundary line was especially difficult to draw. Some
890 baronets and knights and 6,000 esquires were accorded indubitable
gentry status, but many others laid claim to be considered gentlefolk.
To sustain such pretensions successfully, however, it is suggested,
an income of £1,000 a year would be expected in England at the close
of the eighteenth century. Some 700–800 families might be considered
to fall within the higher gentry, receiving £3,000 or more, with another
3,000–4,000 families of lesser gentry, with estates sometimes confined
to a single substantial residence and a couple of farms capable of
being let.[11] As well as exercising their rights as property holders,
the nobility and gentry also enjoyed influence over all those who
were in some sense their clients or dependants. Patronage was
extended to cover virtually all positions in society, extending even
to the poorest through the disbursement of charity to the deserving.
The proper exercise of such responsibilities was regarded as a major
legitimation of landowners' authority and in return such families
claimed and usually received due deference. These relationships were
strong enough to survive a long-standing tendency on the part of
the wealthy to detach themselves from too intimate an involvement
in village life, as they set themselves apart in walled acres of parkland,
and, as well, their seasonal migrations to London and sundry watering
places for months at a time.

   Among the tenantry too, there existed many gradations of status.
When the youthful Marquis de la Rochefoucauld was being conducted
by Arthur Young on a tour of East Anglia he visited a number of
large holdings including a 3,000-acre farm at Rougham (Norfolk),
employing forty-seven persons, and another at South Creake consisting of 1,300 acres with a regular staff of thirty-six, in this case farmed
by a tenant who owned another, even larger, farm elsewhere. Not

[11]   *Ibid.*, p. 23.

surprisingly the young Marquis was impressed by the answers given by such men to Young's questions, which were replied to 'with more intelligence than one would expect from peasants'.[12] It was men such as these who were thought especially at risk from burgeoning social pretensions. Young begrudged no efficient farmer a roomy kitchen, a roaring fire, a bottle of good port after dinner when company was being entertained, and a good nag. But his strictures against *'shew of any kind'* faithfully reflected prevailing conceptions of society: 'all these things imply a departure from that line which separates these different orders of beings, let all these things and all the folly, foppery expense and anxiety that belongs to them remain among gentlemen'.[13] As we have seen, however, tenant farmers on the grand scale were by no means typical. The extensive farms of west Norfolk were balanced by numerous small ones especially on the wetter soils of the east, and readers of the *General Views* of agriculture published from the 1790s were left in no doubt about the inefficiency and precariousness of farmers of another sort – the 'miserably indigent' of north Devon; or the little farmers of Herefordshire who often lived less comfortably than cottagers and whose only advantage over the latter was that they could be idle for a day when they pleased.

Finally, important distinctions may be drawn among the hired hands at the bedrock of agrarian society. One lay between living-in servants who accounted for between one third and one half of all farm employees in an array of parish listings made between 1599 and 1796.[14] For most, farm service was an interlude entered into at adolescence, for although the life-long farm servant was no figment of the imagination, the majority left upon marriage. Nevertheless, among married labourers occupying farm cottages there remained important distinctions based on acquired specialist skills. Horsemen, ploughmen, and shepherds commanded higher levels of remuneration and perquisites, and could rely on greater security of employment than day-men, increasingly likely to be paid by the piece. The existence of positions of special responsibility afforded a social ladder of a limited sort, although with the long-run trend to the reduction of small farms, opportunities to climb out of the ranks of agrarian wage earners were

[12] S. C. Roberts, ed., *A Frenchman in England, 1784: Being the 'Mélanges sur l'Angleterre' of François de la Rochefoucauld* (Cambridge, 1933), pp. 173, 217, 229, 233-4.
[13] A. Young, 'Gleanings in an Excursion to Lewes Fair', *Annals of Agriculture*, 27 (1792), pp. 152–7.
[14] A. Kussmaul, *Servants in Husbandry in Early Modern England* (Cambridge, 1981), p. 4.

scant. A rare study of mobility indicates that at Carlton Husthwaite (Yorkshire) twenty-one of twenty-six farmers had fathers who had been farmers, and only three had fathers who were labourers; at Raskelf all but one of twenty-five were farmers' sons and if anything, the tendency was for younger sons to descend into the ranks of labourers.[15] The position in large farm districts must have been still more unfavourable.

Viewed from another angle, all agriculturalists fell within the embracing concept of an 'agricultural interest' which in principle extended from the richest landlord to the humblest day-labourer. The theory was expressed by Nathaniel Kent, in 1796:

> In the prosperity of agriculture there are three persons who have a natural tye upon each other: the gentleman of landed interest – the farmer – and the labourer. Their degrees of interest are different, but their connection must be permanent as they cannot subsist without the aid of each other. Protection is due from the first – humanity from the second – and obedience from the third.[16]

Moreover the concept of an 'agricultural interest' may be extended to cover a wide range of occupations and so enables our discussion of rural society to be broadened beyond the agrarian elements who, so far, have held the centre of the stage. The outlays of farmers and landowners supported a wide range of services in villages and country towns. Their variety and sophistication varied according to size of settlement, but even villages with a population of 500 or so usually exhibited a group of craftsmen or retailers including the ubiquitous blacksmith, carpenter, miller, publican, shoemaker, and tailor. Often, tradesmen would combine these activities with running smallholdings and their status fell usually between that of the farmer and the cottager or better-off labourer. At a higher level of population, for example at Petworth (Sussex), with 2,000 souls, were to be found more specialised tradespeople such as four bakers, six butchers, a brewer, three maltsters, four saddlers, and even a couple of clock and watchmakers. Here also were two surgeon-apothecaries who today would be distinguished as 'professionals' although such claims might then have been sustained more easily by attorneys, or land agents and surveyors entrusted with the affairs of estates both great and small. A county town with a higher population again, though still dependent on rural

[15]   B. A. Holderness, 'Personal Mobility in Some Rural Parishes of Yorkshire, 1777–1812', *Yorkshire Archaeological Journal*, 42 (1971), pp. 447–50.
[16]   Quoted in E. J. Hobsbawm and G. Rudé, *Captain Swing* (1969), pp. 47–8.

demand, might be expected to feature all these trades and professions and some of an altogether more exotic nature. Thus, in the 1770s York (population about 16,000) could boast booksellers, engravers, jewellers, musicians, tobacco-pipe makers, and an optician.[17] The social standing of tradespeople varied enormously according to their wealth, whether they actually handled processed goods, and on the range of their social connections. We may be sure that relatively little was normally accorded to itinerant vendors, who still accounted for a sizeable proportion of all retail transactions, through peddling and hawking, and attendance at country fairs.

The church, too, blended into the contemporary social landscape. Benefices worth several hundred a year were comparatively rare and, much in the way that progressive farmers sought to add one holding to another, clerics engaged themselves in the vigorous pursuit of plural livings. Several choice ones, especially if held in conjunction with a cathedral office, could yield an income handsome by any standards though on the other hand James Hakewell in Oxfordshire, holding four, could still attain only £117 per annum in the 1780s.[18] To achieve advancement, connections were all-important, and non-residency left many parishes tended only by curates subsisting on tiny stipends who could be regarded as a clerical proletariat. Whilst the degree of attention given to the souls under their care by eighteenth-century clergymen defies easy generalisation, Parson Woodeforde of Weston Longueville in Norfolk is often taken as typical. His extensive diaries[19] bear witness to an absorbing interest in food and in fostering close relations with Squire Custance. They also suggest a humane disposition towards low-ranking villagers, but very little of a penchant for spiritual reflection. As a whole, the church perfectly mirrored the salient features of eighteenth-century rural social structure. By virtue of the tithe, the clergyman was a part of the agricultural interest, and the church maintained an hierarchical structure which fitted perfectly into the pyramidical conception of English society. In 1800, William Scott defended the manifestly inequitable distribution of its revenues arguing that 'the clergy, as a profession, find an easy and independent access to every gradation of society ... Alter the mode of distribution, and you run the risk of producing a body of clergy

[17] G. H. Kenyon, 'Petworth Town and Trades, 1610–1760', *Sussex Archaeological Collections*, 95 (1958), p. 63; P. M. Tillott, ed., *Victoria County History: City of York* (1961), p. 219.
[18] D. McClatchey, *Oxfordshire Clergy, 1777–1869* (Oxford, 1960), pp. 42, 53.
[19] J. Beresford, ed., *The Diary of a Country Parson*, 5 vols. (Oxford, 1924–31).

resembling only the lower orders of society.'[20] His argument implied that as well as offering spiritual guidance, the clergy had a leading role to play in promoting social cohesion.

This task was not easily discharged, for apart from individual short-comings among the clergy, villages were more diverse in character than is usually assumed. There were, indeed, numerous settlements dominated by a single landed proprietor, where villagers acquiesced in his authority without demur. A few such proprietors followed a conscious policy of 'closing' their parishes to outsiders. One means of achieving this was to pull down vacant cottages that might harbour potential paupers. In this the objective of the landlord might agree with that of the overseers representing village ratepayers, and there was a side-benefit to landlords in that their grip on village society was thereby likely to be enhanced. Yet no village, however tightly run, could be entirely self-sufficient and, certainly, none were charac-terized by a total lack of mobility, which was particularly marked among young farm servants who were renowned for their roving disposition albeit over short distances. Moreover, the very success of some landlords in closing their parishes implied the existence of a very different type of settlement, usually in the near vicinity. 'Open' parishes were characterised by a multiplicity of small freeholders, where village tradesmen followed their short-term interests by run-ning up rows of cottages or patching up hovels which a respectable landlord would certainly have regarded as a blot on his estate. Such places were often nests of nonconformity and were also regarded as places of refuge by poachers and petty criminals.

Another category of villages having much in common with 'open' agricultural settlements were those primarily concerned with manu-factures. Though the maypole on the village green symbolised the still essentially rural nature of Burslem in 1750, nineteen years later Arthur Young reckoned that hereabouts pot-manufacture provided work for nearly 10,000 persons.[21] Some 50 miles to the east, lay numerous villages devoted to framework knitting, which, it had been discovered, could be performed here more cheaply than in London. By 1782 the three counties of Nottinghamshire, Leicestershire, and Derbyshire accounted for over 85 per cent of 20,000 frames in the United Kingdom[22] and Chambers's pioneering work on the buoyant

[20] W. R. Ward, *Religion and Society in England, 1790-1850* (1972), pp. 106–7.
[21] J. Thomas, *The Rise of the Staffordshire Potteries* (Bath, 1971), pp. 7, 9.
[22] J. D. Chambers, *Nottinghamshire in the Eighteenth Century*, 2nd edn (1966), pp. 94–5.

population growth of the industrial villages of the East Midlands has received confirmation from more recent work, notably in an exhaustive study of Shepshed (Leicestershire). In this village, consisting of unregulated freehold land, a population of some 600 or 700 in the seventeenth century rose about fivefold by 1812, at which date about 1,000 frames were in use.[23] Ironically, the new factory villages associated with the first, water-powered phase of the industrial revolution in textiles from the 1770s resembled more closely the character of tightly controlled estate villages. A case in point was Mellor in Cheshire, where Samuel Oldknow controlled and directed the lives of a whole community by the exercise of benevolent despotism. Here the master cotton spinner could be seen, each Sunday morning, escorting his parish apprentices to Marple church, well breakfasted and dressed in their best clothes. Equally patriarchal were the mill communities of the Derwent valley in Derbyshire. Although firm discipline was enforced outside the factory walls as well as within them, usually by fines, employers such as the Strutts paid considerable attention to the material as well as the moral welfare of their workpeople. At Cromford, Arkwright annually entertained his people to a feast and was generous in distributing bonuses, receiving due deference in the form of choruses with a positively 'feudal' ring:

> To our noble master, a Bumper then fill,
> The matchless inventor of this cotton mill.[24]

Whilst acknowledging the existence of tendencies towards a simplification of its agrarian core, our portrayal of English rural society has stressed its heterogeneity and emphasised the existence of a series of gradations of status and rank. Contemporaries, it seems, had yet to learn the language of class. However, influenced by Marx's suggestion that the history of all hitherto existing society is the history of class struggles, some suspect that the underlying realities are obscured by uncritically adopting the vocabulary of social gradation. In a recent contribution to the debate E. P. Thompson has argued that conventional models of eighteenth-century society do not take account of the common people's perceptions and that it is the business of the historian to articulate their views by decoding their behaviour. He

[23] J. D. Chambers, *The Vale of Trent, 1670–1800* (*Economic History Review*, Supplement No. 3, 1957), pp. 19–35, 53; D. Levine, *Family Formation in an Age of Nascent Capitalism* (1977), pp. 4, 6.

[24] G. Unwin, *Samuel Oldknow and the Arkwrights* (Manchester, 1924), pp. 135, 159, 174; R. S. Fitton and A. P. Wadsworth, *The Strutts and the Arkwrights* (Manchester, 1958), pp. 99–100, 232–9, 249–60.

goes on to discuss evidence of the existence of a lively plebeian culture which the 'hegemony' of the gentry did not succeed in stifling, through paternalism, or repression, and suggests that we may 'read eighteenth century social history as a succession of confrontations between an innovative market economy and the customary moral economy of the plebs'. Here, he concludes, is evidence of class struggle which preceded the formation of self-conscious classes in the nineteenth-century sense.[25] Certainly there is no shortage of instances of conflict, and attention has focussed chiefly on the crowd disturbances provoked occasionally by the operations of the Militia Acts, enclosures, or turnpiking, but especially (in two cases out of every three) by sudden rises in the price of food.[26] Problems remain in assessing the broader significance of such incidents, however, and amongst historians opinion ranges from those who are persuaded that there was class conflict in the eighteenth century, through those who think the evidence 'fragmentary, but enough to leave a question-mark against the "classlessness" of the eighteenth century'[27] to others sceptical of the value of such an approach because it embodies such venturesome inferential leaps. Given the subjective nature of this debate, there is a strong case for deferring further discussion of class at this point, and for turning to a less shadowy engine of change.

Despite experiencing net losses of population by migration, even counties relatively untouched by industrialisation experienced considerable population increases from the mid-eighteenth century. Between 1751 and 1789 sixteen such counties exhibited an increase of the order of 22 per cent.[28] This was part of a national increase which has been traced recently to a fall in mortality, but more especially to an increase in fertility consequent upon a rising incidence of and falling age at marriage.[29] Whether the balance of these influences was similar in town and country, and as between industrialising and predominantly agricultural districts, remains to be seen.

[25] E. P. Thompson, 'Eighteenth-Century English Society: Class Struggle without Class?', *Social History*, 3 (1978), pp. 33–65.

[26] See G. Rudé, *The Crowd in History, 1730–1848* (1964), pp. 33–7, and A. Charlesworth, *An Atlas of Rural Protest in Britain, 1548–1900* (1983), pp. 83–106.

[27] R. J. Morris, *Class and Class Consciousness in the Industrial Revolution* (1979), p. 18.

[28] W. A. Armstrong, 'La Population de l'Angleterre et du Pays de Galles, 1789–1815', *Annales de Démographie Historique*, 1 (1965), pp. 184–6, using the list of counties identified as agricultural in P. Deane and W. A. Cole, *British Economic Growth 1688–1959* (Cambridge, 1962), p. 103.

[29] E. A. Wrigley and R. S. Schofield, *The Population History of England, 1541–1871: A Reconstruction* (1981), pp. 240-4.

Long-term shifts in the structure of rural society may well have served to weaken traditional constraints on marriage and procreation. Thus, at Terling (Essex), which in the early seventeenth century already showed large farms and many landless labourers, stable and moderately youthful ages at marriage were the order of the day until 1775, after which they fell. Yet they were even lower (twenty-three for men, twenty-two for women) at Melbourne, an open or 'peasant' village set in the corn-growing area of Cambridgeshire which remained unenclosed until 1839.[30] Obviously much work remains to be done in clarifying the links between socio-economic change and marriage and fertility. Moreover, the part played by falling mortality may also have been considerable in rural areas. A valuable study of infant mortality in rural north Shropshire has shown that it ran at 200 per thousand at risk between the mid-sixteenth and early eighteenth centuries, falling to 160–70 in the mid-eighteenth century and to 130 before its close.[31] Whatever the provenance of the rural upswing in population, it could hardly fail to swell the number of labourers and to weaken their market position. Already, from the middle of the century more elaborate arrangements for the relief of the poor were seen to be required in some districts, as evidenced in the building of new workhouses in Dorset, Norfolk, and Suffolk. In some parishes, well before the French Wars, recourse was had to the 'roundsman' system which appeared to involve an undesirable element of wage subsidisation calculated to lower the recipients' self-respect and make for indifferent standards of performance. The twin impact of population growth and price increases made itself apparent in a doubling of per capita relief in many English villages, for example at Melbourne, between the 1750s and the 1780s. Both causes were acknowledged by the rector of Barkham (Berkshire), in a famous treatise which also adduced as factors, enclosures, engrossing, ale-houses, an insufficiency of employment for men in winter, and for females at all seasons. It included a novel series of family budgets which mostly showed deficiencies when annual incomes were compared to annual outlays.[32] This approach

---

[30] Levine, *Family Formation*, pp. 120–4; D. Mills, 'The Quality of Life in Melbourne, Cambs., in the Period 1800–50', *International Review of Social History*, 23 (1978), p. 402.

[31] R. E. Jones, 'Infant Mortality in Rural North Shropshire, 1561–1810', *Population Studies*, 30 (1976), p. 313.

[32] D. Davies, *The Case of the Labourers in Husbandry Stated and Considered* (1795), pp. 50–66, 78–94, 130–200.

was emulated by Eden who substantially endorsed Davies's conclusions so far as the southern labourer was concerned, but stressed that the northern labourer was better placed with respect to reliability of employment, wage levels, and diets,[33] a view which is supported by modern work on dietary patterns, wage levels, and the regional incidence of poor law relief.[34]

Such was the state and condition of English rural society at the onset of the French Wars. Between 1789 and 1815 the rural population increased by a further 26 per cent, but the influence of the demographic factor was overlaid by the dramatic impact of inflationary wartime conditions upon agriculture. Farm prices, having gently ascended for some time, rose smartly, in the case of wheat by some 106 per cent if 1790–4 is compared with 1810–14; though any such figure may mislead, because in years of bad harvests, such as 1795-6, 1800–1 and 1812-13, prices rose very high indeed. The pace of agrarian improvement likewise quickened. About 49 per cent of all land enclosed under parliamentary acts between 1750 and 1829 was dealt with during the war years, involving some 2.9 m acres in addition to other areas enclosed under private agreement. These activities were particularly marked in eastern England, but were by no means confined there, nor to open field arable. An increased proportion consisted of commons and wastes, as more marginal land was brought into use, such as Sherwood Forest (Nottinghamshire), Enfield Chase (Middlesex), Canford Heath (Dorset), and Bexley Heath (Kent).[35] In the early years of the war farmers prospered: as one, from Northumberland, put it, 'The farmers in ye district are full of money . . . as every thing the farmers have to sell are at a higher price than I ever knew before.'[36] In due course, landlords moved to tap the increased revenues of their tenants, and with much variation from one estate to another, it is thought that rent increases over the war years averaged about 90 per cent.[37] Moreover, despite the impression given by some authors, it

[33]   F. M. Eden, *The State of the Poor*, 3 vols., vol. 1, pp. viii, 496–548.
[34]   See the discussions by W. A. Armstrong and J. B. Huzel in G. E. Mingay, ed., *The Agrarian History of England and Wales*, vol. 6: *1750–1850* (Cambridge, 1989), pp. 696–8, 738–40, 762–6.
[35]   Turner, *Parliamentary Enclosure*, pp. 71, 77–9; A. Redford, *Labour Migration in England, 1800–50*, 2nd edn (Manchester, 1964), pp. 72–3.
[36]   Quoted in S. MacDonald, 'Agricultural Response to a Changing Market during the Napoleonic Wars', *Economic History Review*, 2nd ser., 33 (1980), p. 64.
[37]   F. M. L. Thompson, *English Landed Society in the Nineteenth Century* (1963), pp. 218–20.

is not obvious that the position of the farm labourers deteriorated absolutely in consequence of the wars. To some degree, they were protected by payments in kind from the worst of the price fluctuations, and they did not feature to any great extent in the disorders arising from food prices, in 1795, 1800, and 1812. The diversion of many men into the armed services (amounting to 430,000 by 1809) tended to curtail the growth of labour supply at a time when the demand was relatively buoyant, and brought many complaints of seasonal labour shortages. In these circumstances, wages broadly kept pace with prices and, though variable, may in many cases have matched the doubling experienced by landlords and farmers.[38] Such a conclusion would be consistent with evidence collected by the Board of Agriculture, which suggested the expenses of cultivating 100 acres attributable to rent (21 per cent), tithes and rates (9 per cent), and labour (21 per cent) was virtually the same in 1813 as it had been in 1790.[39]

This said, it was inevitable that a doubling of money incomes all round would serve visibly to increase discrepancies in life style and enlarge the social distance between major constituent elements in rural society. Some landlords laid themselves open to charges of rapacity in exploiting the tenantry while at the same time, it was held, becoming less mindful of their social obligations, and tart observations on the demeanour of progressive farmers became commonplace. However, the bulk of recorded criticism was aimed at the lower orders and at changes in the institutional arrangements for the relief of the able-bodied poor, notably against the 'Speenhamland system' instituted by a group of Berkshire magistrates in the crisis year of 1795 which came to be widely imitated in southern and eastern England in the years that followed. Under this system relief payments were tied to the price of bread and the size of a man's family. Though humane in intention, it was thought to further demoralise the poor and, as well, to encourage reckless breeding. Looking back, it is now evident that contemporary fears were exaggerated. Not only is there no evidence linking Speenhamland with excessive procreation, the increase in the poor rates (which reached £5.7m by 1815) was general throughout England and not especially marked in the 'Speenhamland'

[38] M. W. Flinn, 'Trends in Real Wages, 1750–1850', *Economic History Review*, 2nd ser., 27 (1974), pp. 404, 407; P. H. Lindert and J. G. Williamson, 'English Workers' Living Standards during the Industrial Revolution: A New Look', *Economic History Review*, 2nd ser., 36 (1983), pp. 10, 13.

[39] Calculated from the table in Chambers and Mingay, *Agricultural Revolution*, p. 118.

counties.[40] Moreover, modern research on three of them (Kent, Sussex and Essex) suggests that the real incidence of poor law relief barely rose once the impact of price changes and population growth are taken into account.[41] Such nice calculations were not within the competence of anyone to make at the time, when it was commonly suggested that the poor were simply 'more importunate than their necessities required' or that increases in poor law expenditure reflected 'a relaxation of discipline and a corruption of morals'.[42] In short, while the war years scarcely transformed the character of English rural society, they certainly provided a setting within which some souring of social relationships is likely to have occurred.

II

'Between 1813 and the accession of Queen Victoria', wrote Ernle, 'falls one of the blackest periods of English farming. Prosperity no longer stimulated progress . . . falling prices, dwindling rents, vanishing profits . . . crushed the spirit of agriculturalists.'[43] Enquiries conducted by the Board of Agriculture in 1816 and by parliamentary Select Committees in 1821, 1833, and 1836 produced supporting evidence of widespread distress. To be sure, modern research has modified these impressions of sustained and comprehensive adversity. Within the arable sector, the greater adaptability of light soils as against cold wet claylands has been stressed by agrarian historians. Moreover, it has been shown that the animal rearing and dairy districts, particularly those adjacent to large urban markets, were not nearly so seriously affected; indeed it is suggested that they barely suffered depression at all.[44] Despite these important reservations, the climate of deflation was a disagreeable experience against a background of forty years of rising prices, and was particularly hurtful to those who had incurred heavy commitments under the assumption that swollen wartime prices would be permanent. The Corn Law of 1815, which

[40]   J. B. Huzel, 'The Demographic Impact of the Old Poor Law: More Reflexions on Malthus', *Economic History Review*, 2nd ser., 33 (1980), pp. 369–75; J. D. Marshall, *The Old Poor Law, 1795–1834* (1968), p. 23.
[41]   D. A. Baugh, 'The Cost of Poor Relief in South-East England, 1790–1834', *Economic History Review*, 2nd ser., 28 (1975), p. 60.
[42]   Correspondent to the *Gentleman's Magazine* (1792), pp. 1194–5; T. Ruggles, 'On the Police and Situation of the Poor', *Annals of Agriculture*, 16 (1791), p. 367.
[43]   Lord Ernle, *English Farming, Past and Present*, 5th edn (1936), p. 319.
[44]   E. L. Jones, *The Development of English Agriculture, 1815–73* (1968), pp. 12–13.

sought to protect agriculture by forbidding the importation of wheat when the market price was below 80s. a quarter, turned out to be less effective than had been hoped and periodic clamours for a higher level of protection were a feature of the period. It was pressure from a new Association of Agriculturalists claiming to represent fifty local groups in twenty English counties that brought about an enquiry into the operation of the corn laws in 1821. Again, in the years after 1832 when prices staged a fall coinciding with the advent of an enlarged electorate (the Chandos clause of the Reform Act having enfranchised the £50 tenant), a rash of agricultural associations flourished, whilst in 1843–4 a lively anti-league which sought to combat the arguments of the Anti-Corn Law League was busy in the rural constituencies. Within protectionist circles Peel's repeal of the corn laws (January 1846) was viewed as an act of betrayal and when prices once again fell sharply at the close of the decade, huge meetings and even one or two farmers' riots occurred, causing Greville to note in his diary 'there is good reason to fear ... that they will ... break through all the old patriarchal ties and go to any lengths which they may fancy they can make instrumental to their relief'.[45] This, no doubt, was an exaggerated view. In retrospect it can be seen that support for protection among farmers waxed and waned with price fluctuations; that the economic interests of cereal producers and livestock farmers were not identical; and that these movements did not seek to supplant existing 'natural' leaders but merely to press them to bear in mind their responsibilities towards the land. At the same time farmers evinced a capacity for independent thought and action which amply demonstrated that their opinions need not passively reflect the wishes of their landlords.

If agricultural deflation was one prime determinant of conditions in the English countryside down to the mid-century, the other was the continuing growth of the rural population. In Norfolk, Suffolk, and Essex, each of the fifty-six registration districts exhibited increases in 1811–21, 1821–31 and 1831–41, with only four showing decreases in the following decade. In Devon, Wiltshire, and Somerset the number of districts indicating declines rose from two (1821–31) to four (1831–41) and rather noticeably, to twenty-four (1841–51). Overall the rural population continued to swell in numbers. Altogether, the counties

---

[45] T. L. Crosby, *English Farmers and the Politics of Protection, 1815–52* (Hassocks, Sussex, 1977), pp. 37, 84–5, 101, 130, 162.

identifiable as primarily agricultural in 1811 increased their aggregate population by no less than 53 per cent in the ensuing forty years.[46]

In some districts the number of small occupations was further reduced. Without producing any figures, Davies suspected that numerous small owners paying from 4s. – £10 in land tax, succumbed in the bleak years which followed the cessation of hostilities.[47] In Cumberland Graham described how consolidation was applied to his 30,000 acres between 1822 and 1827 and by 1850 the Lowther and Carlisle estates had also succeeded in reducing the number of individual tenancies, in one case forming a 300-acre farm out of eleven small-holdings. On the Leveson-Gower estates in Staffordshire the proportion of holdings over 200 acres in size increased from 52 to 59 per cent between 1807–13 and 1829–33 at the expense of those in the range 20–100 acres.[48] How common such tendencies were remains unclear, but at least we may be sure that increased sub-division did not occur. Consequently, it was inevitable that the number seeking employment would increase in circumstances that were far from propitious. Shifts in the balance of farm employment were encouraged. Contrary to popular belief, servants were not generally ousted from farmhouses during the French Wars; it was in the postwar situation of labour abundance that the pent-up desire of farmers to rid themselves of servants made rapid headway. By 1851 indoor servants as a proportion of the hired agricultural labour force were reduced to 4 and 7 per cent in Hertfordshire and Northamptonshire, and in only six English counties (Devon, Cornwall, Cumberland, Staffordshire, Westmorland, and the East Riding) did they exceed 40 per cent.[49] Although an approximation to farm service conditions continued to exist for choice men (hired on a yearly basis, with a cottage, higher wages, and some perquisites), the decay of indoor service could serve only to increase the social distance between master and man. Further, it was conducive to demographic increase; this is strongly suggested by a modern study in which average age at marriage is

[46]   G. B. Longstaff, 'Rural Depopulation', *Journal of the Royal Statistical Society*, 56 (1893), pp. 385–6; B. R. Mitchell and P. Deane, *Abstract of British Historical Statistics* (Cambridge, 1962), p. 20, using data for the counties mentioned in n. 28, above.

[47]   E. Davies, 'The Small Landowner, 1780–1832, in the Light of the Land Tax Assessments', *Economic History Review*, 1 (1927), p. 112.

[48]   B. A. Holderness, 'The Victorian Farmer', in G. E. Mingay, ed., *The Victorian Countryside*, 2 vols. (1981), vol. 1, p. 230; J. R. Wordie, 'Social Change on the Leveson-Gower Estates, 1714–1832', *Economic History Review*, 2nd ser., 27 (1974), p. 596.

[49]   Kussmaul, *Servants in Husbandry*, pp. 20, 125.

estimated to have been lower by two years (males) and seventeen months (females) in rural registration districts characterised as under 15 per cent 'traditional', i.e. where labourers were abundant and correspondingly fewer of the labour force consisted of farmers, their relatives, and servants.[50]

For the day-labourer these were years of unusual difficulty in retaining regular employment. With the coming of peace the problems of reintegrating men discharged from the forces were frequently remarked upon and the cry of 'surplus population' came to be widely voiced. We meet it, for example, in the evidence given by two Bedfordshire magistrates to the 1817 Select Committee on the Poor Laws. The 'superfluous part of the population' was said to be due in part to persons marrying imprudently, and it was feared that the population was 'likely to increase beyond the employment, and perhaps more in agricultural parishes than in most others'. Their worst fears were fulfilled in certain of the years that followed, especially in 1829–32. Thirteen parishes of the Redbornestoke hundred exhibited as many as 523 'almost wholly in the hands of the overseers' in 1829 whilst at Westoning late the following year only 20 men and a similar number of boys out of a total available of 90 labourers, were in regular employment.[51] Detailed evidence for Kirdford (Sussex) shows 118 labourers on the parish in the winter of 1830–1 leaving only 72 to work 12,000 acres of cultivated land and woodland. Meanwhile at Pulborough 130 labouring men from 308 (including artisans) were out of work for nine months, whilst at Wisborough Green the average number of unemployed in five winters previous to that of 1831–2 was 80.[52] Winter unemployment was commonplace also in Wiltshire, Buckinghamshire, Kent, Surrey, and East Anglia, proving persistent in many villages throughout the 1840s and beyond, if not on the horrendous scale of 1829–32.

The years immediately following the war saw considerable increases in expenditure on the poor. An index of real per capita relief suggests that if the years 1820–34 are compared with 1792–1814, expenditure ran 20 and 30 per cent higher in Sussex and Essex respectively, and

[50] M. Anderson, 'Marriage Patterns in Victorian Britain: An Analysis Based on Registration District Data for England and Wales', *Journal of Family History*, 1 (1976), pp. 65, 76.

[51] N. Agar, *The Bedfordshire Farm Worker in the Nineteenth Century (Bedfordshire Historical Record Society*, 60 (1981), pp. 50, 52, 56, 78; A. F. Cirket, 'The 1830 Riots in Bedfordshire', in *Bedfordshire Historical Record Society*, 57 (1978), pp. 77–8.

[52] N. Gash, 'Rural Unemployment, 1815–34', *Economic History Review*, 6 (1935), pp. 90–1.

by as much as 54 per cent in Kent.[53] A spate of pamphlets dwelt upon the deficiencies of the relief system and on the moral defects of the labourer who, in the words of David Ricardo, was all too frequently 'cruelly calumniated'.[54] The 1820s saw considerable local variations of practice. Following a Select Committee in 1817, legislation was passed empowering parishes to appoint select vestries to supervise the work of the overseers, and in some places, notably at Southwell and Bingham in Nottinghamshire, draconian policies aimed at the abolition of outdoor relief were pioneered. Elsewhere recourse was had to the roundsman system, the levying of a 'labour rate' (under which occupiers were assessed as liable to pay a certain sum in wages, or, failing this, to remit the difference to the overseer), and to scale allowances. However, no decisive steps were taken before 1834 when, following the recommendations of a Royal Commission obsessed with the problem of the able-bodied, the Poor Law Amendment Act remodelled the system. Parishes would henceforth be grouped into unions administered by elected Boards of Guardians which, it was assumed, would offer relief on a rigorous basis incorporating, for the able-bodied, the infamous principles of the workhouse test and less-eligibility. The new arrangements were opposed with vigour in northern industrial areas and also, to a degree which is sometimes underestimated, in the south. Popular resentment taking the form of demonstrations or riots occurred in several counties, most notably perhaps in the Milton union of Kent in May 1835.[55] In the event, existing practices did not necessarily change so radically as had been intended. In East Anglia, for example, the guardians reverted within a few years to the policy of proffering outdoor relief under various guises, from mixed motives of economy and humanity.[56] Nevertheless, as the system settled down, reductions in aggregate expenditure did occur, by some 26 per cent if the public outlay of 1840–4 is compared with that of 1830–4. How far this was due to the salutary disciplines of the new poor law, as against a perceptible (though incomplete) strengthening of the labour market due to factors such as railway building from the late 1830s, it would be difficult to say.

Since the official view of the new commissioners was that the surplus

[53]   Baugh, 'Cost of Poor Relief', p. 62.
[54]   J. R. Poynter, *Society and Pauperism: English Ideas on Poor Relief, 1795–1834* (1969), p. 240.
[55]   N. C. Edsall, *The Anti-Poor Law Movement, 1834–44* (Manchester, 1971), pp. 27–31, 36–9.
[56]   A. Digby, *Pauper Palaces* (1978), pp. 109–13.

population was a mirage, it is not surprising to find that they responded cautiously towards alternative steps proposed by some landlords to ease the problems posed by the labour glut in the south. During the early months of 1835 they agreed to act as intermediaries in the locally initiated transfer of several families from the parish of Bledlow (Buckinghamshire) to mills at Styal (Cheshire) and Bolton. Others were soon passed from the Bedfordshire parishes of Cranfield, Woburn, and Ampthill to Clayton's mill at Mellor. Ultimately the commissioners appointed two full-time agents under an official scheme which lasted until May 1837. A subsequent analysis of 4,684 migrants indicated they were drawn chiefly from Suffolk (49 per cent), Norfolk, Buckinghamshire and Bedfordshire.[57] Of much greater significance than these short-lived schemes was assistance given to send individuals and families abroad. Already in the 1820s parish authorities were adopting this policy, notably in Wealden Kent, and subsequently the initiatives of local associations in which contributing landlords and clergymen could nominate prospective emigrants were supported by the new poor law authorities. They assisted some 14,000 persons to migrate to the colonies between 1836 and 1846, so complementing the work of the Colonial Commissioners of Land and Emigration, set up in 1842 to assist selected persons using funds raised from the sale of crown lands in the colonies.[58] However, these expedients were not conducted on a scale such as to have more than a marginal effect on the rural labour market and down to the mid-century wages moved as might be expected at a time marked by deflation and labour abundance. The average earnings of agricultural labourers in England and Wales sank from 105 (1806–12) to a nadir of 72 (1824) and thereafter averaged 77 over the next twenty-eight years.[59]

Against this background, it is not surprising that many felt that the fissures in English agrarian society were being opened up. From Burghclere (Hampshire) it was reported to the Poor Law Commission that 'All friendly relation between the farmers and the poor ceases', whilst the same source spoke of a 'spirit of revenge' and 'want of good feeling' at Bramshaw and Minstead in the same county. In the 1840s labourers in the neighbourhood of Bury St Edmunds told a

[57]   Agar, *Bedfordshire Farm Worker*, pp. 129–32; Redford, *Labour Migration*, pp. 102, 108.
[58]   C. Erickson, *Emigration from Europe, 1815–1914* (1976), pp. 121, 127; D. Woodruff, 'Expansion and Emigration', in G. M. Young, ed., *Early Victorian England*, vol. 2 (Oxford, 1934), pp. 359–60.
[59]   A. L. Bowley's figures, in Mitchell and Deane, *Abstract*, p. 349 (1891=100), and see Lindert and Williamson, 'Living Standards', pp. 7, 13.

Morning Chronicle investigator that the farmers would seldom conde-
scend to speak to them, except in terms of reproach or abuse, and
the Rev. Sidney Godolphin reckoned that among the labourers of
the West Country, attachment to their superiors, respect for their
employers, loyalty to their rulers, was 'fast passing away'.[60] For both
contemporaries and modern historians, changes in the incidence of
rural crime are thought to provide a barometer of social malaise, and
although the statistics relate to committals rather than offences, they
leave little room to doubt that crime was increasing faster than the
rural population, especially after 1815.[61] Although many felonies were
perpetrated by the poor against the poor, others fell 'within a broad
definition of social crime in that the object was a particular target
of community grievance and the action had broad based community
support'.[62] This was undeniably true of poaching which in the eyes
of the common people did not constitute a crime, it being assumed
that wild creatures were free for anyone who could catch them. There
was more to this issue than the taking of an occasional hare or rabbit
for the hungry labourer's pot. Ever since 1755, when Parliament had
ill-advisedly attempted to ban trading in game, so making innkeepers
and urban poulterers dependent on illicit sources of supply, a lively
commercial trade had flourished. Yet the problem does not seem to
have significantly increased during the war years, perhaps because
military service siphoned off many potential poachers. Thereafter
committals soared dramatically. In Wiltshire the average annual
number during the war years was about twelve rising to ninety-two
by the early 1820s. In Bedfordshire over 1,300 persons were imprisoned under the game laws in the years 1815–30, more than twice
the number committed in the previous fifty years. While doubtless
there was no single grand cause of poaching, any more than there
was one for smuggling or pickpocketing, these increases were linked,
in the eyes of observers such as Lord Caernarvon and Sir Thomas
Baring, with want of employment.[63] Yet however infuriating to the

[60] Hobsbawm and Rudé, *Swing*, p. 61; P. E. Razzell and R. J. W. Wainwright, eds.,
The Victorian Working Class: Selections from the Morning Chronicle (1973), p. 51; *Report
of Special Assistant Commissioners on Women and Children in Agriculture*, PP 1843, XII,
p. 77.
[61] Hobsbawm and Rudé, *Swing*, pp. 77–8; J. Glyde, *Suffolk in the Nineteenth Century*
(1856), pp. 116–17.
[62] J. Rule, 'Social Crime in the Rural South in the Eighteenth and Early Nineteenth
Centuries', *Southern History*, 1 (1979), p. 140.
[63] P. B. Munsche, *Gentlemen and Poachers: The English Game Laws 1671–1831* (Cambridge,
1981), pp. 138–9, 147–8.

gentry, poaching at least appeared to embody the intelligible pursuit of self-interest, whereas incendiarism lacked any semblance of rationality. In the 1820s, but more especially in the 1830s and 1840s, unpopular farmers, poor law guardians and unfeeling clergymen as well as landlords were prime targets. Rural incendiarism in Norfolk and Suffolk has been traced in detail in a study which discovered no fewer than 1,745 cases for the period 1830–70. The peak incidence occurred in 1843–4 with over 300 fires recorded, which coincides with reports in *The Times* newspaper of incendiarism in Bedfordshire, Essex, Kent and Nottinghamshire.[64] By July 1844, the Norwich Union Fire Office was instructing its surveyors to enquire into labourers' wages in villages where incendiarism had taken place and three years later the village of Withersfield was blacklisted due to the poor relations existing between farmers and labourers, so that no farmer could take out a new policy. At no time thereafter was incendiarism perpetrated on quite this scale, although no fewer than 39 per cent of rural prisoners in the gaols of Bury St Edmunds and Ipswich in 1848–52 were arsonists.[65]

By its very nature, fire-raising was usually the work of an isolated individual fearful of open confrontation. The first generalised disturbances of the period took place in East Anglia in 1816, a year of widespread unemployment coupled with high prices. Pressure for reductions at Haverhill, Brandon, and Ely was in line with eighteenth-century traditions of popular protest; however, demands for money with menaces, and the destruction of threshing machines also occurred. At least one person died in the most serious outbreak of violence at Littleport and of the seventy-five prisoners subsequently brought to trial, mostly labourers, twenty-four were capitally convicted. Of these, five were hanged, nine transported and ten imprisoned for twelve months.[66] Further attacks on threshing machines occurred in the neighbourhood of Diss and Eye in the third week of February 1822 and were met by the raising of a force of 250 special constables and by troop movements.[67] Perhaps the labourers were cowed by these displays of a determination by the civil authorities in East Anglia. At all events, the centre of gravity of the much better known Swing riots of 1830–1 lay further to the south; 60 per cent

[64] J. E. Archer, 'Rural Protest in Norfolk and Suffolk, 1830–70' (unpublished PhD thesis, University of East Anglia, 1982), pp. 163–5; *The Times*, 30 Dec. 1843.
[65] Archer, 'Rural Protest', pp. 186, 191; Glyde, *Suffolk*, pp. 144–5.
[66] A. J. Peacock, *Bread or Blood: The Agrarian Riots in East Anglia, 1816* (1965), p. 127.
[67] Charlesworth, *Atlas*, p. 122.

of 1,475 incidents examined in the modern standard account occurred in five counties (Berkshire 165, Hampshire 208, Kent 154, Sussex 145, Wiltshire 208). On the other hand, comparatively few were located in the Midlands and the north (Warwickshire 2, Shropshire 4, Nottinghamshire 5, Cheshire 4, etc.).[68] The Swing riots were triggered by exceptional cold, hunger, and unemployment during the fearsome winter of 1829 and another modest harvest in prospect must have increased the labourers' pessimism during the summer of 1830, coupled, it is thought, by vaguely stirred expectations turning on events across the Channel (the July Revolution) and talk of radical reform. When asked on a semi-systematic basis two years later for their views on the causes of the 1830 riots, local worthies concentrated overwhelmingly upon low wages and unemployment and to a lesser extent on the operations of the poor law, though Hobsbawm and Rudé tend to see these as merely symptomatic of long-run tendencies towards proletarianisation and the degradation of the labourers' position.[69] Yet Swing-related incidents were far from being universal even in villages of the south and east, and in assessing the factors predisposing some to riot and not others, it is generally agreed that much work remains to be done to isolate the relevant causes. Very much clearer is the form that action took; it was again directed chiefly against the threshing machine which had spread with rapidity during the war on account of labour shortages and continued to do so (in the interest of speed in getting grain on to the market) in the years that followed, to the detriment of winter employment among the labourers. Despite the blood-curdling nature of some of the Swing letters, not a single life was lost among the gentry, clergy, and farmers. Notwithstanding this moderation, and the obvious hardships which had impelled the labourers to such drastic courses of action, stern retribution was meted out both in the regular courts and at the hands of special commissioners. Among 1,976 Swing rioters brought to trial, 7 were fined, 1 whipped, 644 gaoled, and 505 were sentenced to transportation. Another 252 were sentenced to death, and execution was actually carried out in 19 cases.[70]

As we have seen, covert protest continued for some time to come, but nothing in the nature of a cohesive social movement occurred

[68]   Hobsbawm and Rudé, *Swing*, pp. 304–5.
[69]   *Ibid.*, pp. 81–2.
[70]   *Ibid.*, pp. 308–9.

among farm workers before the advent of unionism in the 1870s. To explain why the Swing riots did not presage a series of ever-deepening conflicts a number of explanations may be considered. One has been characterised as the 'jackboot' theory, wherein forcible repression looms large.[71] This may be illustrated by reference to the retribution following the riots; to the role of what remained in the postwar period of the Yeomanry, and *ad hoc* civil defence forces formed in 1830; to the appearance of the police forces which county authorities were empowered to set up after 1839; and to the occasional invocation of the law in a palpably unjust way, notably in the famous case of the Tolpuddle Martyrs in 1834, when at the instigation of a particularly vigorous magistrate half a dozen leading spirits in an embryonic village union were convicted and transported for administering 'secret oaths' under an act passed in 1797 to combat naval mutinies. Yet as Hobsbawm and Rudé point out, even at the height of the Swing riots responses to the labourers' actions were 'uncertain and divided',[72] and a more plausible view is that in the post-Swing era social tensions were contained by more subtle means of paternalistic social control. For example, the distribution of charity lay in the hands of Anglican parsons as trustees or administrators and in the later reflections of Joseph Arch, 'with bowed head and bended knee the poor learned to receive from the rich what was only their due, had they but known it'.[73] The device of allotments was used to similar effect. These had long been advocated by well-intentioned persons, but it was no coincidence that Parliament decided, in October 1831, to extend the existing scope for parishes to form allotments, whilst numerous private landlords took similar steps in the immediate aftermath of Swing. The upshot was that allotment schemes were known in 42 per cent of English parishes by 1833 and in some instances (e.g. Oakley in Bedfordshire) had been introduced with the avowed aim of 'curing the place'.[74] Whatever benefits were conferred on the labourers (and in certain circumstances these could be considerable) proponents of the thesis of social control tend to see in allotments yet another lever over the conduct of the men selected. Another agency conducive to

---

[71] F. M. L. Thompson, 'Landowners and the Rural Community', in Mingay, ed., *Victorian Countryside*, vol. 2, p. 457.

[72] Hobsbawm and Rudé, *Swing*, p. 258.

[73] J. G. O'Leary, ed., *The Autobiography of Joseph Arch* (1966), p. 24.

[74] D. C. Barnett, 'Allotments and the Problem of Rural Poverty', in E. L. Jones and G. E. Mingay, eds., *Land, Labour and Population in the Industrial Revolution* (1967), p. 172; Agar, *Bedfordshire Farm Worker*, p. 22.

social discipline was the village school. At the beginning of the nineteenth century many parishes lacked a day school, and the Sunday schools which had recently sprung into existence in large numbers were often opposed by the clergy, suspicious of the motives of the nonconformists who usually ran them. Increasingly the view gained ground that schooling should be encouraged so as 'to communicate to the poor generally . . . such knowledge and habits as are sufficient to guide them through life in their proper stations . . . and to train them to a performance of their religious duties by early discipline'.[75] Progress was especially rapid from the 1820s. In Devon nineteen schools were established, chiefly under the auspices of the National Society, in 1821-30, forty-three in 1831-40 and sixty-four in 1841-50,[76] a trend general in England to a greater or lesser extent. The nonconformists played a more significant role in Sunday school provision although, it may be argued, their essential objective was the same: to prepare the offspring of labouring men to meek acceptance of a life of honest toil. Yet, it seems, landlords were erratic supporters of village schools and many farmers remained positively hostile to the idea that education could be of value to the labouring poor. The clergymen who played a disproportionate role in initiating and sustaining schools often had to fight a constant battle against apathy and shortages of funds, all of which poses a question mark over the persistence with which the goal of social control was positively pursued. Indeed it has been suggested that a great many, perhaps the silent majority, of landlords were simply not sufficiently active, imaginative, or responsible to try to use their position to massage the rural community in any systematic way.[77]

A Professor of Sociology has suggested that in gauging the potential of peasant movements, it is important to assess 'the *number* . . . who *might* be conscious of the communality of their problems, and the *quality* of that consciousness . . . as compared with the number who *are* thus conscious'.[78] This approach, as well as throwing some light on the modest achievements of the Swing rioters, offers a third explanation of the relative quiescence of the ensuing decades. To begin

---

[75] *First Annual Report of the National Society for Promoting the Education of the Poor in the Principles of the Established Church*, 1812, quoted in P. Horn, *The Rural World, 1780-1850* (1980), p. 134.

[76] R. R. Sellman, *Devon Village Schools in the Nineteenth Century* (Newton Abbot, 1967), p. 25.

[77] Thompson, 'Landowners and the Rural Community', pp. 458-9.

[78] H. A. Landsberger, ed., *Rural Protest: Peasant Movements and Social Change* (1974), p. 20.

with, it is easy to underestimate the number of those whose interest
(whether correctly perceived or not) lay in upholding the forces of
order and stability. They included as well as all landlords, clergymen,
and farmers, the great majority of professional men, tradespeople,
and craftsmen who were in a minority at the level of the individual
village, but abounded in even minor market towns and thus formed
a considerable proportion of the population of every rural district.
Like the shopkeepers of Oldham who were reluctant to offend their
working-class customers,[79] these men had to consider the mainstay
of their activities. To court the disfavour of a landlord was unlikely
to be helpful at the renewal of a lease and even where a man was
a freeholder there was nothing to be gained from giving offence to
his best customers. These tacit alliances were cemented in church
and in chapel. In the predominantly Anglican counties of southern
England such lay offices as the Church of England provided were
monopolised by tradespeople and farmers, and the position was
scarcely different in those parts of the country where nonconformity
was more strongly entrenched. Thus, among the Wesleyan congregations of South Lindsey, craftsmen and shopkeepers accounted for
35 per cent of all circuit stewards and 34 per cent of class leaders
in 1851, closely approaching the number of office holders who were
farmers. At Bardney in the same district, some shrewd men were
said to attend both church and chapel, 'for the sake of custom'. Even
among the Primitive Methodists, craftsmen with farmers accounted
for 49 per cent of local preachers and 58 per cent of chief supporters
identified.[80] Among these numerous people, we may be sure, the
perpetration or encouragement of acts of social protest was rare indeed
and, although Hobsbawm and Rudé identify 142 craftsmen among
1,000 Swing prisoners whose occupations were analysed, we may
surmise that these were journeymen and, perhaps, out of employ,
for the trades were not immune from the economic pressures of the
time. As a whole, their figures serve as a reminder that the episode
was, as the Hammonds characterised it, essentially a labourers' movement[81] and to these men we may now turn our attention with Landsberger's words in mind.

First, the agricultural labourers were not in a majority in rural

[79] J. Foster, *Class Struggle and the Industrial Revolution* (1974), pp. 150, 169–70.
[80] J. Obelkevich, *Religion and Rural Society: South Lindsey, 1825–75* (Oxford, 1976), pp.
     195, 202, 239.
[81] Hobsbawm and Rudé, *Swing*, p. 245; J. L and B. Hammond, *The Village Labourer*,
     new edn (1978), chaps. 10, 11.

England. Although they were the largest single occupational group in the countryside, their numbers were increasing only slowly and they did not predominate absolutely over all other categories, a point which is sometimes overlooked when attention is focussed on high labourer – farmer ratios at the village level. Taking the fifteen English counties deemed primarily agricultural by Deane and Cole, in only two (Bedfordshire and Suffolk) did agricultural labourers, as a proportion of males over the age of twenty, reach 51 per cent in 1831. For the rest the proportion averaged 45 per cent and in most English counties it was much lower.[82] Secondly, distress was strongly regionalised. For reasons already touched on, wages in the north were consistently better; in 1851 they were accounted by Caird to be 37 per cent higher north of a line falling between the Wash and the Dee estuary. Students of the position of the labourer in Lancashire, Nottinghamshire, and Cheshire have inferred increases in real wages among farm workers through the years of the agricultural depression, due chiefly to price movements,[83] and that argument appears capable of being extended to those southerners (a minority, no doubt, but perhaps more substantial than is sometimes assumed) who, as 'constant men', could depend on regular work. Moreover, among the day-labourers, it is almost certain that those most vulnerable to underemployment or unemployment were the aged or semi-infirm and young men who, not having families to support, were accorded lowest priority and suffered the most inconsiderate treatment at the hands of the poor law. Youths feature prominently in many contemporary accounts of the Swing riots, though not to the same extent among those brought to trial, and among the arsonists who appeared before the assizes in 1844, the *average* age of those convicted was only 24.3 and of those acquitted, 22.3.[84] Taken together, these points somewhat narrow the scope for contemporary recognition of the 'communality of problems' in rural England, and it remains to add that the quality of the

[82] *1831 Census of Great Britain, Enumeration Abstract*, II, relating (by county), 'Labourers Employed in Agriculture' to 'Males Twenty Years of Age'. All towns of 10,000 or more are excluded from these calculations.

[83] J. Caird, *English Agriculture in 1850–51*, 2nd edn (1968), pp. 511–12; J. D. Marshall, 'The Lancashire Rural Labourer in the Early Nineteenth Century', *Transactions of the Lancashire and Cheshire Antiquarian Society*, 71 (1961), pp. 115, 117; J. D. Marshall, 'Nottinghamshire Labourers in the Early Nineteenth Century', *Transactions of the Thoroton Society*, 64 (1961), pp. 60–1, 69; C. S. Davies, *The Agricultural History of Cheshire, 1750-1850* (Manchester, 1960), p. 86.

[84] Hobsbawm and Rudé, *Swing*, p. 247; D. Jones, 'Thomas Campbell Foster and the Rural Labourer: Incendiarism in East Anglia in the 1840s', *Social History*, 1 (1976), p. 20.

consciousness of even the most desperate was low. Essentially, all that they sought was greater security of employment at a modestly improved wage level. There was no vision of overthrowing the rural social order and, in particular, no call for the expropriation and redistribution of the land. Consequently, it is not surprising that the foundations of English rural society survived their most searching test in modern times, substantially unaltered.

III

About 1851 the number engaged in British agriculture reached its recorded peak, at 2.0m or 19.4 per cent of the occupied population and then fell to 1.38m in 1911. Meanwhile, although the real output of agriculture continued to increase (modestly in aggregate although, obviously, much more rapidly on a per capita basis), it contributed a diminishing proportion to the national income, reducing to under 6 per cent by the first decade of the twentieth century.[85] Such were the secular trends; however, when attention is focussed on variations in the prosperity of farming it is usual to distinguish three broad phases. The first, often characterised as the 'Golden Age' of farming, commenced early in the 1850s. It featured corn prices which were at least remunerative despite the abolition of the corn laws and the enlargement and consolidation of holdings, improvements in manuring, drainage and farm buildings, and a brisk trade in machinery. Money poured into land, and rentals rose while still allowing farmers to make profits. Modern authors have stressed the critical significance of buoyant meat and dairy prices backed by rising urban demand. These induced a discernible shift towards livestock production based on intensifying animal enterprises within mixed farming, using considerable quantities of grainstuffs grown with the aid of heavy costs for labour and artificial inputs to fatten stock.[86] However, adjustments to changing price-relativities were by no means complete, and many farmers were left with an overcommitment to cereal production which they would come to regret when, during the ensuing period of the 'Great Depression', a flood of imports, facilitated by massive reductions in freight rates by land and sea, led to a collapse of prices. Between 1873 and 1894 the price of wheat fell from 57s. 8d. to

[85] F. D. W. Taylor, 'United Kingdom: Numbers in Agriculture', *The Farm Economist*, 8 (1955), pp. 38–9, related to total occupied population in Mitchell and Deane, *Abstract*, p. 60; Deane and Cole, *British Economic Growth*, p. 175.

[86] Jones, *Development of English Agriculture*, pp. 17–25.

22s. 10d. per quarter and the area under corn cultivation in England shrank by some 24 per cent. Undoubtedly the Royal Commissions on the State of Agriculture (1879, 1892) were biased towards large-scale cereal producers and the fall in corn prices certainly worked to the advantage of those livestock farmers for whom grainstuffs were simply an input. They also served to benefit the urban consumer by giving him an extra margin for expenditure upon foodstuffs other than bread.[87] It is true that these expanding markets had to be shared with foreign producers, as the advent of refrigeration brought rising importations of dead meat from America, New Zealand, and the Argentine from the 1880s. Even so there is no doubt that the 'Great Depression' was uneven in its incidence on both a sectoral and regional basis. After 1894 the corner was turned as world demand for grainstuffs began to catch up with the vast increases in supply that had come about since the 1870s. A slow but steady advance in farm prices was evident, and reflected in a stabilisation of cropping aggregates in grazing and arable districts alike. However, by the Edwardian period British farmers retained a monopoly of the home market in only milk and market garden produce. By 1905–9 home producers supplied only 25 per cent of the wheat, 60 per cent of barley, and 74 per cent of oats consumed in Britain, and some 47 per cent of beef, mutton, and lamb, 76 per cent of cheese, and 87 per cent of butter was imported.[88]

In the eyes of agrarian historians, the years from the Great Exhibition to the First World War thus showed a diversity of experience, yet from the standpoint of the social historian the period has a certain unity, viewed from at least three angles. Just as agriculture was left to its own devices, to respond or not to market conditions under free trade, so also was laissez-faire the order of the day in relation to rural social affairs. The major reordering entailed in the 1834 reform of the poor laws was not matched by further changes of significance until the advent of county councils (1888) followed soon by rural district and parish councils (1894). Otherwise, the only important legislation passed with specifically rural problems in mind related to the use of the labour of minors, in the Gangs Act of 1869 and the Agricultural Children's Act of 1873. The agencies which positively shaped changes in rural society were, first, urban-industrial influences

[87] T. W. Fletcher, 'The Great Depression of English Agriculture, 1873–96', *Economic History Review*, 2nd ser., 13 (1961), pp. 418–19, 423–4, 425–30.
[88] Ministry of Agriculture, Fisheries and Food, *A Century of Agricultural Statistics, Great Britain, 1866–1966* (1968), pp. 47, 57.

including improved systems of distribution in which the railway was especially important and secondly, the persistent drain of population from rural areas to the town, often referred to as 'The Flight from the Land'.

By 1850, although aggregate railway mileage was still only 6,200, the main lines were already laid and the second half of the century saw a great multiplication of local and feeder services which approximately tripled railway mileage in Britain by 1900. Everywhere railways were welcomed as the very symbol of progress. They gave farmers easier access to urban markets and reduced costs. Increasingly the railway became the essential link between the rearers of store cattle and sheep in the hill districts and lowland fatteners, whilst the latter stood to gain also from economies made in despatching the beasts to their final destinations. John Hudson, a major tenant of Lord Leicester at Holkham told Caird that his sheep had lost an average of 10 lb and bullocks 28 lb on their journeys to London, costing him some £600 per annum, which loss was virtually eliminated with the advent of the railways.[89] Their second effect was to improve the prospects of dairymen as more remote districts were put in touch with potential urban markets. The cattle plague of 1865–6, which swept away many urban cowkeepers, coupled with the increasingly busy activities of public analysts and medical officers of health, prompted milk dealers to seek supplies from distant sources, a trade soon facilitated by special milk trains carrying tin-plated metal churns which rapidly replaced wooden tubs for convenience of handling. Jefferies instanced the 'general stir and movement' imparted to the western dairy districts, and in the north, the coming of the railway to Wensleydale in 1877 created a new market in Leeds, Newcastle, and Liverpool for milk that would previously have been made into butter and cheese.[90] Other benefits directly attributable to the railways included the arrival in the south of cheaper coal; great improvements in postal services (the penny post would not otherwise have been possible); cheap rates for the transmission of newspapers in bulk and the growth of the telegraph system, originating in the need to transmit information about the movement of trains. All these served to reduce rural isolation and the horizons of villagers were broadened by the availability of

[89]   Caird, *English Agriculture*, pp. 169–70.
[90]   R. Jefferies, *Hodge and his Masters*, new edn (1979), p. 296; P. S. Bagwell, 'The Decline of Rural Isolation', in Mingay, ed., *Victorian Countryside*, vol. 1, p. 37.

cheap day tickets to town, to market, and, from time to time, by organised excursions. By 1892, it was said, in the village public house the absorbing topics were 'no longer bucolic themes, but reminiscences of the latest trip to town'.[91] Finally, the railway provided a source of new jobs. This occurred first in the initial stages of construction; the railway, it is claimed, first gave the Norfolk labourer an opportunity to escape his unenviable lot, with the Norwich–Brandon and Wymondham–Dereham lines of 1845 and 1846 respectively.[92] They also offered permanent posts with unusual security, which were among the most attractive alternatives to work on the land.

However, it became increasingly apparent that, like enclosures, the railways were not an unmitigated boon. It was not their impact on existing systems of transport which gave cause for concern, for although coaching soon succumbed and numerous inns descended to the status of pot-houses, the railways expanded the local carrying trade.[93] Rather, the problem lay in the exposure of village shopkeepers and craftsmen to the draught of urban and factory competition. In principle, the growth of retail shopkeeping was favoured not only by the expansion of the market but also by a persistent long-term decline in the number of fairs, whose numbers are calculated to have declined in England and Wales from 1,691 in 1792 to 1,055 in 1888, a goodly number failing to survive the Fairs Act of 1871 which enabled local authorities, with the consent of the Home Secretary, to abolish them.[94] However, the benefits to retailers were unequally distributed. Small village shops continued to play a significant role, not least (like the corner-shops of large cities) by extending credit to their humbler patrons, but inevitably they charged prices considerably higher than those ruling in the towns, a point remarked on by, among others, Maude Davies comparing Corsley (Wiltshire) and York in 1909.[95] Yet increasing proportions of perishable goods and factory-made products came to be sold across the counters of shops in such regional centres as Canterbury, with a population of 22,000 in 1889. Here were, *inter alia*, fifty-eight grocers and tea dealers (including

---

[91] P. A. Graham, *The Rural Exodus* (1892), pp. 77–8.
[92] L. M. Springall, *Labouring Life in Norfolk Villages, 1834–1914* (1936), p. 48.
[93] A. M. Everitt, ed., *Perspectives in English Urban History* (1973), chap. 8, offers a useful study of the village carrier in Leicestershire.
[94] R. H. Rew, *An Agricultural Faggott* (1913), pp. 44–5.
[95] M. F. Davies, *Life in an English Country Village: An Economic and Historical Survey of the Parish of Corsley in Wiltshire* (1909), p. 140.

a branch of the International Tea Company); sixteen men's clothiers and outfitters; thirteen boot and shoe 'warehouses' including a branch of Freeman, Hardy, and Willis; five dealers in lamps, oil, and paraffin; four sewing machine agents; a bicycle shop; three precocious antique dealers; and, happy to note, a 'cricket bat, ball and stump warehouse'. With railways feeding customers into Canterbury from five directions, it was well placed to serve many of the needs of dozens of villages.[96]

In the sphere of production the broad-based technological changes of the Victorian age tended not only to undermine the position of the village craftsmen, but also favoured concentration into larger units, not least in industries processing farm products. At Horsham, Henry Mitchell brewed about 400 quarters of malt annually in the 1830s and by 1868, 3,075; during the intervening years he had acquired a new brewery, enlarged twice and adapted to steam, a new malthouse, and a succession of tied public houses. At Banbury, Hunt's brewery by 1900 had taken over four smaller enterprises and acquired at least 114 tied houses.[97] Corn milling, too, was transformed. In 1850 there were a few steam-powered units in the larger towns, but most flour was still ground in mills reliant on wind and water power. After 1875 the industry was virtually revolutionised by roller milling, which was found necessary in order to take advantage of the seemingly illimitable supplies of American wheat and to beat off the threat of foreign millers unloading flour on the British market. The first automatic roller mill in Britain was opened at Manchester in 1879 and increasingly the industry came to be concentrated in the more important market towns, large cities, and, above all, the ports. Meanwhile the number of independent country mills rapidly declined. At Bridlington where there were no fewer then ten mills in 1853, only three were operational by 1900.[98] In the boot and shoe industry, the clearest case of concentration comes from Somerset. At Street, C. and J. Clark succeeded by using mechanised methods in quadrupling their annual production (to 800,000 pairs) between 1861 and 1901. This was accomplished with only a modest increase in the labour force, from 900 to 1,250. Significantly, they employed in 1909 over half the shoemakers in the county, whose numbers in the aggregate had declined from 5,029 in 1841

[96] *Stevens' Directory of Canterbury and Neighbourhood* (1889), pp. 183–210.
[97] C. W. Chalklin, 'Country Towns', in Mingay, ed., *Victorian Countryside*, vol. 2, p. 284.
[98] *Ibid.*, p. 283.

to 2,226 in 1901.[99] The list of crafts affected directly by new, usually urban-based, industry is virtually endless. With the coming of the railway, local potters about Farnborough (Surrey) found it increasingly difficult to compete with producers on the scale of Doulton's of Lambeth. The use of new building materials such as concrete, mild steel, and galvanised roofing sheets, and the rise to prominence of large-scale brick-fields and slate quarries, increasingly took toll of local brick-makers and thatchers. Almost universally, craftsmen had recourse to non-local sources of semi-finished products such as iron axles, lead piping or saddler's ironmongery, while in *The Wheelwright's Shop* Sturt noted the use of deal from Norway in place of locally sawn elm boards for the floors of carts and wagons.[100]

In most cases, male-dominated crafts were coming under serious pressure for the first time during the second half of the nineteenth century. With female employment in the outwork industries the chronology of decline was more attenuated. Already, from the late eighteenth century cottage industry had been profoundly affected by the transition to machine spinning in the textile trades, and from one end of the country to the other came complaints that work of this kind was either disappearing or else being offered at only derisory wages. Other industries showed more pronounced capacities for survival and some regions continued to feature marked concentrations of female outwork. A case in point was gloving in Worcestershire and Somerset. In the 1860s the manager of one of the largest London warehouses referred to 'whole villages of born glove makers . . . we have had as many as 6,000 women on our books . . . in any one year' and as late as 1907, the *Select Committee on Homework* claimed that in order to supplement low agricultural wages, 'every house was gloving' in the Yeovil district.[101] Another was pillow lacemaking, favoured by an insatiable demand for lace of all kinds and qualities. A decline in the number of lacemakers in the south Midland counties and in Devon was staved off for longer than might have been expected, there being still some 25,000 in 1871; however, by the 1890s the increasing sophistication of machine-made lace, importations from France

[99] M. A. Havinden, 'The South-West: A Case of De-Industrialisation?', in M. Palmer, ed., *The Onset of Industrialisation* (Nottingham University, Department of Adult Education, 1976), p. 6.

[100] G. Sturt, *William Smith, Potter and Farmer* (1919), p. 221; J. A. Chartres and G. L. Turnbull, 'Country Craftsmen', in Mingay, ed., *Victorian Countryside*, vol. 1, pp. 326-7; G. Sturt, *The Wheelwright's Shop* (Cambridge, 1923), pp. 64-5.

[101] D. Bythell, *The Sweated Trades: Outwork in Nineteenth Century Britain* (1978), pp. 117-18.

and Belgium, and a capricious turn of fashion against lace coupled with difficulties in obtaining fresh recruits, had decidedly reduced the importance of the industry.[102] Straw-plaiting, particularly concentrated in Buckinghamshire, Bedfordshire, Hertfordshire, and Essex, also declined in the closing decades of the century in the face of cheap imports of Far Eastern origin and a shift in fashion towards hats made from other fabrics. Bedfordshire's 20,701 female plaiters of 1871 were reduced to 485 by 1901, working for wages far below those ruling in the 1860s.[103]

From the standpoint of the economist, many of the changes described can be interpreted as straightforward cases of industrial rationalisation, and in some villages, new growth was the order of the day. For example, it was rapid in the neighbourhood of the great brickworks around Peterborough and in south Bedfordshire, and along the Medway valley with its profusion of cement works, found also around Portland Bill and near Rugby. Here and there food processing plants of a decidedly modern nature made their appearance. The first British cheese factories were established in Derbyshire in 1869–70, and by 1875 nineteen were either in operation or under construction in five counties.[104] Also noteworthy were the integrated enterprises of soft fruit culture and preserves of Wilkins of Tiptree (Essex) and Chivers at Histon (Cambridgeshire) where Rider Haggard was impressed by the employment offered to 1,000 outdoor hands and 250 women, and by the factory with its silver-lined boilers, patent filling apparatus, tramways, and packing and printing plant, all lit by electricity.[105] Foundries and agricultural machinery enterprises, often initiated by enterprising blacksmiths, might flourish modestly in situations far removed from the industrial heartlands of Britain, for example the Reeves family business at Bratton (Wiltshire) which gradually expanded its range of activities, acting as 'a meeting place of old and new, of traditional village skills and attitudes and the advancing machine age'.[106] Two of the most important agricultural machinery makers, Garretts of Leiston and Smyths of Peasenhall, were located in what could still be described as villages. All were able to hold

---

[102] G. F. R. Spenceley, 'The English Pillow-Lace Industry, 1840-80: A Rural Industry in Competition with Machinery', *Business History*, 19 (1977), pp. 69, 79–82.

[103] P. Horn, 'Women's Cottage Industries', in Mingay, ed., *Victorian Countryside*, vol. 1, p. 348.

[104] C. S. Orwin and E. H. Whetham, *History of British Agriculture, 1846–1914* (1964), pp. 146–7.

[105] H. R. Haggard, *Rural England*, 2nd edn, 2 vols. (1906), vol. 2, p. 52.

[106] M. Reeves, *Sheep Bell and Ploughshare* (1980), p. 131.

their own with moderate success in face of urban-based enterprises such as Ransomes of Ipswich and Rustons at Lincoln.

The salient features of migratory movements, based on the analysis of census returns and the civil registration details which became available after 1837, are as follows.

(i)   Only five Welsh (Anglesey, Brecknockshire, Cardiganshire, Pembrokeshire, Radnorshire) and four English counties (Cornwall, Herefordshire, Huntingdonshire, Rutland) showed absolute decreases between 1851 and 1911, but such figures obscure the factor of urban concentration within counties. Thus, in Norfolk, the aggregate population of the main urban centres (Norwich, Yarmouth, King's Lynn) grew by 84 per cent, 1851–1911, whilst the remainder fell by 10 per cent.

(ii) At the scale of the registration districts, numbering several hundred, one calculation suggests that the aggregate population of 'residual' rural areas (that is, after subtracting predominantly urban registration districts and those with extensive collieries) was actually rather higher in 1911 (by 18.5 per cent in the north, 9.2 per cent in the south) than in 1841. However, their net losses by migration had been considerable, amounting to some 79 per cent of calculated natural increases (births minus deaths) in the north and 89 per cent in the south.[107]

(iii) At a smaller scale again, cases of absolute decline were quite common. For example, Truro, Chichester, and St Ives, all of which had doubled their respective populations between 1801 and 1861, sustained losses of 11–14 per cent in the ensuing thirty years; and at the level of the individual village, the trend could at times be very spectacular, as in the case of Cerne Abbas (Dorset) where the population grew to reach 1,341 in 1841 but would decline to 582, including 46 in the union workhouse, by 1912.[108]

The fall in the number of agriculturalists was far more spectacular than the rural figures as a whole might lead one to assume, although there was no significant reduction in the number of farmers. While there are many indications that the rate of turnover of tenancies

[107] Mitchell and Deane, *Abstract*, pp. 20–7; A. K. Cairncross, *Home and Foreign Investment, 1870–1913* (Cambridge, 1953), p. 78.
[108] T. Welton, 'On the Distribution of Population in England and Wales, 1801–91', *Journal of the Royal Statistical Society*, 63 (1900), p. 539; H. Aronson, *The Land and the Labourer* (1914), p. 18.

increased, for example on the Holkham estate from the 1880s, the aggregate number identified in the 1911 census of England and Wales was, at 229,000, within 8 per cent of that of 1871 or, indeed, 1851.[109] However, the number of their employees, if we exclude family labour, fell by 46 per cent from its mid-nineteenth-century peak. For this reason most contemporary discussions of 'rural depopulation' focussed upon the agricultural labourer. Other things being equal, shifts in land-use patterns towards pastoral activities would serve to reduce the amount of labour required; moreover mechanisation was a factor, some claimed, working to depress the number of farm workers. Here we have to reckon with, chiefly, the appearance of mowing and reaping machines from the 1850s and 1860s, and the advent of the self-binding reaper in the 1880s, while sets of steam-ploughing tackle, still something of a rarity in the 1860s, became comparatively commonplace by the end of the century. In his *History of the English Agricultural Labourer* (1894) Hasbach supported the view that mechanisation had an inexorable tendency to reduce the demand for labour, although there was no uniformity of contemporary opinion on this matter. Indeed R. C. Little, surveying a massive body of evidence in the final report of the Royal Commission on Labour (1894) was inclined to think that the reduction of farm staffs was a consequence and not the cause of migration.[110] This is not to deny any impact of mechanisation on the farm labour force: it certainly assisted farmers to cut down on the number of casual workers used at critical times in the year and reduced the seasonal work available to the wives and children of farm workers, so tending to bring down the harvest earnings of the regular labour force.

There is a considerable literature on other causes which disposed the labourer to turn his back on the land. Among those adduced by various contemporaries were the poor condition of farm cottages, comparative level of farm wages (too low), hours of work (too long), and, more generally, 'want of outlook', i.e. the very limited prospects of social mobility or betterment for the farm worker. An equally rich but inconclusive literature was addressed to its effects. These were said to include a deterioration in the quality of farm staffs ('We retain the sediment . . .'; 'Few except the doodles remain . . .' and much more

[109]   S. W. Martins, *A Great Estate at Work* (Cambridge, 1980), pp. 111–12; Taylor 'Numbers in Agriculture', p. 38.
[110]   W. Hasbach, *A History of the English Agricultural Labourer* (1894; Eng. edn 1908), pp. 256, 258; *RC on Labour: The Agricultural Labourer*, V (I), *General Report*, PP 1893–4, XXXVIII, p. 40.

in the same vein).[111] Yet farmers had always complained that each generation of workers was inferior to its predecessor and would continue to voice such views far into the future. The only solid fact in this area is that there were definite signs of aging among agricultural workers. In 1891 elderly employees (those aged fifty-five and over) were 59 per cent more numerous on the land than in the rest of the male labour force, and approximately three times more common than among railway employees or coalminers. The implications for labour efficiency remain somewhat uncertain, for, as Canon Bury contended, although the older man might be a little weaker in bodily strength, his experience was more valuable than hitherto 'because of the advent of machinery'.[112]

At least there is no reason to doubt that the outflow was beneficial to those who remained on the land as, by degrees, 'the plethoric population bogey of 1830' came to be 'replaced by the lean-exodus skeleton of 1902'.[113] Prior to 1870 it is probable that improvements in earnings were modest, and contingent upon greater regularity of employment together with an increasing solicitude for the welfare of labourers on the part of more enlightened landlords and employers.[114] Between 1867–70 and 1907 earnings moved up noticeably in all regions of England and Wales, by some 30 per cent on average, and by more than that in terms of their purchasing power, given contemporary trends in prices. Moreover, there is evidence to suggest that migration contributed fairly substantially to the erosion of regional differentials in agricultural wage levels which were substantially reduced between the two dates.[115] Even so, farm workers' wages remained barely half those earned by the average industrial worker, and in the Edwardian period prompted several pioneering investigations into the extent of poverty in rural England.[116]

Comparatively little work has been done on the declining numbers of rural craftsmen. However, a recent study covering several English

[111]   Board of Agriculture and Fisheries, *Report on the Decline of the Agricultural Population of Great Britain, 1881-1906*, PP 1906, XCVI, pp. 11–21; W. A. Armstrong, 'The Flight from the Land', in Mingay, ed., *Victorian Countryside*, vol. 1, pp. 120–4.

[112]   W. A. Armstrong, 'The Workfolk', in Mingay, ed., *Victorian Countryside*, vol. 2, p. 502; *RC on Aged Poor*, PP 1895, XIV, p. 239.

[113]   Haggard, *Rural England*, vol. 2, p. 565.

[114]   E. L. Jones, 'The Agricultural Labour Market in England, 1793–1872', *Economic History Review*, 2nd ser., 17 (1964), pp. 328–32, 338.

[115]   E. H. Hunt, *Regional Wage Variations in Britain, 1850-1914* (Oxford, 1973), pp. 59–64, 248–9.

[116]   Most notably Davies, *Life in an English Country Village*; H. H. Mann, 'Life in an Agricultural Village in England', *Sociological Papers*, 1 (1905); B. S. Rowntree and M. Kendall, *How the Labourer Lives: A Study of the Rural Labour Problem* (1913).

counties has confirmed that in most cases the incidence of country crafts in relation to population was falling after 1861 or 1871, and in many from as early as 1851, whilst emphasising the comparative resilience of blacksmiths and wheelwrights whose activities related directly to the still expanding numbers of horses used in Victorian and Edwardian England.[117] Even less attention has been paid to the migratory patterns of women. Yet a noteworthy feature of the rural exodus was that females played the larger role statistically, so that by 1911, the sex ratio in the fifteen to nineteen age group stood at 864 and 1,062 females per 1,000 males in rural and urban registration districts respectively.[118] Adolescent girls were channelled in droves into domestic service. Characteristically, they were first found places locally in the households of tradesmen, bailiffs or schoolmasters which were considered a stepping-stone to service further afield. No doubt this reflected the absence of alternative sources of female employment but it was at least as well marked in Wales, a bastion of 'peasant' agriculture, as in the rural southern counties of England.[119] It was considered natural that the vast concentration of female servants in towns would serve to 'act as magnets to the lads they leave behind them', and noticed that once they had acquired a taste for town life, few relished the idea of returning to the hardships of life as farm labourers' wives. Consequently, their influence tended to be 'thrown decidedly into the scale in favour of migration'.[120]

The interaction between town and country cannot be summed up by simply setting the tide of factory-made products in one direction, against that of human resources in the other. Some account needs to be taken of the ever-increasing infiltration of urban values into the remotest corners of English rural life. Their absorption began in the schools when country-bred children came into contact with teachers from an urban background, dedicated to the task of improving their youthful charges. One manifestation of this was attempts to make children adopt standardised English. 'There's wor Alice', complained one Northumbrian, 'she's learnin' me to talk like a priest

[117] Chartres and Turnbull, 'Country Craftsmen', pp. 318–25.
[118] J. Saville, *Rural Depopulation in England and Wales, 1851–1951* (1957), p. 110.
[119] Snell, *Annals of the Labouring Poor*, pp. 51–7, 317; A. W. Ashby and I. L. Evans, *The Agriculture of Wales and Monmouthshire* (Cardiff, 1944), p. 76.
[120] M. Winstanley, *Life in Kent at the Turn of the Century* (Folkestone, 1978), p. 27; *RC on Labour: The Agricultural Labourer*, I, England, *Report of W. E. Bear*, PP 1893–4, XXXV, p. 18.

... teacher says *yebble* is not a word. You must call it able.'[121] However, in the long run changes in the pattern of employment did more to erode local dialects than the efforts of the schoolmasters, and much more insidious, in the eyes of many critical landlords and farmers, was the tendency of teachers to provide an 'irrelevant' curriculum. Arguments to the effect that village elementary education should be given an explicit rural or vocational bias were countered by the view that any such principle would be 'acknowledged as absolutely vicious for the children of the rich'.[122] No resolution of the problem was forthcoming either before or after 1914, and children continued to be taught without a significant positive rural bias, which may have improved the prospects of the smarter girls and boys, but left others reflecting on the uselessness of their pre-1914 schooling and looking forward to leaving so that they could get educated.[123] Institutions serving the needs of adults also developed along the lines of urban models. An obvious case is that of the friendly societies. Already, at the close of the eighteenth century these had abounded in the villages, but soon the village clubs had to meet the competition of landlord-sponsored 'county' societies, the first of which was founded in Essex in 1818 followed by eight more within the next forty years. More detrimental still was the rapid diffusion of the great affiliated orders, epitomised by the Manchester Unity of Oddfellows. Dorset may be taken as a case in point: by 1872 the County Society accounted for about a fifth of total membership and the remainder was shared between a vastly increased number of 'lodges' operating from small towns such as Bere and Blandford and surviving local clubs in villages such as Melbury Abbas and Motcombe.[124] Doubtless the affiliated orders offered some major advantages including their seemingly unquestionable stability and, by virtue of their dispersed lodges, the flexibility valuable to potentially migratory young males. There was, however, some social loss. With the collapse of local clubs older members were often left outside the affiliated orders and the jollifications associated with club anniversaries and public house meetings withered away. However, what should be emphasised here is that the changes were an instance of the displacement of a myriad of local initiatives by a standardised, more bureaucratic model.

121   Graham, *Rural Exodus*, pp. 34–5.
122   E. N. Bennett, *Problems of Village Life* (n.d. 1913?), p. 101.
123   R. Blythe, *Akenfield* (Harmondsworth, 1972), pp. 36–7.
124   P. H. J. H. Gosden, *The Friendly Societies in England, 1815–75* (Manchester, 1961), pp. 66–7.

The onward march of the affiliated orders was not likely to be opposed by landlords and farmers, favourable as they frequently were to promoting the ideals of individualism and self-help. Far less welcome was the intrusion of trade unionism into agriculture. Although disputes between farmers and their employees resulting in the cessation of work at harvest time were far from unknown, the view common among established labour leaders of the capacities of the agricultural labourer was condescending to a degree: 'In intellect he is a child, in position a helot, in condition a squalid outcast ... the squire is his King, the parson his deity, the taproom his highest conception of earthly bliss.'[125] Ironically, a month after these words were written, the first quasi-national labourers' union led by the Warwickshire hedger, Joseph Arch, was born in February 1872. Initially, success was achieved in raising wages on a rising market, but the union's inability to resist an organised employers' lock-out in Suffolk in 1874 soon led to disillusionment, while relations were never good with contemporaneous but rival organizations such as the Lincolnshire Labour League and the Kent and Sussex Labourers' Union. By 1879 membership of Arch's National Union is believed to have declined by as much as two-thirds from its 1874 peak of 79,000, and the attention of the unions was focussed to a very great extent on the promotion of emigration. This tactic, which helped to promote a far greater outflow than in earlier decades may have worked to the advantage of the labourers who remained, but it also had a considerable potential to affect union membership adversely.[126] Another fillip was imparted to unskilled unionism on all fronts by the Dockers' Strike of 1889 and in agriculture there is evidence, by 1892, of the existence of six further unions as well as those already mentioned. However, within a couple of years all had either disappeared, including the remnants of the National and Kent and Sussex Unions, or were moribund.[127] At no time had they made any significant headway in northern England or in Wales where farm servants continued to be hired on long contracts. Invariably the arable districts were more

---

[125] Lloyd Jones, former Owenite and advocate of trade unionism, writing in *The Beehive*. Quoted in R. Groves, *Sharpen the Sickle: The History of the Farm Workers' Union*, 2nd edn (1981), p. 36.

[126] J. P. D. Dunbabin, 'The Incidence and Organisation of Agricultural Trades Unionism in the 1870s', *Agricultural History Review*, 16 (1968), pp. 117–18, 138; and *idem*, 'The Revolt of the Field: The Agricultural Labourers' Movement in the 1870s', *Past & Present*, 26 (1963), p. 85.

[127] Hasbach, *Agricultural Labourer*, p. 302; F. E. Green, *History of the English Agricultural Labourer, 1870-1920* (1920), p. 140.

receptive and in the new century trade unionism was almost wholly confined to Norfolk, where George Edwards led an Eastern Counties Labour League numbering, in 1912, 4,000 members. In the present context interest attaches chiefly to the way in which agricultural unionism seemed, in the eyes of its enemies, to call into question the integrity of rural society and to be succoured by alien, predominantly urban, influences. Thus in 1872 we find the Wainfleet branch of the Lincolnshire Labour League acknowledging small donations from such quarters as the Nottingham Dyers Association, the Circular Hosiery Society and the Lace Association from the same city. Meanwhile the National Union drew voluntary subscriptions from as far afield as Bournemouth and Worthing in the south and Jarrow and Manchester in the north as well as on the active support of Birmingham Liberal politicians. Again, in 1890–2, agents of the Dockers' Union busied themselves setting 'men against masters and masters against men' in Lincolnshire, Oxfordshire, and elsewhere.[128] In truth, the support of urban trade unionists was fitful, but to many it seemed most objectionable. Moreover, the histrionic fury with which the unions were assailed, especially in the early 1870s, was attributable to the fact that in recent years philanthropy had been practised to an unprecedented extent, and that 'instead of being met with gratitude it was encountering rudeness and a new kind of demand'.[129] This comment takes us to the heart of the deep offence which unionism gave even to those numerous landlords and farmers who were ready to admit that the labourer's condition left much to be desired. By its very nature trade unionism in agriculture appeared to deny implicitly any local community of interest. The point was neatly put by a Bedfordshire landlord, Capt. Polhill-Turner, at his harvest home in 1874, who drew a contrast between the sort of unionism about which so much had been heard lately and 'the happy bond and unionism they had at Renhold – unionism between landlord and tenant, master and men'.[130]

These explicit examples of the penetration of urban influences certainly do not exhaust the theme. Undoubtedly more important than agents of the Dockers' Union in the dissemination of urban values

---

[128] R. C. Russell, *The Revolt of the Field in Lincolnshire* (Lincoln, 1956), p. 37; *RC on Labour: The Agricultural Labourer*, I (II), *England, Report of C. M. Chapman*, PP 1893–4, XXXV, p. 56.

[129] M. S. Gretton, *A Corner of the Cotswolds through the Nineteenth Century* (1914), pp. 183–4, and see Jones, 'Agricultural Labour Market', pp. 330–2.

[130] Agar, *Bedfordshire Farm Worker*, p. 195.

and modes of thought were those caught up in a contraflow of population from town to countryside. In the closing decades of the century the social structure of rural England was beginning to be noticeably affected by residential growth. The dispersion of persons who had been citydwellers all their lives, or at least had substantial experience of urban life, took many forms. We may instance the extremely rapid rate of growth of country towns such as Watford (which quadrupled in size to reach 29,000 by 1901), or the Surrey towns described as becoming 'as countrified as Wimbledon or Blackheath', but the spread of villadom also affected the villages. Considering Farnham (Surrey), which also quadrupled in population to reach 2,000 between 1891 and 1911, Sturt remarked on the way in which allotments received by cottagers at its recent enclosure (1861) were often sold for building plots: 'the stealthiness of the process, however, blinded us to what was happening'.[131] Such changes were most obvious within commuting distance of London, but were also apparent further afield, for example around the fringes of the New Forest where 'weird bungalows and suburban cottages of the dreariest red brick' were springing up by 1910.[132] Indeed even very modest towns far removed from London were beginning to develop small suburbs, or else to colonise neighbouring villages into which the retired and wealthy could withdraw, as their centres were increasingly given over to offices, shops, workshops, and hotels. A further feature was the tendency of farmers to let their better cottages to 'weekenders', for example around Epping and Billericay in Essex. Writing in 1915, Savage thought that the rediscovery of the country by those with no immediate concern with the land had been a notable feature of the preceding thirty years.[133]

If it is accepted that the diffusion of urban ideas, values, and life styles was making headway in rural England, then *per contra*, we might expect to find evidence of the decay of traditional rural culture, using the term in a broad, anthropological sense to encompass norms of behaviour and received wisdom. Such, indeed, appears to have been the case and many authors alluded to a softening of manners. Village children in the Cotswolds were less given to the 'ceaseless baiting of the village idiot and cripple and cruelty to every bird and beast

[131]   R. E. Pahl, *Urbs in Rure* (1965), pp. 19–20; G. Sturt, *Lucy Bettesworth* (1913), p. 264; *idem, The Memoirs of a Surrey Labourer* (1907), p. 133; and *idem, Change in the Village* (Readers Library edn, 1920), p. 6.
[132]   A. D. Hall, *A Pilgrimage of British Farming, 1910–12* (1912), pp. 33–4.
[133]   J. C. Thresh, *The Housing of the Agricultural Labourer, with Special Reference to Essex* (Chelmsford, 1919), pp. 73, 74; W. G. Savage, *Rural Housing* (1915), pp. 135-6.

in their range'. Others commented on the greater consideration shown by men towards their wives and children, while by the Edwardian period Sturt wrote of a 'surprising equality' and 'dogged companionship' among married couples.[134] Polite forms of address were rapidly replacing the use of nicknames so that even the humblest labourers and their wives increasingly expected to be addressed as Mr and Mrs. It is possible, of course, to view these developments in a less than favourable light: Obelkevich holds that a more privatised family life was a facet of the triumph of capitalist individualism and had been achieved at the expense of loyalty to 'the crowd' though not, he thinks, of class.[135] Be that as it may, more civilised behavioural patterns were paralleled by a decline in the incidence of rural criminality. Labourers now invariably helped to extinguish fires, and reported cases of sheep stealing declined from 649 in 1857 to 119 in 1892 while even poaching diminished, though not to the same extent. Figures for 1891–1901 comparing eight agricultural counties with certain manufacturing towns showed markedly lower rural rates in respect of drunkenness, homicidal crime, and assaults and suicide.[136] Since under-thirties had always featured disproportionately in the criminal statistics, some part of the decrease was doubtless attributable to migration.[137] Concurrently there was a considerable erosion of vernacular customs, traditions, and beliefs. Conscious, perhaps, of an acceleration in the rate of their decay, urban Victorians made vigorous attempts to record them, especially after the formation of the Folklore Society in 1878. Their interests were decidedly antiquarian and their work unsystematic, so that no clear picture of the rate of decline of ancient rituals and beliefs can be arrived at. Much of what was passing away was represented by progressives as primitive superstition, although today's historians are more likely to refer cautiously to 'the prior culture' or 'pre-scientific attitudes of mind'.[138] Many of these observances were quite harmless if ineffectual, such as belief in the efficacy of horseshoes and rowan twigs to ward off evil and bring good fortune. Others were hard on animals, for example the ritual remedy reported

---

[134]   Gretton, *Corner of the Cotswolds*, p. 213; Sturt, *Change in the Village*, pp. 39, 44.
[135]   Obelkevich, *Religion and Rural Society*, pp. 100–2.
[136]   P. Horn, *Labouring Life in the Victorian Countryside* (Dublin, 1976), p. 227; W. Sullivan, *Alcoholism* (1906), cited in D. J. Davies, 'Condition of the Rural Population in England and Wales, 1870–1928' (unpublished PhD thesis, University of Wales, 1931), p. 157.
[137]   Archer, 'Rural Protest', pp. 274–5; Glyde, *Suffolk*, pp. 130–1.
[138]   E.g. C. Phythian-Adams, 'Rural Culture', in Mingay, ed., *Victorian Countryside*, vol. 2, pp. 617, 623.

from the Lake District and Cornwall in the 1860s against brucellosis among calving cows, which involved either the live burial or roasting of young calves. Least regrettable of all, perhaps, was a decline of belief in witchcraft, which Glyde believed to have prevailed among three-quarters of Suffolk labourers even in the 1840s; and which as recently as 1826, had resulted in an elderly bent man at Wickham Heath being 'swam' for a wizard on the village pond.[139] In later times, belief in witchcraft became an increasingly private matter and never resulted in communal action of this kind. It is probably safe to infer that the structure of ancient beliefs and observances survived most strongly at the level of the cottage and that migration must have considerably interrupted their transmission through the generations, as well as acting simply to reduce the number of people available to hold them in common.[140] In addition, some powerful forces were ranged against the 'prior culture'. Schools tended to oppose themselves, as Hardy observed, to the 'fast-perishing lumber of superstitions, folk-lore, dialect and orally-transmitted ballads',[141] as did men of the cloth, Anglican and nonconformist alike. By the second half of the nineteenth century plural livings and non-residency had very largely vanished, and many of the clergy were distinguished by personal austerity and seriousness of purpose springing from evangelical influences. Bell-ringing, for purposes unconnected with summoning people to church, was a target of some clergymen fearful that the ringers would spend the money so earned at the ale-house. Another objective was the reform of church music, entailing the ousting of fiddle-players and other self-taught (but adult male) musicians in the interest of greater decorum, and it was noticeable that women and children made up the greater part of the church choirs and organ players who replaced them.[142] Some customs were laundered and indeed annexed at the instigation of the clergy: the classic case was the transformation of the raucous harvest home traditionally given at farmhouses, or as was sometimes the case with even worse moral consequences, at public houses. From the 1840s date the first harvest thanksgiving services, originating, it is thought, at East Brent (Somerset) and Morwenstowe (Cornwall) and 'Come ye thankful people

[139] J. Glyde, *Autobiography of a Suffolk Farm Labourer* (East Suffolk Record Office, q. S9), pp. 25–6.
[140] Phythian-Adams, 'Rural Culture', pp. 623–4.
[141] T. Hardy, *Tess of the d'Urbervilles*, new edn (1974), p. 50.
[142] B. Bushaway, *By Rite: Custom, Ceremony and Community in England, 1700–1880* (1982), pp. 49, 51–6, 248; A. Jessopp, *Arcady: For Better for Worse* (1887), p. 233.

come' and 'We plough the fields and scatter' were first published in, respectively, 1843 and 1861.[143] Complementary social arrangements increasingly tended to take the form of a parish feast or supper conducted with propriety, and by 1889, the Rev. Baring-Gould could write, 'The harvest home is no more. We have instead harvest festivals, tea and cake at sixpence a head in the school-room, and a choral service and a sermon in the church.'[144]

Unfortunately, the moral earnestness exhibited by an increasing proportion of rural clergymen, now on a par with that of ministers of the nonconformist churches, was not conducive to strengthening the appeal of the church to village populations at large. Despite the ire aroused against individual clergymen-magistrates in the 1820s and 1830s, and the resentment caused among many farmers by the workings of the tithe system prior to the commutation measure of 1836, the 1851 religious census showed that attendances may have been as much as 42 per cent higher in rural areas and small towns than in those of over 10,000 in size, taking all denominations together.[145] No comparable census was taken subsequently, but educated guesses suggested some decline in percentage if not in absolute terms. Bennett reckoned that church and chapel attendance in the villages in 1913 did not normally exceed 25–35 per cent of the adult population, and even these were unlikely to be a representative cross-section of villagers.[146] In the 1890s Graham's characterisation of a typical Anglican congregation was one which included, if not the squire, then at any rate the ladies and servants of his household; most of the larger tenants and their dependants; estate functionaries such as the gamekeeper (evincing loyalty to the established order) and the very poor, hobbling up the aisle and 'making a fine show of rheumatic pains and not forgetting the prospect of Christmas coals'. At the chapel, meanwhile, one might encounter some smaller tenants, artisans, and shopkeepers together with a sprinkling of free labourers and farm servants.[147] Although some resentment was caused by the failure of the Anglican

[143]   Bushaway, *By Rite*, pp. 265–71; J. Julian, *A Dictionary of Hymnology* (1907), pp. 237, 254.
[144]   S. Baring-Gould, *Old Country Life* (1913), quoted in Bushaway, *By Rite*, p. 272.
[145]   K. S. Inglis, 'Patterns of Religious Worship in 1851', *Journal of Ecclesiastical History*, 11 (1960), p. 80.
[146]   Bennett, *Problems of Village Life*, p. 122.
[147]   Graham, *Rural Exodus*, p. 52.

clergy (with a few honourable exceptions) to side openly with the labourers at the time of their 'Revolt' in the 1870s, it is generally agreed that positive anti-clericalism in the continental sense was rare. But some felt that the low church party had done immense harm 'by suppressing all genial jovial natures and making a bleak parsonic gloom the passport to Christianity' and by the Edwardian period there was 'a general feeling' that the church with its incomprehensible liturgies and ancient formularies was quite out of touch with the times.[148]

Part of the difficulty lay, no doubt, in the fact that parsons were still closely associated with the gentry and thus socially distanced from those occupying the lower reaches of village hierarchies whose existence was still accurately reflected in, say, nice distinctions in the fox-hunting field or even in the degree of attention that callers at a solicitor's office might receive.[149] This is not to suggest that the rural social order was immutable, however, and in some respects changes were especially visible at its apex. Increases in rents were the order of the day until the Great Depression began to bite in the mid-1870s, and sample studies have shown that the average decrease which ensued down to the mid-1890s was about 26 per cent, though very much greater in the south and east of the country (41 per cent) than in the north and west (12 per cent).[150] Such a fall could seriously embarrass even members of the aristocracy but those most severely affected were the gentry in the arable districts who in many cases found that their reduced incomes could no longer stretch to cover the full range of activities expected of them. In cases where estates were sold, they were likely to pass into the hands of industrialists or financiers such as the Bradford manufacturer who bought a 7,000-acre estate in Lincolnshire from the Marquess of Ripon in 1889.[151] Several consequences followed. There was some blurring of the concept of gentility. More than ever, the chink of ready money came to count for more than long descent, heraldic quarterings, or ancestral crusaders. Devoting more time to their private business interests or to the pursuit of company directorships, the higher gentry became more remote, only occasionally flitting across the village scene with their gorgeously attired families, 'like kingfishers crossing a flock of

---

[148]   G. Cresswell, *Norfolk and its Squires, Clergy, Farmers and Labourers* (1875), p. 23; Bennett, *Problems of Village Life*, pp. 134–5.

[149]   D. C. Itzkowitz, *Peculiar Privilege: A Social History of English Foxhunting, 1753–1885* (Hassocks, Sussex, 1977), pp. 25–6, 65, 101, 177; Jefferies, *Hodge*, pp. 176–7.

[150]   Thompson, *Landed Society*, p. 310.

[151]   *Ibid.*, p. 319.

hedgerow sparrows'.[152] To some extent, the older generation lost their appetite for assuming the burdens of social and political leadership, whilst the new men would shoulder them only if they pleased rather than recognising any strong obligation to do so. These are, of course, gross generalisations. There were numerous villages where tight squirearchical control remained in evidence, displaying that mixture of beneficence and firmness which, in the eyes of hostile critics entailed the forfeiture of every particle of freedom.[153] Yet, taken as a whole, there is no doubt that the gentry were playing a diminishing public role. The proportion of MPs who were landowners was reduced from roughly two-thirds to one third between the 1850s and 1890s, and to some extent they also relaxed their grip on local government. Since 1834, the tedious administration of the poor law had been left increasingly to farmers and tradesmen, and fears were expressed that the county councils of 1888 would fail to attract gentlemen apprehensive of undergoing triennial elections contested by their social inferiors. In the event, large numbers did submit themselves to this indignity and were rewarded for their public-spiritedness by being duly returned.[154] However, gentlemen were far less in evidence on the rural district councils of 1894, and would be represented by a bailiff or agent, if at all, on the humble parish councils instituted in the same year. Yet, despite some tendency for their direct participation in politics to be reduced, the influence exercised by landlords remained enormous. Throughout the Victorian age tenant farmers looked to them for guidance in the exercise of their votes. Cases of direct intimidation, through threat of dismissal, etc., were not unknown, although it took a very determined tenant and an equally obdurate landlord before matters came to such a head. They rarely did so, especially after the introduction of the secret ballot (1872) and the passing of the Corrupt Practices Act of 1883, the reason being that most farmers accepted 'the premise of the social superiority of the gentry and regarded deference as a natural element of good grace' as it has been neatly put.[155]

More vulnerable to wild ideas, it was feared, were the labourers newly enfranchised in 1884. Being but semi-literate, they were frequently judged to be incapable of holding independent political

[152]   F. Thompson, *Lark Rise to Candleford* (1954 edn), p. 278.
[153]   See comments of the *Daily News* reporter on Ardington and Lockinge in M. A. Havinden, *Estate Villages* (1966), pp. 113–17.
[154]   D. C. Moore, 'The Gentry', in Mingay, ed., *Victorian Countryside*, vol. 2, pp. 395–6.
[155]   Holderness, 'The Victorian Farmer', p. 232.

opinions and, though not by nature fanatical, open to the appeals of demagogues. Certainly they were canvassed with vigour, especially in the early 1890s when, coinciding with the brief revival of agricultural unionism, urban radicals sent out into the villages a stream of red (Land Restoration League) and yellow (Land Nationalisation Society) vans manned by speakers openly saying that landlords were robbers who had stolen the land from the people, and calling for fair rents, fair wages, and the land for all. Occasionally they were turned away by landlords, but mostly went unmolested, continuing until their momentum and funds ran out. By and large the Liberals expected to gain most from the extension of the vote to the labourers, though to a considerable extent their hopes were disappointed. This is well illustrated in the voting figures relating to Joseph Arch's contest on behalf of the Liberals for north-west Norfolk in 1885. Here, many of the 8,282 electors who voted were labourers and Arch did well to secure 4,461 votes to Lord Henry Bentinck's 3,821. His triumph, however, was destined to be short-lived and when this result was reversed in the following year, intimidation of the labourers was said to have been practised, especially by Tory farmers.[156] This was a common complaint by Liberal writers down to the war and no doubt there is truth in many of the instances given of union or radical activists being denied work or otherwise intimidated. However, many labourers deferred instinctively to the wishes of their employers. Some of the men with whom Holdenby came into close contact told him that they never used their vote: 'I know's as 'e be t'other way o' thinkin' and I would no' like to 'urt 'is feelin's.'[157] In other respects, too, apprehensions of the imminent politicisation of the labourers had been exaggerated. Financial considerations prevented them from standing for county or district council elections, and although there was some initial enthusiasm for parish councils (fifty-four labourers were elected to office in Warwickshire in 1894[158]), this soon evaporated when their very limited powers of effecting change in the village stood revealed.

To sum up the condition of English rural society on the eve of the Great War would be no easy task. The dynamic forces of change may be identified readily, but they had operated unevenly. Some districts had been more troubled by the vicissitudes of agricultural

[156] P. Horn, *Joseph Arch* (Kineton, Warwicks., 1971), pp. 170–1, 183–4.
[157] C. Holdenby, *Folk of the Furrow* (1913), p. 226.
[158] Horn, *Labouring Life*, pp. 142–3.

prosperity than others. Some villages remained relatively immune from urban influences on account of poor accessibility, even in the age of the railway. Many, on account of rural de-industrialisation had become more exclusively agrarian and others, in an occupational sense, more cosmopolitan. Against 'open' settlements which preserved elements of an unspecialised, 'peasant' economy to a late date and then in some cases succumbed rapidly to suburbanising influences might be set estate villages featuring enduring 'feudal' relationships, while there were many variations lying between these extremes. The heterogeneity of English villages, which some believe to have been greater than ever, gave enormous scope, of which contemporaries took advantage, for contrasting portrayals of the quality of country life. But it was universally recognised that rural society had lost some of its vitality, and, certainly, much of its capacity for independent development as the British industry-state, still barely adolescent in 1851, moved rapidly towards maturity.

IV

In November 1914, the *Farmer and Stockbreeder* forecast that 'Agriculture of all industries is the least likely to be affected by the war.'[159] In the event, though not before 1916 by which date the retail food price index had risen by some 60 per cent and a more serious view was taken of the German submarine threat, the war necessitated a reversal in the traditional posture of laissez faire towards agriculture. The government then put together a food production programme featuring a system of guaranteed prices, announced in February 1917 and followed in August by the Corn Production Act which set minimum prices, on a declining scale, to extend to 1922. It also assumed unprecedented powers to control cropping, stocking, and the allocation of labour, machinery, and scarce fertilisers through hastily formed County Agricultural Committees consisting of leading landowners and farmers. By the close of the war British agriculture was effectively feeding the population for the equivalent of 155 days in the year compared to 125 at its outbreak. However in 1921, the government dropped guaranteed prices, a step which was bitterly resented as an act of betrayal. Throughout the 1920s, apart from an exceptional measure to subsidise sugar beet production in 1924, agriculture was left

[159]   E. H. Whetham, *The Agrarian History of England and Wales*, vol. 8: *1914–39* (Cambridge, 1978), p. 70.

to its fate in a context of falling prices which between 1920 and 1933 sank from 292 to 107 (1911–13 = 100).[160] A Diss auctioneer recollects that men 'farming land that was a bit ugly went under by the scores. Even on the good land where the farmer hadn't enough capital to look after it and have it properly drained he couldn't hold on ... a good deal of the land went back.'[161] The de-rating of agricultural land and buildings in 1928 was not enough to prevent bankruptcies among English and Welsh farmers from averaging 397 in 1921–31, rising to a peak of 600 in 1932.[162] Thereafter, some support was forthcoming, because it would have been invidious to ignore agriculture when the new National Government was busy erecting a comprehensive system of import tariffs in the wake of the economic blizzard of 1931. In 1932 came the Wheat Act assuring producers of a guaranteed price (45s. a quarter) while horticultural produce received a measure of protection under the Import Duties Act of 1932. By 1937, compared to 1927–9, total food imports from foreign countries had been reduced by 21 per cent in volume, although under imperial preference arrangements a 42 per cent increase in imports from the Empire offset this, so that, overall, imports were 3 per cent higher.[163] Another interventionist step, under an act of 1931, enabled two-thirds of the producers of any agricultural commodity to control output as well as set prices. By 1934 the first marketing boards, for hops, potatoes, milk, and bacon, had appeared, to be characterised by varying degrees of success.

These measures did not succeed in lifting prices to levels at which profits could be easily won, for in 1937–9 they remained 10 per cent below even the level of 1927–9, and in 1938 the total acreage of agricultural land under crops or grass was 6 per cent lower than in 1920.[164] Nevertheless they did betoken the final dethronement of laissez-faire in the sphere of agricultural economics, even before the exigencies of the Second World War were confronted. Wartime strategy was directed towards achieving a coherent food programme and minimising the use of scarce shipping resources for food imports. Agriculture was obliged to concentrate on grainstuffs, potatoes, and milk and with increasing expertise, the government deployed a variety of

[160]   *Ibid.*, p. 230.
[161]   G. E. Evans, *Where Beards Wag All* (1970), pp. 108–9.
[162]   Whetham, *Agrarian History*, p. 238.
[163]   K. A. H. Murray, *Agriculture: History of the Second World War, Civil Series* (1955), p. 31.
[164]   Ministry of Agriculture, *Agricultural Statistics*, pp. 85, 93.

monetary incentives and direct subsidies to reach its goals. Once again land utilisation was put under the control of War Agricultural Committees, and on this occasion the government recognised from the outset that its plans would require considerable labour inputs, so that farm workers were largely exempted from military service and effectively locked into agriculture by orders of 1940 and 1941. Working alongside them were green-jerseyed landgirls and Italian and German prisoners of war and between them these categories made up nearly one sixth of a whole-time labour force that increased by nearly 20 per cent during the war. By such means, coupled with lavish increases in the amount of fertiliser used and increased mechanisation (there were ten tractors to every seventeen British farms by 1945), real net output was raised by between 8 and 20 per cent (depending on how inputs are evaluated).[165] Not unjustifiably, farmers were proud of their achievement and hoped that this second demonstration of agriculture's indispensability within a generation would result in a new appreciation of its importance to the nation. In this they were not disappointed. Urgent balance of payments problems necessitated that imports should be strictly held down. It was against this background that the Labour government passed an Agriculture Act of 1947 which set up the postwar framework for agriculture and comprised an annual price review and guaranteed market for the most important farm products.

Through these years of war and peace, the pace of change in rural society accelerated, yet it is striking how far the direction it took followed lines already clearly laid down before 1914. The introduction of death duties (1894), their strengthening (1908), and the incremental value and undeveloped land duties proposed in Lloyd George's 'People's Budget' of 1909 quickened apprehensions about the likely trend of Liberal legislation and already, in 1910–14, prompted nervous persons to sell. The Great War brought a conjuncture of circumstances calculated to hasten the break-up of estates. Among junior officers, casualties on the Western Front were especially high and estates passed often to distant relatives with no special local ties, who were particularly vulnerable to death duties which were raised to alleged 'confiscatory' levels of up to 40 per cent on estates valued at £2m and over, in 1919. The impact of higher taxation generally had also

[165]   Ibid., pp. 19–20, 22, 62, 71–2, 79; Murray, Agriculture, p. 243. The tractor–farm ratio given here excludes holdings with 5 or less acres of crops or grass, and the real net output figures relate to the United Kingdom.

been keenly felt; on the Wilton and Severnake estates land tax, rates and income tax rose from 9 per cent of gross rental before 1914 to some 30 per cent by 1919.[166] On the other hand, wartime rents did not rise so fast as prices, and the eagerness which farmers showed to purchase land in 1919 and 1920 was remarkable. An avalanche of sales took place in 1919 and at the close of 1921, the *Estates Gazette* estimated that as much as one quarter of England must have changed hands in the preceding four years.[167] In these circumstances it is unsurprising that what was left of the concept of 'stewardship' was in rapid retreat and a moral superiority over the other inhabitants of the rural world could no longer be claimed so confidently by inheritors or purchasers of land in the interwar period. Old-fashioned demeanours were coming to be considered 'more grotesque than intolerable, for in 1925 their "inferiors" laugh'.[168]

For a time the number of owner-occupiers increased rapidly: in 1927 the proportion of English and Welsh agricultural land so held was 36 per cent, against 11 per cent in 1914.[169] However, the trend could scarcely be expected to continue indefinitely, given the state of agriculture, and a fall in land values occurred, from 134 in 1920 to a nadir in 1929 of 82 (1937–9 = 100).[170] The Lofts Hall estate at Elmdon, Essex, passed through the hands of two speculative purchasers, in 1927 and 1929, one of whom ripped out the Elizabethan panelling in the mansion, which ended in the Hearst collection in America; although the farms and cottages were eventually sold off at rock-bottom prices, it is significant that none of the tenants actually bought their farms, though several continued to occupy them.[171] A census of farm land taken in 1941 would reveal that the proportion held by owner-occupiers scarcely changed after 1927, which attests also to the limitations of the smallholdings movement so dear to the hearts of the Liberals, who had long favoured their extension as likely to encourage the growth of a class of voters free from subservience to mainly Tory landlords. Little had come of Acts of 1892 and 1908 which empowered county councils to create such holdings, nor did any great success attend the 1919 Act which aimed to provide smallholdings for

[166] Thompson, *Landed Society*, pp. 321–2, 327–30.
[167] *Ibid.*, p. 332.
[168] J. W. Robertson-Scott, *England's Green and Pleasant Land* (1925), p. 35.
[169] Whetham, *Agrarian History*, pp. 160–1.
[170] J. T. Ward, 'Changes in the Sale Value of Farm Real Estate in England and Wales', *The Farm Economist*, 7 (1953), p. 151.
[171] J. Robin, *Elmdon: Continuity and Change in a North-West Essex Village, 1861–1964* (Cambridge, 1980), pp. 65, 73.

ex-servicemen. Throughout its history the movement had been criticised as backward-looking and liable to produce dangerously unviable
holdings and in the economic circumstances of the interwar period
it is not surprising to find that the rate at which small farms disappeared into larger units exceeded that at which new ones were created
using public funds. In England and Wales, holdings in the range 1–5
acres decreased by 18 per cent between 1914 and 1925, and by a further
8 per cent by 1935; and those of 5–50 acres by 5 and 9 per cent respectively.[172]

Thus, the retreat of the squirearchy and decline of the landed estates
increased the number of owner-occupiers; but reductions in the
number of small farms made it less likely than ever that an ordinary
worker could ascend the agricultural ladder by becoming established
as a small farmer. The *Land Worker*, a newspaper published by the
National Agricultural Workers' Union, viewed smallholdings with
predictable scepticism and sought to contrast employers who were
up-to-date and 'employed science and forethought' with the other
sort who dragged down the average and made profits look bad. This
said, it did not hesitate to criticise the conduct of individual farmers,
and made a point of monitoring the size of farmers' wills. In the
seven years ending April 1933, 1,815 each bequeathing £8,000 or more
left in total £39.4m: 'If we reckon that there are 86,600 farmers in
England, Wales and Scotland with farms over 100 acres, we estimate
that half of them who die leave fortunes of more than £5,000 each.'[173]
Whatever the merits of these calculations, it is clear that valid generalisations about the position of farmers in the interwar period are difficult to make. In Devon, the percentage in a sample of 186 farmers
who owned motor-cars rose from thirteen in 1928 to thirty-four in
1934, by which date one in two holding over 150 acres used them.[174]
A farmer's life style might convey the impression that he was doing
well when, considered from another standpoint, the return on his
capital employed was rather low thus enabling him to grumble publicly about the unremunerative business of farming. At all events,
those who survived the interwar period found greater prosperity during the war, which, according to a Norfolk woman who spoke for
many, 'made most of them'. Beyond a doubt farmers' net incomes

[172]   Whetham, *Agrarian History*, p. 45.
[173]   *Land Worker*, October 1927, December 1931, April 1933.
[174]   W. H. Long and S. H. Carson, 'Farmers and Motor Cars', *The Farm Economist*,
1 (1935), p. 243.

rose more rapidly than wages in general (including farm workers' wages), salaries, professional earnings, and company profits, and approximately doubled their share of the national income.[175] Nor did farmers share fully in the privations of the rest of society. Though harassed by a variety of orders concerning the killing of and disposal of animals and petrol allocations, there is ample testimony that these were not difficult to evade.

Despite the long-standing drift from the land, the ratio of employees to employers remained of the order of 3:1 in 1911. During the Great War thousands of younger men were drawn into military service, though not with quite the effect once believed, for in one way or another, about 97 per cent of total labour input of the pre-war period was still being achieved in 1918. Adult male workers who remained on the farms experienced initially a fall in real wages of about 13 per cent by the end of 1916, due in part to the under-cutting of their position by the use of auxiliaries.[176] Thereafter they benefited from the operations of an Agricultural Wages Board introduced along with the Corn Production Act, so that, overall, wartime increases in earnings (some 95 per cent) kept pace with prices. Trade unionism boomed concurrently and NUAW membership rose from only 4,000–5,000 in 1914 to reach 93,000 by 1920.[177] At about this date, an Essex labourer expressed his satisfaction: 'all my life the farmer's bin sittin' on we, an' now its our turn an' we're sitting on the likes of him'.[178] Such optimism was destined to be short-lived. With the repeal of the Corn Production Act came the replacement of statutory wage-fixing machinery by voluntary county conciliation committees; these proved to be disastrously ineffective, the average cash wages of ordinary workers falling from 37s. in 1921 to 28s. the following year, as farmers sought to retrench. Wages were particularly low in Norfolk where, in 1923, a further attempt was made to reduce them, to $5\frac{1}{2}$d. an hour, which would have yielded a wage of 24s. 9d. on the assumption of a full fifty-four-hour week which, however, employers would not guarantee. The ensuing strike marks another famous chapter in the history of agricultural trade unionism, and saw intimidation on both

[175]   N. Longmate, *How We Lived Then* (1971), p. 235; Murray, *Agriculture*, pp. 289–90.
[176]   P. E. Dewey, 'Agricultural Labour Supply in England and Wales during the First World War', *Economic History Review*, 2nd ser., 28 (1975), pp. 104, 107–8.
[177]   H. Newby, *The Deferential Worker* (1977), p. 228. See also A. Howkins, *Poor Labouring Men: Rural Radicalism in Norfolk 1870–1923* (1985), chaps. 7, 8.
[178]   S. L. Benusan, *Latterday Rural England* (1927), p. 24.

sides, the use of blacklegs, some limited violence, and numerous cases of victimisation in the aftermath of a settlement which, since it featured a 25s. weekly wage for a guaranteed week of fifty hours, could be represented by the NUAW as successful. Yet the episode served also to indicate the weakness of agricultural trade unionism. In this, the strongest district of the country, only about a quarter of the men called upon to do so actually struck, and the benefits payable to those who did cost the union the equivalent of two years subscriptions.[179] However, the strike helped by its impact on public opinion to pave the way for the restoration of statutory wage legislation in agriculture by a Labour government the following year. The rates agreed by county wage committees thereafter did not always hold in face of often genuine ignorance on the part of employers and employees, for in 1935–6 the proportion of English workers still underpaid was probably as high as 21 per cent.[180] For all that, the decision to resurrect wage-fixing machinery was helpful to the farm worker: in particular, wages were held steady in 1931–4 when they would otherwise have tumbled, and by the later 1930s cash wages had lifted a little. Average earnings of ordinary workers stood at 35s. 3d. in 1936–7, with those of specialist workers some 3–5s. higher. In view of contemporary movements in the cost of living, their real value may have increased by as much as 20 per cent between 1925 and 1938 while farm workers' birth rates were also coming down (by 21 per cent between 1921 and 1931) albeit more slowly than in most other occupational groups.[181] These gains were to some extent reflected in rising standards of consumption. Margaret Ashby allowed that their homes by the thirties were 'all well-equipped with cooking utensils whereas in pre-war years frying pan and saucepan were all that were available. Improved soaps, the mantle lamp, the oil stove . . . are not despicable as contributions to the decent life.'[182] Raleigh bicycles complete with Dunlop tyres and Sturmey-Archer three-speed gears were being advertised at £8. 10s – or 12s. a month – in the pages of the *Land Worker* in the 1920s, and many younger men in the 1930s acquired motor-cycles,

---

[179] Newby, *Deferential Worker*, p. 225.

[180] A. W. Ashby and J. H. Smith, 'Agricultural Labour in Wales under Statutory Regulation of Wages, 1924–37', *Welsh Journal of Agriculture*, 14 (1938), p. 20. In Wales the proportion was still higher.

[181] W. H. Pedley, *Labour on the Land* (1942), pp. 35, 38; J. W. Innes, 'Class Birth Rates in England and Wales, 1921–31', *Milbank Memorial Fund Quarterly*, 19 (1941), p. 87.

[182] M. K. Ashby, 'Recent Rural Changes as they Affect the Younger Generation', *Journal and Proceedings of the Agricultural Economics Society*, 2 (1933), p. 229.

if usually second-hand ones. During the Second World War minimum wages were revised in line with farm product prices, and rose to 72s. 2d. with many men earning over £4. Even so the farm worker remained relatively poorly paid. Thus the average wage in seven skilled industrial occupations in 1937 was rather over double what the ordinary agricultural worker could expect to receive, whilst unskilled labourers working for local authorities and on building sites earned 53–4s. and on the railways, 47s.[183] It is not, therefore, surprising that the historic trend towards the reduction of farm staffs continued, until interrupted by the restrictions of the Second World War. From 1921 the outflow can be monitored from the Agricultural Returns, which show, in the 1920s, a marked decline in farmers' reliance on casual labour, both male and female, although not, at that stage, of regular male workers; thereafter, however, their numbers plummeted by some 17 per cent in nine years, 1930–9.[184] Certainly desperate efforts to seek economies in expenditure on labour were made as farmers strove to respond to changing price relativities by shifting the composition of farm output away from cereal production. In East Anglia the cost of poor law relief quadrupled between 1931 and the year ending March 1933.[185] However, in general, those who left the land did so because they wanted to. There were some interesting variations on this ancient theme. By the interwar period depressed conditions in heavy industry, mining, and textile production severely limited the extent to which the remaining labour on the land was drawn away in the north, while in Wales after 1926 there was a positive backflow into agriculture. However, in districts characterised by a mixture of old and new industries (such as Birmingham, Coventry, or Rugby), farmers continued to feel some competition for labour[186] and above all, it was in southern counties, far removed from the traditional industrial heartlands, that losses of labour were now most considerable and well above any necessitated by changes in agrarian practices. In Oxfordshire, which sustained the greatest loss in 1921–38 (48 per cent) one survey showed that only a quarter of agricultural labourers' sons were succeeding their fathers' occupations, and here, the Morris works at Cowley were a strong attraction. In Berkshire the MG plant at Abingdon played the

---

[183] Pedley, *Labour on the Land*, p. 13.
[184] Ministry of Agriculture, *Agricultural Statistics*, p. 62.
[185] Whetham, *Agrarian History*, pp. 236–7.
[186] Ashby and Evans, *Agriculture of Wales*, pp. 80, 231; W. Irons, 'Agriculture in Warwickshire', *Journal of the Royal Agricultural Society*, 91 (1930), p. 48.

same role on a smaller scale, while in Buckinghamshire, substantial numbers of men were lost to furniture factories at High Wycombe, paper mills and brickworks.[187] Moreover, as a study set in the Cotswolds remarked, residence in a rural area was 'now very far from being synonymous with employment in agriculture'. Based on an analysis of children who had left village schools at the age of fourteen, it followed the careers of thirty-six men, half being the sons of agricultural labourers. Ten years on, the thirty-six included only eleven agricultural wage earners (nine at home and two away); those absent included two soldiers and two policemen in Birmingham, and those remaining at home but not employed on farms included two estate gardeners, one groom, one footman, one independent grocer, a garage mechanic, a lorry driver, three road workers, and three handymen.[188] There is a conspicuous absence of mention of rural crafts of a traditional sort. Between 1911 and 1931 the number of rural craftsmen was still falling, in the case of Rutland by some 42 per cent[189]; and it was increasingly felt that their 'moribund condition ... may have to be recognised as the price of industrial progress in other centres'. The study prefaced by these words made particular reference to the virtual ending of outwork industries for women. Lacemaking was considered a craft doomed to extinction so far as working women were concerned; like handloom weaving, it would remain only as a 'delightful hobby for leisured people' attracted by its artistic possibilities.[190] Wherever possible, girls, too, were looking for something more modern. The artistic possibilities offered in the two factories of the Ambrosia Milk Co. in Devon were presumably limited, but the girls were reported to be taking home an average of £1 7s. 6d. a week, and in some cases more than their fathers working on farms.[191]

Relevant to the falling numbers in agriculture was an increasing gap which appeared to be opening up between the levels of rural and urban amenities. This is not to say that those available in rural areas were

[187]   Pedley, Labour on the Land, p. 5; Viscount Astor and B. S. Rowntree, British Agriculture (1938), p. 308; Ministry of Agriculture, Fisheries and Food, Report of Proceedings under the Agricultural Wages (Regulation) Act, 1924, for the Two Years Ending 1931 (1931), pp. 116–34.
[188]   M. A. Abrams, 'A Contribution to the Study of Occupational and Residential Mobility in the Cotswolds, 1921–31', Journal and Proceedings of the Agricultural Economics Society, 2 (1932), pp. 64–5, 68.
[189]   Saville, Rural Depopulation, p. 74.
[190]   H. E. Fitzrandolph and M. D. Hay, The Rural Industries of England and Wales, vol. 3 (Oxford, 1927), pp. vi, 70–1.
[191]   F. G. Thomas, The Changing Village (1939), pp. 116-17.

devoid of improvement. One obvious gain came with the proliferation of bus routes covering many villages not already served by railways. Where services were sufficiently frequent, village employment patterns were considerably enlarged and even where they were only occasional, they made town shopping and access to urban entertainments such as cinemas a great deal easier for rural folk. A considerable improvement occurred in library services. In 1915 Professor Adams's report to the Carnegie Trust suggested that only 2.5 per cent of the rural population, as against 79 per cent of townsfolk, had access to public libraries. The Trust proceeded to offer grants to county councils to inaugurate services, and subsequently under the Public Library Act of 1919 county authorities were permitted to support libraries from the rates. All but three counties were doing so by 1931, usually by distributing book-boxes to village schools: under these arrangements, some 48 million issues were made to 2 million registered borrowers from over 17,000 centres in 1934–5.[192]

More significant than the advent of new amenities, though, was the extremely slow rate at which old ones were improved. A case in point was education. That the standards of village schools were lower than those of the towns was suggested by the fact that while only 34 per cent of all certificated teachers in public elementary schools were employed in rural areas, over 71 per cent of uncertificated, and 87 per cent of supplementary teachers, were employed there. Although many made up in dedication for what they lacked in formal qualifications, some of the old barriers to progress, such as erratic attendance, were still in evidence. Moreover, despite the Hadow report of 1926 which recommended splitting elementary education between junior and senior schools, in 1936 about 65 per cent of rural children were still educated in all-age schools.[193] The war limited further progress and indeed brought new problems with the sudden appearance of urban evacuees, and shortages of equipment and staff. Further education in rural areas was likewise limited and strongly orientated to agriculture. Although by 1938 it was possible to undertake degree and diploma courses in agriculture at seven universities, or to take advantage of the facilities of forty-three Farm Institutes or Experimental Stations run by local authorities, few students emerged from among farm workers' children; the cleverer children were in any case those most likely to be drawn out of agriculture.

---

[192] Pedley, *Labour on the Land*, pp. 127–8.
[193] *Ibid.*, pp. 113, 117.

However, the most obvious rural disamenities related to housing. Few farm workers were able to afford to buy, or even rent, living accommodation in the 871,000 new houses constructed in rural areas (mostly adjacent to towns) between 1919 and 1943. Nine out of ten relied on existing stock, including many tied cottages, which often had been neglected for years and remained so despite the advent of grants for reconditioning in 1926. As yet, few cottages boasted electricity and this was by no means their most conspicuous deficiency for in 1939 no fewer than 25 per cent of English parishes still lacked a piped water supply while progress was still slower with respect to modern sanitation. Wells, cess-pools, and earth closets were becoming widely regarded as relics of a barbarous age and were especially resented by women.[194] Again, the war did nothing to help matters. The weakness of institutions thought essential to the maintenance of social cohesion, was another theme popular in contemporary discussions of the problems of village life. Most agreed that the fortunes of the churches were by now at a low ebb. All too often, said the report of a committee appointed by the Archbishop of Canterbury in 1920, the clergy had evinced a 'blind indiscriminating solidarity of views with the representatives of property'.[195] The roots of this problem lay far back in time and an attitude of suspicious indifference was not to be wondered at, observed the *Land Worker* in a review which contrasted the record of gluttony in Parson Woodeford's recently published diaries with the picture of the late eighteenth century revealed by the Hammonds.[196] Such an attitude was difficult for even the most dedicated and sincere parson to break down, and the more he strove to do so the more unpopular he might well become with the chief supporters of the church who, whatever their defects of character and understanding, did most to keep it going. Moreover, although old animosities were rapidly abating, the chapels scarcely fared any better, for nonconformist membership figures were also declining after 1927.[197]

In other respects village life continued to exhibit a greater air of liveliness. Although many old games had fallen into disuse, organised

---

[194]   Ministry of Health, *Rural Housing. Third Report of the Rural Housing Sub-Committee of the Central Housing Advisory Committee* (1944), p. 10; Pedley, *Labour on the Land*, pp. 72–3, 94, 99–100.

[195]   Pedley, *Labour on the Land*, pp. 145–6.

[196]   *Land Worker*, April 1926.

[197]   R. Currie, A. Gilbert and L. Horsley, *Churches and Churchgoers: Patterns of Church Growth in the British Isles since 1700* (Oxford, 1977), pp. 25, 31.

sport, particularly football and cricket, was well supported. Indeed, easier transport provided better opportunities for inter-village contests, and the generalisation of the half-holiday, extended even to farm workers in 1938, ushered organised sport into its golden era extending from the 1930s through to the advent of television in rural areas in the mid-1950s. No doubt sport could dispel status distinctions more easily than anything else. Likewise, the Young Farmers' Clubs, initiated in 1922 by Lord Northcliffe and numbering 400 by 1939, were open to all with an interest, aged ten to twenty-one, and their Saturday night dances and recreational activities certainly attracted youths and girls from all social levels. On the other hand, the agricultural training element of their programme was calculated to appeal to the sons and daughters of farmers and in 1940 Pedley warned against a certain cliquishness, and a tendency for the movement to develop into a 'youth branch of the National Farmers' Union'.[198] Most nearly approaching universality were the Women's Institutes which originated in Canada and rapidly extended in England and Wales after 1915. In the 1920s the *Land Worker* darkly warned that attempts to instruct workers' wives how to make a hat from the sleeve of a jacket, or trimmings for their bonnets from the edges of discarded shirts were but part of a preparation for reduced wages for their menfolk.[199] Yet the fact that the institutes were usually led by ladies of position did not prevent total membership rising to 328,000 by 1939, when there were nearly 6,000 separate institutes.[200] If only a quarter of these were labourers' wives, the resultant figure would be twice the contemporary membership of the NUAW.

It should be noticed, however, that these more successful village organisations tended to segregate villagers on the lines of generation, occupation, or sex. The only fresh development which had some potential to strengthen the overall cohesion of rural social life was the appearance of village halls. These should not be confused with 'reading rooms', a legacy in some favoured parishes of nineteenth-century landlord benevolence, which had usually degenerated by the interwar period into places where men played darts or billiards to while away long evenings. Village halls proper were usually acquired for the first time in the 1920s, many being ex-army huts, and were encouraged by new voluntary rural community councils which were

---

[198] Pedley, *Labour on the Land*, pp. 152–4.
[199] *Land Worker*, May 1922.
[200] Pedley, *Labour on the Land*, p. 148.

to be found in twenty-one counties by 1939. Using Carnegie Trust Funds and limited subventions from local authorities, these councils assisted local initiatives with grants and by the late 1930s were processing some 200–300 such applications per year. At that date village halls were still far from universal; however, where they did exist, they appear to have been well used. One unnamed hall in Gloucestershire hosted in 1939 ten concerts, forty-eight dances, fifty whist drives, four first-aid classes, air raid wardens' lectures, five educational lectures and children's dancing, amateur theatrical, and keep fit classes.[201] There was an obvious contrast between busy villages of this kind and others, poorly served by communications and almost entirely dependent on agriculture as a means of support, whose vitality ebbed as young people drifted away and reductions in the birth rate occurred even among the farm workers. 'There is not a quarter of the men in the village there used to be look at the big familes [sic] there used to be ... now there is hardly any youngsters on the farms' wrote Frederick Swaffield of Stoke Abbott, Dorset, about 1924, while even in Warwickshire, seventy-seven parishes with a population below 500 in 1851 showed a 30 per cent decline by 1931 and forty-four continued to do so down to 1951.[202] This suggested to some that, by dint of selective migration, rural feeble-mindedness was on the increase and intelligence on the decline. Doubtless this view accorded well with the general impressions of rural primitiveness common among urbanites, but the evidence scarcely stood up to critical scrutiny. Although IQ tests seemed to concur in assessing rural schoolchildren as 'a year behind' their urban counterparts, well before the war thoughtful men were already beginning to question their validity as measures of inherent ability, noting the difficulty of making them free of culture-bias and the effect of the application of differential teaching resources.[203]

V

In his *Problems of the Countryside* (1945) Orwin imagined a modern Rip van Winkle arising from a sleep lasting since 1880. Visiting the village of his boyhood, Rip would find the lanes, fields, and hedgerows

---

[201]   *Ibid.*, pp. 159–60, 162.
[202]   'Reminiscences of Frederick Swaffield, 1895–1924' (Dorset Record Office, D459/1) (unpaginated); Saville, *Rural Depopulation*, p. 87.
[203]   See B. S. Bosanquet, 'Quality of the Rural Population', *Eugenics Review*, 42 (1950), pp. 78, 82–90.

substantially unaltered, and recognise at once most of the farmhouses and buildings, perhaps a little shabbier than he had known them in his youth. He might wonder what had become of the windmill, why nettles were growing in the wheelwright's yard and the blacksmith's shop was shuttered or where all the young people were, but the only things to surprise him would be passing motor vehicles and tractors. By contrast, were he to visit the nearby town, plate-glass frontages, new shopping districts, and factories would make him feel a stranger, while the household amenities taken for granted in modern housing estates would certainly astound him. Pursuing the contrast, Orwin argued that the smallness of many English villages and their tendency in recent years to shrink was fundamental to their lack of virility and inability to keep abreast of changing standards in society at large. Likewise, in agriculture, he considered anything below 250 acres to be inefficient and outmoded, favouring the establishment of larger units which would afford greater scope to management and better opportunities to labour. Rural reconstruction could not be led by private landowners, many of whom had disappeared; indeed it seemed likely that the remaining country houses would be 'as obsolete, before long . . . as the medieval castles which many of them had superseded'. Rather, revitalisation would require the decentralisation of industry and comprehensive planning and control to fuse town and country elements into one community for social purposes.[204]

Orwin's criticisms were pertinent enough. When, about 1950, a pioneering attempt was made to quantify the extent of rural disamenities in Wiltshire, an 'index of social provision' showed a regular relationship with size and dropped below half the maximum 36 points at a population level of 500–600.[205] Moreover, the average size of farms remained modest by international if not by continental European standards; in 1951 only 3,500 English and Welsh farms included 500 acres or more of land devoted to crops and grass and in 1946 horses were still two and a half times as numerous as tractors.[206] Country houses showed every sign of further decline; thus, by 1951 only one third of the gentry families of 1871 in the counties of Essex, Oxford, and Shropshire still retained their seats.[207]

For all that, strands of progress and returning confidence were

[204] C. S. Orwin, *Problems of the Countryside* (Cambridge, 1945), pp. 1–4, 11, 45, 99–100.
[205] H. E. Bracey, 'Rural Planning: An Index of Social Provision', *Journal and Proceedings of the Agricultural Economics Society*, 9 (1951), pp. 210–21.
[206] Ministry of Agriculture, *Agricultural Statistics*, pp. 19, 55, 61.
[207] Thompson, *Landed Society*, p. 342.

interwoven with those of decay, making a complex tapestry. In the public sphere rural transport facilities were moving towards their apogee at this time, in terms of the frequency of bus and rail services. The almost universal conveyance of children to secondary schools in the larger villages or towns afforded to adolescents, especially those considered to be sufficiently able to qualify for selective places in grammar schools, a wider range of opportunities. Although left outside the umbrella of earlier welfare provision for too long, farm workers were full participants in the post-Beveridge era and by 1951 a much higher proportion of their homes was watered, drained, and lit than in 1939. Under the shelter provided by post-war strategies for strengthening agriculture, their industry was buoyant. The net income generated by agriculture continued to increase, by some 32 per cent between 1945 and 1950, and the value of land was rising, reaching an index of 252 in 1951, against 82 in 1929 and 100 in 1937–9. Most remaining craftsmen had plenty of work and agricultural engineers gained from the wider diffusion of machinery: the number of tractors on British farms increased by 129,000 between 1946 and 1950 and surpassed the aggregate number of horses used, for the first time, in that year. Moreover, agriculture was giving more employment. The number of regular workers, in 1949, was 685,000 or 12 per cent higher than in 1939, and the number of casuals or part-timers, at 171,000, was 55 per cent up. Between 1938 and 1950, though the purchasing power of the pound had approximately halved, farm wages virtually tripled to give about a 43 per cent gain in real terms.[208] In these circumstances membership of NUAW rose significantly and in 1948 an all-time peak membership was reached at 137,000, or over three times the level in 1938.[209] However, militancy was not the order of the day. Since the early 1930s the executive had increasingly sought common cause with the National Farmers' Union on agricultural policy matters. The war had seen further signs of rapprochement and it is not going too far to say that the notion of an 'agricultural interest' was partially rehabilitated. When, in 1951, Stanley Evans, Parliamentary Secretary of the Ministry of Food in the Labour government, made his famous comments on the 'feather-bedding' of farmers, the NUAW General

[208] Ministry of Agriculture, *Agricultural Statistics*, pp. 62, 71, 73, 76; Ward, 'Real Estate', p. 151; E. Mejer, *Agricultural Labour in England and Wales*, Part II, *Farm Workers' Earnings, 1917–51* (Nottingham University, Department of Agricultural Economics, 1951), pp. 94, 107.
[209] Newby, *Deferential Worker*, p. 228.

Secretary complained through his Executive Committee and publicly in a speech castigating Labour's farming critics.

Standards of consumption were rising. A government enquiry into the household diets of heavy manual workers carried out in the late 1940s showed that their energy value and nutrient content was scarcely any different for farm workers than among comparable urban groups,[210] and further interesting details of rural consumption patterns emerged from a survey of 1948. Very few rural housewives at any social level now baked their own bread, or made their own clothes. Greater mobility was reflected in the high proportion of consumer goods, such as saucepans and bed linen, purchased in the market town or nearest large city, as were irons and fires, the likely first purchases of those newly linked with the electricity grid. The ownership of bicycles, cinema attendances and football pool 'investment' all ran highest among those in social categories D and E, who, however, were much less likely to take holidays, and twenty-six times more likely to read the *News of the World* than the *Daily Telegraph*. Such 'class' based differences were not always paramount: with respect to the use of lipstick, nail varnish and permanent waves, younger women in rural areas behaved like their urban counterparts, any rural–urban differences being due largely to 'the resistance to change of the over-45 age group in rural areas'.[211] These elements of decay and progress were mirrored in Betjeman's poem, *The Dear Old Village*, a perspicacious if heavily ironic and value-laden evocation of village life about 1950.

As we now know, the rural world was teetering on the brink of changes of lightning rapidity and for the time being these may be left to sociologists and economists who are taking an increasing interest in the field.[212] About 1950 it stood at a crossroads from which the historian may conveniently gaze back down the path traversed over two centuries or more. Despite variations in agricultural conditions and practices and the widely acknowledged heterogeneity of English villages, it is generally agreed that the drift of social change

---

[210] Ministry of Agriculture, Fisheries and Food, *Studies in Urban Household Diets, 1944–9. Second Report of the National Food Survey Committee* (1956), pp. 62–5.

[211] J. W. Hobson and H. Henry, *The Rural Market: A Compilation of Facts Related to the Agricultural Industry and Rural Standards of Living and Rural Purchasing Habits* (1948), pp. 85, 86, 93, 100, 103, 104–5, 110–13, 121.

[212] Of particular value are the works of H. Newby including *The Deferential Worker* and *Green and Pleasant Land? Social Change in Rural England* (Harmondsworth, 1980).

was not directionless, and that economic progress along capitalistic lines was in some sense purchased at the cost of the destabilisation of an older order. For many, the nature of these changes is aptly summarised by the subordination of 'community' to 'class'. The first of these concepts, which are in the nature of abstractions rather than historical facts, connotes the existence of stable, harmonious, and orderly relationships between individuals of widely differing status, acted out in the small-scale environment of the village; the second implies a recognition of division of interest and is essentially conflictual. At one time it seemed possible to talk in terms of a stark dichotomy and indeed to pin-point the change with accuracy. As an anthropologist put it in 1922, 'with the enclosure of the Common Fields and Waste the community life of the village came to an end. Village society became divided into two camps, often two hostile camps.'[213] Today's historians prefer to view changes in village society as the consequence of capitalist developments in agriculture going back to the late Middle Ages. They are likely to know that the concept of community has been defined in at least ninety-four different senses[214] and will certainly be aware that lamentations about the lost 'organic' social relationships of 'old England' are a movable feast, capable of being traced back in literature to the sixteenth century at least.[215] The concept of class gives rise to equally fierce difficulties. Although most sociologists respect the Weberian differentiation between class and status, everyday English recognises no nice distinction; in ordinary parlance the word 'class', ever since its nineteenth-century introduction, has been used by many as a synonym for status-ranking.

Notwithstanding such pitfalls, the emergence of class has remained a central theme in some of the most influential modern works on rural social history. Thus Hobsbawm and Rudé see the labourers as already constituting a class in the eighteenth century and, as we have seen, interpret the events of 1830 as a spontaneous response to oppression and proletarianisation. However, this reaction was archaic and a more modern form of movement, built in part on village nonconformity and presaged by the organisation of friendly societies, emerged only with the labourers' unions in the 1870s. In the meantime,

---

[213] H. Peake, *The English Village: The Origin and Decay of its Community* (1922), p. 214.
[214] G. A. Hillery, 'Definitions of Community: Areas of Agreement', *Rural Sociology*, 20 (1955), cited in C. Bell and H. Newby, *Community Studies* (1971), pp. 27–9.
[215] R. Williams, *The Country and the City* (1973), pp. 18–22.

endemic acts of terrorism reflected a spirit of hatred and revenge which, they say, was 'universally felt'.[216] In a less widely known but extremely able study Obelkevich suggests that classes were forged not only by men acting on the basis of common economic interest but also by their withdrawal from the village community and retreat into the private life of the family. The first class to do so was the gentry, emparked at some distance from the villages whose destinies they nevertheless controlled; next came the farmers (at least, the 'new-style' progressives), busy distancing themselves during the first half of the nineteenth century, by expelling their servants, removing their children from village schools, retreating into isolated farmhouses surrounded by ring fences, etc. This isolated the labourers, who were objectively a class but subjectively unsure of their position *vis-à-vis* the other classes, whose behaviour frequently disappointed and sometimes infuriated them. By degrees as they became more literate, disciplined, and self-reliant, they too developed 'something of a class consciousness' and unionisation in the 1870s marked the consummation of their emergence as a class.[217] This phasing of the evolution of class society accords rather neatly with that put forward by Perkin in a more general study of modern English society, and to some extent is reflected in the work of other modern historians. For example Mingay writes that towards the end of the nineteenth century the country labourer was 'no longer a member of the lower orders but of the lower classes, and a world of difference is reflected in that slight change of terminology'.[218]

In many respects, among which very limited opportunities for self-advancement and low wages were the most obvious, the situation of the farm labourer remained disadvantaged compared to that of workers in other industries, who, indeed, were prone to judge their own social and economic progress by the extent that they distanced themselves from his style and standard of life. To the extent that a sense of inferiority was borne in on the labourers it is scarcely surprising that they developed a form of class consciousness, in the sense of showing an increased awareness of their lowly status. However, there are few indications that class consciousness of that kind carried over into active class hostility. According to Holdenby, many

---

[216]   Hobsbawm and Rudé, *Swing*, pp. 287, 292.
[217]   Obelkevich, *Religion and Rural Society*, pp. 25–6.
[218]   H. J. Perkin, *The Origins of Modern English Society, 1780–1880* (1969), chap. 9; G. E. Mingay, *Rural Life in Victorian England* (1977), p. 226.

Edwardian labourers took a pride in their local gentry, and Green could not believe that 'those who tie their trousers with string ... are filled with class hatred for the booted and spurred'. In the same vein Sturt claimed that against the rich the labourers had 'no sort of animosity' and evinced little hostility even towards their employers (although, sadly, the converse was not true); while at Sledmere (Yorkshire) Fairfax-Blakeborough remarked on the way in which the gentry at the Hall were still looked up to in 1929 with 'almost feudal homage' by the inhabitants of the village.[219] Lest all these observers are considered suspect by virtue of their own class affiliations, we might note also how, at Tysoe, Joseph Ashby found it difficult to maintain a host's courtesy when faced with the 'politics of class and hate' preached by students (mostly young urban trade unionists) brought back by his son Arthur from Ruskin College; the observation (by a Labour party organiser) that in interwar Sussex there was class differentiation, but no class feeling; and the conclusion of Winstanley, based upon oral evidence from Kent, that although labourers were conscious of their class, few showed open hostility.[220] When in the late 1960s Newby investigated with all the finesse of the modern sociologist the images of society held by farm workers in Suffolk he found a morass of views and ambivalent attitudes. The number of classes distinguished ranged from nil to five and there were twenty-four distinguishable types of nomenclature, though with some heaping on a 'dichotomous ascriptive model' (59 per cent). Nearly all those interviewed regarded class differences as inevitable and most reserved their criticism for snobbery, i.e. the flaunting of social distinctions or inconsiderate demeanour, especially if exhibited by the new village middle class.[221] These findings, Newby thought, reflected very recent changes which had brought employers and their much reduced numbers of workers closer together, in face of the new intruders into village life. The farm worker's perception of his economic interest as contrary to that of his employer had thus been clouded, and consequently class conflict and class consciousness had diminished. Some historians might wonder how characteristic it had ever been; Kerridge,

---

[219]   Holdenby, *Folk of the Furrow*, pp. 226-7; Green, *English Agricultural Labourer*, p. 224; Sturt, *Change in the Village*, pp. 104-5, 161; J. Fairfax-Blakeborough, *Sykes of Sledmere* (1929), p. 183.

[220]   M. K. Ashby, *Joseph Ashby of Tysoe, 1859-1919* (Cambridge, 1961), p. 258; P. Ambrose, *The Quiet Revolution: Social Change in a Sussex Village, 1871-1971* (1974), p. 56; M. Winstanley, 'Voices from the Past: Rural Kent at the Close of an Era', in Mingay, ed., *Victorian Countryside*, vol. 2, pp. 633-4.

[221]   Newby, *Deferential Worker*, pp. 335-6, 361, 387-8, 391-5, 408.

for example, insists in a review of a recent compendium of rural social history that England had no classes in the Marxist sense and that attempts to interpret her history in the light of class struggles are foredoomed to failure.[222]

This is not to say that the concept of class has no part to play in furthering our understanding of rural social change. Rather, it is suggested that future research strategies should follow Newby's recommendation that instead of concentrating upon the attitudinal attributes of individuals from which their putative behaviour is then inferred, it is more important to study the situational factors which typically confront them and how these affect the nature of the relationships in which they are engaged.[223] This advice is offered to sociologists, but is no less relevant to historians. The analysis of local labour markets, patterns of residential persistence and migration, marriage horizons (in both a geographical and social sense), family composition, and kinship networks, to mention just a few possibilities, should throw considerable light on social attitudes through the behavioural patterns they reveal. *A priori*, it might be suspected that social tensions tended to run higher in the south and east than the north and west and were more likely to be articulated in terms of class. Or it might be supposed that, regardless of broad regional divisions, village typologies have most to tell us. At all events, until much more work has been carried out on the lines suggested it will remain impossible to generalise with any great confidence about historical trends in social perceptions, and in the meantime, broad interpretations of rural social change may be pivoted more safely on agrarian conditions, the impact of industrialisation, and associated demographic changes.

---

[222] Review of Mingay, *Victorian Countryside*, in *Economic History Review*, 2nd ser., 35 (1982), p. 314.
[223] Newby, *Deferential Worker*, p. 385.

CHAPTER 3

Scotland
1750–1850

ROSALIND MITCHISON

I

In spite of a continuing sense of national identity, Scotland in the eighteenth century was a country of marked regional and ethnic differences. The major division was between the English-speaking areas, all in what is called the Lowlands, and the area of Gaelic usage, the Highlands. The line dividing English from Gaelic speech had been narrowing down the Gaeltacht for centuries, and by the mid-eighteenth century lay very near to the great geological fault which makes the highland edge, though even so there were English-speaking areas to the north of the fault: most of the plain forming the southern coast of the Moray Firth, the town of Inverness, the triangle of Caithness lying beyond the county of Sutherland. The division was not simply one of speech, but of culture, social structure and the means of disseminating culture. There were, before the 1780s, practically no printed books in Gaelic: a translation of the psalms existed, but was not readily available, since it had never been properly distributed. The lack of an Old Testament in Gaelic meant that the imageries used in Scottish and in Gaelic literature were totally separate. Few even of educated men in the Highlands could express themselves in Gaelic on paper with accepted orthography. Gaelic culture was mostly conveyed in song, and usually by the physical presence of the singer. The poetic base of these songs might be the creation of either sex, though male assumptions have sometimes left the name of women poets unknown. The highland area was poor and economically backward, feeding itself marginally on its own grain and the erratic supply of milk and blood from its cattle. Difficulties in land transport perpetuated poverty. Yet within the Highlands there were considerable differences in prosperity. Some places, such as the island of Tiree, had good soil and relatively low rainfall and the coastal strip everywhere was fertile, though in many areas very narrow.

The social and political organisation of the Highlands, the clan, had developed in the absence of effective central government. It was a fictitious 'family', combining social and political dominance in the chief, and, if only for self-protection, clansmen had to be ready to follow their chief in military ventures and private quarrels. This necessary obedience in a region outwith the influence of the crown had been exalted by a tradition of honour into an acceptance of the duty of self-sacrifice for the chief, though this did not prevent clansmen evading their explicit instructions. Clanship as an organisation was broken by the government after the rising of 1745, by the life-long exile of the chiefs involved, by the confiscation of a sample of estates, by the compulsory purchase of feudal franchises and by the presence of government force. But much of the positive support for the institution among clansmen had already evaporated. Knowledge of opportunities outside the Highlands and the pressures of many chiefs for higher money rents had been increasing during the previous fifty years. The success of the 'pacification' of the area, not the immediate and often brutal occupation by soldiery, but the longer term assimilation of the area into law, order, religious discipline and some element of economic enterprise, was so rapid that it is difficult to escape the idea that clanship had already worn pretty thin before 1745. But the clan divisions that had existed left one enduring mark. Highlanders, though prepared after 1750 to go long distances for temporary work in the Lowlands or for the driving of cattle, and also to join the army or emigrate, were relatively unused to the pattern of small-scale mobility so conspicuous in the lowland peasantry. Formidable geographic barriers and frequent inter-clan rivalries meant that there was no history of movement, either as tenant or farm servant, from one agricultural settlement to another.

It is often forgotten that besides the obvious Anglo-Saxon and Celtic cultures in Scotland, there is a third, the Norse. In Lewis this element had become submerged in Gaelic culture, but in Caithness and still more in the Northern Isles it was assimilated only partially to English-speaking lowland norms. The distinctness, in particular, of Shetland society, depended on its use of the sea as a resource, but also partly on the hostility of the bulk of the population to the governing group of intruded Scottish landowners. In both Orkney and Shetland the memory of links with Norway was kept alive by patterns of life and landowning, and also by trading contacts.

Even within English-speaking lowland areas there were sharp

dividing lines, sometimes from past religious or political adherence, sometimes from the variations in exposure to the influence of central government in a state where feudal judicial franchises had been abolished only in the 1740s. The city of Aberdeen had a distinguished intellectual tradition, and had experienced the steady shift of political, ecclesiastical and economic power from the north of Scotland to the south over the last century and a half. Galloway had a tradition of religious and political extremism, and a reputation for lawlessness and banditry. The Borders had had their incipient clan system broken comparatively late by the crown, and were an area of combined thievery and a more than usually market-oriented society. In the Lothians the peasantry were conformist and energetic. The local patterns of social variation in Scotland were to leave traces into the second half of the nineteenth century in the range of size and structure of landownership units, in educational achievement, in vocabulary and accent and in sharply differentiated levels of marital and non-marital fertility.[1] It is therefore not surprising that the cities and larger towns of Scotland came in the nineteenth century to be socially very distinct. Part of this variety came from local recruitment of their population, part from differences in economic function. Altogether as a small population, not much more than one and a quarter million in the mid-eighteenth century, dispersed through a relatively large area of land with poor communications, Scotland must be seen as a varied group of cultures held together by strong national consciousness.

The 1740s saw the start of a long-term movement of population growth. Current opinion is that by 1740 numbers had barely risen enough to recreate the level of population that had existed before the great famine of the 1690s. In Aberdeenshire the population still stood below the level of the early 1690s. After 1740 growth accelerated, so that by the end of the decade and in the early 1750s it was only a little under 0.5 per cent a year. The evidence for this comes from parish information collected through the church by the enterprising Dr Alexander Webster who combined information from all parishes into a census in 1755.[2] It is supported by the evidence of the sharp

---

[1] L. Timperley, 'The Pattern of Landholding in Eighteenth Century Scotland', in M. L. Parry and T. R. Slater, eds., *The Making of the Scottish Countryside* (1980); L. J. Saunders, *Scottish Democracy, 1815–1840* (Edinburgh, 1950), pt 1; M. W. Flinn, ed., *Scottish Population History from the 17th Century to the 1930s* (Cambridge, 1977), pt 5, chaps. 3 and 4.

[2] Flinn, ed., *Scottish Population History*, pt 3, chap. 7, pt 4, chaps. 3 and 4.

drop in the grain exports of the country in the mid-1740s which, occurring in years free of harvest failure, suggests a general rise in demand.

It seems likely that this population growth was related to the expansion of linen as the major domestic industry, but it is notable that many economic concerns moved into a higher level of activity in the late 1740s and early 1750s, for instance the tobacco import and re-export trade, malt manufacture, papermaking.[3] Linen was already in 1740 the dominant industry, with ramifications all through the Lowlands, and the sale of products from this industry expanded sharply at this time. Of course the linen which came to sale on the open market was only a fragment of the total produced, for many households either produced directly for their own needs or made private contracts with spinners and weavers. It was linen as much as any commodity which sustained the new industrial planned villages of the mid-eighteenth century.[4] The significance of the development of textile industries was that they created both new full-time employment and peripheral part-time earnings. Men went into weaving full time; the labour force of a bleachfield, mainly female, would be from thirty to sixty in the summer months, but many fewer in winter; the printing of linen, an area of expansion in the late 1750s and afterwards, was a source of relatively high wages for full-time work. There were also the initial processes of flax preparation which were moving from being part-time activities of cultivators to concentration in mills. Most branches of work gave full-time opportunities, and so did the supervisory and instructional work promoted by the Board of Trustees. A sign of the way that men were committed to weaving came in the recession of the 1750s, when unemployed male weavers in the east of Scotland chose to enter the army, a move which, given the contemporary opinion of the soldier, indicates that there was no alternative source of income. By contrast spinning gave women mainly part-time work. Some of this was done for the home, some for the market, some with the spinners as the employees of weavers. All spinning for wages was underpaid for the hours involved. A few full-time women could exist on this alone, but the tendency for

[3] H. Hamilton, *An Economic History of Scotland in the Eighteenth Century* (Oxford, 1963), chap. 5 and apps.
[4] T. C. Smout, 'The Landowner and the Planned Village in Scotland, 1730–1830', in N. T. Phillipson and Rosalind Mitchison, eds., *Scotland in the Age of Improvement* (Edinburgh, 1970).

production to fall off as prices, and hence wages, rose, shows how long the hours necessary for subsistence were. Every home for which we have an inventory of furniture contained a spinning wheel. Textiles, especially linen, but also the stocking knitting particularly associated with Aberdeenshire, raised the cash incomes of many agricultural families, and thereby their standard of living, and gave specific employment slots to a wide range of workers. Both aspects of these industries would play a part in encouraging population growth, but probably the latter was the more important. We cannot prove, for Scotland in general, that the development of domestic industry raised population by encouraging earlier marriage, but in the only parish in Scotland for which evidence of the age of marriage exists, Kilmarnock, a centre of woollens in Ayrshire, there was already in the 1730s and 1740s a low marriage age, with the median just under twenty-two, for girls in the industrial sector marrying men in the same sector, whereas in the rural part of the parish the median age for girls was over twenty-seven.[5] Many mid-eighteenth-century sources refer to the beneficial effects of the textile industries on employment for the poor, often stressing the moral advantages of hard work and the social advantages of the reduction in begging and stealing, features which may well have been of more direct interest to their superiors than to the workers, but these sources also recognise the improvement in standards of living.[6]

Even with the advantages of money from domestic industry material conditions of the bulk of the population remained poor for the central decades of the eighteenth century. Diet was narrow in its range, mostly based on oatmeal with the addition of kail and small amounts of dairy produce. Even the special occasion dish of haggis, Burns's 'great chieftain of the pudding race', is unmistakably the food of a poor nation. The occasional devastations of epidemics suggest a population at risk from undernourishment: for instance the outbreak of measles in Edinburgh and Kilmarnock in the early months of 1741, after the disastrous crops of 1740. That smallpox killed many children under the age of two in outbreaks every four years, is not a proof of malnutrition, but that in Kilmarnock the measles epidemic of 1752 took a disproportionate share of the children of the industrial side of the parish suggests that these families suffered from poor

---

[5] Flinn, ed., *Scottish Population History*, pt 4, chap. 5.
[6] P. Lindsay, *The Interest of Scotland Considered* (Edinburgh, 1733); A. J. Youngson, *After the Forty Five* (Edinburgh, 1973), chap. 2.

nourishment: the crop of 1751 had not created particularly high prices. In years of known shortage there is evidence of starvation in the remoter areas. It looks as if Dumfries had a typhus epidemic in 1741 and Durness one of dysentery, while in 1772 Thomas Pennant touring the Highlands was deeply moved by visible starvation in the Small Isles.[7]

Poverty shows in comments on the standard of clothing, on the wearing of harn shirts by even fairly substantial farmers, on the habit of women who did not do the type of field work that needed shoes of keeping their single pair for best. It is possible that the rise of spinning for the market reduced the standard of a family's clothing by deflecting the work of the women for cash. Poverty is more conspicuous in comments on housing. In the early eighteenth century glass was coming in for use at least in the windows of the bigger farmhouses, as well as in churches, and was becoming more common in the towns, but was still not within the scope of the smaller tenants or cottars. George Robertson was later to describe the cottar houses of the 1760s as 'mean hovels' put up in a single day, measuring about 12 foot square inside, with walls of 5 foot height, a roof of straw and turf laid over rough branches, and by no means always a chimney.[8] Almost all were of one room only. Where efforts were made for something better, for instance by the officials of the Annexed Estates, there was great trouble in getting reliable performance by workmen. But improvements in furniture reveal the existence of some choice in expenditure. In the 1740s it was common for the best possession to be a mirror. Tables and chairs were often present, and hardwood might be used in chests or tables. Mahogany and oak figure in the equipment of the better farmhouses. If a cottar in a house without glazing did not possess a chest he would have no dry place in which to keep any book or paper, a fact which has a bearing on the limited value that might exist in acquiring the skill of writing.

Urban housing was of stronger construction than was rural, if only from the Scottish tradition of life in tall tenements. 'Relief land' in Inveraray, put up by the Duke of Argyll in 1770, is a good example of this tenement type.[9] Skilled craftsmen and clerks can be seen from the evidence of Edinburgh inventories to have lived with their

[7] Flinn, ed., *Scottish Population History*, pt 4, chaps. 2 and 7; T. Pennant, *Tour in Scotland and Voyages to the Hebrides, 1772*, 2 vols. (1790), vol. 1, pp. 312, 353.
[8] G. Robertson, *Rural Recollections* (Irvine, 1829).
[9] I. G. Lindsay and Mary Cosh, *Inveraray and the Dukes of Argyll* (Edinburgh, 1973), pp. 259–63.

families often in two rooms, perhaps with additional space in a corridor. They would be able to afford some good furniture, large stocks of linen, a range of cooking utensils and even some silver objects. The limitations of this type of housing were not so much of space, for many citydwellers all over the world have used no more, but the lack of sanitary facilities and water supply. Water had to be bought off travelling caddies, and all refuse had simply to be put in the street or alley at night: neither of these features was allowed on Sunday.

The expansion of textile industries had more subtle effects than simply that of raising standards of living. It brought the rural population closer to the market and encouraged the use of cash, meeting the efforts of many landowners to increase the share of money in rent payments. The market was reaching out into the agricultural sector. Without becoming rich more people would often handle money. Commutation of services for cash reduced contact between tenant and landowner, but rural wages continued to be made in kind except for the extra work of the harvest period. That there was often, though not invariably, money in the houses of the farm population is shown by the surprisingly large sums that parishes could produce in response to special appeals from the church; for instance a single farm in the 1680s in Yester (East Lothian) had subscribed over £5 to an overseas cause. In 1764 the relatively poor upland parish of Daviot in Aberdeenshire gave a subscription to the Aberdeen infirmary £5. 1s. 7½d., and contributions on this scale were not unusual.[10]

Expansion of the market aspect of life went with reduction in the claims of lordship. Members of the aristocracy still thought of themselves as heads of surnames. In 1746 the brother of the Earl of Marchmont, a staunch Whig, was prepared to use influence to save the life of a rebel Jacobite of his surname, and in 1732 the Earl had obtained a reprieve for a convicted murderer, a total stranger, whose relatives appealed to him as leader of the Name.[11] In 1726 the exiled Earl of Mar could write in his 'legacie' to his son, a long letter of advice:

Clanshipe in our country is what ought to be encouraged and keept up as much as possible ... You are to be at the head of one which tho not so numerous as those in the highlands, is perhaps as old ... I doubt not but that all of them will be assisting to you ... Endeavour to keep them united.

[10]   Scottish Record Office (hereafter SRO) CH2/377/2 and CH2/549/1.
[11]   Historical Manuscripts Commission, *Report on the Manuscripts of the Right Honourable Lord Polwarth*, vol. 5 (1961), pp. 32–41, 182.

In 1767 the young James Boswell, in a fit of romantic reverence for family rites, invested his younger brother with a ring in a formal ceremony, and extracted in return an oath of faithfulness to the 'ancient Family'.[12] Richer landowners might indulge in the fancy of holding the kin together as a unit of power and lordship, and indeed in politics it was still normal for a man to follow the lead of the head of his name. Yet even at the beginning of the eighteenth century Hamilton palace, the home of the Duke and Duchess, bearers of a widespread surname, was noted as making little use of servants and office holders of the Name.[13] There are no signs that the bond of the surname meant much to the lowland peasantry, or that distant kin links were preserved. The relationship of peasants to landowners was expressed in the paying, usually belatedly, of rent and, very belatedly, the performing of labour services. Within landowning society the powers of the aristocracy, as feudal superiors, were being systematically reduced. The judges, mostly landowners of moderate rank, had decided that rights of this kind were an anachronism, and were freely remaking the law to reduce them. While claiming to administer the law, they assessed that law in relationship to reason and utility: these principles had a strong tendency to agree with the advantages of their own social order. Law was recast as it was enlarged to meet new needs. A judgment of 1744 stated that 'it is the privilege of property, that the proprietor can be put under no restraint'. This statement did not record the existing state of things, but the intention of the judiciary. This intention was to destroy the older pattern of lordship and the special rights of magnates.[14] The process had gone so far by the rising of 1745 that it was generally held by lawyers that no great lord had the right to call up his tenantry to oppose the rebel army. No militia or voluntary force could be raised until the crown gave special permission some three months after the rising got under way.[15]

This does not mean that the citizens of mid-eighteenth-century Scotland had equal rights. It was as landowners, or 'heritors' – that is proprietors of land which carried the burden of supporting the parish

12   S. Erskine, ed., *The Earl of Mar's Legacies to Scotland*, Scottish History Society (hereafter SHS), 26 (Edinburgh, 1896); F. Brady and R. A. Pottle, eds., *Boswell in Search of a Wife, 1766–1769* (1957), p. 102.

13   Rosalind Marshall, *The Days of Duchess Anne* (1973), p. 81.

14   Rosalind Mitchison, 'Patriotism and National Identity in Eighteenth Century Scotland', in T. W. Moody, ed., *Nationality and the Pursuit of National Independence* (Belfast, 1978).

15   Rosalind Mitchison, 'The Government and the Highlands, 1707–1745', in Phillipson and Mitchison, eds., *Scotland in the Age of Improvement*.

church and minister – that men had privileges, not, except in the right to vote in county elections for Parliament, as feudal superiors. The judges were restricting the rights of superiors over the marriages of their vassals and over alienation of land. In 1747 the heritable jurisdictions, which many superiors owned, were bought up by the crown, leaving only the baron courts, with reduced powers, as remnants of the system of feudal franchises. In the same decade the owners of feudal superiority began making nominal allocations of it to owners of mere property, to create fictitious votes and build up electoral support in line with their own landed significance.[16] Influence, partly purchased in this corrupt way, had replaced power.

Proprietors had a special status in local government, for not only did they sustain the parish but they provided such county administration and justice as there was. Local authority could be retained only by regular work. In the first half of the eighteenth century the organs of county government were becoming effective. Considerable influence rested with the sheriffs, and they and two other bodies of men, often overlapping in membership, made the effective decisions. These were the justices of the peace and the commissioners of supply. These were appointed from owners of land worth respectively £200 and £100 Scots a year. The commissioners controlled the assessment for the basic tax on land, the cess, and also raised money for local purposes, as 'rogue money' for arresting offenders, and 'road' money for repairs. They had a fairly free hand in the way this money was used and so provided a genuine element of county government, in the end to be its most important element.[17] As yet, mid-eighteenth century, the power of this group was approximately equal to that of the justices. The justices spent most of the money raised by the commissioners, and met and acted more frequently than they. For the most part the meetings of the commissioners were scantily attended and routine in activity, but they became more lively in war time, since the commissioners had to find the compulsory army contingents from each county, and would be richly attended by all the local great men when a general election was inevitable in the following year, for on their decisions over valuation depended the vote carrying capacity of the fictitious allocations of superiority.

County government was also sustained by 'county meetings' of

16   William Ferguson, *Scotland, 1689 to the Present* (Edinburgh, 1968), chap. 5.
17   Ann E. Whetstone, *Scottish County Government in the Eighteenth and Nineteenth Centuries* (Edinburgh, 1981).

all substantial landowners. It was such a body in Midlothian in the food shortage of 1740 that raised £2,000 to bring in grain and sell it below cost to the parishes. A similar meeting for Aberdeenshire in 1782 provides us with an accurate description of the shortfall of the harvest.[18] In 1760 similar meetings, the composition of which was undefined, met to protest against the demands made by unruly servants for 'vails' (tips) and to petition Parliament for a Scottish militia. As the century went on such meetings had become more frequent. They might concert plans to deal with strikes by agricultural labourers, address the crown patriotically over the American issue, or, less patriotically, about the price levels at which the corn laws intervened, urge modification of the system of entail, discuss the need to control the issue of notes by banks, or evolve schemes for the maintenance of the poor. They had no executive power, and financial control over only the funds they raised themselves, but they filled an important gap in local government and in the voicing of upper-class opinion.

The new system of county government by justices and commissioners was replacing the older system of rule by territorial magnates, but in ways not particularly painful to the magnates. Of the great men, some were fully occupied on the political scene in England, notably the Dukes of Argyll and Hamilton; some such as the second Duke of Queensberry on the London social scene.[19] Intellectual limitations prevented the Duke of Gordon from having local influence, and the second Duke of Atholl, though keen to preserve his local importance, could not give it much of his time since he too was more interested in London. The great houses painlessly divorced themselves from the domination of their regions in favour of the attractions of the capital. The lesser nobility liked to play a part in county as well as in national politics, and for this it had to cultivate the richer lairds, using and creating their votes, building up parties by patronage and persuasion. When the franchise holders lost their heritable jurisdictions in 1747 the cash given in exchange more than made up for the disappearance of courts through which in the Lowlands they had long ceased to exert power.

After 1747 the one remaining private court was that of the barony. This had limited criminal powers, being mostly involved in issues

---

18 L. M. Cullen and T. C. Smout, eds., *Comparative Aspects of Irish and Scottish Economic and Social History, 1600–1900* (Edinburgh, 1977), p. 27.
19 J. S. Shaw, *The Management of Scottish Society 1707–1764* (Edinburgh, 1983), chap. 1.

such as local brawls, slanging matches between the wives of the peasantry and the enforcement of statutes in which the baron had a strong
sporting interest, such as that prohibiting the soaking of lint in
salmon rivers (bad for the fish), or the burning of moors late in the
spring to promote better grazing (bad for fledgling gamebirds). There
was also, often within the baron court, the birlaw court which sprang
from the necessities of farm co-operation and the promotion of good
neighbourhood. Most of the business of these courts was verbal and
has left little record, but the scraps which survive suggest that this
type of court had closer connections with the mainsprings of local
life than had the baron court. The baron court continued to be the
place for the settling of farming issues, enforcing the type of decision
which unfenced or intermixed farming made necessary, but the spread
of single-tenant farms, already dominant in the south-east and in
Aberdeenshire, reduced this need. After 1747 its minor criminal
powers were very small and the civil cases it could handle were of
less value than 20s. Restriction and farming changes led to atrophy.[20]

Even before the changes of 1747 the barony had ceased to be an
effective social unit. The men of a barony would get together grudgingly to perform certain necessary duties, such as the bringing in
of new millstones or the regulation of the celebrations of weddings,
but early in the eighteenth century many of the old functions of the
barony had been spontaneously transferred either to the sheriff courts,
if secular, or to the lowest unit in the church court system, that of
the kirk session. These changes seem to relate to the Act of Union
of 1707, which was followed by the disappearance of the Privy Council,
in the past the supervisor of the franchise courts. In the 1690s when
a parish decided that it had to implement the poor law by imposing
rates, it sometimes simply gave the owners of the baronies within
the parish a list of the needy on their land, and left to them the duty
of furnishing adequate support. Parliament decreed that the landowner could raise half his contribution from his tenants, and he was
left to administer their and his own money. By the 1740s the parish
had, in most areas, assumed this duty: if assessment became necessary
a special committee of heritors and kirk session would be created
to raise and distribute money. This system would then be used to

---

[20] S. Davies, 'Law and Order in Stirlingshire 1637–1747' (unpublished PhD thesis,
St Andrews University, 1984); D. G. Barron, ed., *The Court Book of the Barony of
Urie*, SHS, 12 (Edinburgh, 1892), Introduction.

care for the cases of long-standing poverty, widows and orphans, the insane or the permanently incapacitated, the 'ordinary' poor, while more temporary or casual needs, people suffering from illness unlikely to be terminal, or from other afflictions such as the death of a work horse or the destruction of a house by fire, and vagrants, would be supported as in an unassessed parish by the kirk session directly. Yet in some areas, notably on the Atholl estate, the authority of the landowner was strong enough still for his agent to act as he would have done in the seventeenth century.

The role of the kirk session was a survival of the seventeenth-century enthusiasm for government by committee. The session supervised the parish school, finding the schoolmaster, paying him his small fixed salary, (between £5 11s. and £11 2s. a year) as well as fees for the teaching of poor children, and sometimes laying down regulations about teaching. It also supervised morals and acted as a legal court over particular breaches of rule, such as failure of Sunday observance, gross drunkenness and sexual irregularities which ended in unmarried pregnancy. It could use strong weapons of discipline, not only censure but fines and formal penance in church: the sanction of referral to the sheriff court had been abolished in 1712, but general acceptance of the session's authority continued until the 1770s. The session did not have the power of the baron court of ending the tenancy of a troublesome tenant, but it had a negative power, for it could make it very difficult for a man to move to another parish if it denied him a 'testificate' of good conduct. It had also, besides discipline, the opportunity for rebuke and persuasion, which if persistently used could wear down resistance. For instance, in the 1760s and 1770s the kirk session of Mauchline, Ayrshire, would draw up each year a list of couples who would not be allowed to take communion unless they were 'reconciled' to the church and then apply continuous personal pressure to them until they gave way and accepted its rulings.[21] Church discipline was not as powerful a weapon as it had been in the seventeenth century and the area in which the session would operate had been narrowed, but it was still an important feature of rural life in the third quarter of the eighteenth century.

In directly ecclesiastical matters the session was subordinate to the court of a larger area, the presbytery. The presbytery had the power

---

[21]   SRO CH2/896/4.

of excommunication, and to it difficult cases of discipline were referred – men apparently guilty of fornication but willing to take an exculpatory oath, cases of persistent adultery, practices which seemed derived from witchcraft, and gross breaches of marriage promises such as the selling of a wife. But the formality of the records of this court, except in cases of the deviance of ministers from orthodoxy, show that it did not have the vigour of the kirk session.

There were areas of government where there could be clashes between the structure of church courts and the lay organisation of society. Parishes depended on landowners, as 'heritors', discharging their financial duties in paying the ministers' stipends, the schoolmasters' salaries and maintaining the fabric of church, school and manse. Where relations were bad or landowners high in self-esteem and short of money there could be friction from long delays in payment. Presbyteries had sometimes to put pressure on heritors to set up a school, and there had been a steady demand for manses to be rebuilt to higher standards. In the 1750s an attempt by the church to obtain higher stipends had been frustrated by the landowners. But it was the pressure of the lay authorities, justices of the peace and sheriffs, which had made the parishes improve the poor law and which had ensured that it could deal with food shortage. In many lowland counties these authorities had periodically set up county schemes, ordering parishes, and the parish landowners, to control vagrancy and to support the local poor. Insofar as these were activities statutorily given to the kirk sessions, the lay powers had no direct authority for such orders. Such schemes covered much of lowland Scotland in the 1750s, and though this generation of schemes faded there was a renewed enthusiasm for setting up such structures in the 1770s. Clashes between the two systems of authority were reduced by the fact that they were not completely separate. Landowners might act in the church courts as 'ruling elders', but in the later eighteenth century this became less common as landowners increasingly were non-resident, and even if resident, increasingly drawn to adherence to the episcopal instead of the established church.

Most Scottish parishes did not, mid-eighteenth century, have a nuclear village, but were instead collections of farms, 'muckle towns' in some cases, which would include several families, some as tenants or sub-tenants and some as cottars. It was normal for the parish to arrange for each significant settlement to contain an elder, who would make the round of his 'bounds' collecting money for the general parish fund which, though called the 'poor's money', was used for all manner of purposes, and sometimes for special collections recommended by the higher courts of the church. He would also receive information for the parish's disciplinary side, visible cases of unmarried pregnancy, audible and unmistakable evidence of bad neighbourhood, rumour of unsuitable Sunday activities. It was usually he who brought to the needy the support allotted. He might have to collect oatmeal for them, but more often relief came in the form of cash. It is one of the remarkable achievements of the sessions that their monetary affairs, the raising of collections, retention of it by the elder who acted as treasurer, and distribution, led in the course of the eighteenth century to only a handful of allegations of embezzlement. Most men of sufficient local weight to be elders were by mid-century literate and the treasurer capable of keeping somewhat disorderly accounts of incoming and outgoing money. In a ministerial vacancy most sessions would keep up their records fairly coherently for six or nine months.[22] During this time besides carrying on the business of the poor and the school the session had to arrange for occasional visits by a neighbour minister to take services, and to hire a horse for him. Local government within the church's realm required and received a high level of conscientious effort.

Landowners often held the position of elder, though this did not mean that such men would be active in parish affairs: their use to the parish was as 'ruling elder', that is the delegate to higher courts. The social pattern of the eldership varied from region to region, and in many places a considerable proportion of the landowners had moved out from the established church to become episcopalian dissenters. In many of the eighteenth-century cases of dispute between landowners and kirk sessions, over for instance the management of the poor's money or the appointment of a new minister, there was an element of this dissent. Some landowners were non-resident. A series of disputes between 1749 and 1752 established the right of landowners to inspect the records of parish expenditure and laid down that the poor's money could not be used for anything but the support of the poor, but it is clear from subsequent court cases that this restriction of use of parish money was impracticable. It also was brought home to landowners that if they interfered too much in kirk session

---

[22] H. Paton, ed., *The Session Book of Rothesay 1658–1750* (privately published, 1931), pp. 471–82.

business they might get involved in the practical doling out of money to the poor and that this could not be worked effectively from their social level.[23]

The receipt of poor relief did not yet establish a social gulf between the bulk of the parish and its poor. For one thing the poor's money often contributed to a bursary for university education run by a group of parishes. Such an award could make for a small chance of upward social mobility, but usually led to the youth returning to the rural scene as a schoolmaster. Other uses of parish money would be the wet-nursing of a motherless baby, a surgeon's fee, aid in disasters, and into the first decade of the nineteenth century a parish might, in years of high prices or trade dislocation, give out money to house-holders who were not without employment. Most holdings were still fairly small, and it was a rare family which could count itself comple-tely secure on its own resources. Subscribing to the poor's money could be seen as a form of insurance. Incomes which did not make it possible for all in a family to receive an adequate diet did not prevent expenditure on charity or on schooling of children for a few years. These payments enabled a family to regard itself as respectable, where-as children brought up without at least the ability to read were at a social disadvantage.

In local affairs, in education and in work women were regularly at a disadvantage. The figures for the proportions of both sexes who could sign their names show this disadvantage at its most severe: for the 1750s those who lacked this skill have been given as 22 per cent of men and 77 per cent of women, though of course there were considerable regional and occupational differences, and the figures do not acknowledge any distinction between lowland and highland culture. But ability to read, which could be acquired in about two years of schooling, often at an age when children were not likely to be of economic use, or which might be picked up afterwards for economic or religious reasons, was more evenly possessed between the two sexes. For instance all the 'converts', those who experienced grace, at the Cambuslang revival of 1742 and were subsequently asked to give an account of their conversion, could read,[24] approximately

---

[23] Rosalind Mitchison, 'The Making of the Old Scottish Poor Law', *Past & Present*, 63 (1974).

[24] R. Houston, 'The Literacy Myth? Illiteracy in Scotland, 1630–1760', *Past & Present*, 96 (1982); T. C. Smout, 'Born again at Cambuslang: New Evidence on Popular Religion and Literacy in Eighteenth Century Scotland', *ibid.*, 97 (1982).

two-thirds of these were women, mostly of low social status. Many tasks in agriculture relied on female labour, particularly dairying and the unpopular work of ewe milking. Spinning was expected of all women when not otherwise occupied. Illustrations of farm labour show us women helping with the sowing and also hay making and harvest.[25] At these peak times of yearly effort their wages most nearly approached those of men. Mid-century in the harvest team of the bandwin, women reapers would get 5d. a day, men reapers 6d. and the man who bound the sheaves for six reapers would get 7d. The later eighteenth century seems to have been a period when in relative terms women's earnings fell off, though since it was generally a time of rising standards of living, their actual purchasing power may have improved. Agricultural improvement in the last quarter of the century increased the value of the tasks which were regarded as male, such as the care and use of horses, and male labour became more attractive to employers. Figures from the 1790s show women in agriculture working for between 42 and 48 per cent of men's wages, but these figures apply only to the minority of workers called labourers who were rewarded entirely in money, and this minority was on the whole one of low status.[26] More of the labour force either lived and worked as cottars, or as servants, that is living within the household of their employer. How large a section of the agricultural population was in either category has not yet been determined, and probably varied regionally. We have occasional glimpses: in Tranent (East Lothian) in the 1760s 25 per cent of the men were called labourers, but this was a small town as well as a parish with farms. Barr, in Ayrshire, had in 1745 eighty-one households of cottars to thirty-one tenants, Roberton, in Lanarkshire, in 1747 had thirty-seven to forty-three, Dairsie, in Fife, in 1740 had fifty-one cottars to thirty-four tenants and tradesmen, and already the risks of the two positions had separated sufficiently for the cottars to be the only people receiving poor relief.[27] Cottars were clearly a large part of rural society but one on which most forms of local record keeping are silent. The children of cottars and some of the tenants provided the class of farm servant, not always entering on this form of labour with enthusiasm, as the orders

[25]   A. Fenton, *Scottish Country Life* (Edinburgh, 1976), chap. 3.
[26]   V. Morgan, 'Agricultural Wage Rates in Late-Eighteenth Century Scotland', *Economic History Review*, 2nd ser., 29 (1971).
[27]   Rosalind Mitchison, 'Death in Tranent', *Transactions of the East Lothian Antiquarian and Field Naturalists Society*, 16 (1979); SRO CH1/2/85-7, CH2/427/2.

of the justices of the peace of Dunbartonshire in the 1750s to particular adolescents to leave home and hire themselves as servants imply.[28]

The orders of the justices reflect a continuation into the mid-century of the concept that the deployment of labour and its reward needed government intervention. Wage control seems always to have meant forcing wages down, not up, and it seems to have gone on longer in the west than in the east. There was also pressure to make servants hire themselves for the whole or the half year, instead of trying simply to pick up wages in the harvest period. But all over the country the tendency of those in authority was to support the interests of tenants against those of their employees. It was, for instance, most unusual in a case where a tenant, his son or his servant had roughly seduced a woman servant and made her pregnant for the kirk session to require that the woman leave the employment. The risk of further illicit sexual encounters was less important than the risk to a farmer of being short-handed.

Yet in other ways the church treated the sexes more equally than it had in the seventeenth century. Investigations into sexual irregularities bore more inexorably on women than on men because it was usually initiated when pregnancy was visible and there was no room for denial. The man, on the other hand, might deny accusations, and his persistence, even when the case went higher up the system, would frustrate discipline. The session would pursue the man as far as it could, and try to impose the same penalty on him as on the woman. But the language in which the two sexes were reproved would differ: it would be much more condemnatory and aggressive to the woman. The church had an incipient double standard: overt sexuality was to be taken for granted only in men.

In other social matters the church aimed at equality between the sexes. Though poverty struck more often at women than men, perhaps because it was harder for a woman to earn enough for saving, relief was not discriminatory, either in quantity or in availability. Schooling was an expected parental obligation, but one seen as modified by financial need. A session would urge parents to send children to school, but it would not discipline them for failure to do so. It would make sure that the orphans it was rearing could read well. It is clear that many families made more effort to pay for schooling for boys than for girls, but this discrimination was not overtly sanctioned by

[28] SRO JP6/2/1.

the church. The parish school system could not, given the area covered by many parishes, offer education to all children, but there were often also supplementary parish schools, charity schools or privately run 'adventure schools'. These were particularly necessary in the larger burghs, for burgh councils were more interested in the grammar schools they sustained than in spreading basic literacy. As the towns expanded in the early nineteenth century and the opportunities for child labour in factories increased, the educational attainment of the bulk of the population declined. By the 1830s, in spite of a wide spectrum of available schools, only about a third of Glasgow's children of school age were at school. Yet conceptually even in the nineteenth century Scottish education was more generous than English. The Scottish middle class did not hold that the acquisition of literacy would encourage working-class radicalism, and though opportunities for working-class children to attain higher levels of education were narrowed, they were never completely closed.

By the mid-eighteenth century lowland parishes had developed a system of coping with the problems of poverty which meant that destitution was fended off, but the standard of living of the poor was low and depended partly on casual aid. It was accepted that the recipient of relief would also beg. This recognition was sufficiently explicit, in spite of various statutory prohibitions of begging, for parishes to raise the level of the normal dole when a pauper had become too infirm to leave the house. Most of the lists of the poor were elderly spinsters or widows with young children, but there were often orphans and the insane. There might also be comparatively young people who were recognised, whether for mental or physical reasons, as unable to keep themselves supplied. To these, and the insane, parishes were often very generous. Orphans and foundlings were usually supported until the normal age of apprenticeship. Often their care was handed over to some woman already being supported, as a way of reducing the total cost.

The legal basis of the poor law had changed from that laid down in the formative statute of 1579. It had become accepted that the requirement, there set out, of assessment, might not be carried out. A parish would adopt it if it felt that it could not manage without, but the decision of whether voluntary sums would suffice was its own. There was no external check on the level of relief. Pressure from justices of the peace might be brought to bear on a delinquent parish which allowed its poor to beg elsewhere and there were surges of pressure on all parishes to conform to county schemes which combined efforts to make relief more adequate with instructions on the control of vagrants. Such surges can be found in many areas in the 1750s and again in the 1770s. But the justices had no executive authority to back them.

There was considerable variation in the way that assessments were made. Most parishes laid the burden on all land by formal valuation, but in some it lay only on the resident landowners. There was also developing a system of voluntary contributions which were not rates but which the landowners agreed to and made on the basis of the valued rent. The advantage to landowners was that this could be stopped whenever there was felt to be no need without discussions with the kirk session: the disadvantage was that landowners could not legally place half the burden on their tenants.

Parishes' power was limited. There was no statute empowering the removal of paupers to places where they had a settlement, or of removing potential paupers. Tranent in 1750 decided to remove a woman who had come to dwell with her son and who might have become chargeable, but it was acting as a burgh, not as a parish. In 1759 the rural parish of Straiton applied to the justices of the peace for Ayrshire for authority to remove two elderly people who had not yet achieved the three years' residence which would give a settlement but who begged occasionally, but the action was suspended when a couple of parishioners guaranteed to provide support. The case illustrates the way in which parochial relief could shade into private charity. The same parish in 1767 obtained the removal of a raving lunatic to gaol in Glasgow because he was dangerous. Instances can also be found of parishes paying for relief to people who had a settlement elsewhere, but more usually they held by the idea that the money subscribed for the poor was to be used within the parish.[29]

Before the surge of county schemes in the 1770s it is probable that fewer than 10 per cent of parishes normally carried assessment, but already this figure included many of the towns. In rural parishes in the economic tranquillity of the eighteenth century if a parish found it necessary to assess itself, it was unlikely to be able to revert to a purely voluntary relief system. In the towns where assessment was often joined to managing a poor house, and thus removal of the poor from visibility, this was even more true. Glasgow had set up a united

[29] SRO CH2/357/19, CH2/533/1, CH2/334/9.

system for its varied parishes in the 1730s, using a central town's hospital, and in 1774 this system was based on assessment. Edinburgh had decided to assess for its Charity Workhouse in 1740, but had not united its parishes in support, and never succeeded in raising enough money. An attempt in Stirling in 1739 to raise funds both from the parishes and the town council foundered on the recalcitrance of Ebenezer Erskine, leader of the newly created dissenting communion, the Associate Presbytery, who refused to acknowledge the elders of the established church.[30] It was a sign that dissent and parochially based poor relief were ultimately incompatible. Dissenting communities had to use whatever money they could raise from their membership primarily for the support of the ministry, and tended to leave the established church to support the poor of the dissenting groups.

Dissent had become a feature of Scottish religion in the 1730s, mostly as a consequence of refusal to agree to the acceptance of upper-class power in the practice of lay patronage in church appointments. Some dissenting groups also felt that the moral discipline of the established church was not strict enough. But there was also a new stream in the evangelical message: that grace was arbitrary and irresistible and that people not necessarily regarded as respectable members of society might be numbered among the elect. At one extreme this opinion was Arminian, holding that there were instruments for the reception of grace which should not be neglected. A small group of dissenters led by John Glass took a less extreme stand, but refused to acknowledge the authority of the Westminster Confession or the existing church government as non-scriptural. They made a group of pious but passive separatists. More serious in numbers and influence was the Erskinite secession of 1733, over the church's differential attitudes in cases of alleged heresy. Erskine had combined a series of denunciatory sermons with a refusal to apologise to anyone, and in the end he and his supporters founded a presbytery which they held to be the true church. In theology this group held to standard neo-Calvinism, that is they believed that grace was limited to the apparently godly, but opposed the willingness of groups within the church to compromise with society and the state, and since this attitude inspired the Moderate party, influential in the church after 1750, they were unwilling to re-enter into communion with it. Moderatism's key theme

---

[30]   R. A. Cage, *The Scottish Poor Law 1745–1845* (Edinburgh, 1981), chap. 3; National Library of Scotland MS 1506 (Mackenzie of Delvine papers).

was that, since the church lived in the world, it should co-operate with the various manifestations of secular authority. One of these manifestations was patronage, so this church party tended to sustain the power of landowners. Subsequent schisms in the church involved further breakaways on the topic of patronage, and though the Moderate party, never more than a minority group within the ministry, manipulated the General Assembly to end its routine protests about patronage, the issue was not killed and remained a source of disquiet and division.[31]

II

The pressure of rising population on grain prices and the example of English landownership combined to encourage agricultural reorganisation and 'improvement' in late eighteenth-century Scotland. The new experimental and exploitative approach had by the 1770s become common in the south-east. It meant both different methods of farming and different social and tenurial relationships. Tenures usually changed before techniques, since the latter involved a drastic reorganisation of time and labour acceptable only to farmers with some security. The single-tenant farm, already common, became the norm all over the Lowlands,[32] and the new farms were larger than in the past, usually of over 150 acres (60 hectares), enclosed, which in Scottish terminology means composed of fenced or walled rectangular fields, and with rotations using all suitable land as arable. There were to be no cottars or sub-tenants. Farm steadings were centrally grouped, often large and specialised. The lease would often be for nineteen years. Rents were raised in acknowledgement of the higher capital value of the unit, and increasingly were expressed in money only. Servitudes of 'carriages' or of peat cutting went out, and though the restrictions of thirlage were harder to abolish, in the early nineteenth century legal changes got rid of it.

Tenants did not necessarily pass all these changes on to their labour force. The work was now done by 'farm servants' who might be 'hinds', that is married men settled in cottages, or there might be a

---

[31] T. C. Smout, *A History of the Scottish People, 1560–1830* (1969), chap. 9; Ian D. L. Clark, 'From Protests to Reaction: The Moderate Regime in the Church of Scotland 1752–1805', in Phillipson and Mitchison, eds., *Scotland in the Age of Improvement*.

[32] R. A. Dodgshon, *Land and Society in Early Scotland* (Oxford, 1981), chap. 7; I. D. Whyte, *Agriculture and Society in Seventeenth Century Scotland* (Edinburgh, 1979), chap. 6.

preponderance of unmarried men, living in separate 'bothies', squalid dormitories, or under the 'chaumer system' eating with the farmer. There were also day-labourers hired for particular tasks. Hinds were usually paid mainly in grain, potatoes and grazing, and had the obligation of providing a woman worker, a 'bondager' for particular tasks or seasons. The relationship of a hind to the farmer carried many of the characteristics of the older cottar class, and meant that this group was relatively immune to sharp fluctuations in grain prices. Employment was fixed at the annual hiring fair, a system which, by making it clear to the labour force exactly how many full-time jobs there were, prevented overpopulation of rural communities and subsequent unemployment, by ruthless pruning. There was still some winter unemployment in many parishes where the bulk of the farming was arable, and there was a drastic selection of the type of population to suit farming needs. Thus while in the Lothians, because of the use of women for root crops, the married hind was the preferred type of regular labour, in the central areas of Scotland, such as southern Perthshire, the demand came to be for single men only.[33]

The changes to the new farming and hence the new social systems did not happen at once. The Borders had already early in the eighteenth century been geared to market forces,[34] and the effects of the new techniques and concentration was to make for more specialisation in sheep farming and hence depopulation, since better transport made it possible to bring in grain. In Aberdeenshire and other northern areas improvement was on a small scale, until the nineteenth century, and even when it occurred in some parts of the north it did not so much force out the old peasant system as intermix it with larger farms. Even in parts of the central valley, for instance in southern Ayrshire, there were still areas unimproved in the 1790s.[35] Yet elsewhere specialised dairy farms were being developed. In the Highlands the new specialised system of sheep farming had begun to penetrate some areas, notably Ross and Argyll, before the end of the century, but further north its advent was later.

---

[33]   Malcolm Gray, 'Scottish Emigration: The Social Impact of Agrarian Change in the Rural Lowlands, 1775–1875', *Perspectives in American History*, 8 (1973), pp. 132–8.

[34]   R. A. Dodgshon, 'Agricultural Change and its Social Consequences in the Southern Uplands of Scotland, 1600–1780', in T. M. Devine and David Dickson, eds., *Ireland and Scotland 1600–1830* (Edinburgh, 1983).

[35]   Ian R. Carter, *Farm Life in North East Scotland, 1840–1914* (Edinburgh, 1973), chap. l; W. Fullarton, *General View of the Agriculture of the County of Ayr* ... (Edinburgh, 1793), pp. 17ff; W. Aiton, *General View of the Agriculture of the County of Ayr* (Glasgow, 1811), pp. 695–7.

The collection of parish reports made in the 1790s, comprising *The Statistical Account of Scotland* (the *OSA*), give us a good basis for study of the degree of change achieved by that decade and what it meant for the people involved.[36] In many parishes in southern Scotland it is clear that farms had become fewer and larger and in some areas there are reports of the deliberate destruction of cottages. Where either process had taken place the rural population had come under control in the interests of profitability for the farmer, reflected in the number of families able to remain. In most cases this was achieved by degrading part of the workforce in status, from tenant to labourer, or from cottar to labourer or servant. Probably this change was accompanied by an improved standard of living, for food supplies became more reliable. The natural increase of population had to find jobs elsewhere, and this dispersed families. Opportunities for upward mobility in the farm sector were rare, since the capital necessary for the farming of the new type of farm was about £5 an acre. The gap between tenant farmer and his workforce had become permanent.

The view that material conditions had not deteriorated in the Lowlands gains indirect support from the striking lack of protest over reorganisation. The instances of resistance are so few as to be trifling, in sharp contrast to the reactions to enclosure acts in midland England or to the nineteenth-century highland clearances. If the change of status had involved material loss one would have to postulate an unusually subservient rural population. It is clear that the wages of day-labourers went up faster than the cost of living between 1760 and the 1790s,[37] and the increase was enough to compensate families for the loss of domestic textile industry to the factories in the 1790s.

Yet if the standard of living had not gone down, it was still uncomfortable and unhealthily low. In the best paid areas of southern Scotland diet was not such as to meet the full needs, even in calories, of a married couple with three children, even for the holder of the most prestigious position within the labour force, that of hind. Insofar as the income of the wage earner had improved over the eighteenth century this had been largely not in the grain allowance, except for

---

[36] *The Statistical Account of Scotland*, usually referred to as the *Old Statistical Account (OSA)* to distinguish it from the *New Statistical Account (NSA)* published in the 1840s, was brought out haphazardly in 21 volumes from 1791 to 1799. A new edition, arranged into regional volumes and given valuable introductory essays, is being produced under the general editorship of Donald J. Withrington and Ian R. Grant, from 1973. Unless otherwise stated references here will be to the original and complete edition.

[37] Morgan, 'Agricultural Wage Rates'.

the inclusion of potatoes, but in the money fee. For any family with children some part of this fee would have to go on food purchases; otherwise the hind was immune to inflation.[38] By contrast the day-labourer, who had had conspicuous increases in pay, was fully exposed to the price rise of the 1790s and the later fluctuations. The difference in real terms was that the hind was likely to suffer chronic minor undernourishment while the day-labourer could have periods of sudden hardship.

Neither sort of hardship would, in most years, bring these families into the sphere of poor relief, but in exceptional years of high prices, parish aid backed often by county pressure would be made available. For instance in Prestonkirk (the modern East Linton) in 1800 in response to county pressure an elaborate scheme was set up to allow specific quantities of subsidised grain to be bought by households of low income. 'Single women, widows, the old, those who are unable to or cannot procure work and labourers and tradesmen whose wages are at or below 1s. 4d. per day' formed the group allowed most generous quantities of cheap food, and the classification tells a lot about where hardship was assumed to lie.[39]

Bad harvests were still, at the end of the century, the main source of hardship, and the blending of 'official' and 'unofficial' aid which made up a relief system, and the mixture of assessment and voluntary aid which paid for it, did not prevent some real threat to standards of living. A bad year would lead to the incurring of debts which might permanently lower a family's status, or lead to long-term impoverishment. The *OSA* shows in reports for the parishes of Tranent and St Ninians (Stirlingshire) a rise in paupers after the 1782 harvest failure which lasted for eight or nine years, and the census of 1811 records for Insch, Aberdeenshire, the permanent loss of holdings.[40]

Already in the 1780s the Edinburgh newspapers were carrying correspondence critical of the poor law, occasionally with the argument that relief sapped the spirit of independence in the labouring class. This may have been a response to the attack on the English poor law launched in 1786 by Joseph Townshend, rather than a

[38] M. Goldie, 'The Standard of Living of Rural Labourers in Selected Counties of Scotland as Shown in the *Old* and *New Statistical Accounts*' (unpublished MPhil. thesis, Edinburgh University, 1971).

[39] *Caledonian Mercury*, 5 Dec. 1800.

[40] *OSA*, vol. 10, p. 96, and vol. 18, p. 401. British Library, Add. MS 6897 (this document is the explanations by returning officials of the census of 1811 to the difference between their figures then and those for 1801. These returns cover about two-thirds of Scottish parishes).

response by the upper class to an increasing burden.[41] Indeed, examination of the level of poor relief in twelve parishes which were conscientiously carrying out their duties in the central decades of the eighteenth century shows that the burden did not rise in real terms. What had increased, though, was the number of parishes assessed. This was partly because some parishes relatively neglectful of their duties mid-century were, by the last decade, making more effective intervention, and calling on the landowners for gifts or assessment.

The 1790s saw complaints about assessment, but not in the form that it was crippling landowners, rather that it was bad for the moral character of the labourer. Occasionally a complainant might go further and claim that this damage to character might weaken the urge to save, and so increase the number needing relief. Some ministers writing in the *OSA* trod the delicate path between complaining about the lack of charitable aid from non-resident landowners and a distaste for any system of assessment which would make them contribute.

The restriction of the population wanted on the farms and the decline of domestic industry consequent on the spinning mills, as these developed in the 1790s, sent the spare population to the towns. We have little critical estimate in the *OSA* of how the towns were coping with their expansion: the urban parishes could not be adequately understood by their ministers. It is most unlikely that housing was being provided rapidly enough to prevent overcrowding. We know that some of the smaller towns, such as Forfar, were facing a new scale of need for relief.[42] Glasgow was recording a death rate of over twenty-five per thousand, and the analysis of specific diseases in their contribution to child deaths made for that city for the years 1783–1813 strongly suggests widespread undernourishment.[43] Children poorly fed were liable to succumb to the first serious disease they encountered: until vaccination was introduced into the city on a large scale in 1805 this was likely to be smallpox. Even before 1805 measles was rising in its impact, and from 1807 took over as the leading cause of child death. In 1808 it killed 260 children in a single month in the city. We cannot tell whether the people who migrated to the city were poorer than they had been in the country; we can see the

---

[41] Debate in letters to the *Caledonian Mercury*, March and April 1786; Joseph Townshend, *A Dissertation on the Poor Laws*, 2nd edn (1787), Section XIII.

[42] *OSA*, vol. 6, p. 525.

[43] *Ibid.*, vol. 5, p. 511; Robert Watt, *An Inquiry into the Relative Mortality of Children in Glasgow* (Glasgow, 1813).

epidemiological evidence simply as clear evidence of the existence of undernourishment.

One area of Scotland was resolutely by-passed by prosperity. This was the Highlands. The basic problem here was that the people were much more fertile than the land. The total population of the areas geologically and geographically Highland had gone up from 115,000 in 1755 to nearly 201,000 in 1831. The birth rate was higher than elsewhere in Scotland in spite of the emigration of young adults.[44] Yet most highland areas had poor soil, and not much of it. The highland techniques of using the foot plough and spade cultivation by lazy beds (making enough soil in strips by taking up the soil on the ground between) are not ones which would be adopted where natural provision was generous. Efforts to develop other resources had had only two successes: the cattle trade, which went into depression in 1815, and the kelp industry, for which prices slumped after 1810 and which was rendered obsolete by the repeal of the salt duties in 1825. There seems also to have been an unwillingness on the part of landowners to invest in the productivity of their estates, so that occasional periods of high revenue, such as that experienced by seagirt estates during the kelp boom, had not enhanced productivity.

The *OSA* reports show that already by the 1790s the area was under stress. From many parishes there were reports of emigration, sometimes in parties led by the tacksmen (members of the gentry), resentful of raised rents which came from the landowners turning their aims from power to profit. The considerable drafts of manpower which went into the highland regiments, disproportionate to the share of the Highlands in total population, were a form of emigration. The shift from communal farming to individually managed crofts, which was happening from the 1790s, left many holdings no larger than 3 or 4 acres of arable, and a large number of cottar plots even smaller.[45] The only way in which a family could subsist on such a small patch of land was by the creation of a potato economy. A part, in support, was also played by temporary migration: from the 1750s the Highlanders had followed the pattern of upland peoples in other parts of Europe in taking their appetites and work capacity elsewhere for part of the year, most conspicuously to act as harvest labour in the

---

[44] F. Fraser Darling, ed., *West Highland Survey* (Oxford, 1955), pp. 80–3; Flinn, ed., *Scottish Population History*, p. 270.

[45] Malcolm Gray, *The Highland Economy, 1750–1850* (Oxford, 1955), chap. 2.

south. But it was the potato which gave the highland economy a breathing space of half a century, from the 1780s to the 1830s.[46]

This interlude was not used to set the economy on a stronger footing, if such a thing had been possible. In many areas highland society had been made more vulnerable by the disappearance of the intermediate class of lesser gentry, the tacksmen, either by estate policy or by bankruptcy. The passing of this group left highland society split into a large body of very poor cultivators, using Gaelic language and its oral culture, and a few isolated individuals who might or might not be able to speak Gaelic but whose main instrument of communication was English: ministers, officials, those landowners who were resident and the factors of those who were not. Perhaps it was the sense of a culture under stress which encouraged the adoption of a severe form of evangelicalism. Instances of this, and in some places the appearance of a group of self-selected individuals who attained a reputation for eminent piety by a policy of separation and criticism (later to be known as 'the Men'), are to be found before 1800, and evangelical feeling about a ministerial appointment was part of the inspiration for a riot in Assynt in 1813.[47] A widespread acceptance of evangelicalism of an austere kind, coupled with extreme sabbatarianism and hostility to the traditional Gaelic expression of culture in music and song, developed in the early nineteenth century. This movement, by its fierceness and austerity may have given individual Highlanders assurance of salvation, but it did so at the cost of narrowing their cultural inheritance.

The deterioration of highland standards of living raises the general problem of whether economic growth in one area not only widens the gap in living standards between that area and those more backward but also means actual impoverishment of the latter. For the Highlands it is not clear that the agricultural and industrial developments of the south made for enhanced poverty, but they made it harder for any new industry to start up and catch up in the remoter districts. Overpopulation seems to have been the main cause of enhanced poverty, and this was to some degree relieved by the capacity of the more advanced Lowlands to use highland labour, either on a temporary or a permanent basis. But the lowland expansion

---

[46] Flinn, ed., *Scottish Population History*, pt 5, chap. 7.
[47] A. J. Drummond and J. Bulloch, *The Church in Victorian Scotland, 1843–1874* (Edinburgh, 1975), p. 322; R. J. Adam, ed., *Papers on Sutherland Estate Management*, SHS, 2 vols. (Edinburgh, 1972), vol. 2, pp. 194–5.

of textiles and the urban demand for meat certainly contributed to the smallness of many holdings after 1790, by encouraging landowners to withdraw the use of large parts of the land for sheep farms. These farms used not only hill grazing, but also some of the valley land capable of supporting crops. The kelp industry, also developed for lowland demand, had encouraged the movement of population to the coast, but also its settlement on very small holdings; inland sheep farms and eviction led to the same end, and further compulsory movements of people shorewards were made as landowners began to face the problem of supporting their peasantry in times of crop failure. These movements were on such a large scale that the word 'clearances' has been taken to cover them and also other mass evictions. There is a specialised historiography of the whole series of events, containing a hard core of social dislocation and distress, on which is built much bitterness and some historical myth.[48] Here it is enough to say that the Highlands provide an area where economic change was accompanied by the lowering of material standards and the distortion of social structure.

The people no longer wanted by the new types of agriculture moved of course to the towns. No numerical definition of town can be found which does not exclude some small places of definitely urban culture, but setting the dividing line at 5,000 inhabitants, it was not until the 1881 census that the urban population in Scotland outnumbered the rural. The expansion of trade and its concentration built up the big cities; Glasgow with her suburbs had by the 1790s more than 60,000 people, and would soon overtake Edinburgh in size. It also enlarged the lesser centres. By 1821 Dunfermline had added about 5,000 and Perth about 10,000 to populations which had been around 9,000 in the 1750s.[49] The greatest expansion was in Paisley, where the new cotton industry came to settle and which grew from a little over 4,000 in the 1750s to 24,000 in 1800 and 47,000 in 1821. Already by the time of the *OSA* Paisley was conspicuous for fine fabrics and the luxury trade.[50]

Among the industries expanding in the towns the most conspicuous was textiles, particularly the weaving of cotton. There were said to be 4,000 weavers in Paisley in the 1790s. Still a handcraft, it sustained

[48]   E. Richards, *A History of the Highland Clearances: Agrarian Transformation and the Evictions, 1746–1886* (1982), pt 4; J. Hunter, *The Making of the Crofting Community* (Edinburgh, 1976), chap. 3.
[49]   Smout, *History*, p. 261.
[50]   R. Brown, *The History of Paisley* (Paisley, 1886); *OSA*, vol. 7, pp. 87–8.

a comfortable standard of living for the weavers, on relatively leisurely hours of work. Weavers were the cultural leaders of the labour force, enjoying good material standards and a consciousness of skill. Their efflorescence produced several 'weaver poets' responsible for small volumes. One of these described Paisley as a 'perfect aviary crowded with singing birds', a phrase which reminds that most birdsong is fairly stereotyped. The most celebrated of the poets, Robert Tannahill, wrote little lyrics on scenery, frustrated courtship and local sentiment, sustained by obvious imagery, and kept a substantial following happy. A higher quality of writing was achieved by William Thom of Inverurie, whose adult life was passed in the time of depression for his craft. Thom described the weaving trade as 'mere permission to breathe'. These men are interesting not simply for themselves but because they participated in the same tradition of popular vernacular culture as Robert Burns, and because they found a market within the working population.[51] But these weaver poets were not as well educated as Burns, and lacked also the range of mood from satire to sentiment.

The weaving golden age was the product of the technological gap between the mechanisation of spinning and of weaving. The power-loom did not become common until the 1820s. Well before then the craft of weaving had been shown as too open. Weaving of coarse fabrics was easily learnt by migrant workers from rural Scotland or from Ireland, the occupation became oversubscribed and wages fell. There were about 25,000 weavers altogether in 1780, 58,000 at the turn of the century, 78,000 in the 1820s, and the number did not fall until the later 1840s. Even before the powerloom turned the hand-loom weaver into a mere supplement to factory production, numbers had forced wages down. Wages then approximately halved in real terms between 1809 and 1816.[52] The more highly skilled work held its value for a while, but the increasing capability of machinery and changes in fashion struck eventually at this sector.

Weavers were involved in all the early radical movements. Political radicalism was not a native Scottish activity: there was a general acceptance in the eighteenth century of the concentration of economic and political power in the narrow class of landowners, and those

---

51 R. Tannahill, *Poems and Songs, Chiefly in the Scottish Dialect* (1815); W. Thom, *Rhymes and Recollections of a Hand Loom Weaver* (1843); D. Craig, *Scottish Literature and the Scottish People* (1961), chap. 3.

52 N. Murray, *The Scottish Hand Loom Weavers 1790–1850: A Social History* (Edinburgh, 1971), p. 23.

movements which resisted authority did so within religion rather than politics. As early as 1762 the particularly marked overt manipulations or patronage in the Drysdale affair in Edinburgh had united in protest a wide range of the lower orders,[53] but the issues of the American War and Economical Reform made little stir. Insofar as there was pressure for an improved electoral system it was from landed gentry who disliked the way the franchise was manipulated by spurious qualifications. Any disturbances, such as the weavers' strike in Glasgow in 1787 over a drastic cut in wages, rose from direct economic pressure.

The more vociferous national movements of the 1790s brought political radicalism into Scotland. There was a riot in 1792 over the official celebration of the King's birthday, from hostility to organised authority rather than on alternative opinions.[54] In the ensuing year various radical organisations based elsewhere produced participation in Scotland. Trees of Liberty were planted, to be dug up again by supporters of government. A society of the Friends of the People in Scotland was formed at a lower social level than the English Society which inspired it, and its branches were linked to the London Corresponding Society. The subscription could be as low as 3d. a quarter, so these groups were open to artisans and servants. Tom Paine's *Rights of Man* circulated freely and a link was formed with the society of the United Irishmen. A government spy reported that the Perth Friends of the People were artisans, mostly weavers, and this may well have been the case elsewhere. Yet the agitation cannot be taken as one by a conscious working class, but rather as the small-scale extension of political interest into a wider section of society.

What is striking in the story of this early radicalism is not its willingness to criticise, for in fact it tried hard to keep within the law and made no attack on social inequality, but the panic it produced in those above. A fully orchestrated response was made. The worlds of law and of politics, always close together in Scotland, united. The legal system allowed considerable scope for the handpicking of juries, so convictions for sedition were easily obtained. The most famous of the victims was Thomas Muir, a young advocate, in 1793. He may

---

[53]   Richard B. Sher, 'Moderates, Managers and Popular Politics in Mid-Eighteenth Century Edinburgh: The Drysdale Bustle of the 1760s', in J. Dwyer, Roger A. Mason and Alexander Murdoch, eds., *New Perspectives on the Politics and Culture of Early Modern Scotland* (Edinburgh, 1982).

[54]   Smout, *History*, chap. 17; K. Logue, *Popular Disturbances in Scotland 1780–1815* (Edinburgh, 1979), chap. 5.

have been selected simply because of his incautious recommendations of the work of Paine, but it is note-worthy that he did not truly belong to landed society as did almost all advocates and could be treated as an outsider. Yet even outsiders were gentry, and Muir's transportation to Australia was as a cabin passenger.[55]

The ranks of property closed against political innovation, even though some voices queried the legality of Muir's sentence. It is clear from the tone of the *OSA* volumes produced in and after 1794 that the clergy joined in support to the system. Only occasionally was there disagreement such as that of Alexander Carlyle of Inveresk, who was bold enough to suggest that even in those dangerous times there was no justification for the Scottish system of burgh government by small, self-perpetuating cliques which excluded most of the 'respectable' citizenry. A much more typical comment is that of the minister of Lanark who excepted from his general approval of his parishioners the one or two who from ignorance, violence of temper or lack of religion, agreed with 'the ravings' of the Friends of the People.[56]

All through the volumes of the *OSA* in lowland parishes the reports show both the buoyancy produced by economic growth, and the recognition that economic change was creating new social pressures. The new farming knew what sort of labour force it wanted and forced the rest away. Some part of the movement of people was from the positive draw of the towns. In places where labour-intensive crops, such as turnips, were part of the rotation, the labour force was retained, but not allowed to increase. In Calder (Lanarkshire) the schoolmaster, who wrote the report, gave a general warning of the neglect of educational investment. In Nielston (Renfrewshire), where there were already in 1791 two cotton mills, a printfield and 152 looms, the minister felt that the rate of change was dangerous; industry raised agricultural wages and allowed the introduction of luxurious habits, and the mill children were not getting any schooling, inhaled cotton fluff and lived in clothes impregnated with machine oil. He had fears for their physical and moral health.[57]

It was common for those with good incomes to equate morals with social and political conformity and to regard high wages as a danger to both morals and the economy. Many of the working class appear to have accepted these views. There is no sign of underground

[55] Christina Bewley, *Muir of Huntershill* (Oxford, 1981), chap. 8.
[56] *OSA*, vol. 16, p. 48, vol. 15, p. 42.   [57] *Ibid.*, vol. 8, p. 480, vol. 2, pp. 62–3, 154–5.

radicalism continuing after the trials of 1793, except for a small body, the United Scotsmen, a secret society imitating the Irish model and aiming at the standard feature of annual parliaments. We do not see in the record of its activities, even allowing for the fact that secret and illegal societies leave bad records, any sign of artisan activity in it, or any link between political agitation and the two main causes of popular disturbance during the war period, resistance to conscription to the new militia and trade union activities. Evangelical objections to the exercise of lay patronage in the church, which became more marked as the Moderate movement deteriorated into mere subservience to property and power,[58] also did not establish a link between the religious and political varieties of radicalism. But the tendency for the industrial parts of the country to have a varied pattern of dissenting sects, shown most conspicuously at Paisley, was a likely future source of this link, for dissent in Scotland opposed patronage and state control of religion and criticised the behaviour of the upper ranks by austere Calvinist standards.

In the later 1790s more general and conspicuous unrest than radicalism could produce came from the immediate pressures of food shortage and conscription. Food prices stood high, particularly in 1796 and 1800, causing riots in the towns over the movement of grain to other centres. More serious were the largely rural protests over the militia in 1797: this force was to be selected by balloting from lists of young men without serious family or professional responsibilities, to serve for the duration of the war. Crowds gathered and tried to destroy the lists and nervous authorities called in the military to keep order. In the worst episode, at Tranent, the Deputy Lieutenant and the army grossly overreacted, and slaughter of men and children resulted.[59] The disturbances belong to the early tradition of riot as a demonstration aimed at persuading a government to abandon some innovation, not to the nineteenth-century pattern of it as a demand for radical change.

In 1812, though, a major issue did for a time polarise opinion as if on a class basis: this was the case of the cotton weavers in the west of Scotland. These men had obtained a declaration of minimum wages for their work from the Glasgow magistrates; the employers appealed against this to the central court of session and lost, yet were successful in refusing to pay by the scale approved as reasonable and

---

[59]   Clark, 'From Protests to Reaction'.   [59]   Logue, *Popular Disturbances*, chap. 3.

just. A massive strike resulted, it is said, of as many as 40,000 workers. To get such figures there would have been some intimidation; there was also some sabotage. The employers turned for support to Westminster. One of the most powerful tycoons, Kirkman Finlay, urged the government to declare that justices of the peace had no power to regulate wages in the cotton industry, and to bring in a combination act. There were no real grounds for doubt about the power of justices over wages, for they had been exercised for varying occupations in the eighteenth century. It was also pointed out to the government that the employers as well as the men had been operating a combination. In the event the law was manipulated in favour of property: there was no prosecution of the employers but the leading weavers were tried for combining, and the law allowing for the control of wages was repealed. Even with relatively light sentences and the declaration by the Lord Advocate that there would be no further prosecutions, the story clearly shows gross distortion of law by class interests. The effect of the story may have been further enhanced by a weak judgment, given at almost the same time, against two cotton manufacturers who had been defrauding their weavers by false measurements.[60] It is not surprising that surreptitious trade unionism continued, nor that its most effective sector, the cotton spinners, when the searchlight of justice was next switched on for the industry, should be found using violence, even murder, and intimidation. Respect for the law had got the weavers nowhere.

In the dispute authority had also used a particularly powerful weapon, the ambiguities of the Scottish poor law. When starving weavers had wandered through Glasgow begging, the sheriff produced a proclamation stating that those in health and able to procure work were not entitled to poor relief, and that begging was illegal. This ignored the ambiguous status of the unemployed. There was no clarity in statute law on the issue, and genuine division of opinion. An important legal decision of 1804 held that relief should be given to all in genuine need, whatever was the cause of the need. But since that date the views of Malthus, as expressed in the second edition of his *Essay on Population*, had entered Scotland, and there was an increasing weight of political opinion behind efforts to restrict the total level of poor law expenditure.

This opinion was to be found in the rising group of professional

[60] A. Aspinall, *The Early English Trade Unions* (1949), pp. 138–60; *Scots Magazine* (May 1813).

men in burgh life, law and the church who made up the core of the
Whig party and who were gaining ground. The conspicuous land-
marks of their advance were the establishment of the *Edinburgh Review*
in 1802, which rapidly became the leading intellectual journal, and
of *The Scotsman* in 1817 as a Whiggish Edinburgh paper. These men
made possible the reopening of the debate on political reform silenced
since 1794, and the force that could be brought to it was enhanced
by the collapse of the burghs into corruption and bankruptcy. One
after another the burghs were failing, yet they were a key part of
the government's control over the parliamentary system.

The needs of a demanding war had done much to reduce the wastage
of government funds which had supported the system of 'old corruption' at the central level. The same pressures had not been felt in
local affairs. For the most part the royal burghs were not those parts
of the economy experiencing rapid growth, or, if they were, the thriving new activities did not belong to the group which held local power.
This group had found less arduous ways of making money than manufacture or trade. While burghs did not supply aid which effective
government could give, in regulations on activity and standards of
sanitation, their governors were dining out on the common good,
paying themselves for services which might or might not be carried
out, and selling to themselves at cut prices the town's property. By
1819, for instance, Dunfermline royal burgh was in debt to something
over £20,000 with a normal revenue of a little over £1,000 and the
burgh council had not seen any accounts. Aberdeen had been bankrupted by a debt of nearly a quarter of a million; before that it had
been kept apparently solvent by members of the council drawing
accommodation bills upon each other. Fortrose was under the control
of a boss who lent himself the burgh's money and kept various books
of fictitious accounts.[61] Some of this malfeasance in the burghs might
be seen as simply criminal, but in the capital Edinburgh the bankruptcy
had been achieved for political purposes. Yet some small towns
managed to carry on into the mid-nineteenth century with very
little in the way of governing apparatus. Galashiels had no police,
court house or jail. Kirriemuir had no income and no debt: its streets
were kept in repair by statute labour money. Huntly had to rely on
voluntary subscriptions for its minimal needs.[62] But these were not

---

[61]   SC on Petitions from the Royal Burghs of Scotland, PP 1819, VI; RC on Municipal Corporations, PP 1835, XXIX.
[62]   Saunders, *Scottish Democracy*, pt 2, chap. 4.

places of rapid expansion, where problems of poverty, public health and crime were coming to the fore, or places which needed investment in docks or drainage to maintain their activity.

Burgh collapse was usually met by the creation of a governing 'police' commission, and some part of this new governing body would have to be elected. The portion of the elected element increased with the later bankruptcies, and any popular element was an affront to the established system of power. The whole series of episodes was a visible demonstration of the incompetences of this system and an illustration that it was weakening.[63]

III

The rising group of young Whigs was of able and articulate men, some connected with land, but usually with law as well, regarding themselves as professional income earners. Most of them would not get into Parliament until the surge of support from Whiggery in 1830, by which time they were a powerful and closely united group. They saw no reason to maintain the existing political system, and though they wished one with a wider base, saw no need to include more than the level of moderate property or income. As 'self-made' men they had little interest in those less successful, particularly in the problems of the unemployed poor. Raising rates was to them an attack on their own pockets. They had little trace of the paternalism which led many of landed society to use the device of 'voluntary' contributions. It was a Whig landowner Member of Parliament, young Kennedy of Dunure, who in 1815 had a questionnaire sent out by sheriffs to all parish ministers asking about poor law expenditure over the last twenty-six years, apparently to show that the burden of relief on landowners was rising: indeed in money terms, though not in real terms, this was true. The use of a secular official for an ecclesiastical inquiry shows the dangerous insensitivity of upper-class society to the claims of the church to be independent of the state. Kennedy went on to an unsuccessful attempt in Parliament to destroy the right of appeal against parish decisions. This was too overt an attack on the relief system and it failed.[64]

The rise of the young Whigs removed the gag on Scottish political

---

[63] W. L. Mathieson, *Church and Reform in Scotland* (Glasgow, 1911), pp. 170–6.
[64] *SC on the English Poor Law*, PP 1817, VI, summary of the returns to the enquiry, pp. 145–53.

expression, but the movement of the workforce into the realm of politics was still hesitant. There was an inefficient Glasgow plot revealed by spies in 1816: it involved the usual paraphernalia of secret oaths, passwords and attempts to link up with radical groups in England, as well as extreme incompetence in the prosecution.[65] More significant was the Scottish response to the situation of 1819, a year of post-war slump and, in England, political agitation. There was severe depression in cotton, particularly in Paisley where a body of unemployed weavers, numbered by different sources at 850 and 1,000, obtained a sheriff court decision overruling the parish refusal of relief. The parish took the case to the court of session which decided, in spite of a healthy list of precedents, that the sheriff court had no jurisdiction over kirk sessions. The decision did not touch the substantive question of whether the unemployed were entitled to relief, but destroyed the efficacy of the poor law in a far more fundamental way, since it left the individual kirk session entirely to its own direction, usually under heavy pressures from landowners, on whether any relief, and if so how much, should be given to claimants. Henceforth the only external appeal was to the court of session. Appeal there was impractical for the destitute since it took time and money. The parishes, which in terms of assessment meant the landowners, were left as sole judges as to what relief to pay. It was a neat manoeuvre by Whig landowners for the change of law without application to Parliament.[66]

The Paisley petitioners had been careful, during their appeal, to give no support to radical agitation. Yet since the year was 1819, this took place there and elsewhere, in the aftermath of the violent dispersal of the crowd at 'Peterloo' in August. 'Peterloo' produced protest meetings and demonstrations in Glasgow and Paisley, which were not entirely peaceable. Reform societies expanded and became overt. The government response was an attempt to repeat the repression of 1793 by the prosecution of a liberal-minded Angus gentleman, George Kinloch, a parlour pink who had made an indiscreet speech denouncing the government. Genuine popular indignation mostly stayed well within conformist norms, but this did not prevent an upper-class panic about a possible rising. There was at least one real

---

[65]   Smout, *History*, p. 446; W. M. Roach, 'Alexander Richmond and the Radical Reform Movement in Glasgow in 1816–17', *Scottish Historical Review*, 51 (1972).

[66]   Rosalind Mitchison, 'The Creation of the Disablement Rule in the Scottish Poor Law', in T. C. Smout, ed., *The Search for Wealth and Stability: Essays in Economic and Social History Presented to M. W. Flinn* (1979).

plot, which government spies easily penetrated, and a botched upris-
ing in central Scotland. A few hundred weavers and other artisans
got together and managed to have a fight with the local yeomanry.
More advanced was the secretly organised outbreak of posters in Glasgow calling for a general strike. These appeared overnight and
obtained a response: 60,000 are said to have stopped work.[67]

The events of 1819–20 show that the working class in Scotland,
for the most part, wished to move only within the law, gave general
support to the idea of a wider franchise, but was only to a limited
degree prepared to get involved in organisations to this end.
Quiescence may have partly been due to the relatively slight part
in the economy of large units of employment. Mining was expanding,
but more slowly than in England, heavy industry still awaited the
discovery of the hot blast in 1828. The major employer, cotton, which
was said in 1812 to have a workforce of 150,000 had only about 20,000
of these, mostly women and young people, gathered in factories.
Many of these factories were still in the country. But another reason
was surely the long tradition of authority in church and state. Even
with a reforming body of upper-class men in existence, the bulk of
Scottish people accepted the structure of control, but their sense of
common interest was increasing.

One area conspicuously did not contribute to the disturbances and
demonstrations and this was Edinburgh. The city lacked large manufacturers and the cohesion they could give to the working population.
The manufacturing towns in the east also were relatively quiet, though
involved in the depression.

Unrest and disturbance, but for different reasons and without proletarian overtones, manifested themselves in the Highlands. Early in
the century there had been 'clearances' of the eviction type, simply
telling the inhabitants to get out, on various estates, those of Mackenzie of Coull, Lochiel and Lovat. In these cases the people had been
left to fend for themselves while the land was made into sheep farms.
From 1808 to 1821 the great Sutherland estate, almost the whole of
the modern county, was the scene, area by area, of the more enlightened but equally unpopular policy of clearance for resettlement and
reorganisation. The people were moved, often at very short notice,
from the inland straths to new coastal settlements. Here they were
expected to mix small-scale farming with fishing, and to work as

[67] H. Cockburn, *Memorials of his Time* (Edinburgh, 1909), pp. 342–5; Smout, *History*,
pp. 447–8; Mathieson, *Church and Reform*, pp. 157–62.

labourers in industry. The scale of movement was immense: 600 families were said to have been moved from Lairg and Rogart in 1808,
while more certain because better documented was the movement
of 700 families from various valleys in 1819. Many thousand people
in these movements had to change their location, often to somewhere
they had never seen, their conception of their own status from that
of farmer to labourer or cottar, and to acquire and use totally new
skills. The planning of these forced migrations was crude and dilatory,
because the conceptions which inspired it were oversimplified. It was
assumed that population was the same as labour force, and that labour
could be applied to any task. The lack of skill and experience, the
existence of elderly tenants who could survive as farmers on minimal
activity but not as fishermen, were facts ignored. The provision in
advance of houses, fishing boats and equipment, harbours, even land-
marks, was not made, and in some cases the time available for the
whole transformation was too short because the estate and some of
the factors had an interest in the immediate use of the land vacated.
In Strathnaver, one of the most bitterly resented depopulations, the
people had ten days actual notice in 1814, though they had been
given general warnings in the previous winter.[68]

For the estate it can be said that there had been increasing emergen-
cies and the need to bring in food supplies – difficult when the people
lived inland. The old system was not sustaining the people it had
bred. If the estate was ever to become truly productive change was
inevitable. It was thought that, reorganised, it could hold its own.
There was no intention of sending the people away, though many
fled up the coast to occupy small crofts and hamlets in Caithness.
But the main justification, that the estate would have put forward
if asked, was the concept of absolute property rights, against which
the social standing and way of life of the peasantry had no weight.
The policy was to do in an authoritative way what was thought would
make people happier as well as more productive; the estate did not
feel obliged to ask for agreement or for approval by the people or
the outside public.

In the Lowlands the reorganisation of the work, location and life
style of the peasantry which had made for more prosperous and productive farming, had not been prefaced by discussion, yet had been
carried out peaceably. But there was repeated resistance in the High-

---

[68]   Richards, *History,* chaps. 9–11.

lands. There was a spirited attempt in June 1792 to drive out the new sheep flocks from Ross and Sutherland. It was put down by bringing in the military.[69] There were riots in Assynt in 1813 at the installation of a minister which were as much against the landowner as against the minister. The Highlanders came to face 'clearance' with a mixture of non-cooperation and semi-violent demonstration of a traditional kind, with the women in the front of the protesters in order to prevent retaliation. Officers of the landowner or the state would be humiliated, demonstrations would verge on the violent with ineffective stone throwing, but no serious fighting would take place, and no savagery would be exercised on the hated and intruded sheep. It would be left for the parish minister to obtain some marginal modification to the planned clearance, and peace, coupled with resentment, would reign. The demonstrations and riots had been an appeal to outside public opinion, a statement that the 'right' use of land was to support the traditional life of the peasantry, not the extraction of profit.[70] Of long-term social significance was the fact that the 'cleared' Highlanders retained an attachment to the land they had occupied, and built up a theory of historic rights to it and of a golden age in the past which could be an excuse to evade economic effort.

The different course of agrarian history and the differences in material resource meant that by the 1840s the extremes in types of agrarian structure could be found in Scotland, from the large farms of the Lothians, as further increased in the 1820s, which needed four or five horse teams constantly at work, through the smaller large farms of Aberdeenshire, still often meriting the term 'muckle toon', to the south-west where even the larger farms were usually between 100 and 200 acres. In Galloway, Caithness, the Northern Isles and Aberdeenshire the larger units were interspersed with small farms or even farms so small as to be called crofts. On these, though the methods of farming had changed by the use of better equipment, and by the ending of intermixed strips, the life of the people was much as it had been a hundred years before, with the family providing most of the labour and eating most of the produce. 'Improvement' meant less scourging rotations, better stock and more regular work. For the big farms improvement meant a sharp social gulf between the farmer, a mini-capitalist, and his family on one side and the hired labour

[69] Logue, *Popular Disturbances*, chap. 2.
[70] E. Richards, 'Patterns of Highland Discontent', in R. Quinault and J. Stevenson, eds., *Popular Protest and Public Order* (1974).

force on the other. In the Lothians, and to a lesser degree in central Scotland, this gulf had become permanent. The same was true between crofter and sheep farmer in the Highlands. There the crofter now worked his individual piece of land, but hill pasture was usually in common, which made any selective stock breeding impossible. It would have been difficult for any Highlander to exploit his land more effectively than was the common style, but since the attitude of the Highlanders to suggested improvements had, from the mid-eighteenth century on, been one of passive non-cooperation, the economic gulf merely enhanced an existing cultural gulf. But there were parts of lowland Scotland where, before the more intensive farming of the later nineteenth century increased the need for capital, some part of the agricultural labour force could aspire to move into possession of small farms.

In the Highlands the first half of the nineteenth century saw deteriorating material standards of living, even though public concern and fund raising prevented actual starvation. By the second decade potatoes were the main food for three-quarters of the year in many areas, and this domination seems to have extended even farther by the 1840s. The potato is the only food by itself adequate to maintain adult health, but dependence on it is physically inconvenient, and as a single crop it was increasingly dangerous. The crop failed partially in 1836 and 1837, and this meant severe hardship. The administrators of a relief subscription which raised £50,000 reported of the outer isles 'people . . . in the very extremity of human wretchedness', and of Ardnamurchan as 'desperate' in its state.[71] Life on the coast made it possible to augment diet with small amounts of fish, but overcrowding on the grazing reduced the element of dairy food and occasional meat in the diet. To pay rents the people had to restrict their purchases of food or to sell some of their produce, so they benefited little from the new more commercial economy into which they had been forced.

Elsewhere real incomes were, for most groups, improving after the early decades of the century, with the striking exception of the hand-loom weavers. Yet weaving numbers had risen until the 1840s. It was difficult for a weaver to manage without a juvenile, and this led children to follow their parents into poverty. The most prosperous workers were those in skilled work within the new technology; the

[71]   *Letter by Robert Graham on Distress in the Highlands of Scotland*, PP 1837, LI; *SC on Emigration, First Report*, PP 1841, VI; *Transactions of the Highland and Agricultural Society of Scotland*, new ser., XI (1837).

Glasgow spinners, or calico printers, for instance, might earn enough with the wages of their older children to support a family with some money to spare for meat or other good food or comforts. The risk to these people was from injury or illness preventing work, or a downturn in trade causing unemployment. Numerous friendly societies existed to reduce this risk, and men might belong to several at the same time, but the limited actuarial knowledge of the day meant that individual societies were often short-lived. Miners also enjoyed a good family wage, and were often criticised for the rapid expenditure of it, but these wages relied, at least until 1842, on the work of wives and children. Masons represented a long-standing aristocracy of skill, but with short life expectancy from inhaling stone dust. Below these came agricultural workers, who, if hinds, had usually to see their wives work for at least part of the year. Mere day-labourers on the farm also needed a contribution from women and children for the family to get by.

For many of these groups, though not for the skilled man, income at best meant a diet predominantly of cereal or potato, and it was still rare for the cereal element to have much wheaten bread in it. Fish was available in most towns, and townsfolk and many countrymen could afford tea and sugar. The proliferation of ale-houses and licensed shops – in the central belt of Scotland by 1843 at the rate of one such outlet to every 150 inhabitants or fewer – shows that beer and spirits played a big part in diet. Fuel was available and fairly cheap; in much of the central valley there was coal either locally produced or imported from Tyneside; in the Borders it came from the Tyne at higher cost. Elsewhere there was peat, labour intensive, but at no other cost.[72] Rents were not high in terms of family income though they might be so in terms of the space and amenity provided: this was markedly so for the factory worker, who, even if working at a rural mill, would have to fit his family into a single room in a large tenement block. The Livingstone memorial at Blantyre shows an unnaturally clean, tidy and well-furnished version of such accommodation, in memory of David Livingstone's childhood there in the 1820s. We know from other accounts that the women were often fiercely proud of how well they could keep a cramped house, whether the single room or the 'but and ben'.[73] Most of the working class

---

[72] I. Levitt and T. C. Smout, *The State of the Scottish Working Class in 1843* (Edinburgh, 1979), chap. 3.

[73] David Fraser, ed., *The Christian Watt Papers* (Edinburgh, 1983), pp. 5, 74–5.

had to spend over two-thirds of income on food but still found a few pence every week for schooling, pew rents or other good causes.

Below the various groups of skilled and unskilled earners came the real poor, those who through physical or mental inadequacy, the wrong skill, accident, bereavement or trade depression did not command even the income which could support a purely potato diet. For these Scotland was a harsh environment, and becoming harsher.

In a rural parish the restrictions of the poor law were not rigidly adhered to. Only half of the church collections had to be handled as by law, so small sums could be given from the other half to cases of obvious need. Ministers and elders could know about their parishioners, and ministers would act on their own initiative and give help. But such minor aid was usually late in coming. If there was a general source of distress the minister and elders might call on landowners to raise extra money. Unless estates were in the hands of trustees or of people permanently absent, there was usually response to such requests, but one very late outbreak of food rioting, in Ross in 1847, where the landowners were almost entirely absentees, shows that there was still some popular sanction.

The readiness of rural parishes to help their unemployed, at least if the lack of work lasted for more than a few weeks, was clearly shown in the evidence published by the Royal Commission on the Poor Law (Scotland) in 1844. In almost all parts of Scotland – the exceptions were the Highlands, the north-east and some small enclaves in the Borders and Galloway – the majority of parishes admitted that relief for the unemployed was needed, yet in many areas more than half the parishes which made this admission did not give such relief.[74] A detailed study in 1841 of one of the most generous areas, Berwickshire, showed that in half the parishes (sixteen out of thirty-two) there had been no unemployment for the last ten years, or that if there had been unemployment it had not been recognised. But in six parishes there had been aid to the unemployed from subscription and from poor law funds. Yet all the parish ministers' returns denounced the idea of giving the unemployed a right to relief.[75] Much of the misery of early nineteenth-century Scotland can be ascribed to the inability of men, such as these ministers, to correlate the social facts that they saw with the social theories with which they had been imbued.

[74]   Levitt and Smout, *Scottish Working Class*, pp. 152–78.
[75]   *Report on the State of the Poor in Berwickshire* (Edinburgh, 1841).

If things could thus be hard for the unemployed in the country, where they were individually known, and where the impact of cyclical depression was muted, they were far worse in the towns. Subscriptions were set up during depression, but not before unemployment was widespread and long-standing. By such a time most workers laid off had sold up their furniture and were starving. This pattern of belated charitable activity bears the appearance more of a safety valve against riot and disturbance than an attempt to succour real need.

Even without depressions there was a continual layer of destitution and squalor in the larger towns. Some of the people involved were simply not attractive as labour: widows with children, the old, drunks, immigrant Irishmen, the weak-muscled and weak-minded throw-outs of the new agriculture. Even if medically infirm many of these would not qualify for relief for it took three years' residence to establish settlement. In any case, in Glasgow, parish boundaries were often crossed in the search for rock-bottom rents, so that establishing settlement might be impossible. This dreadful stratum of poverty and its links with alcohol and crime were shown up for Edinburgh in the Burke and Hare case in 1828, which revealed the business of providing by murder fresh corpses for medical dissection. The memory of this recent scandal over corpses may explain the social disturbances that accompanied the cholera epidemic of 1832, which were much more violent in Scotland than in England. In Paisley the riot caused by the discovery of empty coffins, and the assumption built on it that the doctors were hospitalising cases for the purpose of getting corpses, led to the calling in of the dragoons. But it may also be that cholera struck with exceptional ferocity in the Scottish towns. Certainly the only reliable mortality figures, those for Glasgow, show a death rate enhanced by about 70 per cent for the cholera year.[76]

Chadwick's famous *Report on the Sanitary Condition of the Labouring Population of Great Britain* of 1842 marks out the public health problems of the Scottish cities, Edinburgh, Dundee and Glasgow, most particularly the last, as markedly worse than those of any English town.[77] This may have stemmed from housing limitations. The economic growth of Scotland in the later eighteenth century had not led to

---

[76] R. J. Morris, *Cholera 1832* (1976), chaps. 5 and 6.
[77] E. Chadwick, *Report on the Sanitary Condition of the Labouring Population of Great Britain* (1842; reprinted, M. W. Flinn, ed., Edinburgh, 1965), pp. 78, 97–9.

the bulk of the working population enlarging their ideas of suitable housing before the rapid urbanisation that followed on industrial development. People carried the one-room house standard into city life, but also accepted the tradition of tenement-building. The result was a density of population which put a strain on any system of water standpipes and the collection of waste. As middle-class suburbs developed, the use in them of piped water often led to reduced water pressure elsewhere and cuts in the public provision. All these features contributed to a high likelihood of gastro-intestinal infection.

But the comments and criticisms of the urban crisis which was developing in Scotland do not confine themselves to the results of overcrowding, nor was it simply water-borne disease which made for the high death rates. Though the term 'fever' was used still to cover several different diseases there is no doubt that the most likely cause of epidemics of it requiring hospital treatment was in this period typhus – a sure indication of extreme poverty. 'Fever' cases in the Glasgow Royal Infirmary had risen by 1830 from 10 per cent of admissions at the beginning of the century to 50 per cent. The death rate for the city of Glasgow rose from just under twenty-five per thousand in the late 1820s to just under forty in the later 1840s.[78]

A powerful voice was heard in the 1840s asserting that this level of disease and death was the direct result of the high incidence of total destitution. This view was stated in a series of pamphlets by Dr W. P. Alison, Professor of the Institutes of Medicine at Edinburgh University. Destitution was the result of the inadequacies of the poor law, the absence of external force to make parishes treat the poor more generously, and relatively little charity for the relief of simple poverty, partly because mass destitution dulled the urge to give relief.[79] There was, by the 1840s, a wide range of charitable organisations, medical, educational and religious.[80] There was strong religious pressure on the better-off to participate in these and a firmly held doctrine that voluntary giving was in every way a better form of transfer of resource than state relief. In minor matters this may have been true, for the societies could afford to look for the right recipients and provide appropriate aid, but it did not meet the basic issue of

---

[78] Flinn, ed., *Scottish Population History*, p. 389; R. Cowan, *Statistics of Fever in Glasgow* (Glasgow, 1838).
[79] W. P. Alison, *Observations on the Management of the Poor in Scotland* (Edinburgh, 1840).
[80] O. Checkland, *Philanthropy in Victorian Scotland* (Edinburgh, 1980).

survival. People subscribed to the charities which they found inspirit-
ing, and the routine task of keeping the dirty and destitute alive did
not rouse enthusiasm. Alison in fact argued that the middle classes
in Scotland were, by international standards, ungenerous. Quoting
the treasurer of a large-scale charity he said 'the grand object kept
in view by almost any parish is the possibility of *evading*, as far as
their power admits, the duty of relieving the poor . . . The Managers
. . . will bury the father and mother of a young family and never inquire
about the orphans.' He went on to show that almost every other
advanced country made better provision.

Behind this attack lay changes in law and opinion. The lawyer Whigs
had stamped their version of the substantive law on poverty into
the legal textbooks, where it was given a retrospective sanctity as
what had always prevailed. Destitution without disablement now did
not qualify for relief. The Scots had thus carried out, between 1819
and 1825, a 'reform' of their poor law far more drastic than that
achieved in 1834 in England.[81] The other change was in the opinion
of the ministry, who were decisive in the actual provision of relief.
These men had absorbed, at various times since the 1790s, the
influence of frightened conservatism, the concern and propaganda
in England at the level of poor relief there, and at the temporary
system of using rates to supplement wages, the arguments put forward by T. R. Malthus that poor rates were liable to increase the
quantity of poverty and the political agitation in England in the years
after the war for the total abolition of the poor law. In the early parts
of the *OSA* a few of the ministry still held the views which had acti-
vated many of them earlier in the eighteenth century, that it was
desirable to keep pressing the claims of the poor on landed society,
and were not content with a system in which relief in an unassessed
parish was merely the transfer of funds from the needy to the very
needy. But this stance is rare in the later volumes. In the poor law
inquiry of 1815, the 20 per cent or so of the ministry who answered
(and of course this may not be a true cross-section of opinion) deplored
assessment as leading to the decline in the ancient virtue of independence and in the industry of the lower classes.[82] By the time of the

---

[81] Mitchison, 'The Creation of the Disablement Rule'.
[82] An *OSA* report urging more adequate relief was that for Burntisland (Fife): vol. 2,
pp. 431–2. The returns for the 1815 enquiry are in the possession of Lord Moncrieff
of Tulliebole, at Tulliebole Castle, and he has kindly allowed me access.

New Statistical Account, mostly written in the 1830s, almost all ministers accepted a highly loaded question to this effect, and confirmed it.[83]

Politics had played its part in this change, particularly the postwar agitation in England, in which Scottish propagandists took up a position they were to adopt often in the nineteenth century, asserting the superiority of Scottish institutions and, in particular, the contribution of the Scottish system of education to social well being. The decisive influence on the opinions in the church was that of Thomas Chalmers. Chalmers, through oratory, a strong sense of contemporary political and moral issues, a deep conviction of an understanding of God's will and enormous energy at least at the initiatory period of any scheme, had become the dominant voice in the church. His influence lies across the whole of nineteenth-century Scotland. He had absorbed the dogmas of political economy, in particular the views of Malthus on the dangerous nature of poor relief, and like Malthus he saw political economy as a series of laws laid down by God. The church, he held, had been in retreat for a generation, and it was his duty to call upon it to reassert its place in political and social life, and lead response to the changes which had overtaken economy and society.[84]

The church had certainly let go much of its moral discipline as far back as the 1780s, partly because the upper classes, which even before then were not answerable to this discipline, were stressing the right to privacy in matters of moral judgment and behaviour above the claims of the church. There was also a long-standing anti-clericalism in landed society. And there was the development of scientific and philosophical thought in the later eighteenth century which turned some men's minds from the idea of a God monitoring personal behaviour and intervening to bring home His views, to the alternative idea of a God ruling by general laws. By the early nineteenth century there was a complex spectrum of secession churches, some of them influenced by the evangelical revival, and popular evangelicalism was being organised on a congregationalist pattern by the Haldane brothers.[85] The success of the laymen in building up a new structure showed, inevitably, the problems of making the church establishment fit the needs of the new distribution of population.

[83] A striking exception to the general line is the report of the minister of Fala and Soutra (Midlothian): *NSA*, vol. 1, p. 540.
[84] Stewart J. Brown, *Thomas Chalmers* (Oxford, 1982), esp. chap. 5.
[85] A. J. Drummond and J. Bulloch, *The Scottish Church, 1688–1843* (Edinburgh, 1973), chap. 7.

Chalmer's own specific contribution was both backward and forward looking. On poor law matters he held that what he believed was the traditional rural system of management, taking all possible ways of persuading those in need to look for private rather than parochial aid, could be made to work in a modern industrial city. Only a small residue of cases would need parish help from church collections. To prove this he had a large parish – St John's – set up in Glasgow, in 1819, and built up a structure of deacons to supervise and keep down the claims of the poor. The experiment was inherently fraudulent, and did not convince anyone not already in agreement. St John's was not a purely working-class area but a suburb; it was also not the home of a separate population. While the 'experiment' which Chalmers had already described as successful was in operation, relief demands rose within the neighbouring parishes. It is clear that the deacons, mostly middle-class men brought in from outside, were helping from their own pockets.[86] The experimental system died in recrimination after a few years. But Chalmers had fastened one element of evangelical thought on the Scottish church – the idea that relief based on legal claims was socially and morally pernicious.

On the forward-looking side Chalmers pushed the Church of Scotland into a programme for the creation and support of new parishes: 'Church Extension' it was called. For this he had to develop techniques of appeal and raise funds, pioneering what all churches since then have done, both to give themselves money without strings attached, and also to encourage participation. Chalmers put forward 'penny a week' programmes for the poorly paid, and it is a striking tribute to his powers as organiser and inspirer that he extracted pence from families living below any 'human needs' income. His attempts to bring such families more closely into the life of the church, to have them attend services, for instance, at a time when a pew rent for a year might cost a week's wage, failed. The new churches might be placed in the poor areas, which were becoming clearly defined within the cities, but their congregations came mainly from the middle and lower middle classes, and their eldership was recruited entirely from the middle class.[87] In this they followed the path of dissent. Yet the language of public agitation and working-class debate shows a

---

[86]   R. A. Cage and O. Checkland, 'Thomas Chalmers and Urban Poverty: The St John's Parish Experiment in Glasgow, 1819–1837', *Philosophical Journal*, 13 (1976).

[87]   Brown, *Thomas Chalmers*; A. A. MacLaren, *Religion and Social Class: The Disruption Years in Aberdeen* (1974).

working population, at least in the first two-thirds of the nineteenth century, fully accepting the Calvinist dogmas and prejudices on which it had been reared.

The evangelical party came to dominance in the politics of the church in the 1830s, and signalled its power in 1834 by an Act of the General Assembly attempting to limit patronage. This, known as the Veto Act, declared that if the majority of male heads of communicating households would not sustain a candidate for the ministry, his appointment should be blocked. In this the Assembly took the monitoring of appointments away from the presbyteries and further stretched its powers by setting up new parishes without obtaining the agreement of the landowners, on whose financial support the parochial system was based.

In the course of the next ten years the church was to discover that campaigning for the rights of congregations could bring it into conflict with the rights of property and the anti-clericalism of landed society. Patronage was part of the law, could be defended in the civil courts in the ensuing series of clashes, and was. The church ignored the fact that the establishment depended on the civil court, the courts the fact that it was not the function of judges to decide who was or was not allowed to preach in a parish. Passion led to escalation of local issues into constitutional ones, and all came to a head in the General Assembly of 1843 when about a third of the ministers broke with the establishment and set up the Free Church of Scotland.

In one sense this was a valuable demonstration that the church should belong to the people. But it forced the church to surrender its governing functions in morals, welfare and education, since these could no longer be sustained by a body comprising only about a third of the nation, sharing with Old Dissent and the Free Church on fairly equal terms. The split enhanced the gulf between landowners and peasantry in the Highlands for almost all the peasantry went into the Free Church. The social cleavage was enhanced when owners of large estates made it difficult for the Free Church to get feus of land for churches and manses, and of course the determination of the Free Church to imitate the established church made it unwilling to countenance the idea that God could be worshipped and the ministry housed in anything less solid than stone-built buildings in permanent possession.[88] The Free Church, while claiming to be the true

---

[88]   SC on Sites for Churches in Scotland, PP 1847, XIII.

Church of Scotland, had to base its activities where funds and potential elders could be found, and this tied it to the middle class. It became cut off from working-class participation, and this led it to place undue emphasis on moral issues attractive to the middle class, such as the repression of drunkenness and drastic observance of Sunday, in both of these areas finding itself in opposition to easy forms of working-class recreation.

Well before mid-century Scotland had become marked by a reputation for drunkenness. The country by the early years of the century was turning from beer drinking, generally regarded as a desirable practice, to whisky, deplored by all social commentators. From 1829 she was to provide in John Dunlop one of the earliest campaigners against the use of spirits. Dunlop, who did not wish to promote total abstinence, made his main attack on what he called 'artificial and compulsory drinking usages', the conventions which brought dram drinking into all sales, changes of job, starts of journeys, wage payments, funerals, etc. In Scotland the temperance movement was to become closely associated with the dissenting churches; its leaders were middle class. Whisky drinking became an issue of sharp division within Scottish society, and some element within the polarisation was from class.[89]

Scotland experienced the effects of the Whig political victory of 1830 in parliamentary and burgh reform, but neither set of measures was well thought out in terms of Scottish law and social needs, and as a result both had limited effect. The Reform Act of 1832 broke the system of political dominance through closed and corrupt burghs by widening the voting base to some degree, and giving some new, expanding burghs a share in elections. In the country the opening of the vote to the more substantial farmers meant that these were herded by the landowners to the polls; misapplied votes could lead to eviction, a naked use of power rare in England. Control thus remained in the hands of the landowning class, but this was a wider section of society than the old group of feudal superiors. The methods by which voting power was exercised were somewhat less dishonest and illegal than they had been, but were still a distortion of the law. In burgh reform so much collapse had already taken place that it seemed simplest in the Act of 1833 to carry on with the method of

---

[89] *SC on Drunkenness*, PP 1834, VIII; John Dunlop, *Artificial and Compulsory Drinking Usages in North Britain* (Greenock, 1836); Bernard Aspinwall, *Portable Utopia: Glasgow and the United States, 1870–1920* (Aberdeen, 1984), chap. 4.

elected 'police' burghs, and these were inserted in parallel with the existing burgh councils, with wide powers. The Royal Commission which looked into burgh government a year later, preparing for the Act that recreated urban government in England, found that rulings made by the 1833 Act to clean up the existing burghs were being ignored, but nothing was done. The old burgh councils were allowed to lapse into the inactivity their bankruptcies made inevitable, and the new police burghs gave some minimal effective provision for urban needs. The dual system continued almost to the end of the century.

In the 1830s, when there were signs of precocious class consciousness in Britain, the working class in Scotland did not yet show a wish to hold by different standards from the rest of society. The riots over the cholera epidemic sprang from traditional views on the seemly way of caring for the dead. Chartism, when it belatedly arrived, in 1838 (for in the pre-railway era contact with the south of England by workers was sporadic), was entirely of the moral force variety, perhaps because it brought Edinburgh back into the centre of radical activity, and Edinburgh's traditions were law-abiding.[90] The high priority given by the working class to religious issues is shown in the fact that there were Chartist churches, about twenty of them: formally created Chartist congregations and lay and ordained preachers. A minister of the established church, Patrick Brewster of Paisley, preached Chartist sermons of an unusually intemperate variety,[91] and attacked the failures of the Scottish poor law in terms which brought down a formal reproof from the presbytery where he was preaching.

The idea of Scottish working-class legalism is opposed by the evidence produced by an inquiry into trade unions in 1838. The sheriff of Lanarkshire held that though the workmen in different industries in Glasgow did not have a confederacy of unions, they all acted together because they were guided by the same interests. A worker put up against this the claim that during strikes the masters and the local authorities and magistrates were themselves in alliance.[92] It is clear that the Cotton Spinners Association had been maintaining its power by illegality and violence, but this had probably started long before, at a time when mere trade unionism itself was illegal.

---

[90]   A. Wilson, *The Chartist Movement in Scotland* (Manchester, 1970).
[91]   P. Brewster, *The Seven Chartist and Military Discourses Libelled by the Marquis of Abercorn* (Paisley, 1843); Drummond and Bulloch, *The Scottish Church*, p. 55.
[92]   *SC on Combinations of Workers*, PP 1837–8, VIII; *Scotsman* (January 1838).

There is also evidence of a discreet and surreptitious trade unionism of long-standing in the mines. Altogether there are signs that the localisation of power and wealth in the middle class was producing illegal organisation, antagonism and eventually class consciousness in a period of relative prosperity.

The 1840s were to prove, like the 1740s, a period when decisions were made with long-term effects. The Disruption of the church would eventually have forced a reformulation for the Scottish poor law as it existed after the surreptitious changes of the 1820s, but the renewed depression in Paisley which began in 1841 brought the matter to a head even before the church divided. The slump from 1841 to 1843 put over 14,000 on relief in a town where assessment was so badly organised as to be based on about only half the real property. All local resources were soon exhausted, and a fund contributed to on an international basis also ran out. In the second year of depression weekly allowances had to be cut to derisory levels: a weaving family of five were receiving less than 3s. a week, and even this would soon have to stop. Bankruptcy had struck not only many of the manufacturers but also the pawnbrokers.

The response of the government to appeals for help was twofold. A civil servant was despatched with a sum based on private subscriptions from the cabinet, which he applied not in cash but in basic stores. This meant that the sum lasted longer, but gave no help to the small shopkeepers, who were also in distress. Grudgingly also the government put reform of the Scottish poor law on its legislative programme, and set up a Royal Commission to advise it.[93]

The reform when it came, in 1845, was administratively clever: it set up a system of checks and balances under a central Board of Supervision, which ensured that those entitled to relief would get adequate support, in particular that medical aid was provided for the sick. But it accepted the myth that the Whigs had fastened on the law, that the poor law in Scotland had never supported the able-bodied, and perpetuated this principle. In spite of Dr Alison's urgings, the view of the comfortable middle class, that moral virtue lay in self-support, and that private charity could take the edge off severe distress, prevailed. In law, therefore, Scotland had a relief system unsuitable for an industrialised country where large numbers could be affected by

[93]   T. C. Smout, 'The Strange Intervention of Edward Twistleton: Paisley in Depression, 1841–3', in Smout, ed., *Wealth and Stability*.

cyclical depression. Yet in practice the central Board, and the medical profession who worked for it, were anxious to increase its powers, and this meant that various ways of bending the law could be found.[94] Because the new system forced home responsibility for the sick poor, a large number of parishes which had been shirking their legal duties now had to assess themselves to meet them.

Each parish had to have an inspector and a Poor Law Board, and if the parish was assessed this Board had to include all the heritors. Its constitution would be so rigged by the central Board as partly to balance this landed element with a small elected portion, not enough to open the control of policy to the working class but enough to block landowner resistance to necessary expenditure. The pattern of automatic landowner presence on local government was later taken over for other services as these became inescapable. Sanitary needs and highway needs borrowed the system. Only when the recognition that urbanisation had effectively destroyed the working of the parish school system brought in the Education Act of 1872 did the Liberal government omit this built in position of property ownership.

The new poor law was hardly set up, and certainly not working smoothly, when Scotland was faced with the potato blight, which struck the Highlands in 1846, destroying the crop and with it the food of the people for nine or more months in the year. In any case the new poor law was not designed to help with disasters of this mass kind, since the people were 'able-bodied', any more than it was to cope with the urban destitution caused by renewed depression in 1846–7. Highlanders were sustained through the famine year by a mixture of charitable effort, government administration and landowner paternalism. The government stationed two depot ships on the coast (and by now most of the population lived there) and gave out food in response to promises to pay from landowners.[95] Hardship was no worse than usual for many of the people, which is not to say that it was not severe, and indeed, because most of the landowners accepted the obligation of support, the destitute crofter was better sustained than the destitute industrial worker of the towns. But the process bankrupted some estates, and led many landowners to decide to reduce population. It also left the crofters with a burden of debt and on ground which would never again yield a reliable

---

[94]   T. Ferguson, *Scottish Social Welfare, 1864–1914* (Edinburgh, 1958).
[95]   Flinn, ed., *Scottish Population History*, pp. 432–6.

subsistence. Emigration, whether enforced or voluntary, also meant hardship and stress.[96]

So by mid-century long-term structural changes in Scotland were beginning. An administration of a national sort, and some sort of local government, in parochial Poor Law Boards, had been set up. Other services would soon be found to need similar central and local machinery, though none would be made to carry as miscellaneous a collection of functions as this pioneer one. The shape and character of the cities had been formed. The shift of population to the central valley was accelerating, as the farming systems controlled the numbers allowed to remain in the rural areas. Cotton had ceased to expand, but heavy industry in the west was supplying the new industrial spurt. Religious issues could still raise more heat than secular ones, and the political spectrum of Scotland until the end of the century would be dictated by allegiances forged during the Disruption. The urban working class was ceasing to produce active church membership. Middle-class control of society had kept the country tranquil but it was ceasing to be silent.

[96] Hunter, *Crofting Community*, chaps. 4 and 5.

Scotland
1850–1950

T. C. SMOUT

I

In 1935, George Malcolm Thomson, journalist and friend of the recently formed Scottish National party, wrote the following perceptive passage about the recent history of his country:

The belt of coal mines, blast furnaces, factories, shipyards, docks and railways uniting one grim-faced town to another across the desecrated countryside – this may be a part of our country which the alien visitor traverses with averted eyes and all possible speed. But to us it is the outward and visible sign of the labour, the courage, the foresight, the inventive genius of our nation. Our political independence is gone, and we assure one another that we are all the better without that for which our fathers in their folly fought during a thousand years. The men are lifted from our glens like ripe berries by the pickers, and we admire the enhanced desolation of the scenery. The poorer quarters of our cities are a dishonour to God and a disgrace to man, but they serve to set off for us the sharpness of the spiritual tension in which, with no time to spare for less urgent things, we completed the building of our great industrial structure. But tell us that the great structure is itself in decay, convince us that our place among the thriving and busy of the earth, won at such cost, is ours no longer, show us that the hands of the clock have begun to move backwards, that there are no more high cards left in the pack, and where can we look for comfort? . . . finis has been written to a chapter two hundred years long. A new chapter begins. There are grand dividing lines drawn in red ink across the history of all nations. In Scotland there was the arrival of Queen Margaret in the year 1068, the battle of Flodden Field in 1513. In Ireland there was the Famine of 1846. In England there was the last of the Viking raids in 1066. The turn of the industrial tide in Scotland must inevitably be for the Scottish nation an event of such proportions.[1]

These remarks were entirely appropriate. That 'grand dividing line drawn in red ink' came at the end of the First World War, and our examination of the economic structures on which the social history of Scotland rests must divide at 1918. Before that, all was confidence

[1] G. M. Thomson, *Scotland, that Distressed Area* (Edinburgh, 1935), pp. 4–6.

and the expectation of further enrichment, whatever shortcomings there may have been in fact in the distribution of wealth and levels of deprivation in town and country. After it, all was despair and the assumption that, in the natural order of things, Scotland would always need special care and attention. That conditions continued to improve for most Scots in the last third of the century 1850–1950, just as they had done in the first two-thirds, but often more dramatically, was generally overlooked.

Table 3.1 (cols. 1–4) shows the changing structure of employment and total population in Scotland, 1851–1911, during the classic period of expansion. Over the period the population of Scotland grew by 65 per cent, and the employed population by 62 per cent. Neither rate of increase was anything like as fast as those of the United Kingdom as a whole, where population grew by 96 per cent between 1851 and 1911, and total employment by 95 per cent. The major reason for the difference was Scottish emigration to other parts of the UK and to the USA and the white Dominions, itself a reflection that whatever the success of the Scottish economy within this period compared to previous experience, it was still judged by many Scots not to provide as good a living as the world outside.

The general trends evident from Table 3.1 were the same as those evident for the United Kingdom as a whole – a very marked fall in the numbers of those employed in agriculture and textiles, with a concomitant rise in heavy industry and the service sector. In Scotland, however, agriculture was always proportionately more important and the drift from the land, though scarcely less rapid, lagged twenty years behind that of the UK as a whole.[2] Conversely, services were always much less important: the proportion reached in Scotland in this sector in 1911 had already been achieved for the UK as a whole forty years earlier. In the manufacturing sector, Scotland depended proportionately more on textiles at the start of the period than did the UK as a whole (20.2 per cent compared to 13.8 per cent), but proportionately more on heavy industry at the end (19.0 per cent compared to 13.6 per cent). These comparisons suggest features of the Scottish economy in the late nineteenth and early twentieth centuries at once rather more backward and certainly more unbalanced than

---

[2] The proportion employed in agriculture in the UK was: 1851, 22.0 per cent; 1871, 15.2 per cent; 1891, 10.7 per cent; 1911, 7.8 per cent. The proportion in Scotland in 1931 using the Series B classification was 9.0 per cent compared to a 1911 Series B figure for the UK as a whole of 8.1 per cent.

Table 3.1 *Percentage of employed population engaged in various occupations, 1851–1971, all Scotland*

	1 1851	2 1871	3 1891	4 1911	5 1911	6 1931	7 1951	8 1971
Agriculture	24.9	22.2	14.0	10.6	11.0	9.0	7.3	4.1
Heavy industry	8.1	12.1	13.8	19.0	16.9	16.5	15.7	10.5
Textiles	20.2	15.1	12.0	9.5	8.3	6.8	5.4	3.5
'New' industry	n.a.	n.a.	n.a.	n.a.	1.6	2.9	4.7	6.5
Transport and services	19.9	21.7	26.2	28.0	34.9	44.6	44.8	52.2
Total employed population (000s)	1,271	1,464	1,748	2,056	2,067	2,221	2,195	2,164
Total population (000s)	2,889	3,360	4,026	4,760	4,760	4,843	5,096	5,229

Notes: 'Agriculture' includes fishing. 'Heavy industry' includes mining and quarrying, metal manufacture, mechanical engineering and ship-building. 'Transport and services' includes transport and communications, distributive trades, insurance, banking, finance and business services, professional and scientific services, miscellaneous services (including domestic service) and public administration and defence. '"New" industry' in columns 5–8 includes chemicals, instrument and electrical engineering and vehicles. The data originates in census material, and the difficulties of a consistent interpretation are fully discussed in C. H. Lee, *British Regional Employment Statistics 1841–1971* (Cambridge, 1979), pp. 1–24. Perhaps the main point to be borne in mind is that while a fairly consistent series 1851–1911 is possible (cols. 1–4), and another 1911–71 (cols. 5–8), it is not possible to obtain consistency over the entire century due to alterations in definitions, particularly with regard to the distributive trades. Whereas in the nineteenth century the manufacture and distribution of many commodities were often carried on by the same person, today this is much less frequently the case. By modern standards, therefore, the nineteenth-century definitions used by Lee in compiling his Series 'A' tables (cols. 1–4) would understate the service sector and slightly overstate manufactures: this can be seen by comparing cols. 4 and 5 for 1911, which show that by using twentieth-century definitions there would have been 16.9 per cent in heavy industry (not 19 per cent), 8.3 per cent in textiles, (not 9.5 per cent) and 34.9 per cent in services (not 28 per cent). The main cause of distortion in cols 5–8 arises from the fact that in 1911, 132,000 people were 'not classified'; by 1931 this had fallen to 33,000 and by 1951 to 1,600. Most in this category, however, seem to have been subsequently classified in the service sector, which would have the effect of understating the true extent of services, earlier, especially in 1911.

Source: Calculated from Lee, *Regional Statistics*. Series 'A' (cols. 1–4) and Series 'B' (cols. 5–8).

that of the national economy. It has been argued elsewhere that Scottish GNP per capita may have come to within 95 per cent of the United Kingdom figure by 1911, and that 'Scotland then stood near the historic peak of her economic performance relative to that of the other regions and nations of the British Isles'.[3] She stood, however, on a perilously narrow base from which it proved only too easy to knock her down when international trading conditions altered after the First World War.

It may, of course, fairly be objected that there was not one Scottish economy but several, and that some of these show little dynamism either as regards industrialisation or growth of population. Tables 3.2 and 3.3 (cols. 1–4) break down population and employment statistics, 1851–1911, to a regional level, and show both the truth of this observation and its limitations. On the one hand the seven regions show distinctive structures of employment (persistent over long periods) and varying demographic experiences ranging from a net increase of 118 per cent in Strathclyde to a decline of 13 per cent in the Highlands. On the other, they all, from the most rural to the most urban, shared the experience of dramatic decline in the proportion employed in agriculture and clear growth of the proportion in the service sector.

The central belt of Scotland was dominated by three urban-industrial regions. Dominant overall was Strathclyde, its share of total Scottish population growing from a little over a third to a little under a half between 1851 and 1911. It contained the great conurbation of Glasgow, claiming to be the second city of the Empire by 1900; to the west lay the Clyde shipyards where one fifth of total world tonnage was launched by 1913, the nearby textile towns of Paisley and Kilmarnock and the engineering centre of Greenock; to the east were the crowded Monklands parishes, producing iron, steel and coal around the towns of Airdrie, Motherwell and Coatbridge. Strathclyde also had a rural penumbra in south Lanarkshire, Ayrshire and Argyll where dairy farming (even crofting on the islands to the north) was locally the dominant activity.

This region, even in 1851, was clearly Scotland's industrial core, containing more than half the textile employment (then so clearly

[3] In L. M. Cullen and T. C. Smout, eds., *Comparative Aspects of Irish and Scottish Economic and Social History, 1600–1900* (Edinburgh, 1977), p. 14. A suggestion by Rondo Cameron that already by 1850 Scotland was 'nearing the peak of its greatest relative prosperity' does not seem soundly based on any statistical evidence, and is unlikely. See R. Cameron, *Banking in the Early Stages of Industrialisation* (Oxford, 1967), p. 94.

Table 3.2 *Percentage of Scottish employed population and Scottish total population in different regions, 1851–1971*

	1 1851	2 1871	3 1891	4 1911	5 1931	6 1951	7 1971
A Employed population							
Strathclyde	37.6	40.8	43.9	47.5	49.4	49.8	48.5
Lothian	11.4	11.8	13.0	13.5	14.1	14.2	15.4
Central and Fife	8.8	8.0	8.4	9.3	9.5	10.4	10.7
Dumfries, Galloway and the Borders	8.9	7.7	6.8	5.6	5.1	5.1	4.6
Tayside	12.5	11.7	10.9	9.4	8.9	8.3	8.2
Grampian	11.1	11.1	10.0	9.0	8.5	8.2	8.4
Highland	9.5	8.9	7.0	5.7	4.6	4.0	4.2
B Total population							
Strathclyde	35.7	39.9	43.6	47.5	49.3	49.2	48.9
Lothian	11.3	12.1	13.0	13.3	13.5	13.9	14.5
Central and Fife	9.1	8.2	8.5	9.7	9.8	10.4	11.1
Dumfries, Galloway and the Borders	9.4	8.1	6.9	5.5	5.2	5.0	4.6
Tayside	11.7	11.1	10.1	8.7	8.2	8.0	7.9
Grampian	11.8	11.4	10.6	9.6	9.0	8.9	8.4
Highland	10.9	9.0	7.4	5.9	4.9	4.5	4.5

Notes: The regions approximate to the prevailing local government regions as defined in April 1975, with the following main differences: Dumfries and Galloway is amalgamated with the Borders, and Central Region with Fife; the areas covered by the Island authorities of Orkney, Shetland and the Outer Isles are subsumed under the Highlands. See Lee, *Regional Statistics*, pp. 39–45.
Source: As Table 3.1.

dominant in the industrial sector), and about 60 per cent of employment in heavy industry. By 1911, when the relative importance of textiles and heavy industry had been reversed, Strathclyde's share of the latter had risen to 68 per cent, though she still had 40 per cent of all Scottish textile jobs. But the dominance of coal, steel, engineering and ships over every other activity after about 1880 also made the region the *locus classicus* of the strong, skilled male worker. Whereas in 1851 a third of all the industrial jobs in Strathclyde in these two sectors combined had been for women, by 1911 the proportion was a sixth. Glasgow was a man's world.

The next largest region was Lothian, containing the one big city of Edinburgh (with Leith), itself surrounded by organic mineral deposits of coal and shale and by some of the finest and most advanced farming land in Britain. Population here almost doubled between 1851

Table 3.3 *Percentage of Scottish employed population engaged in various occupations, 1851–1971, by regions*

	1 1851	2 1871	3 1891	4 1911	5 1911	6 1931	7 1951	8 1971
A Strathclyde								
Agriculture	13	9	5	4	4	3	3	1
Heavy industry	13	20	21	27	24	23	20	14
Textiles	28	18	11	8	7	6	5	3
'New' industry	n.a.	n.a.	n.a.	n.a.	2	4	6	8
Transport and services	18	21	25	26	34	44	43	50
Total employed population (000s)	478	598	768	977	979	1,097	1,093	1,050
Total population (000s)	1,032	1,341	1,754	2,259	2,259	2,389	2,507	2,558
B Lothian								
Agriculture	15	10	7	5	5	5	4	2
Heavy industry	8	11	11	15	13	13	12	7
Textiles	4	2	3	3	1	2	1	1
'New' industry	n.a.	n.a.	n.a.	n.a.	2	3	4	6
Transport and services	34	34	35	36	44	53	52	61
Total employed population (000s)	145	173	228	277	277	313	312	333
Total population (000s)	326	407	524	631	631	655	707	760
C Central and Fife								
Agriculture	19	18	12	8	8	6	5	3
Heavy industry	12	15	19	30	28	27	26	13
Textiles	29	23	16	11	10	6	4	3
'New' industry	n.a.	n.a.	n.a.	n.a.	1	2	4	7
Transport and services	16	18	22	22	28	39	38	48
Total employed population (000s)	112	117	146	192	192	211	228	231
Total population (000s)	263	277	342	460	460	475	532	582
D Dumfries, Galloway and the Borders								
Agriculture	41	38	29	27	27	25	24	15
Heavy industry	4	4	3	4	3	3	4	3
Textiles	10	10	16	15	14	14	13	12
'New' industry	n.a.	n.a.	n.a.	n.a.	1	1	1	4
Transport and services	20	23	26	28	25	42	42	47
Total employed population (000s)	113	113	118	115	115	113	109	100
Total population (000s)	273	272	279	260	260	251	256	240
E Tayside								
Agriculture	22	19	13	12	12	11	11	7
Heavy industry	4	5	6	6	5	5	7	8
Textiles	35	33	32	30	29	24	15	9
'New' industry	n.a.	n.a.	n.a.	n.a.	1	1	2	6
Transport and services	16	18	22	25	32	42	47	52
Total employed								

Table 3.3   *(contd.)*

	1 1851	2 1871	3 1891	4 1911	5 1911	6 1931	7 1951	8 1971
E Tayside								
population (000s)	159	172	191	193	194	198	183	179
Total population (000s)	339	377	407	413	413	398	410	413
F Grampian								
Agriculture	43	46	30	27	27	24	20	12
Heavy industry	4	4	5	6	3	3	5	4
Textiles	8	6	5	5	4	3	3	2
'New' industry	n.a.	n.a.	n.a.	n.a.	1	2	2	1
Transport and services	21	21	31	30	37	48	50	55
Total employed								
population (000s)	142	163	174	185	186	188	181	181
Total population (000s)	340	385	425	458	458	436	454	441
G Highland								
Agriculture	57	61	47	41	44	36	28	13
Heavy industry	2	2	2	2	1	1	2	3
Textiles	4	4	7	5	5	2	3	2
'New' industry	n.a.	n.a.	n.a.	n.a.	1	1	1	1
Transport and services	18	18	25	30	32	42	49	61
Total employed								
population (000s)	121	130	122	118	124	102	87	90
Total population (000s)	316	302	296	280	280	238	231	234

Notes: See notes for Tables 3.1 and 3.2.
Source: As Table 3.1.

and 1911 and Table 3.3 shows the usual trends in the structure of employment – a relative decline in agriculture and textiles (the latter never very important here), and a growth in heavy industry as mining developed. The strength of some of the smaller consumer goods industries like printing, brewing and rubber is unfortunately not reflected in the table. The most striking feature, however, was the almost constant share of the service sector at around 35 per cent, very much larger than in any other region in 1851, though less decisively so sixty years later. This demonstrates two main features of the capital city, its great importance in the provision of professional services – law, banking and insurance – and the high proportion of wealthy middle-class families resident within it and able to employ a staff of servants.

Central and Fife are our third region in the industrial central belt; they also held important coalfields in Stirlingshire and west Fife, balanced by textile towns and rich agricultural land and fishing in east Fife. The switch to heavy industry was as marked as in Strathclyde but it came twenty years later, around the turn of the century when the exploitation of the Fife coalfield intensified. Population growth was similarly inconsiderable between 1851 and 1871, but then rose by two-thirds before 1911.

These three contiguous industrial regions were flanked to the south and north by four other regions where industrialisation, where it occurred at all, was restricted to narrow enclaves. Dumfries, Galloway and the Borders was the region to the south: here total population stagnated and then actually fell after 1891 as manufactures and services proved incapable of taking up all the surplus shed by farming, which despite quite heavy falls was still employing a much larger percentage of the population in 1911 than any of the three central belt regions had done even in 1851. Heavy industry hardly existed: the only signs of industrialisation were in the late-developing Border towns where the textile phase of the industrial revolution was beginning to arrive in the last quarter of the century, anachronistically, and on a very limited scale, a hundred years after it had begun on Strathclyde.

Tayside, to the north of the central belt, was less backward and increased its overall population by a fifth. It contained a group of large towns, especially the city of Dundee, but also Perth, Arbroath and Forfar, which had formed an enclave for important textile manufactures, particularly linen and then jute, from before the middle of the nineteenth century. The absolute number employed in textiles remained roughly constant over the period, though there was some concentration on Dundee and the sex ratio altered: men had been nearly as numerous in Tayside textile jobs in 1851, but by 1911 were outnumbered almost two to one. Dundee therefore became a woman's town almost as much as Glasgow was a man's one. There was only a little significant heavy industry, and the main alteration in the overall structure of employment was the switch from agriculture into transport and services common to all the regions.

Grampian, too, had its urban-industrial enclave in the city of Aberdeen, and increased its population overall by a third. Superficially it appears as emphatically and persistently agricultural as the extreme south, but something of this is due to the fact that fishing is subsumed under the general heading 'agriculture' in the industrial classification, concealing the growth of the prosperous deep sea trawling industry as a staple of Aberdeen and the concomitant enlargement of many of the smaller fishing communities all round the coast. The proportion employed in heavy industry and textiles together remained constant at the very low figure of 10–12 per cent, though Aberdeen, like Edinburgh, had consumer goods industries (like papermaking) that do not show up on the tables.

Finally there was the highland region, the most remote, least urbanized and most persistently agricultural of all, with no less than 41 per cent of its occupied population still in farming as late as 1911. This was, admittedly, a third less than the proportion of 1871, the usual growth in transport and services accounting for most of the difference, since industry in all its forms was very underdeveloped, discouraged both by the absence of minerals and by the distance from urban markets. The Highlands, of course, experienced a drop in population: yet the decline, 13 per cent over sixty years, was relatively modest and, contrary to general belief, probably had very little to do with the highland clearances. The drop over the period 1851–71, was smaller, in percentage terms, than that in the period 1891–1911, though in the former the crofters were unprotected from eviction and in the latter they enjoyed security of tenure under Gladstone's Crofters Act of 1886.

What sort of a living did the Scottish economy yield? Dr Rubinstein found six Scots among the forty largest British fortunes, 1809–1914, of which only one, the third Marquess of Bute (d. 1900), made his money substantially outside Scotland – in his case on urban and mineral property in South Wales. The others consisted of two Lanarkshire ironmasters, William Baird (d. 1864) and William Weir (d. 1913), two Paisley sewing-thread magnates, Peter and James Coats (both d. 1913), and a Glasgow chemical manufacturer, Charles Tennant (d. 1906). All died worth more than £2 million, and all made their fortunes in Strathclyde. At a less plutocratic level an indication of middle-class wealth is provided by the Schedule D income-tax assessments: Dr Rubinstein's examination of these assessments in London and in the British provincial towns of over 100,000 inhabitants in 1879–80 shows the Scots relatively well placed. Edinburgh, with its lawyers and bankers, was by this measure the third wealthiest British town paying £21.1 per inhabitant, and Glasgow with its merchants and manufacturers, the fifth, paying £16.4.[4] Behind them by a large margin came Aberdeen at £9.3 and Dundee at £8.4, but even these exceeded English cities like Leeds and Sheffield, just as Glasgow very

[4] W. D. Rubinstein, 'The Victorian Middle Classes: Wealth, Occupation and Geography', *Economic History Review*, 2nd ser., 30 (1977), pp. 614–18.

comfortably exceeded Birmingham and Newcastle (though not Manchester or Liverpool). There is no reason to think of the Scottish Victorian middle class as the poor relation of the English provincials.[5]

For the working class the situation was rather different. In the middle of the nineteenth century one of the attractions of Scotland for capital was the cheapness of industrial labour in mine, mill and shipyard. It was a situation that altered only slowly. When Edward Young made his report on international wage levels to the American Congress in the early 1870s, he went in person to John Elder's yard in Glasgow and subsequently commented: 'The great demand for Clyde-built ships has not been caused by their superiority . . . but from the fact that they can be built at less cost, owing in part to the cheapness of materials, but chiefly to the abundance of skilled workmen and the low rate of wages paid to them.'[6] The words 'mere pittance' came readily to the US consuls of that period when they considered Scottish wages, and they regularly listed rates for joiners, blacksmiths, carpenters, rivetters and labourers significantly below those of London or Newcastle.[7]

In 1886 the first British UK wage census gave, in R. H. Campbell's words, 'an unequivocal interpretation of Scotland as a low-wage economy', though E. H. Hunt takes a slightly more optimistic view, regarding wages in central Scotland as then 'near the national average', and indicating a substantial improvement in the region's relative position since 1850.[8] Certainly the average annual earnings of cotton workers in 1886 were well below the UK average (£28 compared to £36), partly because of the higher proportion of women workers in Scotland. The same low earnings were found, less markedly, for shipyard workers (£70 compared to £76) and in many other trades, such as building (£62 compared to £66) and printing (£46 compared to £53 in large works). In some other significant Scottish industries, however, there were either no differences (engineering, distilling, carpet manufacture)

---

[5] In absolute, instead of per capita, terms, Glasgow was the fourth wealthiest city in Britain and Edinburgh was the fifth, according to the Schedule D assessments. London was, of course, the first.

[6] *Labour in Europe and America* (Government Printing Office, Washington, DC, 1876).

[7] The consular reports for Scotland are available in Edinburgh University Library. See T. C. Smout, 'U.S. Consular Reports: A Source for Scottish Economic Historians', *Scottish Historical Review*, 58 (1979), pp. 179–85; T. C. Smout, 'American Consular Reports on Scotland', *Business History*, 33 (1981), pp. 304–8.

[8] R. H. Campbell, *The Rise and Fall of Scottish Industry, 1707–1939* (Edinburgh, 1980), p. 80; E. H. Hunt, *Regional Wage Variations in Britain, 1850–1914* (Oxford, 1973), pp. 50–3.

or a very slight advantage in Scotland's favour: coal and iron-ore mining (£53 compared to £52), the manufacture of pig iron at the blast furnace (£74 compared to £73) and linen (£26 compared to £25).[9]

By the time of the next wage census in 1906, however, most of the ambiguity had disappeared. Cotton, certainly, was still a low-wage industry in Scotland, continuing to employ a large proportion of ill-paid women. But in four vital fields of heavy industry – iron and steel manufacture, light iron castings, shipbuilding and (less markedly) engineering and boilermaking – Scotland in general and the Clyde in particular reported average earnings and wage rates well above the UK average. On the other hand, there is some indication that coal mining (the only evidence is from Lanarkshire) had not kept up with the national level. But Campbell is in no doubt that Clydeside had by then become a high-wage region in the leading sector industries, and E. H. Hunt puts central Scotland as one of the four highest-wage regions in Britain.[10]

This finding, if correct, implies that in thirty years industrial Scotland had gone from a low-wage to a high-wage area, and also that the figure generally accepted for overall improvements in real wages in Britain between 1850 and 1900 – about 80 per cent – would be substantially larger in the Scottish case. Before drawing the conclusion that the typical Scottish worker was particularly prosperous at the start of the twentieth century, however, certain other factors have to be considered. First, even in 1900 there were large remaining sectors in textiles where the characteristic employee was a badly paid girl. Secondly, the heavy industries supported not only skilled workers whose wage rates were extensively reported to the census but substantial numbers of labourers about whose earnings little is known except that they were low, and that the gulf between the skilled and the unskilled was always obvious and great. To Harry McShane, who worked in the shipyards as a boy before the First World War, it was symbolised by the skilled engineers' weekend dress of a blue suit and a bowler hat compared to the rough clothes of the labourers.[11] Thirdly, the only detailed account of Scottish wages in shipbuilding in the quarter-century before 1914 shows that the employers deliberately exaggerated the average earnings of rivetters in their reports to outsiders and to the Board of Trade for the census, and that in

[9] Campbell, *Rise and Fall* p. 190.
[10] *Ibid.*, pp. 84–8, 191–4; Hunt, *Wage Variations*, pp. 50–3.
[11] Harry McShane and Joan Smith, *No Mean Fighter* (1978), p. 42.

1906 the average earnings per week were not 47s. 11d., as reported, but 36s. 4d., fully 25 per cent less. Between 1900 and 1910 half the rivetters earned less than £2, and a quarter less than 30s.[12]

There is, however, little doubt that employers did feel the steady pressure of rising wage costs on their profit margins and therefore on their ability to compete world-wide in the production of ships even before the First World War. They tried every device to keep the wage bill down, for example by employing a high ratio of apprentices to qualified journeymen, and by enforcing wage cuts in times of depression, as in 1908–10; conversely, the workers defended their jobs by opposing every new attempt to introduce a technology that might threaten their jobs. That such opposition was not empty is illustrated by the US consul's report on an important trial of American pneumatic rivetting tools that took place at the works of Scott of Greenock in 1902. The trials lasted six weeks, but the consul observed:

speaking generally, the experiments appear to have given every satisfaction and to have demonstrated the fact that a great saving in time and labor could be effected. However, the use of these machines is not favored by the labor unions, and with native labor they accomplish little, if any, more than is accomplished under the present system.[13]

Much of the class bitterness that was to grow in the first two decades of the twentieth century along the Clyde can be considered in the light of these opposing pressures on the returns to capital and labour.

The foregoing discussion of wages relates mainly to the industrial belt of central Scotland. Hunt's investigation of rural southern Scotland – Dumfries, Galloway and the Borders – suggests substantial relative and absolute gains for agricultural labour (the main occupation) between 1850 and 1870. By the latter date agricultural workers here were already paid 5 per cent above the British average for their occupation, and they enjoyed further substantial gains to 1907, when the area was one of the four best paid in Britain for farm work. On the other hand, agricultural labour generally was badly paid in relation to industrial labour, of which there was little, though textile wages in the eastern Borders were not inferior to those in the West Riding of Yorkshire.[14]

North of the central belt the position deteriorated. Tayside and

---

[12] S. F. Price, 'Rivetters' Earnings in Clyde Shipbuilding 1889–1913', *Scottish Economic and Social History*, 1 (1981), pp. 42–65.

[13] Cited in Smout, 'American Consular Reports', p. 307.

[14] Hunt, *Wage Variations*, pp. 47–50.

Grampian's level of agricultural earnings were about 3 per cent below the British average in 1867–70 but 1 per cent above by 1907. The city of Dundee was dominated by low-paid female jute workers whose average earnings in 1886 were even lower than those of the Strathclyde cotton workers. Though men in most trades in Dundee seemed to have earned as much as those in Glasgow, there was a margin between both those cities and the lower wages earned in shipbuilding and engineering in Aberdeen. The highland region, however, was much the worst of all: still overwhelmingly dominated by agriculture, farm earnings remained 14 per cent below the British average in 1867–70 and 13 per cent below in 1907. The crofting counties certainly had the lowest incomes of any region in Great Britain; the drift of people from the area even after the land reform needs no further explanation.[15]

The second part of our period has to be considered separately. After the end of the First World War, Scotland along with the other traditional British regions of staple industry entered the bleak years of the depression which seemed to George Malcolm Thomson to mark so decisive a break in national history; and although rearmament and the Second World War revived employment and profits in the traditional sectors, there was still, even by 1950, little growth of new industry. It is no doubt true, as Neil Buxton has persuasively argued, that the initial cause of Scotland's disastrous performance lay in the structure of the Edwardian economy, with too large a proportion of her resources tied up in what were to become irretrievably depressed staple industries, and that 'there was little that individual entrepreneurs could have done to ameliorate the effects of the depressed inter-war market. They were overwhelmed by market forces beyond their capacity to control.'[16] Yet it is also true that in the longer run the 'Scottish economy has dramatically failed to come to terms with the economic world of the twentieth century'.[17] Such a failure was part and parcel of the general British failure, but it was much more acute in Scotland, and had profound social and political effects, as well as the obvious economic ones.

[15] *Ibid* ., pp. 53–6.
[16] N. K. Buxton, 'Economic Growth in Scotland between the Wars: The Role of Production, Structure and Rationalization', *Economic History Review*, 2nd ser., 33 (1980), pp. 538–55.
[17] S. B. Saul, 'The Shortcomings of Scottish Industry', *Scottish Economic and Social History*, 1 (1982), p. 76.

One of these has been to make many question the Union relationship. For a few, the whole value of 'rule from London' has come to be doubted. For the majority (including, paradoxically, most of those in the first category), the feeling has been that Scotland, as a relatively poor region, has a right to demand more from central government than it ever received in the past: insofar as this demand is conceded, it makes Scotland more, and not less, dependent on Union than ever it was in the past. In any case, the easy self-confidence of the nineteenth-century Scots as (in their own eyes) the most deservingly successful nation in Britain has been replaced by a twentieth-century image of the Scots as well balanced, like the Australians in the joke, by a chip on each shoulder.

Table 3.1 (cols. 5–8) shows the changing structure of employment and total population in Scotland, 1911–51, with an additional column for 1971 to bring the story more up to date. Over the sixty-year period, population in Scotland grew by a mere 10 per cent compared to a 32 per cent growth for the UK as a whole. The rate of population increase in Scotland was thus much less than it had ever been since the country started to industrialise, and in one decade, it was even slightly negative: Scottish population dropped between 1921 and 1931 by 40,000. Migration to more prosperous regions in England and abroad was the main cause: no less than 70 per cent of natural increase was lost in this way between 1911 and 1951.[18]

The growth of employed population actually ceased in Scotland after 1931, though in the UK as a whole it continued to grow by 17 per cent between that date and 1951. Thus Scotland's problems were compounded by a contracting workforce obliged to support an increasing number of dependants. This in turn was due mainly to alterations in the age structure of the population, because many young earners left the country. It was also a reflection of the fact that relatively fewer women of working age followed gainful employment in Scotland than in England, largely because the continuing dominance of heavy industry and the decline of textiles left fewer openings for them until further changes in industrial structure after 1950. In 1911 there were 2.5 male jobs in Scotland for every female job: the ratio was still as high as 2.3 in 1951, but had altered to 1.7 in 1971 – the last figure was the most favourable for women since records began in 1841.

[18]   D. J. Robertson, 'Population Growth and Movement', in A. J. Cairncross, ed., *The Scottish Economy* (Cambridge, 1954), p. 13.

The general trends in the structure of employment after 1911 were a combination of old and new. As in the previous period, agriculture and textiles continued to shed labour, though both sectors were still relatively more important in Scotland than in England at the end of the period. There was again a lag of two or three decades between Scotland and the rest of the UK in this respect, the proportion employed in agriculture in Scotland in 1951 being much the same as that achieved nationally in 1921, and the proportion employed in textiles in Scotland in 1951 only a little smaller than that achieved nationally in 1931. Similarly in the service sector, though the proportion thus employed continued to increase significantly in Scotland as it had done before 1911, the figure reached in 1951 had been achieved in the UK as a whole by 1921.[19] On the other hand the steady increase in the proportion of the population engaged in heavy industry came to a halt in 1911, but only very gradually began to fall. The rise of 'new' industries (chemicals, instrument and electrical engineering, vehicles) was, however, extremely slow in Scotland: again, the UK as a whole had achieved twenty years earlier the proportion reached in Scotland by 1951.[20]

When these figures are disaggregated to the Scottish regional level (Tables 3.2 and 3.3, cols. 5–8), an immediate contrast is evident between the three regions of the central industrial belt and the four outside it. Those in the central belt continued to increase their share both of employed population and of total population, while all the others declined on both counts. Indeed, nowhere outside the central belt were the numbers either in employed population or total population higher in 1951 than in 1911, though only in the Highlands was the absolute fall substantial. Here employed population fell by 30 per cent but total population by only 18 per cent, imposing a special burden on the region.

At first sight the distribution of decline may seem surprising, as the industrial central belt was the heartland of the coalfields, shipyards and heavy engineering shops where depression, unemployment and failure of international markets were most notorious in the interwar

---

[19] In the UK as a whole the figures are as follows: in agriculture, 1921, 7.2 per cent; 1951, 5.1 per cent; in textiles, 1931, 5.9 per cent; 1951, 4.5 per cent; in services, 1921, 44.2 per cent; in 1951, 47 per cent. There are particular difficulties in calculating the service sector discussed in the notes to the tables.

[20] The UK figures for employment in 'new' industry were 4.9 per cent in 1931, 8.3 per cent in 1951.

years. Yet it is clear that the proportion of the employed population engaged in most of these activities remained remarkably constant, partly because of the practical difficulties for skilled adults like blast-furnacemen and boilermakers transferring to alternative jobs, and partly because the main response of Clydeside employers was to hold on and hope that something would turn up in the end – which indeed it did, as a palliative, in the shape of rearmament in the late 1930s. In addition, insofar as there was any new industry in Scotland at all before 1951 it was concentrated (as the tables clearly show) in the central belt, and these regions (especially Strathclyde and Lothian) were also the main source of service employment. Positive shedding of labour, in fact, took place most notably not in the activities that dominated the central belt (apart from mining) but in agriculture in Grampian and the Highlands, and in textiles in the very depressed jute industry of Tayside.[21] At the height of the depression there was a very clear rush out of the rural north. Thus in ten years after 1921 Shetland lost no less than 17 per cent of its population, Ross and Cromarty 12 per cent and Caithness 11.5 per cent; but the four largest cities in the same decade increased their aggregate population by 4 per cent. 'Love on the dole' in the towns was a lesser evil than the 'idiocy of rural life'.

This process left Scotland in 1951 with 74.4 per cent of its employed population, and 73.5 per cent of its total population, in the three regions of the central belt, compared to 57.9 per cent and 56.1 per cent respectively a century earlier. As a long-term change this had all sorts of implications. Just as Scotland as a whole was losing her self-confidence and sense of entirety with the accelerated drain of population and prosperity to the south of England, so the peripheral areas of Scotland, left with an ageing and independent population, resented the drain of their life blood to Glasgow and Edinburgh. A fear of the 'dominance' of Strathclyde in national and local politics became, for the outlying counties at least, as real as a fear of the 'dominance' of London.

The altered relative prosperity of Scotland within the United Kingdom was clearly shown in the statistics of unemployment. As early as 1923 unemployment in Scotland stood at 14.3 per cent compared

---

[21]   The labour force in Scotland, 1911–51, fell in agriculture from 219,000 to 162,000 (29 per cent); in textiles from 172,000 to 118,000 (33 per cent); in mining from 156,000 to 99,000 (36.5 per cent).

Table 3.4 *Percentage of Scottish insured population unemployed, 1927–39*

	In United Kingdom	In NE England	In Scotland
1927	9.7	13.7	10.6
1928	10.8	15.1	11.7
1929	10.4	13.7	12.1
1930	16.1	20.2	18.5
1931	21.3	27.4	26.6
1932	22.1	28.5	27.7
1933	19.9	26.0	26.1
1934	16.7	22.1	23.1
1935	15.5	20.7	21.3
1936	13.1	16.8	18.7
1937	10.8	11.0	15.9
1938	12.9	13.5	16.3
1939	10.5	10.1	13.5

Source: Ministry of Labour Gazette.

to 11.6 per cent in the UK as a whole, and at the bottom of the slump, 1931–3, more than a quarter of the workforce in Scotland was out of a job, compared to a little over a fifth in the UK. Up to this point, however, it is possible to argue that Scotland was not badly off compared to other regions with a similar dependence on the traditional staples. As Table 3.4 shows, until 1933 the nearest neighbouring region, north-east England had consistently higher unemployment.[22] After that date, however, though Scotland approximately halved her unemployment rate under the pressure of rearmament to 13.5 per cent by 1939, her relative position worsened. In Scotland between 1927 and 1929, unemployment had been only about a tenth higher than the UK average: between 1937 and 1939 it was a third higher. She failed in particular to maintain her position compared to the north-east, where unemployment by 1939 had actually fallen below the national average. This suggests that there were particularly serious inbuilt rigidities in the Scottish economy: and that seemed to be confirmed again after the Second World War when unemployment north of the border, though temporarily wiped out as a serious social

[22] Wales was very much worse off, with an unemployment rate in excess of 20 per cent for a whole decade after 1928, rising to almost a third in 1931–3: her position *vis-à-vis* Scotland had scarcely changed by 1939.

problem, and standing in Scotland at a mere 2.9 per cent, was never-theless twice the UK average.

What kind of a living did this unfamiliar, depressed Scotland pro-vide for its inhabitants after 1918? There was certainly slippage in Scotland's share of UK national income. We have suggested that in the first decade of the century Scotland probably earned at least 95 per cent of the British average. A. D. Campbell's calculations are avail-able from 1924, and suggest a figure for the period to 1950 averaging at best around 92 per cent of the British equivalent, and dropping to as low as 87 per cent in 1931–3.[23] He attributed the low share of Scotland after 1945 to the inferior level of earnings, the higher rate of unemployment and the smaller proportion of income earners in the total population: 'the deficiency due to the low level of wage-earnings was more than twice the size of the deficiency caused by the higher rate of employment and between one and two times greater than the deficiency due to the relatively low proportion of wage-earners'.[24] In the interwar years, of course, the contribution of unem-ployment would have been relatively greater, but that of the burden of unearning dependants less.

Campbell found the lower level of earnings to be common both to salaries and wages, but it was especially marked in salaries. This was partly because of the growth in external control of business by companies operating from England (or even from abroad after 1945), which had tended to concentrate the best-paid top jobs and most enterprising middle managers in the south, thus depressing the aver-age salary level.[25] The lower level of wage earnings could not, by 1950, be attributed to lower wage rates in Scotland, as it could a hundred years before: trade-union strength from 1914 onwards has resulted in progressive erosion of differentials both between Scotland and England and between different cities and regions within Scot-land.[26] Rather it was due to a high proportion of Scottish workers concentrating in what were becoming, by 1950, low-pay and low-productivity sections of industries, like Dundee jute and Border

---

[23]   A. D. Campbell, 'Income', in Cairncross, ed., Scottish Economy, pp. 46–64, contains slightly lower 'preliminary estimates', suggesting an average of around 90 per cent. The estimates quoted here are from his article 'Changes in Scottish Incomes, 1924–1949', Economic Journal, 65 (1955), pp. 225–40; but in fact the lower figure corresponds best with Gavin McCrone's findings for personal income per head in 1949–51, Regional Policy in Britain (1969), p. 163.

[24]   Campbell, 'Income', p. 56.

[25]   See J. Scott and M. Hughes, The Anatomy of Scottish Capital (1980).

[26]   D. J. Robertson, 'Wages', in Cairncross, ed., Scottish Economy, pp. 149–69.

hosiery among textiles, and heavy rather that light engineering on Clydeside.

The relative fortunes of salaries and incomes – and by implication those of the middle and working classes – also varied.[27] Between 1924 and 1929 the total of Scottish wage income remained stagnant but the total of salary income rose by 10 per cent. Both then dropped to 1933, but then increased in money terms to 1949, by about two and a half times, total wage income actually growing about a fifth more than total salary income.[28]

It was, however, very easy in these years, as since, to be over-impressed by tartan Jeremiahs of press and hustings who bemoaned the failure of Scotland to 'keep up with English prosperity' – by which they usually meant the prosperity of the English south-east. In real terms Scottish incomes rose by about 20 per cent even in the depression years 1924–37, and by about 40 per cent over the whole period 1929–50 – making possible a very substantial improvement in the general standard of living. By 1950, though it was undeniable that Scottish personal incomes were fully 10 per cent below those of the UK as a whole, they were actually no worse than those in the north of England, and a good deal better than those in Wales or south-west England: they were a third above those of Northern Ireland.[29] It is easy to have some sympathy with those civil servants who maintained that what the Scots had become most skilled at manufacturing since the First World War was a stream of complaints. Whether these appeared justified depended largely on whether you were sitting comfortably at Westminster or on a slightly harder seat in Scotland. But everyone was better off than had been dreamt possible in 1850, or even thought likely in 1900.

---

[27] Campbell, 'Changes in Scottish Incomes', p. 226.

[28] In an intriguing article, 'An Index of the Poor and Rich in Scotland, 1861–1961', *Scottish Journal of Political Economy*, 18 (1971), pp. 49–67, Lee Solow argues that evidence from housing (the number of rooms occupied by each family) indicates that relative inequality decreased only by 5–10 per cent from 1861 to 1901, but has accelerated until 'today's inequality is but half that of a century ago'. The point is interesting, but as council house building policy has become the main determinant of house size in Scotland by the middle of the twentieth century it would be hard to accept this as any measure of the inequality of wealth distribution.

[29] McCrone, *Regional Policy*, p. 163, gives the following estimates of personal income per head in the British regions outside the south-east in 1949–50, as percentages of the UK average: Scotland and northern England, 90 per cent; north-west England, 100 per cent; Wales, 81 per cent; south-west England, 82 per cent; Northern Ireland, 58 per cent.

II

The major feature of Scottish political life in the first half of the century after 1850 was the loyalty of the voter to the Great Liberal Party. It was as much a sociological as a political phenomenon.[30] Liberalism in Scotland, even more obviously than in England, was a coalition of groups who often had manifestly opposing interests, and occasionally opposed each other at the polls, especially where the risk of a Tory taking the seat was small. The social apex of the Liberals was formed by the Whigs, heroes of 1832, aristocrats and gentlemen, strongly represented in the legal profession: in fact, in social terms they were not obviously different from the backbone of Scottish Tory support. The Whigs instinctively believed that the extension of the franchise had always gone far enough; they deplored ideas on licensing reform; they were against meddling with the church. As time passed their influence declined, but for many years they were in great demand as candidates for constituencies where their type of Liberal was heavily outnumbered: Glasgow, for example, the largest and most loyal Liberal conurbation in Britain, long preferred gentlemen and orators to be their representatives. Anyone too obviously provincial in speech or outlook would have embarrassed them.

The middle-class radical Liberals were epitomised by their distinguished leader Duncan McLaren (MP for Edinburgh and brother-in-law of John Bright), self-made man, dissenter, temperance reformer, who had come up the hard way through municipal politics and made a reputation first as Lord Provost. The middle-class radicals were characteristically small businessmen and free churchmen; and it was a distinct advantage to the Liberal party that after the Disruption of 1843 a minority of the Protestant population claimed allegiance to the old Church of Scotland. The political divide in Scotland often split exactly on the line of church allegiance: in the election of 1868, 1,221 Church of Scotland clergy out of 1,288 voted Conservative, 1,468 dissenting Presbyterian clergy out of 1,536 voted Liberal.[31] The radicals were anxious (ferociously anxious after 1876) to disestablish the Church of Scotland, to Gladstone's considerable embarrassment.

---

[30] The following three paragraphs owe much to I. G. C. Hutchison, 'Politics and Society in Mid-Victorian Glasgow 1846–1886' (unpublished PhD thesis, Edinburgh University, 1974), now incorporated in his recent book, *A Political History of Scotland, 1832–1924: Parties, Elections and Issues* (Edinburgh, 1985).

[31] A. J. Drummond and J. Bulloch, *The Church in Late Victorian Scotland, 1874–1900*, *(Edinburgh, 1978)*, p. 90.

They wished for anti-drink legislation, holding that most poverty was caused by intemperance. On the other hand they considered the factory acts unnecessary, and the idea of allowing trade unions to picket, absurd. They also deplored the idea of non-sectarian Board-school education which both the Whigs and the working-class Liberals were keen on.

The working-class Liberals, the 'Lib-Labs', were the third main faction, without a vote before 1868, though certainly not without influence. Their candidates in Scotland seldom reached the ticket in national elections and not often in local elections, but the Lib-Labs were the dominant force in the trades councils. The politically active fractions of the working class were the skilled men, stubborn in defence of trades-union rights and ready to press for extensions of the mines and factories acts or workmen's compensation legislation, urging extensions of the franchise and supporting the Whigs over education. Though often individually strong believers in the temperance movement, they were 'moral suasionists', anxious to reform by example and persuasion rather than by legislation. They were, on the other hand, allies of the middle-class radicals in efforts to keep down the poor rates, believing no less fervently than McLaren that a man should take care of his own social security by the systematic practice of thrift. The unskilled Irish voter, whose earnings were so low or irregular that thrift was irrelevant, were also normally Liberals, labouring under the belief that Gladstone was about to grant Ireland home rule. Though heavily discriminated against in the electoral system (the simple rule in the Second Reform Act that a householder could not exercise his vote unless he had already paid his rates regularly disenfranchised two-thirds of the Irish householders in Glasgow) the Irish were not entirely without muscle. In 1874, a year when other working-class Liberals were disillusioned with their party over its reluctance to legalise picketing, the Glasgow Irish decision to vote Tory as a protest against Liberal coercion over the water resulted in victory for a single Conservative, their only gain in that city between 1832 and 1886.

In these circumstances it is easy to see what occasionally tore Liberals apart, but more difficult to identify what (apart from religion) held them together behind the banners of free trade and reform. There were perhaps three main elements. The first was reference to a common ideology of 'standing on your own two feet' which the lawyer, the big employer, the self-made shopkeeper and the respectable workingman could all admire. John Vincent writes primarily with reference to England, but his description of Liberal ideology applies with equal force to a Scotland where thriftiness was next to Godliness:

For the nineteenth century man, the mark or note of being human was that he should provide for his own family, have his own religion and politics and call no man his master. It is as a mode of entry into this full humanity that the Gladstonian Liberal Party most claims our respect ... the great moral idea of Liberalism was manliness, the rejection of the various forms of patronage, from soup and blankets upwards, which had formerly been the normal part of the greatest number.[32]

It was Gladstone's great gift, or trick, to appear to embody these impalpable yet vital 'principles of right'.

The second bond was nationalism. 'I am a Liberal because I am a Scotchman' exclaimed Taylor Innes in 1887, summing up the sentiment of many of his fellow party loyalists.[33] The identification of the Conservatives with imperialism, the Church of England and state interference in ecclesiastical affairs in Scotland before the Disruption, and the opposite identification of the Liberals with sympathy for nationalist movements in Europe, for a measure of home rule for Ireland and greater respect for the traditions of the provinces, tended to line up Scottish identity with Liberalism; in fact, Gladstone was as slow as Disraeli or any other nineteenth-century Prime Minister in recognising that Scotland might have special legislative needs due to its heritage of different law and tradition. Scottish nationalism in the nineteenth century was a mild phenomenon in the sense that few wanted home rule, or wanted it fervently, but it nevertheless expressed a powerful ethnic consciousness, hostile towards those who in matters great and small unthinkingly regarded Scotland as part of England. It was this sentiment the Liberals so effectively harnessed, and success bred success: the more the Liberals swept the board in Scotland, the more they were regarded as the 'natural' Scottish party.

The third and most interesting bond among the Liberals was class consciousness, surprising for a party that proclaimed the brotherhood of man, but perhaps not more surprising than the same juxtaposition among socialists, though they defined terms in a different way. The

[32]   J. R. Vincent, *The Formation of the Liberal Party, 1857–68* (1966), pp. xiii, xiv. This passage is quoted in Joan M. Smith, 'Commonsense Thought and Working Class Consciousness: Some Aspects of the Glasgow and Liverpool Labour Movements in the Early Years of the Twentieth Century' (unpublished PhD thesis, Edinburgh University, 1981), p. 96. I am deeply indebted to this work for much of the illustration in the next few pages.

[33]   H. J. Hanham, *The Scottish Political Tradition* (Edinburgh, 1964), p. 23.

Liberals sometimes liked to express it as 'the class versus the masses' meaning by 'the class' the body of privileged landowners and their toadies and by 'the masses' everybody else – the people. This is how Gladstone put it in a speech in Glasgow:

You are opposed throughout the country by a compact army, and that army is the case of the class against the masses . . . and what I observe is this, when a profession is highly privileged, when a privilege is publicly endowed, it is in these cases you will find that almost the whole of the class and the professions are against us.[34]

It was a formula that could powerfully unite the middle-class radicals with the working-class Liberals in a common hatred, though it ultimately alienated most of the Whigs. It was confirmed and inflamed every time a landlord denied the Free Kirk ground for a church, and every time evictions swept men from the glens to the towns. It also covered a multitude of shortcomings in the economic system. In 1884 the Glasgow Trades Council circularised all known trades councils in the British Isles for their opinions on the causes of the depression of 1879: the unanimous response was that the 'land laws', the special privileges of the landed aristocracy, were responsible – though the Glasgow Council itself astutely observed that that could hardly be the whole explanation, as the depression had also involved the USA which had no land laws.[35]

The great reform processions of the trades in Edinburgh and Glasgow, especially those of 1866 and 1884 on the eve of the Second and Third Reform Bills, were marvellous visual demonstrations of the character of proletarian Liberalism. They at once encapsulated class hostility against the landlords, and were expressions of craft pride and a sense of belonging to a coherent tradition of reforming zeal that stretched back at least a century. The Glasgow demonstration of 1884, intended to put pressure on an obstructive Tory House of Lords, involved 64,000 in the procession and another 200,000 gathering to greet them on Glasgow Green. They carried countless pictures of Gladstone and many of Bright, a flag from 1774, banners from 1832 and from Chartist days, and models and mottoes old and new. The French polishers, for example, carried a miniature wardrobe first borne in 1832, and a flag with a motto 'The French polishers will polish off the Lords and make the cabinet shine'. The upholsterers had a sofa first carried in 1832, the potters a model kiln with the words

---

[34] Quoted in Smith, 'Commonsense Thought', p. 98.   [35] *Ibid.*, pp. 105–6.

'we'll fire them up', the sawyers a banner with the device of two circular saws and the words 'The crooked Lords – we'll cut them straight'. The executive of the Scottish Land Restoration League passed with the motto 'God gave the land to the people, Lords took the land from the people'. The employees of Charles Tennant carried a dozen flags and banners, with a model of a cooper at work made in 1754 and borne in the demonstrations of 1832, 1866 and 1883. The fleshers simply led an ox with a placard round its neck, 'the House of Lords'. The basic message was clear – the 'class' obstructed reform, the 'masses' are here to demand it.[36]

In fact the demonstration of 1884 represented almost the last occasion at which it would have been possible to rally such a strong, almost unanimous show of working-class support for Liberalism. The Gladstonian party was challenged in 1886 on the right by the Liberal Unionists over the Irish question, and on the left by the Crofters' party, and, two years later, by Keir Hardie in the Midlanark election which led directly to the formation of the Scottish Labour party and then in 1893 to the foundation in Bradford of the ILP. The Liberal Unionists attracted many who had had increasing doubts not only over Ireland but over excessive democratic tendencies and sectarian enthusiasm for disestablishment. They did not do as well in Scotland as in England, but they helped to give the Tories their first national electoral victory in 1900, and in doing so shook the image of Scotland as a one-party state. For the first time substantial numbers of business-men were voting against the Liberal party, and in 1912 the Liberal Unionists formally merged with the Conservatives to form a Scottish Unionist party.

Of the challenges on the left, that from agrarian radicalism had some more immediate success but was far less serious than the socialist challenge in the long run. Four highland seats fell to the Crofters' party in 1886: the party originated from the campaign to force concessions over land legislation from the Liberals, and has some claim to be considered the first mass working-class party in Great Britain. But the Crofters' party did not last beyond the 1890s – the Highlanders started to vote Liberal when it became clear the Whig landowners were turning Tory.

The challenge of urban socialism was another matter. Keir Hardie had little success in 1888 and there were no Labour MPs until two

---

[36] *Ibid.*, pp. 188ff.

were returned in 1906. But their relative electoral failure belied the public excitement the socialists created from the 1890s onwards. Churches, municipal authorities and the political parties all in different ways tried to make a fitting response to the allure of the left, the churches by parading for the first time an active social conscience, and town councils by emphasising their schemes for municipalisation (and calling forth a ratepayers' backlash), the political parties by schemes for welfare legislation. By the early twentieth century the ILP had made considerable inroads into Glasgow municipal politics, and had nineteen members on the town council at the outbreak of war.

The success of the socialist movement can be explained partly in terms of the dynamism and talent of the young leadership who had the world at their feet – R. E. Muirhead, Tom Johnston, John Maclean, James Connolly and John Wheatley made the Scottish Liberal leaders of their generation look grey old bores. Socialism came in many shades of red, from the purer Marxism of bodies that had evolved from Hyndman's original London-based SDF (the SSF of Connolly, the BSP of Maclean and the syndicalist-inclined SLP) to the evolutionary socialism of the ILP.[37] The ILP, however, was the group with the widest appeal to the working class, precisely because it shared in, and gloried in, the political and cultural heritage of Liberalism at least as much as in the new socialist revelation. The leading Scottish socialists, for example, were almost all personal abstainers.[38] The ILP in particular believed the cause of socialism was the cause of morality and reason, so their favourite weapons were the *Forward* newspaper (founded in 1906 with Tom Johnston as editor) and socialist evening classes,

[37] The SSF was the Scottish Socialist Federation: 'Despite its name this was mainly a local Edinburgh body, and was a product of the split which had occurred in the British Social-Democratic Federation in 1884. The Edinburgh section eschewed the factious concerns of its metropolitan leaders and constituted itself as an autonomous "Scottish Socialist Federation"'; it re-affiliated to the SDF in 1895: O. D. Edwards and B. Ransome, eds., *James Connolly, Selected Political Writings* (1973), pp. 15–16. The BSP (British Socialist Party) was a London-based development of the mainstream SDF, founded in 1912. The SLP (Socialist Labour Party) was a Scottish-based breakaway group that left the SDF (with Connolly's help) in 1903: it became attracted to the 'industrial unionist' ideas of Daniel De Leon and had considerable importance despite its sectarianism and small membership. 'There can have been scarcely a single person involved in the foundation of the Communist Party of Great Britain who was not, at some time, influenced by the SLP and its literature': Walter Kendall, *The Revolutionary Movement in Britain 1900–21* (1969), p. 69.

[38] Out of fifty-two Labour MPs elected before 1945, thirty-two were abstainers, two were not, and for eighteen their habit is not known: W. Knox, ed., *Scottish Labour Leaders, 1918–39: A Biographical Dictionary* (Edinburgh, 1984), p. 23.

rather that the barricade and the political strike. In the best radical Liberal tradition they hated the landlords: Tom Johnston's *Our Noble Families*, a bitter lampooning attack on the acquisition of hereditary wealth by the aristocracy, was both a best-seller and a much more venomous criticism than anything *Forward* ever launched on industrial capitalism, although from 1908 the newspaper was clearly identifying the capitalist as the enemy alongside the landlord. Like the Liberals, the ILP believed in 'Home Rule All Round'. And they believed in the march of progress as much as the Liberals did, or even more. Indeed, in a sense the party was the inevitable outcome of the question that the Glasgow Trades Council asked itself at a meeting immediately after the achievement of the Third Reform Bill – where do we go from here in the crusade to widen the political representation of the people? For middle-class radicals and Whigs, 1884 was the end of the road: for working-class Liberals it seemed to be the beginning of real political representation, but only if they began to work outside the party.

It is doubtful, however, if socialism would have made even as much headway as it did before the First World War unless its basic message to the urban working class, that capitalists were with the landlords and against the masses, had not struck root in ground made more fertile by altered working-class experience. Almost certainly, at the end of the nineteenth and early twentieth centuries, the perceived gulf between capital and labour grew wider, and the gap within the working class between craftsman and labourer smaller. It was more difficult for a journeyman to become a small employer, work became more rushed and demanded less skill in occupations like mining, engineering and shipbuilding which were the backbone of the economy, unemployment when it came affected skilled as well as unskilled, units of production grew larger, unions more popular and defensive, management more professional and aggressive. It is easy to exaggerate the extent of this, and one does well to remember that most of the working class that had the vote continued normally to use it to identify with the traditional consensus and to vote Liberal at general elections. But the trend towards heightened class consciousness was undoubtedly there.

It took concrete form in, for example, the wave of unemployment that struck the economy in the depression of 1908. Glasgow was one of the most seriously affected cities in the UK: *The Times* reported 16,000–18,000 on the verge of starvation in Govan parish alone by

September. The SDF and ILP organised a Right to Work demonstration which was reminiscent, on a smaller scale, of 1884: 35,000 marched, 'each organisation carried a banner, or symbols of its trade, craft or purpose', the joiners, for example, bearing an 1832 banner with the motto 'they are unworthy of freedom who hope for it from hands other than their own'. But in the speeches on Glasgow Green the message was not praise for the Great Liberal Party. John Hill, a boilermakers' leader, expressed the despair of his craft in these words:

Only a few years ago unemployment had no terrors for well-organised skilled trades ... now the tables are turned. With improved machinery our craft is at a discount, and a boy from school now tends a machine which does the work of three men ... It is mostly machine minders who are wanted, and a line from some well-known Liberal or Tory certifying that you are not an agitator or a Socialist is the chief recommendation in the shipbuilding and engineering trades. Thus today we find the ranks of the unemployed largely recruited by men of intellect, men of genius and men of high character and independent means.[39]

It is against this background of rising insecurity and resentment by the skilled men that the cataclysmic change in class politics that accompanied and followed the First World War must be understood.

The events of Red Clydeside during and immediately after the First World War attained such fame, or notoriety, that it is easy to misinterpret them.[40] For some of those caught up in the peak of the excitement on either side Scotland seemed to be on the point of spontaneous combustion. Of the demonstrations and confrontations with the police in George Square, Glasgow, during the Forty Hours Strike of 1919, William Gallacher, the strikers' leader exclaimed afterwards: 'A rising was expected. A rising should have taken place. The workers were ready and able to effect it; the leadership had never thought of it.' The Secretary for Scotland told a meeting of the war cabinet at the time: 'In his opinion it was more clear than ever that it was a misnomer to call the situation in Glasgow a strike – it was a Bolshevist rising.'[41]

---

[39] Smith, 'Commonsense Thought', pp. 319–24.
[40] For useful accounts from differing standpoints see Kendall, *Revolutionary Movement*; James Hinton, *The First Shop Stewards' Movement* (1973); Iain McLean 'Popular Protest and Public Order, Red Clydeside 1915–1919' in R. Quinault and J. Stevenson, eds., *Popular Protest and Public Order* (1974), pp. 215–39; R. K. Middlemas, *The Clydesiders* (1965); C. Harvie, *No Gods and Precious Few Heroes, Scotland 1914–1980* (Edinburgh, 1981), chap. 1; J. Melling, 'Scottish Industrialists and the Changing Character of Class Relations in the Clyde Region, *c.* 1880–1918', in T. Dickson, ed., *Capital and Class in Scotland* (Edinburgh, 1982).
[41] Quoted in McLean, 'Popular Protest', pp. 215, 231.

It is easy to show that these interpretations of that particular event were totally wrong. Gallacher, who had reacted on the spot with horror rather than with revolutionary enthusiasm to the police confrontation, found that the strikers had lost their taste for praxis and returned to work within a few days. The government, in turn, had simply been misled by the head of the Special Branch, Basil Thomson, whose profession it was to find reds under every bed. But much of the writing on Red Clydeside since has been dominated by those wishing to prove the depth and spontaneity of revolutionary class consciousness on the Clyde, or by those who, conversely, wish to play the whole thing down and suggest that there was no fundamental radicalism or affection for socialism on the part of the working class.

The events themselves were comparatively simple, and limited in number. During the war, and mainly between February 1915 and April 1916, there were a series of strikes in the munitions works along the Clyde that hinged partly on the question of wage levels but more on the attempt under the Munitions Act to bring in women to do the work of skilled men in the engineering shops for the duration of the war – the 'dilution' question. These strikes mainly involved the engineers themselves, and only on one significant occasion (in August 1915 at Fairfields) brought in the shipyard workers. Although the innovations struck at the heart of craft privilege, ASE officials were reluctant to act and leadership fell into the hands of an unofficial body of shop stewards, the Clyde workers committee, heavily influenced by activists from the SLP and described as 'mostly revolutionary syndicalists of one kind or another'. The strikes led to a visit from two cabinet ministers at Christmas 1915 attempting to explain dilution:

The visit spectacularly misfired. On Christmas Day, an impatient audience of shop stewards listened to Arthur Henderson explaining at some length the justice of the war on behalf of the 'brave and independent' Belgians ('Oh heavens! How long have we to suffer this?') and to Lloyd George asserting with passion that the responsibility of a Minister of the Crown in a great war was not a light one ('The money's good', and laughter).[42]

Forward printed an accurate account of the meeting, and an outraged Lloyd George had it instantly suppressed. The government used the strong arm of the emergency laws on several occasions in the next three months, suppressing two more socialist newspapers, imprisoning several who had been involved in their publication, including

[42] *Ibid.*, p. 218.

Gallacher and the socialist educator John Maclean, and deporting from the Clyde area ten CWC leaders for fomenting a strike at Beardmore's Parkhead forge. This did not end the tradition of militancy, but from then until the end of the war threats of serious industrial trouble were bought off by concessions and wage rises.

There were two other related sets of events during the war. One was the rent strikes of 1915, led very effectively by ILP women in the shipyard and engineering districts where the rents of working-class tenements had been pushed to exorbitant heights by firms of factors acting for small private landlords: the protests were so menacing and effective that the government introduced wartime rent control to secure peace in an area already rocked by industrial trouble.[43] The second set of events were the demonstrations of 1917 and 1918 (still more alarming to the government) in favour of the Russian Revolution and urging a negotiated peace. On May Day 1918 some 100,000 struck work to attend a meeting on Glasgow Green, the largest contingents coming from the engineers, the railwaymen, the ILP branches and the 'No Conscription Fellowship'.[44] The government replied by arresting (and imprisoning for the second time) John Maclean (who had been appointed Soviet Consul in Glasgow), and by police raids to destroy printing machinery at the SLP headquarters where translations of Lenin's pamphlets were being published. More significantly, however, the revolutionary socialists like Maclean and the SLP proved quite unable to organise any prolonged industrial action against the war, and the ILP also failed to provide a united front about the best way to end it. John Wheatley of the ILP characteristically declared himself 'opposed to the use of armed force in the establishment of Socialism in this country because I regard it as immoral and impracticable', which indicated how completely the largest faction in Red Clydeside was committed to the evolutionary line and democratic processes.[45]

Immediately after the war, Red Clydeside reached its climax (or its anti-climax) in the Forty Hours Strike of January 1919; the police charge in George Square was followed next day by the occupation of the area by English troops (dispatched north on the overnight sleepers by Bonar Law against the judgment of Winston Churchill),

---

[43] J. Melling, 'Clydeside Housing and the Evolution of State Rent Control 1900–1939', in J. Melling, ed., *Housing, Social Policy and the State* (1980), pp. 139–67.
[44] Smith, 'Commonsense Thought', pp. 506–9.
[45] Quoted, *ibid.*, pp. 512–13.

deploying machine gun nests on the roofs and tanks in the streets. The cabinet had overreacted, but the strike failed to get official backing and the whole thing was called off, following the arrest of the leadership, after sixteen days.

What did it all amount to? It is easy to see that the government and the would-be local Bolsheviks were wrong to imagine Glasgow as a second St Petersburg. But it is equally wrong to see in Red Clydeside nothing of fundamental significance. The conduct of the First World War presented to the workers an extraordinary demonstration of ruling-class stupidity and selfishness. It was, however, commenced with an enthusiasm that the working class shared to the full. Harry McShane, one of the socialists who opposed the war from the start, recalled its early days:

It was believed that the war would last six weeks, six months at the most, and then the British army would march past the Kaiser in Berlin to celebrate the British victory. Nobody even thought about removing the Kaiser; he was just going to be there to see the Germans defeated . . . A terrible war fever developed. Men rushed to join the army hoping that the war wouldn't be all over by the time they got to the front; they had to march in civilian clothes because there weren't enough uniforms to go round. Many young people, particularly those who were unemployed, were caught up in the adventure of the thing. On every hoarding there was a picture of Kitchener . . . pointing his finger and saying 'Your Country Needs You'. There he was, and then along came daft middle-class women with white feathers trying to drive young men into the army.[46]

There is plenty of evidence that at the outbreak the Scots were especially enthusiastic. The Highland Light Infantry was largely recruited from the 'pals battalions' of the slums of Glasgow; one battalion was recruited solely from the employees of the corporation tramways by their manager, taking his men to war rather in the spirit of an eighteenth-century chief leading his tenants in battle. Over a quarter of all Scottish miners joined the forces, and two-thirds of the fishermen.[47]

With the beginning of the great slaughter at the end of 1915, however, and especially with the campaign on the Somme and the introduction of conscription next year, disillusion set in. Glasgow lost 18,000 dead, probably nearly 10 per cent of the adult male population: Scotland as a whole lost between 75,000 and 100,000.[48] The blame

[46] McShane and Smith, *No Mean Fighter*, p. 62.
[47] Harvie, *No Gods*, pp. 10–15.
[48] *Ibid.*, p. 11.

was put where it belonged: on discredited politicians and ineffective generals; on a church which blessed the war and which met tragedy with hollow sentiment;[49] on employers who used the national crisis to make excessive profits and to introduce new work practices which raised productivity but equally deliberately were designed to destroy long-held craft privilege; on local rationing committees who used their powers to feather their own nests. For example, when margarine was rationed in 1917, the committee charged with distributing supplies in Clydebank (characteristically dominated by local tradesmen), allocated eight out of fifteen hundredweight to one retailer, who happened to be the convener, but only three hundredweight to the co-ops, although they had 60 per cent of existing trade.[50] Yet it was impossible to blame individuals – there were too many of them: it began to be perceived as the corruption of a class, of 'the system'.

So the First World War did result in the appreciable heightening of class consciousness, especially among skilled workers. In a sense it confirmed their growing sense of doubt about the ultimate benevolence of 'the system', and gave credence to the socialists' identification of the Liberals as humbugs and of capitalism as fundamentally exploitative. But the revolution hoped for under the ILP version of socialism, while basic enough in that it envisaged limited programmes of nationalisation, state aid for council housing, and home rule for Scotland, also owed a great deal to the old Liberal radical faith that when the people ('the masses') came to impose their will upon Parliament, the system would, in a fairly unspecific but quite sweeping way, be altered for the better. Few expected that it would be necessary to change parliamentary democracy itself, or use force to attain their ends, or to abolish property. It would be enough for working men to capture Parliament and a brave new world would follow.

The first fruits of this new mood were seen after the Representation of the People Act of 1918 had greatly increased the working-class electorate, and after the old political parties had further discredited themselves by postwar infighting. In 1922, twenty-nine Labour MPs and a Communist were elected out of Scotland's total of seventy-two, gaining 33.6 per cent of the votes cast compared to 28.9 per cent

[49] P. Matheson, 'Scottish War Sermons', *Records of the Scottish Church History Society*, 17 (1972), pp. 203–13. The clerical principal of Aberdeen University described the war as 'a sacrament, and a sacrament in the full sense of that name as we Scots have been brought up to understand it': *Ibid.*, p. 207.

[50] J. Kinloch and J. Butt, *History of the Scottish Co-Operative Wholesale Society Limited* (Glasgow, 1981), p. 277.

for the left-wing parties in England.[51] What was distinctive about the Scottish MPs, however, was the reputation of the ILP Clydesiders led by James Maxton, John Wheatley and Tom Johnston as men of the left who kept themselves deliberately apart. Beatrice Webb said of Tom Johnston:

The dour Scot objects to any social intercourse; we are to meet only at public meetings and committees and in the lobbies of the House of Commons. The private houses of rich members of the Party are anathema, and any club to which these members and their wives belong is almost equally objectionable.[52]

The group certainly brought an unfamiliar element of proletarian rage into the House of Commons, most famously during a debate on the Scottish estimates when Maxton called the Tories in general and Sir Frederick Banbury in particular, 'murderers' for threatening the lives of children by making cuts in health expenditure by local authorities. He was suspended, with three other Clydesiders who supported him, after he refused to apologise.

From 1922 onwards Labour went from strength to strength, though not in a linear direction. Thus their numbers were reduced to seven in 1931 (though on the same percentage share of the vote as in 1922) and they did not obtain an absolute majority of Scottish seats until 1945. But even at their low point, gains were being made in other directions: the capture of Glasgow City Council in 1933 was of enormous significance, and after the Second World War all the Scottish cities apart from Edinburgh came normally to have Labour majorities on their councils. Other left-wing groups had very little success after the failure of the General Strike, though William Gallacher captured Fife coalfield for the Communist party in the general election of 1935 and held the seat for fifteen years, and the Communists remained strong in the trades councils, some unions and a few local authorities, the 'Little Moscows' in Fife and the Vale of Leven.[53] They certainly cast a red glow over the west, Baedeker in 1937 interrupting its description of the Firth of Clyde with the observation that 'Clydeside is the chief stronghold of Communism in Great Britain'.[54] Meanwhile, the Liberal party, already reduced to eight seats by 1924, was not represented at all by 1945. The real change was that 'Good Old Labour'

[51] J. G. Kellas, *The Scottish Political System* (Cambridge, 1973), pp. 106–7.
[52] B. Webb, *Diaries 1924–32* (1956), p. 12.
[53] S. Macintyre, *Little Moscows: Communism and Working-class Militancy in Inter-War Britain* (1980).
[54] K. Baedeker, *Great Britain: Handbook for Travellers*, 9th edn (1937), p. 577.

had replaced 'The Great Liberal Party' in the hearts of the Scottish working class, while the middle class had gone unequivocally Tory. In that sense class politics had clearly arrived.

The character and appeal of 'Good Old Labour' had, however, become by the start of the second half of the twentieth century, different in several important respects from that of the old Clydesiders. For one thing, commitment to home rule for Scotland had gone out of the window: in 1918 such nationalist sentiment had been not merely an important inheritance of the ILP from Liberalism but, since Scotland was more obviously left-wing than England, an attractive way to achieve 'socialism in one country'. With the failure of Home Rule Bills sponsored by Scottish Labour members in 1924 and 1929, the collapse of the export-oriented economy in the 1920s and 1930s, and finally the achievement of a majority Labour government at Westminster in 1945, it seemed pointless to try to go it alone.[55]

Tom Johnston's later career exemplifies some of the changes. He was selected by Churchill to be Secretary of State for Scotland in the Second World War, partly on the grounds that the erstwhile poacher from Red Clydeside would make a good gamekeeper on labour matters – as he did. Johnston's politics had become those of the consensus, a significant throwback to the Liberal roots of the ILP: he was to say in his autobiography that he regarded himself as a 'moderate extremist', and one who believed 'that in co-operation and mutual aid and not in fratricidal strife can we win through to material plenty for all, and to a spiritual and cultural development and greatness for each of us'.[56] His commitment to home rule of the Scots by the Scots had become transmuted to a commitment to organise Scottish advisory committees to strengthen the hand of the Secretary of State in governing Scotland and dealing with London. He had moved from democratic socialist to quango-man. His successor in turn found himself bitterly opposed to the home rule movement when in 1949 John MacCormick's Scottish Covenant Association marshalled two million signatures to a document calling for a Scottish Parliament within the framework of the United Kingdom 'with adequate legislative authority in Scottish affairs'. Scottish Labour members, once in power, found themselves not opposing the system, but becoming it.

The class war and the nationalist tradition in Labour politics was

[55]   M. Keating and D. Bleiman, *Labour and Scottish Nationalism* (1979).
[56]   T. Johnston, *Memories* (1952), p. 249.

thus heavily played down in the 1940s compared to the 1920s. Nevertheless, the power of the Labour party in Scotland rested unequivocally on two distinctively Scottish class facts – living in a council house and the threat of unemployment. Labour became the party of housing and jobs.

The importance of housing to the Labour cause dates back to the initiative of Glasgow Trades Council in 1900 in forming a Scottish Housing Association which 'made a clear call for state provision of housing in 1908' and to the ILP campaign to force the council to build and let at rates subsidised from the profits of the municipally owned tramways £8 Cottages for Glasgow Citizens, to quote the title of a celebrated pamphlet written by John Wheatley in 1913.[57] The connection was strengthened in the First World War by the rent strikes and the case for government intervention made impelling by the Royal Commission on Housing in Scotland of 1917, which revealed how 'the people of Glasgow were packed into their homes to a degree unimaginable even in the larger English cities'; there were over two persons per room in 55.7 per cent of Glasgow's houses but in only 9.4 per cent in English cities.[58]

These pressures were a major part of the Housing and Town Planning Act (Scotland) of 1919, which introduced state subsidies, greatly strengthened in 1924 when John Wheatley became the Minister of Health in the first Labour government. The effect of this and subsequent legislation was that council house building and slum clearance were begun in earnest, council houses being constructed in Glasgow at eight times the rate of private houses in the interwar years, and after the Second World War the private sector was for a time deliberately denied materials and building permits to allow council housing to increase its share still more substantially. The end result was that by the late 1960s Scotland was building more of her housing in the public sector than any other country in Europe, Russia included.[59] The verminous old slums had been destroyed; new housing estates of low rent, low quality construction, poor amenity and novel types of social problem had been created – and the inhabitants voted Labour to keep things as they were.

Labour's reputation as defender of jobs developed more slowly,

---

[57]   S. Damer, 'State, Class and Housing: Glasgow, 1885 – 1919', in Melling, ed., Housing, Social Policy, p.90.
[58]   S. G. Checkland, The Upas Tree (Glasgow, 1977), p. 20.
[59]   D. Niven, The Development of Housing in Scotland (1979), p. 34.

as during the interwar years employment vanished from the heavy industries so rapidly that neither left nor right had any clear notion of what to do about it, other than providing the palliatives of dole money. The initial steps to attract new industry to Scotland were taken under the National government in the 1930s with the passage of the Special Areas (Development and Improvement) Act of 1934, and after the Second World War the Labour government used planning controls to determine the location of industry in a more positive way. Although the great age of pumping money into dying industries was to come in the 1960s and 1970s, the trend was firmly set by 1945 against the free market and towards central direction. A vote for Labour was coming to be seen as a vote for the right to live where you had always lived and to work where you had always worked. The welfare state and the mixed economy would join hands to look after you.

The results of all this look odd, in the long perspective. In the 1870s the working man voted Liberal to declare his sense of manhood, his detestation of patronage and his determination to control his own destiny; in the 1920s he voted Labour to declare a newly emphasised sense of class solidarity and again to express his determination to control his own destiny; by 1950 he voted Labour primarily to allow experts to keep the status quo slightly in his favour. A self-help ideology distrustful of the system survived until the mid-1920s and then became transmuted into one where the system was expected to help the self. The class animosities sanctioned by radical politicians changed between the Third Reform Bill and the First World War from anti-landlordism to anti-capitalism: but by the 1940s positive class animosities of any kind were regarded as 'fratricidal strife', bad form in political life. If there had been one individual among the Clydesiders who could perhaps have recalled the Scottish Labour movement back to its self-help and socialist traditions it was James Maxton, who survived until 1946. But he hopelessly isolated himself by withdrawing a remnant of the ILP from the Labour party after the disasters of 1931. The disaffiliated ILP and the Communists jointly organised the Hunger March among the unemployed in 1932 and 1933, but little substantive could be done outside the main movement.

The average Scot in his everyday non-political life, of course, had obviously not eschewed class animosities of a defensive kind: in industry, especially in the west of Scotland, the record of strikes, go-slows, restrictive practices and absenteeism remained extremely bad from

Table 3.5 *Percentage of Scottish population living in communities of different sizes, 1861–1951*

	1,000 +	5,000 +	50,000 +	500,000 +
1861	57.7	39.4	27.8	0.0
1891	70.6	53.5	32.2	14.0
1911	75.4	58.6	39.8	19.9
1931	80.1	63.1	43.6	22.6
1951	82.2	64.0	42.3	21.4

Source: Census of Scotland for years cited; M. W. Flinn, ed., *Scottish Population History from the 17th Century to the 1930s* (Cambridge, 1977), p. 313.

the 1920s onwards; management and labour's mutual distrust almost amounted to a suicide pact in a modern competitive economy. But in Scottish politics the fire in the belly had gone out, quenched by the interwar experience of unemployment and economic defeat and by the subsequent acceptance of Keynes and Beveridge as better mentors than Gladstone or Marx.

III

In this section we consider the towns. For the Registrar General for Scotland anyone living in a community of 1,000 souls is counted among the urbanised; for the editor of *Scottish Population History* only centres of 5,000 and over are satisfactorily described as towns; for other purposes it may be more relevant to know how many lived in settlements with many tens of thousands, or hundreds of thousands, of inhabitants. Table 3.5 lays out the Scottish data under various headings at selected dates.

From this it is plain that by any criteria rapid urbanisation was a marked feature of the second half of the nineteenth century, but that the rate of concentration into towns (especially large towns) has dramatically slowed since the First World War. Table 3.6 lays out the data for settlements of over 5,000 by geographical area and emphasises a second and no less striking feature – that the experience of urbanisation in Scotland has been exceptionally uneven over space as well as over time. Some regions remained very rural and urbanised late. In the predominantly rural far north, the Highlands and the Borders, while the proportion living in towns roughly tripled between 1861 and 1939, they were not even at the latter date even half as urbanised

Table 3.6 *Percentage of Scottish population living in communities of over 5,000, by geographical area, 1861–1951*

	Far north	High-lands	North-east	W. Low-lands	E. Low-lands	Borders
1861	7.0	6.3	21.7	62.2	41.6	9.9
1891	8.8	15.2	29.8	72.1	55.0	21.7
1911	10.6	18.6	39.9	72.2	59.3	25.2
1931	17.0	21.7	43.3	76.7	60.3	28.3
1951	18.8	21.1	44.5	74.4	64.1	28.7

Note: The 'geographical areas' are defined as containing the following former counties:
  Far north: Orkney, Shetland, Caithness
  Highlands: Sutherland, Ross and Cromarty, Inverness, Argyll, Bute
  North-east: Nairn, Moray, Banff, Aberdeen, Kincardine
  Western Lowlands: Dunbarton, Renfrew, Lanark, Ayr
  Eastern Lowlands: Perth, Angus, Fife, Kinross, Clackmannan, Stirling, East Lothian, Midlothian, West Lothian
  Borders: Berwick, Peebles, Selkirk, Roxburgh, Dumfries, Kirkcudbright, Wigtown.
Source: Flinn, ed., *Scottish Population History*, pp. 313–15.

Table 3.7 *Population of the six largest Scottish towns, 1861–1951* (000s)

	Glasgow	Edinburgh and Leith	Dundee	Aberdeen	Paisley	Greenock
1861	394.9	201.6	90.4	73.8	47.4	42.1
1891	565.0	328.9	153.1	121.6	66.4	63.1
1911	784.5	400.8	165.0	163.9	84.5	75.1
1931	1,088.5	439.0	175.6	167.3	86.4	78.9
1951	1,089.8	466.8	177.3	182.7	93.7	76.3

Notes: There are always substantial difficulties in estimating the true size of towns because of boundary changes, and different definitions could produce substantially different results; for example, the inclusion of the contiguous Abbey parish in Paisley in 1861 and of Govan and Partick in Glasgow in 1911 would have increased the population of both those cities by a fifth or more. As it is, the populations given here are of 'Parliamentary burghs', as defined at different census dates to 1911, and thereafter 'Entire County of City and Parish', as similarly defined.
Source: Census of Scotland for years cited.

as the western Lowlands had already been in 1861. In the industrial central belt the dominant experience was not coming to live in towns *per se*, but coming to live in towns of great size. Table 3.7 gives the population of the six largest towns at selected dates. By 1951, out of a total Scottish population of about 5,000,000, two-fifths lived in the densely developed Clyde basin. Of this, Glasgow's share was about 1,000,000, i.e. 21 per cent of the total population (London had only 8 per cent of the total population of England and Wales). While it has always been true that in Scotland a slightly smaller proportion of the total population lived in towns than in England, the really significant feature in Scotland has been these extremes of low levels of urbanisation in the north and south combined with very high levels in the centre.

Urbanisation, especially the headlong growth of Glasgow and other towns in the west, continued to pose enormous problems throughout the period, though the sense of panic which so often swept contemporaries when they considered the cities in the 1830s and 1840s receded in the decades that followed.

The formal machinery for governing the towns in the second half of the nineteenth century was hampered by its own complexity. It began by following the lines established by the burgh reform statutes of 1833, two of which abolished the corrupt old closed corporations in favour of election of councils by £10 householders, and the third allowed such householders in a royal burgh or burgh of barony to by-pass (but not supplant) the existing councils by adopting a parallel 'police system', whereby elected magistrates and commissioners of police were given powers to raise rates for watching, lighting, paving, cleansing, draining, bringing in a water supply, and similar functions. Most large Scottish towns – Glasgow, Edinburgh, Leith, Aberdeen, Dundee, Greenock – worked under their own Police Acts, and in 1862 Lindsay's Burgh Police Act enabled communities of no more than 700 inhabitants to make building and sanitary bye-laws of their own, though it remained, in Professor Best's words, 'nobody's official business, until the nineties, to make sure either that the bye-laws which were needed were made, or that, having been made, they were enforced'.[60]

The mid-Victorian years, the 1850s to the 1880s, were a period of administrative confusion in local government in Scotland to an even greater degree than in England.[61] For example, in 1845 the belated

[60]   G. Best, 'The Scottish Victorian City', *Victorian Studies*, 11 (1968), pp. 329–58. See also I. H. Adams, *The Making of Urban Scotland* (1978), chap. 7.
[61]   The best survey is G. S. Pryde, *Central and Local Government in Scotland since 1707* (Historical Association Pamphlet No. 45, 1960).

reform of the Scottish poor law resulted in the creation of a Central Board of Supervision and a multiplicity of parochial boards: the former became in 1867 a kind of central sanitary office (though with quite feeble powers); the latter had a paid inspectorate that became loaded with all kinds of responsibilities other than looking after the poor – for example, auditing registrars' accounts (1854), enforcing vaccination (1855), dealing with lunatics (1857), public health duties (1867), licensing pawnbrokers and raising the education rate (1872). Again the commissioners of supply had existed in Scotland since the seventeenth century to do many of the things for which the quarter sessions had responsibility in England: they were given control over the county police forces when they were made obligatory (in 1856–7) and came together with burgh magistrates in many *ad hoc* authorities – for example, district boards of control over lunacy in 1857, the prison commissioners in 1877 and the county road trustees in 1878. In 1872 the establishment of the Scotch Education Department and a local network of elected School Boards added further to the tangle.

Order began to be imposed on this welter of conflicting responsibilities with the creation of popularly elected county councils in 1889 (absorbing the powers of the commissioners of supply and many of the specialised authorities), and the replacement in 1894 of the Board of Supervision and the parochial boards by a more authoritative Local Government Board with parish councils. Meanwhile, in town government proper, the Burgh Police Act of 1892 ended the system of dual responsibility (so that henceforth a town might be governed either by provost, baillies and councillors, or by police magistrates and commissioners, but not by both). The Town Council (Scotland) Act of 1900 logically completed the process by insisting on uniform constitutions in all burghs under provost, baillies and elected councillors.

The major reform of the first half of the twentieth century was the local government legislation of 1929 which set up three types of burgh: four 'counties of cities', twenty 'large burghs' (with populations of *c*. 20,000) and 171 'small burghs'. The four cities were largely self-administrating, with wide powers over education and police. The large burghs also controlled their own police, but power over education within them resided in county councils. The small burghs were responsible only for housing and for some local services such as lighting, cleansing and drainage: everything else in them fell to the county councils. The basic difference in local administration was well summed up by Professor Pryde's remark that between the nineteenth and twentieth centuries 'the *ad hoc* gave way to the *ad omnia* body'.[62]

Given the extent of overlapping and ineffective authority, it might be imagined that the Scottish Victorian town was almost incapable of effective government. The problem was exacerbated because many statutes intended for the better government of towns throughout the entire United Kingdom simply could not be imposed on Scotland because they had been drawn up without any regard to the singularities of Scottish law. The Sanitary Act of 1866 was a case in point: it was designed to establish machinery to compel local authorities to improve sanitary provision, but it proved inoperable in Scotland because the ultimate means of enforcement was by appeal to the Court of Queen's Bench which had no jurisdiction north of the Border. It reveals the poor quality of Westminister's care for Scotland in this period that when this and similar anomalies were discovered nothing at all was done for many years to remedy the matter. Indeed, not until the Public Health (Scotland) Act of 1897 did Scotland catch up with England in the matter of sanitary legislation, and 'Scotland was, by then, a long way behind'.[63] The disadvantage was felt most sharply in smaller and middle-sized burghs – communities like Motherwell and Port Glasgow – where even at the beginning of the present century the laissez-faire squalor of Chadwick's world seemed to have been less mitigated than elsewhere, except by the provision (often belatedly) of piped water. In the great cities, however, as Professor Best has emphasised, urban government was neither impotent nor unimaginative in the face of these handicaps. Ruled by Police Acts, and driven by a mixture of civic pride in the populace and authoritarian tradition in the councils, they proved themselves capable of innovation. Edinburgh, for all the sanitary horrors of its old wynds, had, even in the 1850s, the best scavenging service and the most universally available medical service (through the doctors of the Royal Infirmary) of any city in Britain. The collapse of an old tenement in the High Street with the loss of thirty-five lives led in 1862 to the appointment of Henry Littlejohn as the first Medical Officer of Health in Scotland. His report in 1867 on every aspect of the sanitary condition of the capital, and in particular on differential mortality in its various quarters, provided the kind of quantitative backing for future reform that Chadwick had provided for England and Wales in 1842, and

[62] *Ibid*. p. 22.   [63] Best, 'Scottish Victorian City', p. 334.

was just as famous on its narrower stage. The building of Chambers Street in the name of a reforming Lord Provost was a first attempt to drive a swathe through the slums that hemmed in Edinburgh University.[64]

This initiative was generally followed in the 1870s and 1880s by the reconstruction of most of the area round the Royal Mile, the Cowgate and the Grassmarket, destroying in the process one of the most remarkable late Renaissance cities in Europe and replacing it by a Victorian *pastiche*. If it also wiped out the worst corrosions of endemic disease and crime, it did nothing to help rehouse the displaced poor. The invisible hand found a more acceptable solution when, with rising real wages in the last decades of the century, affluent artisans who had hitherto lived in the centre began to move out from among the company of the poorest in the old town to privately built rented tenements constructed in new working-class suburbs at Gorgie-Dalry and Easter Road. The football teams, Heart of Midlothian and Hibernian, followed their supporters out to new stadia in each location. Thus the architectural expression of social division which began in the eighteenth century with the movement of the upper classes to the new town was completed in the late nineteenth when the least skilled were left in possession of the old town.

It was Glasgow, however, rather than the capital, which in the second half of the nineteenth century won the more widespread reputation for dynamic government. Like Edinburgh, it was blessed with pushy and effective Medical Officers of Health; the first appeared immediately after Littlejohn's appointment, and the most famous, Dr J. B. Russell, was a power to be reckoned with in the land. In 1859 Glasgow broke new ground by bringing the highland waters of Loch Katrine to the city – the first municipality in Britain to harness abundant natural supplies in this way: the contrast can be made with Dundee, which in 1861 was said to have only five waterclosets for a population of 92,000 and all its water came from carts or wells – of which the largest was heavily polluted from a slaughterhouse.[65] The wisdom of Glasgow was perhaps demonstrated in 1865–6 when it largely escaped the fourth cholera epidemic, suffering only fifty-three out of some four hundred deaths in Scotland, whereas in the

[64] H. Macdonald, 'Edinburgh with Special Reference to the Work of Dr Littlejohn as Medical Officer of Health' (unpublished PhD thesis, Edinburgh University, 1972), is the best account.
[65] Adams, *Urban Scotland*, p. 136.

previous (and more severe) epidemic of 1853–4 it had suffered 4,000 out of a Scottish total of about 6,000. Other towns followed her example, Edinburgh obtaining water from St Mary's Loch and Dundee ultimately from the Loch of Lintrathen. In the smallest burghs the struggle between those willing to pay for pure water flowing down from a reservoir in the hills and those who believed it would be sufficient to pump it cheaply up from the nearest (but generally polluted) river was often fierce: in Selkirk the town was so divided in a bitter contest to elect a council of 'Gravitationalists' over 'Pumpers' that the annual rite of the Common Riding had temporarily to be abandoned.[66]

Glasgow's tradition of decisive, not to say totalitarian, action was demonstrated again in 1862 when the city obtained extraordinary *ad hoc* powers (copied throughout the other Scottish cities before the First World War, though vary rare in England) of 'ticketing' houses; i.e. of fixing metal plates to the walls of houses of a certain size indicating how many occupants were allowed, and accompanying this by peremptory searches if overcrowding was suspected. Such behaviour by the authorities certainly harassed the Irish, the poorest and most overcrowded of the Glasgow slum-dwellers, and the thump of the police on the door at midnight became a commonplace working-class experience. In one year 55,000 'night inspections' revealed 7,000 houses breaking the law, about 13 per cent of those investigated.[67] This kind of action had more to do with social control than concern for welfare, and the same spirit too often informed the treatment of the destitute under the 1845 Scottish Poor Law, which until the 1920s continued to deny the able-bodied unemployed any entitlement to relief while subjecting all paupers to minute and often degrading inspection and regulation. And not for nothing did Glasgow Council in 1878 appoint from 100 applicants at a salary of £100 a year as superintendent of the model lodging-houses a former drill sergeant of the Third Argyll Rifles.[68]

---

[66] I am grateful to Dr Gwen Neville, Emory University, for this detail from her unpublished research.

[67] J. Butt, 'Working Class Housing in Glasgow, 1851–1914', in S. D. Chapman, ed., *The History of Working-Class Housing* (Newton Abbot, 1971), pp. 57–92; Damer, 'State, Class and Housing', pp. 73–112.

[68] J. Whiteford, 'The Application of the Poor Law in Mid-Nineteenth Century Glasgow' (unpublished PhD thesis, Edinburgh University, 1982); I. Levitt, 'The Scottish Poor Law and Unemployment, 1890–1929', in T. C. Smout, ed., *The Search for Wealth and Stability: Essays in Economic and Social History Presented to M. W. Flinn* (1979), pp. 263–80; Butt, 'Working Class Housing', p. 68.

Slum clearance began in Glasgow on a large scale, as so often in Victorian towns, when the railway termini demanded extensive land near the centre. Then in 1866 the Glasgow Improvement Act established the Improvement Trust to carry on slum clearance in a more planned way, aiming to destroy a 'moral sewer of the most loathsome description . . . degraded by drunkenness and every attendant form of vice and profligacy': a large area round the Saltmarket that was then to be redeveloped by private interests. Much was cleared but little was rebuilt for the poor who were evicted, and the Trust allegedly exacerbated overcrowding until the recession of 1878 put a stop to any further work for a decade. From 1888, however, the corporation revived its activities and went into building and owning property on municipal account. By 1914 they had built 2,199 houses and 78 lodging-houses – housing little over 2 per cent of the population, but a notable precedent for the future.[69]

The tradition of public ownership of utilities in Glasgow fed on a non-party mixture of municipal pride and public dismay at the frequent inefficiency of private enterprise.[70] The Loch Katrine water scheme had been followed by municipalisation of the gas supply in 1867, by which the city halved the price, committed itself to public lighting of courts and tenements, and connected more households to the public mains than in any other in the world. In the 1870s the city built the tramlines, and in 1894, took over management so effectively that the trams seemed for a time (especially to the ideologically committed ILP) a model of how a service could be run by and for the public. Nor did public ownership stop there: its ramifications by the opening of the twentieth century were described by one enthusiast in these words. In Glasgow a citizen:

may live in a municipal house; he may walk along the municipal street, or ride on the municipal tramcar and watch the municipal dust cart collecting the refuse which is to be used to fertilise the municipal farm. Then he may turn into the municipal market, buy a steak from an animal killed in the municipal slaughterhouse, and cook it by the municipal gas on the municipal gas stove. For his recreation he can choose amongst municipal libraries, municipal art galleries and municipal music in municipal parks. Should he fall ill, he can ring up his doctor on the municipal telephone, or he may be taken to the municipal hospital in the municipal ambulance by a municipal

---

[69] C. M. Allan, 'The Genesis of British Urban Redevelopment with Special Reference to Glasgow', *Economic History Review*, 2nd ser., 18 (1965), pp. 598–613; Butt, 'Working Class Housing', pp. 60–4; Whiteford, 'Application of the Poor Law', p. 223.

[70] W. H. Fraser, 'Municipal Socialism and Social Policy' (unpublished paper), is the best account. I am deeply grateful to the author for allowing me to use it.

policeman. Should he be so unfortunate as to get on fire, he will be put out by a municipal fireman, using municipal water; after which he will, perhaps, forego the enjoyment of a municipal bath, though he may find it necessary to get a new suit in the municipal old clothes market.[71]

Glasgow's municipalisation was indeed by then the most extensive in Britain, and it differed (as did that of other Scottish cities) from English examples like Birmingham in that in Scotland municipal enterprises were not expected to make a profit or to subsidise the rates: they were simply expected to make specific services cheaper and better for the citizens. A ratepayers' backlash in the early twentieth century called a halt to what many Liberal Unionists and Conservatives in the city were coming to regard as the creeping socialism of the New Liberals and the ILP, thus introducing a novel element of party politics into municipal affairs. But it remained true that public utilities had a better record than private ones: while Glasgow possessed the only underground railway outside London, it was privately run from its opening in 1897 until its municipalisation in 1922, and quite failed to compete in that period with the corporation trams.[72]

Was all this activity of the councils more than marginal to the welfare of the great body of the citizens? The central problems of the towns in the 1840s (apart from the relatively simple one of public order which was, in fact, clearly contained by the police) had been the appallingly high death rates from those diseases rooted in bad sanitation as well as in poverty, and shocking housing conditions rooted in overcrowding. Scotland shared in the general reduction of the crude death rate from the 1870s, and most of the fall before 1900 was due to a reduction in deaths from tuberculosis (which remained, however, a very major killer still accounting for 13 per cent of deaths in the 1890s), from the typhus group of diseases, from scarlet fever and from diphtheria. Of these, the clearest marker of bad sanitary conditions is the typhus group, which accounted for 5 per cent of deaths in Scotland in the 1860s but only 1 per cent in the 1890s. Interestingly, in view of what has been noticed above about the energy of big towns compared to small ones in overcoming administrative and legislative handicaps, mortality from typhus was, at least from the 1870s, consistently lower in the cities than in small towns. The attack on the sanitary problem must thus be adjudged at least a partial success in Scotland as it was

---

[71] I am indebted to Dr Fraser for this quotation, which is from R. E. C. Lond, *Fortnightly Review* (Jan. 1903).
[72] Adams, *Urban Scotland*, p. 119.

Table 3.8 *Persons per room in Scottish houses, 1861–1951*

	Persons per room	Intercensal decrease
1861	1.79	—
1871	1.69	5.6
1881	1.59	5.9
1891	1.52	4.5
1901	1.48	2.6
1911	1.45	[2.0]
1921	1.42	2.1
1931	1.27	10.6
1951	1.05	8.7*

Note: Up to and including the census of 1901 the statistics of occupation of residential premises were given not in relation to houses only but in relation to all residential premises including hotels, boarding houses, institutions, etc. This affects the comparison between figures up to 1901 and figures after it but the degree of variation involved is not such as to vitiate the broad general comparison.
* This figure is halved (in the absence of a census in 1941) to make it comparable to those above.
Source: 1951 Census of Scotland, p. lii.

in England, though the obstacles to be overcome had been even larger. On the other hand, it was only partial. The record of infant mortality, in Scotland as in the south, showed no improvement before the twentieth century, and then dropped more slowly than in England. In Scotland, in the nineteenth century, infant mortality had, on average, been appreciably lower than in England (perhaps because of generally lower levels of urbanisation, perhaps because of better infant feeding customs by weaning children on to porridge). In the twentieth century the reverse has been the case – though in both countries the rates of infant mortality have dropped dramatically, the fall has been greater in the south. As early as the 1920s Scotland began to experience a higher rate than England.[73]

The conquest of bad housing and overcrowding was, as Tables 3.8 and 3.9 show, far more incomplete. The contrast is particularly striking with England: as early as 1911 the English had already attained a lower density per room than the Scots reached even in 1951 (0.95 compared to 1.05); in 1951, 26 per cent of the Scottish population still lived in one- or two-room houses, compared to 2.6 per cent in England; and in 1951 only 37.4 per cent of Scottish homes yet had

[73] M. W. Flinn, ed., *Scottish Population History from the 17th Century to the 1930s* (Cambridge, 1977), pp. 396–420.

Table 3.9 *Percentage of Scottish population in houses of different sizes,*
1861–1951

	1 room	2 rooms	3 rooms	4 rooms	5 rooms
1861	26.2	37.7	12.7	6.4	3.7
1871	23.7	38.3	13.9	6.7	3.8
1881	18.0	39.5	16.1	7.6	4.2
1891	14.3	39.4	17.9	8.3	4.6
1901	11.0	39.5	19.9	9.1	4.9
1911	8.7	40.9	21.9	9.9	5.6
1921	8.4	40.8	22.1	10.5	5.8
1931	7.1	36.9	26.1	12.0	6.2
1951	3.5	22.3	31.2	25.2	8.8

Note: The figures for 1911–51 refer to population enumerated in private households only, but those of earlier censuses include the entire enumerated population, viz., those in institutions, lodging houses, hotels as well as in private
homes.
Source: 1951 Census of Scotland, p. 76.

more than three rooms, compared to 84.7 per cent of English ones.
Or – to compare the largest cities in each country – in 1951 in Glasgow,
half the houses were of one or two rooms, in London only 5.5 per
cent; in Glasgow, a quarter of the population were living more than
two to a room, in London only 1.7 per cent.[74] Such differences were
not new. The Scottish housing problem over the whole of this century
was of a different order of magnitude from the English.

The question of why this should be so has often been raised, but
is not as readily answered. The native feuing system, by which a
piece of land was 'sold' in return for a lump sum down and a fixed
quit rent in perpetuity, has frequently been blamed for encouraging
speculative builders to crowd as many homes as possible into the
traditional tall stone tenements. But it is hard to see why it should
have this effect more than say, an outright sale or a very long lease
as common in English law. Only a lease for a limited term of years
during which the original landowner retained an interest in 'respectable' long-term development (exceptional in either country) was
proof against the uncontrolled greed of the building speculator, who
will build as badly as he can get away with as long as it pays him.
It is wiser, therefore, to look to some combination of economic, social
and environmental factors to explain the demand for a small home
in a tenement. It is certainly relevant that the Scots were a very much

[74] T. Brennan, *Reshaping a City*, (Glasgow, 1959), pp. 20–1.

poorer people than the English in the early and middle nineteenth centuries when the patterns of urban development were established, and, if poorer, could afford lower rents. To live in one or two rooms (as 64 per cent of Scots did in 1861, and 49 per cent as late as 1921) also effected substantial savings in heating and lighting in a cold and dark country, especially in the tenements where the contiguous houses (*anglice* 'flats') kept one another warm.

It is also true, however, that the Scots over a long period have proved unwilling to pay as large a proportion even of their lower incomes towards housing costs as the English and most other Europeans. It is again hard to say why. There may be an element of inertia: if a population becomes accustomed to living in small, poor-quality homes at low rents (as private tenants or as council tenants) it may seem a disproportionate sacrifice of other items of consumption to pay much higher rents for larger houses. This explanation in turn seems superficial, however, for why have others been more willing than the Scots to improve their housing expectations from low levels? However, among the historical reasons for the reluctance of the working class to put as much money into their homes as the English may be welfare insecurity: as long as the Scottish poor law refused to give any help at all to an able-bodied man out of work the Scots worker had to save more than the English against a rainy day: thrift and bad housing, in fact, may have been complementary before 1914.

Whatever the cause, however, one should be very wary of saying that the Scots lived in bad tenement housing 'because they liked it'. On the contrary, there is much evidence (at least in the twentieth century) of enormous resentment by the working class at being trapped in the verminous slums. The rise of the ILP in Glasgow before the First World War was largely due to the appeal of Wheatley's campaign for good houses, which in turn was based on an idea of an immigrant engineer, John Burgess, who believed that Scottish councils could and should build English-type cottage homes for the workers.[75] The first government-assisted council houses built in the city after the First World War were obviously influenced by this model, though the traditional tenement also went on being built by councils because it was cheap. It was not, however, preferred. Brennan, writing in 1959, found that most people wanted a house with its own front door, and if possible a bungalow, 'that is, a house as unlike a tenement

---

[75] *Minutes of Evidence Taken before Glasgow Municipal Commission on the Housing of the Poor* (Glasgow, 1904).

flat as possible'.[76] Whether it was ever practicable to build this kind of house in the public sector on a large scale is another matter.

Against this background it is difficult to assess the absolute achievement of Scotland in its housing record over the entire century. As Table 3.8 shows, the biggest improvements in overcrowding per room before 1914 came in the 1860s and 1870s and to a lesser extent the 1880s. This period coincides with the first blitz on the classic slums of the 1840s, and the private construction of new working-class suburbs for the better paid. The very serious slowing down that followed from the 1890s to the close of the First World War seemed to show that capitalism left to itself had no solution; though in fact the percentage of families in one-room houses actually halved even in this period. The success of the ILP, not least when backed by the rent strikes that made the government exceedingly nervous in the war, leant political weight to the sombre findings of the Royal Commission on Housing in Scotland, published in 1917.

The age of the state-subsidised council house followed the Scottish Addison Act of 1919, and the general history of legislation thereafter broadly follows the English pattern.[77] The Scots, however, became much more deeply committed to council housing than the English, partly because the interwar depression and the drift of better-off Scots to the south profoundly discouraged the private sector in Scotland, and partly because the Labour party in the councils largely owed its appeal to local housing programmes. Altogether, between 1919 and 1939, 213,000 council houses were built in Scotland, compared to 104,000 private houses (and even of these 43,000 were built with state assistance): this was 67 per cent of the total, compared to 28 per cent in England.[78] Even this, however, seemed a totally inadequate effort in the face of manifest need, and at the close of the Second World War the Labour government again placed a very high priority in solving the housing problem through the state. In the next six years, 106,000 permanent and 32,000 temporary prefabricated public sector houses were built, while private enterprise was so starved of building permits, labour and materials, and so discouraged by rent controls, that it could only manage 6,000.[79] By 1956 one third of all the houses in Glasgow were municipally owned.

[76] Brennan, *Reshaping a City*, p. 30.
[77] R. D. Cramond, *Housing Policy in Scotland, 1919–64* (Edinburgh, 1966).
[78] C. Miller, 'The Scottish Economy and the Post-War British Governments' (unpublished MPhil. thesis, St Andrews University, 1981), p. 170.
[79] *Ibid.*, p. 167.

The result of the council house movement between 1919 and 1951 can be partly judged from Tables 3.8 and 3.9. Overcrowding was reduced at more than four times the rate of the previous period when provision had been left entirely to the market, and the proportion living in one- and two-roomed houses was halved: the one-room house, indeed, nearly disappeared, and for the first time in 1951 there were more people living in three-room houses than in two-room houses. These, of course, are national figures: in individual cities, especially Glasgow, the overall position was always a good deal worse, and it never crossed anyone's mind in 1951 that the housing problem was in any sense 'solved'.

The building of the new council estates (like Pollock, Knightswood, Mosspark and Blackhill in Glasgow or Pilton and Craigmillar in Edinburgh), combined as it was with slum clearance in the inner city, brought its own obvious problems in its train. One was to transform the traditionally compact nature of the Scottish town by vast spatial expansion at a time of little or no demographic growth: the sprawling new estates, combined with the bungaloid character of such private building as there was, cut off the bulk of the urban population from their traditional easy access both to city centre and surrounding country, while municipal tram and bus services poorly compensated for this loss of convenience and community. The Glasgow councillor who responded to the palpable need of poor people around him by exclaiming 'tae hell wi' planning' was only saying aloud what most politicians thought privately; but the result was often to construct ghettos of fearsome ugliness, few amenities and concentrated deprivation.[80]

Not all council estates, of course, were equally poor, for there was a world of difference in Glasgow in the 1930s between respectable Knightswood and the razor-gangs' Blackhill. That itself created problems. Who decided where an applicant for a council house was to go? And on what grounds? The creation of a municipal bureaucracy with power over the people in the name of the people was one inevitable and unhappy consequence. Then the need to stay in the same town to accumulate enough official points to qualify for a house, and the difficulty of swapping a council house in one place for a similar house in another, helped to immobilise the population at times, especially after 1945, when geographical and occupational mobility

---

[80]   Brennan, *Reshaping a City*, p. 27 and *passim*; Checkland, *Upas Tree*, pp. 35–40, 63–80.

Table 3.10 *Numbers of males employed in agriculture, 1881, 1911 and 1951, as a percentage of the numbers employed in 1851*

	1881	1911	1951
Great Britain	80	75	55
Scotland	82	76	57
Highland	89	80	42
Borders and south-west	76	73	68

Source: Lee, *Regional Statistics.*

in labour was most to be desired if Scotland was to achieve a more modern and flexible economic structure.[81]

Such costs as these could not be easily, or quickly, perceived, still less quantified. But they were there, and they were heavy. The bad housing of the nineteenth century has proved a burden to the twentieth century of incalculable magnitude. We are no surer how to carry it now than we were in 1919 or 1945, but we have been crippled in bearing what could not be ignored.

IV

Agriculture has always been slightly more important to the Scottish economy than to the economy of Great Britain as a whole: in 1851 employment in farming, forestry and fishing was 22 per cent of the total employment for men in Great Britain, but 25 per cent in Scotland; by 1951 the figures were 5 per cent and 7 per cent respectively. Similarly, the decline in agricultural employment has been everywhere a major cause of depopulation and its associated problems in rural areas, hardly worse in Scotland than elsewhere.

Table 3.10 shows how the decline went over the century 1851–1951. Compared to the starting date, numbers in agriculture in Great Britain and Scotland alike had dropped by about a fifth in 1881, by a quarter by 1911 and by between a third and a half by 1951. The more significant variation however, is between two deeply rural areas of Scotland: the Highlands – where decline was well below average before 1881 and to a certain extent before 1911, but catastrophic between 1911

---

[81] R. Baird, 'Housing', in Cairncross, ed., *Scottish Economy*, pp. 193–211.

and 1951 – and the Borders and south-west – where decline was much sharper down to 1881 and 1911, but very much less from 1911 to 1951. Many Scots would find these figures amazing. Clearances, after all, were a feature of the Highlands, not of the Lowlands, until the land reforms of the 1880s; and the corpus of crofting legislation built up between 1886 and 1911 was designed to stop the depopulation of the north, not of the south whose farmers and farm labourers did not come under its sway. The obvious conclusion is that evictions were not the main cause of depopulation nor legislation any protection against it.

What happened in the Highlands in the century after 1850 was the creation and demise of an economy supported on one leg by crofting and on the other by the earnings of migrant labour. To go south in search of harvest work, navvying or military service had long been a tradition of the Highlanders, but after the blights and famines of the 1840s remittances back from the Lowlands became the only way to ensure that rents for the croft would continue to be paid. Dr Devine has shown how the population was maintained at its exceptionally high levels by crofters working for part of the year on southern farms, or by sons working in factories, on construction jobs or on the boats, or by daughters working as domestic servants, field hands and fish gutters – but all returning to be reunited on the croft in due course.[82] By the 1880s farm mechanisation was eating into some jobs, and the industrial dislocation of that period helped to precipitate the poverty and discontent that accompanied contemporary land agitation. But there was as yet no permanent shortage of industrial openings: there were still rivetters on the Clyde who went back to their island holdings for seed time and harvest, and were perhaps in due course entered as crofters by the census men.

Consequently, despite a century of the most bitter complaint of men being driven from the land by sheep farms and deer forests, the total population of the Highlands contrived to remain much higher in the second half of the nineteenth century than it had been in 1801, and in 1901 it was still only 11 per cent below its all-time peak in 1841. This figure, however, masks a great deal of redistribution. In the Outer Hebrides a population explosion was still actively taking place, probably the only part of rural Britain where this was the case

[82]   T. M. Devine, 'Temporary Migration and the Scottish Highlands in the Nineteenth Century', *Economic History Review*, 2nd ser., 32 (1979), pp. 344–59.

– on Lewis and Harris, for instance, numbers stood at 21,500 in 1841 but 35,000 by 1911. Conversely, in the Inner Hebrides, there was a collapse – population on Skye, Islay and Mull fell from 46,700 to 23,600 over the same dates.[83] The basic distinction was that in the Outer Hebrides, but not in the Inner, there were excellent prospects for jobs on east-coast fishing boats that put into Stornoway and Castlebay on Barra, and which took the girls to the gutting at Wick, Peterhead and places south.

The First World War and its aftermath, however, brought disaster to this economy throughout the Highlands. An abnormally high proportion of the young men died in the trenches and at sea. The herring fishing was ruined by the collapse of its East European market, farming was shedding labour, domestic service declining and the shipyards laying off men by the thousand. So severe was the dislocation of the local economy in the short term that civil servants in the 1920s were soberly warning Edinburgh and Whitehall that there might be an actual return to famine in the islands, as though the clock had gone back to 1846.[84] The population of the Highlands fell more abruptly than at any time in the nineteenth century, the Hebrides as a group losing 28 per cent of their inhabitants between 1911 and 1951. The return to full employment in the Lowlands after the Second World War was incapable of restoring the migrant economy. The young weighed the traditional life against the world portrayed by the cinema and the radio, found it wanting, and left.

It might indeed be cogently argued that what was truly distinctive about the Highlanders compared to the other inhabitants of rural Britain in the later nineteenth century was not that they were exposed to crueller pressures but that they resented them more. Sir John MacNeill, secretary to the Board of Supervision of the Scottish Poor Law, reporting on the aftermath of the famine in 1851 marvelled at the Highlanders' 'tenacity of their attachment to their native soil' which 'years of intercourse with the more advanced districts seems to produce no desire to change', and cited the example of a Skye crofter who 'travelled about 600 miles, separated himself from his family and worked hard for six months every year, that he might continue to enjoy his croft and comparative idleness for the other half-year

[83]   Flinn, ed., *Scottish Population History*, p. 306; W. H. Murray, *The Islands of Western Scotland* (1973), pp. 308–9.

[84]   I. Levitt, 'The Scottish Poor Law and Unemployment, 1890–1939', (unpublished paper presented at SSRC Conference on History and Social Policy, Manchester, 1976).

in Waternish. And such was the feeling of everyone.'[85] The world view of the man from Waternish obviously conflicted with that of the lairds and political economists, who believed that only permanent emigration would cure what they termed 'congestion' and a new start for the crofters became possible in a better and more enriching environment outside the Highlands. It was not that Highlanders were averse to enrichment in itself: there was no consumer resistance to better clothes or imported food, and some of the complaints of the 1880s are related to failure to get enough of these good things for themselves over the past half-century. But, broadly speaking, the nineteenth-century crofter put home before wealth, the certain possession of land before the dubious opportunity to gain enrichment by a better income as an industrial worker at home or even as a landholder overseas. Consequently he was prepared to share the holding with his grown-up sons and their families rather than oblige them to leave the settlement for ever, to live for years on the brink of subsistence rather than to commit himself irretrievably to the dangerous currents of urban life. In some respects these sentiments begged almost as many questions as those on the other side, for what would happen if crofting lands were so constantly divided that income levels were driven below mere subsistence? Anyone with a knowledge of Ireland in the 1840s could see this was not entirely an idle question, and it was not convincingly answered by those crofters who said that the return of grazing land under sheep or deer would solve the problem of land-hunger for all time.

In the event, large-scale eviction, as Dr Richards has shown, came to an end with a series of incidents in the late 1840s and early 1850s, such as those at Suishnish on Skye, Knoydart and Coigach on the western mainland and Greenyards in Easter Ross, for the most part 'ugly scenes, marked by panic, hysteria, anger, rough handling and pitiful suffering'. They were also exceptionally well reported – indeed, sensationalised – by an anti-landlord press with an increasingly avid Liberal readership in the towns. The force of public opinion, together with partial recovery from the economic traumas of the famine decade, discouraged lairds from trying the like again. Nevertheless, there was a good deal of small-scale moving on and surreptitious encouragement to leave, 'invisible pressure on the people to ease them out of the

---

[85] *Report to the Board of Supervision by Sir John McNeill, GCB, on the Western Highlands and Islands* (Edinburgh, 1851) p. xii.

region', though there is no reason to believe it was worse here than elsewhere in Great Britain or Ireland.[86]

Then, in the 1880s there was a sudden turning of the tables; the crofters took the initiative and began to press their claims not merely for legally guaranteed security of tenure but also for action to return lands that had been lost to sheep or deer to the grazing of the townships.[87] The reasons for this burst of political self-help from a hitherto unpoliticised section of the nation were complex: the example of Irish land agitation was clearly important, as was help provided by middle-class outsiders including influential enthusiasts of the Celtic cultural revival at Edinburgh University and elsewhere.[88] Disorder in Skye, resulting in the despatch first of a contingent of the Glasgow city police to Braes near Portree, and then, even more improbably, of a gunboat full of marines to Glendale, was avidly reported in the urban Liberal press. One upshot was the return to Parliament in 1885 of four MPs of an independent Crofters' party, on a platform of returning the land to the people: 'it has some claim to the title of the first mass political party in Britain'.[89] Another was the establishment of a Royal Commission, under Lord Napier, to enquire into conditions in the crofting counties. Its monumental report showed considerable and unexpected support for the crofters, perhaps because Napier's experience as a senior civil servant in agrarian India had accustomed him to pay patient attention to far more things in heaven and earth than were ever dreamt of by conventional political economists. The ensuing legislation, however, owed more to Gladstone's Irish Land Act of 1881 than to any other model, giving the crofters heritable security of tenure in their holdings and establishing a rent review body – the Crofters' Commission – to determine the fair level for rents. In the crofting areas, it outlawed evictions. It was a staggering interference with the traditional rights of landowners in mainland Britain, justified largely on the historical grounds that crofters had had a raw deal in the past, and it was followed in due course by legislation in 1897 and 1911 which empowered the state to buy up

[86] E. Richards, *A History of the Highland Clearances: Agrarian Transformation and the Evictions, 1746–1886* (1982) pp. 233–43, 444–74.

[87] J. Hunter, *The Making of the Crofting Community* (Edinburgh, 1976), pp. 107–64.

[88] C. Dewey, 'Celtic Agrarian Legislation and the Celtic Revival: Historical Implications of Gladstone's Irish and Scottish Land Acts, 1870–1886', *Past & Present*, 64 (1974), pp. 30–70; H. J. Hanham, 'The Problem of Highland Discontent, 1880–1885', *Transactions of the Royal Historical Society*, 4th ser., 19 (1969), pp. 24–30.

[89] D. W. Crowley, 'The "Crofters' Party", 1885–1892', *Scottish Historical Review*, 35 (1956), pp. 110–26.

land under sheep or deer and return it to crofting agriculture. The consequences were neither instantaneous nor revolutionary, but between 1886 and the early 1950s some 52,000 acres of arable land and 732,000 acres of pasture were added to the area occupied by crofters, a process which involved the creation of over 2,700 new holdings and the enlargement of nearly 5,200 existing crofts. By the end of the 1920s anyone who wanted a croft – or a larger croft – could be fairly sure of getting one.[90]

As we have seen, however, the new corpus of land law was powerless to prevent depopulation, and it has often been argued that the legislation of 1886 and its successors froze the structure of the Highlands in a way that inhibited development: 'change is now frustrated by the high degree of security which the crofters enjoy, as well as the essentially communal nature of the system, which allows a conservative minority to obstruct the progressive majority'.[91] Since, however, it was the aim of Gladstone to concede security rather than opportunity to the rural population, he can hardly be blamed for not foreseeing that in the long run the Highlanders, like everyone else, would be seduced by the gospel of private enrichment and economic growth.

The rural problems of the Lowlands, if less well reported than those of the Highlands, were no less pervasive, especially in the lean years for farming in the last quarter of the nineteenth century and again in the interwar years. The incidence and effects of the agricultural depressions varied markedly. The slide in wool and grain prices after 1875 had a particularly bad effect on the Borders and the south-west where the population of Berwickshire dropped by 20 per cent and Wigtownshire by 28 per cent between 1851 and 1911. In the Lothians, on the other hand, the main visible result was to drive to the wall the old tenant dynasties who had created the heavily capitalised high farming of 'Lothian husbandry', and to replace them by 'new men . . . a rather different class . . . hard working grieves who had saved money, merchants' sons with capital ready to risk': they pulled the area through by increased mechanisation and potato husbandry, shedding labour heavily as they did so.[92] In the north-east, buoyant prices for good-quality Aberdeen Angus meat kept the larger farmers

[90] Hunter, *Crofting Community*, pp. 205–6.
[91] For a sensitive study at the close of our century, see A. Collier, *The Crofting Problem* (Cambridge, 1953).
[92] A. G. Bradley, *When Squires and Farmers Thrived* (1927), p. 86.

prosperous, but marginal farmers and upland crofters (excluded from the protection of the Crofters Holding Act of 1886 which applied only to the western Highlands) suffered badly. Ian Carter has eloquently described how such small men, pinched between high rents and falling profits, and driven to exploit the labour of their own families more and more intensively, finally succumbed to the economic realities.[93] He quotes J. R. Allan's 'exquisite elegy for the northeast peasantry':

As you walk across the lower slopes of the hills you may find a heap of stones that was once a house, and trace among the bracken the rectangle that was once a field. They are melancholy things, witnessing that courage, determination and all the ancient virtues are not enough to bring life out of a stone. A hunger for land drove the people there, and the insatiable hunger of the soil drove them away again. Those ruins are the stony limit where a human tide spent itself before it began to ebb away.[94]

Not everyone in this position, though, went bankrupt, emigrated or left for the towns. It has been argued that the rarity of owner-occupation was a strength of Scottish farming at the time, as it did not tie a man to the land and 'young, enterprising glen farmers were nothing loth to better themselves by leasing farms in kindlier areas'. Thus tenants in the upper parts of Tay, Dee, Don and Spey valleys moved downstream to their more fertile straths, and their sons perhaps moved again to still more productive land. Men from the south-west came eventually to the Lothians, Berwickshire and Fife, while Banff-shire and Aberdeenshire men came to Moray, Kincardineshire and Angus, and men from Caithness to Ross: 'the harder upbringing experienced on stock-rearing or dairying farms stood the migrants in good stead'.[95]

In the very different circumstances of the twentieth century much of this flexibility was lost. The Agriculture (Scotland) Act of 1948 gave all farmers that heritable security of tenure for which they had striven for seventy years. Many landlords then sold. Farms with vacant possession were soon commanding twice the price of those without, very few farms to rent were available and the capital cost of running a farm greatly increased. Farmers' sons therefore found it very difficult to get an independent start off the parental holding.[96]

[93] Ian R. Carter, *Farm Life in North East Scotland, 1840–1914* (Edinburgh, 1973), esp. chaps. 3–6.
[94] *Ibid.* p. 160.
[95] J. A. Symon, *Scottish Farming Past and Present* (Edinburgh, 1959), p. 198.
[96] *Ibid.*, p. 267.

The life of the farm worker in the century after 1850 was transformed out of all recognition by labour-saving machinery and gradually rising wages. It has to be remembered, though, that only in a few parts of nineteenth-century Scotland – pre-eminently the Lothians and Berwickshire – did the labour input from hired hands decisively exceed the input from family members. More typical were the north-eastern counties of Aberdeen, Banff and Kincardine, where between 1851 and 1911 the family regularly supplied 35–45 per cent of the male and often 80 per cent of the female labour.[97] Again, only in a few areas like the south-east was the farm worker normally a married man in the 1850s: in Aberdeenshire, Lanarkshire and Ayrshire, for instance, the traditional pattern was for him to be a bachelor boarding around the farm, who would leave to take up his own holding or to go to the town as a carter or industrial worker on marriage. As time went by, this changed, partly because small farms became less attractive, partly because moving to the town became more so. Farmers found that to keep labour they might have to build a cottage for the ploughman after marriage. In the bothy districts of Angus and Perthshire there was a similar transformation, though the squalid barracks for young horsemen continued to be used until after the First World War.[98]

Even in the Lothians and the south-east, the *locus classicus* of Scottish capitalist farming, where farm labour was the most proletarianised from the early nineteenth century, the years after 1850 brought enormous alteration. The characteristic work unit at mid-century had been a 'hind', or ploughman, assisted in the field by a teenage son or 'half-hind', and married to a 'bondager', whose work at harvest and other times paid the rent of their cottage to the farmer and left a little over. Seasonal work was done by highland girls housed in female bothies, and at harvest by itinerant Irish bands. The female workers of the south-east were a very important and highly regarded part of the labour force, 'Amazons with the faces of a harvest moon and the muscles of a prize fighter', paid about 1s. a day in cash.[99] Many of the hinds received little in money, but a relatively high wage in kind: in Roxburghshire as late as 1870 a ploughman might receive only £5 a year in money, 'the rest of this wage consisting of a cottage

97 Carter, *Farm Life*, p. 104.
98 Gavin Sprott, 'A Weel Plou'd Rig: The Era of the Working Horse on the Farms of the East Coast of Scotland', in B. Kay, ed., *Odyssey* (Edinburgh, 1980), pp. 99, 109.
99 Bradley, *Squires and Farmers*, p. 80.

and garden, rent free, the keep of a cow, carriage of fuel, potato ground, and certain allowances of oats (or oatmeal), barley and peas'. This contrasted with what contemporaries called the 'meal and milk system' of Perthshire and Fife, where ploughmen got an allowance of oatmeal and a Scotch pint of milk daily, with £20 in cash – but the workers of the south-east were regarded as better-off.[100] One characteristic that was emphasised by the Royal Commission on the Employment of Children, Young Persons and Women in Agriculture (1867) was that farmers and workers alike had a much greater enthusiasm for education in Scotland than in England. A mother in Berwick told the commissioners that she wanted to make her children 'good scholars, I don't want them to be hinds draggling on the land all their lives if they can better themselves', and they heard of shepherds in remote hill farms banding together to employ a tutor if there were five or six families to share the expense.[101]

By the First World War most of the distinctive features of this society had gone. The number of female labourers, both highland and bondager, was very much reduced – as, indeed if A. G. Bradley is to be believed, was their physique: 'They had begun to think of their complexions, and chewed rice to modify the gorgeous hues thereof, just as they eschewed porridge to the sapping of their splendid strength.' The fact was that as soon as their own wages went up, hinds tried to withdraw their women from the bitter toil of hoeing in the fields. Irish itinerant labour was largely replaced by the self-binding reaper at harvest time. The system of payment in kind increasingly gave way to payment in money as diets changed: 'oatmeal disappeared ... home-baked bread went the same way. The cow and the milk was commuted for cash allowance. Tea and anaemic baker's bread and the grocer's cart with tinned stuff took their place.'[102] Enthusiasm for education did not long survive compulsory attendance at the Board schools after the Act of 1872 – the Royal Commission on Labour of 1892 could find little trace of the once-famed zeal for reading and learning.[103]

By the interwar years, Scottish rural communities of many kinds appeared singularly demoralised, although the standard of living of

---

[100]   C. S. Orwin and E. H. Whetham, *History of British Agriculture, 1846–1914* (1971). p. 216.
[101]   *Ibid*, p. 215.
[102]   Bradley, *Squires and Farmers*, p. 80.
[103]   *RC on Labour: The Agricultural Labourer*, III (II), *Scotland*, PP 1893–4, XXXVI, especially pp. 67, 121–2, 179.

individuals in most of them had obviously markedly improved since Victorian times. Partly it was a problem of depopulation, and the skewed age distribution of those who remained. Especially in the Highlands, but also in many of the more remote lowland counties, the young voted *en masse* with their feet against the boredom and lack of opportunity in rural life.

Farming, of course, was in bad shape between the wars: so were fishing and coal mining, two other stand-bys of the rural economy of great local importance. Other occupations that had usefully varied the rural economy in the middle of the nineteenth century had long since vanished, like lead mining in Dumfriesshire and Lanarkshire, and the very last vestiges of handloom weaving were dying out in Fife and the Borders in the 1920s (though in Harris and Lewis hand-made tweed had a significant interwar revival). If some compensation was beginning to come from the tourist trade, it was not yet enough in most areas to erase the impression that the countryside had become Cinderella to the town.

The 1940s, however, helped a little to redress that balance by bringing full employment, fuller wage packets and much more self-respect for the three main rural occupations, when society, through war and crisis, learnt renewed dependence on home-produced food and fuel. After the war, too, wider car-ownership and an efficient network of rural bus services started to break down the sense of isolation which the countryside had come to feel and to resent. The costs in integration and prosperity in terms of the sacrifice of local identity were inevitable, and no less so the expressions of regret which accompanied them:

There are still great contrasts between such communities as Cowdenbeath and Crail, or even neighbours like Inverkeithing and Aberdour. Yet perhaps the most striking thing is how alike they have become in much that is fundamental. For an increasing number of people, the houses in which they live, the broad conditions under which they work, the educational system by which they are taught, and the type of entertainment they seek, have become very similar. As a result, there has been a standardisation of dress, of speech, of manners and of the whole attitude to life. Increased travel has worked in the same direction . . . With this standardisation, opportunities and creature comforts have both become more plentiful, but whether happiness has increased is a point on which few people could care to make a firm pronouncement.[104]

In history, though, you cannot have your cake and eat it.

---

[104] A. Smith, *The Third Statistical Account of Scotland: The County of Fife* (Edinburgh, 1952), p. 83.

V

The problem of the survival of identity to which the commentator on Fife referred was an illustration on the local scene of an anxiety more often voiced nationally. Would Scotland herself survive as an identifiable entity? Or would she irretrievably become what the nationalist poet, Tom Scott, in the 1960s referred to as 'Scotshire', a mere northern extension of a flavourless English culture? It was an old worry, often voiced then by nationalists, but never confined to them. Henry Cockburn, whose drafting of the Great Reform Bill for Scotland in 1832 had done much to encourage the convergence of Scottish and English political systems, could still write that 'the prolongation of Scotch peculiarities, especially of our language and habits, I do earnestly desire', though in the next phrase he declared 'nothing can prevent the gradual disappearance of local manners under the absorption and assimilation of a far larger, richer and more powerful kingdom'.[105] Almost a century later his words are echoed by Edwin Muir:

What makes the existence of the mass of the people in Scotland so unsatisfactory, apart from their economic plight ... is not the feeling that they are being subjected to English influence, but rather the knowledge that there is no Scottish influence left to direct them. They are not English, and they are ceasing to be Scottish for lack of encouragement.[106]

Yet Muir was to incur the wrath of Hugh MacDairmid by denying that the older Scottish tongue any longer formed a vehicle in which anything of importance could be said to the people of Scotland.

Formal nationalism in the political and intellectual sense was, at least in European perspective, a late and weak growth in Scotland. The National Association for the Vindication of Scottish Rights, founded in 1853, was mainly antiquarian, seeking the restoration of the Scottish Privy Council abolished in 1708 and the rectification of trivial abuses of the Union, such as flying the wrong flag on royal visits. The Rosebery Liberals successfully extracted the concession of a Scottish Office from London in 1885, and their successors, most notably the Young Scots between 1900 and 1906 were enthusiasts for the Liberal programme of 'Home Rule All Round' – though unprepared to go to any lengths at all to secure it. The foundation of the Scottish National party in 1934 (an amalgamation of two groups formed in 1928 and 1932) marked the belated arrival of a conventional

105   *Journal of Henry Cockburn, 1831–1854*, vol. 2 (Edinburgh, 1874), pp. 301–2.
106   Edwin Muir, *Scottish Journey*, ed. T.C. Smout (Edinburgh, 1979), pp. 27–8.

nationalist party, though one with little electoral success before the late 1960s.[107] The intellectual equivalent was the poets of the Scottish Renaissance, above all Hugh MacDairmid who in the 1930s was brilliantly reinventing his country and its culture, with all the passion and imagination of a nineteenth-century Bohemian in Prague, or Finn in Helsinki.

This delay in the emergence of nationalist politics and culture almost to the point of anachronism has been related by both Nairn and Harvie to the consistent success of the Scottish middle classes and the intelligentsia within the British state for a long period from 1750, which meant that the nineteenth-century 'springtime of nations' had little appeal until after the First World War, and being then without roots, only a limited one thereafter.[108] This did not, however, at all preclude the survival of an intense popular self-awareness, a refusal of Scots to call themselves English whatever the outside world might do. As we shall see, in the Victorian years some symbols of Scottishness weakened, especially the church. Others were, however, invented, or adapted to cover the entire country instead of a part of it, such as the association of the whole of Scotland (instead of just the Highlands) with tartan and bagpipe. In this respect nothing was more important than sport, especially the schism between the Football Association and the Scottish Football Association in 1887, which led to the firm foundation of a separate Scottish League.

This had an important secondary effect in helping to preserve a characteristically Scottish media in the twentieth century. As Kellas has pointed out, as late as 1970 no daily newspaper published in England took more than 3 per cent of the adult readership, and the *Sunday Post* and *Sunday Mail* (published in Dundee and Glasgow) took 79 per cent and 53 per cent of Sunday readership respectively.[109] The reasons for this are clearly connected with advertising revenue and coverage of local news as well as with sport. There was, however, little point in the Glasgow man buying the *Daily Mirror* or the *Daily Telegraph* if his main interest in life was to follow Rangers or Celtic, and to relish fully the triumphs of Scotland over England at Hampden Park: that needed properly impartial reporting, such as only the *Daily Record* or the *Glasgow Herald* were qualified to provide.

[107]   H. J. Hanham, *Scottish Nationalism* (1969).
[108]   T. Nairn, *The Break-Up of Britain*, 2nd edn (1981), pp. 92–195; C. Harvie, *Scotland and Nationalism* (1977).
[109]   Kellas, *Scottish Political System*, pp. 178–91.

From the middle nineteenth century, however, the underlying forces of assimilation grew slowly stronger. The coming of the penny post, the completion of the railway links with London, the telegraph, the telephone and, in the first half of the twentieth century, the trunk-road network and the wireless set, created a communications revolution in which the control of Scotland from a remote external centre became possible for the first time. There is a sense in which the Incorporating Union of 1707 only became operationally possible about one hundred years ago. The growth in the size of firms and of the public sector gradually produced a shift in the effective control of the Scottish economy away from Glasgow and Edinburgh towards London and beyond, though it was not until the 1950s that English and American ownership of Scottish companies became a very marked feature of the Scottish economy.

The growth of the state itself worked mainly in the same direction. At first government interference wore a Scottish face – the 1845 reform of the poor law, the 1872 Education Act, the 1867 and 1897 public health reforms all took explicit account (though with varying competence) of the peculiarities of the Scottish institutions they were intended to regulate, and in this they were typical of Victorian government. Nevertheless, they did represent the intrusion of Westminster into spheres hitherto left solely to local discretion. In the twentieth century practice varied – unemployment benefit and old age pensions were directed from London, but housing was left largely to local government and when the National Health Service was set up in Scotland after 1945, it came under the control of the Secretary of State. The movement of the Scottish Office to St Andrews House in 1939 and the subsequent vigorous exercise of the power of the Secretary of State by Tom Johnston began to create a Scottish government bureaucracy, but one directly answerable to London, not Edinburgh. The simple fact that what the state did in 1950 mattered so much more than what it did in 1850 made the Union vastly more important in everyday life than it had been a century earlier.

Two interlinked spheres in which the guardianship of the Scottish sense of identity was traditionally strong, religion and education, altered profoundly in the century after 1850. The monolithic face of Presbyterianism broke at the Disruption: before 1843, probably at least three-quarters of the Scots belonged to the Church of Scotland – after it, their allegiance split three ways between the Church of Scotland, the Free Church and the United Presbyterians (itself an amalgamation

Table 3.11 *Percentage of marriages in Scotland taking place in churches of different denominations, 1861–1950*

	1861–1870	1881–1890	1901–1910	1921–1930	1941–1950
Church of Scotland	44.3	46.2	45.3	44.5	60.6
Free Church	23.5	20.3	26.6	20.5	
United Presbyterians	14.3	11.6			
Roman Catholic	9.2	9.9	10.5	11.6	13.1
Scottish Episcopalian	2.1	2.8	2.9	2.8	3.1
Other religious forms	5.9	6.7	8.3	8.8	8.0
Non-religious forms	0.2	2.5	6.4	12.7	15.1

Note: The majority of the Free Church joined with the United Presbyterians to form the United Free Church in 1900; the majority of the United Free Church joined the Church of Scotland in 1929. Some of those under the heading 'Other religious forms' after 1901 are due to the residue of these churches remaining outside the unions. 'Non-religious forms' are irregular marriages up to 1940, civil marriages thereafter. For an explanation, see T. C. Smout, 'Scottish Marriage, Regular and Irregular, 1500–1940', in R. B. Outhwaite, ed., *Marriage and Society: Studies in the Social History of Marriage* (1981), pp. 204–36.
Source: Annual Reports of the Registrar General for Scotland.

of eighteenth-century seceder groups). Sectarian bitterness character-ised much of the century, and the damage was only partly rectified by the union of most of the Free Church and the United Presbyterians in 1900 and the subsequent reunion of most of that grouping (United Free Church) with the Church of Scotland in 1929. The revival of a strong Roman Catholic church to minister to the Irish community and their descendants was confirmed by the re-establishment of the hierarchy in 1878.[110] Table 3.11 shows how the formal allegiance of the population changed, as indicated by the churches to which they went to be married. The number of people prepared to be married outside any church had steadily increased but was still relatively small even in the 1940s.

How far did religious allegiance ever go beyond respecting the rites of passage? The results of the religious census of 1851 suggest at first sight that more people attended church in Scotland than in England, nearly a third of the entire population in the north attending morning service, but only a little over a quarter doing so in the south. But, as Table 3.12 shows, the evidence is ambiguous: obviously evening

[110]   A. J. Drummond and J. Bulloch, *The Church in Victorian Scotland, 1843–1874* (Edinburgh, 1975), and *idem, The Church in Late Victorian Scotland*; D. McRoberts, ed., *Modern Scottish Catholicism, 1878–1978* (Glasgow, 1979).

Table 3.12 *Percentage of the population attending church in Scotland and England, 30 March 1851*

	Scotland	England and Wales
Morning	32.7	25.9
Afternoon	21.5	17.7
Evening	6.5	17.1

Source: John Highet, 'The Churches' in A. J. Cairncross, ed., *The Scottish Economy* (Cambridge, 1954), p. 307.

services were unpopular in Scotland, and it is possible that the impression of greater Scottish attendance is false, at least if many English and Welsh went in the evening who had not been in the morning or afternoon. On the other hand, there were in Scotland church seats for 63.5 per cent of the population (as opposed to 57 per cent in England), though contemporaries estimated that only 58 per cent would ever be in a position to attend church at any one time, the rest being too young, too old or too sick.

A hundred years later, social surveys suggested that regular churchgoing had dropped substantially, from around a third of the population to around a fifth. Highet, however, produced evidence to show that the number of people claiming church membership did not significantly vary between 1871 and 1951, being around 60 per cent of all adults throughout the period: if so, they must have become less keen on going to church.[111]

These figures, for all their ambiguities, suggest two conclusions that fully justify the dominant note of pessimism that was heard whenever churchmen opened their mouths. First, even at the start of the period, the 'unchurched masses' were enormous, possibly as many as 45 per cent of all those who could have gone to church. Secondly, over the years the situation deteriorated, until by 1951 about two-thirds of those who could have attended church were not doing so. For the Protestants, the rot began in the labouring classes and worked up. Long before 1850 Thomas Chalmers and others were expressing their anxiety at the failure of the kirk to keep up with the expansion of the population in the cities, but the Free Church at least began life after the Disruption with substantial backing from the skilled,

[111] J. Highet, 'The Churches', in Cairncross, ed., *Scottish Economy*, pp. 297–315.

urban worker as well as from the crofter. MacLaren has suggested that the artisan was subsequently largely alienated by incessant demands on his pocket. As the Free Church called for funds to build as many and as fine churches and schools as the established church, the middle class who paid the piper called the tune.[112] In any case, the ethos of the Presbyterian churches in the third quarter of the nineteenth century – puritan, condescending, sabbatarian and Chalmerian in their view that the poor were mainly to blame for their poverty – must have helped to distance them from the masses. By the 1880s there was a new gospel of social responsibility, preached in all the kirks, and especially in the United Presbyterian: it had its effect, certainly, in influencing the new labour leadership, many of whom emerged from a background of lower middle-class Calvinistic piety. Not for nothing, when the Clydesiders were returned to Parliament in the election of November 1922, was their triumph celebrated by a service at St Andrew's Hall, Glasgow, when 'the pealing organ crashed its paens . . . the audience sang the Old Hundred and Twenty-fourth Psalm . . . which still possesses the power to "tirl the he'rt strings a' to the life" and quicken the souls of men who value liberty more than life'.[113]

By then, however, the church was beginning to bemoan the falling off of large sections of the middle class as well as of the working class from the regular ordinances of religion. Alternative attractions developed as popular recreation spread – in the 1890s ministers were deploring the new habit of farm workers in going on cycle rides on Sundays instead of coming to church; by the 1930s the Scots were more devoted to the cinema than people in any other section of the British Isles. Football, it was said time and time again and with good reason, was the new religion. By the 1950s there was still probably more church-going among the Scottish middle class than among the English; if one church member in four was now Catholic (in 1871 it had been one in ten) a third of the school-age population was even then going to Sunday schools run by the Church of Scotland. Nevertheless, the church was quite dethroned from the central position it had occupied in Scottish affairs in the middle of the nineteenth century: politics, pleasure and its inability to answer the great eschatological

---

[112] A. A. MacLaren, 'Presbyterianism and the Working Class in a Mid-Nineteenth Century City', *Scottish Historical Review*, 46 (1967), 115–39.
[113] G. McAllister, *James Maxton, the Portrait of a Rebel* (1935), p. 100.

questions about where we come from and where we are going in the face of modern scientific enquiry and biblical criticism had shorn it of most of the power if had gathered to itself since the Reformation.

It cannot be said, however, that the decline in the influence of the church was accompanied by any measurable increase in immorality – at least as conventionally regarded and denounced. Illegitimacy, running at 9.85 per 100 births in 1866–70, had declined by a third to 6.26 by 1936–9; consumption of whisky per head, 1.65 gallons in 1871, was a mere 0.40 by 1931. There is some reason to suppose that the most 'religious', and certainly the most sternly Presbyterian, part of Scotland remaining in 1950 was the northern Highlands. Illegitimacy in Ross and Cromarty, however, rose from 4.85 per 100 births in 1866–70 to 8.35 by 1936–9; though we know less about the regional distribution of whisky consumption, the 'Wee Free' island of Lewis was notorious for its level of alcoholism after the Second World War.[114]

Changes in education over the century were no less sweeping than changes in church life. Mid-Victorian Scotland was proud of its educational provision, but critical minds were also well aware of defects. The First Report of the Registrar General for Scotland showed that in 1855, 11.4 per cent of males and no fewer than 22.8 per cent of females could not write their own names in the marriage registry: the regional variation swung from a trifling 1.2 per cent illiteracy both of men and women in lowland Berwickshire, to an appalling 36.7 per cent of men and 49.4 per cent of women in highland Ross and Cromarty; Lanarkshire, with its heavy concentration of urban industrial workers, had 15 per cent illiteracy for men and 30.2 per cent illiteracy for women. The Argyll Commission in 1867 showed that the position was much the same a decade later – elementary school provision was good in the rural Lowlands, and very bad in the rural Highlands; in the big cities it varied from fair to awful. Over the whole of Scotland 18 per cent of children aged between four and fourteen were not on the school roll: in Glasgow the percentage varied from 29 per cent in middle-class Blythswood to 72 per cent in the slums of Tradeston. Obviously there were very large holes in the net of the Knoxian ideal of education for all. Some comfort was drawn from the fact that while in England only one child in 1,300 went on

---

[114]   Flinn, ed., *Scottish Population History*, pp. 350–1; G. B. Wilson, *Alcohol and the Nation* (1940), pp. 344–5.

to enjoy any form of secondary schooling, in Scotland the proportion was one in 140.[115]

Urbanisation had caused grave problems for the traditions of educational provision in both halves of Great Britain, exacerbated in Scotland by the paralysing split in the kirk in 1843 just when urgent co-ordinated action was most needed. The obvious solution appeared to be to remove control over parochial schools from the church to the state, which was achieved in Scotland in 1872 by the creation of School Boards, two years later than the equivalent English measure. At the same time a Scotch Education Department was created, though at first this was 'simply a room in Whitehall with the word "Scotland" painted on the door',[116] with the same president and vice-president as its English equivalent: only slowly did it attain independence, and not until 1921 was its main headquarters established in Edinburgh. The 1872 Act was an obvious move to the centralised secular direction of education, but arguably a more important shift in that direction had already been made in the application of the Revised Code to Scotland in 1862, 'imposed on Scotland entirely on the result of inquiry into the condition of elementary English schools', as one embittered inspector put it: it lasted until 1885 and had the effect of concentrating learning on the mechanical acquisition of the 'three Rs', at the expense of everything more intellectual or broadly based.[117]

The next half-century certainly saw an improvement in formal school attainments. By 1917, illiteracy as measured by failure to sign the marriage register was down to less than 1 per cent for both sexes, and even in Ross and Cromarty was only 2.5 per cent. Nevertheless, it is questionable whether Scotland shone any longer above England as a centre of educational excellence. That 'zeal for learning' which had once seemed to be characteristic of the Lowlander, and which the Argyll Commission had still regarded as alive and well in the rural areas in the 1860s, was not very obvious in Royal Commission enquiries in the same areas in the 1890s: working-class apathy towards the acquisition of education was more evident still by the 1950s. A. S. Neill, a young village schoolmaster in 1915, found the whole Scotch Code enervating and depressing:

[115]   J. Scotland, *The History of Scottish Education*, 2 vols., (1969), vol. 1, p. 184; G. S. Osborne, *Scottish and English Schools: A Comparative Survey of the Past Fifty Years* (Pittsburg, 1966).

[116]   Scotland, *Scottish Education*, vol. 2, p. 5.

[117]   J. Kerr, *Memories Grave and Gay* (Edinburgh, 1903), p. 58.

What does it all mean? What am I trying to do? These boys are going out to the fields to plough; these girls are going to farms as servants. If I live long enough the new generation will be bringing notes of the pleese-excuss-james-as-I-was-washing type ... and the parents who will write them went out that door five minutes ago. I can teach them to read, and they will read serials in the drivelling weeklies: I can teach them to write, and they will write pathetic notes to me by and bye; I can teach them to count, and they will never count more than the miserable sum they receive as a weekly wage ... My work is hopeless, for education should aim at bringing up a new generation that will be better than the old. The present system is to produce the same kind of man as we see today.[118]

His own later experiments at Summerhill and elsewhere, among the most daring and innovative in the English-speaking world, seemed to hold few lessons from which the ruling mandarins of Scottish education could learn. They continued to believe in more conventional virtues than liberation. They could not afford Utopia, and they would not have liked it anyway.

After 1885, the possibility present in the 1860s and 1870s that Scottish education would soon be forced to become formally identical with English passed. The general steps in the direction of extending educational provision were, however, similar in both countries, but with Scotland leading in innovation as often as England. Thus primary education became compulsory in Scotland in 1872, in England in 1880; it became free in Scotland in 1889, in England in 1891; the school-leaving age was raised from thirteen to fourteen in Scotland in 1901, in England in 1918; and in both countries effectively to fifteen in 1945. In secondary education the right to free schooling was admitted in Scotland in 1918 and in England in 1944, while reorganisation of secondary schools was achieved in two steps in Scotland in 1936 and 1945, in England in 1945. School Boards were not abolished in Scotland until 1918, when they were replaced by thirty-eight elected local education authorities, only for these to be superseded in 1929 by the education committees of the city and county councils.[119]

Both countries clearly profited from each other's experience in going down the same path. Nevertheless, Scottish school education remained distinctive at several levels. It aimed to be broader and less specialised at secondary level. It relied more on the use of corporal punishment. The tawse was more often in the hands of university graduates: in 1938, 70 per cent of the men and 32 per cent of the women teachers in Scotland were graduates, whereas in England the

---

[118]   A. S. Neill, *A Dominie's Log* (1915), pp. 11–12.
[119]   Scotland, *Scottish Education*, vol. 2; Osborne, *Scottish and English Schools*.

percentages were 16 and 14 per cent respectively. Finally, it was effectively controlled by a narrow circle composed of principals of the Scottish Education Colleges, inspectors from the Scottish Education Department and teachers who belonged to the Educational Institute of Scotland, especially headmasters from the east of Scotland, who were out of touch with the realities of teaching the deprived urban proletariat of the west.[120] The leaders of Scottish education put an especially high premium on maintaining the profession as a closed shop for those trained in Scotland. It was not very distinctive or distinguished in any more important ways.

Higher education did not share with the schools the policy of keeping jobs for the Scottish boys, but maintained an open door to recruitment for 'best applicants' irrespective of their training or domicile; consequently, the universities became in the course of time the most anglicised sector of Scottish education. Legislative provision in any case pressed Scotland in that direction. The Universities (Scotland) Act of 1858, was partly a consequence of the disappointing performance of Scottish candidates in the new competitive examination for the Indian Civil Service, a branch of the Empire that the Scottish middle class had hitherto looked on as peculiarly its own: it altered much, but left intact the concept of a philosophy-based general arts course as a central part of a Scottish university degree and a preliminary to specialised study. The Universities (Scotland) Act of 1889, however, raised the average age of entry from about fifteen to seventeen, and introduced a four-year honours degree as an alternative to the general degree – it differed from the English model only in being a year longer and involving more study outside the main subject.[121] When the University Grants Committee was set up in 1919, Scottish universities came under its sway rather than under a Scottish body, and they have remained outside the orbit of the SED or the Scottish Office: an increasingly English professoriat has been anxious that they should remain so. As Table 3.13 shows, in the provision of university places, Scotland remained well ahead of England in proportion to her population, though not to the same degree as in the earlier nineteenth century.

How good or bad an education system is cannot be judged outside

[120] A. McPherson, 'An Angle on the Geist: Persistence and Change in the Scottish Educational Tradition', in W. M. Humes and H. M. Paterson, eds., *Scottish Culture and Scottish Education, 1800–1980* (Edinburgh, 1983), pp. 216–43.
[121] For a stimulating, if controversial, survey, see G. E. Davie, *The Democratic Intellect* (Edinburgh, 1961).

Table 3.13 *University places in England and Scotland, 1830–1950*

	1830	1900	1938	1950
England	3,000	13,200	56,000	63,600
Scotland	4,400	6,000	10,000	15,000
Places per 000 population				
England	0.22	0.40	1.35	1.45
Scotland	1.47	1.34	2.00	2.96

Source: G. S. Osborne, *Scottish and English Schools: A Comparative Survey of the Past Fifty Years* (Pittsburg, 1966), p. 25.

the context of the purposes for which it was designed, and there is no evidence that any part of its purpose was to make the Scots aware of their culture or their own distinctive identity. Scottish history received scant treatment in the schools past the stage of tales of adventure at primary level: in the universities there were only two chairs in 1950, and for most students 'British History' was *de facto* English history. The Scottish dialects of the Lowlands were discouraged in the classroom as uncouth, and Scottish literature in the universities was treated with even more devastating contempt than Scottish history. In the Gaelic-speaking Highlands teaching in and of the native language was first discouraged and then (under pressure from the Celtic movement from the 1880s) allowed; but it was given little emphasis, largely because Gaels themselves wished their children to be given the expertise of speaking and writing in English to equip them for life in the Lowlands or abroad.[122]

At the level of popular culture, what was lost was appreciation of a heritage, apart from an extraordinarily resilient and widespread affection for Burns in all classes, and a good knowledge of Scott until around 1950 in the middle class. But for most people, by the mid-twentieth century, being Scottish was mainly a matter of identifying with tartan and bagpipes (to previous centuries merely highland symbols), with the accordians of BBC Scotland's 'Scottish country dance music', and with certain football teams.

In high culture, however defined, the Scottish achievement over

---

[122]   C. W. J. Withers, *Gaelic in Scotland, 1698–1981: The Geographical History of a Language* (Edinburgh, 1984); V. E. DurKacz, *The Decline of the Celtic Languages* (Edinburgh, 1983).

the century was large, much larger than generally realised by those who assumed that everything stopped with the end of the Enlightenment. Something certainly did stop, especially in philosophy and the social sciences, where the eighteenth-century Scots had shone so astonishingly. Yet, for the century after 1850, Lister and Simpson in medicine, Clerk Maxwell, Thomson (Lord Kelvin), Bell, Baird, Fleming, Boyd Orr and Fraser Darling in science, Geddes in planning, the Glasgow colourists in art, Rennie Mackintosh in architecture and Robert Louis Stevenson, Hugh MacDairmid, Edwin Muir, Sorley Maclean and Grassic Gibbon in literature are merely the greatest names in a long roll of distinction. Most, however, had little specific impact on Scotland. The doctors and scientists gave to the entire world their innovations of anaesthesia, penicillin, telephones and television; it was international physics, food science, ecology and town planning that were enriched by Scotsmen; on the other hand, the literati of the twentieth century were little known and less liked on their hearthrugs, even when they won the plaudits of international criticism.

It was, not surprisingly, the writers of the interwar years who were most aroused by the deracination of the Scots at all levels, Hugh MacDairmid to a brilliant anger, Edwin Muir to a sombre analysis. The identity of Scotland seemed to them to have almost disappeared. Muir said of Edinburgh:

The actual town, the houses, streets, churches, rocks, gardens, are there still; but these exist wholly in the past. That is a national past; the present, which is made up of the thoughts and feelings and prejudices of the inhabitants, their way of life in general, is as cosmopolitan as the cinema. This is not universally true; but it applies to the populace, rich and poor, the great multitude who have been Anglicised and Americanised, whether by the film, the Press, the radio, the lending library or the public schools ... the present inhabitants of Edinburgh are as different from the inhabitants of fifty years ago as the Americans now are from the English. They are better in some ways, no doubt, less rigid and hard, and less bigoted; but they do not think in what one might call an Edinburgh way, as their forefathers did.[123]

There is much the historian might want to put on the balance on the other side, the improvements in welfare, the loosening of ecclesiastical bonds, the greater facility in a cosmopolitan life of enjoying cosmopolitan pleasures, but it was hard to argue honestly that the

[123] Muir, *Scottish Journey*, pp. 23–4.

century from 1850 to 1950 had made it easier for most Scots to live their personal lives more richly or more freely. Edwin Muir can be left with the final verdict.

> . . . the powerless dead,
> Listening can hear no more
> Than a hard tapping on the sounding floor
> A little overhead
> Of common heels that do not know
> Whence they come or where they go
> And are content
> With their poor frozen life and shallow banishment.[124]

It is left for the century after 1950 to see if it can do better.

[124] *Ibid.*, p. 39.

CHAPTER 4

Wales

D. W. HOWELL and C. BABER

'Modern Wales' emerged in these years with the transition from a predominantly rural society at the outset to an increasingly industrial and urbanised one and the replacement of the old social and political dominance of the landed classes by freedom and democracy. This transformation from a traditional to an urban world was, of course, a British phenomenon but, for all that, Welsh society was to exhibit characteristics which were to contrast with its English counterpart. Accordingly, a principal aim of this chapter will be to explore and explain those distinctive aspects of Wales's culture and society. Nineteenth-century Welsh society was shaped above all by its pervading nonconformist ethos and, closely bound up with it, the Welsh language. Such separate traits as emerged were to be largely neglected by successive English governments down to the 1880s, not to mention the ill-natured ridicule of things Welsh by the London press, a state of affairs which, indeed, did so much to fuel the nationalist drive of the 1880s and 1890s for securing recognition of Wales's separate identity. This distinct nationality notwithstanding, increasing industrialisation locked Wales more and more into a 'fated mutuality' with the English,[1] and another aim will be to show how growing English influence had profound implications for the survival of the traditional 'Welsh way of life'. While declining everywhere from the 1920s, this traditional 'Welsh' culture, based on the language, chapel and class harmony was, indeed, from the opening decades of this century to be increasingly jettisoned by the vigorous, rapidly anglicising coalfield society of South Wales, and a further concern will be to analyse the equally distinctive culture that came to replace it, a culture characterised by its remarkable degree of class and community loyalty. The treatment will begin with an examination of the economies, social

[1] Bud B. Khleif, *Language, Ethnicity and Education in Wales* (The Hague, 1980), p. 1.

structure and standard of living of rural and industrial Wales respectively before proceeding to investigate the culture and politics of the Welsh people.

I

Agriculture's role in the Welsh economy, as for that of Britain as a whole, declined over the course of the nineteenth century, increasingly so from the 1850s onwards. One index for measuring this decline is the labour force. The population of Wales and Monmouthshire rose dramatically in the nineteenth century, increasing between three and fourfold over the period to 1911 from under 600,000 to over 2 million. This increase was not shared over the Principality. Although there occurred a fast rise in the population of all Welsh counties down to 1841, nevertheless the rate of increase in the agricultural counties was falling. Montgomeryshire and Radnorshire reached their peak levels at the 1841 census and thereafter Welsh rural counties soon experienced decreases in their total numbers, all before 1881. These falls were due to people leaving the countryside, most ending up in the industrial areas of South and North Wales. The profound change in population distribution is reflected in the fact that whereas at the beginning of the nineteenth century over 80 per cent of Welsh people inhabited rural areas, by 1911 fewer than 20 per cent did so. In the depression of the interwar years the net outflow from the Welsh countryside continued on a similar scale as before 1914, although, predictably, it was the central upland region that lost people most heavily. This exodus meant that the numbers involved in Welsh farming decreased by 31.4 per cent between 1851 and 1911 (from 169,191 to 116,147), and by 26.8 per cent between 1911 and 1951, the latter year registering just 89,724 people.[2]

More useful in pointing to the diminishing role of agriculture is a statement of the proportion of occupied population engaged in farming between 1851 and 1951. While 33.1 per cent of the total Welsh labour force was occupied in farming in 1851, by 1911 some 11.3 per cent was so engaged. Likewise, between 1911 and 1951 the proportion

[2] B. Thomas, 'Wales and the Atlantic Economy', in B. Thomas, ed., *The Welsh Economy* (Cardiff, 1961), pp. 15, 18; *idem*, 'The Industrial Revolution and the Welsh Language', in C. Baber and L. J. Williams, eds., *Modern South Wales: Essays in Economic History* (Cardiff, 1986), p. 6; J. G. Thomas, 'Population Trends in Wales', *Welsh Anvil*, 3–4 (1951–2), pp. 87–97; calculations from figures provided in L. J. Williams and T. Boyns, 'Occupations in Wales, 1851–1971', *Bulletin of Economic Research*, 29 (1977).

of the working population engaged in agriculture dropped from 12 per cent to 8.2 per cent.[3]

Physical factors dictated that for much of Wales farming was mixed, with an emphasis on store animals and dairy produce. In this way, the structure of Welsh farming as a region (though it is emphasised that certain favoured lowland areas like Flintshire, the Vales of Clwyd and Glamorgan, and south Pembrokeshire were exceptions) was clearly different from that which obtained in the south-east and Midlands of England. Economic conditions in the second half of the nineteenth century, in particular high labour costs and (slightly later) falling cereal prices of the last three decades, saw a still greater concentration on grass farming. Between 1870–2 and 1912–14 the area under permanent grassland increased from 57.3 per cent to 75.2 per cent of the total cultivated area of Wales.[4]

During the war years, 1914–18, prices for agricultural products soared and Welsh arable farming underwent a short revival. However, the repeal of the Corn Production Act in 1921 resulted in a sharp fall in cereal production in the years down to 1939. In the depressed years of the 1920s and 1930s the proportion of arable land dropped by almost a half, most of the gain accruing to rough grazing. The fall in arable acreage occurred mainly within tillage. Although Welsh farmers as pastoralists did not suffer as much as their corn-growing counterparts in eastern England in the early 1920s, prices fell also after 1920 in other farm produce and lasted with varying degrees of intensity in some products down to the early 1930s and in others to the mid-thirties. Probably most Welsh farmers managed to make profits down to the mid-1920s. The only bright ray in the midst of this depression in the 1920s and 1930s was the establishment of the Milk Marketing Board in 1933, a scheme facilitated by the growth of motor transport. The number of registered milk-producers in Wales grew by 92.4 per cent between 1934 and 1939 and there had occurred another 40 per cent increase by 1947, which meant, of course, that the traditional livestock rearing and making of butter declined.[5]

In the 1930s, sales of crops off Welsh farms were negligible compared

[3] Williams and Boyns, 'Occupations in Wales'.
[4] D. W. Howell, *Land and People in Nineteenth-Century Wales* (1978), pp. 14–15.
[5] A. W. Ashby and I. L. Evans, *The Agriculture of Wales and Monmouthshire* (Cardiff, 1944), pp. 15, 19–21, 50–4, 61–2; A. Martin, 'Agriculture', in Thomas, ed., *The Welsh Economy*, pp. 76, 82–3; B. Jones, 'The Present Agricultural Position', *Welsh Outlook*, 10 (1923), p. 175; A. W. Ashby, 'The Agricultural Depression in Wales', *Welsh Outlook*, 16 (1929), pp. 335–8.

with those of livestock and its products, which accounted for around 95 per cent of the total income of the Welsh farmer. The war years, 1939–45, witnessed a ploughing-up campaign which, together with high prices, saw more than a doubling in the proportion of arable between 1939 and 1946, from 11.9 per cent to 26.4 per cent of the total agricultural land. By 1959 the arable area had fallen back to 21.8 per cent.[6]

Down until 1920 the production of almost every type of commodity on the small, largely self-sufficient family-run holdings shielded the Welsh farmer from the drastic price fluctuations experienced in the Midlands and the south-eastern counties of England. Even so, it would be wrong to conclude that there was absence of hardship in the 'distempered' times of the early 1780s, during the three decades or so up to the mid-nineteenth century, during the 'Great Depression' of the last decades of that century and during the 1920s and 1930s. Welsh farmers were generally poor, able to scrape a living only by dint of hard work and a frugal life style, and adverse economic conditions brought distress and sometimes failure. The Welsh problem was, indeed, that of the typical peasant economy – poverty, overpopulation and land-hunger, aggravated to some extent in Wales by a cultural and political divide between landowners and peasantry.[7] These features were to have profound implications for the type of rural society which was to unfold over these years.

Welsh farming outside the few favoured areas could never have been a handsomely profitable enterprise. Store livestock, which continued as the staple output of Welsh holdings even after the coming of railways (the latter nevertheless doing much to increase sales of surplus produce to the best English markets and industrial towns of South Wales), could only yield limited profits, for the turnover was too slow and labour contributed too small a share to the value of the product.[8] During the late eighteenth and nineteenth centuries, however, Welsh farming was 'lower' than it need have been, and this persisted despite the improvements which came in from the 1870s. It has been widely held that the system of land tenure had much to do with this backwardness. Arguably, however, the cultural, religious and political differences between landlords and their tenants

---

[6] Ashby and Evans, *Agriculture of Wales*, pp. 72–3; Martin, 'Agriculture', pp. 76–7.
[7] E. J. Hobsbawm, *Industry and Empire* (1968), p. 254.
[8] D. Jenkins, *The Agricultural Community of South-West Wales at the Turn of the Twentieth Century* (Cardiff, 1971), pp. 40–1.

did not wholly give rise to the unfortunate economic consequences that were widely alleged at the time by nonconformist radical leaders within Welsh society. Indeed, tenants on large estates of over 3,000 acres farmed under positively favourable conditions. Under a system of increasing yearly tenancy as the nineteenth century advanced, virtual hereditary succession prevailed amidst acute land-hunger and tenants felt no strong sense of insecurity. In certain instances they were charged fair and often lenient rents, although even on large estates land sometimes went too high because of competition, landowners being led to believe that lands were of greater value than they actually were. Large landlords also effected considerable improvements – especially from the late 1860s – with only small returns on their outlays, and tenants' improvements were not automatically confiscated in higher rents. Conditions on small estates, however, which covered the largest spread of the land area, were far less advantageous. Tenants paid competitive rents, very likely feeling insecure in the process, and received little in the way of improvements. Their owners were concerned to take as much from the land and return as little as possible. Albeit, lesser owners of Welsh stock were hardly rapacious, for if they took the offers made they probably withheld from squeezing the last penny. Poverty prevented the small owners from maintaining their estates in good repair. Exploitation was rather the practice of the newcomer from business, who felt none of the traditional ties.

Although feelings of insecurity of tenure prevailed on lesser estates and tenants there were unwilling to improve for fear of high rents, and, although again, lack of compensation for unexhausted improvements (if never the constraint it was made out to be) was a genuine grievance of tenants in land-hungry Wales when properties of under 1,000 acres of large and small estates alike were being sold from the 1870s, there were other more basic obstacles to improvement. These included poor communications with commercial centres, the language barrier which hampered knowledge of progressive farming, wide tracts of unenclosed moorland hindering improvement in livestock breeding, tenants' want of capital and the peasant mentality unwilling to invest. Perhaps the last was the crucial constraint. Peasant-tenants were preoccupied with farming as cheaply as possible, which stemmed only in part from a concern for low-risk farming. Low expenditure mainly involved keeping the rent at its traditional level. Thus tenants were concerned to do as little as possible to manifest signs of prosperity. Although large owners neither evicted tenants nor increased rents automatically upon tenants' improvements, yet the slightest 'possibility' that rents might be raised was sufficient to paralyse all efforts. There was thus a total inhibition against all improvements. Fear of rent increases was the greatest obstacle to improvement, and though on small estates this arose in part from the tenants' justifiable fear that improvements would lead to increased rents, it stemmed basically from the peasant mentality for farming cheaply. An additional factor explaining the peasant's reluctance to invest was simply his lack of faith in the development of land as a commercial speculation.[9]

There was a considerable extension of freehold farming in Wales following the sale of a number of landed estates after 1910, landowners selling partly out of fear of Lloyd George's proposed land taxes and, more importantly, because of the decline of status conferred by land-ownership. Disintegration of estates reached a dramatic level only from 1918, many owners now being heavily in debt. They could take advantage not only of the higher prices prevailing but also, for various reasons, of their tenants' keen desire to purchase their farms. Fewer sales occurred after the mid-1920s with the land market becoming depressed. This break-up of estates was more thorough than in England. The proportion of Welsh land owned by the occupier rose from 10.2 per cent in 1909 to 39 per cent in 1941–3; the equivalent figures for England were 12.4 per cent and 33 per cent. It was soon apparent that many of these occupying-owners had taken on heavy financial burdens in a time of inflated prices, for soon the value of capital sunk in agriculture by owner-occupiers was to drop steeply. No adequate substitute had been found as yet for the landlord's capital and estate management. Mortgages became too heavy to bear; some sold to their neighbours while the farms of others were taken over by their mortga-gees, often solicitors and estate agents. Those who struggled on were able to do so by dint of the unpaid work of the family and were to be ultimately rescued by the inflation of the 1940s.[10]

It may have been that these new owner-occupiers were worse farmers than tenants of landlords. However, whether under free-holders or tenants, standards of farming continued to be generally

---

[9]   Howell, *Land and People*, pp. 85–92.
[10]   J. Davies, 'The End of the Great Estates and the Rise of Freehold Farming in Wales', *Welsh History Review*, 7 (1974), pp. 186–212; A. W. Ashby, 'The Peasant Agriculture of Wales', *Welsh Review*, 3 (1944), p. 211.

poor, suffering under the constraints of lack of capital, the uneconomic size of holdings, occupants clinging to traditional farming methods, and a lack of suitable education. Nevertheless, there was some improvement: thus between 1871 and 1921 the total increase in productive efficiency of farm organisation, measured 'per hour of labour', was around 40–5 per cent and the same process was continuing at a like, perhaps accelerated, rate between 1921 and 1928 and to some extent up to 1930; again, pastures of upland sheep walks were improved in the 1930s and 1940s so that more sheep could be carried.[11]

At the apex of Welsh rural society until the turn of the twentieth century were the aristocracy and gentry. However, increasingly from the late eighteenth century onwards they were ceasing to be an organic part of rural society; more and more so, they were in but not of the community. Already by the late eighteenth century, they had become largely anglicised, had adopted English fashions and values and lacked real concern for their native language and literature. Besides, their falling numbers, consequent upon the high rate of failure of male heirs, with estates thereby being merged through frequent marriage with heiresses, together with the growing incidence of absenteeism among the better-off families, meant that the traditional hospitality of gentry families and, indeed, as T. M. Humphreys indicates, their role as leaders of their communities, was in decline.[12] This division was reinforced in the nineteenth century, first, by the massive growth of nonconformity and, secondly, by the emergence of radical Liberalism. Although the gentry dared not repeat the vengeful political evictions visited upon 'ungrateful' Liberal voters in the wake of the 1868 election, those evictions became fiercely etched in the folk memory and landowners never lived them down. Again, if an impressive number of landlords, for sentimental and diplomatic motives, did grant leases for erecting nonconformist chapels, and if they did not generally distinguish between churchmen and nonconformists in

---

[11]   Davies, 'End of the Great Estates', p. 204; C. B. Jones, 'Some Welsh Rural Problems', *Welsh Outlook*, 17 (1930), p. 301; J. M. Jones, 'Agricultural Co-Operation in Wales, 1902–26', *Welsh Outlook*, 15 (1928), pp. 308-11; A. W. Ashby, 'Some Characteristics of Welsh Farming', *Welsh Outlook*, 20 (1933), p. 294; E. G. Bowen, 'The Heartland', in E. G. Bowen, ed., *Wales: A Physical, Historical and Regional Geography* (1957), pp. 279–80.

[12]   P. Morgan and D. Thomas, *Wales: The Shaping of a Nation* (Newton Abbot, 1984), p. 46; Glanmor Williams, *Religion, Language and Nationality in Wales* (Cardiff, 1979), p. 22; T. M. Humphreys, 'Rural Society in Montgomeryshire in the Eighteenth Century' (unpublished PhD thesis, University of Wales, 1982), pp. 84, 89–90; D. W. Howell, *Patriarchs and Parasites: The Gentry of South-West Wales in the Eighteenth Century* (Cardiff, 1986), pp. 222-3.

letting farms, others, as their critics insisted, did, as late as the 1880s and 1890s, favour churchmen. Perhaps most odiously in the eyes of many rural dwellers, they resisted the erection of Board schools after 1870, though here, again, the issue was not wholly clear-cut, for some of the middling groups in rural society, including farmers, were opposed to them or wished to restrain the scale of their activity in order to keep down the rates.[13]

Although the gentry's politics, religion and lack of Welsh obviously reduced their standing and influence, it is emphasised that until the 1880s they were still generally well regarded as landlords by the tenantry and popular in their communities on a personal level. The gulf, however, widened significantly in the 1880s upon their becoming accused of economic exploitation. The depression in farming, together with the examples of the Irish and Crofter movements and the landlords siding with the clergy over the tithe issue, led to a severe attack on landlords as failing to provide adequate rent reductions and other satisfactory conditions of tenure. The division between owners and tenants in language, creed and politics, it was alleged, prevented that 'community of feeling' between the parties which was a prerequisite for profitable agriculture.[14] Although, as we have argued, large land-owners were hardly guilty of economic oppression alleged against the landlord class in general, and justifiably so with regard to the numerous small gentry, the charges levelled against landlords as a class served to break down the old bonds even further. By the early 1890s support for land reform was widespread and Charles Fitzwilliams of Cilgwyn (Cardiganshire) was left ruminating: 'The old ways are things of the past, landlords and tenants are not now the same to each other.'[15]

[13]   K. O. Morgan, *Wales in British Politics*, 2nd edn (Cardiff, 1970), pp. 26–7, 45–6; R. J. Colyer, 'The Gentry and the County in Nineteenth-Century Cardiganshire', *Welsh History Review*, 10 (1980–1), pp. 504–5; J. E. Vincent, *The Land Question in North Wales* (1896), pp. 183–4; Howell, *Land and People*, p. 67; National Library of Wales, Voelas and Cefnamwlch MSS: letters of 28 October and 1 November 1892, 22 May 1893 of J. Bovill and of 9 January 1871 of A. Trethwy; *Carnarvon and Denbigh Herald*, 23 September and 11 November 1892; D. A. Pretty, *Two Centuries of Anglesey Schools* (Llangefni, 1977), pp. 198–9.

[14]   Morgan, *Wales in British Politics*, pp. 53–9; idem, *Rebirth of a Nation, Wales 1880–1980* (Oxford and Cardiff, 1981), pp. 9–10; Jane Morgan, 'Denbighshire's *Annus Mirabilis*: The County and Borough Elections of 1868', *Welsh History Review*, 7 (1974), p. 66; Howell, *Land and People*, pp. 86–7; *House of Commons Debates*, Tenure of Land (Wales) Bill, 16 March 1892.

[15]   Cited in J. H. Davies, 'The Social Structure and Economy of South-West Wales in the Late Nineteenth-Century' (unpublished MA thesis, University of Wales, 1967), p. 87.

Yet, notwithstanding the institution of local land leagues in Caernarfonshire and Flintshire in early 1886 and plans for them in Cardiganshire and Carmarthenshire, the break-down of landlord–tenant relations on an *individual* basis was not always evident. It was indeed the case that on some large hereditary estates and on those of 'old' Welsh families in Carmarthenshire 'good feeling' and loyal sentiments prevailed into the 1890s despite the widespread clamorous agitation for land reform and the wholesale political rejection of landowners. But just how general the popularity of large owners was among their tenants, notwithstanding their liberal treatment of the latter, is problematic. It was alleged by the pro-landlord spokesman, J. E. Vincent, that in Caernarfonshire, where the bulk of the land was owned by Lord Penrhyn, Lord Newborough and Mr Assheton Smith, large owners were necessarily out of touch with their tenants and that the agents were 'cordially disliked'. Despite the consideration shown for the tenants on these large Caernarfonshire properties, there was no feeling of personal affection for their owners. Vincent indeed observed: 'I have almost invariably found it to be the case that the tenant of a small landowner whom he knows is better contented with his position than the man who never communicates with his landlord except through the channel of the agent. Commercially and practically speaking the latter (the tenant on large estates) is far more fortunate.'[16] Paradoxically, if the hereditary small owners were less generous to their tenants they may have been more popular. Yet, given the widespread support for land reform, how else can we explain such a claim of continuing satisfaction on the part of certain tenants with their landlords except on the basis that for some at least, it was possible at one and the same time to dislike landlords as an exploitive class while remaining content with one's own landlord? Another paradox is encountered when considering the political rejection of the Welsh gentry at the local government elections of the 1890s, for insofar as south Cardiganshire at any rate was concerned gentry candidates 'remained as personally popular after the elections as they had been before'.[17] Thus the personal popularity within their communities we

---

[16]   R. Douglas, *Land, People and Politics* (1976), pp. 98–9; *RC on Land in Wales and Monmouthshire, Evidence*, PP 1895, X1, qq. 38,826, 38,970–1; Anon., *Letters from Wales* (1889), p. 4.

[17]   A. Bainbridge, 'The Agricultural Community in Carmarthenshire c. 1876–1896' (unpublished MA thesis, University of Wales, 1975), p. 83; Davies, 'The Social Structure and Economy of South-West Wales', p.102; Jenkins, *Agricultural Community*, p. 278.

noted for the pre-1880s era seemingly persisted to the close of the century, albeit, it is supposed, on a waning basis.

In the absence of a well-defined and sizeable middle class in the countryside before the end of the nineteenth century, there was only one main social group below the gentry, namely, the peasantry, all members of which were linked together by the one paramount factor in their lives, the land. This class was, however, divisible into the two clear categories of farmers and, beneath them, cottagers or the 'people of the little houses', who comprised farm labourers, non-agricultural labourers as road menders, quarrymen, gardeners and coalminers, and also craftsmen, as weavers, shoemakers, blacksmiths and the like.[18] It is here in the rural areas during the nineteenth century that Hechter's concept of a cultural division of labour was probably most in evidence, a clear distinction obtaining between the anglicised gentry and the Welsh peasantry.[19]

Although farms in Wales were normally small and their occupants worked the land alongside their labourers and there was little difference between them in their standard of living, yet the farmers' ownership or, far more commonly, occupancy of land bestowed status and independence. They possessed a strong group sense of their superior social standing. If intermarriage was not entirely absent, nevertheless farmers' children were expected to marry among their own kind, just as farm labourers were expected to marry maidservants.[20]

Nevertheless, down to the close of the nineteenth century farmers and cottagers were closely linked. The close-knit nature of local neighbourhoods was to a considerable extent a consequence of the relative poverty, isolation, backwardness and low production of much of the Principality, and the persistence of semi-subsistence farming, since these prevented the appearance of wide income disparities and encouraged mutual help in major farming operations. Small farms perforce relied upon co-operation at all seasons between neighbouring farmers themselves and also between farmers and local cottagers. Indeed, farmers and cottagers were mutually dependent upon one

[18]   D. Parry-Jones, *My Own Folk* (Llandysul, 1972), pp. 49–50; Jenkins, *Agricultural Community*, pp. 12-13.
[19]   Charlotte Aull, 'Ethnic Nationalism in Wales: An Analysis of the Factors Governing the Politicisation of Ethnic Identity' (unpublished PhD thesis, Duke University, 1978), p. 191.
[20]   *RC on Employment of Women and Children in Agriculture*, PP 1870, XIII, Appendix N, p. 30; Parry-Jones, *My Own Folk*, pp. 50–1; Jenkins, *Agricultural Community*, pp. 100–1; A. B. Williams, 'Courtship and Marriage in the Nineteenth Century', *Montgomeryshire Collections*, 51 (1949), p. 120.

another. For those cottagers with a little land, help from local farmers by way of ploughing and carting was repaid by assistance at harvest, so vital to the farmer, who generally could not afford to hire extra labour. Even cottagers possessing only a garden were clearly linked with local farms, in south-west Wales the old practice of cottagers 'setting out potatoes' in farmers' fields involving, indeed, a definite and specific labour 'debt' to be performed at harvest, often by the cottagers' wives.[21] Besides economic interdependence, farmers and cottagers were further linked by the ties of the Welsh language, attendance at the same nonconformist chapels, personal friendship and kinship. Kinship, above all, was the vital mutually supportive group within this rural society of close-knit, autonomous communities and, despite rural migration depleting numbers of related households, was to remain a significant element down to the close of our period.[22]

At the specific level of farmers' relationships with their indoor servants and outdoor labourers, these, with the exception of areas like Anglesey, the Lleyn Peninsula, the Vale of Clwyd and the Vale of Glamorgan where large farms were to be found, were reasonably close down to the end of the nineteenth century (even if they were growing somewhat less intimate from mid-century consequent upon the better bargaining position of the workforce): farm labourers in Wales were mainly of the indoor-servant type and, a peculiar Welsh feature, in most districts outside the favoured 'English' lowland areas outdoor labourers were boarded at the farms. Such close social contact and, associated with it, the lack of conflicting economic interest between the classes, together with the dispersed labour force and the language barrier isolating Welsh labourers from knowledge of union activity outside, explain the virtual absence of labourers' protest and trade-union activity throughout the nineteenth century.[23]

This kind of rural community was slowly changing around the turn of the twentieth century. Scarcity of labour and the attempt during the 1880s and 1890s to cut down on production costs by reducing

[21] J. Ceredig Davies, *Welsh Folk Lore* (Aberystwyth, 1911), p. 78; *RC on Labour: The Agricultural Labourer, II, Wales*, PP 1893–4, XXXVI, p. 165; Jenkins, *Agricultural Community*, pp. 43–4, 51–3, 58; idem, 'Rural Society Inside Out', in D. Smith, ed., *A People and a Proletariat* (1980), pp. 114–26; *Wages and Conditions of Employment in Agriculture in Wales*, PP 1919, IX, pp. 61, 124.

[22] Jenkins, *Agricultural Community*, chap. 7; E. Davies and A. D. Rees, eds., *Welsh Rural Communities* (Cardiff, 1950), pp. 10, 187–9.

[23] *RC on Labour, Wales*, PP 1893–4, pp. 8, 29–31; but for activity in Radnorshire and Monmouthshire, W. H. Howse, *Radnorshire* (Hereford, 1949), pp. 91–2; *Labourers' Union Chronicle*, 21 June, 18 October 1873, 27 February 1875.

labour bills led to new forms of machinery, which had an impact socially. Thus machinery restricted and eventually destroyed the ancient practice of co-operation at hay harvest while the corn-binder wrought a revolutionary impact upon rural society in south-west Wales by allowing farmers to discontinue the potato-setting group, which had been the connecting link between farmers and cottagers. This dissolving of the ties between farmers and cottagers was complemented from the other side by common people becoming by the 1880s far more independent, their economic emancipation resulting from higher money incomes and the spread of far more local shops with more and better food than hitherto. To repeat, all this meant that local communities lost much of their peasant characteristics based on near-subsistence, interdependence and isolation, and with its passing went, too, many of the old folk customs.[24]

From the opening years of this century there also occurred a widening in the relationship between farmers and their labourers, the latter maintaining that their employers were not allowing them a share in the comparative prosperity they had enjoyed in the revival of farming after its long period of depression. The failure of wages to keep pace with the rapid rise in the cost of living during the First World War increased the sense of antagonism. Such hostility was particularly in evidence in Glamorgan and Monmouthshire, contact there with industrial trade unionism providing the added militancy. The widening gulf between the classes saw the growth of labourers' unions in most Welsh counties towards the end of the war, by which time farmers, in Cardiganshire and Carmarthenshire at least, had also become unpopular with other groups like ministers of religion, schoolmasters and shopkeepers. In Monmouthshire, Glamorgan, Anglesey and Denbighshire, especially, class feeling between farmers and labourers was pronounced, but elsewhere, despite the beginnings of unionism, it could still be maintained that, with farmer and labourer meeting at meal times and fraternising at religious and social gatherings, 'social intimacy exists which would never be found in the richer farming districts of England'.[25]

Social classes and their relationships apart, what were the distinctive features of Welsh rural society over these 200 years? An important

[24] Jenkins, *Agricultural Community*, pp. 55, 257–8, 264; Howell, *Land and People*, p. 157; T. M. Owen, *Welsh Folk Customs*, new edn (Llandysul, 1987), p. 22.
[25] Anon., 'Rural Labourers' Movement', *Welsh Outlook*, 4 (1917), p. 381; *Wages and Condition of Employment*, PP 1919.

feature of Welsh farming compared with the overall English situation was the large number of farmers, the high amount of family labour and the small hired labour force: whereas in England in 1891 the ratio of farmers, their relatives and hired labourers was 20.5:6.5:73.0, the corresponding figures for Wales were 38.9:12.7:48.4. The ratio in Wales was moving in favour of farmers and relatives from mid-century, for the fall in numbers within Welsh farming in the century following 1850 occurred mainly among the hired labour force. The migration of young women even exceeded that of young males from many parts of rural Wales, so that by the interwar period very few women were engaged in field labour apart from helping out in the busy seasons. All this meant that while the typical Welsh farm continued to be throughout these years a family farm, its organisation changed significantly between 1851 and 1931. Whereas around 1851 there had been on average rather more than two male farm labourers to each male farmer, by 1931 there was less than one. More and more so, the characteristic Welsh farm was becoming a one-man concern, the farmer depending chiefly upon the assistance of his wife and family.[26]

Migration from the countryside occurred, in the first place, because of the 'pull' of the industrial areas, where higher wages, shorter hours of work and more varied social facilities were all attractions. To a certain extent, however, rural dwellers were 'pushed' out by adverse conditions. Even with the improved conditions following the mid-nineteenth century, there remained 'push' incentives: cottage accommodation was atrocious, the monotony of the countryside was implanted into children's minds by the system of elementary education after 1870, the employment of boys from reformatory and industrial schools in England on Welsh farms, especially in the south-west, in the 1890s as cheap labour during the depression, to some extent drove married labourers from the countryside, and in the interwar years fresh 'push' factors were provided by the concentration on milk production and growing mechanisation.[27] The continuing haemorrhage of population furnished a poignant indicator of the deep

[26] *RC on Land in Wales and Monmouthshire*, PP 1896, XXXIV, *Report*, p. 599; Ashby and Evans, *Agriculture of Wales*, pp. 76, 85.

[27] *Report on the Decline of the Agricultural Population of Great Britain, 1881–1906*, PP 1906, XCVI, pp. 9–10, 15; *RC on Land in Wales*, PP 1896, pp. 601–2; *Welsh Land: The Report of the Welsh Land Enquiry Committee, Rural* (1914), p. 195; G. Davies, 'The Agricultural Labourer in Wales', in Anon., *Social Problems in Wales* (1913), pp. 90–104; D. Williams, *Modern Wales* (1950), p. 289.

impoverishment of Welsh rural communities. Such deprivation remained the case throughout these two centuries, although considerable improvements took place in many aspects of life from the mid-nineteenth century. While farmers themselves did not generally migrate, they were an impecunious class, down to the close of the nineteenth century (and doubtless beyond), having to live frugally and, indeed, frequently having to struggle as hard, if not harder, for existence than the cottagers, who had their weekly wages to rely on, and certainly harder than the artisans or miners in their neighbourhood. The relative poverty of the Welsh farmer can be seen from the fact that the average farmer's return from the United Kingdom as a whole in 1950 was rather over three times the Welsh amount.[28]

Down to the mid-nineteenth century the Welsh agricultural labourer in the purely agricultural districts removed from mines and quarries earned a mere pittance, necessitating either some form of supplementary income from activities like knitting of stockings, gleaning and seasonal migration for work elsewhere or, as in Cardiganshire, dependence upon the 'potato system'. And, for all the improvement in money wages that came in with the railway – only some of it before the late 1870s being cancelled by the rising cost of living – down to 1918 the labourer in the farming areas away from industry remained very impoverished, earnings proving inadequate for a decent subsistence. Thus most farm servants in Cardiganshire in 1918 handed over the bulk of their cash earnings for the use of their families back home, for only by virtue of such supplementary incomes were the majority of cottagers able to survive. Similar assistance was given their families by farm servants in Carmarthenshire and Anglesey. 'Decided progress' occurred in both money wages and real earnings over the course of the interwar years, but for all that, remuneration of farm labourers fell far behind that of town workers.[29]

From the 1870s the earlier strenuously long hours of work, also,

---

[28]   7th Report of the Medical Officer of the Privy Council, 1864: Dr Hunter's Report on South Wales, PP 1865, XXVI; RC on Women and Children in Agriculture, PP 1870, Appendix A, i, p. 101; RC on Land in Wales, PP 1896, p. 632; Ashby, 'Peasant Agriculture of Wales', p. 210; Martin, 'Agriculture', p. 81.

[29]   RC of Inquiry for South Wales, PP 1844, XVI, q. 5566; J. Williams-Davies, 'Merchedd y Gerddi: A Seasonal Migration of Female Labour from Rural Wales', Folk Life, 15, (1977), pp. 12–26; RC on Women and Children in Agriculture, PP 1870, Appendix O, p. 40; Report on the Earnings of Agricultural Labourers in the UK, PP 1900, LXXXII, pp. 58, 108; Wages and Conditions of Employment, PP 1919, pp. 31, 51, 63; Ashby and Evans, Agriculture of Wales, p. 88.

were gradually lessened. Nevertheless, the long working day was still a grievance in 1918. Further improvements had been introduced by the late 1930s, although at fifty-two hours for an average working week hours of labour remained long. Likewise, the labourer's diet gradually improved in the late nineteenth century, especially with regard to more regular consumption of meat, but it was still deficient in the 1890s. The practice in Wales of boarding labourers meant that down to the opening decades of the twentieth century their families at home lived on extremely meagre diets.[30]

Rural accommodation remained atrocious down to the Second World War, with hardly any improvements taking place. Worst of all was that provided for indoor servants in the lofts over the stable or cowhouse. Albeit, male servants preferred sleeping in these filthy outbuildings because they were free to come and go as they pleased, perhaps, in particular, to practise the custom of 'bundling' or courting in bed. Cottages of married labourers were wretched abodes. The percentage of working-class houses overcrowded in the late 1930s in England and Wales was 2.9: England alone was 2.8 and Wales 4.0. Anglesey and Caernarfonshire had a high degree of overcrowding, Anglesey showing 9.5 per cent and Caernarfonshire 6.2 per cent. Overall, in the rural districts of Wales the position was far from satisfactory.[31]

Poverty and deprivation within Welsh rural communities led to a high incidence of tuberculosis, Dr Hunter reporting on its prevalence in Carmarthenshire and Cardiganshire in 1864. In response to tables of mortality from the disease showing some Welsh rural counties always occupying a position of pre-eminence, the Welsh National Memorial Association was founded in 1910. In spite of its efforts tuberculosis remained a terrible scourge, high rates of incidence obtaining in Pembrokeshire and especially Cardiganshire in 1918. Figures for mortality rates from tuberculosis between 1930 and 1936 reveal that Welsh counties held the first seven highest places in England and

---

[30] *RC on Labour, Wales*, PP 1893–4, pp. 16, 19–20; *RC on Land in Wales*, PP 1896, pp. 610–11; *Wages and Conditions of Employment*, PP 1919, pp. 14, 19, 51, 63, 128; Ashby and Evans, *Agriculture of Wales*, p. 88; *RC on Women and Children in Agriculture*, PP 1870, Appendix, part ii, A.19, p. 107; *Hunter's Report on South Wales*, PP 1865.

[31] R. C. Davies, 'The Present Condition of the Welsh Nation', *Red Dragon*, 4 (1883), p. 350; *RC on Land in Wales*, PP 1896, p. 703; *RC on Labour, Wales*, PP 1893–4, p. 22; *Wages and Conditions of Employment*, PP 1919, pp. 20–1; Anon., 'Hovels and Houses in Wales', *Welsh Outlook*, 1 (1914), pp. 10–11; D. Rocyn-Jones, 'Public Health in Wales', *Welsh Review*, 1 (1939), pp. 19–20.

Wales: Caernarfon, Merioneth, Anglesey, Cardigan, Pembroke, Glamorgan and Carmarthen. Undoubted factors in causing this high incidence were the appalling housing and sanitary conditions, ill-effects that were exacerbated by overcrowding. Conditions of the rural schools were bad – old, small and insanitary – particularly those in the remoter villages of the purely agricultural areas.[32]

Poverty meant that the rural community was often under pressure, understandably more so in the early nineteenth century than later. The food riots of the 1790s and early 1800s, enclosure riots, the limited number of labourers' disturbances in east Glamorgan and Monmouthshire in 1830–1, and, above all, the Rebecca rioters in 1839 and 1842–3 – farmers squeezed in the remorseless pincers of falling prices and rising costs but finding no conciliatory and helpful response from the gentry – saw the peasantry resist with the only means at their disposal, violence.[33] (Having given their support to the Rebeccaite farmers, Carmarthenshire and Cardiganshire labourers held their own meetings in late August 1843 to remind farmers of that fact and to complain against the paltry way the latter were treating them – an indication that, close social ties and the absence of any real class antipathy notwithstanding, there was an element of exploitation in the relationship.)[34]

Although material conditions improved from mid-century, protest by no means disappeared, although, as shown, there was hardly any trade unionism in the late century. The significant protest was over tithe and the land question. Although pinched by depression, farmers were really motivated by religious and nationalist sentiment in their opposition to tithe. That landlords did not face similar direct action protest over high rents can be explained on the grounds that conditions on most Welsh estates were not so adverse as in Ireland; certainly as a class they were more popular than the clergy and were acknowledged as having done something to alleviate their tenants' suffering, and, of course, they were at hand to retaliate effectively

---

[32] *Hunter's Report on South Wales*, PP 1865; *Wages and Conditions of Employment*, PP 1919, pp. 51, 127; HMSO, *Report of the Committee of Enquiry into the Anti-Tuberculosis Service in Wales and Mons.* (1939); National Library of Wales, T. Mervyn Jones papers, 2/18; J. E. Tomley, 'The Inquiry into the Anti-Tuberculosis Service in Wales and Monmouthshire', *Welsh Review*, 1 (1939), pp. 278–9; F. Evans, 'The Problem of the Rural School', *Welsh Outlook*, 15 (1928), p. 126.

[33] The standard works are D. J. V. Jones, *Before Rebecca* (1973); D. Williams, *The Rebecca Riots* (Cardiff, 1955).

[34] *The Times*, 5 September 1843.

whereas the clergy were more vulnerable. Nevertheless, frequent attacks were made by large groups throughout the century on land-lords and their lackeys over enforcement of gaming rights both on land and on rivers, and also over enclosure of upland commons (albeit on another level permanent fences stopped bickering between farmers and shepherds), so that even if rural Wales by virtue of the chapel influence was reasonably peaceful and free from crime and growing more sober in the later decades of the nineteenth century (and this was partly because indoor servants were forced to attend the chapel by their 'patriarchal' masters), we should not ignore these particular sources of underlying tension and open hostility.[35]

An anti-English element played a part in some of these protests: part of Rebecca's wrath was turned against English toll farmers and land stewards; some of the supporters of the 'second' Rebecca rioters, who poached the Wye for salmon in the late nineteenth century, thought they were resisting the foreign capitalism 'of the English Low-lands' and its alien rights and, similarly, Cardiganshire fishermen were praised in 1867 for standing up to 'Saxon oppression' in the form of recent river fishing Acts.[36]

The agricultural community, of course, formed only a part of the total rural community. Thus in 1851 the agriculturalists in the rural counties of Anglesey, Merioneth, Montgomery, Cardigan, Pembroke and Radnor formed 46.7 per cent of the total labour forces of those counties taken together. Moreover, increasing diversification was occurring, a growing proportion of the aggregate population of those counties following other than agricultural occupations over the years: by 1891 the proportion engaged in farming had dropped to 31.8 per cent and by 1951 to 29 per cent.

Down to the beginning of the First World War, and to a much lesser extent until 1939, Welsh rural communities were largely self-sufficient. Accordingly, craftsmen were to be found in abundance in the rural towns and villages, and included those who processed raw materials, like corn millers, tanners, curriers, spinners and weavers, and those

---

[35] J. P. D. Dunbabin, *Rural Discontent in Nineteenth-Century Britain* (1974), p. 293; D. J. V. Jones, 'The Welsh and Crime, 1801–1891', in C. Emsley and J. Walvin, eds., *Artisans, Peasants and Proletarians* (1985); idem, 'Crime, Protest and Community in Nineteenth-Century Wales', *Llafur*, 1 (1974); S. H. Jones-Parry, 'Crime in Wales', *Red Dragon*, 4 (1883); RC on Labour in Wales, PP 1893–4; RC on Land in Wales, PP 1896.

[36] D. J. V. Jones, 'The Second Rebecca Riots', *Llafur*, 2 (1976), p. 53; *Cardiganshire Advertiser*, 1 November 1867 – reference kindly provided by D. L. Baker-Jones.

who produced tools and equipment, like blacksmiths, wheelwrights, carpenters, saddlers, turners, coopers, basketmakers, bootmakers, stonemasons, tailors and hatmakers. Many were closely connected with farming, so that the distinction between the agricultural and wider rural community was by no means clear-cut. Craftsmen like blacksmiths, wheelwrights, carpenters, coopers, saddlers and millers were vital to the running of local farms and, besides, these and others more independent of farming like shoemakers, tailors and masons were often craftsmen–smallholders who, as we have shown, were intimately stitched into the fabric of mutual interdependence between smallholdings and larger neighbouring farms. When the factory system led to mass production of goods and implements, the Welsh craftsman increasingly went out of business, particularly after 1914. Craftsmen's workshops were centres of intellectual liveliness in eighteenth and nineteenth-century Welsh rural communities and craftsmen played a crucial part as leaders of both Older Dissent and Methodism in the years 1650–1850.[37]

Others within the rural community not categorised as having 'agricultural' occupations were, likewise, close to the land. Thus, as shown, non-farming cottagers were bound up in the huge embrace of economic interdependence between farmers and cottagers, such ties dissolving only in the closing years of the nineteenth century. Even workers in extractive industries were not wholly independent of farming, slate quarrymen of Merioneth and Caernarfonshire, anthracite colliers of Pembrokeshire, and Cardiganshire lead miners all farming smallholdings which provided a supplementary income. (Crucially, insofar as labour relations in north-west Wales were concerned, the fact that quarrymen were smallholders did not inhibit their class consciousness for they thought of themselves principally as quarrymen.) On the other hand, upon the growth in the early nineteenth century of coastal villages like Aberporth, Llangrannog and New Quay in southern Cardiganshire into truly seafaring villages (and remaining as such down to 1914), there grew up a complete

---

[37]   J. G. Jenkins, 'Rural Industry in Cardiganshire', *Ceredigion*, 6 (1968–71), pp. 90–1; A. D. Rees, *Life in a Welsh Countryside* (Cardiff, 1950), p. 27; Edgar Chappell, 'The Development of Rural Industries', *Welsh Outlook*, 10 (1923), p. 304; J. G. Jenkins, *Welsh Crafts and Craftsmen* (Llandysul, 1975), pp. 5-10; A. W. Ashby and J. M. Jones, 'The Social Origin of Welsh Farmers', *Welsh Journal of Agriculture*, 2 (1926), p. 32; I. C. Peate, 'Welsh Rural Crafts', *Welsh Outlook*, 16 (1929), pp. 140–1; D. Jenkins, 'The Part Played by Craftsmen in the Religious History of Modern Wales', *Welsh Anvil*, 5–6 (1953–4), pp. 90–7.

separation between the outward-looking seafaring community and the surrounding inward-looking rural neighbourhood.[38]

When considering the non-agricultural groups, one vital remaining component requires investigation, namely, the townspeople. Country towns in late eighteenth-century Wales were generally 'small and unimpressive' but, for all that, they were important as market centres. Urban growth had been restricted by the sparsely populated country-side and by poor communications, but from the late eighteenth century onwards certain towns, many of them on the coast or tidal rivers, were to experience significant growth as a consequence of a quickening of economic life and improved communications. Excluding those towns which grew up as industrial centres like Swansea, Newport and Wrexham, especially important as regional and metropolitan centres by 1831 were Carmarthen (9,955 inhabitants), Caernarfon (7,642), Cardiff (6,187), Haverfordwest (5,787), Monmouth (5,446), Brecon (5,026), Abergavenny (4,953) and Aberystwyth (4,128). All were important market towns, centres of trade and handicrafts, professional and banking centres and some had permanent theatres. These centres housed a middle class and supported an urban life. Although at a lower level, the towns of Denbigh, Pembroke, Welshpool, Bangor, Chepstow and Llandovery, all with populations ranging roughly from 2,000 to 5,000, also functioned as regional service centres. One other similar rural-based town was Newtown, but it owed its importance to the woollen industry. Its pre-eminence as the 'Leeds of Wales' was, however, to be short-lived, for the foolish attempts to compete with Lancashire and Yorkshire flannels by imitating their products spelt decline from the 1860s, the new centres of Welsh weaving shifting to villages in south-west Wales where prosperity lasted till 1920. Below this group came smaller towns like Bala, Machynlleth, Dolgellau, Pwllheli, Llanidloes, Hay and Llandeilo, essentially local in nature, lacking regional administrative functions but still, through their economic activities, playing a useful role in servicing the countryside. In this group, too, came towns like Holyhead, Milford and Amlwch, as centres of either transport or industry. Finally, at the bottom were those many small, entirely local and limited

---

[38] G. Davies, 'Community and Social Structure in Bethesda, 1840–70', *Carnarvonshire Historical Society Transactions*, 41 (1980), pp. 126–7; Merfyn Jones, 'Class and Society in Nineteenth-Century Gwynedd', in Smith, ed., *A People and a Proletariat*, pp. 206–7; M. R. C. Price, *Industrial Saundersfoot* (Llandysul, 1982), p. 32; W. J. Lewis, *Lead Mining in Wales* (Cardiff, 1967), pp. 275–6; J. G. Jenkins, *Maritime Heritage: The Ships and Seamen of Southern Ceredigion* (Llandysul, 1982), p. 4.

market towns like Builth, Presteigne, Knighton and Lampeter, with populations of under 1,500.[39]

Although many of the rural towns remained closely bound up with the character and fortunes of the local agricultural economy and, indeed, their large numbers of craftsmen were closely connected with farming, nevertheless traders like bakers, milliners, grocers, drapers, chandlers and chemists, together with the growing numbers of professional people like lawyers, surgeons, schoolteachers, clergymen, printers, booksellers, postmasters and bankers, were clearly, independent of agriculture. I. G. Jones has perceptively pointed to the crucial importance of these rural towns as providing the seed bed of political radicalism in the countryside, for it was only here in their socially more diversified and mobile societies that there could emerge the rural leadership drawn from the ranks of the craftsmen, tradesmen and small shopkeepers, many associated with the nonconformist chapels which were vital in producing distinctive and independent rural elites.[40]

II

The transformation of a nation of poverty-stricken, politically subservient peasants into a modern and democratic society, it will be apparent, was engineered by industrialisation, by the rapid expansion of mining and manufacturing activities throughout the later eighteenth and nineteenth centuries which not only diametrically altered the economic bases of the two coalfields upon which it largely occurred, but due to its impact upon the internal migration of population was to have a profound influence upon the life of an ever-increasing proportion of Welsh people. Whereas mid-eighteenth-century Wales was overwhelmingly rural with a population of less than 300,000 scattered widely over the face of the Principality, by 1951 there were over 2.5 million inhabitants, three-quarters of whom lived in the two coalfield areas, which together constitute only around 10 per cent of the total land area.[41]

Wales, before the later eighteenth century, was Britain's least likely

---

[39]   H. Carter, 'The Growth and Decline of Welsh Towns', in D. Moore, ed., *Wales in the Eighteenth Century* (Swansea, 1976), pp. 48–51; H. Carter, *The Towns of Wales* (Cardiff, 1966), pp. 50ff; Jenkins, *Welsh Crafts and Craftsmen*, pp. 12–16.

[40]   I. G. Jones, *Explorations and Explanations* (Llandysul, 1981), pp. 280, 287.

[41]   Indeed, the population of Wales, which had stood at 2,656,000 in 1921, in fact fell to 2,487,000 by 1939. By 1951 it had increased again to 2,598,000.

industrial candidate, her lack of an industrial tradition starkly contrasting with Britain's other industrialising regions.[42] Apart from its mineral wealth, as yet largely untapped, Wales was in the eighteenth century singularly unsuited and ill-prepared for industrialisation, and when the process did gather pace in the later years of the century, it was to require considerable reinforcement from outside the coalfields: particularly the movement of people from the rest of Wales and later from England, and the substantial influx of English capital and enterprise so vital in the initial stages. This, perhaps more than any other single feature of its industrial growth, coloured the social history of Wales. If industrialisation 'modernised' Wales, it also saw Wales becoming increasingly integrated into the greater British economy as its heavy industries provided a vital component for overall expansion.

There is, of course, no guarantee that a coalfield, more than any other region, should be endowed with all the ingredients necessary for industrialisation, nor that its population be concentrated geographically. The Welsh coalfields were no exception, and remained overwhelmingly rural until the industrial revolution, which was already transforming large parts of England, sought to exploit Wales's resource potential. Wales, then, somewhat belatedly because of its geographic isolation, began to experience that 'scattering of men, driven by the urge for self-assertion, no less than by the prospect of money gain, which became active over the face of Britain making new combinations of ideas, of things, of forces and of other men'.[43] It was, of course, in its effect upon the new combinations of men, of their relationship with one another, with their new places of living and working, and with the entrepreneurs who fashioned the new economy, that industrialisation was to have its profound social impact. In particular, because of its lateness, and the consequent scale of change, it was to exert sudden and therefore dramatic implications for the social context which it moulded.

Although coal mining was to eventually dominate the economic prosperity of Wales, the first phase of industrialisation, which lasted roughly up to the middle of the nineteenth century, was characterised

---

[42] A. H. John, *The Industrial Development of South Wales* (Cardiff, 1950), pp. 1–21; A. H. Dodd, *The Industrial Revolution in North Wales* (Cardiff, 1933), pp. 1–30, both referring to the 'Old Order'.

[43] S. G. Checkland, *The Rise of Industrial Society in England, 1815–85* (1964), p. 3.

more by metal smelting. In South Wales two distinct industrial districts were emerging by the end of the eighteenth century. The first saw the easily mined coal of the south-west corner of the coalfield attract a number of copper-smelting concerns to the district, particularly to Swansea, which was South Wales's first significant urban centre. By 1800 Swansea was firmly established as Britain's major copper-smelting centre and of the twenty-one works responsible for nearly 85 per cent of national output in 1830, only four had been in existence in 1760. Most of the works were established by concerns, or with capital, from outside the region. Although the smelting of both lead and spelter, the beginnings of tinplate manufacture and a bituminous coal export trade had all, by 1850, helped create a varied industrial base, copper smelting dominated the urban growth of the south-west parts of the coalfield with Swansea's population in particular increasing from under 2,000 in 1750 to over 30,000 in 1851.[44]

The other early industrial concentration saw the north-east rim of the coalfield emerge as Britain's foremost iron-smelting region. Between 1760 and 1830 a number of English entrepreneurs, attracted by the juxtaposition of easily mined ironstone and good coking coal, established some twenty ironworks along an 18-mile stretch from Hirwaun to Blaenafon. Early growth was stimulated by the demands of war, while Henry Cort's invention so advantaged the iron manufacturers of the region that it became universally known as the 'Welsh Method'.

Merthyr Tydfil became the industry's main centre, but works were also set up at many other locations including Ebbw Vale, Nantyglo and Tredegar. By 1850 the works of the northern rim of the coalfield were producing around 370,000 tons, 40 per cent of Britain's total: an expansion largely stimulated by the concentration of the larger works on rail manufacture. As with copper smelting, almost all the iron works were established by entrepreneurs from outside the region, as the Guests, Crawshays, Homphrays and others brought a new industry to a bleak, uncharted terrain, thereby suddenly creating an entirely novel pattern of economy and society with dramatic results. Thus by the early nineteenth century a string of 'New Towns' stretched across the north of the coalfield with Merthyr Tydfil the undisputed

---

[44]   R. O. Roberts, 'The Smelting of Non-Ferrous Metals since 1750', in A. H. John and Glanmor Williams, eds., *Glamorgan County History*, vol. 5: *Industrial Glamorgan* (Cardiff, 1980), pp. 47–96.

capital, and the largest town in Wales, boasting a population of 46,378 in 1851.[45]

At the end of the eighteenth century a few canals were built from the northern rim to the coast thus affording better access for the iron to its outside markets.[46] These in turn saw the growth of towns along the seaboard as the early emergence of Swansea and Neath as ports and non-ferrous metal-smelting centres was consolidated in the west, while Cardiff and Newport, along with the respective Glamorganshire and Monmouthshire canals, provided the eastern half of the coalfield with vital commercial centres and an effective infrastructure. The growth of these early nineteenth-century industrial towns and ports was to constitute a major transformation of Welsh society and this aspect will therefore merit particular attention later in this section.

Although it saw fairly extensive coal mining during the late eighteenth century, particularly around Brymbo and Bersham where John Wilkinson had applied Abraham Darby's coke-smelting process to ironmaking, the North Wales coalfield experienced a more limited industrial birth and it has remained overshadowed by its southern counterpart ever since. Generally, industrial growth has always been more sporadic than in the south, with small urban communities, such as Wrexham, Rhos, Mold and Holywell, dotted piecemeal over the face of the coalfield.[47]

A second 'phase' of industrial growth, beginning around the middle of the nineteenth century, saw the insatiable demand for coal alter the face of South Wales as the region took on the identity that was to, for ever, symbolise its history in the public mind. As steam coal transformed both inland and ocean transport, so did the smokeless coals of Glamorgan become especially prized in world markets, and as will also be shown in the later discussion on towns, the narrow valleys, still essentially rural in 1840, were quickly transformed into ribbons of life and activity. Although they continued to grow and remain the region's major urban centres, the focus of growth moved from the ports and from the iron towns of the northern rim to the coalfield itself, as the output of coal increased from 4.5 million tons

---

[45] See especially M. Atkinson and C. Baber, *The Rise and Decline of the South Wales Iron Industry, 1760–1880* (Cardiff, 1987).

[46] C. Baber, 'Canals and the Economic Development of South Wales', in Baber and Williams, eds., *Modern South Wales*, pp. 24–42.

[47] For a comparison of different rates of industrial development between North and South Wales see F. Holloway, 'The Inter-War Depression in the Wrexham Coalfield', *Denbighshire Historical Society Transactions*, 27 (1978), pp. 52–6.

in 1854, to 18 million tons in 1879, to 39 million tons in 1900 and to 56 million tons in 1913. The expansion of overseas markets was especially significant and by 1913 exports comprised nearly 60 per cent of the market for Welsh coal.[48]

Although the industry came to dominate most parts of the coalfield after 1840, it was the eastern half, and especially the steam coals of the Rhondda Valleys, which saw the most dramatic exploitation. From a largely rural setting in 1840, the Rhondda had, by the end of the century, become one of the world's most productive coal-mining areas. By 1913 the Rhondda boasted fifty-three pits, with a total output of over 9.5 million tons of coal, where eight out of ten men were employed underground. Although perhaps exaggerating the narrowness of the region's economic structure, the Rhondda did, nevertheless, most fully exemplify its productive character as all the valleys of the coalfield were, to varying degrees, reliant on the exploitation of their coal resources.[49]

The South Wales coal industry experienced substantial growth between the mid-nineteenth century and 1914, transforming the very nature of the coalfield in creating one of Britain's foremost economic regions. By the outbreak of the First World War, around 210,000 men, some 40 per cent of the region's total were employed underground compared to less than 40,000 a half-century earlier.[50] By the same date South Wales was producing more coal than any region of Britain and nearly half of this was exported. This expansion occasioned, and was in turn stimulated by, a growth in the scale of coal mining's ownership pattern. Although the average colliery in 1914 was still relatively small by the standards of most other British coalfields, with the typical pit of 600 or so miners providing the economic basis of almost every valley community, a certain degree of concentration of ownership had occurred. Three companies, Powell Duffryn, Ocean and the Cambrian Combine between them controlled almost 20 per cent of the total output by 1914 (a trend which was to gather momentum in the interwar years) thus effecting an increasing influence upon the region's economy. This paradox of increasingly large concerns

---

[48]   The South Wales coalfield was significantly more dependent upon foreign markets than other British coalfields.

[49]   E. D. Lewis, *The Rhondda Valleys* (1959).

[50]   J. Morris and L. J. Williams, *The South Wales Coal Industry, 1841–1875* (Cardiff, 1958); L. J. Williams, 'The Coal Industry, 1750–1914', in John and Williams, eds., *Industrial Glamorgan*, pp. 155–209.

controlling many, but relatively small, productive units together with the coalfield's complex physical structure was to form the basis of the difficulties which lay ahead.[51]

Although coal provided the economic lifeblood of South Wales, exerting a profound influence upon the entire region, and upon other industries, along the coast from Llanelli to Newport a range of activities were attracted by the more diverse needs of the ports. In particular Cardiff, in addition to the concentration of food-processing industries such as flour milling and brewing, emerged as a significant ship-repairing and marine engineering centre, while Swansea in the west in addition to its metal industries also benefited from a reasonably diversified industrial structure.[52]

With the advent of Bessemer's converter in 1856 and the introduction of the open-hearth method by Siemens at Landore in 1866, steelmaking rapidly expanded in the period up to the Great War as the main industrial complement to coal mining. In the northern parts the dominant wrought-ironmakers were faced by the need to exploit the superior properties of steel. Some like Dowlais and Ebbw Vale did so rapidly, a few others, Tredegar for example, rather more tardily, but most, largely because of the financial burdens involved, simply went out of business. But only six of the district's iron works converted to Bessemer steel and only three were to continue production into the twentieth century. The decline of steelmaking along the northern rim was almost as inevitable as the growth of ironmaking had been a century earlier. Steel necessitated the importation of non-phosphoric haematite, initially from Cumbria, but increasingly from abroad, especially Spain, and the relative transport costs of coal, ore and the finished steel increasingly favoured a coastal location. However, it was only Dowlais of the original concerns that set up a coastal site at Cardiff in 1890.

In the western parts of the coalfield, however, the greater flexibility of the open-hearth method saw the rapid expansion of sheet steel manufacture as the basis of a tinplate industry which quickly replaced the district's declining copper smelters, as changing market forces began to favour location close to ore sources. Although the industry

---

[51] See T. Boyns, 'Labour Productivity in the South Wales Coal Industry, 1874–1913' (unpublished PhD thesis, University of Wales, 1982).

[52] C. Baber, 'The Subsidiary Industries of Glamorgan, 1760–1914', in John and Williams, eds., *Industrial Glamorgan*, pp. 211–75.

suffered a severe blow in 1891 when the McKinley Tariff spelt the loss of its major overseas market, the USA,[53] by 1911 there were around eighty works in south-west Wales, mainly in Swansea and Llanelli (Tinnapolis) producing over 800,000 tons of tinplate and providing employment for over 22,000 men.

The economy of South Wales was seemingly on the crest of a wave in 1913, with production and exports of coal, steel and tinplate all running at record high levels. But the reality was somewhat different. Coal had serious productive problems, particularly a low level of mechanisation, and therefore productivity, occasioned by complex geological conditions, and a multiplicity of small productive units failing to exploit both productive and distributive economies.[54] Both steel and tinplate also suffered from a relatively low level of productivity, but as with coal, buoyant markets disguised these underlying weaknesses as they did the chronic economic narrowness of the whole region.[55] But for the record, South Wales's economy successively exceeded past achievements right up to the Great War.

Although the North Wales coalfield continued to expand its range and scale of activities as the nineteenth century progressed it was increasingly overshadowed by the south. Coal mining, though on a far lesser scale, also formed the basis of the north's industrial advancement and had given rise to the development of various metal-smelting and working activities including brass, lead, copper and silver, though these suffered contraction towards the latter part of the century. The trade in coal was enhanced, particularly with the Irish market, by the opening up of the Flintshire coalfield, which also saw the growth of brick and potterymaking around Buckley. On the whole, however, industrial developments in the north tended to be far more piecemeal despite the coalfield's more limited extent. Connah's Quay had emerged as the 'Cardiff' of the northern coalfield during the nineteenth century, a position it was soon to lose in the present century to Mostyn. The major industrial event came in 1896, with the erection of John Summers's steel works at Hawarden which provided a major industrial nucleus for the twentieth century. In 1917 the Courtaulds Company introduced the new synthetic fibre industry which was to

[53] In 1891 the USA was taking 325,000 tons of the total exported of 450,000 tons.
[54] L. J. Williams, 'The Road to Tonypandy', *Llafur*, 1 (1973), pp. 41–52.
[55] See W. E. Minchinton, *The British Tinplate Industry: A History* (Oxford 1957), and T. Boyns, D. Thomas and C. Baber, 'The Iron, Steel and Tinplate Industries, 1750–1914', in John and Williams, eds., *Industrial Glamorgan*, pp. 97–154.

form the basis of significant economic security for the area as it replaced the declining manufacture of chemicals.[56]

With the coming of the Great War there was an increased pressure of demand on the basic industries and at the same time a fall in the available labour force as the call to arms mounted. Together these resulted in a frantic rush to increase output at any cost, especially the cost of wasteful mining methods with little heed of the implications for future development and the overuse of existing plant and machinery with scant replacement or technological improvement. Thus by 1918, though the war had been won, the economic future of South Wales was by no means a sure one. In addition to the underlying productive problems, the buoyant markets facing the main industry had contracted as alternative fuels and new sources of coal saw the output of South Wales fall to just over 30 million tons in 1921. A temporary respite occurred as various impediments limited the extent of international competition,[57] but by 1925 coal, as well as steel and tinplate, had fallen to a new productive low which was to prevail throughout the interwar period. The 1920s were replete with industrial crises as Britain's commitment to the international gold standard accentuated the lack of competitiveness of South Wales's industries, while a stubborn failure or inability to diversify provided no apparent solution to the problem. The General Strike of 1926 symbolised the situation and fully illustrated the intractable nature of the region's economic circumstances.

The industries of South Wales were chronically overstaffed in the light of the market conditions prevailing in the interwar years and, as a result, completely lost their competitive edge. In particular, coal mining, which suffered from a low level of mechanisation, was to provide the main source of the most glaring manifestation of the region's economic ills, labour unemployment. Between 1925 and 1938 the average level of unemployment remained consistently above 20 per cent and in the peak years such as 1932 and 1933 it stood at 37.4 per cent and 34.9 per cent respectively. But in the all too numerous blackspots, invariably those districts most narrowly dependent on coal mining, the incidence of the problem was much greater. Thus in 1931 Merthyr Tydfil, with a population of 71,000, suffered an unemployment rate of 49.6 per cent, which had worsened to 62.3 per cent by

---

[56] Morgan, *Rebirth*, pp. 63–4; Holloway, 'Inter-War Depression', pp. 52–6.
[57] A strike of coalminers in the USA and the French occupation of the Ruhr delayed the full force of international competition until the end of 1923.

1932, while in the smaller valley towns the situation was even bleaker. In 1932, the worst year for many places, Ferndale and Bargoed experienced rates of 79.7 per cent and 68.2 per cent respectively. In comparison to the other industrial regions of Britain, South Wales suffered most profoundly. Between 1927 and 1937, whereas the average level of unemployment for the 'distressed' regions varied between 15.2 per cent in the better years and 25.8 per cent in the worst, for South Wales the comparable figures were 20.3 per cent and 37.4 per cent.[58]

While the social implications of unemployment were manifest, the overt economic effects tended to compromise the region's material progress. The heavy incidence of unemployment, which was in itself the symptom of a more deep-rooted economic malaise, saw a progressive deterioration of the region's urbanised infrastructure which further diminished the capacity for spontaneous recovery.[59] With the negative multiplier of economic decline which consequently resulted, the economic potential of South Wales sunk to ever lower levels. For many the only seeming solution was to leave the region, and indeed between 1921 and 1939 probably upwards of 430,000 left Wales mainly for the industrial Midlands and the south of England, especially London.[60] Although this obviously eased the position in the short run, it further weakened the region's development as a disproportionate number of those leaving were in the young, active age groups.[61] The trend was ever downwards as the region suffered profoundly from an increasing sense of economic hopelessness.

Elsewhere in Wales conditions during the interwar years were not so hopeless. Thus the depression in north-east Wales as a whole was not so intense as in the south. The north-east coalfield weathered the 1920s relatively well owing to the fact that this small and localised coalfield exported insignificant amounts. But fortunes changed from 1931 owing to the impact of world depression from 1929 and because no new pits were opened to take up the labour from closed mines. By 1935 structural unemployment reached levels experienced in the South Wales coalfield. The greater diversification of industry in Flintshire saw the county from 1933 – paralleling the wider British

---

[58]   The incidence of unemployment varied both between and within the main economic regions of Britain, and South Wales tended to do worse on both counts.

[59]   See especially C. Baber and D. Thomas, 'The Glamorgan Economy, 1914–1945', in John and Williams, eds., *Industrial Glamorgan*, pp. 519–79.

[60]   B. Thomas, 'The Influx of Labour into London and the South-East, 1920–1936', *Economica*, 4 (1937), pp. 323–36; *idem*, 'The Influx of Labour into the Midlands, 1920–37', *Economica*, 5 (1937), pp. 410–38.

[61]   Baber and Thomas, 'Glamorgan Economy'.

recovery – becoming relatively prosperous on the basis of the thriving steel, rayon and building industries.[62]

The international economic crisis of 1929–32 hit South Wales as it did the rest of Britain, though more so, but it did see the flickerings of a new attitude on the part of the government towards the intractable problems of the traditional industrial regions. In addition to the ending of the gold standard and the beginnings of protectionism, legislation was enacted, which, though limited in extent at the time, did point the way forward to more conscious rationalisation in the basic industries. Further horizontal integration in coal mining and the beginnings of a move towards integrated steel plants with the extensive modernisation at both Cardiff and Port Talbot (as a result of the formation of the Guest, Keen and Baldwins (British) Company in 1930) spelt progress in this direction. The decision, in the light of government pressure, to construct Britain's first integrated steel works at Ebbw Vale in the mid-1930s was, however, a crude retrograde attempt at putting the economic clock back for the sake of social priorities, though at the time it was seen by many as the rebirth of the northern rim of the coalfield.

It was more in the attraction of new industries into Wales, or rather of laying the ground rules for the future, that the 1930s saw the government step into the regional economic breach. Although it disappointed some contemporaries, and has been seen by subsequent commentators as being both atrophied and inadequate, the Special Areas legislation of 1934–8 did mark the beginnings of a new approach to the problem – of taking work to the workers. The creation of the Treforest Trading Estate in 1936, though initially concerned largely with providing a haven for refugee entrepreneurs from Central Europe, proved both a symbol for the future and for the greater diversification of the South Wales coalfield, and in itself a highly attractive and convenient location for new industrial concerns. It is nevertheless important not to overstate the extent to which industrial diversification had modified the industrial complexion of Wales before the 1950s. The beginnings of the recovery of the Welsh economy had to await the later 1930s and the mobilisation associated with the Second World War.

Indeed war preparedness and the war years were to achieve far more for Wales's economic progress than the combined efforts of

---

[62] Holloway, 'Inter-War Depression', pp. 49–85.

market forces and government had during the previous two decades.[63] Because of its relatively isolated location Wales provided a real attraction for a varied range of industries which sought refuge from Hitler's bombers, a trend enhanced by the establishment of a number of Royal Ordnance Factories in various locations. The war also occasioned a resurgence in the demand for the products of the old basic industries, particularly coal and steel, as the need to manufacture ever more quantities of armaments and fighting vehicles and machines mounted. Female employment, which in Wales had traditionally been limited due largely to the 'heavy' nature of industry, significantly increased as the loss of men to the armed forces coupled with the more varied (lighter) industrial requirements suddenly created an entirely different employment situation. In essence the war dispelled the myth that Wales was in economic terms a 'finished place'.

The ending of hostilities in 1945 saw a very different economic future ahead compared even to that which had been apparent only eight years earlier. In particular the immediate postwar years saw a scarcity in labour supply nationally which helped to ensure the direction of new industries to Wales. Industrial prospects were indeed bright as the British economy expressed an excess demand for productive resources and Wales was able to supply ample reserves of the key factor in critically short supply. In addition, the beginnings of the rationalisation of the basic industries which were to be a leading factor in the following decades was witnessed with the completion of the mammoth steel strip mill at Port Talbot in 1951.[64]

It has been emphasised that industrial and commercial development saw the growth of towns and ports; indeed, the pattern of settlement in south-east Wales was influenced more by industrialisation than by any other factor. Two main types of settlement were to grow up in the late eighteenth and early nineteenth centuries: first, the iron towns which in 1840 generally varied in population between 4,000 and 10,000 and comprised a line of 'manufacturing or mining camps' stretching eastwards from Hirwaun along the bare northern outcrop of the coalfield to include Aberdare, Merthyr, Penydarren, Dowlais, Rhymney, Tredegar, Sirhowy, Ebbw Vale, Nantyglo and Blaenafon. Their rate of population increase had been nothing less than phenomenal – faster than in most other areas of England and Wales – Merthyr

---

[63]   D. A. Thomas, 'War and the Economy: The South Wales Experience', in Baber and Williams, eds., *Modern South Wales*, pp. 251–77.
[64]   B. Thomas, 'Post-War Expansion', in Thomas, ed., *The Welsh Economy*, pp. 30–54.

growing from a hamlet in 1750 into a town of 7,705 by 1801, so outstripping Swansea, and, in 1831, with 27,000 people, was twice as large as the latter and four times the size of Cardiff. The iron works comprised the nucleus of each settlement around which grew up a cluster of workmen's stone houses built in rows, sometimes two to five deep, and, for want of any other space, these rows of terraces ran longitudinally along the steep valley sides. The second type of settlement on the 'Black Domain' was the colliery village to the south of the iron towns; containing only a few hundred people, they were smaller than the iron towns and healthier places to live in.[65]

The exploitation of the steam coal seams in the eastern part of the coalfield from the 1850s led to the rise of many new towns and ports. The largest and most colourful coalfield community was the 'Rhondda', where the savage winning of steam coal from the mid-1860s meant that the population increased from under 1,000 in 1851 to over 152,000 by 1911. In particular, the years of the coal boom between 1881 and 1911 saw the population nearly treble, a phenomenol increase which produced chronic overcrowding. Whole new mining communities developed around the spate of pits that were being increasingly opened up, communities like Maerdy, Ferndale, Tylorstown, Treherbert, Treorchy, Tonypandy, Porth, Pentre and Llwynypia. If less spectacularly, towns and villages alike, for example, Bargoed, grew up in the other narrow river valleys that sliced through the central and eastern parts of the coalfield plateau, valleys which included Neath, Afan, Garw, Ogmore, Llynfi, Cynon, Taff, Rhymney and Ebbw. As we shall see, the terraces climbing up the slopes of these valleys, for all their monotony and drabness, contained houses that were a distinct improvement on the two-roomed cottages of the earlier iron towns.[66]

The fact that by 1871 Cardiff (including Llandaff) with a population of 56,911 had overtaken Merthyr in size to become the largest Welsh town is a reflection of the shift of the centre of gravity in the South Wales economy to coal mining. Between 1851 and 1911 Cardiff's

[65] J. W. England, 'The Inheritance', in G. Humphrys, *Industrial Britain, South Wales* (Newton Abbot, 1972), pp. 17–18; *Minutes of the Committee of Council on Education, Part II, App. II, Commissioners of Inquiry into the State of Elementary Education in the Mining District of South Wales*, PP 1840, XI; D. J. V. Jones, *The Last Rising* (Oxford, 1984), pp. 13–15; idem, *Before Rebecca*, pp. 86–7; Carter, *Towns of Wales*, pp. 308–11; G. A. Williams, *The Merthyr Rising* (1978), pp. 26–7.

[66] England, 'The Inheritance', pp. 20–3; Morris and Williams, *South Wales Coal Industry*, p. 115; K. S. Hopkins, ed., *Rhondda Past and Future* (Rhondda Borough Council, 1975), p. 111; Carter, *Towns of Wales*, pp. 312–13, 322.

nine-fold rate of growth from 20,000 to 182,000 was unusually rapid and, indeed, was only surpassed in Britain by Middlesbrough. In the later decades of the century Cardiff emerged both as the leading port in the eastern half of the coalfield – it was, indeed, the largest coal-exporting port in the world – and the unrivalled commercial centre. Other coastal ports either developed for the first time or grew apace to cater for the huge demand for South Wales coal: thus additional docks to those at Cardiff were constructed at Barry, which grew into a town following the opening of the first dock in 1889 so that its population of just 500 in 1881 had grown rapidly to 33,763 in 1911, at Penarth, where a dock was opened in 1865, at Swansea and at Newport, from which last two ports coal had, of course, been shipped in sizeable amounts from the early century. The ports and the multitude of coal-mining villages, linked by the all-important railways, though poles apart in terms of social and urban sophistication, were inextricably united by common economic interests.[67]

In the western part of the South Wales coalfield the industrial towns of Swansea, Morriston and Llanelli grew on the foundations of the thriving copper industry and the associated exploitation of coal for smelting purposes. Fortunately, the impact of the decline of the copper industry from the 1860s on the area was eased by the development of tinplate manufacture and there now developed in the late nineteenth century a number of self-contained tinplate townships. Besides the largest, Llanelli, others included Pontardulais, Morriston, Gorseinon, Pontardawe, Briton Ferry, Neath and Port Talbot. As little technological change occurred within the tinplate industry in this region down to the 1950s these townships retained many of their traditional, largely rural, modes of life.[68]

The exploitation of the anthracite seams of the western part of the coalfield from the last quarter of the nineteenth century witnessed the expansion of small rural villages into larger mining villages (in some of which tinplate works were also located). In these mining areas of the western coalfield the valleys, like the Amman and the Gwendraeth, were wider and, in contrast to the ribbon development further eastwards, the villages were clearly physically separated from

[67] M. J. Daunton, *Coal Metropolis: Cardiff, 1870-1914* (Leicester, 1977), pp. 11, 33ff; England, 'The Inheritance', pp. 23–4; D. Moore, ed., *Barry: The Centenary Book*, 2nd edn (Barry, 1985), pp. 211, 271–2; Morgan, *Rebirth*, pp. 66–7.

[68] W. E. Minchinton, ed., *Industrial South Wales, 1750-1914* (1969), pp. xxiv–xxx; England, 'The Inheritance', pp. 22–3; T. Brennan, E. W. Cooney and H. Pollins, eds., *Social Change in South-West Wales* (1954), pp. 13–17.

one another. These small pit villages were closely integrated with the surrounding pastoral farming economy – indeed, not uncommonly a miner was a smallholder – and as such we shall see that the tempo of life was slower and more congenial.[69]

These industrial towns and villages were in large measure peopled by migrants from outside the vicinity. As on the other coalfields of Britain, the bulk of the unskilled labour which comprised the greater part of the labour force was drawn in from the neighbouring agricultural counties – particularly from Carmarthenshire, Pembrokeshire, Cardiganshire and Brecknockshire – and from the Vale of Glamorgan itself, but some came from the neighbouring English counties of Staffordshire, Shropshire, Gloucestershire, Somerset and Herefordshire.[70]

Most Welsh migrants in the late nineteenth century went to the Welsh coal-mining valleys and not to the coastal ports like Cardiff and Swansea, whereas, on the whole, the position was reversed for English migrants. This concentration of Welsh incomers was to influence crucially the survival of a distinctive Welsh culture in the mining communities down to the 1880s and beyond. Equally significant for the survival of the language is the fact that between 1901 and 1911 an unprecedented number of non-Welsh migrants found their way to the predominantly 'Welsh' coal-mining valleys of Glamorgan. The coming of young English migrants, too, certainly had something to do with the changing climate of labour relations after 1898. By way of contrast, migrants to the anthracite pit villages of the western part of the coalfield continued throughout to be drawn from neighbouring Welsh communities, English migrants rarely penetrating so far westwards. One other aspect of this migration was to have important social implications, namely, the influx of the Irish element onto the coalfield, who differed in their religion and wholly different standard of life. They settled mainly in the iron-mining centres and the ports.[71]

Industrial development outside the South Wales coalfield also saw the emergence of towns. Thus in Anglesey, Amlwch grew up as a result of the important copper industry based on the Parys and Mona mines and in Caernarfonshire and Merioneth the towns of Bethesda

[69] Brennan *et al.*, eds., *Social Change*, pp. 15–17.
[70] Minchinton, ed., *Industrial South Wales*, p. xvi; John, *Industrial Development*, p. 63.
[71] B. Thomas, 'The Industrial Revolution and the Welsh Language', in Baber and Williams, eds., *Modern South Wales*, pp. 16–17; Brennan *et al.*, eds., *Social Change*, p. 14; John, *Industrial Development*, p. 68; Jones, *The Last Rising*, pp. 20–1.

and Blaenau Ffestiniog grew up as slate towns. Both the slate and copper industries were early capitalist modes of production and developed precisely because this area of Gwynedd was *not* remote, good communications intimately linking it to the advanced economy of south Lancashire and north Cheshire. Further east, the towns of Wrexham and Flint were both given impetus by the coming of industry and Holywell paralleled Merthyr Tydfil, growing up from a very small settlement to becoming the centre of the textile and metallurgical industries of the Flintshire section of the North Wales coalfield. Smaller colliery villages also grew up, like Ruabon, Brymbo, Gwersyllt, Bagillt, Coed Talon and Rhosllanerchrugog.[72]

The growth of industrial towns and cities, together with railway communication, also stimulated the rise of Welsh holiday resorts. It was the North Wales coast which was to develop into Wales's premier holiday area, accessible as it was to become to the industrial masses of Birmingham and Merseyside by the completion of the Chester to Holyhead railway in 1848, and unspoiled, too, by neighbouring industrial workings. Llandudno, Colwyn Bay and Rhyl were all to become important resorts. Tourism developed to a lesser extent along the Cardigan Bay coastline, notably at Aberystwyth, and, in the southwest, at Tenby. Further east, Porthcawl and Barry rapidly expanded in the last quarter of the nineteenth century. Rail communication also saw Llandrindod Wells, and, to a lesser extent, Llanwrtyd and Llangammarch, reach popularity in the late nineteenth century.[73]

Finally the question must be raised whether there were any significant social and cultural factors which help explain why South Wales remained simply an exporter of coal, pig iron, sheet steel and tinplate for others to process and failed to develop secondary engineering industries for much of this period. The basic explanation, let it be stressed, lay in the absence of an industrial tradition in South Wales. Thus Merthyr failed to establish manufacturing industries because the requisite existing labour skills for the various metal trades were lacking, local capital was unavailable for small or new firms given that no local financial agencies were to hand and that ironmasters took no interest in developing other industries, and even had there been access to capital the relative absence of 'middling' social categories

[72]   Jones, 'Class and Society', pp. 199–214; Carter, *Towns of Wales*, pp. 62, 74, 331–2.
[73]   W. J. Anthony-Jones, 'The Tourist Industry in Wales', *Welsh Anvil*, 3–4 (1951–2), pp. 101–4.

between workers and the handful of capitalist families told against the emergence of entrepreneurs. In this last respect, of course, a social factor did to some extent retard development of manufacturing industries. What had happened in the case of the iron industry held good later on for coal, tinplate and steel, for although in the case of coal the entrepreneurs (and capital) were drawn from within South Wales yet they, too, looked for the greatest and most immediate profits which were patently yielded by the heavy industries, and so they, like the early ironmasters, neglected the development of other industry. In considering Cardiff's failure to become a manufacturing centre, especially for shipbuilding, M. J. Daunton points to the port having enjoyed many advantages over Merthyr in the supply of resources, but, for all that, 'its development ... was fundamentally constrained by the earlier failure of Merthyr to break with the established pattern'.[74]

When consideration is given to whether cultural factors played a part in all this, a number of possibilities have been suggested. The Welsh are a people, it has been claimed, with a talent for talking rather than doing, excelling rather as teachers, preachers, politicians, actors and singers than as businessmen. J. W. England has suggested that: 'It may be that [this] national temperament, together with the conservatism of a peasant people, the other-worldly influence of the chapel, the educational system, and the egalitarian spirit of Welsh society, have combined to give the professions a status above mere "business" in South Wales.' Drawing on W. E. Minchinton's study, he proceeds to argue that cultural constraints seem to have played a significant role in the tinplate area of west South Wales until well into the 1930s, the small local investors there allegedly lacking the singlemindedness and aggression of the typically successful entrepreneur in their looking to the works as a security for capital rather than as a means of making profits. If these are intriguing claims, they nevertheless, in some respects at least, need to be viewed with some scepticism. In particular, England's contention that 'religion was a cause which attracted much money [in the way of chapel building and maintenance] which otherwise might have been available for industrial investment' is difficult to accept. Again, if his reference to the Welsh educational system is to an extent valid insofar as the

---

[74] Daunton, *Coal Metropolis*, p. 52; England, 'The Inheritance', p. 32.

preoccupation of the new system of Welsh intermediate schools from the 1890s with narrow academic-based examination results – which in the eyes of nonconformist parents afforded the sweet prospect of entry to the white-collar professions which bestowed status and security – led to the neglect of the needs of the local economy and community and so failed to raise 'Welsh boys and girls to be leaders and pioneers in science, industry and commerce', yet the nineteenth-century educational system was not wholly unsuited for training children for careers in industry. For the larger and more important of the copper and iron 'works schools' provided instruction in unusually advanced subjects like land surveying, algebra, geometry and chemistry.[75]

When we turn to examining the social structure of the industrial communities we move over to a different world, for while the rural societies were stratified hierarchically into estates and, down to the 1870s at least, deference worked a social harmony between unequal groups, in the towns communities were stratified along class lines and class consciousness informed relationships.[76] The upper classes in the iron towns comprised a dozen English families, some living away from the coalfield, who exercised a tight control over their workforce. In contrast to the smaller sale-coal villages southwards, which were essentially one-class settlements, there existed in the iron towns a more complex middle class, small in numbers and largely drawn from outside, which included tradesmen, engineers, works managers, surgeons and Anglican clergymen, who occupied houses of 'decent exterior'. Beneath them came the mining population, most of them Welsh by birth and speech, though some, we have seen, were immigrants from outside. They were certainly not a homogeneous workforce: iron workers were divided into a whole complex of differing craft groups each with its own wage and status and separate housing quarters, while there was, too, a fundamental division of working and living conditions and consequent separation of outlook as between those who worked for the iron companies on the one hand and the sale-coal colliers on the other. Besides the generally bitter feelings harboured by this workforce towards their employers, a point to which we shall return later, the ethnic differences within the work-

---

[75] England, 'The Inheritance', p. 30; G. Perrie Williams, *Welsh Education in Sunlight and Shadow* (1916), pp. 24–5; G. E. Jones, *Controls and Conflict in Welsh Secondary Education, 1889–1944* (Cardiff, 1982), pp. 66, 72–4; L. Wynne Evans, *Education in Industrial Wales, 1700–1900* (Cardiff, 1971).
[76] Jones, *Explorations and Explanations*, p. 286; Morgan, *Rebirth*, p. 10.

ing population was also an important source of tension and troubled the authorities. In particular, anti-Irish feeling was rampant, especially during the opening and closing years of the 1840s.[77]

Certain distinctive features about the social structure of the eastern steam coal mining valley communities from the mid-nineteenth century need highlighting. Down to the 1880s the upper class of coal-owners, unlike the earlier ironmasters, were mostly Welshmen, frequently nonconformist, resident and, to some extent at least, paternalistic. From the 1880s, however, they were to play an increasingly diminishing role in the local administration and government of the coalfield, many moving away from the collieries to live, and, with the growth of combines, they became increasingly remote from coalfield society. Beneath the masters there was emerging in the later decades of the century, as in Britain generally, a more developed middle class of small businessmen, shopkeepers, merchants, solicitors, journalists, accountants, surgeons, bankers and nonconformist ministers, typically inhabiting large terraced houses with bay windows and keeping servants. This new middle class in industrial society was immeasurably strengthened by the educational opportunities afforded by the Forster Education Act of 1870. In what, indeed, amounted to a social revolution in terms of the emergence of a new, thrusting elite, they came to hold influential public positions in the expanding domains of sanitation, public health, education and the like, and provided the leadership of the Liberal party in South Wales. We shall see how in the middle and later decades of the century, unlike the earlier Chartist phase, the working class came to espouse a similar outlook to that of the middle classes and to co-operate closely with their representatives in parliamentary and local politics. Apart from the realm of workers' trade unions towards which the middle classes grew increasingly unsympathetic, the convergence of the two classes was to be marked; indeed, as I. G. Jones argues, in the crucial area of public health the lower classes, given the qualifications for election to a local board before 1882, had no choice but to co-operate with enlightened members of the middle and professional classes, such as were to be found noticeably so in Cardiff among its 'wharf gentry', Swansea (whose middle class was less wealthy than Cardiff's) and,

[77] Jones, *The Last Rising*, pp. 16–21; G. L. Williams, 'Plutocrats and Proletarians' (unpublished MA thesis, University of Wales, 1984), pp. 41–2; *State of Elementary Education in South Wales*, PP 1840; John, *Industrial Development*, p. 68.

to a lesser extent, Newport. Only in the years after 1900 was this Liberal consensus (slowly at first) to disintegrate.[78]

In the iron towns the collier had belonged to but one occupational group among several, such as those of the skilled iron worker and the iron-stone miner. Hence he had tended to provide his own forms of social relaxation and self-improvement, living in his own neighbour-hoods and having his own pubs and friendly societies. In contrast in the new colliery villages one community of colliers was the norm. Not that hierarchical differences in the workforce were thereby negated; on the contrary, the collier prided himself on his skill and felt superior to the day-wage men as repairers and hauliers. Thus if the dangerous work of the collieries together with their smallness of size nurtured a strong sense of community, and if it is legitimate to perceive these colliery communities as 'working class', there were nevertheless subtle status differences, relative gradations in the social hierarchy that were intuitively comprehended and sought after. Chapel offices were in this way keenly aspired to, and the prevalence in these villages of home ownership, as distinct from tenancy of houses in the earlier iron towns, facilitated the expression of these grades of respectability. In these collier villages, too, there was less availability of alternative employment than in the iron towns. And when a fall-off in trade stilled the colliery hooter all members of the community jointly suffered and shared privation, not just those of one occupation or inhabitants of one section of the town.[79]

These valley towns also differed in social structure from that which obtained in the coastal ports. The latter were generally devoid of an industrial base and their workforce was mainly occupied in servicing and in transporting minerals produced in the valleys. As such they were to show a different response to economic fluctuations from that engendered among the industrial valley communities. The society of the ports was, too, far more anglicised and cosmopolitan than (especially down to the 1880s) the predominantly Welsh communities of iron towns and coal-mining villages alike. It will be shown later

[78] L. J. Williams, 'The Coalowners', in Smith, ed., *A People and a Proletariat,* pp. 106ff; Morgan, *Rebirth,* pp. 68–9; Jones, *Explorations and Explanations,* pp. 289–90; *idem,* 'The People's Health in Mid-Victorian Wales', *Transactions of the Cymmrodorion Society* (1984), pp. 146–7; N. Evans, 'The Welsh Victorian City: The Middle Class and Civic and National Consciousness in Cardiff', *Welsh History Review,* 12 (1985).

[79] I. G. Jones, 'The South Wales Collier in Mid-Nineteenth Century', in *Victorian South Wales Architecture, Industry and Society* (Victorian Society 7th Conference Report, 1969), pp. 34–51; *idem,* 'The Valleys: The Making of a Community', in P. H. Ballard and E. Jones, eds., *The Valleys Call* (Ferndale, 1975), pp. 55–67.

how the anglicised nature of the ports was to have profound implications for the fortunes of Cymru Fydd in the 1890s. Cardiff in 1911
– prosperous as the 'Chicago of Wales', possessed of magnificent
civic buildings and wide streets and, from the last quarter of the century, downright boastful – was the most cosmopolitan centre in Wales
and, indeed, stood second only to London in the proportion of its
inhabitants who were foreign-born. Tiger Bay by the late nineteenth
century was a multi-racial community. Predictably, in times of economic difficulty coloured sections were made scapegoats; in particular,
postwar economic and social dislocation saw whites identifying blacks
as the reason for their unemployment and want of houses, such feelings erupting into violent racial disorder in Newport, Barry and,
especially, Cardiff in June 1919.[80]

Any survey of the living conditions in emerging industrial communities over the course of the nineteenth century must differentiate
between the early iron towns together with Swansea on the one hand
and the later coal-mining valley towns on the other.[81] The former
had been shaped by employers who for the most part adopted a
laissez-faire approach, which produced wretched and overcrowded
housing, lack of fresh water, deplorable sanitation and abysmal street-
paving and lighting. Merthyr's dirtiness around mid-century was
allegedly without parallel elsewhere in Britain. Likewise, in the north-
east Walian colliery villages, coal and ironmasters were indifferent
to the condition of their workforce and Rhosllanerchrugog may have
suffered even worse degradation than Merthyr. Small wonder that
diseases like smallpox, typhus and scarlet fever took their toll, that
cholera claimed deaths in South Wales in 1832 and, far more devastat-
ingly, in 1849, and that death rates in 'normal' years were high.[82]
Government legislation from the Public Health Act of 1848 onwards
met with varying degrees of success: in the iron towns, where there
was virtually no form of town government, a reflection itself of the
absence of an independent middle class between master and labourer,
delays in providing public health facilities were 'incredible'. By way
of contrast, in the municipal corporations of the older boroughs of

[80] Morgan, *Rebirth*, p. 67; Evans, 'The Welsh Victorian City', p. 352; *idem*, 'The South
      Wales Race Riots of 1919', *Llafur*, 3 (1980).
[81] Jones, 'The Valleys', p. 57.
[82] *Report on the Sanitary Condition of Swansea and Merthyr Tydfil*, PP 1845, XVIII,
      pp. 131–50; *State of Elementary Education in South Wales*, PP 1840, pp. 207–16;
      A. H. Williams, *Public Health in Mid-Victorian Wales* (Cardiff, 1983); E. Rogers, 'The
      History of Trade Unionism in the Coal Mining Industry of North Wales to 1914',
      Denbighshire Historical Society Transactions, 15 (1966), pp. 135–42.

Newport, Cardiff, Swansea and Neath, housing upper middle-class families aping the gentry and a more variegated lower middle class than in the iron towns, far more was achieved in the way of providing water supply, sewerage and gasworks by the 1870s. But the smaller industrial townships adjacent to the old boroughs lying within what were designated 'rural areas' again suffered from a lack of administrative structure, and reform, as at Ystalyfera, was consequently slow.[83]

The new south-east valley towns growing up in the late nineteenth century escaped the awful conditions of the older communities; they were healthier places and they improved still further following the legislation of 1875–6. In line with towns elsewhere in Britain, houses were better constructed, particularly from the mid-1870s, and did not in fact become overcrowded until the fast inflow of population in the 1890s. Moreover, they were not built by the colliery owner, so that the collier, we have seen, unlike the earlier iron worker, was not a tenant of his master.[84] From 1899 higher real incomes down to 1921 led to a massive increase in house-building together with a vastly improved standard of house size and design. At the same time, after 1900 there was a marked shortfall in housing provisions: a deficiency of 40,000 to 50,000 dwellings existing by 1914. Under these circumstances, overcrowded houses were further swollen by male lodgers. If we instance Cardiff, the fact that three-quarters of the houses had been built since 1871 meant that around 1914 there were no slums, but for all that the fact that the houses erected were too large and expensive meant that single working-class families could not afford to rent them so that there was a large amount of sub-letting, families being compelled to share rented dwellings with other families.[85] Improvements on early nineteenth-century conditions notwithstanding, in the years spanning the late century down to 1914 the mining valleys of South Wales and the poorer quarters of Swansea and Cardiff had a lower standard of material existence – as in their sub-standard housing, overcrowding and chronic ill-health – than most parts of Britain. Nevertheless, it is noteworthy that in the western anthracite coalfield – not really developed till the 1880s – the growth of communities was less hectic, more sober and orderly, and more

[83] I. G. Jones, *Health, Wealth and Politics in Victorian Wales* (Swansea, 1979), pp. 15–21; G. D. Fielder, 'Public Health and Hospital Administration in Nineteenth-Century Swansea' (unpublished MA thesis, University of Wales, 1962), pp. 68–76.

[84] Jones, 'The Valleys', pp. 57–61; P. N. Jones, *Colliery Settlement in the South Wales Coalfield, 1850–1926* (Hull, 1969), p. 12.

[85] Jones, *Colliery Settlement*, pp. 14–16; Daunton, *Coal Metropolis*, pp. 97–101.

congenial to live in, the smaller and more scattered colliery villages exhibiting a continuing strong rural ethos.[86]

During the depression from the early 1920s conditions deteriorated. According to Allen Hutt writing in 1933 the worse dereliction was to be found in the old iron towns along the northern rim of the coalfield. Thus at Blaenavon, no new houses were being erected, most had been built sixty or seventy years previously and were generally dilapidated and chronically overcrowded. Westwards in Merthyr and Dowlais, likewise, no advances had been made and houses were out-of-repair and overcrowded. Though housing conditions were often better in the Rhondda than in the older industrial towns, poverty had produced overcrowding through resort to sub-letting. In the western valleys of Monmouthshire, poverty in Abertillery had similarly produced overcrowding and Ebbw Vale had a number of sub-standard houses. The sub-standard housing and appallingly low standard of public hygiene in places like the Rhondda in the 1930s were inevitably reflected in the poor standards of health of the industrial communities; malnutrition and death rates here were the worst in Britain. In particular, TB was a 'Welsh scourge'.[87]

The atrocious living and working conditions of the early nineteenth-century iron towns of south-east Wales led to endemic unrest. Indeed, they were the most unsettled part of the United Kingdom. As such, they stood in contrast to the Swansea copper area where peaceful labour relations prevailed, a reflection of the more integrated social structure of that area. The most militant areas of the south-east were the sale-coal villages of the lower valleys of Monmouthshire, which, we have shown, were smaller and possessed of a class structure even more monolithic than the mining towns further north and suffered more than elsewhere from irregularity of work. Everywhere, the isolated pockets of settlement in the industrialised 'Black Domain' of the south-east were characterised by squalor, discomfort and insecurity; true enough, in times of full employment wages were high, provisions plentiful and houses contained costly furniture but, apart from some skilled men at the iron works, work for most people was irregular – especially for those in the sale-coal villages – and at times of short-

[86] Morgan, *Rebirth*, p. 71; Thomas Jones, *Welsh Broth* (1952), p. 126; Brennan *et al.*, eds., *Social Change*, pp. 12–17; Jones, 'The South Wales Collier', pp. 35–8.
[87] Allen Hutt, *The Condition of the Working Class in Britain: South Wales* (1933), pp. 8–16; Morgan, *Rebirth*, pp. 233–5; for TB in the mining valleys see South Wales Miners' Library, Hendrefoilan, Swansea: transcript of tape of Dr D. A. Thomas.

time working, lay-offs and wage reductions, poverty and indebtedness were rife.[88]

All-important in shaping this new society was the domination of the masters over every aspect of the workers' lives, amounting in most instances to a regime of fear and terror. This control was bitterly resented by the workmen, no ingredient of it more so than the 'long pay' and truck system. Matters were made worse insofar as this unbridled power was generally in no way tempered by a sense of responsibility for the welfare and morality of the workforce who, left to their own devices, were frequently steeped in 'sensuality', 'ignorance' and 'improvidence'. With few exceptions, notably at the great iron works of Dowlais and Cyfarthfa, employers saw their only responsibility as paying wages. The class hatred which generally characterised relations between workmen and masters down to the late 1840s (though there was certainly some show of deference in the aforesaid Merthyr iron works in 'good' times) was attributed by contemporaries to this neglect of their duty on the part of the employers. The fact that ironmasters were English and Anglican served to further intensify the social division between them and their Welsh-speaking, often nonconformist workforce. Relationships were allegedly rendered more difficult by the virtual absence of a middle class outside Swansea and Merthyr.[89]

Given this unrest, how much working-class solidarity was there achieved in these early years? Working-class consciousness was evidenced in the 1820s, 1830s and 1840s in the Scotch Cattle movement; in the Merthyr Rising of 1831 in which workers, excited by the reform crisis, struck out in a natural justice riot for reform, which they peculiarly construed in terms of toppling the town's middle class – ironically their erstwhile 'moderate' political mentors but whom they had

[88] Williams, 'Plutocrats and Proletarians', pp. 1, 5, 12-13; Brennan *et al.*, eds., *Social Change*, pp. 22–3; G. A. Williams, 'Locating a Welsh Working Class', in Smith, ed., *A People and a Proletariat*, p. 26; Jones, *Before Rebecca*, pp. 87, 91–3; *idem*, *The Last Rising*, pp. 19, 39–40; *Commissioners of Inquiry into the Employment of Children and Young Persons in Mines*, PP 1842, XVII; *Sanitary Condition of Swansea and Merthyr Tydfil*, PP 1845.

[89] Jones, *The Last Rising*, pp. 25, 34–6; Williams, 'Plutocrats and Proletarians', pp. 4, 25–35, 56; E. L. Edmunds, ed., *I Was There: The Memoirs of H. S. Tremenheere*, (Windsor, 1965), pp. 37–8; P. E. Razell and R. J. W. Wainwright, eds., *The Victorian Working Class: Selections from the Morning Chronicle* (1973), p. 37; *Report of the Commissioners of Inquiry into the State of Education in Wales*, PP 1847, XXVII, Part 2, p. 293; *Employment of Children in Mines*, PP 1842, p. 481; *State of Elementary Education in South Wales*, PP 1840, p. 216; T. Phillips, *Wales* (1849), pp. 36, 47.

finally come to lose faith in – and winning for themselves freedom and control over their workplace, industry and communities; and in Chartism, the latter movements in aiming at workers' control over production representing a significant advance on the earlier strikes and riots which were traditional-type consumer movements.[90] Albeit, this working-class movement lacked both complete unity and continuity: witness the want of involvement of *all* Merthyr workers in the 1831 Rising, the refusal of Merthyr men to adopt the Scotch Cattle organisation and the split between Merthyr and Monmouthshire men during the Newport Rising of 1839. Such weakness emanated from a number of factors such as the overwhelming power of the employers, the lack of a trade-union tradition amongst labourers only recently loosed from their rural moorings, the division into different trades within the workforce – divisions exploited by the masters – a want of strong leadership, and the hindrance to working-class awareness, respectively, of chapel and public house.[91]

Although labour relations in the iron industry in the two decades after the mid-1840s were harmonious – reflecting the more paternalistic approach of the masters after the Chartist troubles[92] – the 1840s to the mid-1870s were characterised by strife amongst the South Walian colliers over wage fluctuations and safety conditions. The three major strikes of the early 1870s under the aegis of the Amalgamated Association of Miners were to give way to an era of peace, however, with the institution in 1875 of the Sliding Scale whereby wages were to be regulated according to the selling price of coal. Mabon, the attractive miners' leader, and his fellow-agents, Lib-Lab in their belief in the identity of interest between capital and labour, had an appreciation of the employers' difficulties and were ready to compromise. His personal influence meant that the mechanism, for all its defects in frequently reducing wages to subsistence level, was accepted by

[90] Williams, 'Locating a Welsh Working Class', pp. 28, 36, 38; Jones, *Before Rebecca*, pp. 108–9, 154–5, 157–8; Williams, *The Merthyr Rising*, pp. 131–3, 224, 227–8; Williams, 'Plutocrats and Proletarians', p. 40; A. V. John, 'The Chartist Endurance', *Morgannwg*, 15 (1971), pp. 24, 29–35; Jones, *The Last Rising*, pp. 113, 207–8; *idem*, 'Chartism in Welsh Communities', *Welsh History Review*, 6 (1973), p. 255.
[91] K. Strange, 'The Condition of the Working Classes in Merthyr Tydfil, c. 1840–1850' (unpublished PhD thesis, University of Wales, 1982), pp. 494–502; Williams, 'Plutocrats and Proletarians', pp. 40–3, 50; Williams, 'Locating a Welsh Working Class', p. 38; *idem*, 'The Emergence of a Working Class Movement', in A. J. Roderick, ed., *Wales through the Ages* (Llandybie, 1960), vol. 2, pp. 140–2; Morris and Williams, *South Wales Coal Industry*, p. 270.
[92] *RC on Trades Unions, Fifth Report*, PP 1867–8, XXXIX; Phillips, *Wales*, pp. 38–9.

the workforce for a long time, the men becoming disgruntled only in the 1890s.[93]

South Wales was clearly a slow starter in terms of the development of an industrial labour movement. That no effective coalfield-wide union was to be achieved before 1898 was principally due to district particularism, which was exacerbated by the physical isolation of each valley. Moreover, the Sliding Scale itself removed the essential need for a trade union. Again, the phenomenal rate of growth of the industry after 1875 demanded a steady inflow of outside labour, often rural, which added to the problems of organisation. Nonconformist chapels, too, continued in their opposition to unions while the power of the employers militated against a strong, centralised union. Likewise, among the small, primitive pit villages of north-east Wales unionism was very weak till the 1890s, although thereafter the sterling leadership of Edward Hughes was to mould the North Wales Miners' Association between 1898 and 1914 into a strong body.[94]

The souring of industrial relations on the South Wales coalfield in the 1890s erupted in the strike and six-month lock-out of 1898 when the miners denounced the Sliding Scale. Out of their defeat and sense of bitterness and humiliation – which had significantly been absent in their 1875 defeat – came a new order, the South Wales Miners' Federation with over 100,000 members. A sea-change in labour relations on the coalfield was marked by 1898, for conciliation gave way to militancy.[95] The new mood of the 1890s in the south-east was paralleled in the slate-quarrying industry of north-west Wales. The Penrhyn quarrymen, passionately Welsh in language and national sentiment, strongly nonconformist, remarkably cultured and, from the early nineties, increasingly class conscious, were driven into a principled, grim but hopeless struggle in 1896–7 and 1900–3 for the very right of combination itself against a 'feudal-minded', reactionary employer, Lord Penrhyn, who incredibly extended his aristocratic

---

[93]   Morris and Williams, *South Wales Coal Industry*, pp. 248–84; E. W. Evans, *The Miners of South Wales* (Cardiff, 1961), pp. 65–116, 137–9, 227; *idem, Mabon* (Cardiff, 1959), pp. 2–14; Lewis, *The Rhondda Valleys*, pp. 167–8.

[94]   Evans, *The Miners of South Wales*, pp. 122–6, 216–17; *idem, Mabon*, pp. 18–19; L. J. Williams, 'The Strike of 1898', *Morgannwg*, 9 (1965), p. 63; E. Rogers, 'The History of Trade Unionism in the Coalmining Industry of North Wales to 1914' (unpublished MA thesis, University of Wales, 1928); T. McCay, 'Edward Hughes, 1856–1925, North Wales' Miners' Agent', *Llafur*, 2 (1979), p. 48; *Carnarvon and Denbigh Herald*, 18 November 1892.

[95]   Williams, 'The Strike of 1898', pp. 77–9; Morgan, *Rebirth*, pp. 77–8.

philosophy of the sacred freedom of contract in agrarian tenurial relations to cover 'free labour' in the industrial field.[96]

The full implications of the new mood among South Wales miners heralded in 1898 was to be seen in the years 1908–14, for now the mining areas there became a cockpit of class war, witnessing in particular the year-long Cambrian Combine strike of 1910–11 in the Rhondda which spilled over into the notorious Tonypandy riots of 7–8 November 1910. Conflict basically grew out of the new situation facing owners and colliers because of declining productivity – owners were thus seeing their costs rising while colliers faced an erosion of earnings. Coalowners, in a bid to lower them, sought to reduce the customary allowances made for working in 'abnormal places' while workers responded by insisting on a minimum payment for this disadvantaged work. Given that technological improvements had not come about to raise productivity, the two parties were set on a collision course. The increasing tendency towards the large combine heightened the potential for conflict. In their situation of exploitation, the militancy of the miners also owed much to the influence of new ideas on left-wing socialism. Vital in disseminating these doctrines of class struggle was the Central Labour College and its tutorial classes founded on the coalfield and, closely associated with the CLC movement, the Plebs League, based in the Rhondda, although it has been contended that the Marxist ideas stemming from these classes were not so much causing as reinforcing a trend towards a more class-conscious Labour movement that had emerged before the Ruskin College strike. Although some members of these socialist classes were attracted to ideas of revolutionary syndicalism, many more, while Marxists, sought to apply their gospel through conventional political and trade-union channels. Even though the militants furnished Marxist trade-union leadership, the growth of Marxist classes on the coalfield before 1914 must not be overstated; K. O. Morgan demonstrates that most miners before 1914 embraced either the constitutional gradualism of the Labour party or Liberalism. Heightened consciousness was to be seen also amongst other industrial workers: the new unions and trades councils of the 1890s survived into this century to provide the power

[96] This is based on the fine analysis of R. M. Jones, *The North Wales Quarrymen, 1874–1922* (Cardiff, 1982).

house of a new working-class aggressiveness, manifested above all by the Welsh railwaymen.[97]

Faced with the continuing long-term problems of the fall in real wages and the tendency towards large combines and the immediate wartime problems like high prices and profiteering, the miners' militancy was profoundly sharpened during the war; valley communities by 1916–17 were awash with class antagonism, each side viewing the other with equal hostility.[98] This tide of militancy flowed out of the war years and ran ever stronger to 1921. Marxism had by now taken a firm hold on the coalfield and there was a heady whiff of revolution and the overthrow of capitalism in the air. But this confident, assertive militancy was to take a battering following the onset of industrial depression from 1921. The year 1926 was a climacteric in the Welsh Labour movement, demonstrating the arrival of an 'alternative cultural pattern' severed from the old nonconformist Liberal consensus founded on deference, conciliation and harmony, an alternative cultural pattern having no counterpart elsewhere in industrial Britain. So it was that this uniquely radicalised, internationally orientated working class, bolstered by the militant Miners' Minority movement of 1924–5 and by an increasingly implacable SWMF executive, more so than elsewhere defiantly resisted, in the face of awful odds, the attack on living standards. Perhaps the tragedy was, as Thomas Jones saw it, that both sides were led by uncompromising, 'confrontation' men.[99]

By December 1926 it was all over; the miners returned to lower

---

[97] D. Smith, 'Tonypandy 1910: Definitions of Community', *Past & Present*, 87 (1980), pp. 158–84; G. A. Williams, *When Was Wales?* (1985), pp. 241–2, 249; Morgan, *Rebirth*, pp. 75–6, 145–54; H. Francis and D. Smith, *The Fed* (1980), pp. 5–8, 10, 13, 15; D. Hopkin, 'The Llanelli Riots 1911', *Welsh History Review*, 11 (1983); Williams, 'The Road to Tonypandy', pp. 41–2; R. Lewis, 'Leaders and Teachers: The Origins and Development of the Workers' Education Movement in South Wales, 1906–40' (unpublished PhD thesis, University of Wales, 1979), pp. 151–3, 220–6, 230–43; P. Stead, *Coleg Harlech* (Cardiff, 1977), p. 8; L. J. Williams, 'The New Unionism in South Wales', *Welsh History Review*, 1 (1963), pp. 413–29.

[98] Morgan, *Rebirth*, pp. 172–4; Francis and Smith, *The Fed*, pp. 22–3; J. L. Rees and N. Nicholas, 'The Policy of the Colliers', *Welsh Outlook*, 2 (1915), pp. 375–7; National Library of Wales, Edgar Chappell papers, box 7: evidence of Frank Hodges before Commission into Industrial Unrest, 1917; *Commission of Inquiry into Industrial Unrest. Report of Commissioners for Wales*, PP 1917–18, XV, pp. 20–4; Anon., 'The Unrest in the Coalfield', *Welsh Outlook*, 3 (1916), p. 379.

[99] Francis and Smith, *The Fed*, pp. 28, 52–6; Williams, *When Was Wales?*, pp. 250–1, 266–7; Morgan, *Rebirth*, pp. 194–7, 284ff; Lewis, 'Leaders and Teachers', pp. 363, 439; Gwyn Jones, *Times Like These* (1979), p. 165; Anon., 'The Mind of the Miner', *Welsh Outlook*, 3 (1916), p. 279; H. Francis, 'South Wales', in J. Skelley, ed., *The General Strike* (1976), pp. 240–1; Stead, *Coleg Harlech*, p. 19.

wages and longer hours and their union, their great anchorsheet and support at all levels during the struggle, was smashed until the mid-thirties; union officials and 'trouble-makers' were victimised, the SWMF membership fell dramatically as many, particularly middle-aged, men, who were all along moderate in outlook, bitterly blamed the left-wing militants for their parlous condition after 1926. Poverty and emigration, too, eroded its ranks as also did the development of the hated company unionism, which in the mining villages of Bedwas, Bedlinog, Trelewis, Nelson and Treharris fissured class and community solidarity. In north-east Wales the resistance of miners led to a sharp and permanent fall in the union's strength.[100]

By the mid-thirties, however, the community consciousness of 1926 was once again surging through the valleys with militancy and unrest once again to the fore, contrasting with the defensive position of the coalfield since 1926. It contrasted, too, with the lack of real militancy among North Wales miners, strikes in the 1930s playing but an insignificant role. Now, in 1934, the SWMF began to involve itself directly in the 'unemployed' struggle, co-operation between employed and unemployed showing itself in the public outcry against Part II of the Unemployment Insurance Act which, it was claimed, through the implementation of the household means test would have led to the break-up of the revered family itself. United Front action in the form of massive demonstrations and marches (which surpassed for sheer breathless scale of communal action similar marches elsewhere in Britain), culminating in the monster marches of Sunday, 3 February 1935, forced the government to capitulate. Such morale-boosting action, coupled with the expunging of the 'Scab' union, meant that 1935 was indeed a watershed year in the South Wales Labour movement.[101] The latter, led by Communists and left-wing activists, now re-established its leadership over the valley communities and the initiative in community action was wrested from those active in the social service response to unemployment and who, embracing the

[100] Francis and Smith, *The Fed*, pp. 55–9, 65–6, 78; South Wales Miners' Library, Swansea, oral testimonies of O. Morgan, R. Fine and O. Powell; Francis, 'South Wales', p. 250–2; C. E. Gwyther, *The Valley Shall Be Exulted* (1949), pp. 22–3; H. W. Edwards, *The Good Patch* (1938), p. 143; Morgan, *Rebirth* p. 287; *The Colliery Workers' Magazine*, 5 (1927), p. 43; R. M. Jones, 'A Note on 1926 in North Wales', *Llafur*, 2 (1977), pp. 59–60.

[101] Francis and Smith,*The Fed*, pp. 113–38, 202–3, 216–17, 224, 245, 253–4, 258, 275, 282–9; Williams, *When Was Wales?*, pp. 262–4; Jim Griffiths, *Pages from Memory* (1969), pp. 42–3, 137–8; South Wales Miners' Library, oral testimony of Mavis Llewellyn.

ethos of the WEA, had sought to replace class conflict by an outlook based on co-operation and reconciliation.[102]

Amidst all the drama of strikes, marches and demonstrations we must not lose sight of the people themselves, those brave, 'simple, faithful' folk of Idris Davies's depiction, whose menfolk were proud of their work-skills, of their family and home. Material conditions of housing and health deteriorated and social outlets, such as chapel activities, musical activities in general, miners' institutes and libraries, and rugby teams, all dramatically declined. There is no escaping the fact that long years of unemployment, despite the brave front to poverty, led to periodic bouts of depression among the ordinary workers. While the over-forty-fives got used to the 'thirty shillings-a-week' standard, there was nevertheless resentment at idleness; according to Jennings 'an abiding sense of waste of life' was felt by nearly all. Nevertheless, involvement in schemes such as the unemployment clubs (associated with the various voluntary bodies backed up financially from the mid-thirties by the National Council of Social Services, such clubs simply concerning themselves with the problem of 'time to spare') destroyed apathy and hopelessness. For the unemployed young adult there was a sense of fatalism about the chances of employment, even that fate itself had decreed his predicament. Certainly, the industrial depression increased the feeling of solidarity and brought shopkeepers and teachers into the fold. Nevertheless, it is debatable as to just how 'political' the valleys were: it is likely that although passions ran high at times of lock-outs and strikes, in normal times only a minority were 'single subject' men; most were milder, middle-of-the-road Labour supporters, whose politics were just one element in their lives – by the demanding standards of the left they were politically apathetic. Even if social life was truncated, most still found some outlets to relieve the gloom; some in the social and cultural activities of the chapels; some in the unemployed clubs and many more in the miners' institutes and libraries (the latter before 1937–8 frowning upon the clubs as merely designed to keep workers quiet); some in the brass bands and choirs; some in the dance-halls and the 'pictures'; some in sport like running in the Cambrian Dash and the Pontypridd Powder Hall, boxing and rugby; and some in walking alone or in groups on the mountains and in working their allotments. Even if reading of serious literature was falling off by the mid-thirties,

[102] Lewis, 'Leaders and Teachers', pp. 553–5, 562.

that decade could nevertheless still boast of a laudably cultured group of workers. Life in the big towns of Cardiff and Swansea in particular was fairly robust; Swansea, escaping the full blight of depression, was a lively and quite sophisticated town in the 1930s. So life was not unalleviated misery or exclusively spent in political activity. Throughout, the womenfolk shouldered much of the burden and, despite the physical toll on them, never lost courage.[103]

III

Central in shaping the distinctive character of Welsh society, both rural and urban, down to the close of the nineteenth century and (if to a lesser extent) beyond, were nonconformity and the Welsh language. The two were to be closely associated, for the chapels were fiercely Welsh in character – indeed, it was held that the very survival of religion was dependent on the continuance of the Welsh tongue. The nineteenth century was to witness a dramatic growth in nonconformity, so that by mid-century, despite the fact that only something like a third of the Welsh population attended a place of worship (albeit, the Welsh people, particularly its poorest groups, were a great deal more religious than the English), those who did were overwhelmingly nonconformist. Its growth had much to do with the fact that the established church, based on the pre-industrial parish unit, was too administratively cumbersome and inflexible to cope with a fast rising population and, dominated by the landowning classes, its undemocratic ethos and English outlook could not compete with the opportunities offered by the chapels for fellowship and lay participation, their emotional hymns and sermons and wholly Welsh atmosphere. This last evangelical, emotional trait had been imparted to Old Dissent by the Methodist revival; it was this which constituted Methodism's most important contribution and more than outweighed its negative

---

[103] Jones, *Times Like These*, foreword by Glyn Jones and pp. 16–17; South Wales Miners' Library, oral testimonies of Phil Abraham, Trevor Davies, Bryn Thomas, O. Morgan, W. Rosser-Jones and R. Fine; 'Nantyglo: Portrait of a Mining Town', *Fact*, Nov. 1937, pp. 37, 39–40, 48, 76–7, 237; H. Jennings, *Brynmawr* (1934), pp. 140–1; A. Lush, *The Young Adult in South Wales* (Cardiff, 1941), p. 31; *Fourth Report of the Commissioner for the Special Areas*, PP 1937–8, XII, p. 787; Morgan, *Rebirth*, p. 239; P. Stead, 'And Every Valley Shall Be Exalted', *Morgannwg*, 34 (1980), pp. 87–8; Edwards, *The Good Patch*, pp. 151–4, 159–60, 162, 177, 182–4; *Third Report of the Commissioner for the Special Areas*, PP 1936–7, XII, p. 661; P. Stead, 'The Swansea of Dylan Thomas', in *A Memorable Year 1977–8* (Dylan Thomas Society Wales Branch, 1978).

impact in helping undermine the old fun-inducing, joyous customs of the peasantry.[104]

While in industrial areas the chapel's influence was noticeably to decline from the close of the First World War, religion continued to play a great part in the lives of Welsh rural dwellers down to the 1940s, especially in the remoter 'Welsh' counties, albeit the old puritanical ideal was softening. Nevertheless, the wireless, cinema, the development of bus services and the secularising influence of the schools were all eroding the old cultural isolation and dogmatic beliefs, and the hold of the chapel suffered accordingly. Moreover, increasingly from the last decades of the nineteenth century people were being appointed deacons because they were of the emerging middle class and others passed over because of poverty and this doubtless contributed to the chapel's decline.[105]

At the height of its influence down to the turn of the present century, chapel services in rural Wales were held three times a Sunday, and week-night meetings would include a *seiet*, a prayer meeting, an occasional sermon, sometimes a lecture or a musical evening, and, in the Welsh-speaking districts, a literary society during winter.[106] Sunday schools, attended by adults as well as children, played a vital part in chapel life and gave those of lowly occupational status a chance to show their intellectual and 'public' gifts. Thus in Cardiganshire in 1918 a large proportion of Sunday school teachers were farm servants. The Calvinistic Methodists there held scripture examinations annually and presented medals to the best performers in each class, on a number of occasions farm labourers winning the gold medal given to the most successful in the adult class.[107] Arguably, Sunday schools had an even more profound influence in the rural towns and countryside than the *eisteddfodau*. 'Their gifted teachers and perfect organisation have made the Welsh nation a nation of students', wrote

[104]   Williams, *Religion, Language and Nationality*, pp. 25, 104; Jones, *Explorations and Explanations*, pp. 21, 26–7, 221, 225–7; E. T. Davies, *Religion and Society in the Nineteenth Century* (Llandybie, 1981), chap. 1; E. D. Evans, *A History of Wales, 1660–1815* (Cardiff, 1976), p. 95; Owen, *Welsh Folk Customs*, pp. 23ff.

[105]   Rees, *Life in a Welsh Countryside*, p. 118; Davies and Rees, eds., *Welsh Rural Communities*, pp. 40–1, 194–6; Morgan, *Rebirth*, pp. 198–9; L. Morgan, 'The Future of Welsh Nonconformity', *Welsh Outlook*, 18 (1931), pp. 176–7; I. Peate, 'Society in Wales', in B. Jones, ed., *The Anatomy of Wales* (Cardiff, 1972), pp. 51–2; J. E. Southall, *Wales and her Language*, 2nd edn (1893), p. 215.

[106]   *RC on Land in Wales*, PP 1896, pp. 645–6; *RC on the Church and Other Religious Bodies in Wales*, PP 1910, XIV.

[107]   *Wages and Conditions of Employment*, PP 1919, p. 51.

Owen M. Edwards towards the close of the nineteenth century in referring to Bala, and accounted for the fact that Wales had perhaps a more flourishing literature than any European country of its size. An instance was recorded in 1918 of a Cardiganshire labourer who, having been given a heifer as a reward for seven years' service, sold it and spent the proceeds on buying books.[108]

The periodic competitive meetings between chapels did much for the intellectual improvement of the rural peasantry. Festivals were of two kinds, *cymanfa ganu* (a singing festival) and *cymanfa bwnc* (a meeting held for the purpose of catechising Sunday schools on a specific portion of Scripture). These festivals were held by a group of chapels of one denomination and at one level fostered competition between chapels of the same denomination. But at the other level they were the occasion of co-operation between chapels of the same denomination to provide a festival that would match or surpass the corresponding festival held by other chapels of a different denomination. This friendly rivalry (or so it was ideally!) between different denominations cannot be denied, but although membership of different denominations gave people a sense of belonging to distinctive groups such groups felt more in common with one another than with the 'world'.[109]

Throughout the nineteenth and early twentieth centuries contemporaries recognised a fundamental social distinction in the rural community between those who belonged to 'the church' and those who belonged to 'the world'.[110] The characteristics of those belonging to 'the church' were regular attendance at services and the various activities of the chapels and (established) churches, total abstinence from alcoholic drink, thrift, respect for education and a desire to 'get on'. Those of 'the world', on the other hand, even if some of them did attend chapel or church, did not support it in all its activities, did not keep the Sabbath but rather were prepared to enjoy secular recreations, frequented public houses, were inclined to spend on immediate pleasures and did not value education and 'getting on'.

---

[108] *RC on Labour, Wales*, PP 1893–4, p. 40; *Wages and Conditions of Employment*, PP 1919, p. 51.

[109] *Wages and Conditions of Employment*, PP 1919, pp. 51, 75; Jenkins, *Agricultural Community*, pp. 197–205; *idem*, 'Aberporth', in Davies and Rees, eds., *Welsh Rural Communities*, p. 53.

[110] Davies and Rees, eds., *Welsh Rural Communities*, pp. x–xi; but note that Jenkins in *Agricultural Community*, pp. 210ff, distinguishes between members of a chapel and 'hearers' who attended chapel services. The latter were of 'the world'.

David Jenkins and others have demonstrated that high social status was chiefly determined by membership of the 'religious group'. At the same time, they recognise a social stratification based on occupation. The awkward circumstance could sometimes arise within a chapel of a lowly cottager holding an office granting authority over a farmer, so a tendency developed of accommodating relationships in the one field to those in the other, relatively more farmers becoming deacons than those holding lower-status occupations.[111]

Chapel activities in rural areas – religious, cultural and social – provided the best forum for *whole* families of a neighbourhood to meet right down to the 1940s.[112] Nevertheless, there is no mistaking the appeal to individual family members by then of such secular activities as the Women's Institute, which had taken hold by the early 1920s, *Urdd Gobaith Cymru* (Welsh League of Youth), the Young Farmers' Club, the cinema, the YMCAs and the WEA classes. The manifestation of the spread of new recreational facilities not based on the chapel was the building of 'village' or 'memorial' halls after the First World War.[113]

The contribution of nonconformity to Welsh industrial society was immense and in large measure beneficial. Initially, nonconformity performed an inestimable service in providing the newcomers with the means of grace in a form that was familiar and precious to many of them and giving them a feeling of belonging and sense of friendly community within this hostile 'frontier' society. It taught the working classes of the valley towns and ports the virtues of thrift, sobriety, cleanliness and honesty in an environment of pervading squalor, drunkenness and careless abandon – most sensationally though uncharacteristically manifested in Merthyr's 'China' and, later, in

---

[111]   Jenkins, 'Aberporth', pp. 14ff; see also essays on Tregaron and Glanllyn in Davies and Rees, eds., *Welsh Rural Communities*; Jenkins, *Agricultural Community*, p. 193; G. Williams, 'On Class and Status Groups in Welsh Rural Society', in G. Williams, ed., *Crisis of Economy and Ideology* (Sociology of Wales Studies Group, 1983), pp. 134–86.

[112]   T. Owen, 'Glanllyn', in Davies and Rees, eds., *Welsh Rural Communities*, p. 205; Parry-Jones, *My Own Folk*, p. 157.

[113]   Rees, *Life in a Welsh Countryside*, p. 139; Jenkins, 'Aberporth', p. 20; W. King, 'The Adolescent in Rural Wales', *Welsh Outlook*, 10 (1923), pp. 330–2; T. Jones Hughes, 'Aberdaron', in Davies and Rees, eds., *Welsh Rural Communities*, p. 175; E. Matthews, 'Anglesey Union of Village Halls and Societies', *Welsh Outlook*, 10 (1923), pp. 17–19.

Cardiff's Butetown and Splott. Through its democratic organisation in chapel and Sunday school it also provided an opportunity for personal status for talented working-class people, who were otherwise denied it. Indeed in rural and industrial Wales alike, possibly nonconformity's greatest contribution, argues Charlotte Aull, was its furnishing 'the basis of a new status system, divorced from English social structure, that produced a new Welsh elite'. Finally, the nonconformist Sunday schools, more so than any other agency down to the close of the nineteenth century, were responsible for teaching the ordinary people in their native tongue.

The chapel was far more than a means of spiritual support, for the secular activities of the working classes in the towns, as the *eisteddfodau*, literary societies, concerts, penny readings, and *cymanfaoedd* (singing festivals) were often associated with the chapels. It is indeed vital that we recognise the tremendous hold of the *eisteddfod* – usually chapel-based – and of choral singing in both the old and new towns over the course of the mid- and late-nineteenth century. The *eisteddfod* by mid-century had become a widespread, popular, highly democratic public event and, along with the chapel, was a major agent of adult education. The chapels, too, saw the rise of marvellous choirs, often temperance ones, from the 1850s onwards, trained in the tonic sol-fa system. As membership of chapels grew in the late decades of the century it became a matter of self-esteem to put on an annual oratorio, and even the less ambitious congregations had to attempt a sacred cantata. In the chapels and *eisteddfodau* countless ordinary people could achieve a measure of self-expression and personal dignity; indeed, claims I. G. Jones, it was in the *eisteddfod* that the working man 'discovered his self-consciousness'. It was, the same authority reminds us, because of their very 'social' dimension that people were drawn to the chapels. And, he again insists, the chapels and their associated secular activities were the people's own creation, a claim that holds much truth although we would caution that the contribution of the late nineteenth-century coal owners in financing chapel-building should not be lost sight of. These various chapel activities in truth satisfied the people's keen desire to get together, and even if there were rivalries and jealousies engendered between choirs at the innumerable *eisteddfodau* and singing festivals nevertheless such inter-chapel activities gave the separate mining townships a chance to break down their sense of isolation by joining with neighbouring villages in a common, organic culture. Indeed, insofar as rivalry was concerned, this was perhaps overall a good thing for it might be argued that each separate village and township could only establish its own identity by such rivalry which extended not only to choral singing but to rugby as well.[114]

For all the benefits conferred by nonconformity, its leaders in the industrial communities of South Wales have nevertheless been criticised on the grounds that their Calvinistic individualistic theology rendered them preoccupied with personal salvation and the after-life and largely indifferent to contemporary social problems. In particular, it is stressed, nonconformity frowned upon early working-class movements such as trades unions, benefit societies and Chartism.[115] There is much truth in this criticism (although it is as well to bear in mind that certain keen chapel members were to be found among the marchers on Newport in 1839). For all that, it can still be claimed that nonconformity, and to a lesser extent the church, played a vital, positive role in shaping the new industrial environment, in civilising that society.[116] While recognising this magnificent contribution, it remains unfortunately true that nonconformity's hold on urban and rural Welshmen alike did rather induce a nervous and apologetic tone when alluding to pleasurable pastimes and an excessive feeling of guilt over small transgressions, and there was certainly the danger of self-righteousness, conceit and priggish censoriousness creeping in in nonconformity's total abstinence not only from alcohol but from all kinds of sport.[117]

During the last two decades of the nineteenth century a new mood

[114]   Jones, 'The South Wales Collier', pp. 46, 49; *idem*, 'The Valleys', p. 62; W. Lambert, 'Some Working-Class Attitudes towards Organised Religion in Nineteenth-Century Wales', *Llafur*, 2 (1976), p. 5; *State of Education in Wales*, PP 1847, Part 1, pp. 5–8; E. T. Davies, *Religion in the Industrial Revolution in South Wales* (Cardiff 1965), pp. 54, 92; *idem, Religion and Society*, p. 64; T. J. Morgan, 'Peasant Culture in the Swansea Valley', in S. Williams, ed., *Glamorgan Historian*, vol. 9 (Cowbridge, 1973), p. 118; T. Jones, *Rhymney Memories* (Newtown, 1938), p. 131; Aull, 'Ethnic Nationalism in Wales', p. 78; E. D. Lewis, 'Population Changes and Social Life 1860–1914', in Hopkins, ed., *Rhondda Past and Future*, pp. 120–2; D. Smith, *Wales! Wales?* (1984), p. 34.

[115]   Davies, *Religion and Society*, pp. 76ff; Lambert, 'Some Working-Class Attitudes', pp. 9–11; C. Gwyther, 'Sidelights on Religion and Politics in the Rhondda Valley, 1906–26', *Llafur*, 3 (1980), pp. 32–3.

[116]   Jones, *Explorations and Explanations*, pp. 233–4; Williams, *Religion, Language and Nationality*, p. 141.

[117]   W. G. Roberts, 'Nonconformity: A Force in Welsh National Life', *Young Wales*, 9 (1903), pp. 87, 91–2.

set in among the working class of industrial South Wales. The negative attitude on the part of nonconformity to the workers' problems, the preoccupation on the part of Liberal leaders and nonconformist preachers (many of whom had rural backgrounds) with the problems of rural Wales and the by now middle-class composition of the colliery-manager chapel-deacon out of touch with the feelings of the workers (the early-century deacons had been drawn from among the working-class population) led increasing numbers to abandon the chapels in favour of trade unionism and socialism, which they perceived as the best representatives of their true interests. The many miners' institutes founded across the coalfield in the two decades up to 1910, each housing a reading room and library, where men became well versed in science, poetry, religion, philosophy and economics, were increasingly to appeal to the young and to draw them away from the out-of-touch chapels. Welsh nonconformist chapels were antagonistic towards the new labour movement partly because they conceived socialism to be an ungodly movement and partly because, as ever, they were suspicious of English influences. Socialism's hold was significantly strengthened during the First World War, the chapel's standing now being dented by its support for the war. By this time, the decline of the Welsh language was also posing a problem for the chapels. After the war, more and more so socialism and trade unionism, with the fellowship of their institutes and miners' welfare halls, constituted attractive alternatives to religion, and leisure pursuits, too, it will be shown, from the 1890s posed strong counter-attractions. All-important, the cinema had come in by 1914. Innovation in travel, too, allowed for Sunday excursions to Barry Island or Swansea, while the radio from 1923 effected a veritable social revolution in broadening people's outlook. The old hell-fire, fundamentalist character of nineteenth-century nonconformity commended itself less and less to the young. Furthermore, chapel members were migrating to jobs elsewhere in the 1920s and 1930s and, moreover, given that religious observance was in part bound up with respectability, the depression meant that people lacked suitable clothes for chapel attendance. Some, too (in Brynmawr at least), during the depression were disillusioned at the way certain ministers had rejected the offer of a bare maintenance grant and had moved to churches that could pay the usual salary. The Sunday schools declined partly because their teachers were unable to relate to the problems of the young, who were now being weaned away from the old puritanism by secular education.[118]

Decline was mirrored in the overcapacity and overlapping of chapels in Wales evident by 1910 and even more so by 1929. Nevertheless, that decline should not be exaggerated. Membership remained large down to the Second World War, numbering well over 400,000 in the 1920s. We have seen that attendance remained strongest in rural areas where right down to the 1940s and even into the post-1945 era the chapel influence was still a very important force, and here it is vital that we appreciate that at a time when religious conviction was in retreat the continuing strength of kinship and compelling awareness of a personal obligation to maintain the tradition of a family with a particular Bethel motivated continuing attendance. Even with regard to industrial South Wales, religion remained an important, if declining, force down to the Second World War, and that this was particularly so as late as the 1920s doubtless owed something to the religious revival of 1904–5. Even in the sphere of the labour movement, the fact that enlightened social attitudes were coming increasingly to prevail meant that in the Rhondda a number of active members of the SWMF and the mid-Rhondda Trades and Labour Council remained attached to the chapels and that in the 1920s and 1930s many chapels there, notably the Methodist Tonypandy Central Hall under Rex Barker, did valuable work in helping alleviate distress and were a part of the United Front response.[119]

If the chapel played an inestimable role in industrial society throughout the Victorian era, nevertheless there were a number of other recreations far removed from the ethos of the chapel which the industrial worker could enjoy. The main alternative social outlet for the worker during his few leisure hours was the smoke-filled, badly-lit public house. Not that chapel and pub were mutually exclusive, however,

---

[118]   Davies, *Religion in the Industrial Revolution*, pp. 160–1, 166–7; *idem*, *Religion and Society*, pp. 75–7; Lambert, 'Some Working-Class Attitudes', p. 14; D. B. Rees, *Chapels in the Valley* (Wirral, 1975), pp. 148, 184–5, 193, 197; Gwyther, 'Sidelights on Religion and Politics', p. 35; B. Richards, *History of the Llynfi Valley* (Cowbridge, 1982), pp. 250–1; Lewis, 'Population Changes', p. 312; Morgan, *Rebirth*, pp. 197–9; Edwards, *The Good Patch*, pp. 81–2; B. Thomas, 'Organisation of Religion in Wales', *Welsh Outlook*, 16 (1929), p. 365; *Third Report of the Commission for the Special Areas*, p. 7; Lush, *The Young Adult*, pp. 47–8; Jennings, *Brynmawr*, p. 142; T. N. Williams, 'The Sunday School: Its Failure and Future', *Welsh Outlook*, 17 (1930), pp. 6–9.

[119]   Thomas 'Organisation of Religion', pp. 364–5; Morgan, *Rebirth*, p. 199; Owen, 'Glanllyn', p. 195; Rees, *Chapels in the Valley*, p. 157; Gwyther, 'Sidelights on Religion', pp. 36–8; *idem*, *The Valley Shall Be Exalted*, pp. 21–3, 71; Edwards, *The Good Patch*, pp. 143–4, 168–72; Francis and Smith, *The Fed*, pp. 256ff.

for some colliers at the close of the nineteenth century were to be found going to the pubs on week-days and to the chapel on Sundays. On Saturday nights, especially pay-Saturday nights, and particularly at the local fairs, drunkenness and fighting were common, even the womenfolk fighting one another with bare fists. Another source of popular entertainment in the valley towns and villages between mid-century and the late 1870s and, to a lesser extent, down to 1914, were the portable theatres which visited the numerous fairs. Not surprisingly, their vulgarity and sensationalism rendered them unpopular with the chapels. For all that, they provided a welcome touch of gaiety to the harsh lives of the working classes, allegedly drew the workers out of the pubs, and were to make the same kind of warm appeal as was to be later found in the music halls of the valley towns and ports of the Edwardian era. By the opening years of this century those still in business were being increasingly converted to cinemas. The permanent theatres, both those of the county towns and seaside resorts which had been established from the turn of the nineteenth century and those later ones established in the major industrial towns and ports, also provided an important opportunity for the Welsh people to enjoy, above all, melodrama, but also some opera and Shakespeare. Predictably, nonconformity opposed them as the home of frivolity and even vice. In the century or so down to 1880 the highest standards of theatre in Wales were to be found at Swansea but there-after theatre at Cardiff grew from strength to strength.[120]

Besides the pubs, theatres and (later) music halls, there were the visiting circuses and travelling fairs, the latter holding out for the youth the special attraction of the boxing booths. Weekly bare-fist, £1-a-side boxing and wrestling bouts also occurred on the hillsides of the Rhondda. Very popular there, too, were the horse-racing and foot-running contests at the Partridge Field, Llwynypia, and other recreations among Rhondda miners were rounders, quoits, whippet racing and particularly hand-ball.[121]

A significant extension to leisure activities, and, with it, increasing secularisation of society, came from the 1890s, with organised sport

[120] Jones, 'The South Wales Collier', p. 47; Wil Jon Edwards, *From the Valley I Came* (1956), pp. 7, 66; Lewis, 'Population Changes', p. 116; C. Price, 'Portable Theatres in Wales 1843–1914', *National Library of Wales Journal*, 9 (1955–6), pp. 65–92; idem, *The Professional Theatre in Wales* (Swansea, 1984). Mr Peter Stead made helpful suggestions for this paragraph.
[121] Lewis, 'Population Changes', p. 125.

now playing a vital and increasing role in South Wales's industrial society. Big crowds met to watch wrestling, boxing, rugby and soccer matches. In the Edwardian era South Wales was, indeed, to produce some outstanding boxing and wrestling champions. Most spectacularly, 'Freddie Welsh' and Jimmy Wilde were to become world boxing champions. Rugby became a passion that gripped a large section of the population of Edwardian South Wales like a spell – some contemporaries would have said an evil spell. During the 1870s and 1880s it was, however, very much a middle-class game and was, moreover, often played by men of non-Welsh birth from the neighbouring West Country strongholds of the game who, from the 1860s, had gone west to make their fortunes as professional people in the bonanza society of industrial South Wales. By the early 1890s the numerous villages in coalfield society had come to boast their own clubs containing working-class players and at the same time the longer-standing clubs of the larger towns began to recruit workingmen. Moreover, the national side by the late 1890s had come to include heavy working-class 'Rhondda Forwards' (a term actually embracing tinplatemen, steel workers and dockers, as well as colliers), who played an important part in securing no less than six Triple Crowns between 1900 and 1912. Rugby thus came to act as a social solvent by cutting across class barriers and bringing together working and middle-class players and spectators alike. Just as importantly, it became by 1900 a 'focus for nationality', a (pleasing) means for asserting Welsh national identity. Although rugby was the dominant sport in South Wales, soccer, too, had a wide appeal among the South Wales industrial communities from the 1890s, and between 1890 and 1906 (before the full implications of professionalism were felt) the four most successful clubs were Rogerstone, Treharris, Aberdare and Barry. Indeed, in *geographical* terms, soccer won wider appeal amongst the Welsh than rugby.[122]

A further touch of colour and diversion was afforded Welsh society, particularly after the coming of rail communication, by visits and excursions to seaside resorts and inland spas. Thus railway excursions to Swansea were becoming common among Merthyr workmen in the 1850s while, from the 1880s, colliers from the Welsh steam coal valleys went on day excursions by rail to Barry and Porthcawl. Simi-

---

122   *Ibid.*, pp. 125–6; Morgan, *Rebirth*, pp. 133–4; Smith, *Wales! Wales?* pp. 35–7; B. Lile and D. Farmer, 'The Early Development of Association Football in South Wales, 1890–1906', *Transactions of the Honourable Society of Cymmrodorion* (1984), pp. 193–215.

larly, the industrial population of North Wales, together with those of Lancashire, were drawn increasingly from the 1860s to the resorts of Llandudno, Colwyn Bay and Rhyl. Visits were also made by members of South Wales industrial society to the inland spas of Llandrindod Wells and Llanwrtyd.[123]

Class stratification of leisure was here apparent in the tendency for certain resorts to cater for a particular type of visitor. Thus it was the middle classes who spent their summer holidays at Llandrindod Wells while working-class colliers went to Llanwrtyd. Likewise, in the south, the bourgeoisie visited Penarth whereas the working classes made day excursions to Barry, and, in the north, Llandudno attracted the middle classes – mainly from Lancashire – and Rhyl the working classes. Class stratification of leisure could be seen, too, in sport; rugby, we have shown, was at first a middle-class game and cricket, too, was played by the middle classes. On the other hand, the native Welsh game of hand-ball was played by the working classes in the tavern yards of the industrial villages of South Wales.[124] There was, too, class stratification of other more serious facets of culture: in the pre-1880 years the secondary schools of Wales were the preserve of children of the middle classes while it will be apparent that whereas the Church of England in the early nineteenth century had been a church of the landed gentry, industrial magnates and the traditional, established middle classes, the chapels in rural and urban Wales were solidly working class in composition. From mid-century, however, this earlier class stratification was slowly to dissolve: true enough, the landed gentry and the old, traditional middle classes continued to dominate the Church of England in rural areas while the peasantry attended the chapels, but now there grew up gradually within both rural and urban nonconformity a middle-class leadership, and, within urban nonconformity, many of the coalowners of the late nineteenth century were nonconformists.[125]

If nonconformity was a crucial marker of Welsh ethnic identity, of even greater importance in this respect was the Welsh language.[126]

[123] A. V. John, 'The Chartists of Industrial South Wales' (unpublished MA thesis, University of Wales, 1970), pp. 178–9; Morgan and Thomas, *Wales* p. 124; P. Stead, 'The Town that had Come of Age, 1918–39', in Moore, ed., *Barry*, p. 380; I. W. Jones, *Llandudno* (Cardiff, 1975).

[124] Morgan, *Rebirth*, pp. 128–9; Morgan and Thomas, *Wales*, p. 209.

[125] Davies, *Religion and Society*, p. 17; *idem, Religion in the Industrial Revolution*, pp. 148–51.

[126] Khleif, *Language*, pp. 34ff; Aull, 'Ethnic Nationalism in Wales', pp. 77–8; Wyn Griffith, 'What is the Welsh Way of Life?', *Welsh Outlook*, 52 (1965).

While industrial development had a beneficial influence in prolonging its life, argues Brinley Thomas, by dint of concentrating the bulk of Welsh-speaking, rural migrants within the South Wales industrial valleys (though Dudley Baines has (perhaps unconvincingly) contended that Thomas has overestimated the extent of this Welsh migration there), it nevertheless hastened its decline in the long run by attracting 'outside' English-speaking migrants. The crucial turning point was 1901–11: up until then, Thomas and others claim, these incoming migrants had been successfully absorbed by the Welsh-speaking population (though the claim by a knowledgeable contemporary that by the mid-1880s 'children in the Rhondda speak English habitually in the play-ground; this results from the immigration of English people' casts some doubt as to the total validity of this contention), but the decade 1901–11 attracted such large numbers from England that they could not be successfully absorbed: henceforth the language was fatally in retreat, the percentage of Welsh-speakers in Wales falling noticeably after 1901 and, crucially, *absolute* numbers dropping after 1911.[127]

Even if absolute numbers of Welsh-speakers rose in the nineteenth century, there was, nevertheless, already from the early nineteenth century a proportional decline in this group. Economic pressures led to a growth of bi-lingualism which in the nature of things led on to anglicisation.[128] Welsh parents by the 1840s were anxious for their children to learn English in order to 'get on' and by that decade (if not earlier) down to the early 1890s, when it was almost obsolete, the punitive 'Welsh not' ensured that children did not speak Welsh during school hours. Down to the 1880s the English government neglected the language, the 1861 Revised Code ignoring its existence and thereby ensuring its banishment from the schools. The extension of elementary education from the 1870s, of course, intensified the Code's adverse effects. The situation was all the more tragic insofar as the supposed safeguard of the Welsh language in the eyes of parents and authorities alike, namely, the nonconformist Sunday schools, were failing to instruct children in proper grammatical usage which meant that by the 1880s Welsh as a *written* language was falling into

---

[127]   Thomas, 'The Industrial Revolution and the Welsh Language', pp. 16–17; D. Baines, *Migration in a Mature Economy: Emigration and Internal Migration in England and Wales, 1861–1900* (Cambridge, 1985); Southall, *Wales and her Language*, p. 127.
[128]   Thomas, 'The Industrial Revolution and the Welsh Language', p. 15.

disuse.[129] School Board managers, inspectors, teachers and parents alike frustrated the implementation of bi-lingual teaching in elementary schools after the (at last) favourable government concessions of 1888; only after the reorganisation of school management following 1902 did bi-lingual schemes become adopted but even then they were not pushed through.[130] Perhaps even more harmful were the effects of the much-lauded Intermediate Education Act of 1889 – itself mainly the outcome of the passion for education among the poorer classes induced principally by nonconformity and unrivalled amongst the English lower classes – for the new 'county' schools failed to encourage the teaching of Welsh. Many of their products, especially in rural areas, left Wales to enter the professions in English towns and cities; while a marvellous new social mobility was thus achieved this nevertheless had dire results for the language. Migration drained the Welsh areas, urban and rural, of their most talented people and so left them culturally impoverished.[131] (Another unfortunate result of the academic bias of these secondary schools was that the interests of the majority were sacrificed and this may have been a major reason for the high percentage of working-class children in Glamorgan leaving before reaching the higher forms.[132])

From the early years of this century other influences have harmed the language, so that whereas in 1891, 54 per cent could speak Welsh, by 1911 this had fallen to 44 per cent, by 1931 to 37 per cent and by 1951 to 29 per cent. Besides the unprecedented number of English immigrants already referred to, other factors hastening anglicisation were the decline of nonconformity, and, associated with this, the decline in vitality of local patriotic and literary societies; the economic dislocation of the 1920s and 1930s which drove thousands out of rural and older industrial communities either into the more anglicised coastal areas of the new metal industries or out of Wales altogether; the growth of the mass media which, together with increased social

---

[129] Southall, *Wales and her Language*, pp. 76, 84–5, 113ff, 191; *idem, Bi-Lingual Teaching in Welsh Elementary Schools* (Newport, 1888), pp. i–ii; M. J. Evans, 'Elementary Education in Montgomeryshire, 1850–1900', *Montgomeryshire Collections*, 63 (1973–4), pp. 15–16; HMSO, *Welsh in Education and Life* (1927), p. 150; Williams, *Religion, Language and Nationality*, p. 145.

[130] *Welsh in Education and Life*, p. 70.

[131] *Ibid.*, pp. 61–2; Williams, *Religion, Language and Nationality*, pp. 145–6; G. E. Jones, *Controls and Conflicts*, pp. 83–4, for an excellent discussion; J. R. Webster, 'The Place of Secondary Education in Welsh Society, 1800–1917' (unpublished PhD thesis, University of Wales, 1959), pp. 171–90.

[132] P. Stead, 'Schools and Society in Glamorgan before 1914', *Morgannwg*, 19 (1975), pp. 49–51.

mobility deriving from motor transport, fatally undermined the old and self-perpetuating linguistic and cultural autonomy of local areas; the development of tourism; and contraception.[133]

If the language for most Welsh people in twentieth-century Wales has been English, so, too, has been their literature. In earlier centuries, however, the most important literary tradition was Welsh. The Welsh cultural revival of the eighteenth century was the work of a group of middle-class literary enthusiasts who, dismayed at the twin adverse cultural impact of the decline of the bardic order and the neglect of Welsh culture by a fast-anglicising gentry, and fired by Augustan neo-classicism, undertook a search into medieval Welsh literature in order to discover classical models that might stand comparison with the work of renowned Greek and Latin authors. That they could publish ancient texts, dictionaries and grammars on such an unprecedented scale was made possible by the vast increase in literacy from the late seventeenth century as a consequence of the religious – Church of England and Old Dissent as well as Methodist – and educational enlivenment of the period. Ironically, the vehicle for much of this enthusiasm for antiquarianism and romantic patriotism – which resorted to much mythical invention in order to give the common people a sense of, and pride in, their past – were the London-based societies founded in the late eighteenth century, societies which, along with the revived *eisteddfod* from 1789, were to continue into the nineteenth century to play a vital role in promoting Welsh culture.[134]

Despite the rapid rise of nonconformity, Welsh culture was to be dominated in the first thirty or forty years of the nineteenth century by romantic Anglican parsons and by the gentry, who were the moving spirits behind the *eisteddfodau* and literary movements. As yet, nonconformity was preoccupied with theological concerns and was, indeed, unsympathetic towards these activities as occasions which led people astray. However, before mid-century it was to relax its previous mistrust of both political involvement and the *eisteddfod* and patriotic societies so that, increasingly, Welsh music and literature came under its dominance. Welsh culture now became a truly

---

[133]   Morgan and Thomas, *Wales*, pp. 53–4; Williams, *Religion, Language and Nationality*, p. 29; Thomas, 'The Industrial Revolution and the Welsh Language', p. 21; A. B. Philip, *The Welsh Question: Nationalism in Welsh Politics, 1945–1970* (Cardiff, 1975), pp. 42–7.

[134]   Williams, *Religion, Language and Nationality*, pp. 22–3, 25, 138–9; Morgan and Thomas, *Wales*, pp. 184–5; Williams, *When Was Wales?*, p. 165; P. Morgan, *The Eighteenth-Century Renaissance* (Llandybie, 1981), pp. 101–35.

peasant' culture, the ordinary working-class members of society organising and creating their own music and literature which in turn produced a level of peasant intellectual and cultural attainment that was not matched amongst English workers. We are now in the heroic age of the chapel choirs and *cymanfaoedd* (singing festivals), which assemblies had become extremely popular throughout Wales by the 1870s. The annual *eisteddfod* meetings held in most Welsh villages from mid-century, many, we have seen, associated with the chapels, and, unlike the provincial *eisteddfodau* and the national *eisteddfod* – the latter dating effectively from 1858 – predominantly Welsh in their transactions, also saw extensive music making, not only sacred but secular also. Both chapel and *eisteddfod* music were to be a highly distinctive element of Welsh culture down to 1914, but thereafter the (interconnected) decline of chapel and the language saw outside influence take over in the form of Anglo-American entertainment.[135]

In a similar vein, the literature of Wales had by mid-century fallen into the hands of 'workers, peasants and preachers'. Those powerful transmuting agencies of nineteenth-century Welsh society, nonconformity and industrialism, whereby Wales was to become morally puritan and sabbatarian, radicalised and increasingly fired with nationalist pride – though in the early decades showing little signs of becoming transmitters of that earlier linguistic and patriotic consciousness – by mid-century were influencing a great outpouring of Welsh literature and Welsh newspapers and periodicals. The huge influx into the South Wales coalfield of Welsh-speaking, nonconformist immigrants created a relatively prosperous and increasingly literate workforce, who came to demand growing numbers of Welsh books and periodicals. The *eisteddfod*, growing ever more popular over the nineteenth century, was the vital vehicle for literary output of an artistic kind. Significantly, from mid-century the mythologising and fantasising of the 'eighteenth-century renaissance' fell away before the new interest in the Welsh literary world in material progress and rational discussion. But, predictably, most of the Welsh literature produced from mid-century was of a religious nature.[136]

---

[135] Williams, *Religion, Language and Nationality*, pp. 140–1; Morgan and Thomas, *Wales*, pp. 163–4, 187, 199; *Welsh in Education and Life*, pp. 75–7; Parry-Jones, *My Own Folk*, p. 47.

[136] Morgan and Thomas, *Wales*, pp. 187–8, 200–4; Williams, *Religion, Language and Nationality*, pp. 141–2; *Welsh in Education and Life*, pp. 76–7; Morgan, *The Eighteenth-Century Renaissance*, pp. 154–5.

From the last quarter of the century, however, as Welsh society became more secular, there occurred a break-out from the previous monolithic literary pattern of puritan piety and radical polemic. Now, for instance, we see essays and novels gaining in popularity. Altogether Welsh literary standards became more critical, scholarly and secular. Crucial in influencing this upgrading were the young students, notably Owen M. Edwards and John Morris Jones, gathered around Sir John Rhys, Principal of Jesus College, Oxford.[137]

During the 1920s there emerged a brilliant, creative group of Welsh writers who specialised in writing critical essays, essays of self-analysis and short stories, outstanding among whom were Saunders Lewis, R. T. Jenkins, W. J. Gruffydd, Kate Roberts, D. J. Williams, T. H. Parry-Williams and D. Gwenallt Jones. Characteristic strands of thought in their works were a more vigorous socialism and pacifism, a new attraction towards medieval Catholicism and a more positive attachment to Welsh political nationalism. It was, however, perhaps the impact of the firing of the Lleyn bombing school in 1936 which provided the vital stimulus into pushing Welsh writers into adopting a heightened radical nationalist stance.[138]

Besides the impressive Welsh publications of the 1920s and 1930s, confined albeit to a middle-class readership, there was also a flourishing Anglo-Welsh school during the interwar years, whose starting point lay in the novels of Caradoc Evans, who bitterly attacked with surely 'savage disproportion' what he saw as the hypocrisy of rural, nonconformist Wales. Anglo-Welsh novelists of the 1920s and 1930s like Gwyn Jones, Glyn Jones, Gwyn Thomas and Jack Jones, mostly natives of the industrial south, reacted against the values of radical and rural nonconformity. In a Wales by now fast becoming peopled by English-speaking Welshmen, they sought to come to terms with the obvious problem of identity and to make sense of their somewhat schizoid existence as English-speaking Welshmen. Many of the novelists were left-wing and wrote out of indignation at the grim tragedy that befell South Wales during the depression.[139]

[137]   Williams, *Religion, Language and Nationality*, p. 17; Morgan and Thomas, *Wales*, pp. 188–9; Thomas Parry, 'The Welsh Renaissance of the Twentieth Century', in Roderick, ed., *Wales through the Ages*, vol. 2, pp. 209–14.

[138]   Morgan and Thomas, *Wales*, p. 190; Morgan, *Rebirth*, pp. 246–8; D. H. Davies, *The Welsh Nationalist Party, 1925–45* (Cardiff, 1983), pp. 165–6.

[139]   Anon., 'Caradoc Evans', *Welsh Review*, 4 (1954), pp. 24ff; Morgan, *Rebirth*, pp. 250, 258ff; Morgan and Thomas, *Wales*, pp. 192–3; Williams, *When Was Wales?*, pp. 284–6; Anon., 'Jack Jones', *Welsh Review*, 6 (1947).

IV

Given its overwhelming nonconformity and major industrial development in the south-east, it is not surprising that the Welsh people
early cast off the centuries-old political control of the landowners and
embraced radical Liberalism. From the 1830s Old Dissent, and from
the late 1840s traditionally conservative Calvinistic Methodism as well,
became increasingly vociferous about the civil disabilities of their sects
who, significantly, were fast becoming the majority of the 'religious'
people of Wales. Their grievances were felt to be those of the people
of Wales and feelings were dramatically heightened by the incredible
insult heaped on the Welsh tongue and nonconformity by the Education Commissioners of 1847.[140] (This development and articulation
of a middle-class self-consciousness around mid-century, it will be
apparent, was growing up alongside and was antipathetic towards
the independent working-class movement enshrined in Chartism and
Rebecca and, as we have seen, from the 1850s the working classes
were to abandon their former independent course of action and
instead come to co-operate closely with the middle class; that this
occurred was largely owing to the influence of the chapel ethos and
growing economic prosperity.[141]) For all the radical leavening of earlier
decades, the real break-through in the politicisation of the Welsh people was only to come in the 1860s, when the incipient middle-class
elite of the chapels were educated in politics; all-important here were
the huge and unprecedented outpourings of Welsh and English newspapers and, vitally, the Liberation Society, whose local-based organisation from the start of the 1860s urged Welsh people to vote into
Parliament members who would represent their true needs by calling
for full civic equality for nonconformists. The 1867 franchise extension,
together with the fact that the 1868 election was fought over Irish
Disestablishment, with which Welsh nonconformists could fully
empathise, saw the first major, if limited, blow dealt political land-
lordism in Wales in the said election. Undoubtedly, the true significance of 1868 lay in the aftermath of vindictive evictions of tenants
by their disappointed and smarting landlords, for consequently the

---

[140] The best coverage is Morgan, *Wales in British Politics*, chap. 1.
[141] *Ibid.*, pp. 15–16; Jones, *Explorations and Explanations*, pp. 290–1; *idem*, 'The South
Wales Collier', pp. 49–51.

previous genuine ties of political loyalty on the part of tenants to their traditional representatives were severely weakened.[142]

The period of Liberal ascendancy in Wales from 1868 down to the close of the First World War, when Labour supplanted it, was a vital one for the development of Wales as a nation. The Secret Ballot Act of 1872, the franchise extension of the mid-eighties and the Local Government Acts of 1888 and 1894 together provided the mechanisms whereby the nonconformist people of Wales were enabled to seize political power from an 'alien' squirearchy and church. Such was the impact of the franchise reform of 1884–5 that the continuing dominance of the gentry in many constituencies was dramatically ended, for in every parliamentary election after 1885 down to 1918 Liberals gained the overwhelming majority of both urban and rural seats, and in the twenty years following 1886 Wales was the most intensely Liberal of any 'region' in the British Isles. Gentry power was felt most intensely, however, in the localities, and here a revolution in local government occurred following the 1888 County Council Act; gentry candidates were rejected wholesale at the polls in favour of the nonconformist middle class and here in Wales, once again more so than elsewhere, the breach with the 'feudal' past was severe. Likewise, the Parish Council Act of 1894, though not so drastic in its impact, further denuded their local authority. In the first council elections the sheer thoroughness of the 'rural revolution' in rural areas of South Wales resembled that of East Anglia.[143]

The 1880s also saw an exhilarating, tempestuous sea-change in Welsh politics, for now the earlier nonconformist Liberalism was being transmuted into nationalism as new, distinctly 'Welsh' issues came to dominate the Liberal party in Wales. (And this new brand of Welshness had a quite different chemistry – more aggressive and powerful – from the earlier Welshness promoted by the eighteenth-century Welsh scholar patriots.) Central to this metamorphosis was the emergence of a whole new group of young nonconformist radical Welshmen, notably David Lloyd George and Tom Ellis, ardently patriotic and zealous to promote the distinctive claims of Wales as a nonconformist nation, a group which replaced the older, elderly Whiggish Liberals. Ellis held that England had hitherto treated Wales 'mainly

---

[142]   Jones, *Explorations and Explanations*, pp. 236–68, 292–8; Morgan, *Wales in British Politics*, pp. 17, 22–7.

[143]   Again, the authoritative treatment is Morgan, *Rebirth*, pp. 26–31, 52–3; *idem*, 'From Cymru Fydd to Crowther', in Jones, ed., *Anatomy of Wales*, pp. 18–19; R. Heath, 'The Rural Revolution', *Contemporary Review*, 67 (1895), pp. 187–9.

with contemptuous neglect'.[144] A Welsh parliamentary party now emerged to lend greater unity and discipline than hitherto. The most cherished among the new issues was that of Disestablishment (itself pushed forward all the more vigorously in the face of the Church of England in Wales having since mid-century pulled itself together) and it is wholly significant that from 1886 onwards, unlike hitherto, Disestablishment was being demanded for Wales on aggressively national grounds.[145] Second to Disestablishment as the burning issue of the 1880s and 1890s was the Land Question, Tom Ellis, Bryn Roberts and others demanding special treatment for Wales along Irish lines to solve the distinctive social and economic grievances of the Welsh tenant farmer – although justice between man and man was seen by farmers as to obtain between landlords and tenants, to the neglect of the labourer. Indeed, in the 1892 election people in the rural constituencies were concerned above all with the Welsh Land Bill. Ellis saw Disestablishment and the Land Question as 'strikingly interwoven': the clergy and landlords having 'fought into one another's hands' the people perforce had to 'strike against both'. That there were grievances within the Welsh land system is clear, but undoubtedly the land issue was played up by radical leaders for political and sectarian advantage.[146] The 'tithe war' was bound up with both the Land Question and Disestablishment. Although agricultural depression triggered it, the driving force in sustaining the hostility was the nonconformist hatred of payment of tithe to an alien church, and when the clergy reacted unsympathetically to their initial request for abatements and the Ecclesiastical Commissioners resorted to distress sales with the help of the police and military, the farmers (doubtless encouraged by their nonconformist leaders) became more extreme, going beyond wanting abatements to opposing payment of tithe as such to an 'alien' church. The anti-tithe movement broadened out so as to include land reform and, it will be apparent, to supporting Disestablishment.[147] Secondary and higher education was, again,

---

[144] K. O. Morgan, 'The Welsh in English Politics', in R. R. Davies, R. A. Griffiths, I. G. Jones and K. O. Morgan, eds., *Welsh Society and Nationhood* (Cardiff, 1984), pp. 237–9; Morgan, *The Eighteenth-Century Renaissance*, p. 160; *Carnarvon and Denbigh Herald*, 28 October 1892.

[145] Morgan, *Rebirth*, pp. 40–2.

[146] *The Times*, 2 September, 29 October, 1886; *Carnarvon and Denbigh Herald*, 16 September, 28 October, 11 November, 1892; Morgan, *Rebirth*, pp. 38–9.

[147] *Inquiry as to the Disturbances Connected with the Levying of Tithe Rent Charge in Wales*, PP 1887, XXXVIII; Morgan, *Rebirth*, p. 40; Dunbabin, *Rural Discontent*, pp. 211–31, 282–96.

seen as an area in which Wales, with its distinctive culture and society, had special claims to separate treatment, and here Welsh Anglicans and the Conservative government, as well as nonconformists and Liberals, adopted this nationalist stance. (By way of contrast, bitter sectarian division raged over the issue of Welsh elementary education, the predominance of church national schools in Wales being resented by nonconformists. Hence the 'Welsh Revolt' over the Balfour Act of 1902, which put church schools for the first time on the rates.[148]) Temperance legislation and reform of the magistracy were also seen as requiring special treatment to accommodate the distinctive needs of Wales. Thus a change in the way that magistrates were appointed was seen as urgent in order to bring in nonconformists to the various Welsh benches.[149]

The Welsh radical programme had some sound achievements, perhaps most of all in the securing of a distinctive system of university colleges (those of Aberystwyth, Cardiff and Bangor) and intermediate schools, which together, Peter Stead pertinently remarks, 'in effect established the basis of modern Welsh society'. Other victories were the 1881 Sunday Closing Act, the gaining government acceptance of the need for appointing Welsh-speakers to many important public positions such as bishops and judges, the founding in 1907 of the National Library of Wales and a National Museum, significant symbols of national distinctiveness, and the long-delayed passing of a Welsh Disestablishment Bill in 1914.[150] Contrariwise, despite the Welsh Land Commission of the early 1890s a Welsh Land Act failed to materialise, largely owing to the return of an unsympathetic unionist government and the lifting of prices by the turn of the century. Again, the 'Welsh Revolt' against rate aid to church schools came to nothing. Certain failures notwithstanding, the period from the 1880s to the First World War was that of the heroic years of Welsh nationhood, so that Wales had by 1914 become accepted as a political reality; even

[148]   Morgan, *Rebirth*, p. 37; *Carnarvon and Denbigh Herald*, 9 September 1892; but note that the Bangor Diocesan Conference in September 1892 resolved to prevent the schemes for intermediate education already published from coming into law – *Carnarvon and Denbigh Herald*, 23 September 1892.

[149]   Morgan, *Rebirth*, pp. 36–7; *Carnarvon and Denbigh Herald*, 16 September 1892; *Hansard*, 16 February 1892, pp. 604–6.

[150]   Morgan, 'From Cymru Fydd to Crowther', pp. 121–2; Stead, *Coleg Harlech*, p. 2; *Hansard*, 19 February 1892.

the unionist-ridden Conservative party had by then been won over to the idea of Welsh nationality.[151]

Although national sentiment ran strong through Welsh politics during the 1880s and 1890s, as through all walks of Welsh life, for example in sport, especially rugby football and in Welsh literature, there was no strong public clamour from the Welsh *gwerin* – the classless 'mass of people' – for self-government. Unlike the Irish, who demanded home rule, the Welsh were 'less obtrusive and exacting', seeking in a remarkably peaceful way merely equality within the United Kingdom, not separation from it. It is true that the *Cymru Fydd* (Young Wales) movement of 1894–6, advocating a measure of home rule, sought to capture the allegiance of the Welsh Liberal party, but in this it failed; for in general Welsh Liberals, even those outside the cosmopolitan ports of the south, had no wish to cut themselves adrift from the mainstream of the British Liberal party, within which they had achieved signal national concessions.[152] (Nor, on the other hand, should the Welsh sentiment among the cosmopolitan Cardiff middle class at the end of the nineteenth century be underestimated, Cardiff's elite claiming their city to be 'the Metropolis of Wales'.[153])

The one serious challenge to the Liberal ascendancy in Wales before 1914 was the Labour movement. In both its industrial and political wings Labour was slow to emerge in a Welsh society dominated by a radical nonconformist ethos whose leaders claimed to represent a classless *gwerin* and who stressed conciliation and co-operation between capital and labour, but this consensus came increasingly under strain from the six-months' stoppage of 1898. In the industrial field, we have shown, there occurred thereafter a growing bitterness and class antagonism. The assertion of a positive and distinct Labour identity was nowhere near as dramatic in the political sphere; indeed, Liberalism and Labour (Lib-Labism) survived as a compromise down to 1910 and even, though more superficially so, down to 1914, for the four Welsh Lib-Lab MPs returned at the 1906 election stood as more than leaders of Labour – rather than being 'sectional' they could identify with the wider principles of Welsh Liberalism. The few ILPers

151 Morgan, 'The Welsh in English Politics', p. 239.
152 Morgan, *Rebirth*, pp. 113ff; *idem*, 'From Cymru Fydd to Crowther', pp. 121–2; Sir R. Coupland, *Welsh and Scottish Nationalism* (1954), pp. 226–32; Davies, *The Welsh Nationalist Party*, pp. 8–9; Morgan and Thomas, *Wales*, p. 142.
153 Evans, 'The Welsh Victorian City', pp. 350–87; G. O. Pierce, 'University College Cardiff 1883–1893', *Transactions of the Honourable Society of Cymmrodorion* (1984), pp. 173–80.

who put up in South Wales against Lib-Lab progressive candidates, who were, importantly, personalities, deeply entrenched in their wider communities, were rejected as sectional and thereby posing a threat to communal concord. Nevertheless, as one authority has recently argued, the Welsh Lib-Labs after 1906 were being forced onto the defensive against ILP argument. And, from 1910 onwards, even if the 'Great Unrest' temporarily halted ILP activity it nevertheless settled the argument for a Labour party; 1913, indeed, was the year when a local Labour party was to become a reality in South Wales and in Caernarfon. Significantly, the SWMF was now in favour of Labour parties in the constituencies and, towards this end, were for the first time co-operating with other unions. So, although the Liberal ascendancy was to all outward appearances to hold intact until 1914, in fact the alliance with Labour in the years 1910–14 was crumbling beneath the surface, and the working class under the trauma of the 'Great Unrest' was sanctioning political independence. Labour had won through, if as yet only at local level.[154]

For all the subterranean encroachment by Labour before 1914, it was the First World War that was to form the great political divide in Welsh politics. The war ushered in a long period of Labour dominance lasting from 1918 down to 1966. Partly this was by default, Labour gaining from the decline of Welsh Liberalism: the strong attachment of Welsh Liberals to Lloyd George meant that they suffered disastrously from his fall in 1922; but, of greater importance, the old society dominated by squire, parson and brewer upon which Welsh Liberalism had thrived as the party seeking social and civic equality was fast dying, and with the passing of the 'old causes' Liberalism's cutting edge was blunted.[155] Besides, the war had inflicted a severe blow upon the nonconformist radical culture, facing as it did nonconformist Liberals throughout Wales with an unaccustomed lack of certainty for now the old moral values of the middle-class elite were put in question and the former confidence and optimism were undermined. Both during and after the war Welsh nonconformists were

---

[154]   P. Stead, 'Establishing a Heartland – The Labour Party in Wales', in K. D. Brown, ed., *The First Labour Party 1906–1914* (1985), pp. 64–88; *idem*, 'Working-Class Leadership in South Wales, 1900–20', *Welsh History Review*, 6 (1973), pp. 331ff; Morgan, *Rebirth*, pp. 143–5.
[155]   Morgan, *Rebirth*, pp. 140–2; *idem*, 'From Cymru Fydd to Crowther', p. 124.

to become aware of loss of faith and decline. Disillusionment with the aftermath of the war further damaged Liberal morale.[156]

But Labour also rose to dominance by virtue of its own appeal. Although we have emphasised the strength of Labour among local authorities, particularly in South Wales, on the eve of 1914, it was nevertheless the war which acted as the vital catalyst in speeding up Labour's advance by giving the Labour party in Wales, as elsewhere, a new organisational structure and a mass following through the growth of trades unions. The industrial militancy surrounding the coal-mining disputes of 1919–21 and the collapse of the postwar boom in 1921 further added to Labour's appeal.[157]

Although the Liberals were successful in Wales at the 1918 general election, the transformation that was taking place was clearly reflected in the 1922 elections, when Labour took from the Liberals eight seats, six in the South Wales coalfield. In all in 1922, Wales had eighteen Labour MPs, six Conservatives, one Independent and eleven Liberals, the latter significantly clinging on in the nonconformist- and Welsh-dominated rural seats. The following year Labour was to win twenty-one seats and by 1929 this had increased to twenty-five, Labour at this last election polling 43.9 per cent of the vote. Although Labour understandably slipped back in Wales in the débâcle of 1931 (though less so than elsewhere), it made up some of the loss in 1935, gaining half of the Welsh seats, and its share of the vote rose to 45 per cent. Besides keeping its hold on the South Wales valleys, it did respectably well in most rural seats so that Liberalism was being eroded in its rural stronghold as well. By 1933 it was becoming clear that the identical political interests of farmer, labourer and small peasant that had obtained under the Old Liberalism could no longer be taken for granted as widening fissures appeared. Nevertheless, until the 1945 election Labour did not succeed in ousting Liberalism from the rural fastnesses of the north, where many stayed loyal to Lloyd George. Indeed, the one challenge to the Labour hegemony in South Wales came from the Communist party: as in Scotland, the party gained a considerable following in South Wales, especially the Rhondda valleys, in the 1920s. Its appeal was reinforced during the 1930s and in fact it mounted a serious though unsuccessful challenge on two occasions for Rhondda East. Significantly, however, those two Labour

---

[156] Morgan, *Rebirth*, pp. 163ff, 188–9; Morgan and Thomas, *Wales*, p. 144.
[157] Morgan, 'From Cymru Fydd to Crowther', pp. 125–6; Stead, 'Establishing a Heartland', p. 85; Morgan, *Rebirth*, p. 191.

victories were to show that the people of South Wales chose to remain within the wider British Labour party. The Labour ascendancy in the interwar years threw up a new kind of Labour MP, closely in touch with his class: many were trade unionists, a lot of them miners, and a few of the miners groomed by the Central Labour College, notably Aneurin Bevan, James Griffiths and Morgan Phillips, formed a distinct elite and were to rise to prominence in the Labour party nationally both before and after 1945.[158]

The social revolution effected by the rise of Labour, however, lay not so much in the election of working-class MPs or even in the kudos given by trade-union leadership operating at a national level but in the opportunity afforded in every town and village for working-class leadership in the running of localities both as local councillors and as trade-union officials. Already by 1916 a great improvement had allegedly come about, especially in relation to public health and the poor law. This monopoly over local government and every area of public life was especially secured, from the early 1920s onwards, in Monmouthshire, Glamorgan and east Carmarthenshire, and these working-class leaders, unlike the earlier Liberal elite, were drawn from the very heart of their communities. At a time of grave social and economic dislocation, these (for the most part) Labour people dedicated their talents to making life bearable. Interestingly from the viewpoint of the level of political consciousness in these monolithic working-class communities, the Labour party councillors in the Rhondda between 1917 and 1921, though satisfactory in the eyes of the general public, were deemed too moderate by the Labour activists within the trade councils and lodges. Indeed, by the mid-twenties the intensifying bitterness between the two groups had largely emasculated Labour party effectiveness in the Rhondda.[159]

Unlike the First World War, which toppled the Liberal ascendancy, the Second World War only served to enhance the standing of Labour in Wales: as over the country in general, here, especially in the relatively less radicalised mid and North Wales, public opinion was pushed leftwards. The war years demonstrated the crucial need for centralised

---

[158]   Morgan, *Rebirth*, pp. 191–2, 274, 280, 282–3; *idem*, 'The Welsh in English Politics', p. 242; T. Huws Davies, 'Politics', *Welsh Outlook*, 20 (1933), p. 340.
[159]   Stead, 'Working-Class Leadership', pp. 345ff; Anon., 'The Mind of the Miner', *Welsh Outlook*, 3 (1916), p. 249; Morgan, *Rebirth*, pp. 291–2, for a generous tribute; Chris Williams, '"An Able Administrator of Capitalism"?, The Labour Party in the Rhondda, 1917–21' (paper read at a Gregynog University of Wales seminar, March 1987).

economic planning. The 1945 general election thus saw the Labour ascendancy in Wales reach new heights and, significantly, after 1945 its hold was at last (and rapidly) extended over the rural hinterland. There was to be no revival of Conservatism in Wales in the 1950s. Throughout the long period of Labour ascendancy from 1918 to 1966, Labour members, unlike their Liberal forbears and, indeed, to an extent Keir Hardie and the ILP, were not so concerned with distinctly Welsh matters. Certainly they had nothing to do with Welsh separatism.[160]

The declining fortunes of the Welsh language and decay of 'the Welsh way of life' led to the founding of a Welsh Nationalist party in 1925. Down to 1945, however, it was 'not really a political party at all but a cultural and educational movement'. Membership remained small, perhaps 2,000 in 1939, and comprised Welsh-speaking college lecturers, schoolteachers, nonconformist ministers and other middle-class professionals. The lack of political activity was shown above all in the failure to contest local and national elections to any significant extent. The Roman Catholicism of its 'angular and uncompromising', albeit revered, poet-leader, Saunders Lewis, and, in the late thirties, the alleged fascist sympathies of the leaders, were not helpful in attracting members. Above all, insistence by the leadership right down to 1939 upon Welsh being the language for the running of party activities, and the fact that the leaders were out of touch with the problems of the south-east valleys, was bound to deter English-speaking Welshmen. The dramatic burning of the bombing school in the Lleyn Peninsula in 1936 did not really have the desired effect of rousing the nation to a new sense of national awareness and urging party members to greater political involvement. In 1939 the party's fortunes were at a low ebb; but, largely because of the experience gained in the 1943 University of Wales by-election, it emerged in 1945 with a renewed vigour and contested more parliamentary seats than the total of the previous twenty years. It had at last come to resemble a real political party, but, apart from two encouraging but illusory by-election results in 1946, the party made little headway in the following twenty years.[161]

A virtual revolution within Welsh society accompanied the new

---

[160] Morgan, *Rebirth*, pp. 296–7; Morgan and Thomas, *Wales*, pp. 147–8; Morgan, 'From Cymru Fydd to Crowther', pp. 127–8; *idem*, 'The Welsh in English Politics', p. 242.

[161] Davies, *The Welsh Nationalist Party*, pp. vii–viii, 71, 73, 112ff, 163–5, 182–6, 197–9, 261, 263, 267–8; Philip, *The Welsh Question*, pp. 14, 17; Morgan, 'From Cymru Fydd to Crowther', p. 131.

affluence of the 1950s and 1960s, for there now occurred a reorientation in people's life styles. The population became significantly better-off and better provided for in terms of housing, health and education. Accompanying this there came a transformation in leisure pursuits: private ownership of cars, the spread of television and consequent greater flood of mass entertainment all eroded the old forms of social participation. The chapel influence further waned, the falling congregations partly a consequence of linguistic ebb. In the industrial south, the new affluence spelt inevitable decline for the old world of intimate community and comradeship, a world remarkable for its rich working-class intellectual vitality. All this was to be replaced by the mindless monotony of the drinking clubs and bingo halls and the relatively cheerless, sanitised housing estates or commuter suburbs. Dai Smith perceptively concludes: 'in retrospect the late 1940s stand out as the last authentic years of that distinctive culture which had been fashioned in South Wales'.[162] However, for all the growing secularisation and anglicisation throughout the Principality, the more remote and western and north-western counties of rural Wales in the 1950s and 1960s, especially outside the towns, could still claim to have a distinctive 'Welsh' culture based on the language, chapel and the *eisteddfodau*, a 'specifically Welsh cultural activity' that was 'reinforced by strong subjective identification with Welshness'.[163]

The issue of language has, we have hinted earlier, given rise from the early part of this century down to the present to a crisis in identity among the people of Wales. While we would not fundamentally disagree with Bud Khleif that 'a shift in language is a shift in identity', it should be recognised that English-speaking Welshmen spiritedly and justifiably counter that, lack of Welsh notwithstanding, they, too, are a distinctive 'Welsh' people, possessed of characteristics which separate them from their English, Scottish and Irish neighbours. For them, it is their separate history, instinctive radicalism in religion and politics, contempt for social pretentiousness, personal warmth and exuberance, sociability, love of music and near-obsession with rugby which mark them out as Welshmen.[164]

[162]   Morgan, *Rebirth*, pp. 340, 345–7, 352–4; Smith, *Wales! Wales?*, p. 124.
[163]   P. J. Madgwick, *The Politics of Rural Wales* (1972), pp. 84–5.
[164]   Khleif, *Language*, p. 35; for a sensitive discussion see Williams, *Religion, Language and Nationality*, p. 147.

CHAPTER 5

The north-west

J. K. WALTON

Conventional wisdom about the fortunes and significance of this region in the two centuries after 1750 comes trippingly off the tongue. Below a thin crust of banal generalisations, however, the questing historian uncovers shifting, unstable strata of diverging and conflicting accounts and interpretations, often venting as emissions of superheated debate which alarm and confuse the innocent bystander, obscuring the view with steam and volcanic gases and dispelling the illusion of clarity, security and control. Explanations of the social circumstances surrounding the spectacular rise, sustained heyday and precipitous decline of the cotton industry and its associated towns form a staple of historical debate, although the first two phases have received much more attention than the third. The early and intensive interaction of the steam engine, the factory system and an unprecedented rate of urban growth, concentrated within a narrow area of south Lancashire and north Cheshire, proved irresistible to social commentators then and has remained so for social historians ever since. Cotton Lancashire became 'the first industrial society' and 'the cradle of the Industrial Revolution'. The cotton industry became a much-debated 'leading sector' in British industrialisation, while at the same time its assumed characteristics tended to be misleadingly paraded as a surrogate for the more complex pattern of changes in British economy and society as a whole. The industrialising experience of a small corner of Lancashire and its adjoining counties became at once exciting exception and all-embracing norm in the treatment of Britain's industrial revolution. Moreover, there were political dimensions to the changes. Here, it seemed, was emerging a new, thrusting, entrepreneurial middle class whose reforming vigour might change the face and direction of the British political system. Here, too, immiseration, exploitation and vile working conditions, themselves a matter of heated debate, appeared to some to threaten – or promise –

355

a much more radical undermining of the established economic and political order.

The industrial revolution in Lancashire thus seemed – and was, and is – nationally and internationally of special significance. This perception has nurtured a self-sustaining and apparently exponential growth in the historiography of the cotton district, as theoreticians of economic growth and analysts of class struggle have sought to test, apply or elaborate their ideas through local or industrial case-studies, occasionally detonating explosive conflicts. Historians and sociologists of all persuasions have produced mutually incompatible versions of changes and continuities in textile town social structure, firm size, living standards, family organisation and social and political relationships. From the Mancunian medical commentators of the later eighteenth century, through the apocalyptic, apologetic and celebratory polemicists of the generation of Engels and Cooke Taylor, to the recent clashes between Foster and Musson, Smelser and Anderson, controversy has fed controversy, and interpreters of Lancashire's industrial revolution cultivate a thickly sown and haphazardly laid minefield. The beginnings of similar debates are apparent as historians are drawn forward into the later Victorian and Edwardian cotton towns, seeking the roots of what seems to be a sudden transition from the political and industrial militancy of the 1830s and 1840s to the controlled industrial relations, social peace and two-party hegemony of the second half of the nineteenth century. The unique extent of women's factory work is also attracting attention, and all these areas are becoming disputed territory, as shown by reactions to the work of Vincent, Joyce and P. F. Clarke. As the historiography of the cotton industry's decline develops in turn, we can expect new areas of controversy to be defined. The cotton Lancashire experience has been too important, in its own right and for our understanding of wider processes, to be left to the cosy atrophy of consensus.

But there is much more to Lancashire than the cotton district. Merseyside, especially, developed a distinctive social configuration of its own, with a historiography to match. Liverpool's version of the commercial revolution has, however, generated less sustained interest and controversy among social historians. Like Merseyside more widely defined, it lacks the magic ingredients of steam-powered factories, early evidence of class conflict in politics and labour relations, and systematic employment of women and children outside the home. But Liverpool's spectacular maritime expansion created deep social divisions which challenge the more famous ones of Engels's Manchester, as prospering merchants retreated to a succession of suburbs and rural mansions, leaving the badly built, insanitary, overcrowded housing around the docks to become a district of deprivation where casual labour and crime existed in symbiosis. Migrants from Ireland, always more numerous than in the cotton towns, added an extra dimension of internal conflict by the 1840s. Higher up the social scale, the lack of a charismatic equivalent of the Anti-Corn Law League has helped to stunt the historiography of Liverpool's ruling classes. We know a great deal more about Liverpool's mercantile middle classes as businessmen than as citizens, and a whole range of roles and relationships remains almost unexplored. This is also largely true of the social circumstances surrounding the rise of the coal, salt, glass and chemical industries of greater Merseyside, stretching to Wigan, St Helens, Warrington and the Cheshire wiches, despite important groundwork in economic history and historical geography.

North of the Ribble we encounter a different set of influences again. Here seaports and pockets of water-powered industry flourished briefly in the late eighteenth and early nineteenth centuries only to fade again in the railway age, and only the variously specialised urban economies of Lancaster, Blackpool, Morecambe and Barrow showed sustained growth over significant lengths of time. As in Cheshire beyond the pull of Merseyside and the cotton towns, agriculture remained predominant here; and throughout the region farming remained important enough to merit sustained attention. On the lowlands, at least, the influence of aristocracy and gentry died hard.

Any assessment of regional social trends in Lancashire and Cheshire must take account of the striking contrasts in sub-regional experiences. It is possible and useful to generalise about the region as a whole in relation to the nation at large, but such statements will need careful qualification. This requirement is particularly pressing when we look at the important and controversial developments of the period conventionally labelled 'the Industrial Revolution'.

I THE TRANSITION TO INDUSTRIAL SOCIETY, *c.* 1750–1850

The century after 1750 saw the rise of the cotton industry in south-east Lancashire and north-east Cheshire. Here the full impact of the transition to the steam-powered factory, with its distinctive form of concomitant urbanisation, was absorbed. In this crucible a new kind of society was forged, although the manner of its transformation ensured that it retained many significant characteristics of the old one.

Lancashire's industrial revolution gathered momentum rapidly in the early nineteenth century, and especially in the 1820s and 1830s, but the initial impetus came in the later eighteenth century. The switch to pure cotton production at this time was accompanied by innovations which took the spinning and preparation processes out of the home, but created an enormous compensatory demand for handloom weavers. The domestic putting-out system was no Utopia of the independent smallholder/craftsman, as pressure on the land increased and families became increasingly dependent on what amounted to piece-rate wages. The spread of hand-operated spinning jennies and machines for carding, roving and twisting occurred unobtrusively during the 1770s, when the large water-frame spinning mills with their 'factory villages' also began to appear. But the main impact of the water frame came after 1785, and country mills employing several hundred operatives remained conspicuous but unusual. Even when water power was applied to Crompton's mule in the 1790s, as the pace of factory-building quickened and the transition to steam began, cotton spinning was still dominated by small units of production, often glorified workshops. Many of Oldham's 'original mills' were established in the 'commodious bedrooms' of dwelling-houses, and converted corn mills were often adapted to house water frames. Capital investment was usually on a limited scale, drawn cautiously from the established resources of existing merchants and manufacturers, their families and neighbours.[1]

These developments ensured the demise of domestic spinning, but otherwise their impact was limited. Urbanisation was not yet spectacular, as population growth spread through the countryside in scattered farmsteads and 'folds' of weavers' cottages, and water-powered mills dispersed in search of suitable upland sites. Manchester's population grew almost fourfold to 70,000 between 1760 and 1801, when adjoining Salford contained another 13,000. Over the same period Bolton almost trebled its population to pass 17,000, but the other cotton towns lagged

---

[1] S. D. Chapman, 'Fixed Capital Formation in the British Cotton Manufacturing Industry', in J. P. P. Higgins and S. Pollard, eds., *Aspects of Capital Formation in Great Britain 1750–1850* (1971), p. 59.

behind. Outside Manchester the sheer scale of urban living was not yet a source of serious social problems.

The really impressive changes came in the first half of the nineteenth century. Retained raw cotton imports increased more than tenfold between 1800 and 1841, especially after 1815. The number of mills grew much less spectacularly, from about 900 nationally in 1797 to about 1,200 in 1834; but this period saw the rapid advent of steam power and mule spinning, with great increases in factory productivity and the concentration of mills on urban sites. The transition to steam was almost complete by 1841. Increases in mule capacity, and the introduction of the self-actor in the 1830s, threatened the privileged status and autonomy of the adult male labour aristocracy of mule spinners, although this was a complex and protracted process. But the scale of workplace organisation did not increase markedly. The ready availability of credit and second-hand machinery, and the sub-division of factory buildings into smaller, rented production units, kept spinning open to the small (but insecure) entrepreneur. By 1841, admittedly, 77 per cent of the factory labour force worked in firms employing more than 150 people, but the few really large concerns were survivors from the early days of the industry. 'Medium-sized' firms employing between 150 and 500 predominated. These were comparatively very substantial, but less daunting to the operative than expectations based on the predominance of 'giant' firms might indicate; and most recruits were socialised into the factory at an early age.[2]

The other major development in cotton was the mechanisation of weaving. Continuing improvements to the handloom, an ample and elastic labour supply and the difficulty of developing a cost-effective and reliable powerloom ensured the continuing expansion of hand-loom weaving into the 1820s. The number of weavers probably trebled to about 225,000 between 1795 and 1811 and stabilised for a decade from the mid-1820s at about 250,000. At its peak handloom weaving dominated the economy of an extensive and thickly populated district of north-east Lancashire and was important over a much wider area. It was an easy trade to enter, apart from certain fancy fabrics. Apprenticeship restrictions had collapsed, basic skills could be learned in

---

[2] V. A. C. Gatrell, 'Labour, Power and the Size of Firms in Lancashire Cotton in the Second Quarter of the Nineteenth Century', *Economic History Review*, 2nd ser., 30 (1977), pp. 95–139; S. D. Chapman, 'Financial Restraints on the Growth of Firms in the Cotton Industry, 1790–1850', *Economic History Review*, 2nd ser., 32 (1979), pp. 50–69; R. Lloyd-Jones and A. A. Le Roux, 'The Size of Firms in the Cotton Industry: Manchester, 1815–41', *Economic History Review*, 2nd ser., 33 (1980), pp. 72–82.

a few weeks, and the labour market became oversupplied. In time of high demand yarn was also exported to be woven and finished on the Continent. During the 1820s piece-rates began to fall rapidly and inexorably. Weavers responded by working longer hours and increasing production at the lower rates, exacerbating a problem which was also being affected by the rise of the powerloom. The putters-out, with their low overheads, continued to make profits into the 1840s, but weavers' children began to enter the factories, subsidising their parents at the loom. Heavy population losses by migration occurred in the weaving villages during the 1830s and 1840s, as the powerloom completed its triumph; but handloom weaving survived tenaciously into the 1850s in many upland areas, especially where it could still be combined with small-scale farming.[3]

Factory weaving provided even more openings for the small entrepreneur than factory spinning. Although many of the powerloom pioneers were large integrated spinning and weaving firms in south Lancashire and north Cheshire, by 1850 the industry was becoming concentrated into north-east Lancashire, and the average number of employees per firm was less than 100. As in spinning, the weaving shed was a highly personalised, far from anonymous working environment. Unlike spinning, women were employed on the same terms as men, though male wages were slightly higher and promotion to the supervisory grades was a male preserve. Even so, the importance of family incomes rather than adult male wages persisted strongly from domestic industry; and powerloom weaving became a predominantly female occupation.

By mid-century the factory textile industry had reached maturity in cotton, with many short-term and sectoral traumas and catastrophes, but with surprisingly few long-term social discontinuities. It might be argued that the most important problems and pressures arose more from population growth and urbanisation than from factory industry in itself.

Between 1801 and 1851 the population of Lancashire and Cheshire increased by 185 per cent, and that of the cotton district more than trebled, while that of England and Wales doubled. Textile Lancashire

---

[3] J. S. Lyons, 'The Lancashire Cotton Industry and the Introduction of the Power-Loom, 1815–50' (unpublished PhD thesis, California University, Berkeley, 1977), pp. 34–99; G. Timmins, *Hand-Loom Weavers' Cottages in Central Lancashire* (Lancaster, 1977), p. 51; D. A. Farnie, *The Lancashire Cotton Industry and the World Market 1815-96* (1979), pp. 276–84.

was already relatively densely peopled in 1801, but the age of the canal and the steam-powered factory brought rapid urbanisation. Over the half-century Manchester more than quadrupled its population to over 300,000, while in 1851 four other towns in the cotton district (including Salford) counted more than 50,000 inhabitants, and five more (including Wigan) topped 20,000. Smaller towns also proliferated. On one definition nearly two-thirds of the area's population lived in its thirty towns by mid-century.[4] This was urbanisation on an altogether novel scale and pattern.

How did this happen? There was some short-distance migration from outside the area, and we must not forget the Irish, especially in the 1840s; but the key to the population increase lay in remarkably high birth rates and fertility ratios, especially in the 1810s and 1820s. Even in the depressed years of 1837–41 the Lancashire birth rate was the highest in England. This fecundity was spread across the county, on Merseyside and in the mainly agricultural west and far north as well as in the textile heartland, suggesting that it was more than just an instrumental response to job and marriage opportunities and the industrial demand for child labour. Death rates were also very high throughout the county, and life expectancy at birth showed no improvement between the 1780s and 1840s. Fleischman comments that in the 1830s 'Lancashire had higher birth, death and marriage rates, shorter life expectancy, and a younger population than any other county in the nation.'[5] Urban populations were already recruiting partly by natural increase by 1800, in spite of high child mortality; but in any case the pattern of migration to towns was predominantly short-distance and even local. Manchester attracted a higher proportion of long-range migrants, and its slum population, in Ancoats at least, was highly volatile;[6] but the cotton towns in general grew in a manner which permitted new urban dwellers to maintain mutually supportive contacts with kin and friends.

We must not exaggerate the importance of cotton as an employer in these towns, although comparatively the degree of specialisation

---

[4] J. T. Danson and T. A. Welton, 'On the Population of Lancashire and Cheshire and its Local Distribution during the Fifty Years 1801–51', *Transactions of the Historic Society of Lancashire and Cheshire*, 11 (1858–9), p. 31.

[5] R. K. Fleischman, jr, 'Conditions of Life among the Cotton Workers of South-East Lancashire during the Industrial Revolution (1780–1850)' (unpublished PhD thesis, State University of New York, Buffalo, 1973), p. 260.

[6] P. Rushton, 'Housing Conditions and the Family Economy in the Victorian Slum: A Study of a Manchester District, 1790–1871' (unpublished PhD thesis, Manchester University, 1977), pp. 99–100.

was very high by any standards. On one calculation the cotton industry consistently employed over one third of Lancashire's total population during the heyday of handloom weaving between the late
eighteenth century and the 1830s. For adult male labour saturation
point had already been reached in the mid-eighteenth century in some
parishes, where between half and two-thirds of the fathers of children
baptised in the parish church worked in the textile industries. In 1841
the urban figures for men over twenty years old were less spectacular.
Manchester in particular was developing quite a diverse employment
structure, as it became more of a commercial centre. In 1841 fewer
than a quarter of the town's adult males worked in textile processes
as such, and just over half of these seem to have worked in factories.
Textile workers were outnumbered by miscellaneous craft occupations. General labourers accounted for nearly 20 per cent of adult
males, and commercial, professional and shopkeeping occupations
were nearly as numerous. In more specialised centres such as Ashton,
Blackburn and Bolton textile workers accounted for between 40 and
nearly 50 per cent of the adult male workforce, and many more of
these worked in factories.[7] The true dependence of these economies
on cotton went much deeper than this, as jobs in all sectors from
labouring and coal mining to building and retailing depended on the
prosperity of the staple industry; and the rapid rise of machine-making
during the 1840s was largely geared up to the needs of local cotton
firms, although a growing proportion of output was for export. But
cotton factories as such still employed a minority of adult males even
in Ashton, where their influence was strongest. In most places they
accounted for a quarter or less of this sector of the workforce.

To assess the full extent of cotton's dominance towards mid-century
we need to consider the distinctive age and sex structure of factory
employment. In 1841 more than 40 per cent of women aged over
twenty in Manchester's workforce were in textiles, two-thirds of them
in factories. For the under-twenties the former figure was nearly 60
per cent. In the really specialised cotton towns the proportions were
much higher: more than two-thirds of the female over-twenties labour
force were in textiles in Blackburn and Ashton, and over 80 per cent
of the under-twenties. Almost all were factory workers. Children

---

[7] V. A. C. Gatrell, 'The Commercial Middle Class in Manchester, c. 1820–57' (unpublished PhD thesis, Cambridge University, 1971), p. 81; Rushton, 'Victorian Slum',
pp. 198–9. In Preston the corresponding figure was only 32 per cent: M. Anderson,
Family Structure in Nineteenth-Century Lancashire (Cambridge, 1971), p. 25.

under the age of thirteen probably accounted for nearly one fifth of cotton factory workers in south-east Lancashire and north Cheshire in 1833, and despite factory legislation the under-eighteens made up over one third of the factory population in 1847. The peak ages for cotton employment, especially in the mills, were the late teens and early twenties. In 1851 nearly 40 per cent of girls aged between fifteen and nineteen in the whole of Lancashire worked in cotton manufacture, and about one in every four boys. This suggests that factory work was an almost universal experience for female teenagers, and very much the norm for males, in the cotton towns themselves. By the mid-twenties the age participation rate was dropping steadily, as men who failed to make the grade sought better-paid jobs in other industries, and women married and started families, for at this stage only the hardest-pressed mothers sought factory work while their children were young. The overall percentage of the adult population working in cotton, including the surviving non-factory sector, ranged in 1851 from 38.3 in Blackburn through 34.7 in Ashton and 29.5 in Preston to 16.5 in Wigan and a mere 16.0 in Manchester itself, with much lower figures for the area north of Preston and negligible ones for Merseyside.[8]

West of Wigan, north of the Ribble and in most of Cheshire the impact of cotton was indeed very limited. The economy of greater Merseyside developed rapidly with little reference to it during the second half of the eighteenth century. Salt, coal and the Atlantic traffic bulked largest at this stage in Liverpool, and slavery brought occasional windfall profits rather than consistent or reliable high returns. Cotton became an important Liverpool trade at the end of the eighteenth century, and by the 1820s it was the most valuable single import; but this was a diversified maritime economy whose own surpluses were invested in inland transport and nearby coalfields rather than the cotton industry as such. Eighteenth-century Liverpool also had a substantial manufacturing sector, with impressive concentrations of coal-using crafts as well as shipbuilding, pottery and chemicals. Early in the nineteenth century these industries declined or migrated to Liverpool's hinterland, as the town's specialisation in commerce and shipping deepened. It still grew significantly faster than Manchester, and by 1851 its population stood at over 375,000. The rise of the coal, salt and chemical industries inland, where

---

[8] Rushton, 'Victorian Slum', p. 198; Lyons, 'Power-Loom', pp. 147–51; Anderson, *Family Structure*, pp. 26–8; Fleischman, 'Cotton Workers', p. 29.

urbanisation (outside Warrington and St Helens) lagged far behind the textile district, created vulnerably specialised local economies with a heavy dependence on unskilled adult male labour, although Cheshire salt, in particular, employed whole families in arduous and unpleasant tasks. In contrast with the textile district, the Merseyside social structure was increasingly characterised by a shortage of skilled industrial work, a chronic lack of female and juvenile employment, and a limited representation of the middle ranks of tradesmen and small manufacturers.

North of Preston the cotton industry sprinkled factory settlements quite thickly over a wide area during its water-powered phase, socialising countrydwellers as well as parish apprentices into factory life; but they were already declining by the 1830s, as the advantages of the coalfield asserted themselves. Mining and quarrying persisted in places, to be revitalised in Furness in the 1840s and afterwards. But the growth of industry in the late eighteenth century was not consolidated subsequently, and decline was apparent in most sectors by 1840. South Lancashire, instead of stimulating economic and social change further north, became a successful competitor for its fruits, enticing the natural increase of the countryside southwards in the process.

In 1850 as in 1750 the social structure of north Lancashire was dominated by agricultural occupations, and farming remained important throughout the north-west. Agriculture accounted for only just over 10 per cent of Lancashire's adult males in 1851, but farmers and farm workers were remarkably thick on the ground; indeed, the Lancashire figure of 29.6 per square mile was substantially higher than the national average.[9] Cheshire's agricultural interest bulked larger in the total population, but the pattern in both counties was similar. Small farms predominated: three-quarters of Lancashire's farms in 1851 occupied less than 50 acres each, and in Cheshire only eleven farmers had more than 500 acres. A relatively high proportion of farmers were owner-occupiers, although their numbers declined after 1815. The landed gentry were strong and well established in lowland Cheshire, but thin on the ground in Lancashire away from the coastal plain. Pastoral and mixed farming prevailed, with an emphasis on cattle rearing and dairying. Much of the labour came from the farmers and their families, although in 1851 agricultural day-labourers and living-in farm servants averaged more than two per farm in Lancashire

---

[9] Danson and Welton, 'Population of Lancashire and Cheshire', p. 33.

and three in Cheshire. The social distance between farmers and labourers was limited, especially in the frequent cases where farm servants were farmers' children saving for a holding of their own, or waiting to inherit. Agricultural real wages were relatively high and tending upwards through the period, especially near the industrial districts. This was a generally stable agricultural system, apart from the progressive sub-division of holdings in south-east Lancashire and north-east Cheshire. It was little disrupted by enclosure (mainly of mosses and upland commons) or innovation, and its perpetuation was aided by the ample scope for surplus rural population to find industrial employment or move to towns which were themselves providing expanding markets for the farmers' products. The farmers themselves were rarely prosperous or even comfortably off, but the rural social system worked well enough to ensure that migration off the land could take place by choice before pressure on the labour market made it a necessity.

How did the changes of the century after 1750 affect the living standards and life styles of the industrial labour force? We must consider two sets of related influences, one emanating from the factory, the other from urbanisation.

Cotton factories imposed long hours of regimented toil, at a pace and rhythm governed by an external motive power and watched over by a hierarchy of supervisors, in an unpleasant and unhealthy environment. Most of these assertions require some qualification, however, and there were benefits to set against the costs. Above all, factory work meant improved family earnings, even when only the children participated. Only a small minority of men graduated to the supervisory aristocracies of mule spinners and overlookers, but there was plenty of relatively well-paid work for women (especially when power-loom weaving expanded), while children could make a useful contribution to the family budget from an early stage, and teenage incomes were high for the age group. Anderson's Preston figures suggest that, in a reasonable year, most young couples and families with children in work at mid-century were safely clear of a poverty-line derived from Rowntree's York. Foster's more pessimistic Oldham evidence indicates that poverty levels compared favourably with the contrasting urban economies of Northampton and South Shields. Most families fell into poverty when the children were young, but the availability of factory work for wives was an additional resource to alleviate this universal problem. Cotton factory wages were relatively regular and predictable, though they were always threatened by the trade cycle and the high turnover of smaller employers. Some attempt at budgeting, saving and insurance was increasingly possible to many, however, and the importance of family rather than individual incomes reduced the potential impact of the illness or death of the main breadwinner.

These material advantages carry more weight relatively than absolutely, and the life styles assumed by the calculators of living standards are very basic indeed. McKenzie's nutritional analysis of working-class budgets in the Manchester area for 1841 applies only to the 'sober and industrious', as do the Anderson and Foster figures. Even then, although the well-paid and fully employed might enjoy a boring but adequate diet based on bread, potatoes and a little meat, similarly virtuous labourers on short time descended to a bill of fare seriously deficient in protein and calories, which was 'very likely' to have 'some immediate effect on health and the ability to resist disease'.[10] These calculations make no allowance for waste or food adulteration, or 'irrational' expenditure on drink and entertainment; and such evidence sets textile Lancashire's relatively high family incomes in perspective. To maintain and safeguard a barely adequate diet it was necessary to adopt an abstemious life style of endlessly deferred gratifications. The proliferation of beerhouses in the cotton towns after 1830 is one indication among many that such sustained self-control was far from the norm.

The factory economy had obvious disadvantages. Working hours were very long for most of the period, and accidents and factory-induced diseases were rife. The work was monotonous and mentally demanding as well as physically debilitating. As Kay remarked, cotton operatives' employment

absorbs their attention, and unremittingly employs their physical energies. They are drudges who watch the movements, and assist the operations, of a mighty material force, which toils with an energy ever unconscious of fatigue. The persevering labour of the operative must rival the mathematical precision, the incessant motion and the exhaustless power of the machine.[11]

Such work imposed its own discipline, which was reinforced by the mill management hierarchy. But one does not have to endorse Andrew

---

[10]   J. McKenzie, 'The Composition and Nutritional Value of Diets in Manchester and Dukinfield', *Lancashire and Cheshire Antiquarian Society*, 72 (1962), pp. 123–40; Anderson, *Family Structure*; and J. Foster, *Class Struggle and the Industrial Revolution* (1974).

[11]   J. P. Kay, *The Moral and Physical Condition of the Working Classes Employed in the Cotton Manufacture of Manchester* (1832), pp. 24–5.

Ure's apologetics, in which factory children were unashamedly likened to 'lively elves' who revelled in their employment, to suggest that the employers' adoption of elaborate codes of factory rules and fines was at least in part a defensive response to the irrepressible indiscipline of a young and resourceful labour force who found ways of lightening the burden of their toil.

In mule spinning at least, adjustment to factory life was made easier by the perpetuation of a family-sized basic production unit (spinner, piecers, scavengers) and a patriarchal authority structure. Sub-contracting was prevalent in spinning as in many other industries, and evidence from the 1830s suggests that two-thirds of male under-eighteen factory workers, and one third of the females, were hired by the operatives rather than the masters. This does not mean that the family units of domestic industry were transferred to the factory *en bloc*: Smelser's assertions to this effect have been successfully challenged by Anderson and others on demographic and empirical grounds, and many handloom weaving economies were being underpinned by children's factory work from the 1820s onwards. But a substantial minority of factory children were being employed and paid by their fathers on a sub-contracting basis, and many others were similarly supervised by other relatives and neighbours. How this system came into operation is still an open question, but Lazonick argues that the factory masters found it convenient to leave the recruitment and discipline of the spinners' assistants to the spinners themselves.[12] The privileged position of the mule spinner was thus safeguarded against dilution and innovation by the need for discipline to be imposed by physical domination and reinforced by the normative sanctions of patriarchal or quasi-patriarchal authority, although such norms must often have shielded the children themselves from excesses of cruelty or exploitation.

The crucial differences entailed by the factory were the separation of home from workplace, and the expression of each member's contribution to the family economy as a separate money wage, except where this was masked by sub-contracting. Work outside the home was the norm in agriculture and many other occupations, of course, but factory work took economically active household members away for very long hours on a regular basis, women included. Contemporaries worried

---

[12]   W. Lazonick, 'Industrial Relations and Technical Change: The Case of the Self-Acting Mule', *Cambridge Journal of Economics*, 3 (1979), pp. 231–62; N. J. Smelser, *Social Change in the Industrial Revolution* (1959).

about the social implications. Here is Engels, at one with Ashley and the factory reformers on this issue:

> The employment of women at once breaks up the family; for when the wife spends 12 or 13 hours every day in the mill, and the husband works the same length of time there or elsewhere ... the children ... grow up like wild weeds; they are put out to nurse for a shilling or eighteenpence per week, and how they are treated may be imagined.[13]

There is much more in the same vein, about children being ruined for family life and moving into lodgings at the first opportunity, about the immorality of factory girls and the painful reversal of sex roles as unemployed men kept house while their wives went out to work. The reality was less apocalyptic. Anderson calculates that in the Preston of 1851 '23% of children who had a co-residing father had working mothers', half of whom were in factory occupations. Most of these children were looked after by relatives and neighbours, and only a tiny minority of infants were left with professional child-minders.[14] The mothers who worked in factories did so to mitigate the impact of the poverty cycle in families headed by low wage earners. Admittedly, Preston's administrative and residential functions probably offered a wider range of non-factory and indeed home-based employment for mothers than did most cotton towns. Moreover, evidence from 1851 may well provide a more stable and reassuring picture than similar sources might have suggested for earlier years. We must not ignore the systematic dosing of children with opiates and the tragically high infant mortality levels for the cotton towns; but such problems were also prevalent elsewhere, and Liverpool, especially, had a much worse child mortality record. As for adolescents leaving home and factory immorality, what evidence we have is at worst inconclusive. We should remember that middle-class observers were easily shocked by female bad language, and all too eager to equate its use with depravity of a more physical kind. Factory work gave women a measure of cultural independence, at least during working hours, and the evidence of this was deeply disturbing to most commentators. The factory must have inhibited the transmission of housewifery skills, and it certainly imposed a 'double shift' of housework and mill work on those wives and mothers who found it inescapable. But the worst effects of the factory on the family arose from child labour, although even this had its antecedents in the domestic workshops of proto-

---

[13]   F. Engels, *The Condition of the Working Class in England* (Panther edn, 1969), p. 171.
[14]   Anderson, *Family Structure*, pp. 73–4.

industrial Lancashire, where hours could be as long and discipline as brutal as in any factory. By the 1830s legislative controls and economic considerations were conspiring to reduce the level of child employment in the youngest age-ranges; and more generally the impact of the factory on the working-class family was cushioned by family and neighbourhood support networks, aided by the short-range nature of most migration and the early emergence of relatively stable working-class areas. Significantly, most of the adverse contemporary comment came from Manchester, whose size and wide migration catchment area made these mitigating factors less effective.

Few experienced the transition to factory and town simultaneously. Many families first experienced factory work in the rural 'industrial colonies', which became staging posts for migrants *en route* to the larger centres. Adult migrants to the cotton towns rarely worked in factories themselves unless they already had appropriate experience. Only children and young adolescents were likely to make both sets of adjustments at once.

The traumas of town life, as such, centred on health and physical environment. Working-class housing in the cotton towns was often of very poor quality. Employer housing was rarely provided for more than ten or twelve key workers, and 'model' housing in the manner of the Ashworths at Egerton and New Eagley or the Ashtons at Hyde was most unusual. Such employers often deducted rents at source and imposed strict regimes of supervision and inspection, while profit bulked larger than paternalism as a motive for provision of this kind. Housing subsidies were unknown.[15] The pressures and risks of the land market and building industry as experienced by the small speculators who predominated, combined with the urge to profit, ensured that tightly packed urban housing was easily and frequently overcrowded by the most basic of public health standards. Families responded to depressions or troughs in the poverty cycle by economising on space, taking in relatives or lodgers to make the rent go further. The lack of untainted water and sewering compounded the problems, especially in working-class areas. The lack of adequate washing facilities encouraged the spread of louse-borne diseases like typhus along with a wide range of other environmentally related

---

[15] S. M. Gaskell, 'Housing Estate Development 1840–1918, with Special Reference to the Pennine Towns', (unpublished PhD thesis, Sheffield University, 1974), chap. 2; L. D. W. Smith, 'Textile Factory Settlements in the Early Industrial Revolution' (unpublished PhD thesis, Aston University, 1976), pp. 38, 42, 202–3.

sicknesses. Squalor and high death rates were the most obvious physical disadvantages of urbanisation, compounded by air pollution and the adulteration of food supplies.

Why did the cotton towns recruit so successfully among short-distance migrants who knew what they were coming to? In the first place, historians are in a much better position to take account of high urban death and disease rates than were contemporary migrants, who seem to have taken little or no notice of this issue, despite growing awareness among sections of the professional middle classes, especially during the 1830s and 1840s. Beyond this, the answer varies according to the origins of the migrant. If they lay in domestic industry, subsistence migration increasingly predominated as life in handloom weaving settlements became more difficult. If in Ireland, the case was even more clear-cut. If in agriculture, the age structure of migrants, concentrated in the teens and twenties, suggests that the cotton towns promised early release from dependence, whether on the family farm or in farm service, especially for those who did not expect to inherit. For such people the towns offered independence, amusement and the prospect of early marriage.

Short-range migration to compact towns of manageable size enabled extended families to provide mutual aid in hard times, and ensured that neighbours were likely to share a common background in experience and culture. Workplace recruitment through personal contacts reinforced these tendencies, and supportive social and familial networks were probably strengthened by the urban milieu, which also provided alternative or additional support systems based on workplace, pub, church or chapel. Customs and traditions were likewise defended and perpetuated: the wakes holidays, for example, might be truncated in time and content, but they survived to enter a new lease of life beyond mid-century, alongside the new commercial influences of singing saloon and music hall.[16] The solidarity and systematic mutual assistance provided by neighbourhood, workplace and extended family in the cotton towns stands out as a positive feature of the response to industrialisation; and the growing strength of the friendly societies reinforced these informal institutions. These arguments are reinforced if we reject Anderson's assumption that this behaviour was largely founded on the coldly rational calculation of

---

[16]   J. K. Walton and R. Poole, 'The Lancashire Wakes in the Nineteenth Century', in R. D. Storch, ed., *Popular Culture and Custom in Nineteenth-Century England* (1982), pp. 100–24.

individual long-term interest, and give normative values and traditional expectations their due explanatory weight.[17]

The impact of large-scale, rapid urbanisation was perhaps more traumatic outside the cotton towns. Liverpool had a particularly sad
record. The decline of manufacturing industry, and the concentration
of employment into transport and services to commerce, meant that
from the late eighteenth century casual workers, and especially
dockers, grew even more rapidly in relative importance than in absolute numbers. By 1851 about 45 per cent of household heads were
in 'unskilled' or 'semi-skilled' occupations. There were few economic
openings for children or married women, and many family economies
depended very heavily on the uncertain incomes of casually employed
dockers and labourers. Housing conditions were especially appalling,
as dockers' housing competed with commercial users for scarce space
near the waterfront, and landowners rationed the supply of development land. Back-to-back courts formed nearly one third of the housing
stock by 1850, and ten years earlier over 12 per cent of the population
of Liverpool parish (the inner city) lived in damp and polluted cellars.
The average working-class cottage occupied only 16 square yards of
land, but high land prices sent overall building costs soaring. In 1845
they were 10 per cent higher than in Manchester and 30 per cent
more than in Bolton or Bury. The combination of low, uncertain wages
and high rents meant large numbers of lodgers and lethal levels of
overcrowding. Death rates rose sharply after 1820. They stayed at
well over thirty per thousand through the 1830s and 1840s, reaching
a gruesome peak of seventy-one per thousand in the aftermath of
the Irish famine in 1847. Liverpool's mortality levels at this period
were the worst in England, and possibly the worst in the world. Long-
distance migration predominated, especially from Ireland, and despite
the Irish tendency to cluster in particular areas, the neighbourhood
solidarity of the cotton towns could not yet be reproduced in the
dockland slums. No wonder contemporaries identified perennial
problems of theft, drunkenness, violence and vice.[18]

Liverpool's urban pathology illustrates the problems of rapid
urbanisation without manufacturing industry. Significantly, the most

---

[17] J. K. Walton, 'Lunacy in the Industrial Revolution: A Study of Asylum Admissions
in Lancashire, 1848–50', *Journal of Social History*, 13 (1979–80), pp. 16–17.
[18] I. C. Taylor, 'Black Spot on the Mersey: A Study of Environment and Society in
Eighteenth- and Nineteenth-Century Liverpool' (unpublished PhD thesis, Liverpool
University, 1976), pp. 124, 196–7.

horrendous areas of Engels's Manchester lay close to the city centre, where factory work was not available and a casual labour market similar to that of inner Liverpool prevailed. The emergent centres of mining and heavy industry in Liverpool's hinterland, however, shared some important characteristics with the cotton towns, as locally recruited labour kept up established festivals and violent sports, outwork survived in watchmaking, toolmaking and nailing (but as yet without the traumas of the handloom weavers), and family incomes in mining could be supplemented by women and children (whatever the other social costs) until the 1840s. Public health problems were universal, and market towns like Ormskirk or emergent resorts like Southport had 'black spots' of their own. In many ways the cotton towns came out best in the longer term from the working-class experience of industrialisation in the north-west. Under prevailing circumstances, the factory became more asset than liability for the life-chances and living standards of the urban labour force.

During this period important changes also took place in Lancashire's propertied and governing classes. The balance of power and prestige tilted towards the industrial and commercial wealth of south Lancashire, and new administrative bodies were colonised by textile magnates and their allies. The rise of the 'cottonocracy' or 'millocracy' in the cotton towns was accompanied by the emergence of new kinds of mercantile wealth in Liverpool and a measure of landed continuity in many rural areas.

Lancashire had its fair share of aristocratic estates, and Cheshire substantially more than that. But the gentry and greater yeomanry were relatively thin on the ground, and very small holdings of less than 100 acres were particularly numerous in south-east Lancashire. Large estates were concentrated disproportionately into the more fertile south and west, and so were gentry residences. Merchants and manufacturers were already taking over the country seats of the textile district by the early nineteenth century, and most of Lancashire's new gentry of the eighteenth and nineteenth centuries rose by this route. The great estates, from the Stanleys downwards, prospered from steadily rising rent-rolls and windfall profits from mining and urbanisation, while the gentry were economically secure unless tempted into injudicious industrial speculation. The landlords themselves were benefiting from the economic changes which produced the challengers to their power.

The substantial factory masters were the most visible and controversial of the new men. Few were abrasive self-made men in the Bounderby idiom. Howe's study of 351 Lancashire textile industrialists finds that between the late eighteenth century and the 1840s only 5 per cent 'definitely rose from the ranks of shopkeepers, artisans and operatives', although a further 21 per cent had unknown origins. The successful ones made substantial fortunes by provincial standards, but could not compare with the richest metropolitan bankers and merchants.[19] Nearly half were Anglicans, and nonconformists (apart from Unitarians and Quakers) were not overrepresented in their ranks. They were not a race apart, but an affluent, distinctive and well-integrated group, linked by cultural, familial and economic ties to the society which spawned them. By 1872, indeed, thirty-nine of Howe's sample (or their direct descendants) owned landed estates of more than 1,000 acres; and many more had a smaller, but significant, stake in the land.

Liverpool merchants and bankers were also acquiring small estates on the urban fringe in this period, and Manchester had a wealthy mercantile group which outweighed most of its manufacturers in prestige. Coal, brewing, chemicals and engineering nurtured successful entrepreneurs, usually from comfortable backgrounds. Everywhere, too, an uneasy, volatile and politically unstable stratum of shopkeepers and small manufacturers proliferated below the rich and relatively comfortable.

Among the substantial merchants and manufacturers there were deep divisions between Tories and reformers, Anglicans and dissenters. In most cotton towns the Tory factory masters were wealthy, well established by the 1820s, and closely linked with the local clergy and landed gentry. The reformers were usually 'new men' with smaller factories, lower status and a narrower, more townbound social outlook. In Liverpool and Manchester Tory elites, entrenched in the old local government institutions, were pitted against nonconformists of more recent origins, led by well-educated and wealthy counter-elites of close-knit Unitarian cousinhoods. Strife between these contending groups was endemic between the 1790s and the 1840s, reaching a climax in Liverpool with municipal reform in 1835 and in

---

[19] A. C. Howe, 'The Lancashire Textile Masters 1830–60: A Social and Political Study' (unpublished DPhil thesis, Oxford University, 1980), chaps. 1–2.

Manchester with incorporation in 1838 and the rise of the Anti-Corn Law League.[20]

Despite their internal divisions, the middle classes were beginning to challenge the dominance of the established landed families on several fronts in Lancashire during the 1830s and 1840s, though not over most of Cheshire. They invaded the county magistrates' bench: in 1831, 60 of the 105 active magistrates were landed gentry, but by 1851 the figure was 144 out of 400. Industry, banking and commerce accounted for twenty-eight JPs (including seven cotton magnates) in 1831 and 187 (109) in 1851, as the millocracy took administrative control of the industrial parts of the county. Lancashire's parliamentary representation was transformed even more remarkably. Between 1800 and 1831 only four of fifty-nine MPs had been cotton masters, and landed influence predominated; but between 1832 and 1852 textile employers accounted for twenty-four of the eighty-five MPs, and landed society claimed only twenty-three, with the balance drawn largely from commerce, other industrial interests and the professions. As well as the boroughs, they invaded the southern division of the county, and had to be conciliated by the Stanleys and Cavendishes even in the mainly agricultural northern division. They made little impact at Westminster, but the implications for Lancashire's power structure and social order were real enough.[21]

Meanwhile, urban local government was passing to new institutions which were dominated by the middle classes to the exclusion of the landed interest. The advent of reformed corporations in Liverpool and Manchester outflanked and defeated the Tory elites there, with their landed connections. But these groups proved strong and resilient, and recovered during the 1840s. The apparent hegemony of the Anti-Corn Law League and the 'Manchester School', of free trade and laissez-faire, was more fragile in Manchester than some have suggested. Toryism remained well entrenched among Manchester's business community, as shown by the even division of elite votes at the 1839 election. But the growing unease of many landed gentry

[20] Gatrell, 'Commercial Middle Class'; *idem*, 'Incorporation and the Pursuit of Liberal Hegemony in Manchester 1790–1839', in D. Fraser, ed., *Municipal Reform and the Industrial City* (Leicester, 1982), pp. 15–60, and B. D. White, *A History of the Corporation of Liverpool* (Liverpool, 1951), chaps. 2–3; S. A. L. Gunn, 'Insiders and Outsiders: The Formation of the Urban Elites and the Struggle for Municipal Power in Liverpool, 1800–35' (unpublished MA dissertation, Lancaster University, 1982).

[21] D. Foster, 'The Changing Social and Political Composition of the Lancashire Magistracy 1821–51' (unpublished PhD thesis, Lancaster University, 1971), pp. 291–2; Howe, 'Lancashire Textile Masters', pp. 108–20.

was understandable. It was easy to equate the outpourings of the Anti-Corn Law League and other pressure groups with the collective voice of a threatening new class of thrusting industrialists. The reality was less disturbing. Many manufacturer recruits to the county bench, and even some millowner MPs, were Tory protectionists who were anxious for acceptance into landed society by the established route, through estate purchase and the adoption of an appropriate life style. Derek Fraser's suggestion that in early Victorian England 'the great political issue . . . was the class struggle between bourgeoisie and aristocracy'[22] expresses the great divide between a vociferous segment of the entrepreneurial middle class on one hand, and the rural landed interest on the other; but it ignores an extensive middle ground of industrialists with landed connections and aspirations, and landowners with industrial interests, which accounted for a large proportion of Lancashire's leading citizens.

These beneficiaries of industrialisation found it increasingly difficult to ignore the problems of towndwellers and industrial workers. Basic to their concern was the need to maintain work discipline and social discipline, to maximise productivity and protect property. Religious and humanitarian impulses often reinforced or camouflaged these goals, or even encouraged deviations from them; but they were rarely far from the surface. By the 1830s most Lancashire employers had accepted and internalised a crude political economy of laissez-faire, individualism and free competition, although this did not inhibit the formation of employers' associations to keep wages low and fight for legislative favours. Many were also willing to act, as individuals or through voluntary organisations, to improve the lot of their workpeople, or of the poor in general; but with rare exceptions they repudiated compulsion, insisting on the autonomy of the individual capitalist and the preservation of the employer's patriarchal dominion over his workforce. Thus employers famed for model housing and generous educational and social provisions might be fined for persistent breaches of the factory acts, or object to proposals for compulsory schooling for factory children. Poverty, disease, crime and social unrest were ascribed to the depravity, incompetence or ill-fortune of individuals, rather than the failings of the wider economy and society. The most acceptable remedies, coercion apart, were religious and educational, suitably blended to reform individuals by teaching

[22] D. Fraser, *Urban Politics in Victorian England* (Leicester, 1976), p. 22.

subordination, acquiescence in the social and political order, and basic life skills to cope with it.

The direct influence of organised religion was weak in Lancashire in the late eighteenth century. The Church of England has been described as 'meaningless and invisible', with its huge sprawling parishes, badly paid curates, pluralism and absenteeism.[23] Pockets of Old Dissent persisted, and the Methodists moved into the religious vacuum in some areas, especially in the textile district in the early nineteenth century. By the 1830s the Anglicans were beginning a major programme of church-building and endowment, stimulated by the rise of evangelical seriousness in their own ranks, and by competition from Roman Catholics, deists and socialists as well as nonconformity. But even in 1851 Lancashire's religious attendances, proportionate to population, were well below the national average for all denominations except the Roman Catholics. Even where attendances were lowest, as in Oldham and Preston, the figures are compatible with fairly regular observance by about one fifth of the population, but the working-class level was much lower. Church or chapel attendance, in itself, can have done little to mould the consciousness of the Lancashire working class in the desired directions.

Religious influences operated most effectively through the Sunday schools. Their numbers and influence increased steadily after the 1780s, reaching a peak in the 1820s and 1830s, especially where children worked in the textile industries during the week. Employers opened their coffers more readily to Sunday school promoters than to church-builders. They hoped to see their young employees taught that God's law enjoined subordination, thrift, self-denial, punctuality and obedience, using appropriate biblical texts, and many reinforced the sabbatarians in their opposition to the teaching of writing and arithmetic. Sunday schools reached vast numbers of children and adolescents, but their impact is debatable. Pupils voted with their feet from schools which ceased to teach useful literacy skills, and the amount of indoctrination that could be packed into a few hours was limited, especially if it ran counter to the norms of home and community. Teachers were difficult to supervise, and most were not the sons and daughters of the middle classes. The Sunday school was not necessary to teach factory discipline to factory children: the factory itself fulfilled that function. Sunday scholars were notoriously

---

[23] J. Addy, 'Bishop Porteous' Visitation of the Diocese of Chester, 1778', *Northern History*, 13 (1977), pp. 175–98.

prone to frequenting fairgrounds and singing rooms, and many Chartist leaders acquired essential literacy skills through the Sunday school. Some working-class children did internalise the values enjoined by Sunday school promoters, but others rejected them or failed to comprehend them. There was an enormous wastage between Sunday school attendance in one generation and adult church attenders in the next, and the overall cultural influence of the schools was probably quite limited.[24] The rise of the church- and chapel-funded elementary day schools, especially in the 1840s as the factory acts began to bite, was much more important in the long run. The Church of England, drawing on donations from London and the Home Counties rather than from factory masters, dominated this aspect of Lancashire education by 1850, exploiting to the full its ability to exercise strict control over trained, salaried, dependent teachers.

Attempts to go beyond a basic level of skill transmission and religious indoctrination were patchier and more controversial. From the mid-1820s the Mechanics' Institutes spread rapidly through the north-west, but Tory employers were often opposed to non-sectarian scientific education, and only a tiny minority of the working class took advantage of lectures and libraries whose content was usually carefully vetted by committees of middle-class patrons. The efforts of large employers to go beyond providing relatively 'efficient' factory schools, by promoting self-improvement and 'sponsored mobility' through reading rooms and institutes in mill colonies, similarly produced a limited response from toil-worn operatives. The provision of 'rational recreations' by employers, religious bodies and the temperance movement expanded rapidly after 1830, offering excursions and tea meetings as well as reading rooms to build bridges between the classes and lure workpeople away from beerhouses, races, fairgrounds, blood sports and gambling. These initiatives proved more popular, but, as with the public parks which began to appear in the 1840s, they were incorporated into an existing recreational pattern, rather than displacing or replacing it.

Joyce has labelled the employer initiatives of the 1830s and 1840s 'the new paternalism', but we should remember the limited success of most attempts to extend employer influence beyond the work-

---

[24] Compare T. W. Laqueur, *Religion and Respectability: Sunday Schools and Working-Class Culture, 1780–1850* (1976), and M. Dick, 'The Myth of the Working-Class Sunday School', *History of Education*, 9 (1980), pp. 27–42.

place.[25] These were anyway the preserve of a few large employers, in mining as well as textiles, with substantial resources and distinct areas of employee housing around their works; and everywhere they were accompanied by an autocratic attitude to trade unions, wage bargaining and the labour process. The employers' willingness to ameliorate their workers' living standards stopped short at wages and rents. Their treatment of poverty took place within a rigid framework of expectation that the price of labour would be ruled by market forces, although they were willing enough to tinker with the labour market by seeking sponsorship for parish-assisted migrants from the rural south, and they were also ready to provide charitable assistance, especially in kind, during trade depressions. This was, after all, voluntary assistance, calculated to preserve the social order, keep the workforce together and forge bonds of gratitude between poor and propertied.

Legislative interference was a different matter. Employer support for the handloom weavers' pursuit of a guaranteed minimum wage fell away rapidly between the 1810s and the 1830s, by which time the weavers' remaining allies were presented as eccentric sentimentalists by their opponents. Factory reform in the 1830s and 1840s attracted the same unorthodox minority. The old poor law was so tightly run in most of Lancashire, including Liverpool and the rural areas, that per capita expenditure was among the lowest in England, although general economic conditions were also obviously important here. The new poor law made very little practical difference to administration or policy. Campaigns for public health reform made little headway in the 1830s and 1840s. Manchester's Longdendale water scheme and Liverpool's public health initiatives of the 1840s were significant straws in the wind, but vested interests, conflicting administrative jurisdictions, faction-fighting, lack of expertise, technological uncertainty, parsimony and the sanctity of private property combined with laissez-faire ideology to make a formidable set of barriers to effective improvement.

Under these circumstances coercion and repression remained central pillars of the social system. Lancashire's rate of recorded crime was consistently well above the national level between 1811 and 1851, and the urban rates must have been higher still. The vast majority of these crimes – and, no doubt, most of the undetected and unreported

---

[25] P. Joyce, *Work, Society and Politics* (Brighton, 1980).

ones – involved theft, usually petty theft. Liverpool, with its distinctive economy, generated a particularly obvious sub-culture of interrelated crime and deprivation, exacerbated by a very high density of drink outlets, coupled with violence and prostitution. Despite occasional alarmist comments, the textile district had nothing to compare with this, though here political unrest also became endemic. But rate-supported police forces were introduced gradually and grudgingly. The county justices, immune from electoral pressure, set up a county police force at the first opportunity in 1839; but the urban areas, which complained most about crime and disorder, also generated angry opposition to the expense and threat to individual and local liberties allegedly posed by the new police. Several towns preferred to operate smaller and cheaper police forces of their own, and low pay, insecurity and bad working conditions ensured that the 'new' police of the 1830s rarely offered much improvement on the old town watchmen. Thus it was understandable that the tradesmen most at risk from crime should still prefer low rates to an increased police presence. The police were used to put down disorderly popular recreations in public places, but their effectiveness in this role may have been exaggerated.[26] Even in the disturbed 1830s and 1840s, the level of crime and disorder did not break down the distrust of Lancashire's propertied classes for the coercive apparatus of central and local government. Many feared that police powers would be abused by their political opponents. Even so, the persisting willingness to rely on voluntary associations, private police forces and, *in extremis*, military force indicates the limited extent of the threat to property and order posed by the industrial population.

In the absence of really effective cultural initiatives from above, the urban working class came to terms with industrial society in its own way, defending living standards and established rights through mutual assistance and the solidarity of kinship, neighbourhood and workplace, increasingly supplemented by and expressed through voluntary organisations. Lancashire already had 452 registered friendly societies in 1796, and they proliferated rapidly thereafter. By 1850 membership levels were close to saturation point in the textile towns. The societies offered health and unemployment insurance, and promised a proper funeral; they offered responsibility and

---

[26] R. Poole, *Popular Leisure and the Music-Hall in Nineteenth-Century Bolton* (Lancaster, 1982); *idem*, 'Oldham Wakes', in J. K. Walton and J. Walvin, eds., *Leisure in Britain, 1780–1939* (Manchester, 1983), p. 85; P. Bailey, *Leisure and Class in Victorian England* (1978), pp. 20–1, 83–4.

prestige to competent and assiduous members; and most met convivially in pubs. The benefits were, of course, in direct proportion to the contributions, which had to be paid regularly; so the better-off worker in regular employment gained the most security, and the societies were much stronger in the cotton towns than on Merseyside.

The friendly societies overlapped with the nascent trade unions, which often offered similar benefits to members while using them as a cloak for industrial activities which the law proscribed. Combinations to advance the economic interests of workpeople against masters fell foul of several statutes, of which the combination laws of 1799–1824 were only the most explicit. Even so, weavers' combinations were already active in the Manchester area in the mid-eighteenth century, as were various trades in Liverpool and Chester. They sought to regulate labour supply through the enforcement of Tudor limitations on apprenticeship, if possible through the courts; but already in the late 1750s rising food prices brought direct wage bargaining into the equation, and the check weavers of the Manchester area sustained a long strike on both issues. The leaders were successfully prosecuted, but the core of the organisation remained intact, enabling it to revive at subsequent points of economic tension. This set the basic pattern of trade-union activity for the rest of the period. Unions lay dormant, sometimes for long periods, to reappear in strength when wage cuts were threatened during depressions or not restored when trade revived, or when the customs of a trade were threatened by new machinery, cheap labour or the erosion of apprenticeship. The factory cotton spinners and engineers organised extensively from the late eighteenth century alongside the older trades. Collaboration between trades and districts was already being canvassed at this time, and several strikes in the early nineteenth century saw attempts at organising general unions, much to the alarm of the authorities. But such ventures could not be sustained long enough to secure tangible and lasting gains. Strikes tended to be caught by downswings in the trade cycle, as well as being vulnerable to repression, sectionalism and organisational problems. The bargaining position of the handloom weavers, especially, deteriorated rapidly after the great strike of 1808, as they lost their fight to enforce the apprenticeship laws and secure a minimum wage. Machine-breaking was a regular occurrence in the cotton industry from the 1760s to the 1820s, and outbreaks among the weavers intensified in violence as negotiation became more difficult. But evidence from Oldham suggests that in those trades where apprenticeship remained a reality, and in some factory occupations, trade unions could mount a formidable challenge to employers and authorities, who found it very difficult to secure convictions on combination charges. Despite their general weaknesses, the existence of continuous trade-union organisations, capable (occasionally) of mobilising mass support beyond the bounds of individual trades and localities, is highly significant. It shows the resilience of important sections of the skilled working class, whose leaders became capable of generating a telling critique of orthodox political economy, stressing the overriding importance of the value of labour, the need to concentrate on the home market and maximise consumption through fair wages, and the deleterious effects of machinery.[27]

This articulate counter-culture within the working class became most influential in the cotton towns, and of little account in the mining districts and on Merseyside; and the same applies to the distinctive educational institutions which supported it, especially in the 1830s and 1840s. Secular Sunday schools, Owenite Halls of Science and less formal mutual improvement groups were numerous enough, and the reading public for the radical press was attentive enough, to give the propertied classes food for thought about the dangerous spread of alternative views of society. But there developed other, sometimes overlapping cultural tendencies within the working class. Some made use of chapel, Mechanics' Institute or temperance society, and many of these accepted the social message along with the cultural medium; others fulfilled themselves through music and singing, as Handel's oratorios gained a mass following in handloom weaving communities. Others again were autodidacts, pursuing knowledge for its own sake as individuals. But above all the sociable appeal of public house and singing saloon, of fairgrounds and wakes celebrations, remained at the core of the predominant working-class way of life, despite the efforts of factory masters and 'rational recreationists'. A deeply rooted participant traditional culture was only just beginning to be affected by the incipient commercialisation of popular recreations in the 1840s.[28] 'Self-improvement' of any kind remained, understandably, a minority preoccupation.

This is not to deny the importance of the political reform campaigns

[27] A. P. Wadsworth and J. de L. Mann, *The Cotton Trade and Industrial Lancashire, 1600–1780* (1931), chaps. 18-19; J. Bohstedt, *Riots and Community Politics in England and Wales 1790–1810* (1983), chaps. 3–7; Foster, *Class Struggle*, pp. 47–50.

[28] Poole, *Popular Leisure*; R. Elbourne, *Music and Tradition in Early Industrial Lancashire 1780–1840* (Woodbridge, 1980).

which attracted mass followings at various times between the 1790s and 1840s. Organised support for equality of political rights first emerged among middle-class groups in Liverpool, Manchester and Chester in the immediate aftermath of the French Revolution, which gave wider relevance and heightened urgency to existing campaigns against unreformed corporations, the slave trade and the political disabilities of dissenters. In the early 1790s some of these reformers moved on to become full-blown Paineites, attacking the war against France, unfair taxation and aristocratic corruption, and urging thoroughgoing parliamentary and constitutional reform. They were suppressed by loyalist associations and church-and-king mobs during 1793–4, never to revive in Liverpool or Chester; but in the Manchester area parallel 'working-class' organisations had emerged and attracted numerous supporters, including weavers, artisans and even factory workers. They produced a core of principled, politically committed activists whose influence extended throughout the cotton district, giving a dimension of political awareness to bread riots and trade-union agitations, and posing a recurrent threat to established authority. Booth has demonstrated the existence of a well-organised revolutionary underground movement, the United Englishmen, in the Manchester area during the traumatic period of trade depression, high prices and food shortages at the end of the eighteenth century. This was less than a mass movement, but it worried those in authority who knew that constitutional loyalism had lost its savour for a hungry and war-weary population.[29]

This was not to be the model for subsequent developments, though there were echoes of it in 1812, when high prices and disrupted trade fuelled food-rioting, machine-breaking and a threat of insurrection, though *agents provocateurs* played their part. Hard times again provided a mass following for radical reformers in the late 1810s, but at this point the tradition of the 1790s resurfaced in more constitutional form, although mass petitions and organised drilling sometimes alarmed the authorities. This phase, which reached its tragic climax at Peterloo, was dominated by the handloom weavers, angry at their failure to secure parliamentary redress of economic and legal grievances.

The weavers and other wage earners were again prominent in the

---

[29]   A. Booth, 'Reform, Repression and Revolution: Radicalism and Loyalism in the North-West of England, 1790–1803' (unpublished PhD thesis, Lancaster University, 1979).

campaign leading up to the 1832 Reform Act, but here the waters were muddied by a middle-class reform movement which was eager to settle a long way short of manhood suffrage and the ballot. They wanted fuller representation for the mercantile and manufacturing interests, with a view to undermining aristocratic corruption, reducing taxes, freeing trade and (in most cases) redressing dissenters' grievances. The working-class reformers' goal of a Parliament which might enact minimum wage legislation, shorten working hours and protect trade unions was not to their taste. The working-class reformers lived to regret their eventual grudging acceptance of the Act, and the legislative record of the reformed Parliament ensured mass support for Chartism in the north-west.

The 1832 settlement gave a new dimension to the politics of reform in the cotton district. Hitherto the enemy had been identified mainly as the London government and its aristocratic supporters. The Peterloo magistrates had been gentry, coalowners and clerics rather than cotton employers, although the latter were apparently prominent among the Yeomanry officers. After 1832 the case became more clear-cut: the larger employers, at least, could be identified as embodiments of political as well as economic oppression, especially as they gained local power as magistrates, poor law guardians and municipal councillors. But the anti-aristocratic political diagnoses of Cobbett and Paine remained at the root of Chartist ideology, in Lancashire as elsewhere, reducing the impact of this transition, although hostility to employers provided an added dimension of direct class conflict at moments of high tension, especially in 1839 and 1842.[30]

Chartism was particularly strong in the north-west. Organisation and mass support were concentrated into the cotton district, where the Whig governments after 1832 seemed to have launched a concerted assault on working-class institutions and local autonomy. The new poor law offered a frightening prospect to working people who were well aware of their vulnerability to cyclical unemployment. The threat of the workhouse was coupled with the reformed Parliament's resistance to full and effective factory reform; the disdainful rejection of the handloom weavers' last plea for legal defences against falling living standards; the renewed attack on trade unions, epitomised most

[30] G. Stedman Jones, 'The Language of Chartism', in J. Epstein and D. Thompson, eds., *The Chartist Experience: Studies in Working-Class Radicalism and Culture 1830–1860* (1982), pp. 3–58; N. Kirk, 'Class and Fragmentation: Some Aspects of Working-Class Life in South-East Lancashire and North-East Cheshire, 1850–70' (unpublished PhD thesis, Pittsburgh University, 1974), pp. 11–12.

cogently by the prosecution of the Glasgow cotton spinners' leaders in 1837–8; and the introduction in 1839 of the new county police force, which was seen as the coercive arm of the factory masters against strikes and disturbances. When these initiatives coincided with cyclical depression and sustained pressure on wage rates, it is easy to understand the huge attendances at mass meetings, and the insurrectionary character of some of the rhetoric. The Charter provided a unifying political goal through which these grievances might be redressed, and it was capable, for a time, of accumulating the momentum from a range of specific but interrelated issues, especially the poor law and factory reform. These issues were most obviously and immediately relevant in the textile district, and it is no surprise to find the north-west's Chartists concentrated there, although the contrasting lack of Chartist activity on Merseyside remains arresting.

Lancashire Chartism recruited across the whole spectrum of working-class occupations, as well as attracting some middle-class support. The handloom weavers maintained their radical tradition, especially in industrial villages like Sabden, although Bolton's relatively prosperous weavers of fancy fabrics were apathetic. Factory workers were becoming increasingly active, alongside artisans and workshop craftsmen of all kinds; and Sykes has shown that trade-union involvement in Chartism was much more direct and sustained than has usually been assumed, with many trade societies affiliating to the National Charter Association in the knowledge that trade-union struggle by itself had been tried and found wanting.[31] Shopkeepers and small employers also figured among the Chartist leadership in places like Oldham and Rochdale, where Paineite radicalism had deep roots and the policies of the Whigs seemed to threaten higher rates and taxes, to undermine local autonomy and to maintain some of the Church of England's much-resented privileges.

The nature and strength of Chartism varied over time and between places. Much middle-class and some working-class support was alienated by the violent language and insurrectionary rumours of 1839 and 1842, and attracted by the divisive blandishments of Peel's government and the Anti-Corn Law League and Complete Suffrage Union. This applied most obviously in Manchester, with its diverse economy and divided working class. Elsewhere Chartism was probably strongest – and most moderate – in towns with many small manufacturers

---

[31]   R. Sykes, 'Early Chartism and Trade Unionism in South-East Lancashire', in Epstein and Thompson, eds., *Chartist Experience*, pp. 152–93.

and a long radical tradition, where a 'union of the productive classes' could be formed to link, but seldom to unite, mutually suspicious working-class and petty bourgeois campaigners against aristocratic corruption and its local manifestations among the 'big bourgeoisie' with their landed connections. Such an analysis fits Oldham's case more convincingly than Foster's vision of an archetypal revolutionary proletariat.[32] Where large employers held a stranglehold over local economies, blacklisting dissidents and attempting to repress independent working-class politics, threats of insurrection and the linking of political and trade-union issues were more likely to develop. Chartism thus expressed class conflict between factory masters and wage-labourers most violently and convincingly in places like Ashton-under-Lyne and Stockport, although such expression was intermittent. The 'Plug Plot' strike originated in this area. There was no simple relationship between industrial structure, size of firm and level of Chartist activity, however, and all generalisations on this score seem vulnerable to counter-examples and counter-arguments.

During the 1830s and 1840s a complex range of interrelated social and political problems created a crisis of early industrial society in the north-western textile district. We must not exaggerate its dimensions. Always, the working class was politically divided. Constitutional loyalists made their presence felt in the 1790s and Operative Conservative Associations recruited in the 1830s. Apathy, resignation and all-consuming efforts to survive at a personal and familial level, without time or energy for outside commitments, must have accounted for most of the population, most of the time. But there existed a substantial core of convinced and committed radical politicians among the artisans, factory workers and petty tradesmen. They were capable of attaching mass support at key moments to campaigns which at very least identified a common class enemy, the corrupt aristocracy and its local allies, and in some contexts mobilised a perceived common working-class interest against the factory masters. These were turbulent and uneasy years for those in authority; but they soon gave way to a long period of relative prosperity and social stability in the north-west, lasting from the mid-nineteenth century to the First World War. Before explaining this enduring resolution

[32] Foster, *Class Struggle*, chap. 5; D. S. Gadian, 'Class Consciousness in Oldham and Other North-West Industrial Towns', *Historical Journal*, 21 (1978), pp. 161–72; R. Sykes, 'Working-Class Consciousness in Oldham, 1830–42', *Historical Journal*, 23 (1980), pp. 167–79.

of the crisis of the 1830s and 1840s, we need to look at economic conditions, employment patterns and living standards in the north-west after the Chartists.

II STABLE PROSPERITY? THE HEYDAY OF VICTORIAN AND EDWARDIAN LANCASHIRE, c. 1850–1914

Between 1850 and 1914 most of the region saw continuing economic growth and urban expansion on an altogether novel scale. Lancashire's population more than doubled to well over four million during the second half of the nineteenth century. By 1911 about half the county's inhabitants lived in urban centres containing over 100,000 people, and over five-sixths lived in towns of over 10,000. This level of urbanisation was unparalleled elsewhere, and its manufacturing and suburban influence extended into north Cheshire. Outside the main industrial areas, Barrow and Crewe showed spectacular mid-Victorian growth from tiny beginnings, and the rise of the seaside resorts, especially Blackpool, provided impressive evidence of growing regional prosperity.

Not surprisingly, the spectacular growth rates around mid-century could not be sustained. During 1871–81 Lancashire's population rose by 22 per cent against 14 per cent for England and Wales; but thereafter the county marched in step with the nation at large, and some urban populations were already declining in the 1890s. Cotton was 'unambiguously holding its own in the growth league tables'[33] right up to 1914 in most places, but some industries were faltering by the 1890s, especially coal and Lancashire chemicals. Growth was punctuated by cyclical depressions, although these became less disruptive as cuts in output were achieved through short time rather than lay-offs, especially in cotton. The late nineteenth century brought problems to most of the staple industries, but falling prices boosted the living standards of their workers. Sub-regional analysis will add substance to these points.

Cotton's expansion continued with remarkable rapidity, although the Cotton Famine of the early 1860s conveniently masked a severe cyclical depression. Foreign competition was emerging in some export markets in late Victorian times, when a squeeze on prices put pressure on profits and margins; but the Edwardian years saw a surge of speculative expansion and mill-building. Major innovations, the ring frame

[33] J. L. White, *The Limits of Trade Union Militancy* (1978), p. 14.

in spinning and the automatic loom, were adopted very slowly, especially by contrast with the United States. But this caution may have been justified by Lancashire conditions, and ring spinning, which used cheap female labour, was readily introduced for new capacity on the coarser yarns where its advantages were most clear-cut.[34] Productivity improvements came mainly from adjustments to existing technologies and working methods. Between 1884 and 1914 Lancashire's spindles increased by 45 per cent and looms by 51.3 per cent, and much of the 1914 output was of higher quality and value, as Lancashire used its skills competitively.

Cotton's fortunes varied between places. The geographical division between spinning and weaving intensified, though it was never complete. Towns developed distinctive products and markets, and the north-east Lancashire weaving centres grew especially rapidly in the late nineteenth century, while Rossendale saw declining urban populations in face of competition from Oldham and overseas in coarse spinning. But machine-making prospered from the growth of overseas textile industries, and most economic indicators in cotton Lancashire still looked favourable to most Edwardians.

Most cotton firms continued to provide working units of manageable size, especially in weaving. Employees per factory still averaged under 200 in the 1890s. Changes in the organisation of the firm carried more social significance than relatively modest factory size increases. Despite the existence of one or two vast combines, there were still about 2,000 firms in Lancashire cotton in 1914. But limited companies were phasing out the older family firms and partnerships, especially in spinning. The rise of the Oldham 'Limiteds' from the 1870s, and the slower and later spread of the limited company elsewhere, had important implications for labour relations and politics in the cotton towns.

Between 1851 and 1911 Lancashire's cotton labour force grew by over 40 per cent to just over half a million. Women workers more than doubled to over 300,000. Despite this, the proportion of Lancashire's population (over ten years old) working in cotton fell from one in five to one in seven. Some of the larger cotton towns were themselves becoming less specialised. But cotton's growth and importance

---

[34] L. C. Sandberg, *Lancashire in Decline* (Columbus, Ohio, 1974), chaps. 2–3; W. Lazonick, 'Factor Costs and the Diffusion of Ring Spinning in Britain prior to World War I', *Quarterly Journal of Economics*, 96 (1981), pp. 89–109.

remained impressive, especially for key areas and age ranges, and it continued to dominate local economies.

Despite changes in the age/sex composition of the workforce, there were important continuities in the labour process. In spinning, despite the triumph of the self-acting mule, the established hierarchy of spinner (or minder), big piecer (a youth or young adult receiving less than half a spinner's net wage) and juvenile or adolescent little piecer, remained almost unchallenged, although other arrangements emerged in a few areas where male recruitment was difficult, and ring spinners were female. The workplace organisation of powerloom weaving was also effectively unchanged. What did alter significantly was the relative importance of women and children.

Child labour declined. Successive Factory Acts raised the minimum working age from eight in 1844 to twelve in 1901, and after 1844 the under-thirteens were required to spend part of the week in school on the 'half-time' system. Meanwhile women were becoming increasingly important in factory work, especially weaving and the spinning preparatory processes. By the late nineteenth century 'it was almost automatic that a working-class girl would go into the mill when she left school'. Many left to get married in their early twenties, but an increasing proportion continued through the early years of marriage and motherhood, leaving the factory in their mid-thirties or afterwards as children began to earn. This pattern became especially prevalent in weaving, where low male wages assumed the factory employment of wives.[35]

Cotton continued to employ up to half the male workforce in the cotton towns themselves. Its influence peaked among teenagers, with much subsequent wastage into other jobs, leaving a residue of well-paid overlookers and spinners, a 'sub-aristocracy' of strippers and grinders in the preparation processes, and large numbers of relatively ill-paid weavers. Textile engineering provided well-paid work for many adults, especially in Oldham and Bolton, and coal mining, wool and papermaking were locally important. Building was a major employer, as were the generally expanding transport, municipal and white-collar sectors. But there were many ill-paid and underemployed general labourers, and Edwardian cotton towns remained overwhelmingly working class, despite incipient suburban spread.

Merseyside, like the cotton towns, kept its distinctive occupational

---

[35] J. Liddington and J. Norris, *One Hand Tied Behind Us* (1978), pp. 58–9.

profile. Casual work for dockers, porters and carters predominated in central Liverpool. Building and shiprepairing craftsmen were better paid but vulnerable to unemployment, as were Birkenhead's shipbuilders. But merchants, professionals, shopkeepers and traders comprised over 20 per cent of householders in 1851. Even so, Liverpool had a high proportion of unskilled and relatively few skilled labourers when compared with York or even Preston. Waged work for women was scarce, domestic service apart, and low, irregular male earnings ensured abundant cheap female labour for the slop clothing trades. Hawkers and prostitutes were numerous, and workless children were often reduced to begging and petty crime. The main late Victorian growth sector was clerical work, but even this was often ill-paid and insecure, especially as a respectable appearance and demeanour had to be maintained. Central Manchester had a similar commercial economy, and similar extremes of mercantile wealth, squalid poverty and insecurity.

In Liverpool's hinterland coal mining and glassmaking boosted St Helens's population sixfold to over 90,000 by 1911. Further south the alkali industry brought a mid-Victorian boom to Runcorn and Widnes, but they stagnated from the 1890s as competitors introduced new processes, including Brunner, Mond on the Cheshire saltfields. Other towns grew less spectacularly, but there was a general predominance of adult male labour, mostly unapprenticed, with relatively high wages and high risks. In glass and chemicals, especially, the trend to oligopoly and large units of production was strong, and by contrast with cotton the gulf between capital and labour was widening rapidly in late Victorian times.

Elsewhere the even more spectacular mid-Victorian rise of Barrow produced another 'overwhelmingly proletarian' town dominated by men's work in iron, steel and later shipbuilding. Skilled workers and long-distance migrants were much in evidence, and most were employed by a few large firms. The railway town of Crewe exhibited many similar characteristics, and at Lancaster specialisation in oilcloth gave great economic influence to two large firms in an older and more diverse economy. By contrast the seaside resorts attracted volatile and insecure populations of small tradespeople, commuters and retired residents, and their seasonal economies generated distinctive social problems.

Agriculture held its own as an employer in much of north Lancashire and mid-Cheshire, although the numbers involved in Lancashire as a whole fell steadily after mid-century. There was increasing specialisation in pastoral farming in north and east Lancashire, while a growing concentration on labour-intensive arable on the larger estates of the south-west was partly offset by farm consolidation and mechanisation. Farm service declined rapidly here in mid-Victorian times, surviving longer in the north; but in general wage rates remained relatively high, small farms relatively numerous, and the transition from labourer to small farmer remained attainable for the fortunate and thrifty. The farmers complained of high rents, precarious tenure and lack of compensation for improvements, especially during the late Victorian agricultural depression; but rent rebates and the proximity of urban markets kept most of them afloat, and the major financial problems of the 'Great Depression' fell upon the landowners. Their eager investment in drainage and other improvements around mid-century had reaped disappointing returns: and their initial response to depression was further investment in the expectation of eventual rent increases. By the 1890s many were faced with mounting debts, unremunerative improvements, and falling land values which reduced borrowing capacity. Even where estates had urban and industrial revenues, retrenchment was necessary, but some heirs preferred conspicuous consumption to careful management. By 1900 the break-up of some major estates was beginning. Landowner paternalism was eroded by economic necessity, and the democratisation of counties in 1889 and parishes in 1894 confirmed the declining power of the gentry, even in the countryside. But landed influence on county councils, and elsewhere, long remained pervasive in Lancashire as well as Cheshire.[36]

Rural labourers' living standards were improving, aided by migration opportunities and alternative rural occupations, especially on the railways and in the police. The trend in industry was also upwards for those in regular work, especially during the late Victorian price fall. In Edwardian times food and commodity prices were cheaper in Lancashire and Cheshire than anywhere else in Britain. The rise of commercialised leisure reflected these trends, and public health improvements reinforced them. But urban poverty and insecurity were far from being conquered by 1914, especially on Merseyside and in Barrow and Lancaster. Even in the cotton towns, improvements in material conditions were dearly bought in other ways.

[36] J. M. Lee, *Social Leaders and Public Persons* (1963), chaps. 2–3; J. D. Marshall, ed., *The History of Lancashire County Council* (1977), chaps. 1, 4.

Cotton Lancashire was a high-wage area for adult males in most occupations, from engineering to building. Cotton itself was less generous, though Edwardian mule spinners and other 'aristocratic' groups took home well over £2 per week. But male weavers averaged only 25s. per week, and big piecers, often young adults, were among Britain's worst-paid male industrial workers. But women's and children's work boosted family incomes to unusual levels of comfort and relative affluence. Weaving was third in the women's industrial wages league in 1906, and women weavers' earnings almost matched the men's. Other factory jobs paid much less, but children's wages soon reached 10s. per week, helping families out of cyclical poverty. After the mid-1860s real wages in cotton increased faster than in most other industries, and the cotton towns became relatively prosperous except during depressions or prolonged strikes. There were relatively few paupers, except in Manchester; but poverty was visibly receding even in mid-Victorian Ancoats, as the incidence of working mothers and shared accommodation declined.[37] Friendly societies flourished, and the Co-op, in shopkeeping rather than Utopian socialist guise, became well established in the 1850s and attracted mass memberships in late Victorian times. Thrift, cash trading, saving and regular budgeting were increasing when they were still luxuries in most Victorian urban economies. Regular, predictable and relatively high incomes allowed growing expenditure on leisure, holidays and domestic comfort alongside defensive thrift through savings and friendly societies. Specialised shops proliferated accordingly, despite the Co-op, selling everything from fruit and confectionery to picture frames and pianos.

The cotton towns led the commercialisation of leisure, which was encouraged by the spread of the Saturday half-holiday after 1850. At mid-century Manchester and Bolton music halls already attracted audiences of a thousand or more, with teenage factory workers much in evidence; and music halls expanded and multiplied steadily thereafter. Late Victorian cotton Lancashire pioneered both the development of professional football as a mass spectator sport, and the working-class seaside holiday. Thrift was harnessed to enjoyment as rushbearings and traditional wakes hospitality gave way to extended seaside visits to Blackpool and its rivals, as unpaid summer holidays were steadily extended. Electric tramways in the 1890s brought parks

---

[37] Rushton, 'Victorian Slum', p. 44.

and countryside into easier reach. All this helped to undermine the centrality of the pub in popular culture. This trend was accentuated by stricter licensing provisions from the 1870s and especially after 1904, reducing pub numbers and checking their spread into newly built working-class areas.

After 1870 improvements in drainage, water supply and building controls began to make an impact on death and disease rates, although their influence is hard to disentangle from other aspects of improved living standards. The mid-Victorian cotton towns had a patchy public health record, as the substantial manufacturers who predominated in local government remained divided, uncertain and vulnerable to pressure for economy from penny-pinching and vulnerable groups of small ratepayers. It was easier to invest in town halls than in controversial sewering and water supply schemes which required the approval of neighbouring authorities, landowners and Parliament itself. But late Victorian municipal governments began to make real headway, prodded from the centre and bolstered by profits from municipal utilities. Water supplies improved, privies and ashpits gave way to water closets, and in Edwardian times controls over milk supply and food adulteration became increasingly effective. Death, disease and infant mortality rates began to fall, although the cotton towns lagged behind the nation at large. Industrial diseases remained rampant and worsening working conditions perpetuated low life expectancies for cotton workers. Industrial needs and influence kept towns smoky and rivers polluted, although overcrowding indices began to fall. But persisting pockets of high mortality and environmental dereliction remind us of the darker side of cotton living standards.[38]

Family incomes depended heavily on women's and children's factory work. Even where husbands helped at home, the 'double shift' was an overwhelming burden. Stress and exhaustion took their toll, exacerbated by pressure to conform to demanding 'respectable' ideals of labour-intensive domestic cleanliness. Convenience foods were widely used, while lack of domestic technology and loss of domestic skills worsened matters.

Cotton workers' families experienced high levels of infant mortality, despite the ready availability of child-minders among family and

[38] J. Garrard, *Leadership and Power in Victorian Industrial Towns 1830–80* (Manchester, 1983); G. Trodd, 'Political Change and the Working Class in Blackburn and Burnley, 1880–1914' (unpublished PhD thesis, Lancaster University, 1978), chap. 4.

neighbours.[39] The stresses are suggested by cotton workers' early recourse to family limitation, which became apparent in the 1860s and was strongly marked by Edwardian times. Abortion was probably prevalent, encouraged by the female factory community, but the methods used must have prejudiced the health of mothers and surviving children. Birth rates, still very high in the 1870s, had fallen by 1900 to around or below the national average. Surviving children were pushed into the factory at the earliest opportunity. The 'half-time' system reached its peak in the 1890s, and was strongly defended by the operatives. It persisted longer in cotton Lancashire than elsewhere, and was not effectively abolished until 1921. The margin above poverty which came from multiple earnings within families, despite overheads incurred on child care and laundry, encouraged competitive consumer spending which may have generated 'secondary poverty' through neglect of essentials. Thus an Oldham observer in 1897: 'They put away £200,000 for wakes week, yet they send their eleven-year-olds into the mill to help earn it.'[40] Whatever the perils of retrospective value judgments, cotton living standards were not unproblematically high.

Liverpool fared much worse. High and rising mid-Victorian rents and food prices ate into even skilled workers' incomes, while casual work and irregular earnings bred casual and irregular spending habits and low expectations among the poor. Friendly societies were ineffectual under these conditions, and the Co-op's development was late and stunted. Pawnbrokers and moneylenders were numerous, as in inner Manchester and Salford. The death rate rose sharply in the 1860s after receding in the 1850s, and infant mortality remained very high. Corporation expenditure on public health bore little fruit, and although most back-to-back courts had been demolished by 1914, the local authority could not provide enough alternative accommodation for displaced inhabitants. Improved living standards and falling death rates appeared later and more tentatively in Liverpool than elsewhere in the north-west.

Liverpool's manufacturing hinterland saw precarious living standards threatened by bad working and environmental conditions. Chemical works labourers lost teeth, appetite and ability to work,

---

[39] White, *Trade Union Militancy*, p. 46, Table 17; M. Cruickshank, *Children and Industry* (Manchester, 1981), p. 105. See also E. Roberts, 'Working-Class Standards of Living in Three Lancashire Towns, 1890–1914', *International Review of Social History*, 27 (1982), pp. 62–4.

[40] Cruickshank, *Children and Industry*, p. 98.

and were disproportionately likely to die prematurely in the work-house. Employers took care to live at a safe distance. Much of south-west Lancashire became a notorious moonscape of dead trees, stinking rivers and chemical waste heaps. Such conditions were not universal, but ill-health and foreshortened working lives prevailed among miners and glass workers as well as chemical workers, and outside mining hours were often very long. The late but rapid development of the Co-op reflected higher and more regular incomes than in central Liverpool, but with heavy social costs.

Barrow and Lancaster were different again. They had important craft elites, but also large numbers of unskilled men whose earnings hovered around £1 per week. Family budgets among the low-paid were eked out by cheap allotment produce, 'living off the land', part-time female employment in the home, and resourceful housewifery. Roberts argues that, with little female factory work, standards of diet, health and domestic comfort were actually better than in the cotton towns. This finding is influenced by external value judgments about life styles and spending patterns, but it reminds us that there is more to living standards than family incomes and consumer spending.[41]

Assertions about rising working-class prosperity must be heavily qualified. Even in the cotton towns, security against old age, long-term sickness or unemployment, and injury were lacking. Friendly societies and saving schemes provided least cover for those who needed it most, and they did not protect against the poverty cycle. At best, even the Edwardian cotton towns offered *relative* prosperity, compared with earlier times and other places. Even Crewe, with its secure and well-paid railway engineers and craftsmen, saw a threatening shrinkage in its job market in Edwardian times. Despite important positive indicators, especially from the 1870s, the rise in living standards in the north-west was too little, too late and too insecure to provide a full explanation for the achievement of social and political stability after mid-century.

Around 1850 the explosive mixture of economic and political threats and grievances, which fuelled Chartism, had lost its potency as its constituents became separated out and isolated. By the mid-1860s contemporaries could remark on the cotton district's 'perfect tranquillity and peace', even in the immediate aftermath of the Cotton Famine. Such views were misleading: industrial strife, sometimes violent,

---

[41] Roberts, 'Three Lancashire Towns', pp. 43–65.

remained close to the surface, and aspects of Cotton Famine relief had provoked angry working-class opposition and occasional disturbances. As Kirk remarks, 'The desire for a more egalitarian and democratic society was still present in the 1860s, albeit in a more etiolated form'; but the cotton district's mid-Victorian Labour movement was 'more interested in coming to terms with and gaining its due recognition from capitalist society than in working for fundamental social change'.[42] This statement holds good in many ways until 1914 and beyond. How should we explain the enthusiastic assimilation of the working class into a two-party political system which cut across class lines, and resisted late Victorian and Edwardian attempts to revive class politics?

Economic stabilisation and rising living standards, themselves problematic, are only part of the answer. We also need to consider the political and social initiatives of employers and others in authority, the adaptation of the labour force to industrial society, and the structural and ethnic divisions in the cotton district's working class.

As grievances were redressed and threats defused, successive layers of Chartist support were peeled off during the 1840s. The poor law, factory reform and trade-union issues retreated from centre stage, and so did the handloom weavers. Government flexibility disarmed the Chartist critique of aristocratic corruption, and corn law repeal ushered in a lasting consensus on free trade economics. For Oldham, Foster shows how Tory initiatives for factory reform and against a borough police force detached one wing of the 'working-class' radicals, while others were attracted to the Liberals by temperance, limited parliamentary reform and opposition to the Church of England. The employers and their allies made concessions to the radicals, but assimilated them, and the new alignments were reinforced by later developments.

'Chartist Lancashire' thus gave way to 'Liberal Lancashire', and then, after the Second Reform Act, to a long spell of Tory predominance. These labels conceal a genuine transition to a two-party system in which contests were generally close enough to sustain widespread participatory enthusiasm. But the heyday of 'Liberal Lancashire' conceals a sharp swing away from the 'Manchester School' during the 1850s, as the 'Imperialism of Free Trade' favoured a Palmerstonian

[42] Kirk, 'Class and Fragmentation', pp. 5, 8.

foreign policy to safeguard expanding eastern markets. From Palmerston to Disraeli was to be a short step, aided by the strong continuity of commercial and manufacturing Toryism in the cotton district through the 1830s and 1840s. The extent of Tory influence on working-class householders was made explicit under the new urban franchise in 1868. In 1865 the cotton constituencies produced six Tory MPs and twelve Liberals, but three years later the Tories led by thirteen to seven. In the spinning towns around Manchester the Liberals declined from eleven seats out of twelve to seven out of fifteen. This was not just an artefact of boundary changes, but a genuine expression of widespread working-class Tory support, which proved to have deep roots. Class conflict was seldom absent, and both parties adopted the language of class when it suited them, but cotton Lancashire's electoral configuration cut across class boundaries. The most important political fault-lines were not those of class. What, then, *were* the main determinants of social and political unity and division in the post-Chartist cotton towns?

Joyce finds the answer in the social and political influence of the factory. He identifies a 'new paternalism' among mill owners in the 1840s, as they accepted responsibilities to their workforces, tried to build bridges between capital and labour, and sweetened their patriarchal discipline with outings and amenities. He sees the workpeople responding positively to these overtures and identifying themselves with employer politics. The workplace became the core of a satisfying system of community loyalties, which found expression in a form of deferential political behaviour, based on a mixture of coercion, calculation and internalised conviction. The 1868 election saw mill communities lining up to vote on the side of their factory patriarchs, Liberal or Tory, and the key social divisions were between factories and factory communities, rather than between classes. The factory, with its authority systems and chain of command, became the crucial instrument of social stability.

This argument works best for large factories with satellite settlements of employer housing. The extent of *new* paternalist initiatives in this setting in the 1830s and 1840s is difficult to prove, and such arrangements remained exceptional. Much of Joyce's evidence comes from Blackburn, where these 'industrial colonies' were uniquely important, and the leading Tory mill owners, especially the squirearchical Hornbys, were closely identified with a beery, sporting popular culture. A concentration on Oldham, with its smaller factories, shortage of employer housing and 'industrial colonies', absentee employers and early introduction of abrasively managed limited companies, would require different explanations for its equally convincing (and equally flawed) post-Chartist stability. Calhoun argues that smaller factories were more likely to generate and sustain a radical political consciousness: if so, the transition to order requires more explanation in an Oldham-type environment than in Blackburn. Moreover, a full paternalist programme was costly, and the effective extent of employers' cultural influence is doubtful: after work the beerhouse was preferred to the reading room or institute, and an extensive range of working-class social institutions lay outside employers' reach, from trade unions to music hall. Excursions and treats were occasional, and limited in their positive impact.[43] Even the voting figures have their limitations, as Joyce admits. Factory communities voted with employers in the ratio of 2:1 or 3:1, rather than unanimously. We cannot be sure what the votes meant, and Joyce's occupational figures are biased towards those householders with deepest local roots, those who qualified for the vote in 1868 and were still *in situ* at the 1871 census. There was considerable mobility between firms, even among spinners, and those who stayed on in employer housing were those most likely to find the regime sympathetic. Many of the householders were not even mill workers, or worked at mills some distance away. Joyce's version of the mill as total institution is beguiling, but flawed.[44]

These criticisms are partly matters of emphasis. Joyce does deal with the world beyond the factory gate, and with continuing efforts by employers and others to use its institutions to mould and manipulate popular consciousness. But here employers operated alongside other, sometimes countervailing influences.

Denominational religious observance had a limited and socially specific impact, as an heroic wave of church- and chapel-building failed to increase working-class attendances significantly between 1851 and 1882. Specific religious attachments helped to define political allegiances, usually Liberal/nonconformist and Tory/Anglican, within an already accepted system, rather than themselves making the system acceptable. A more diffuse attachment to basic Christian teachings

[43] Joyce, *Work, Society and Politics*; C. Calhoun, *The Question of Class Struggle* (Oxford, 1982), pp. 175–8, 198–202; H. I. Dutton and J. E. King, 'The Limits of Paternalism: The Cotton Tyrants of North Lancashire, 1836–54', *Social History*, 7 (1982), pp. 59–74; Poole, *Popular Leisure*.
[44] M. A. Savage, 'Union and Workers in the Cotton Industry of Preston, *c.* 1890–95' (unpublished MA dissertation, Lancaster University, 1981).

underpinned a secular morality of mutual assistance and good neighbourliness in the cotton towns, but this was rational, and morally
validated, on its own terms as well.[45] The political pathology of popular Protestantism, or anti-Catholicism, was a different matter, as we
shall see.

Day schooling was more important than church-going. The Anglicans tightened their grip on elementary education, stepping up school
provision after the 1870 Education Act to keep out School Boards
and obviate the need for Board schools. Factory schools declined in
importance. Roman Catholic provision was locally impressive, but
the nonconformists flagged. Attendances and basic literacy in Lancashire caught up to the national average in the 1850s and 1860s, as
the day schools took over from the Sunday schools in this respect.
By 1901 Lancashire's school provision had overtaken the national average, with two-thirds of the children in voluntary schools, mostly
Anglican. Lancashire was a unique stronghold of religious, and
especially Church of England, elementary education. This must have
affected popular attitudes, and Anglican schools may have nurtured
working-class Tories, but the causal mechanisms are tangled. Most
parents were indifferent to the precise denominational content of their
children's education: most schools served neighbourhoods first, denominations second. Clerics and employers believed schools to be valuable instruments of conformity and social discipline, but their
effectiveness was conditional on, and limited by, the need to work
with the grain of working-class attitudes. Neither religion nor education were necessarily, or even usually, employer-dominated, and
their autonomous influence should not be exaggerated.

Nor was schooling important to the upward social mobility which
may have acted as a safety-valve for the frustrations and aspirations
of the ablest of the workforce. Elementary schools provided basic literacy and numeracy: parents, managers and ratepayers looked askance
at anything more elaborate. Beyond this, education was expensive
and remained the preserve of tradesmen's and overlookers' children.
For most working-class children, what counted was the ability to enter
the factory at the earliest opportunity. Trodd finds some late Victorian
mobility into the growing teaching and white-collar sectors in Black-

---

45   A. Ainsworth, 'Religion in the Working-Class Community and the Evolution of
Socialism in Late Nineteenth-Century Lancashire: A Case of Working-Class Consciousness', *Histoire Sociale*, 20 (1977), pp. 354–80.

burn and Burnley, but even where local authorities took the initiative after 1902, the take-up rate for secondary education remained low.[46] Declining Mechanics' Institutes and narrowly vocational evening classes were of little account.

Thrift, good fortune and entrepreneurial grasp were more important stimulants to social mobility. Workplace promotion offered opportunities to a minority, although it is hard to show that they expanded after mid-century. Small production units and cheap second-hand machinery kept the transition to 'little master' within reach, especially in the late-developing weaving towns of Burnley and Nelson; but increasing capital requirements made it increasingly difficult in the older centres, especially in spinning. The optimistic findings of Chapman and Marquis in 1912 on the recruitment of cotton masters and managers from the workforce are vitiated by methodological flaws. Most successful speculators in the Edwardian boom were tradesmen and small businessmen in other fields, rather than cotton operatives.[47] Belief in upward mobility through hard work and thrift was pervasive, and stabilising in itself; but its actual extent was limited and probably declining.

Many more operatives acquired a stake in the system by supplying share or loan capital to companies, especially the Oldham 'limiteds' from the 1870s. This was usually a speculative, income-maximising response to perceived opportunities, reinforcing a prevalent ethos of individualistic opportunism. It worked alongside corporate institutions of self-help like the building societies and the 'new model' Co-op, making existing conditions more comfortable for those who already had a small surplus. The positive ideological implications were limited.

The prevalence of instrumental responses to cultural initiatives and economic opportunities was general. It applies to leisure: witness the transformation of football from public school-sponsored 'rational recreation' to professional spectator sport, and the introduction of beer and self-government to working men's clubs in the 1870s and 1880s. This ability to seize upon the useful, relevant or enjoyable aspects of a new institution while ignoring or rejecting its ideological packaging was also important to the Co-op's success, as it eventually shed

---

[46] Trodd, 'Political Change'.
[47] Farnie, *Cotton Industry*, pp. 293–4; and see the entertaining comments by B. Bowker, *Lancashire under the Hammer* (1928), pp. 16–18.

most of its Owenite inspiration to become a combination of shop, joint-stock company and savings bank.

By mid-century working-class culture was autonomously adapting to cotton town conditions, and this process continued, with the entrenchment of a distinctive ethos based on custom, mutual assistance, neighbourliness and thrift. Families and supportive neighbourhood groups grew stronger as urban populations became stable and deep-rooted, recruiting by natural increase rather than migration. Consciousness of the value and dignity of labour was expressed as pride in hard work, which was seen as the natural condition of the factory workforce. These attitudes coexisted with insistence on 'fair' wages and conditions, as workers and unions learned 'the rules of the game'; but the overall social and economic system was seen as inevitable. Acquiescence was predicated on tolerable living standards as interpreted by an undemanding workforce, and on perceived reasonable behaviour by employers and the state; but it became the dominant mode of consciousness.

As well as being culturally adaptive, the cotton district working class was structurally divided. There were two major fault-lines: between 'labour aristocrats' and others (with varying implications in different industries), and between militant Protestants and Catholic Irish. These divisions need further discussion.

The 'labour aristocracy' is central to Foster's explanation of the 'restabilisation' of cotton Lancashire. He sees a redefinition of workplace relationships in the key industries during the 1840s, as relatively autonomous craftsmen gave way to supervisory piecemasters and pacemakers, 'bosses' men', who participated in the exploitation of their subordinates. This grouping became culturally distinctive, accepting employer political economy, seeking 'self-improvement' in individualistic ways, and accepting a privileged share of the super-profits arising from the exploitation of overseas markets. Thus the employers buttressed their political control by purchasing the loyalty of a working-class elite and its dependants. This argument is compatible with some of Joyce's ideas about employer paternalism; and there was indeed a shift away from craft skills towards supervision and sub-contracting. But it was neither as sudden nor as all-embracing as Foster suggests.

The all-round craft skills of the millwright were coming under pressure in engineering in the 1830s and 1840s, and in 1852 the newly formed ASE lost a tough struggle against untrammelled piecework,

systematic overtime and 'illegal men'. But 'one-off' jobs and complicated inventories kept skills at a premium, and the sub-contracting
of piecework remained unusual, although more prevalent in south-
east Lancashire textile engineering than elsewhere. Engineering was
certainly not transformed. In cotton spinning, sub-contracting was
long-established, the transition from hand-mule to self-actor was protracted and piecemeal, and mule spinning had always been more a
supervisory occupation than a craft. Technological change here
involved a threat to old methods of working and the replacement
of one elite by another; but the organisation of the workplace changed
surprisingly little. In mining, too, the changes were neither sudden
nor clear-cut, and do not fit Foster's chronology. There was no abrupt
mid-century watershed. Nor can the cultural divisions within the
working class be systematically linked with occupational status, as
Bristow's evidence on Preston illustrates. Decent housing, abstemious
life styles and 'respectable' behaviour were not the sole prerogative
of the skilled and supervisory. The divisions within the working class,
though real enough, involved complex cross-currents of life style and
outlook. Here again, status at the workplace was only part of the
story.[48]

Occupational stratification remained important, of course, even
though its nature was not changed dramatically at mid-century. In
spinning the self-actor minders took the lion's share of the rewards
for increased productivity, although their assistants bore the brunt
of the extra pressure from faster machinery and additional spindles.
Dilution was resisted because the system suited the employers, the
spinners were strongly organised to resist initiatives, the piecers
hoped for promotion or left the industry, and the women who might
have been deployed were relatives or neighbours of the spinners.
The survival of the minder/piecer system became unique to Lancashire, expressing the strength of patriarchal attitudes and a general
social conservatism. In the other branches of cotton, supervisory work
was a male preserve, and in weaving the most productive assignments
were reserved for men. Assumptions about domestic authority were
carried over to the workplace and reinforced there. The cotton working
class was not merely fragmented: it was hierarchically organised, with

[48] B. Bristow, 'An Artisan Elite Residential District in Preston, 1851', *Manchester Geographer*, N.S., 3 (1982), pp. 5–17; Foster, *Class Struggle*, pp. 224–38; and see also Trodd,
'Political Change', pp. 259–64.

overt conflict between the levels of the hierarchy kept to a minimum. This was a powerful influence for stability.

The cotton unions reinforced this pattern. They expanded rapidly in mid-Victorian times as federations of rather insular local organisations, celebrating and codifying their hard-won collective bargaining rights through complex piecework wage lists negotiated by highly trained officials who aimed at accommodation and arbitration. The spinners' union was particularly 'aristocratic', demanding uniquely high dues and paying 'luxurious' benefits. By 1891, 90 per cent of north-western spinners were in the union, and the piecers were held in tutelage, sometimes uneasily, by a kind of associate membership after they threatened to organise separately in the 1880s. The less powerful cardroom workers' (after 1886) and weavers' unions were also dominated by 'aristocratic' elements within their own ranks. Most of their members were women, and they accounted for more than five-sixths of all British female trade unionists in 1896; but the female members had little say in their unions' counsels.

These organisations remained on the fringe of mainstream labour politics, often taking independent initiatives for parliamentary redress of specific grievances. They usually acquiesced in employer initiatives to raise productivity by speeding up machinery and pushing up workloads, the results of which safeguarded the position and earnings of senior members of the workforce. The weavers' unions did campaign against the competitive 'driving' of weavers by aggressive overlookers, and the 'steaming' of weaving sheds through unhealthy artificial increases in humidity. But the cotton unions were run by sectional interests who feared foreign competition and were anxious to perpetuate the existing organisation of production.

Even so, labour disputes on specific issues were endemic. Occasionally they flared into long industry-wide confrontations in spinning or weaving, as in 1853–4, 1878 and 1892–3. These were usually fought on the downswing of the trade cycle, against wage cuts which were held to go beyond the industry's real needs. Violence sometimes erupted, as at Blackburn and Burnley in 1878, when employers' houses were attacked and burned, and Hornby himself was pelted. These events, admittedly aberrant, must be considered alongside Joyce's view of Blackburn's industrial paternalism. But labour leaders retreated from the rhetoric of class conflict, with Chartist overtones, which marked the bitter Preston dispute of 1853–4. Most conflicts were brief and focussed on specific local issues; and attempts to codify industrial relations culminated in cotton Lancashire's talisman of order and control, the spinning industry's Brooklands Agreement of 1893.[49]

The cotton unions' change of posture, which was reciprocated by the masters, was gradual and piecemeal but cumulative and stabilising. Similar processes operated in mining and engineering, and the Tory and Liberal parties penetrated so deeply into the unions' rank and file as to inhibit a separate labour politics. Mid- and late Victorian trade unions expressed the occupational, geographical and political divisions within the cotton Lancashire working class more than they obscured them.

Ethnic divisions also became important in mid-Victorian times, as Irish immigration increased in the 1840s with the advent of poverty-stricken refugees from the famine, who proved particularly hard to assimilate. The Irish were residentially concentrated, culturally distinctive, and posed an apparent threat to wages and jobs. In Stockport and Stalybridge, at least, they invaded the factory workforce in strength during the 1850s, and there was a definite economic dimension to the anti-Irish riots which became endemic after the infamous Stockport disturbances of 1852.[50] But there was also an anti-Catholic dimension, fuelled by militant Protestant and Orange organisations and by Tory defenders of the Church of England. It was later stoked up by the itinerant orator Murphy, who identified Catholicism with an overtly sexual threat to domestic patriarchy, and by controversies about Fenianism and Irish disestablishment, which particularly affected the 1868 election. Subsequently the Irish issue faded in the cotton district, but it added an extra dimension of division to the working-class experience at a crucial period. It was partly spontaneous in origin, and partly fomented from above; and its roots were ultimately economic, nationalistic and constitutional rather than religious. It was probably a consequence rather than a cause of the Chartist collapse, but it encouraged the more jingoistic aspects of 'Tory democracy'. It was at least a significant symptom of changes within the working class, even if we play down its causal influence.

The late nineteenth century saw the revival of working-class movements with broader social and political aims. Their challenge was aided by changes in the established order. The dynastic family firms of the

---

[49] See esp. H. I. Dutton and J. E. King, *Ten Per Cent and No Surrender* (Cambridge, 1981), chap. 3; Trodd, 'Political Change', pp. 288–90.

[50] N. Kirk, 'Ethnicity and Popular Toryism, 1850–70', in K. Lunn, ed., *Hosts, Immigrants and Minorities* (Folkestone, 1980), pp. 64–106.

older cotton centres were giving way to limited companies whose visible greed for profit maximisation removed the cloak of patriarchal authority and gentlemanly mystique from industrial relations. The flight of employer elites to seaside, Lake District or remoter country seats accelerated. In municipal government the mill owners gave way to tradesmen and professionals who lacked their precursors' wider influence and prestige. An abrasive 'New Toryism' attacked trade unions, repudiated paternalist obligations and asserted the neglected claims of employers to control recruitment and work processes. Pressures to boost productivity by speeding-up and 'driving' increased, and working conditions worsened. Real wages suffered a setback in the Edwardian cotton boom, while successful speculators flaunted their wealth. Destabilising technological innovation was in the air. These processes were patchy in their impact: in Blackburn and Macclesfield, for example, old-style employers remained socially and politically powerful, though not unchallenged or invulnerable. But the trends are clear: the vertical ties between capital and labour were weakening, and the barriers between trade-union concerns and wider working-class political activity were beginning to crumble.[51]

Trade unions expanded rapidly from the 1880s. By 1911 the weavers had achieved almost 100 per cent membership in some towns. The employers defeated an attempt to impose the closed shop, but the growth in confidence and aspirations is remarkable. The miners and cardroom workers recruited well, as did several new unions among the unskilled. Textile Lancashire played a lively part in the labour unrest after 1910, as rank-and-file pressure made the cotton unions less conciliatory. The spinners remained determinedly 'aristocratic', but the weavers began to admit women to responsible positions, while the overlookers began to ally with the other weaving trades against the masters. The divisions between and within trades were gradually being eroded.[52]

Socialism was gaining converts, especially in the newer weaving centres. The ILP became well established during the 1890s, especially in Nelson, while Burnley became an SDF stronghold. Several trades councils came under socialist influence, and important unions, including the miners and weavers, adopted some socialist policies intermittently. Socialism was a minority creed racked by internecine strife,

[51] Joyce, *Work, Society and Politics*, pp. 331–42.
[52] White, *Trade Union Militancy*; Trodd, 'Political Change', chaps. 5–6.

but its influence became pervasive enough to worry established authority of all kinds.

The emergent Labour party had a much wider appeal. The legal onslaught on trade unions around 1900 pushed even the cotton unions into support for the Labour Representation Committee, especially after a Blackburn employer gave Lancashire its own Taff Vale case in 1901. Labour experienced several Edwardian near-misses in the cotton district as well as a sprinkling of successes, and Lancashire politics were acquiring an explicit class dimension.

In 1906 the Liberals, in alliance with Labour, ended nearly forty years of Tory domination in Lancashire, and Clarke sees them as the lasting beneficiaries of the transition to class politics, had the war not intervened. But his argument requires an identification between trade unionists, working-class voters and the 'New Liberalism' which is hard to square with other aspects of working-class attitudes. Labour disputes, squabbles over seat allocations and socialist initiatives put the alliance under perpetual strain, and in 1913 the three largest cotton unions voted clearly for the use of trade-union funds for political purposes. This amounted to rank-and-file endorsement of the Labour party.[53] Moreover, Labour and Socialist candidates in local government regularly fought against Liberals as well as Tories, and the labour movement captured Nelson town council in 1906, although in most places it held a fluctuating handful of seats. But the 'progressive alliance' was little in evidence in local government, where Labour was making an independent impact. Lancashire's Liberals may well have held a caretaker role, until further franchise extensions and increased resources allowed Labour to reap its full reward. The popular politics of paternalism, ethnicity, pub and chapel were in decline, and their most threatening challenger was the labour movement, in spite of its internal divisions, cautious leaders and limited expectations.

Labour's strength lay in its defence of trade-union interests. Socialism, as such, remained a fringe creed in most places, innovatory and threatening. Both the SDF and the ILP organised like revivalist sects

---

[53] P. F. Clarke, *Lancashire and the New Liberalism* (Cambridge, 1971), chaps. 1, 12, 15; J. White, 'A Panegyric on Edwardian Progressivism', *Journal of British Studies*, 16 (1976–7), pp. 143–52; A. Fowler, 'Lancashire and the New Liberalism: A Review', *North-West Labour History Society Bulletin*, 4 (1977).

rather than political parties, and like the chapels their viability depended on sociable events which absorbed members' energy and commitment, so that means became more important than ends. The ILP, especially, bore the stigmata of earnest, self-improving nonconformity, and the socialists themselves became imprisoned in the institutions of the old cultural politics.[54] The working-class women's suffrage movement was similarly held back by existing social arrangements, as the 'double shift' made it impossible to convert the tens of thousands of suffrage petitioners into activists, despite the enthusiasm of supporters and the sympathy of the weavers' unions.

Outside the cotton district, post-Chartist stability is easier to explain; indeed, Chartism itself had been weak. Disturbances in Liverpool in 1848 owed more to Irish hostility to the Act of Union than to Chartism, and elsewhere the 1840s saw little threat to the established order.[55] The new political initiatives of the 1890s and after also made less of an impact outside the cotton towns.

Liverpool was a special case. Its Irish population, including many Ulster Protestants, generated formidable ethnic and sectarian conflict, which persisted strongly into the twentieth century. The Tories made use of Liverpool's unique brand of virulent low church Protestantism, although even they sometimes drew back in distaste and dismay from the excesses of demagogues like George Wise. Processions provoked extensive street fighting on the great Ulster anniversaries. This was nationalistic hostility tinged with economic rivalry and clothed in religious garb, though church attendances were unimpressive. The Catholics espoused Irish nationalism, expressed in T. P. O'Connor's long career as MP for Liverpool Scotland. These intractable divisions sufficed to ensure that Liverpool remained infertile soil for class-based socialist or labour politics. The defensive solidarity of working-class communities expressed itself through ethnicity rather than through overt class conflict.

These circumstances did not prevent the New Unionism of dockers and transport workers from becoming established on Liverpool's waterfront; but they reduced its wider impact. Deteriorating industrial relations and working conditions, arising from larger firms, limited

[54] K. Hunt, 'Women and the Social Democratic Federation: Some Notes on Lancashire', *North-West Labour History Society Bulletin*, 7 (1980–1), pp. 60–2.
[55] J. Belchem, 'English Working-Class Radicalism and the Irish 1815–50', *North-West Labour History Society Bulletin*, 8 (1982–3), pp. 9–16.

companies and abrasive management, led to the seamen's and dockers' unions and strikes in 1889 and 1890. The rhetoric of class conflict was explosively deployed in the heat of the struggle, but the main aims involved defensive control over 'hiring procedure and work practices', and there was little mutual assistance between trades. These and other new unions did not disappear, however, and dockers and seamen were again prominent in the great transport strike of 1911, which temporarily transcended sectarian and occupational divisions within Liverpool's workforce. But despite the efforts of an eager group of syndicalists, the strike's objectives remained limited and mundane. In its aftermath seven labour candidates were elected to the city council, and initiatives were developed on the docks for joint negotiating procedures and the amelioration of casual labour. But the solidarity of 1911 proved short-lived, and Liverpool politics soon reverted to type. The unions' challenge to the established order had been evanescent.[56]

Elsewhere, organised labour as a political force did best in areas of mining and heavy industry from the 1890s. The miners took over several south Lancashire coalfield constituencies, and labour representatives made rapid municipal inroads at St Helens. Barrow likewise saw the development of a strong trades council and labour electoral influence. In Lancaster and around Northwich, however, authoritarian paternalist employers in the major industries squeezed out the incipient labour movement, and the small businesses and seasonal economies of the seaside resorts offered little encouragement to organised labour. But in 1912–13 militant trade unionism reached the agricultural labourers of the Ormskirk area, the part of Lancashire where capitalist farming was most advanced. A hard-fought strike in 1913, with help from Liverpool syndicalists and the National Union of Railwaymen, achieved shorter hours while revealing the anger and bitterness which were usually hidden below the calm deferential surface of 'close' agricultural villages like Speke.[57]

The Edwardian advances were usually made by labour representatives rather than socialists; and the Tories remained a force to be reckoned with throughout the north-west, despite their tariff reform election disaster in 1906. Despite changing social and economic

[56] P. J. Waller, *Democracy and Sectarianism: A Political and Social History of Liverpool, 1868–1939* (Liverpool, 1981), pp. 97–106, 230–48; H. Hikins, ed., *Building the Union* (Liverpool, 1973), pp. 99–152.
[57] A. Mutch, 'Lancashire's "Revolt of the Field"', *North-West Labour History Society Bulletin*, 8 (1982–3), pp. 56–67.

conditions, the two-party hegemony was strong and resilient; and despite the declining political role of the local employer and civic patriarch, the politics of culture and community remained important beyond the First World War. Moreover, they were pervasive enough to make an indelible mark on the new politics of labour consciousness. Throughout the north-west, despite pockets of socialist strength such as Nelson and manifestations of labour solidarity like the Liverpool transport strike, the impact of the new politics was still quite limited. Transition was still incipient. There were strong hints in the early twentieth century of more thoroughgoing changes in the economic and political system, but their full impact was reserved for the troubled years after the First World War.

III CRISIS AND DECLINE, 1914–50

Between the wars, the most important sectors of the north-western economy fell into sharp and irreversible decline, generating mass unemployment and occasional angry outbursts of social unrest. But conditions were never as bad as in South Wales or north-eastern England, and after 1931 gloom was relieved by falling unemployment and pockets of industrial prosperity. The Second World War brought full employment, and associated industrial restructuring assisted a widespread medium-term recovery which was evident by 1950. But the relative industrial prosperity and world economic importance of pre-1914 Lancashire evaporated at alarming speed, although the resulting challenge to existing economic and political arrangements was generally lukewarm and limited.

Lancashire cotton appeared to survive the First World War quite well, despite disruptions in cotton supply and export markets; and 1919–20 saw an enormous speculative investment boom, when many firms were amalgamated and reconstructed at nominal values which soon appeared absurdly over-optimistic. The industry was already losing its vital export markets in India (especially), China and the Middle East to local manufacturers and export competition, especially from Japan; and cotton Lancashire never really recovered from the depression of 1920–1, as world depression and rising tariff barriers exacerbated existing trends. British cotton cloth exports never again approached the 1913 peak. In 1929 they were little more than half that level, and the collapse of 1930–1 halved the export yardage again. In 1938–9 cotton exports fell below their mid-nineteenth century level.

Calamity was postponed by systematic short-time, below-capacity working and price-fixing agreements; but ultimately the interwar years saw the effective collapse of the north-west's most important industry, although its death-throes were protracted. Hardly any new textile machinery was ordered, with catastrophic results for the engineering firms; and coal mining also suffered severely as depressed demand was exacerbated by geological problems and low productivity. Liverpool also suffered, and not only from the collapse of the cotton trade, as shipping lines relocated to London and Southampton and the port retained a declining share of falling British overseas trade. Barrow's industries collapsed in the early 1920s but recovered modestly thereafter, and here especially rearmament boosted the economy after 1937.

The damage was worst in the most specialised spinning and weaving centres, especially those producing the coarse yarns and cheap fabrics which were hardest hit by overseas competition. In Oldham, Blackburn, Burnley and their smaller neighbours the collapse of cotton was most complete, and in the weaving area especially, few new industries appeared to fill the gaps.[58] Lancashire's industrial centre of gravity shifted towards the south and west, as new developments in electrical engineering, vehicle-building and garment manufacture became concentrated into a Liverpool–Manchester axis, while glass and chemicals did relatively well in the 1930s, and Ellesmere Port's oil industry began to develop apace. Liverpool itself was attracting manufacturing industry by the 1930s, and there were outposts of growth further north. The Second World War accentuated existing trends. Decisive government intervention hastened the amalgamation and rationalisation of cotton firms, and in some areas the dispersal of strategically important factories brought lasting benefits, as production continued or premises were adapted after the war. By the late 1940s, indeed, there were labour shortages in some of the old staple industries of the cotton district after a long period of low recruitment, and over much of the region significant industrial diversification had been achieved.

The basic causes of the interwar slump were beyond the north-west's control. Changes in world trading patterns and the rise of

---

[58] Lancashire Industrial Development Association, *Industrial Reports* (1948–56); Board of Trade, *An Industrial Survey of the Lancashire Area* (1932); and for a more optimistic view G. Rushton, 'A Geographical Survey of the Changes in the Industrial Structure of Lancashire Towns since 1931' (unpublished MA thesis, University of Wales, 1962), pp. 14–15.

410 J. K. WALTON

protected overseas textile industries made the collapse of Lancashire cotton inevitable, and similar trends hit the other staple industries. Lancashire's reservoirs of skill and experience on the mule and plain loom were outflanked by new technologies, but Sandberg argues convincingly that heavy investment in ring spinning and automatic looms would merely have delayed the inevitable, with serious consequences in technological unemployment and unremunerative investment. Admittedly, the speculative boom of 1919–20 had undermined the industry's finances, and overvalued assets inhibited further investment, while Rochdale's early (for Lancashire) acceptance of ring spinning and artificial fibres gave it a more resilient textile industry than its neighbours.[59] The industry's past successes militated against further adaptation, as managers stuck to trusted formulae and unions resisted labour-saving innovation. But the best possible outcome would still have been an uphill and ultimately unsuccessful struggle, and Lancashire's internal problems were not the authors of its misfortunes. The way forward lay in industrial diversification, rather than the remaking of the prewar economy.

What were the social consequences of the slump? Three themes stand out: the changes in the upper strata of north-western society, the impact on those in employment, and most obviously the implications of mass unemployment and underemployment.

The interwar years saw the culmination of the decline of the landed gentry, and the substantial merchants and manufacturers who had become assimilated into it, as an effective political and social force. Many surviving patriarchal employers sold up and retired to more congenial climes in the postwar boom; and others adopted a more private life style as subordinate directors of financially ailing amalgamations. Urban local government lost much of its autonomy and passed almost completely into the hands of a secondary elite of shopkeepers, tradesmen and a few managers. The county councils were similarly transformed, although a core of active gentry retained disproportionate influence in Lancashire. Agriculture was itself depressed, with poultry-keeping the only growth sector; and county society ceased to function as a distinctive social system during the 1920s,

---

[59] Sandberg, *Lancashire in Decline*, chaps. 6–7; LIDA, *Industrial Report No. 5: The Spinning Area* (1950), p. 26.

as recognition of social obligations of all kinds crumbled before the pursuit of individual pleasures.[60]

Lower down the scale, tradesmen and shopkeepers guarded their living standards carefully, and expressed their preoccupations in penny-pinching local government policies, especially towards the poor and unemployed. The energies of working-class families were channelled into the getting and keeping of employment, although trade unions remained assertive in defence of wage levels and established methods of working. Promotion avenues from piecer to spinner and on into management became blocked in a contracting cotton industry, and aspirations to upward mobility were thwarted as a small and contracting elite reserved positions of authority for relatives and friends.[61] But wage cuts did not keep pace with deflation, and most of those in work experienced gently rising living standards.

But after 1920 many people were not in work. Various work-sharing practices obscured the true extent of unemployment and under-employment in cotton, but even so over 40 per cent of the registered workforce in the weaving area was returned as unemployed in 1931, when figures of between a quarter and one third were commonplace elsewhere in the industrial north-west. This was the worst point in the slump, and matters improved steadily through the 1930s, although Merseyside still had an official unemployment rate of 18.9 per cent in 1939, and most of Lancashire remained well above the national average. Worries about damage to the work ethic among the young unemployed proved short-lived as the job market improved, but long-term unemployment was intractable on Merseyside, among miners and among the middle-aged, especially women. Family incomes, share and property ownership and attachment to skills and neighbour-hood inhibited out-migration from the cotton district, although it was increasing in the 1930s; and low birth rates helped to ensure an ageing, custom-bound, inward-looking, stagnant population. In important respects the Victorian virtues of the cotton labour force had become its interwar vices. In the coal and chemical areas of south-west Lanca-shire a younger population was more adventurous, but here the local

---

[60] P. A. Harris, 'Social Leadership and Social Attitudes in Bolton, 1919–39' (un-published PhD thesis, Lancaster University, 1973), chap. 1; Lee, *Social Leaders*, chap. 4.
[61] Harris, 'Social Leadership', chap. 5.

economy was adapting better to changing circumstances. It took the war, and the alienation of a rising generation from the declining cotton industry, to alter the pattern significantly in the textile heartland.

The interwar years did bring marked improvements in public health and housing conditions, in the north-west as elsewhere. Tuberculosis and infant mortality declined sharply, for example, and Liverpool and Manchester were particularly energetic in their provision of municipal housing, although the spacious new estates were enjoyed mainly by skilled and white-collar workers who could afford the rents and fares. The problems of the inner city slums remained, fuelled by high birth rates among their inhabitants. Medical Officers of Health played down the impact of unemployment on public health, although in 1934 'the general opinion seems to be that parents are sacrificing themselves for their children'.[62] New roads, electricity and increasing mobility brought benefits mainly to the better-off, and much of the industrial north-west remained physically repugnant to outsiders and sensitive insiders alike. Meanwhile, suburban sprawl engulfed agricultural acres in north-east Cheshire and the Wirral, as the lower middle and upper working classes of Manchester and Merseyside voted with their feet.

Despite widespread economic disaster, the north-west between the wars did not become fertile soil for revolutionary socialists or other radicals. The Labour party advanced steadily in Lancashire during the 1920s, and in 1929 it captured forty-one of the county's sixty-six parliamentary seats. But this was the interwar high-water mark, and in 1931 the Conservatives almost swept the board, taking established Labour strongholds such as Gorton, St Helens, and even Nelson and Colne. Labour recovery remained incomplete in 1935. Labour's successes in local government were patchy and limited, and Labour councillors and guardians in Lancashire were unwilling to break out of the constraints imposed by central government. They could be angrily vociferous in opposition, but they had no workable alternative strategy. Liverpool remained *sui generis*, as sectarian conflict refused to evaporate and Labour became the embarrassed legatee of the Irish nationalists, who kept considerable influence in the local party's

---

[62]   PRO MH.66/128, p. vii. Jane Mark-Lawson kindly drew my attention to this source.

counsels.[63] More generally, Labour and the trade unions had a distant and uneasy relationship with the National Unemployed Workers' Movement, which did achieve some intermittent mobilisation of the unemployed in demonstrations and hunger marches. The NUWM had several Lancashire branches, but its Communist leadership attracted little sustained support, and the demonstrations were more successful at stimulating violent reactions from the police than at wringing concessions from the authorities. Significantly, Oldham Trades Council members in 1932 suggested that the troubles of the unemployed arose from their neglect of union membership when in work; and suspicion of the unemployed by their more fortunate neighbours seems to have divided the working class throughout the industrial north-west.[64] Meanwhile, the depression exacerbated the divisions between skilled and less-skilled, and between one trade and another; and those in work preferred safety-first economic policies, preferably tempered by humanity, rather than risking a socialist alternative which was anyway beyond the imagination of most Labour MPs. Despite the ossification of the social structure, and the lack of real opportunities for social mobility, the myth of the open society lived on in the cotton towns; and the hard-won Victorian acceptance of the industrial system had generated values which proved tenaciously pervasive when the system broke down. Labour's lasting breakthrough in Lancashire politics had to wait until 1945, with unemployment in abeyance and a new idealism emerging from the war years. The county council went Labour in 1952, and even Liverpool succumbed in 1955. Cheshire, of course, remained largely immune. But this was emphatically support for social reform rather than revolution; and what is really remarkable is the limited extent of the radical political response to the traumas of the interwar years. Even in 1945 many Labour seats in the cotton district were marginals, and the Conservatives held Bury, Darwen and Stockport.

All this suggests the survival of old political attitudes and behaviour alongside the new. Politics for many postwar Lancastrians were class influenced but not class based. In learning to cope with the industrial

---

[63] Waller, *Democracy and Sectarianism*, chaps. 16–17; A. Shallice, 'Liverpool Labourism and Irish Nationalism in the 1920s and 1930s', *North-West Labour History Society Bulletin*, 8 (1982–3), pp. 19–28; R. S. W. Davies, 'The Liverpool Labour Party and the Liverpool Working Class, 1900–39', *North-West Labour History Society Bulletin*, 6 (1979–80), pp. 2–14.

[64] R. H. C. Hayburn, 'The Responses to Unemployment in the 1930s, with Particular Reference to South-East Lancashire' (unpublished PhD thesis, Hull University, 1970), pp. 292–3.

revolution, Lancashire's working class had evolved a system of values, attitudes and allegiances which resisted the implications of new economic and ideological influences. We have examined the formation of this industrial tradition, with its blend of individualistic opportunism and collectivist mutual assistance, of thrift and hedonism, of earnestness and scepticism, of independence and deference, of hard work and ostentatious leisure. As yet it is much more difficult to chart the decline of this distinctive regional culture, and to explore its implications. Many important themes in the social history of the north-west since the First World War still await scholarly analysis, and the problems of decline and adjustment in this pioneer industrial region are just as interesting, and important, as the problems raised by its development and heyday. Further work on society and politics in twentieth-century Lancashire should be at or near the top of the research agenda for social historians.

CHAPTER 6

The north-east

D. J. ROWE

I THE REGION

Compared with many of the modern economic regions of Britain, which exist more for administrative than any organic reason, the north-east does appear to have some intrinsic merits and historical validity as a region. If we take as the basic region the old administrative counties of Northumberland and Durham, it has reasonably well-defined geographical boundaries with the North Sea, the Scottish border, the central uplands and the river valley of the Tees. It was, therefore, firmly distinguished to the east, to the north (if really only by the ancient antagonisms of race) and to the west by hills which restricted mobility. Only to the south was the region weakly bounded in a sparsely populated agricultural and metal-mining area between the south Durham coalfield and the developing West Riding towns. More than the simple boundaries of regional geography gave the area some unity, however. In an age when overland transport was very costly, the sea was the major highway for the movement of heavy or bulky goods. It was, therefore, inevitable that commercial activity looked to the nearest coast for other than local trade and that towns such as Bishop Auckland, Durham, Hexham, Morpeth (and their environs) should look to the east and the market powers of towns such as Newcastle, Sunderland and Stockton with their river access to the sea. Ultimately (but paradoxically since it covered only a minor part of the region) it was the coal industry which gave unity to the region. In an age when its population was sparse and its other attractions limited, the north-east was to all intents and purposes (and especially to south-eastern intents and purposes) the Great Northern coalfield.

It would, however, be a mistake to regard the region as uniform either at a point in time or over the last 200 years. In terms of land

type and use the region has as much of a mix as may be found anywhere in the country. As a result there have always been sharp distinctions between industrial, mining and agricultural areas. Moreover,
some of these areas have a greater affinity to their neighbours outside
than those inside the region. The agriculture of north Northumberland
(Milfield plain, the valleys of the Till, Breamish and Tweed) was much
closer in the late eighteenth and early nineteenth centuries to that
of south-eastern Scotland than it was to that of central Northumberland. The former areas were advanced agriculturally, adopting new
crops (such as the turnip) and crop rotations and machinery (such
as threshing machines), while the agriculture of central Northumberland was backward. Such distinctions affected the local way of life
and attitudes. Similarly the east Pennines had more to do with the
west Pennines than they had to do with the east Durham coalfield.
The lead-mining communities of Weardale and Teesdale had more
in common with those of Alston and Nenthead in Cumberland than
they had with coal-mining communities (epitomised by the fact that
few lead miners were attracted to work in the coalfield, despite the
attraction of higher earnings, until the collapse of lead mining in the
last quarter of the nineteenth century). In the same way it is clear
that the agricultural north bank of the Tees was more similar to North
Yorkshire than it was to the rest of County Durham, at least until
the 1830s.

To look at the southern end of the region, however, draws attention
not only to the limitations to regional unity at any point in time but
also to the fact that aspects of regional unity change over time. The
completion of the Stockton and Darlington Railway in 1825, linking
the land-locked south Durham coalfield to the sea, was to initiate
the growth of Teesside. Stockton was found to be an unsatisfactory
point on the river Tees for the shipment of coal and in 1830 the railway
was extended to the south bank of the river, where previously a farm-
house had been the only settlement. The result was the growth of
Middlesbrough (along with West Hartlepool, one of the Victorian new
towns created in the region). Spurred by the exploitation of Cleveland
iron ores after 1850, Middlesbrough grew dramatically as the pivot
between those ores and south Durham coking coal. In doing so, not
only did it replace Stockton as the focal point for the lower Tees but
it redefined the north-east. Part of the North Riding now had to be
included with Northumberland and Durham because of the dictates
of industrial logic. Since Stockton, Darlington and other parts of south

Durham developed iron and engineering works it would obviously be nonsensical to exclude the major iron-working area, Middlesbrough, purely because of the arbitrary dictates of administrative and river boundaries. More confusingly, the Cleveland Hills, which supplied Middlesbrough with its iron ore and were firmly anchored to the Tees by railway building, tend to be excluded from the north-east even though their links, for a time while ore and railways lasted, were much stronger there than with the agricultural North Riding.

Region is, therefore, an indeterminate and fluctuating tool with which to attempt to analyse society, even in an area which at first glance and through long historical definition appears to have a unity. Moreover, it is also the case that similar features may do more to lead to rivalry and disharmony than they do to bring unity. Sunderland and Newcastle, for instance, both owe much of their growth to the facilities they offered for the easy and cheap transport of the region's coal but in many senses this did not unite but differentiated them. Collieries between the two rivers shipped their coal either from the Tyne or the Wear and a divide grew up, a divide which to some extent still exists. It is most appropriate that since 1974 the new metropolitan county has been known as Tyne and Wear, which emphasises the two parts, rather than by a unifying name. There is a social distance between Newcastle, the regional metropolis, and Sunderland which feels that life has been unkind to it (as indeed it has) and this is reflected in both corporate and individual attitudes in the two towns. Sunderland frequently tries not to acknowledge Newcastle, as anyone who has tried looking for sign posts to the latter in the former will be aware; its inhabitants prefer the Darlington morning paper to that published in Newcastle. It is not, however, necessary to go to towns so geographically far apart as Newcastle and Sunderland to find disharmony. The river Tyne between Newcastle and Gateshead has offered and continues to offer a boundary more marked than that between any regions. Gateshead has never forgiven the quip that it was 'a long [sometimes the adjective is 'dirty'] lane leading to Newcastle'; it has always suffered inferior provision in social overhead capital to that of its neighbour and has always been very much aware of the fact. As we shall see Gateshead suffered Newcastle's problems without the resources to deal with them: the large shops, offices and industrial firms made their money in and paid their rates to Newcastle while their employees frequently lived in Gateshead, where they placed pressure for poor relief and other payments.

II DEVELOPMENT 1750–1950

At its very simplest one might say that the unifying feature of the region over the period was deprivation as compared with the national norm in economic provision. In the middle of the eighteenth century the northern part of the region was only just beginning to develop after centuries of border skirmishing in which the most northerly town, Berwick, changed hands between England and Scotland on several occasions. The remainder of the region was, with the exception of the margins of the Tyne and Wear, sparsely populated, culturally backward, closer to subsistence agriculture and less innovative than many other regions. One might regard it as 'deprivation with beauty' because of the scenic grandeur of hills and coasts, but the love of the country and the transport facilities with which to enjoy it had yet to appear. During the nineteenth century and especially in its second half the region (or much of it) experienced dramatic mining and industrial development which increased wealth, even for the majority of workers who swelled its population by migration and increased natural growth. The increased wealth (both absolute and relative to other areas) was, however, ephemeral and co-existed with the continuation of deprivation. The industrial areas may have bustled with employment opportunities but their environs were appalling, with conditions of housing and ill-health which deteriorated compared to other areas. The industrial growth even blighted some of the natural beauty, throwing up iron works on desolate marshes and turning beautiful beaches black with coal waste. After 1920 the relative prosperity of the north-east ebbed and, although there was a brief resurgence during and for a decade after the Second World War, it has not returned. Decline in the nineteenth-century staple industries, coal, iron and steel, engineering and shipbuilding, left the region with a surplus of useless labour skills and industrial capital and a deficit in resources with which to change the future. In renewed deprivation there was little but returning beauty (as the industrial landscape reverted to nature) to offset high unemployment, low provision of social overhead capital, low educational provision, etc.

1750–1825

At the beginning of the industrial revolution period the north-east was remote from the major areas of economic growth and population. Internal communications with other parts of the country were poor, it is said to have taken six days by coach to London, and it was only coastal shipping, chiefly for the coal trade, which made the region of any interest to the rest of the country. The region's population was small, with only Newcastle a town of any significance, possessing a merchant community which had developed on the back of the coal trade, and the ability to import and export the needs and the produce of a wide neighbourhood. Sunderland was a small-scale version of Newcastle, drawing the coal supplies of its hinterland and providing services and goods for the surrounding community. It was not, however, on the main road from London to Edinburgh, which, despite the inadequacies of road transport, was clearly a limitation on Sunderland's growth. Other towns were of even less significance, little more than market villages catering for their surrounding agricultural region, drawing in agricultural produce for their own use and more widespread distribution to Newcastle or even London (in the case of the coastal communities such as Berwick or Alnmouth).

Agriculture was indeed by far the most significant occupation throughout the region with the exceptions of narrow corridors a few miles either side of the rivers Tyne and Wear. By and large it was a fairly traditional agriculture which knew little of the techniques brought in by the 'agricultural revolution'. There was a good deal of subsistence farming, with little interest in the market economy, in the remoter areas away from the coast and urban communities. Sheep grazing was common in the upland interior, although little attention was paid to improvements in quality of the animals either for meat or wool. In these remote valleys of west Northumberland, such as Redesdale, life was little removed from the Middle Ages. There were family rivalries which resembled the clan strife of the Highlands, cattle and sheep stealing were common and the illicit distilling of spirits a way of life. Close to the coast and in the sheltered river valleys such as the Tyne, agriculture became more profitable and market orientated with the fattening of sheep and cattle, while in the broad lowlands between coast and hills an unimproved arable farming, concentrating on cheap cereals, oats and rye, with regular fallows, was the norm.

While agriculture dominated land use and employment, it was the coal industry which dominated the rest of the country's perception of the region. Coal was chiefly required for domestic heating and the major source of demand was London, the great centre of population, easily supplied from the north-east by coastal ship, together with many other minor ports from East Anglia to the south coast. While Britain was well endowed with coal only the Great Northern coalfield had immediate access to water transport and no competitors over a coastline of several hundred miles. As a result it accounted for around 25–30 per cent of British output, most of it, over a million tons per annum around 1750, being shipped southwards. Because of the inadequacies of overland transport, this coal was supplied by collieries close to the Tyne and Wear. The very furthest collieries involved in 'sea-sale' to distant markets were no more than 10 miles from the river Tyne and the majority were only a mile or two. This meant that isolated pit communities lined the river banks and a short distance north and south from them, for there was then no continuous urban ribbon along the rivers. Inland from the rivers the exploitation of the coal for a few miles had been facilitated by the development of waggonways (an invention of the Nottingham coalfield soon brought to the north-east in the early seventeenth century), wooden tracks on which horses could haul coal-waggons with greater ease than on mud roads. In the eighteenth century, therefore, the colliery communities were enabled to penetrate further into the coalfield and what had been previously agricultural areas, to places like Tanfield on the north-west Durham hills 10 miles from the Tyne. Beyond this distance on the main coalfield and in outlying places like the south-west Durham coalfield and the Northumberland hills with their lime-stone coal measures, the mining of coal was on a small scale for local 'land-sale' only, a result of the fact that carrying the coal by horse and cart for 10 or 12 miles would more than double its pit-head cost.

Major sources of employment, other than in agriculture and coal mining, were largely linked to the movement of coal. Many hundreds were employed in the waggon haulage from the collieries to the rivers and many more, the keelmen, in the movement of the coal by keel or barge down river to the anchorage points where it could be loaded on to the waiting colliers for transport south. There grew up as a result small tight communities of keelmen and even larger ones of seamen, as at South Shields, with all the problems attached to having the men employed in a highly dangerous occupation which kept them away from home for weeks at a time. The size of the community of seamen in the mid-eighteenth century cannot be given accurately but may be estimated from the knowledge that more than a million tons of coal were shipped annually from the Tyne and Wear in colliers whose burthen perhaps averaged 200 tons and which took five men a month to complete the round trip to London.

There was also a good deal of employment provided along the rivers in servicing the coal trade. Colliers had to be built, wood purchased, iron fittings, ropes and sails made, while the ships had to be provisioned for their voyages. The rivers were already the hub of the region's life and activity , where raw materials for manufacture were most cheaply obtained and where employment and demand for manufactures were high. But to say that is only to make a statement relative to the rest of the agricultural region, for contemporary illustrations show the large part of the banks of the Tyne and Wear to be as nature left them with no industrial intrusion. Apart from their employment activities in servicing the coal trade the river banks also offered employment based on using coal – activities which would not have existed locally but for the availability of cheap coal. Salt, although its local output was already in decline by 1750, was manufactured at the river mouths by the evaporation of sea water in large pans using poor-quality and small coals and Tyneside, to a greater extent than Wearside, was beginning to develop as a centre for glass manufacture, again based on local coal and cheap silica brought as ballast in returning colliers. These apart, the region had little to offer to the national economy and its existence was largely insular. Most employment was in craft skills and labouring capacity which met local demand for housing, food, clothing, household goods for the comfortably off and drink for the majority. Together with and partly a result of geographical isolation this helped to breed an enclosed community reluctant to move away from the region and initially reluctant to accept incomers, instanced by the rules of a number of Tyneside crafts in the early eighteenth century that none of their members should be allowed to take a Scotsman as an apprentice.

This picture of the regional economy in the middle of the eighteenth century is not one which suggests that the north-east would play a major part in the industrial revolution, the gathering zephyr which was, in time, to sweep the country. Not, that is, unless one believes that industrialisation was carried on the back of coal, steam power and technology. But, while there can be no doubt that these factors enabled the eventual continuation of industrialisation in the nineteenth century, the failure of the north-east to rise above the rest of the economy in the late eighteenth century surely denies their too early supremacy. Apart from its remoteness from the major areas of the country's population, and even that was partly offset by the facility of cheap coastal transport, the north-east was, in retrospect, as well placed in the mid-eighteenth century as any other area to lead industrialisation. It had trade (a long-established merchanting tradition), resources (especially coal but also some iron, lead, limestone, wool, timber, etc.), existing industrial experience, but it failed to generate growth, perhaps because of the small size of the local market. The north-east was ultimately to benefit from the long-run changes brought by industrialisation, from wood to coal as fuel and wood to iron as constructional material, but these changes were to come only slowly in the eighteenth and early nineteenth centuries, were to be at high tide in the late nineteenth century and were to ebb rapidly from 1920.

Perhaps the first and most significant piece of evidence for the slow growth of the north-east economy in the eighteenth century is that its population was growing more slowly than the national average. The regions which we link with industrialisation, however, Lancashire, the West Riding of Yorkshire and the Midland counties, had faster rates of growth than the national average. They attracted migrant labour and had higher rates of fertility, factors closely associated with the freedom from old restrictions brought by industrialisation. By contrast the picture for Northumberland and Durham is one of very slow growth and, unless Deane and Cole's detailed figures are wildly inaccurate,[1] slower even than those of most southern agricultural counties which had no industrial stimulus. In both counties the average annual rate of growth of population by natural increase is given as identical for the period 1781–1800 as for the period 1701–50, with in each case a rather faster (but still slow relative to the national position) growth in the decades between those periods. This would suggest that there was some initial stimulus to population growth in the early stages of industrialisation after 1750 (when population began to rise rapidly in the country as a whole) but that it was not followed through in the north-east. Little or no work has been done on the region's population in the late eighteenth century, which makes it impossible to offer any reasons for the slow growth, but there seems no reason to doubt the accuracy of the figures in relation to those

[1] P . Deane and W. A. Cole, *British Economic Growth 1688–1959*, 2nd edn (Cambridge, 1967), pp. 103 and 115. Their estimates give populations respectively for Durham and Northumberland; 1701 112,724 and 118,380; 1751 130,091 and 139,011; 1801 165,479 and 162,115.

for the rest of the country. Equally it is difficult to doubt the statement that a region which saw rates of natural increase of population much the same as a county such as Wiltshire for most of the eighteenth century and slower for the crucial last two decades, was little involved in industrialisation. Indeed, while Deane and Cole place Northumberland and Durham in their category 'industrial and commercial' counties, this attribution can only be based on their subsequent experience and for the eighteenth century they would more appropriately have been placed in the 'mixed' if the 'agricultural' category were felt inappropriate.

Without a considerable increase in its population the only way in which the region could have made a significant contribution to industrialisation was by increasing the per capita output of its existing population. Inevitably it is not possible to produce regional output figures but all the evidence suggests that such a rise in productivity did not occur. There were no new industries developed in the region, such as cotton textiles in which technological change offered the opportunity for massive increase in per capita output from the labour force. Moreover, the existing industrial activities in the north-east were not ones in which marked technological change occurred. It is a commonplace that the coal industry grew by more extensive methods until the early twentieth century and, although this observation may be due to greater concentration on the method of production at the coalface than is strictly justified, it is unlikely to be far from the mark. The Great Northern coalfield was already organised on an advanced commercial and technological basis by 1750. The use of more efficient steam engines and developments in waggonway technology thereafter are unlikely to have made dramatic increases in output per head of the total colliery labour force. If that is true of the region's most significant industry, then it is difficult to see that there could have been sufficient changes in technology elsewhere in the region's activities to have affected total output. Moreover, whatever happened to the total work effort of the labour force in the period of industrialisation (and it is by no means certain that total hours and/or intensity of work increased as a whole) there is no reason to believe that there was an increase which specifically affected the north-east.

If we look at the pattern of industrial growth in the region over the three-quarters of a century after 1750 it will clearly reinforce the picture of growth, but growth in response to what is happening elsewhere in the country rather than any innovative development which would lift the rate of growth of the economy as a whole. The most obvious area in which the rest of the country required the north-east was for its ability to supply coal. For most of this period the major demand was for domestic consumption for heating purposes and this was the prime factor behind London demand which dominated north-eastern shipments. London's population grew rapidly and its inhabitants were increasingly making use of coal fires but there was also a rising demand for metallurgical manufacture and for steam raising. It is easy to forget that London was the country's major industrial centre at this time with numerous non-ferrous metal works, foundries and industries such as brewing which were increasingly using steam power. As a result, coal shipments from the north-east rose from about 1.2 million tons in 1750 to 2.25 million tons in 1800 and 4.25 million tons by 1830. This was a rate of growth which considerably exceeded that of the national growth of population and therefore reflected both more intensive and extensive use of coal. Given the limitations on technological change in the industry it meant an extension of demand for coal-mining labour and a widening of the geographical area of the exploited coalfield (although more effective steam pumps did mean that a number of flooded Tyneside collieries could be de-watered, reopened and deeper seams exploited). Employment statistics for this period are mere speculations but a figure of 13,500 for coal-mining employment in Northumberland and Durham in 1800 has been suggested, which (if later nineteenth-century levels of about 40 per cent of total population in the labour force held for this earlier date) would imply that about 10 per cent of the economically active population was employed in coal mining. By 1851 the census noted some 41,000 whose occupations were returned as in coal mining, about 14 per cent of the total employed population, although these figures considerably underestimate the importance of coal mining since the census listed many labourers, some of whom will have been involved in colliery work.[2] Already by the early part of the nineteenth century it is clear that the region was moving towards a position in which a few industries would have a remarkable dominance in its industrial structure. The growth of coal mining was also extending the differentiation of the labour force. Early coal workings had had to be near

[2] D. J. Rowe, 'Occupations in Northumberland and Durham 1851-1911', *Northern History*, 8 (1973), pp. 119–31. The census used an occupational and not an industrial classification – apart from some labourers the figures also exclude some colliery workers employed in the transport of coal.

the river banks or inland centres of population in order to be viable. As a result the pitmen were part of or closely linked to the urban communities. Increasingly as output expanded the pitmen began to live in more isolated communities and a new image of them began to build up, a somewhat frightening one to many city dwellers.

Other than the rise of coal mining in response to demand in other parts of the country the region saw little notable change in the period to 1825. The salt industry withered and died by 1800 as competition from Cheshire rock salt developed. The steel industry, in which Tyneside dominated a very small total British output in 1750, stagnated while output in Sheffield responded to the growth in national demand and eclipsed Tyneside production. Of these two examples of failure the first might be attributed to fortuitous geographical features and be the disappearance of an unimportant pre-industrial sector. Long term, however, lack of local salt was to be a significant factor in the decline of the chemical industry on Tyneside and Wearside and its being overtaken by Teesside and Merseyside. The relative decline in the Tyneside steel industry is more significant. Although as yet on the fringes of the major metallurgical demands of the period, steel was clearly within the area of output in which the industrial revolution was proceeding. That Tyneside with an initial advantage could not sustain it, points to some failure in the local economy to respond to industrial growth (especially since Tyneside was much better placed than Sheffield to receive the imports of bar iron from Sweden which were used in steel manufacture). It has to be a failure of entrepreneurship on Tyneside and successful recognition of future market expansion by Sheffield entrepreneurs which was responsible for such a change.

Alongside these failures, the areas in which the north-east made a national impact by 1825 are limited and hardly of dramatic significance for economic growth. The most obvious is the glass industry, in which the region did capitalise on its earlier involvement. By 1825 Tyneside and Wearside together were probably the largest single producer of glass in total (broad, crown, flint and bottle) in the country. Glass consumption nationally was, however, insufficiently large for the local industry to have significant impact on employment. The remaining areas of regional employment continued to be those which serviced the coal industry (and its growth meant their expansion in areas such as ropemaking) and those which provided for the needs of the local population. In 1825, other than its shipment of coal, the region remained largely an insular economy, little affected by industrial change and little affecting that change.

1825–1920

Even before the second quarter of the nineteenth century there is some evidence that the north-east was beginning to catch up with the growth rates of more advanced areas in the country. In terms of population, for instance, the rate of growth for Northumberland and Durham was only slightly below the national average for the period 1801–30 and that for Durham alone was slightly higher, reflecting the greater impact of coal mining there than in Northumberland. Nevertheless, it is clear that it is only from about 1825 that the region began to make a distinctive contribution. After 1821 its rate of growth of population was in excess of that of the national average in every decade up to the end of the century.[3] County Durham grew most rapidly, in some decades its rate of growth being at least twice the national average, from 150,000 in 1801 to almost 1.2 million in 1901 while Northumberland's population grew at about the national average (except for the last two decades of the century when it grew very rapidly with the opening of the Ashington area of the coalfield), from 170,000 to 600,000. Increasingly the geographical distribution of population was along the margins of the rivers. The north Tyneside belt accounted for 36 per cent of the population of Northumberland in 1801 and 61 per cent in 1901. This was the most marked example in the region since the rest of Northumberland saw little industrial growth and, therefore, increase in employment opportunities, while population in many rural areas began to decline from the mid-nineteenth century. To a lesser extent, however, the example of north Tyneside was repeated on south Tyneside and, of course, Teesside, each area increasing its proportion of the total population of County Durham at the expense of the rural hinterland. The north-east became, therefore, very heavily dependent on urban dwelling, the distinction between industrial and rural areas becoming very marked, especially in Northumberland.

Population growth was chiefly a result of a rising rate of natural increase (a result almost certainly of both rising birth rates and falling death rates) as compared with the late eighteenth-century position,

---

[3] D. J. Rowe, 'Population of Nineteenth Century Tyneside', in N. McCord, ed., *Essays in Tyneside Labour History* (Newcastle upon Tyne, 1977), p. 21.

but growth was also facilitated by inward migration at certain times. Migration never accounted for more than one third of the region's population growth in any inter-censal period, although it almost reached that level between 1861 and 1871 and was not far short in the previous decade. In these decades employment opportunities in north-east industry really took off and could not be filled by the rise of the indigenous population. For many parts of the region, of course, migration was much more important in particular periods – the new towns such as Middlesbrough and West Hartlepool and the colliery villages – and polyglot (at least in terms of accent) communities developed. Inevitably these communities attracted young men because of their employment opportunities and resembled frontier communities. They had high proportions of men to women; in 1871 Durham had 941 females per 1,000 males (the lowest of any county) against an average for England and Wales of 1,052. As a result the marriage rate was high and there was a very low proportion of women of marriageable age unmarried. A consequence of the low average age of the population in the third quarter of the century was very high birth rates which remained high when the national rate was falling and maintained population growth at a high level up to the turn of the century.

Indissolubly linked with population change was rapid growth in the region's industrial economy. Coal output soared to some 56 million tons by 1913 on the back of an economy which was at last dependent on the fruits of eighteenth-century industrialisation – steam power and iron technology – and also with a large increase in exports of coal. As a result of the extension of the waggonway network, with the development of railways (using stationary and then locomotive steam engines), the whole of the coalfield was gradually opened up. The areas which benefited were south-west Durham, sending its coal to the Tees from 1825 and later from West Hartlepool; east Durham, gradually expanding from 1822, when Hetton colliery was opened, and culminating in the sinking of the coastal collieries in the late nineteenth century; and south-east Northumberland, with the opening of many of the collieries in the Ashington–Bedlington area after 1850. The result was the development of a number of colliery towns, such as Ashington, and many more villages with populations of perhaps 5,000, which were largely or completely dominated by coal mining.

While there were developments in other parts of the country, there can be little doubt that the introduction of railways owed a great deal to experimentation in the north-east, by a number of colliery 'engineers' of whom George Stephenson is the best known. Initially they applied stationary steam power to winding sets of waggons by rope up inclines, enabling waggonways to take more direct routes to the rivers, which horse haulage could not manage. Transport of coal was speeded up and cost reduced. Then followed the introduction of locomotive haulage and from the early 1820s several composite railways were built, using horses, stationary and locomotive engines, from the collieries direct to the ports rather than to the river banks like the old waggonways. A minor point, perhaps, but it reflected the changes which were overtaking the region's established activities. Railways were to provide a new growth point for the region. For a time in the 1820s Robert Stephenson & Co. of Newcastle was the only manufacturer of locomotive engines in the country. Its example was soon followed by R. & W. Hawthorn in Newcastle, while the Bedlington Iron Works built up to a claimed employment peak of 2,000, largely on the base of supplying wrought-iron rails and other fittings for railways as well as some locomotives. In the south of the region the railway expansion on Teesside led not only to the setting up of works by the railway companies, as at Shildon, but also to demand for iron supplies met by the development of firms in Darlington, Stockton and other towns.

As iron became more important, for a myriad of uses beyond the railways, it was inevitable that a region so well endowed in coal would develop in iron manufacture, however limited the local availability of iron ore. Both counties had seen earlier attempts to develop the industry and a number of new, isolated works was established around the 1830s at places like Ridsdale in Northumberland and Birtley in Durham. All were based on relatively insignificant local sources of iron ore and, despite the development of the Derwent Iron Works at Consett during the 1840s to become one of the largest in the country, the region was an insignificant producer. The change came in the 1850s with the exploitation of the huge deposits of iron ore in the Cleveland Hills. From an output of less than 150,000 tons of pig iron in 1850 (around 5 per cent of British output), the region was producing 2 million tons, almost one third of national output by the early 1870s. This development, not the impact of railway-borne coal in the 1830s, really caused the dramatic growth of Middlesbrough, 'the ironmasters' town', from a population of 7,000 in 1851 to 70,000 in 1891.

On the base of local supplies of iron the shipbuilding industry was to expand. The Tyne and Wear had for long been significant producers of wooden vessels, especially colliers, and in the 1830s it was claimed that the Wear produced a bigger output than any other shipbuilding port. The vessels were, however, small and traditional and the change in significance really came with the switch to iron shipbuilding, gaining ground in the 1850s on the Tyne and becoming pre-eminent in the region from the mid-1860s. To Charles Mark Palmer's iron-hulled, steam-powered, water-ballast colliers from 1852 may go the palm for the most obvious emblem of the change, but there were precursors and others who played a major role, including migrant shipbuilders such as Andrew Leslie from Aberdeen. Many firms developed on each of the three rivers, producing a wide range of vessels from warships to oil tankers with the result that while north-eastern yards produced less than 20 per cent of British output in the late 1850s they produced more than 50 per cent in the 1890s.

Along with shipbuilding went the rise of general engineering as the use of iron became more widespread. Even before 1800 there was some regional base in the industry, linked especially to colliery requirements. Firms such as Hawks & Co. of Gateshead produced a wide range of iron goods from nails to anchors but it was in the middle of the nineteenth century that the scope came for notable expansion in the size and numbers of firms. For general constructional work, bridge-building, machine parts, waggons and other colliery and railway equipment, armaments and so on, the demand for iron, and from the 1870s steel, products was almost limitless. Large firms became common such as Abbots of Gateshead and Head, Wrightson & Co. of Thornaby, while the Tyne boasted giant integrated iron and steel, shipbuilding and engineering firms such as Palmers and Armstrongs, the latter with an employment at Elswick alone exceeding 10,000 in the years before 1914.

It is then really in the second half of the nineteenth century that the north-east played a major role in the nation's growth. Nor was it limited to coal, iron and steel, shipbuilding and engineering, since there was a major contribution from the chemical industries, especially the production of alkalis in which the Tyne accounted for up to 50 per cent of British output in the years around mid-century. Even within the period to 1920, however, there were suggestions of fragility in the region's industrial base and prosperity. The Bedlington Iron Works declined from the 1850s and closed in 1867, at Gateshead Abbots closed in 1909 having had a peak employment of 2,000, while the similarly sized Hawks, Crawshay closed in 1889. Of course these may be put down to entrepreneurial failure or inappropriate location but the reasons add up to an inability to compete and without adjustment to changing circumstances eventual failure was inevitable. Already before 1914 the Tyneside chemical industry had discovered this fact. It had declined into a pale shadow of its former self as a result of the introduction elsewhere of more efficient methods of manufacture of heavy chemicals. Moreover, by the early twentieth century competition was not only coming from other regions in Britain but from abroad and the north-east was going to have to be in the forefront of modernisation if its heavy industries were not to suffer the same fate as the chemical industry.

1920–50

Whatever the doubts about rising competition before 1914, they were stilled by the demands of wartime production and, briefly, by the postwar needs of reconstruction. From 1920, however, decline set in. The reduced ability of Britain to supply for export during the war had encouraged many countries to develop their own industries to make up for ships, iron and steel and engineering products which had previously come from the north-east. After the war such countries raised tariff barriers to protect their newly expanding industries and many export markets were permanently lost, the decline in world trade reducing demands for shipbuilding. Coal, previously sent from the north-east to continental countries was to a considerable extent replaced by European output. Moreover, home demand in Britain was no longer rising for many of the staple products of the north-east and could not, therefore, make up for the loss of export markets. Home demand for coal did not rise in the interwar years as other fuels began to compete. Railways suffered from the competition of the internal combustion engine and, apart from one ill-fated venture into automobile production by Armstrongs, the employment effect of the rise of motor transport was not felt in the north-east. Inevitably, the heavy, capital goods industries were hit most seriously by the slump since investment fell more sharply than consumption. Inevitably also, the north-east was hit more seriously than many other parts of the country because of its commitment to the staple industries (in 1911 almost one half of total employment in County Durham lay within four main industrial sectors, coal, shipbuilding, iron manufacture and engineering). At the peak of interwar unemployment in 1932,

22.7 per cent of the insured labour force was unemployed nationally, but 37.4 per cent in the north-east, 45.8 per cent in west Durham and 64.3 per cent in Stanley.[4] Villages and towns dependent on single industries, such as Jarrow on shipbuilding, were worst hit but the interlocking nature of the heavy industries reinforced the decline in demand and the drop in earnings among their employees inevitably led to declines in expenditure on consumer goods.

Of course the decline in the staple industries was not the whole story of the interwar years. New industries developed and with them new employment opportunities. One area into which the north-east began to diversify at the beginning of the twentieth century was electrical engineering and, despite the local dominance of coal and gas for fuel, power and light, before 1914 the region had developed the best organised provision of electricity supply in the country. Linked to this went the manufacture of electrical generating equipment and two firms, A. Reyrolle & Co. at Hebburn and C. A. Parsons & Co. at Heaton, made significant contributions to new employment on Tyneside. Indeed at Hebburn, next door to Ellen Wilkinson's depressed Jarrow, the existence of typical estates of owner-occupied semi-detached houses built in the mid-1930s, points to the prosperity which came to some, even on depressed Tyneside. At the other end of the region, on Teesside, the rise of the chemical industry with ICI's development at Billingham is another pointer to diversification. Overall, however, the new job opportunities could do little to offset the massive declines in old areas. In 1923 the coal-mining labour force peaked at 170,000 in County Durham but in the late 1930s it ran at not much over 100,000.

One result of mass unemployment was huge migration away from the north-east with the young, active adults predominating in the movement and without their presence many communities appeared even more depressed and lacking a future. Between 1921 and 1931 the north-east had net outward migration of almost 200,000, approximately 8 per cent of its 1921 population.[5] The region which had been growing more rapidly than the national average abruptly changed direction. The overall population of the north-east, which had increased by 1 million between 1881 and 1921, rose by only 100,000

[4] G. H. Daysh *et al.*, 'Inter-War Unemployment in West Durham 1929–39', in M. Bulmer, ed., *Mining and Social Change: Durham County in the Twentieth Century* (1978), p. 143.

[5] J. W. House, *North-Eastern England: Population Movements and the Landscape since the Early Nineteenth Century* (King's College, Newcastle upon Tyne, Department of Geography, research series 1, 1954), p. 56.

to 2.5 million in 1951. Towns just ceased to grow, which at least gave them a respite from the rapid increase of their environmental problems.

A second result of mass unemployment was a huge increase in the deprivation which already existed in the region. Survey after survey showed the demoralising impact of long-term unemployment and in an area where jobs were disappearing more rapidly than they were being replaced (because the region's industrial structure was out of date), it was inevitable that unemployment would be long term for the older men, the less than dynamic and those who were merely conservative and home-loving. The worst effects of long-term unemployment were seen in the one-industry towns and especially in the colliery villages. At Crook in 1936 the Pilgrim Trust observers found that 71 per cent of the unemployed had had no work for the previous five years but they nevertheless felt that 'the "atmosphere" in the homes visited in Crook was more satisfactory than anywhere else'.[6] Reference was made to the strength of family life in Crook (even more noticeably than in the Rhondda) as a factor in limiting the insidious effects of unemployment, while the working men's clubs and allotments (this was the time of the rise of the leek competition) made major contributions to stability. There was a sense of solidarity in depression, which must have contributed to the rising dominance of the Labour party in County Durham and which carried over into the more recent period. It is sometimes as if the north-east actually thrives on and enjoys deprivation, if only to scorn the 'soft-living' in 'the south'.

Within a couple of years of the commencement of the Second World War the problem of unemployment had disappeared, actually to be replaced by shortages of labour and the need for more coalminers. The region's industries were once more in demand and this position continued, even more surprisingly, after the war was over and on into the mid-1950s. This was less a result of the much-heralded government commitment to full employment and regional policy than to rapidly rising world trade and growth of new industrial demand at home as yet little affected by foreign competition. Coal-mining employment stabilised at rather over 100,000 in County Durham, shipbuilding benefited from higher demand than in the 1930s, the chemical and engineering industries saw new and expanding

[6] Pilgrim Trust, *Men Without Work* (Cambridge, 1938), p. 74.

demands. New capital investment in buildings and machinery was the order of the day and the north-east's capital goods industries were anxious to oblige. Unemployment in the north-east, still above the national average, was only about 1.5 per cent in the mid-1950s. From the end of the decade the scene changed, however. Competition from new fuels led to the decline of coal (employment in coal mining in County Durham fell by three-quarters to only 25,000 in 1976), ship-building and then many other manufacturing industries felt the chill wind of foreign competition and went into decline. In the 1960s regional policy encouraged industrialists to move to the north-east among other depressed areas but the results were slight in the long term since the branch plants of national firms were the first to disappear in the closures of the 1970s. Can the future hold better prospects? The outlook suggests that it is unlikely. The north-east retains a higher proportion of employment in manufacturing industry than the national average and its relative dependence on manufacturing has been increasing in recent years. Given the greater volatility of manufacturing employment during cyclical downswings and Britain's appalling long-run record in industrial competitiveness, such a dependence is hardly encouraging.

III REGIONAL CHARACTERISTICS

In a single chapter it is possible to do no more than outline the overall development of the region but rather than devote the whole chapter to outline it seemed worthwhile to pick on a number of characteristics and examine them in somewhat greater depth. The obvious point at interest is to attempt to isolate those aspects of life in which the north-east was in some way different from the rest of the country.

Perhaps the general characteristic on which it would be possible to get clear agreement is the remoteness of the region for much of the period covered. To some extent this was offset by the existence of rivers and harbours which provided access to the cheapest of contemporary forms of travel before the railways – the sea. But sea journeys were slow and dangerous in the small ships of the late eighteenth and early nineteenth centuries and were used only for essential travel by the poor and the transport of heavy goods and raw materials. Walking apart, long and expensive coach journeys were the only other method of reaching areas of civilisation (such as Edinburgh and London) and of industrial development. Inevitably such travel was limited to the wealthy and there can be no doubt that geographical isolation was less of an inhibiting factor to the upper middle classes and gentry than to the rest. The large farmers and landowners often travelled to and communicated with their fellows in other parts of the country. In following the progress of George and Matthew Culley, from being small farmers in south Durham in the 1760s to large land-owners and tenants of thousands of acres in north Northumberland by the early nineteenth century, one can see that remoteness, even of the north of the region, was no serious bar for those who wished to communicate.[7] The Culleys made a number of agricultural tours away from the region to explore agricultural innovations, had many visitors from other parts of the country and maintained a voluminous correspondence with farmers and landowners in other regions. Nevertheless, the Culleys frequently noted the limited impact which their considerable contributions to agricultural improvement had on their neighbours. Remoteness may not have prevented development for those with drive and initiative but it may well have hindered the spread of the new ideas of industrialisation and the cultural changes which came with more widespread mobility elsewhere in the eighteenth century.

Parts of the region, away from the coast, experienced a geographical remoteness which has hardly changed in the twentieth century. The growth of lead mining in the northern Pennines in the late eighteenth century led to the rise of villages such as Middleton-in-Teesdale and Nenthead and to small towns such as Alston, described as the highest market town in England. Existence in hilly areas inevitably meant isolation because of transport difficulties. Until well into the nineteenth century transport depended on horse for passengers and pack-horse and mule for goods and the movement of lead. From the 1850s many of these communities and others such as the agricultural and mining ones in the north Tyne valley (Bellingham, Plashetts, etc.) were given a respite from remoteness by the building of a considerable network of railways. North-west Durham could perhaps justify this development on the basis of mineral resources despite its light population density but western Northumberland's railways were largely a white elephant from the beginning, even their ultimate justification,

---

[7] D. J. Rowe, 'The Culleys, Northumberland Farmers 1767–1813', *Agricultural History Review* 19 (1971), pp. 156-74, and S. Macdonald, 'The Role of the Individual in Agricultural Change: The Example of George Culley of Fenton, Northumberland', in H. S. A. Fox and R. A. Butlin, eds., *Change in the Countryside* (1979).

the provision of an alternative through route to Scotland, proving of little value. Nevertheless, the railways made wider use of local coal, iron and limestone resources than could have occurred with road transport alone; they facilitated journeys to local markets and offered mobility to rural dwellers to whom the concept had been previously largely unknown. In doing so they almost certainly led to outward migration, the decline of the communities, especially from the 1870s and ultimately the recognition in the twentieth century of the lack of financial return from rural railways, their closure and a return to remoteness.

The significant question is the extent to which remoteness contributed to regional characteristics. Given the fact that in the eighteenth century the region itself was fragmented, it seems highly unlikely that any cohesive north-eastern characteristic appeared as a result of the region's general remoteness. Agricultural communities, lead villages, market towns and the Tyne and Wear communities had their own distinctive characteristics and their links with one another were largely limited to trade. The nineteenth century did something to modify this picture by placing the regional focus strongly on the areas of heavy industry. As the coalfield area became more densely populated and the three rivers more specialised, a regional identity became more noticeable. Nevertheless, the rural areas remained to some extent divorced, as did the lead dales. In them there was considerable suspicion and dislike of the coal-mining communities to which they were closest, let alone of the large urban developments along the rivers. And while the coal communities had much in common, each had much which distinguished it from its neighbours and there was strong and often violent rivalry between pit villages.

While it might be thought that the influx of migrants into the colliery communities, as coal mining expanded in the nineteenth century, would have destroyed their insularity, it is clear that this was only a temporary phenomenon. In the 'social melting-pot', which was his term for the coal-mining villages,[8] Jack Lawson saw people from various parts of the United Kingdom as being converted over time into pure Durham metal with all the old and some new characteristics. With the end of population growth each community closed in, as did the whole region after about 1910. Outward migration after 1920 did nothing to break down insularity (except to encourage the

[8] J. Lawson, *A Man's Life* (1932), pp. 56–7.

following of the fortunes of those who left by relatives and friends who stayed). Those who went were the young and enquiring while those who stayed were largely those who could not break from their environment and their commitment to it was often reinforced by those who returned from the 'south' having been unable to settle. After the Second World War the situation began to change for the region as a whole and for the coal communities, particularly following the run-down of coal mining from the late 1950s. The old dominance of many villages, with perhaps 75 per cent of their total labour force working at 'the pit', was broken. People had to travel to work (and the motor car has increasingly contributed to the change), while new occupations, often in factories on small industrial estates, to some extent replaced coal. The old pattern of following father into the pit was broken and with it the clannishness of those who lived and talked a mysterious and separate way of life. But while the breakdown of remoteness was most noticeable for the colliery villages, it had a wider impact on the whole region. Prosperity and government regional policy for the 'development areas' brought new firms and (more often) new branch factories of old ones to the region. While much unskilled labour was recruited locally, key personnel, both for shop-floor and management, were often brought in and throughout the north-east introduced new insights and attitudes. Nevertheless, it remains true that a very large proportion of north-easterners are geographically immobile. If they enter higher education on leaving school they are very likely to go to the local college or university rather than further afield, while a high proportion of all north-easterners would not consider moving to a job in another region. Relative to much of the rest of the country the new towns, such as Cramlington, Newton Aycliffe and Peterlee, are in the same tradition of insularity as their mining predecessors. It is a matter of value judgment as to whether insularity is beneficial or detrimental to social life.

There can be little doubt, however, that remoteness has been a significant factor in contributing to another regional characteristic – the image of the north-east portrayed south of Sheffield (some might say south of the Tees). The caricature is of a dirty, grimy industrial region full of pits and blast-furnaces where the men wear caps, drink beer out of straight glasses, grow leeks and race whippets while the women stay at home, wear 'pinnies' and curlers and sand the doorstep. It is an image which is met regularly by those who interview students applying for places at north-eastern universities. 'Where are the pits?'

is a question asked by those who have travelled by train through County Durham for the first time – 'Where is the smoke and grime?' It is easy to explain the decline of heavy industry and point to the impact which clean-air legislation has had on north-eastern towns as on other parts of the country. The removal of pit heaps, the closure of waggonways, the demolition of blast-furnaces and many other changes have made the north-east not dissimilar from any other region. The significant question is the extent to which the north-east did suffer from earlier manifestations of its particular industrial structure.

It has been suggested that industrialisation had made little impact on the natural beauty of the region in 1750 nor was to do so for many subsequent decades. Newcastle was the only large town (earlier in the century perhaps fourth in size to London, Bristol and Norwich in England), but even in 1801 its population was less than 30,000. The problems brought by mass urbanisation, although present, were far less widespread than in many other areas – no north-eastern town grew to huge size nor did any expand at a particularly rapid rate during the nineteenth century. Newcastle reached a population of 200,000 during the 1890s while no other town had done more than struggle to 100,000 by then. Moreover, since much of the growth came in the second half of the century, rather than the first, as with Bradford, for instance, it should have been easier to accommodate as knowledge accumulated. It is also important to note that as well as being relatively small, north-eastern towns were strung out linearly along the rivers with the result that they were not very wide. Few people, even in Newcastle, could therefore have been far from the countryside, a fact which must have limited the prison-like effect of town life. Of course, as population grew and industry expanded in the nineteenth century, the towns became more unpleasant but this must have been mitigated by the ease with which it was possible to get out of them. In the 1870s a London-based journalist wrote of his journey across 'the Tyne to the unlovely town of Gateshead, and so go on, fortunately not far, till we get out of its noise, smells and unmitigated squalor, to the greenfields again'.[9]

If this were true for the major towns, where in addition there were open spaces such as Newcastle's Town Moor and Jesmond Dene, gift to the town in 1883 of Sir William Armstrong, it was even more

[9] *Athenaeum*, 27 Sept. 1873, p. 407.

true of the mining villages. In the lead dales farming and mining had traditionally been combined as occupations, while in coal-mining communities, despite the claustrophobic impact of unbroken terrace rows, it is clear from many accounts that the surrounding countryside was much used. For the children it provided convenient play areas away from the overcrowded houses, trees to climb, rivers to swim in and scope for much fun, which was lacking in Manchester or Birmingham. For the men it offered the chance to walk, court, poach (an endemic activity which provided a useful variation in diet), exercise, race dogs and so on. In addition in the mining communities space was not at a premium as it was in the towns and the colliery terraces often had considerable gardens as well as the availability of nearby allotments. They provide a fascinating contrast to the poky front gardens and back lanes of the terrace rows in the towns, where there was little or no scope for satisfaction out of working hours from growing one's own food. The contrast can only be explained in terms of the relative cost of land and, in the towns, the need to pack working people in as small an area as possible in order to provide accommodation close to their work, in an age of poor and expensive transport facilities. Whatever the reason, the contrast strongly favoured the otherwise disadvantaged colliery villages. It is easy to dismiss (or alternatively concentrate on) them as barbaric outposts, where workingmen were robbed of their humanity by the rule of the coalowners, and aspects of that caricature are true but it misses the fact that there were opportunities for satisfaction outside work (although it is equally clear that as a group pitmen gained considerable work satisfaction relative to factory operatives for instance). Urban workers were far more prisoners of their environment than were the pitmen, despite the unattractive picture drawn by outsiders of pit communities.

The garden and allotment were not just escapes from the employer-dominated working life, they were places where the pitman could establish his own identity, where he could give expression to his own individuality and create. It is noticeable that flowers were much grown and that annual flower shows were an important highlight of the year (a practice with a modern hangover of growing dahlias, chrysanthemums and other flowers, which surprises the more recent middle-class converts to allotmenteering). Of course vegetables were important. They were not widely available as market commodities in remote communities and a private supply was a useful contribution to limited wage incomes. Out of them came an undoubted regional characteristic, leek growing. Leeks were widely grown for eating and for show-ing in the nineteenth century but it was really from the interwar years that the September leek show for 'pot' leeks began to dominate the image of the north-eastern horticultural scene with the development of a prize level out of all proportion to those offered for other exhibits. The reason why of course remains intangible but it was certainly an in-group activity which enabled workingmen to differentiate them-selves, gain respect among their peer group and a life-line on which to hang in a period of potentially crippling change. Once again, how-ever, the present position is different, the leek clubs have become more open and classless and although their exhibits are regarded by outsiders as an epitomisation of the region, this is to generalise fanci-fully from a small group. Far more north-easterners grow kitchen leeks than show any interest in the 'pot' variety for shows. As with much in the field of regional distinction, differences lie in the eye of the media, which is likely to focus on trivialities.

However, the media have pointed out the inadequacies of social overhead capital in the region (and there is some evidence to suggest that these have been worse than in many other areas of heavy indus-try). For the whole of the period under discussion the north-east has been poorly supplied with a whole range of social facilities, which is perhaps the major reason for regarding it as a relatively deprived region over the 200-year period. The road network was poor and con-tributed to regional isolation until serious improvements began to be made in the 1960s. Any effective government policy, aimed at deal-ing with the regional imbalance in economic performance which became obvious by the 1930s, would surely have concentrated on providing a road network which would have made the north-east more attractive to the industrialists whom the actual regional incen-tives were intended to attract. With declining use of coastal shipping and the uncompetitiveness of the railways for goods carriage, no amount of provision of advanced factories, depreciation and tax allow-ances, etc., would have serious impact if the major form of goods communication was inadequate. In the industrial climate of the middle of the twentieth century the north-east had too small a population to provide a viable economic demand and its enterprises had, there-fore, to be competitive in wider markets. While poor road facilities may have been a result of the nineteenth-century concentration on the sea as the major means of transport it is less easy to explain other areas of inadequacy in social provision. The two which are most significant are housing and health, which may be looked at in some depth since they provide major planks in the case for calling the north-east a deprived region. They relate not to superficial characteristics but to matters of crucial and everyday concern to the whole of the population.

Housing

The quality of housing is one of the great factors which differentiates the north-east from other regions. We know little of the state of housing for the majority at the beginning of the period, other than that it was poor, but that was true for the country as a whole. As population increased, from the middle of the eighteenth century, however, it is clear that the majority crowded into existing accommodation. Towns, such as Newcastle and Berwick, only slowly expanded beyond their medieval limits. What new building there was tended to be of an infill type, worsening the spatial overcrowding by reducing the availability of light and air. The central, medieval houses, once the accommodation for wealthy merchants, became tenemented and dilapidation followed overcrowding. In such circumstances the norm of a single room or at most two rooms as a family dwelling became established. In mining areas, probably the result of following the established local agricultural pattern, the single-roomed cottage, approximately 15 feet square was certainly common by the end of the eighteenth century. With many dwellings so noticeably limited in space it was inevitable that high levels of overcrowding would ensue. From the publication of the first census figures for 1801 it is possible to produce figures for overcrowding by dividing total population for any area by the number of dwellings which existed. The results are, however, of little use and are probably not at all comparable between local areas, let alone with figures for other parts of the country. The reason for this statement is that the statistics are unreliable. Apart from the fact that it is known that the early censuses under-recorded the population, it is unlikely that the recorded figures for the numbers of unoccupied houses are accurate while the definition of what was a house remained by no means constant. What was more, it must have been inordinately difficult for census enumerators to make consistent decisions as to what was a separate house in the tenements of Newcastle or Gateshead. For what they are worth the figures show densities per occupied house of 9.0 persons in Newcastle and 8.5

persons in Sunderland in 1801, with some decline to a little over 8.0 in the following two censuses. The significance of such figures depends, of course, on house size but, placed alongside the indications that the number of rooms per house was low, they suggest that very serious overcrowding already existed in the main towns of the region by the beginning of the nineteenth century. While the figures take no account of room size it is difficult to believe that this factor could offset the problem. Although comparisons with other areas are of very little validity it is significant that no other region in England and Wales had figures of density of occupation which approached those in the north-east. As one might expect, the next highest figures related to London and Middlesex, where densities varied from 7.2 to 7.5 in the decades 1801–21. Since more accurate figures for later in the century confirm this pre-eminence of the north-east in terms of overcrowding, it seems safe to say that it was a position which was already established by the beginning of the nineteenth century. The important conclusion which follows is that it pre-dated both any significant growth in the region's population and industrialisation on any scale. Overcrowding in terms of density per house was not, therefore, due to intolerable pressure of growing numbers on the existing house stock with a failure to build enough new houses to cope. Nor was it a result of industrialisation which forced working people to live in limited housing space because of low incomes. It was historically endemic.

Considering the importance of housing to human history it is surprising that so little work has been undertaken to analyse the problems of the north-east and assess why it should have had the worst overcrowding levels in England and Wales. Of the ideas which have been put forward as explanations none is convincing on its own and even cumulatively they hardly appear satisfactory. It has been suggested that the north-east was influenced by Scottish experience but this seems to be based more on the fact that both areas had high overcrowding levels than on any evidence that those levels had a similar cause or that the directional link was from north to south. The policy of colliery companies in the north-east of providing 'free' housing for most grades of adult male colliery workers has also been put forward as a partial solution. It is argued that the companies provided low-cost, small houses which proved inadequate but that their employees would not leave them for better accommodation, partly because there was little alternative but chiefly because they would lose their rent-free accommodation. They were, therefore, tied to overcrowded accommodation. While there is much truth in this argument, which helps to explain why overcrowding continued in the colliery villages throughout the nineteenth century (especially with the practice of families taking in single men as lodgers), it does not explain why it started. The free colliery house was largely a development of the nineteenth century in response to the lack of housing in the remoter parts of the coalfield which were then being penetrated by mining. As such it was a response to the already accepted standards of housing accommodation in the region. It seems unlikely that coalowners deliberately had houses built which were smaller than the norm for the region, which was determined as much as anything by the urban areas close to the rivers where the earlier collieries had been established. High land prices have also been offered as a cause of the building of accommodation of low square footage. Again this seems more likely to have been a causative factor in the continuation of overcrowding in the nineteenth century rather than a reason for its original innovation. In any event high land prices were only of significance in certain areas and had no impact on colliery villages where houses were small but gardens often large.

There are other factors, on whose significance little work has as yet been undertaken, which are clearly relevant to the region's housing structure. The first of these is the level of rents. If rents were higher than in other regions it might be argued that workingmen would purchase a smaller amount of dwelling space than in other regions. For the period when, it has been argued, the region's small size of dwelling became established, there is no convenient source of evidence on rents. For the early twentieth century, however, a Board of Trade survey[10] does show that rents in the north-east were above the average for similar accommodation in other industrial towns in England and Wales. Newcastle had the fourth highest rents out of a list of seventy-three large towns, while Jarrow was sixth and Gateshead eighth. Nevertheless, while the level of rents in those towns ranged from only 66 per cent to 76 per cent of the London figures for similar accommodation, London houses were not normally small. Moreover rents at Sunderland and South Shields were noticeably lower and similar to those in towns such as Middlesbrough, Oldham and Cardiff where houses were on average larger and over-

[10]   *Report of an Enquiry by the Board of Trade into Working-Class Rents, Housing Retail Prices and Standard Rates of Wages in the United Kingdom*, PP 1908, CVII, pp. xiii–xx.

crowding was less significant. Indeed the Board of Trade report noted that while there was some broad correlation between high rents and high levels of overcrowding and vice versa, there were too many towns in which the fit was poor for the correlation to be strong.

The second factor of relevance is income levels in the region. Again too little is known on this subject for the late eighteenth and early nineteenth centuries but it is clear that wage rates were at least equal to those for similar jobs in other industrial areas in the second half of the nineteenth century. Moreover the north-east had a high proportion of its employees in relatively well-paid occupations.[11] While it is possible that unemployment in the region was above the national average and that average earnings might therefore have been lower than would otherwise be expected, there is no reason to think that this would have been noticeably greater than in other areas of heavy industry. A final factor with regard to income was that the opportunities for female and child employment were limited in the heavy industries of the region and that this therefore limited the scope for expanding family earnings. It is, however, unlikely that this was of sufficient importance to have affected the size of the region's houses and it clearly does not explain the fact that female employment was high and male wages were high in agricultural areas of Northumberland but house size was still small.

Neither the relatively high rents of the region nor the probable level of earnings seems likely to have been a determining factor as the cause of the region's characteristically small houses, although it is difficult to be confident on these matters without detailed research on the position in the late eighteenth century. Indeed, it seems unlikely that it is possible to produce any single factor which gave the north-east its unenviable reputation in overcrowding. The occupation of small dwellings (whether they were separate houses or part of a tenemented building) was already established as part of regional standards by the end of the eighteenth century and relative isolation from other communities and other standards of housing provision seems to have maintained it. Even the inward migration of the 1860s and 1870s did nothing to change expectations of housing standards, presumably because the immigrants were workers who could do little but accept what accommodation was available even if it was less spacious than that to which they were used.

[11] E. H. Hunt, *Regional Wage Variations in Britain, 1850-1914* (Oxford, 1973).

The towns had at least the advantage that cellar dwellings were uncommon, a point on which the Tyneside report to the Health of Towns Commission commented in 1845. Of the old mansions near the quayside it did, however, note, 'Some of the finest residences of former Newcastle, the early abodes of the noble and the wealthy, with many of the advantages of modern civilization parcelled into tenements, have been turned into the foulest shelters for the poor.'[12] It was not just the overcrowding of old buildings, since, the report continued, 'At this very moment some of the newest streets of Newcastle and Gateshead are fast becoming as bad as the very worst parts of the old.' In the central Newcastle parish of All Saints 'rooms [are] very commonly inhabited by eight or ten persons; they are so choked up by the crowded contiguous buildings, that any semblance of a window they may possess is useless, and on entering them some minutes must elapse before the eye can distinguish objects'. The report went on to give detailed figures on overcrowding which showed that figures of 4.25–4.5 persons per room was an average density for houses in All Saints, Newcastle, although 'In the worst part of the parish, however, we have very constantly found from six to eight persons inhabiting one room, and frequently 11 and 12. They all sleep in the same room and the average size of each room is 12 feet by 10, and under 9 feet high.' Even in the less crowded parish of St Andrews, to the north of central Newcastle, population density was 3.5 per room on the north side of Gallowgate. Chadwick told the Social Science Association 'that if "Siva the Destroyer" were to require it, we could certainly build a city in which we could ensure a death rate of 40 per 1,000, or far more than double the general mortality of the country. For that purpose we should copy liberally and closely the old parts of Whitehaven, those of Newcastle-upon-Tyne, and the wynds of Glasgow and of Edinburgh.'[13]

Of course other towns could show housing and overcrowding conditions which were equal to the worst which could be shown by Newcastle or Gateshead but not the widespread problem which was apparent in the latter. It is noticeable that Chadwick chose four old-established towns and not the newer ones which had expanded because of industrialisation, which again points to the long-estab-

---

[12]   D. B. Reid, *Report on the State of Newcastle upon Tyne and Other Towns* (1845), p. 89.
[13]   E. Chadwick, 'Address on Health', *Transactions of the National Association for the Promotion of Social Science*, Aberdeen Meeting 1877 (1878), p. 100.

lished nature of the problem in the north-east. It is, therefore, fortunate that the region's population growth came not in the eighteenth
century but in the slightly more enlightened and socially aware conditions from the second quarter of the nineteenth century onwards.
Earlier population expansion, housed to established standards of
accommodation with more primitive building and sanitation techniques, would have produced even more deplorable conditions. As
it was there is some evidence to suggest an overall improvement in
density of housing occupation in the region in the first half of the
nineteenth century. Too much attention should not be paid to the
statistics, which may only reflect changing definition of what was
a separate dwelling, but the 1851 census shows that Durham had
an average of 6.0 persons per occupied house and Northumberland
6.3. These figures were well below that for Middlesex (heavily dominated by London) of 7.9 but similar to that for Surrey (again affected
by London) of 6.3 and they were above the figure for any other
county. While the densities per occupied house were falling, even
for the major towns, they were still very high by national standards.
Between 1821 and 1861 Newcastle's figure fell from 8.4 to 7.8 but
in the latter year it was the highest figure for any provincial town
in England and Wales.

It can, therefore, be shown that overcrowding did not worsen during
the population and industrial growth of the first half of the nineteenth
century. Indeed it seems clear that the heterogeneous collection of
individuals and firms which made up the construction industry
managed to cope with population growth. Housing output responded
with very little lag to population growth and the censuses show many
instances in which, measuring between decadal points, rates of
growth of population and housing stock were very similar. This was
most obvious with regard to colliery villages, of which two examples
from the east Durham coalfield will suffice (see Table 6.1). For the
major towns the correlation is less remarkable but still significant (see
Table 6.2).

Population growth and the building of housing are, of course, flows,
while the censuses only enable us to observe the stock of population
and housing at decadal intervals. Undoubtedly there were, at particular points in time, discrepancies between the two with housing showing a lagged response to population growth. As a result of a sudden
growth of population in a particular community overcrowding conditions would worsen temporarily but the broad picture over time

Table 6.1 *Population and housing stock in two east Durham colliery villages, 1831–81: rates of increase (percentage) by decade*

	1831–41	1841–51	1851–61	1861–71	1871–81
Thornley					
Population	5,460	0.4	20.7	−7.5	2.4
Housing stock	5,856	1.1	19.7	1.4	11.4
Wingate					
Population	2,283	−6.4	−12.7	44.8	91.7
Housing stock	2,241	7.3	−3.4	37.4	80.8

Table 6.2 *Population and housing stock in Newcastle and Sunderland, 1811–71: rates of increase (percentage) by decade*

	1811–21	1821–31	1831–41	1841–51	1851–61	1861–71
Sunderland						
Population	23.1	28.5	30.9	24.8	25.2	22.7
Housing stock	11.7	28.0	38.7	18.7	29.4	22.8
Newcastle						
Population	28.3	28.3	63.7*		24.3	17.7
Housing stock	28.7	38.4	54.4*		33.9	17.7

* The 1841 figure for housing stock for the Tyneside towns is known to be inaccurate and comparison is therefore made between 1831 and 1851.

is one of fairly consistent provision of housing. There were, however, places where there was a considerable deterioration, usually as a result of industrial and urban development in a new area. On Tyneside, for instance, Jarrow's population had been between 3,000 and 4,000 in the period from 1811 to 1851 with a density of population per house ranging from 4.9 to 5.8. From the early 1850s population began to rise rapidly and reached 60,000 by 1901, under the stimulus of the growth of Palmer's works, and between 1861 and 1901 the density figures ranged from 7.1 to 8.1.

In the second half of the nineteenth century the building of new industrial communities tended to maintain overcrowding at a high level, while the populations of older communities expanded to already accepted standards. There were, however, modifications to the old pattern. First, the number of rooms to the average dwelling began to increase. Whereas one or two had been the norm at the beginning of the nineteenth century, the new building after the middle of the century would normally have been of two or three rooms per dwelling. Significantly, perhaps, the change came as a growing proportion of the region's dwellings were structurally separate (if terraced) houses, as against the old tenements. It was less easy to divide a two- or three-roomed cottage into dwellings for more than one family than it had been with older, larger houses. With this development there came the evolution of distinctive housing styles, especially the Tyneside flat but also the single-storied, terraced cottage which appeared in mining villages but especially in Sunderland. Little is known about the reasons for the evolution of regional housing types and no confident explanation can be offered.[14] The single-storied cottage was probably a cheap way of providing a minimum amount of space. It obviously had a long history in the region but had evolved by the second half of the nineteenth century from a single room, the traditional agricultural and mining pattern, to two side-by-side and often a kitchen behind. A further derivation, very common in colliery communities, had been for the unceiled loft above the single room to be converted into sleeping quarters with ladder access, the height of subsequent cottages to be increased to give two full rooms, one-up-one-down and then further expansion to three or four rooms.

The most distinctive house style was, however, the Tyneside flat, beginning to emerge from the 1850s. The name tends to localise the style to too great an extent, since it was also used in Sunderland and West Hartlepool (and even spread to parts of London, although there the flats often had rear gardens to which the upper flat had no access). The Tyneside flat was divided horizontally, with ground and first-floor flats, the upper flat having access to the back yard via a staircase. Initial examples tended to have two rooms in each flat but in later ones there were three rooms in the upstairs flat (the extra one being partially created in the space over the stairs). The Tyneside flat therefore followed the contemporary norm in terms of the amount of space it offered. It is commonly argued that the form it took was a result of high land costs and, therefore, the necessity to house as many people in as limited a space as possible in order to keep rents at a reasonable level. Too little is known to be certain but it seems unlikely that land costs could have been a sufficiently large proportion of total costs of housing to have had such an influence. In addition

---

[14] The overall position is outlined very clearly and the pattern of the north-east discussed in S. Muthesius, *The English Terraced House* (1982).

other factors make the land-cost explanation seem doubtful. The Tyneside flat developed just at the time when house-building on Tyneside was beginning to develop away from the old urban centres and the flats were most common on the fringes of Gateshead, Newcastle, South Shields and so on, where land was presumably cheaper. Secondly, the Tyneside flat was a reversion from the larger houses, divided into tenements, which had been built on presumably more expensive land nearer the centres in the first half of the century. Thirdly, the Tyneside flat existed in Sunderland where single-storied cottages were also built and it is difficult to argue that cost of land was an important factor in such circumstances.

It seems most likely that the Tyneside flat was a response to the need to improve local housing standards, perhaps within the constraints of relatively high-cost land. In this light the flat would be seen as giving larger accommodation than was previously available for many and with the advantage of a self-contained dwelling in place of a tenement. The lack of garden space (and therefore external play area) would obviously be a result of the fact that the earlier tenemented dwellings had given the area no experience of the use or benefits of gardens. Subsequent flat-building followed the pattern of improvement of housing standards with the evolution of a norm of three- and four-roomed flats by the end of the century. This began to ease the overcrowding problems in the major city areas, although only slowly since the smaller, older dwellings remained a large proportion of total stock.

While the increase in number of rooms per dwelling was the first modification to the regional housing and overcrowding problem in the second half of the century, the second was the markedly different pattern which developed in the southern part of the region. While the existing towns such as Stockton and Darlington had the advantage of being small, both they in their nineteenth-century growth and the new towns of Middlesbrough and West Hartlepool managed to house their increasing populations at much lower densities per house than were the norm in the Tyneside and Wearside towns. Darlington had densities of between 6.0 and 6.5 from 1811 to 1851 and below 5.0 by 1900; Stockton had densities below 6.0 throughout the century; and West Hartlepool's only rose a little above 6.0 in two rapid periods of population growth in the 1840s and 1860s. By contrast in 1901 the Tyneside towns varied in densities from 7.5 per house at Hebburn to 8.3 at Wallsend.

Local expectations of housing provision were obviously different in the southern part of County Durham, right from the beginning of the nineteenth century, and these affected the housing which was built even in the rapidly expanding towns. Housing conditions and overcrowding for the Middlesbrough iron and steel workers may have been poor, as Lady Bell showed, but they were still considerably better than in the older parts of the region. And this is a distinction which becomes dramatically clear when we have detailed figures for overcrowding collected from the 1891 census onwards. This was a culmination of a considerable outcry about the conditions of working-class housing on a national scale, which had led to the posing in the census of a question to determine the proportion of the population living at a density of greater than two persons per room. The results confirmed that the north-east had levels of overcrowding which were horrifically worse than any other area: 34 per cent of the population of County Durham and 38 per cent of that of Northumberland living at densities greater than two per room, while the next worse was London which averaged just under 20 per cent. In the next two decades there was improvement and in 1911 the figures were 28.7 per cent for Northumberland and 28.5 per cent for County Durham. While those figures were surprising it was the similarities and differences within the region which were fascinating. First, the distinction between south Durham and the rest of the region was confirmed. In 1911 Barnard Castle (14.8 per cent), Bishop Auckland (18.1 per cent), Darlington (12.8 per cent), Shildon (15.9 per cent), Stockton (10.9 per cent) and West Hartlepool (16.7 per cent) may be simply picked from the list of Durham communities because they were the only places with overcrowding below 20 per cent of their populations. That they had around one half of the regional level of overcrowding points to their distinct experience in housing terms. The second conclusion to which the statistics lead is that for the remainder of the region (other than south Durham) overcrowding levels were generally high. There is no evidence that urban areas had higher levels than rural areas nor that large towns had higher levels than small towns, indeed some of the highest levels in Durham were in small mining communities such as Annfield Plain and Leadgate where small working-class houses made up nearly the whole of the housing stock. Overcrowding was clearly endemic throughout Northumberland and most of County Durham as a result of low expectations. In Northumberland in a market town such as Morpeth, 15 miles north of Tyneside, the level in 1911 was 32.9 per cent as compared with the nearby mining town of Ashington at 32.2 per cent, the small port of Amble at 32.6 per cent, the agricultural village of Belford at 31.3 per cent and the regional metropolis of Newcastle at 31.6 per cent. Of course, those examples have been chosen to highlight the point that communities of totally different size and industrial structure had virtually identical overcrowding problems and it is possible to select areas where the problem was less (or more) marked. Already by the evidence from the 1891 census it is clear that the problem was caused by the large number of dwellings composed of very few rooms. In Glendale, in the rural north of Northumberland, there were, in 1891, 88 dwellings of only one or two rooms, each containing nine or more occupants, while at the other end of the region there were 495 such dwellings in Newcastle. When it is remembered that dwellings of one or two rooms needed respectively only more than two or four and not nine occupants to be classified as overcrowded, the extent of the problem may be imagined. In Northumberland in 1891 dwellings of only one or two rooms comprised 46.3 per cent of the total stock.

In 1901, 77.4 per cent of Durham's and 77.8 per cent of Northumberland's housing stock was of less than five rooms, while the figure for the next worst county, Lancashire, was 49.5 per cent. The figures for the proportion of dwellings of any particular size which were overcrowded show much higher figures for the north-east for dwellings of one to four rooms than any other area, pointing to the fact that the widespread provision of small houses was the cause of overcrowding. The 1921 census, for instance, showed that 538 per 1,000 of Northumberland's housing stock were of only one to three rooms and 458 of County Durham's, while the next highest level for a county in England and Wales was 340 for the West Riding of Yorkshire, followed by 252 for Cumberland.

Growing social concern and the availability of evidence such as that brought forward by the censuses led to a series of social enquiries which further elucidated the problem. This was part of a national movement which included Booth's work on London and Rowntree's on York and in it the north-east figured to only a limited extent. Almost certainly the pre-1914 prosperity of the heavy industries led to the assumption that all was well while the underlying evidence points to the continuation of relative deprivation. It was not until heavy unemployment set in in the interwar years that social investigators paid serious attention to the region and then there were excellent surveys of Tyneside by Mess and Goodfellow,[15] the latter noting that 'Tyneside in the past has suffered from false prosperity . . . High wages did not mean plenty.'[16] The investigators continued to stress the impressive levels of overcrowding, drawing their evidence from each successive census which showed absolute improvement but the continued pre-eminence of the north-east relative to other regions. Mess noted that 'Tyneside homes are exceptionally small'[17] and pointed out that in 1921 the towns of Gateshead, Newcastle, Tynemouth and South Shields had more than 10 per cent of their families living in only one room (against an average for England and Wales of 3.6 per cent) and more than 25 per cent living in only two rooms (England and Wales 10.5 per cent). Conversely, less than 20 per cent of families occupied five or more rooms (against an average for England and Wales of 46 per cent). Tyneside averaged in 1921 an overcrowding level (at greater than two persons per room) of 34.9 per cent of its population, while the worst level in the rest of the country was in two London boroughs, Finsbury and Shoreditch, where 30 per cent was exceeded. At Hebburn (which significantly had the largest proportion of one- and two-roomed dwellings) the region's worst overcrowding level was 46.9 per cent against an average for England and Wales of 9.6 per cent.

Disparities of that order could not be expected to disappear, especially in the depressed years of the interwar period when local authorities in the north-east were among the most hard-pressed in terms of available financial resources and when much of the population was in no position to pay for improved accommodation. Slum clearance did a little to remove the worst of the problem by eliminating many of the old one- and two-roomed tenements in central areas. In addition, probably for the first time, new building, both council and private (which even in the north-east accounted for the majority of all houses constructed in the interwar years), was done to a standard of accommodation similar to that in the rest of the country. The stock of small, old dwellings continued to dominate the situation, however, especially in the large towns which were not experiencing much new building because of stagnation in population size. In a national overcrowding survey published in 1936 north-eastern towns filled the first

[15] H. A. Mess, *Industrial Tyneside* (1928), and D. M. Goodfellow, *Tyneside: The Social Facts* (Newcastle upon Tyne, 1940).
[16] Goodfellow, *Tyneside: The Social Facts*, pp. 18–19.
[17] Mess, *Industrial Tyneside*, p. 77.

six places in a list of the towns with the highest overcrowding levels.[18] Statistical analysis of the figures given in the survey shows that there was only marginal difference between the north-eastern towns and others with regard to distribution of families by size, while far more small families were living in overcrowded conditions in the north-east than elsewhere, pointing conclusively to the significance of house size in causing overcrowding. Similarly the 1951 census showed Gateshead top of a list of 157 large towns in a number of important categories – the number of dwellings of only one to three rooms, density of persons per room, number of overcrowded households, and number of households with more than 1.5 persons per room.[19]

Even in the 1980s the hangover of late nineteenth-century housing still means that provision in much of the region is below the national average in terms of space per dwelling. That many such houses have lasted for a century and in recent years have justified modernisation rather than demolition, does, however, point to their essentially sound quality of construction. Indeed in the 1980s they may, at last, have found their true *métier*, fitting modern family size without causing overcrowding.

Although the region has always had an unusually high proportion of its population in the working classes, for whom tenement dwellings and small houses were the norm, it would be unreasonable to leave the impression that these were the only form of accommodation in the region. By the middle of the eighteenth century both Tyneside and Wearside had well-established merchant and commercial communities, the middle-class members of which could afford housing of high quality. Initially they had lived in the medieval town centres but growing wealth enabled them, and the problems of growing city centre population persuaded them, to move further afield. Large Georgian terraced houses with gardens behind were built on new streets radiating from the old centres, subsequently in the nineteenth century to be converted and then demolished for the purpose of retailing. As the wealthy population spread further afield to maintain its exclusiveness new middle-class terraces were built in the early nineteenth century and onwards, catering also for the rising numbers of

---

[18] Ministry of Health, *Report on the Overcrowding Survey in England and Wales* (1936), p. xvii.
[19] N. McCord and D. J. Rowe, 'Industrialisation and Urban Growth in North-East England', *International Review of Social History*, 22 (1977), p. 62.

businessmen. Newcastle, in particular, went in for such terraces of large, refined but identical houses – homes for professional men, small industrialists, merchants and so on. Frequently these provided the first stage in upward social mobility, to be followed perhaps by a villa in Low Fell, south of Gateshead and then (if fortune continued to smile) by a modest country house with twenty or thirty rooms and a few hundred acres of land.

The country house was an area of accommodation in which the region and especially Northumberland was well supplied (many have now experienced conversion for use as schools, restaurants and offices, as a result of the inevitable shortages and high cost of domestic staff). The region's landowners had the inevitable supply of large houses (showing the fascinating influence of border warfare and its decline in their gradual conversion from fortress, to house-cum-fortress to purely domestic architecture). The largest included houses outstanding by national standards such as Alnwick, Chipchase, Raby and Lumley Castles. But it was less the houses of the old-established landowners than those of the newly developing ones which gave the region such an impressive collection. From early in the eighteenth century, gathering strength during that century and coming to full flower in the first three-quarters of the nineteenth century, there was a massive phase of country-house building based on industrial and commercial wealth. Tyneside merchants, like the Ridleys who built Blagdon, coalowners, like C. W. Bigge who built Linden Hall, and industrialists, like Isaac Cookson and William Cuthbert who built respectively Meldon Hall and Beaufront Castle, all contributed to this efflorescence. Its apotheosis was seen in Cragside, the house built for Sir William Armstrong on a remote, rock and moorland estate near Rothbury. But Cragside (like the earlier modifications to Alnwick Castle) was the work of a London architect, while most of the country-house designs were home-grown. Simple, classical work was inaugurated by Sir Charles Monck in his own Belsay Hall and then in Linden Hall jointly with John Dobson, the doyen of Northumberland architects, whose work in a variety of styles was to provide for the aspirations of many of the industrially rich during the first half of the nineteenth century.

The contrast between the housing of industrialists and of their workers is always startling but it is perhaps more than unusually so in the nineteenth-century north-east. It is also remarkable in that, although the rich and poor had always had accommodation differentiated by their respective wealths, they had in the past not been separated spatially. The managing partner of the Elswick Lead Works near Newcastle, for instance, lived in a house (albeit a very spacious one) in the works until the early nineteenth century, adjacent to the cottages built for his strategic workers. Social pressures and perhaps improving transport facilities meant that this kind of propinquity became much less common as the century progressed.

One final point might be made about housing and that is the relative shortage of middle-class housing in much of the region – one of the great complaints of the business executive of the second half of the twentieth century condemned to a stint in a regional office. There are a number of reasons for this shortage. Prime among them must be the fact that in the nineteenth-century formative period of the housing stock there was a low proportion of professional and higher managerial personnel in the region's population, while the depression of the interwar years, when commuter housing really became important elsewhere, made the region even less attractive to such people. That many of the villages on the edges of the major built-up areas were colliery communities made it difficult to establish middle-class commuter areas based on old agricultural centres. It is noticeable that Newcastle's one significant middle-class commuter village, Ponteland, is to the north-west of the town, off the coalfield. To a great extent, therefore, middle-class housing was dependent on the large terraces of the Victorian and Edwardian years, frequently garden-less, which often did not appeal to the modern businessmen. Lack of 'executive' type house-building in the years before 1939 left the region with an obvious inadequacy which was to prove costly in the third quarter of the twentieth century in terms of failure to attract the more dynamic entrepreneurs to the area. The pattern of housing outlined above has also left the region with a different ownership structure from the national picture. In 1976 the northern region had the lowest level of owner-occupancy (45 per cent) in England (whose average was 55 per cent) and conversely the highest level of local authority housing provision (40 per cent) against an English average of 29 per cent. Although this structure resulted from attempts by local authorities since the 1920s to deal with the previous deprivation in regional housing provision, it does, of course, point to the continuation of a different form of deprivation since owner-occupiers receive higher housing subsidies (through mortgage interest relief) and social status than do council house occupants.

Health

The state of public health is affected to a considerable extent by the home environment, and since a large proportion of the region's population has always lived in housing which was inadequate in terms of space, it cannot be wondered at that it experienced high levels of mortality from those epidemic diseases associated with poor living conditions.

From the beginning of the nineteenth century contemporary social investigators commented on the appalling housing conditions and their likely impact on health, especially on Tyneside where the worst conditions were most widespread.[20] Newcastle's Medical Officer of Health, in writing a survey of the town's sanitary history up to 1881, quoted an account written in 1804:

It is impossible to give a proper representation of the wretched state of many of the habitations of the indigent, situated in the confined lanes from the Quay-side, Castle Garth, and Sandgate, which are kept in a most filthy state, and, to a stranger, would appear inimical to the existence of human beings; where each small unventilated apartment of the house contains a family, with lodgers, in number from five to seven, and seldom more than two beds for the whole.[21]

Such conditions must have led to very high urban death rates, but with low concentrations of urban population and slow population growth rates before 1800, the problem was not particularly serious. Northumberland, in particular, had very low death rates (reflecting its basically rural character) in the period up to the early nineteenth century. It was with population growth and concentration on the major riverside towns that the problems really came. Newcastle's death rate in the years 1841–7 averaged 25.7 per 1,000, sufficiently high to justify intervention by the General Board of Health to set up a Local Board under the 1848 Public Health Act. The strong opposition among local ratepayers and members of the town council to any unnecessary expenditure on social conditions made it clear, however, that intervention under the Act would have been pointless. It is noticeable that towns such as Newcastle and Sunderland suffered severely from the various cholera epidemics. Newcastle experienced 322 deaths from cholera in 1831–2, 412 in 1848 and no fewer than 1,533 in 1853 (ironically the higher number in the latter year being

[20] See J. Smith, 'Public Health on Tyneside 1850–80', in McCord, *Essays in Tyneside Labour History*, pp. 25–46.

[21] H. E. Armstrong, 'Sketch of the Sanitary History of Newcastle-upon-Tyne', *Transactions of the Sanitary Institute of Great Britain*, 4 (1883), p. 84.

partly caused by the recent introduction of a more widespread water supply, partly drawn from the Tyne close to the town). Deaths from cholera were, however, a mere pimple on the mountain of death but the serious impact of the disease in the region's main towns pointed to major problems in public health.

Small dwellings in an agricultural community or in a market town might be acceptable (although their occupants would still be subject to all the social tensions brought by overcrowding), but heaped together in a large town they brought almost intolerable problems. One of the most obvious was sanitation, or rather the lack of it. Sanitary reports up to the middle of the nineteenth century contain horrific accounts of the problems attached to the disposal of human excrement and even worse of the problems caused by the frequent failure to dispose of it. In one of the old streets of Gateshead, Pipewellgate, where the houses had been converted into tenement buildings for the poorer classes, there were in 1843 only three privies although the total population was over 2,000. Mortality in such areas was much above the average for the town.

Despite the overwhelming evidence of insanitary conditions provided by the various enquiries of the 1840s, very little was done in any attempt to improve the situation. Symptomatic of the lack of concern was the failure of either Newcastle or Gateshead to appoint a Medical Officer of Health until 1873 (and even then the latter town's appointment was only of a part-time employee) and South Shields not until 1875, a step which Liverpool had taken in 1845. There was some attempt by most towns to extend local bye-laws to provide the means of control over such matters as new building and public nuisances but little was done which would have any serious effect on the urban environment. There was no significant attempt by any of the local authorities in the region to build accommodation for the working classes under the various enabling acts of the later nineteenth century. Indeed in Newcastle there was strong opposition in the local council to such activity. Of the £4m borrowed nationally between 1891 and 1904 from central government under the 1890 Housing of the Working Classes Act, Newcastle borrowed £5,761 while even Alnwick borrowed £23,000.[22] Even in the obvious areas which had been widely condemned, such as the provision of privy middens, many towns continued to allow their construction for new housing

[22] E. R. Dewsnup, *The Housing Problem in England* (Manchester, 1907), pp. 173–85.

in the third quarter of the nineteenth century. They presented enormous problems of spread of disease through their use by large numbers of persons, while they were infrequently cleaned out and provided an effective breeding ground for disease. In Middlesbrough in 1869 no fewer than 94 per cent of houses had privy middens, the last of which was not abolished until 1914. Although the provision of water closets began to gain ground and was strongly favoured by health reformers, ash closets continued to be built up to the end of the century because they were cheaper. Again the risk of contamination and spread of disease was higher than with water closets and at the beginning of the twentieth century the region's urban areas faced a huge conversion problem. In 1912 there were 15,000 dry closets in Middlesbrough which had a total of 23,000 houses, while Liverpool by that time had largely moved to water-borne sanitation. The back lane, a standard feature of housing in the region, largely necessitated for the emptying of ash closets, was, and is, largely a waste of space which might have been devoted to gardens. It might be said that it provided space and light, previously missing in the older tenemented accommodation, and provided a play area for children. Clearly, however, back lanes were insalubrious places. The Medical Officer of Health for Gateshead commented in 1925 on those areas which had recently been converted to water carriage, that there were 'generally cleaner yards, fewer flies, cleaner back streets, with absence of the unsightly liquid faeces oozing from the closet doors and with it a purer atmosphere'.[23] In 1920 Gateshead had only 6,000 water closets for 27,000 tenancies and only commenced the major campaign to eliminate dry closets in the mid-1920s because of the availability of government grants. Some local authorities, such as South Shields, were even slower than Gateshead to undertake conversion schemes, while the smaller urban areas had large numbers of dry closets in the 1930s.

The north-east's unenviable position with regard to sanitation was repeated in many other areas of social characteristics and the improvements to the housing stock in the interwar years still left its inhabitants in a state of relative deprivation, since other regions did not stand still while the north-east caught up. Even though every house in Middlesbrough was said to have a water closet in 1945, some 50 per cent of them were outside the house, while 50 per cent of

[23] Quoted in Mess, *Industrial Tyneside*, p. 96.

Middlesbrough's houses were without a fixed bath, and in the old working-class wards, such as Cannon and Newport, it was 90 per cent or more while in largely middle-class Linthorpe it was only 9 per cent. In the years 1935–9 Middlesbrough's infant mortality rate had averaged 74.4 per 1,000, the second highest rate of any county borough in the country.

By the interwar years the statistics on public health are reasonably accurate and well documented and there was a wide range of interest in their perusal but, although documentation is less good for the nine-teenth century, enough has been suggested to show that the region could not expect an average standard of health. It is certain that death rates rose in the major urban areas as populations increased in the early part of the nineteenth century. In Newcastle in 1866 the crude death rate was 32.1 per 1,000, the third highest among the large towns of Britain, but Newcastle did not have the problems of huge size and early expansion from which many of the towns suffered. As many contemporary observers noted, Newcastle's problems were of her own making and largely reflected a lack of desire among the middle-class councillors to do anything about them. In the period up to 1914 death rates were consistently above the national average and, more significantly, above the average for large towns. Gateshead's death rate for the years 1881–3 averaged 22.9 against a figure for England and Wales of 19.3 and an average for fifty large towns of 20.2. Newcastle's death rate averaged 28.2 for the years 1867–72, 24.8 for 1874–9 and did not fall consistently below 20 per 1,000 until after 1902, and even then its rate was about two points above the average for seventy-six great towns.

The evidence of the interwar period showed that 'the North-east had one of the worst, if not the worst, health records of any region in England and Wales'[24] and the regional figures were used by the Registrar General to compare with those of the best region, Eastern Rural Districts, and the average for England and Wales. In 1920, for instance, Sunderland's death rate was 16.0 compared with the average of 12.5 for the great towns. In the county boroughs of the north-east male life expectancy at birth in the years 1920–2 was 49.59 years (and male life expectancy at age ten was actually higher at 50.85, reflecting the high infant mortality rates), against a figure of 55.62 years for the average of county boroughs in England and Wales. The average

---

[24]   J Hadfield, *Health in the Industrial North-East* (n.d.), p. 35. The subsequent detail on health in the interwar period is taken from this very useful source.

number of male deaths in the county boroughs of the north-east in the years 1920–2 was 4,810 per annum, whereas the expected number of deaths if the average mortality rates for England and Wales had operated was 3,705. In other words, it might be said that more than 1,000 men died purely because of conditions which were prevalent in the north-east. Of course, that is too simple an analysis since there were many factors involved – some of them linked to other aspects of deprivation in the north-east. One of the reasons for the region's high death rates was the fact that its social structure was skewed, more strongly than the national average, towards the lower social classes with their shorter life expectancy. In 1931 County Durham had 10 per 1,000 of its population in social class I (while Surrey had 56), 70 in class II (Surrey 161) but 313 in class IV (Surrey had 105). Nevertheless, death rates for the higher social classes in the north-east were also above the national average.

While social structure may have had some effect it is difficult to explain the north-east's inferior health record to areas with similar structure, except in terms of absolutely worse environmental conditions. In the years 1920–2 male deaths in the north-east exceeded the national average for county boroughs in a ratio of 1.298 (an excess of nearly 30 per cent more deaths). The next highest level was in the county boroughs of Lancashire and Cheshire where the ratio was 1.256. In urban districts other than county boroughs the picture was the same with the north-east with the highest ratio of deaths to the national average at 1.125 (followed in this case by urban districts in South Wales at 1.098).

The diseases which were most strongly prevalent in the region were those which had a high correlation with environmental factors. Enteric fever and tuberculosis, for instance, had consistently higher attack and fatality rates in the north-east than they had in other regions. Even before 1914 TB rates on Tyneside had been above the national average but the more reliable figures of the interwar years show this to have continued to be true and although the incidence of the disease on Tyneside declined, it did so more rapidly in the country as a whole, leaving the region relatively worse off. In the years 1912–13 Tyneside's rate was 30 per cent above the national average, while from 1935 to 1937 it exceeded the national average by 53 per cent. County Durham had the highest death rates from tuberculosis of any county in England and Wales, with Gateshead and South Shields averaging death rates from the disease some 75 per cent above the national average. In the ten years 1919–28 South Shields was never below the fourth worst position for TB deaths of all county boroughs in England and Wales and was top on four occasions. TB was a disease which was closely correlated with overcrowding, large families and undernourishment and since these were also factors closely linked to infant mortality it is not surprising that the region featured prominently in infant deaths as well. In the years 1920–2 the probability of male deaths during the first year of life was 0.11471 in the north-east against 0.08996 for England and Wales. What is more, although once again the absolute conditions of health were improving, they did so more rapidly in other parts of the country than in the north-east. By the early 1930s the large towns of the north-east had the highest infant mortality rates of twelve groups of large towns in the country, even though they had occupied only fourth highest position in the years 1911–14. For the years 1930–2 the north-east had the highest infant mortality rates in social classes III–V, with the highest figure 130 per cent of the national rate in class V, but for the second year of life the north-east had the highest rates for classes II–V, with the rates ranging from 130 per cent to 155 per cent of their respective class averages for England and Wales.

It would be possible to go on to detail the north-east's unfavourable record for many other diseases compared to the national average and the way they took their toll at all ages and not just among infants. It is much more difficult to be precise about environmental effects on health which did not lead to major disease and death but merely lowered the standard of life in the north-east relative to other regions. A number of references, however, suggest that there were high levels of sickness, low height and weight figures for children and evidence of nutritional deficiency diseases such as rickets and anaemia during the interwar years. Given the fact that smaller proportions of the population of the north-east attended TB clinics than the national average, despite the high regional incidence of the disease, it seems likely that there were fewer facilities for treatment of minor ill-health in the north-east and that its population received less attention for such matters than those in other parts of the country.

There were, of course, major health improvements by the end of the 1930s. The TB death rate fell from almost 2 to only 1 per 1,000 per annum, while infant mortality rates halved between 1900 and the 1930s. These improvements were the result of much increased expenditure on child welfare centres, ante-natal clinics, TB sanatoria, the appointment of midwives, improved sanitation, a considerable extension of hospital facilities, together with many minor developments which included increased dental care, provision of spectacles and meals for needy children and so on. But these were part of national developments and what is important for the regional position is not absolute but relative provision. In the years 1911–13 the average male death rate for South Shields was 134 per cent of the national average, while it was 138 per cent in the years 1930–2; for Sunderland the figures were 128 per cent and 132 per cent; for West Hartlepool 121 per cent and 128 per cent; and for Gateshead 120 per cent and 126 per cent.

Apart from the obvious links between overcrowding and ill-health, the mortality and health statistics of the north-east were strongly affected by the region's industrial structure. Many of the major occupations were among those with the highest health risks. Coal mining and coastal shipping carried particularly high risks of death at work, especially in the eighteenth and nineteenth centuries, while industrial injuries were very prominent in the former. In a period before the introduction of compulsory insurance against industrial injuries, an employee who was temporarily, or even more importantly permanently, incapacitated from work would experience a disastrous decline in already low living standards. Few received significant compensation from employers and it is not surprising that in the mining villages in particular there was strong membership of the friendly societies such as Oddfellows and Foresters. It was not only the obvious industries in which health was damaged, since employment in iron and steel manufacture, in iron foundries, shipbuilding and engineering, as well as the manufacture of chemicals and lead, was also subject to a high level of industrial accidents and to deleterious conditions which provided scope for TB and bronchitis among other diseases. Moreover, in many of these occupations strength and youth were at a premium and older workers experienced lower earnings and, therefore, declining living standards just at the time when their health might be affected by their earlier working conditions. Inevitably, these were factors which were mirrored in all areas where there was a concentration of heavy industry and it is noticeable that although the north-east was prominent among the worst regions with regard to housing provision and mortality rates, its rivals were invariably Lancashire, South Wales and the West Riding of Yorkshire. The north-east's prominence has to be put down to the strong sense of insularity in the region; its unattractive total environment was merely accepted as normal by those who lived and worked in it and was, therefore, not challenged. It needed an influx of outsiders with wider experience and it is noticeable that many of these, especially those concerned with social provision such as doctors, were appalled by what they found in the region. Although many of them worked for change there were too few of them to have any significant impact before the Second World War and, indeed, as they became involved with the north-east they too became insular. They became concerned about absolute improvements in regional conditions and applauded and were often satisfied when these occurred, failing to recognise that the rest of the country was not standing still waiting for the laggards to catch up.

A regional perspective

Many of the general failings of the north-east may, therefore, be regarded as a result of the failure of its leaders to look beyond the regional inheritance of deprivation. For much of the period, of course, this was a result of the existence of an individualist society in which there was neither the institutional means nor the collectivist will among those with power to do anything about the overall environment. This is not to deny that the region had paternalists but merely to state a general fact. As the town environments deteriorated during the nineteenth century the response of the wealthy was to move to more salubrious areas, an option which was not open to the working classes. To move out was to become largely divorced from urban conditions which made it very easy to do nothing about them. The result was that the prosperous years of the late nineteenth century saw little or no attempt at improvement at a time when a town such as Birmingham, under determined leadership, showed that improvement was possible. By the interwar period, when improvement became a nationally accepted theme, the north-east was hardly in the financial position to cope with the general trends of the time let alone eliminate past deprivation.

Many of the people who had made money out of the region's industrial growth had taken it out of the region to live in more favourable climes, while such prosperity as remained existed in pockets isolated from the general depression. This pattern had existed for some time with Gateshead, for instance, being jealous of the fact that many

profitable businesses paid rates to Newcastle while their poor
employees lived in Gateshead in premises of low rateable value. But
the question of rate income became crucial in the interwar years as
both needs and the desire to meet them increased in the poorer areas.
The small, poor authorities such as Jarrow, Hebburn and Wallsend
on Tyneside suffered from low rateable values and therefore low
income. Of the 9,298 occupied persons in Hebburn in 1921, 'Only
44 persons engaged in industry returned themselves in the categories
of employer, owner, agent, or manager . . . there were eleven clergymen and five doctors, but there was no dentist, no solicitor, no barris-
ter, no accountant, no journalist, no social welfare worker . . . no one
over the age of 18 enumerated as a student.'[25] Of neighbouring Jarrow
one commentator wrote at the end of the 1930s:

> It must be one of the strongest manifestations of 19th century civilisation
> that business men were able to construct districts such as Jarrow, themselves
> to live in another town, and then to leave the people of Jarrow to overcome
> typhoid and tuberculosis as best they could on their tiny resources while
> the profits were being spent elsewhere.[26]

The missing middle-class residents frequently lived in Gosforth or
Whitley Bay, where the incidence of overcrowding was more like 3
per cent than 30 per cent, communities which were anxious to maintain their independence and not contribute to the upkeep of the poor
in neighbouring communities. Indeed, Tyneside was one of the worst
examples of class enclaves with resultant massive inefficiency. There
were no fewer than fourteen local authorities on Tyneside in the interwar years responsible for the provision of many social benefits but
with greatly varying resources with which to provide them. As a
result, birth or residence on one or another side of an artificial boundary had a dramatic impact on life expectancy, education provision
and many other services. The discrepancies led to many demands
for a unified Tyneside – 'If a civic conscience is ever to be developed,
the fact must be faced that Newcastle, Gosforth, and Whitley Bay
and Monkseaton must enter a unified Tyneside and give it the benefit
of their rateable value'[27] – but despite the setting up of a Royal Commission on the subject in the 1930s nothing was done.

Naked self-interest may have been an important factor in creating
the industrial prosperity of the late nineteenth century, but it was

[25] Mess, *Industrial Tyneside*, pp. 167–8.
[26] Goodfellow, *Tyneside: The Social Facts*, p. 69.
[27] *Ibid.*, p. 67.

certainly a barrier to dealing with the legacy of industrial depression. But it was not only a failure to unite to deal with the problems – there was a considerable lack of initiative. In 1928 Mess wrote: 'At Gateshead and elsewhere the ruins of buildings stick out as unsightly stumps along the slope of the cliff. These slopes, unsuitable for modern buildings of any kind, might in some cases be planted with bushes, and be converted into hanging parks, with zig-zag paths.'[28] For a long time nothing was done and more than fifty years later some of the areas of river bank are still an eyesore. To take another example, the Town Moor at Newcastle was (and is) used for one week a year for the 'Hoppings' but, at the cost of dispossessing the freemen of their grazing rights, an imaginative use could have been provided by its development as a permanent pleasure and leisure ground. While the terraces of Scotswood had no play areas, Newcastle had the highest ratio of open space to built-up area of any large town – but the use made of the largest area of open space was trivial.

Although they did not apply themselves to improvement of the regional environment it would not do to end this survey without saying something of the people of the region and their activities. First, it is important to draw attention to the impressive stream of invention and innovation which came from individuals in the region – initially from natives but frequently from the middle of the nineteenth century from immigrants as the prosperity of industrial growth acted as a mecca for the dynamic entrepreneur. In agriculture, John Rastrick's thresher, John Common's reaper and the stock-breeding improvements made by the brothers Culley and Colling stand out among the features which made the region significant by the mid-nineteenth century. In industry there were many who made major contributions to knowledge and productive techniques ranging from the well known, such as the Stephensons in railways, Armstrong and Palmer in shipbuilding and engineering, Charles Parsons in marine and turbine engineering and Joseph Swan in electricity, through the slightly known, such as J. W. Isherwood in ship design, to the hardly known, such as Edward Chapman, inventor of the ropemaking machine and John Walker of Stockton, inventor of the friction match. It is difficult to measure a region's inventiveness but during its nineteenth-century expansion those mentioned and many others gave the region a claim to have made a contribution of greater significance

---

[28] Mess, *Industrial Tyneside*, p. 97.

than might have been expected by its size. Many of the men who made noticeable contributions to inventiveness also developed their ideas and created employment opportunities and prosperity. In this area they were joined by numerous entrepreneurs who offered little in the way of new ideas but who had the ability to use the ideas of others to create industrial enterprises. From their efforts resulted the huge iron and steel firms of Teesside and the shipbuilding yards on all three rivers. There were also major contributions in cultural areas. Tyneside was the home of a number of nineteenth-century painters of distinction, among them Carmichael, Perlee Parker, the Richardsons and John Martin, whose works are now collectors' items, while Dobson and others not only bespattered the region with elegant country houses but also designed for Newcastle the finest centre of any industrial city.

What happened to these veins of innovation and entrepreneurial ability after the First World War? It would be pointless and untrue to say that they dried up, for there have obviously been many new ideas produced and successful businessmen established in the region since that time. Nevertheless, it is clear that the north-east has in the last fifty years or so been less dynamic than in her earlier history. Perhaps the depression of the region and the attraction of other areas (especially London and the south-east) has led to the departure of some of the most innovative. It is not difficult to find examples. Isherwood took his ship design ideas to London to develop his practice in naval architecture and Percival Hunting also took his interests in aircraft and petroleum there, from which the Hunting Group of companies developed. In addition the movement away from individual to corporate enterprise has both reduced the attention society pays to individuals and concentrated the power to shape industrial development on London. The north-east was, therefore, likely to attract only factory development, often in the form of branches of national and increasingly international companies (easily closed or their capacity reduced in time of recession), and not the outstanding inventor or entrepreneur.

For much of the period under consideration it was the major industrialists, together with the old-established landowners, into whose ranks the industrialists had been absorbed by the purchase of country estates, who held power in the north-east. In the towns, commercial and industrial oligarchies ran the corporations during the eighteenth and most of the nineteenth centuries. The creators of industrial enterprises like Palmer at Jarrow and Henry Bolckow and John Vaughan at Middlesbrough were frequently among the first mayors of and MPs for their respective towns. As they moved into landed society, leaving a vacuum frequently filled by tradesmen, many of the industrialists joined the landowners as deputy lieutenants and sheriffs for the counties. The contrast which has been seen between agriculture and industry, the country house and urban terrace affected many aspects of the north-east's history. One of the strongest contrasts within the region lay between the traditional power of the landowners and the Church of England and the growing power of the workingpeople. The contrast was marked between the two counties. Northumberland was traditionally a very conservative and backward county in which the power of the landowners was close to feudal even in the nineteenth century. This might be seen in the Charltons of Hesleyside or the Trevelyans of Wallington, men of considerable significance with regard to any development, such as railways, in their local area. But the most significant of all were the Dukes of Northumberland, whose vast ownership of land, both rural and in urban areas, was one reason why Northumberland was the English county which the 1873 survey showed to have the largest proportion of all its land held in large estates. Through their dominance the large landowners ensured the continuance of a traditional rural society, slowing the break-up of old patterns of behaviour. Nevertheless, change came and Northumberland provided, in Thomas Burt, MP for Morpeth, and later Charles Fenwick (another Northumberland miner and ex-Chartist) some of the first working-class Members of Parliament. Somehow, however, the respect for land in Northumberland has remained, evidenced by the fact that a Lord Ridley of Blagdon, descendant of one of the earliest of Tyneside merchants to move into land, could be chairman of Northumberland County Council in the 1970s. By contrast, in County Durham, although there had been great landed power, not least among the clergy, rising industrialisation brought great change. In the middle of the nineteenth century the rector of Stanhope was reckoned to be richer than many bishops because of the mineral royalties attached to his living and the Earls of Durham and Lords Londonderry had enormous power, political, rural and industrial. But it was County Durham in 1919 which became the first county council in the country to have a majority for the Labour party. The gradual movement away from Liberalism, the great political strength of the coalfield, epitomised by 'the Durham thirteen' of 1874, through the election of 'Lib-Lab' MPs, had culminated in a mood of independence brought by the First World War. As Jack Lawson put it, 'the old social superstition of a superior people who are entitled to a superior life has gone forever'.[29] Inevitably, he exaggerated the change; the attitudes of centuries do not disappear in decades but the future great men of County Durham were to be no longer the industrialists but workingmen, like himself and Peter Lee, who found that society could make use of their talents elsewhere than pit-face, furnace and shop-floor.

The mood which elected pitmen MPs and Labour county councillors came out of a recognition of the community of interests and power of the majority of workingpeople, for it was they who created the society which was (and is) the north-east. We are left with the question 'How far were the people of the north-east and their culture different?', in addition to the differences which have been seen in their environment. It is difficult to write much about the period before the nineteenth century, when population was small and divided by poor communications and about which we know so little. In any event, it is to the nineteenth century, with its growth in population and social awareness, to which we need to look for cultural identity. It is in that period that the 'Geordie' concept originated, relating not merely to Tyneside but more widely to the coalfield. To some extent, however, the coalfield and industrial communities were distinct. The very nature of coal mining and its communities meant greater insularity and closeness than could exist in the much more open and changing industrial communities along the river banks. Once a pit was established there was little change in size of community over many years; the pit was the only source of employment – it dominated life. Houses in pit communities were continually open to other members of the community and privacy was impossible (in small houses it was not even possible within a family). Family life was strong, partly a result of the fact that there were no opportunities for female employment, and homekeeping was a respected activity. Despite the distinctive hours of work, whether on the two- or three-shift system, wife/mother would always be up to see her menfolk off to the pit – 'the old law of the colliery woman' – in case she never saw them again. But the distinctiveness of the colliery village was not just made up of fear, dirt (the first pit-head baths in the region were installed at Boldon

---

[29] Lawson, *A Man's Life*, p. 234.

Colliery in 1927) and cramped living conditions. It consisted in an immense amount of pride in the occupation, the skill and independence of 'the big hewer', and the ethos of the village seen in the glorious pit banners. There was rivalry, often fierce, between villages but there was also the communal spirit of mining seen in 'the big meeting', and annual miners' gala at Durham.

It is difficult to be sure whether there were cultural activities which distinguished the mining from industrial communities, since mining commenced on the industrial river banks and only later set up distinctive, more remote communities. Many of the distinctive features of working-class culture of the north-east were found equally in both areas, although the shorter working hours in mining communities (a distinctive north-eastern feature with only seven hours at the pit-face by the last quarter of the nineteenth century) meant that there was greater time to indulge them. Gardening was a notable feature of colliery villages, where there was the space to develop the activity, but one should not underestimate the extent to which the desire to get back to nature survived in all but the most dense brick jungles such as the Scotswood terraces. Religion was certainly a more distinctive feature of the colliery villages than the larger urban areas. The huge chapels, most especially of the Primitive Methodists, still bear witness to the power of nonconformity in Durham mining villages from the 1820s. The chapel, like early political activity in Chartism, gave many workingmen self-confidence, taught them not to honour other men and gave them opportunities for leadership. Presbyterianism, reflecting the closeness to Scotland, was stronger than the national average, as was Roman Catholicism, which had its second highest proportion of adherents in the region (the highest being Lancashire), only partly a result of Irish immigration. Among other leisure activities dog racing, especially with whippets, appears to have been an essentially mining activity.

In the urban communities there was less distinctive community interest, partly because of their larger size and partly because, with exceptions such as Jarrow and Scotswood, they were dependent on a wider range of occupations. There were, however, many common leisure activities which to some extent bound people of otherwise distinct types. Drinking was perhaps the most obvious. In the period of the highest ever national per capita levels of alcohol consumption in the second half of the nineteenth century, the region made a major contribution to the statistics. Heavy labour, as in many of the regional industries, is usually linked to high alcohol consumption and the level of expenditure on drink was one of the reasons for the failure to raise living standards during a period of prosperity. In 1911 Northumberland was the leading county and Durham was second in the number of convictions for drunkenness per 10,000 population. Other activities were less socially divisive. Rowing was the major spectator sport on Tyneside in the mid-nineteenth century – the Thames being the only other river where the sport was as significant. Rowing was to be eclipsed later in the century by the rise of association football in which both amateur and professional clubs in the region were to play a significant part. Horse racing was a popular spectator sport for workingmen, while pigeon-fancying was a common participatory one. The strength of local song (often in dialect) and the music hall are other features of working-class culture in the region. All of these working-class activities add to a culture which was certainly differentiated from that of the middle classes with their Literary and Philosophical Society at Newcastle, professional societies (such as the North-East Coast Institution of Engineers and Shipbuilders), concert societies, lawn tennis clubs and so on. It is more dubious as to whether it differentiated working-class society from its peers in other parts of the country. It seems more likely that the much-famed 'Geordie' culture is merely a carefully cultivated and preserved myth, like the local accents a mere superficiality in the distinctions which make up mankind.

Such superficialities have begun to break down under the widespread influence of the mass media and mobility in the later twentieth century. Some have cultivated new homes in other regions, others have become less strong in their own home area. The distinctions which remain are in the old area of institutional deprivation. In the interwar period social commentators noted the poor standards of educational provision in the region. In the mid-1920s in public elementary schools in all the county boroughs of England and Wales some 22.5 per cent of children were in classes of over fifty children, while in Newcastle the figure was 46.1 per cent; in Hebburn it was 65.7 per cent while the average for urban districts and metropolitan boroughs was 14.0 per cent. In 1926–7 three of the four Tyneside county boroughs were among the fifteen nationally (out of a total of eighty-two) which spent less than £10 per child on educational provision (while the fourth, Tynemouth, spent only slightly more). In the early 1980s, while expenditure on education compares well with the national average, the years of neglect have built a mould of educational expectation which does not break. Consequently, the 1982 edition of *Regional Trends* shows that the northern region had the lowest proportion of children staying in full-time schooling after the age of sixteen when compulsory education ends. The region's figure of 18.8 per cent of the age group compared with a figure of 26.0 per cent for the UK and 32.0 per cent for the south-east. The region also has the lowest levels of achievement of school leavers at public examinations, the lowest levels of the age group going into full-time further education and even the lowest going into non-advanced further education. A larger proportion of school leavers is therefore limited in its horizons and condemned to a narrow range of job opportunities and so the old expectations of education are reinforced in the next generation – home background being the basic determinant of educational performance. In many other areas the deprivation of the region relative to the national position continues – in the numbers of doctors and dentists per 100,000 of the population, in car ownership and in any one of a wide range of statistical comparisons. The 1982 edition of *Regional Trends* shows that telephone possession (at 52 per cent of houses against a national average of 65 per cent) was lower than in any other region; that there were 5,068 persons per dentist (the highest regional figure) against a national average of 3,725; that 46 per cent of dwellings were owner-occupied (the lowest regional figure) against a national average of 57 per cent; and that unemployment was the highest of any region in Great Britain at 1.3 times the UK average.[30]

Whether such relative deprivation (which mirrors that which is increasingly occurring between Britain and other industrial countries) is important can probably not be answered or even comprehended by the individuals (including the writer) involved. Do they affect the basic human activities of living, loving, hating? Does the risk of spelks mean that making love on a board is less pleasure-giving than on a Dunlopillo mattress?

[30] Regional inequalities are usefully outlined in G. Taylor and N. Ayres, *Born and Bred Unequal* (1969). Central Statistical Office, *Regional Trends* (1982), Tables 3.3, 4.9, 6.3, 7.6 and 9.5.

CHAPTER 7

London and the Home Counties

P. L. GARSIDE

INTRODUCTION

The reality of London has never been easy to grasp – the character of this vast city has been shrouded in uncertainty and ambiguity and much has depended on the perspective of the observer. Most obviously, there have been the contradictions arising from London's various, overlapping spatial contexts – London has operated and has been experienced at sub-metropolitan, metropolitan, regional, national and international levels. Each of these arenas has generated a particular 'London view' and much of London's history since 1750 can be seen as a series of conflicts arising from the associated interests and tensions. Yet despite its 'chinese box' character, a fundamental feature of London has been its stability and continuity.

The basis of London's orderliness has, paradoxically, been its continued dynamism, driven by a particular type of physical and economic growth that permitted both interdependence and autonomy. The two centuries between 1750 and 1950 can be regarded as the benchmarks of this inherently stable, though expansionist era for London – after 1950, changed economic and political conditions accentuated the fragility of London, forcing previously hidden and unresolved contradictions in metropolitan life to the centre of the social and political stage.

The prism through which London is viewed in what follows is that of the impact of the metropolis on the Home Counties – that is, its expansion from the old core cities of London and Westminster, through Middlesex, and later Surrey, Essex, Kent and Hertfordshire. The nature of that impact, its causes and consequences cannot, however, be comprehensively assessed. While there are important pointers from the new, quantitative economic history, and from old-fashioned political and administrative history, the sheer scale and diversity of the expanding metropolis appears to have daunted, and

471

even defeated, social historians. London history remains a thing of shreds and patches, lacking overall form. As the London giant grew, neither his own clothes nor those fabricated by historians have been quite able to grow with him.

I LONDON: IMPERIAL CAPITAL AND MERCANTILE
STRONGHOLD 1750–1820

> Oh, London is a fine town,
> A very famous city,
> Where all the streets are paved with gold,
> And all the maidens pretty.
>
> George Colman The Younger, *The Heir at Law* (1797)

The mysterious grandeur of London

The distinctiveness and separateness so emphatically displayed by London in the later eighteenth century both enthralled and alarmed contemporary observers. The scale and complexity of London's myriad worlds was generating a highly diverse, intricate yet interdependent way of life. Approaching a population of 1 million in 1801, London was the nation's foremost milieu for court and high society: it provided the seat of government, a mercantile stronghold for traders, financiers and specialist manufacturers, a cradle for new professions as well as the apogee of the old, and the principal national stage for political movements and entertainers alike. London – the unique city – stood apart in its magnificence and variety, distinct both from the rest of Britain's developing urban hierarchy and also from its immediate rural hinterland. In the Midlands and the north the expanding provincial manufacturing centres were establishing a wholly new 'urban frontier', while in the agricultural areas bordering the metropolis, the contrast with London life was particularly stark: indeed, it has recently been argued that the rural unemployment and low wages of Surrey, Kent, Middlesex and Hertfordshire resulted directly from the capital's own immense, but highly specialised demand for goods and services.[1]

Complexity, ambiguity, specialisation and distinctiveness were the

---

[1] P. J. Corfield, *The Impact of English Towns, 1700–1800* (Oxford, 1982), pp. 9–11. K. D. M. Snell, 'Agricultural Seasonal Unemployment, the Standard of Living, and Women's Work in the South and East, 1690–1860', *Economic History Review*, 2nd ser., 34 (1981), pp. 407–37.

hallmarks of late eighteenth- and early nineteenth-century London. The scale, pace and impact of the capital's growth defied description – indeed our understanding of London's significance and wider influence remains even now partial and inconclusive.[2] The need to evaluate the links between London and the changes underway in the surrounding region, and in the nation as a whole, is one of the major themes to be explored in this chapter. The present state of knowledge, however, means that while we know a considerable amount about certain aspects of London life between 1750 and 1820, the processes connecting these with broader metropolitan, regional and national changes remain enigmatic and difficult to grasp. Historians have begun to explore some of these connections in ways which have proved very illuminating, but for the most part this section must serve simply to highlight those elements of the London scene which seem particularly important in establishing the framework for the subsequent discussions of the dynamics of change in Victorian London.

The first part of what follows seeks to identify those aspects of London which had the most significant social and economic impact on surrounding counties and on national life as a whole. The latter part examines more directly the world of London itself, in particular, the complexities of metropolitan social and occupational structure, its built form, public institutions and cultural life.

London and the national economy

The significance of London in the period 1750–1820 obviously needs to be assessed in relation to the kind of place it was, and the experience it afforded to those living there. To *Angliae Nottia* in 1702, London was the epitome of England, the seat of the British Empire, the Chamber of the King, and the greatest Emporium in the whole world. Indeed, London's heterogeneity and multiple sources of growth confounded the classification systems devised by contemporaries to cope with Britain's burgeoning urban network – spa town, dockyard town, manufacturing town, resort, university town, 'thoroughfare town'. As cartographers and publishers of guides and directories strove to identify London's diverse parts, commentators such as Chamberlayne and Defoe conceded that the contiguous but highly varied built-up

---

[2] Corfield emphasises the enigmatic nature of London's role as both 'exemplar and exception', *Impact of English Towns*, p. 66. London provided both a model for provincial towns, and also a unique configuration which none could hope to match.

areas 'seem to make indeed one City' whose 5,000 or so streets and alleys might one day extend from Chelsea to Deptford Bridge 'which if it should happen, what a Monster must London be'.[3]

London eluded attempts to define it through classifications and systems, as it had earlier eluded attempts at physical confinement. Rudé has illustrated, for example, the inadequacy of both 'traditional' and 'realistic' assessments of London's multiplicity of trades and crafts. John Strype, writing in 1720, concentrated solely on those trades still regulated by the old City companies, and recorded a mere sixty. Even the more extended list of a 'General Description of all Trades' published in 1747 limited its conception to the 135 crafts and 80 other occupations which were organised in the 'traditional' way with small master craftsmen, their journeymen and apprentices. In fact, a growing number of London's industries and services either paid mere lip-service to the regulations of the old guilds or ignored them altogether, being organised 'on almost capitalist lines'. Following Dr George, Rudé suggests that London's occupations are best considered in three broad categories: First, trades catering for London's position as national and international market-place and entrepôt – shipbuilding, refining and processing of raw materials especially brewing, distilling, sugar-refining and dyeing. Second, luxury trades providing for the wealthy consumer market in London and abroad – furniture making, coachbuilding, plate, porcelain, watches and other precision instruments. Third, trades common to any urban area serving the city's everyday needs – construction, food and drink manufacturers and retailers, wigmakers, tailors, shoemakers, carriers, and suppliers of professional and personal services. The range, volume and diversity of economic activity in London was of great social significance. The degree of specialisation between and within crafts and other employment groups gave rise to a complex social structure which was reinforced by spatial specialisation even among comparatively petty trades.[4] Technological developments and capitalist organisation distinguished some major industries and especially brewing and food processing, but other sectors were organised in small traditional

---

[3] Quoted in *ibid.*, p. 190.
[4] G. Rudé, *Hanoverian London 1714–1808* (1971), pp. 25–6. L. D. Schwarz, 'Conditions of Life and Work in London c. 1770–1820, with Special Reference to East London' (unpublished DPhil. thesis, University of Oxford, 1976). J. M. Howe, 'Occupations in Bermondsey 1701–3', *Genealogists' Magazine*, 20 (1982). T. R. Forbes, 'Weaver and Cordwainer: Occupations in the Parish of St Giles, London, in 1654–93 and 1729–43', *Guildhall Studies in London History*, 4 (1980). I. T. Prothero, *Artisans and Politics in Early Nineteenth-Century London* (Folkestone, 1979), chap. 2.

workshops, while in the docks, men were employed predominantly on a casual day-to-day basis.[5] One quarter of London's workforce, 20,000 men, are estimated to have been employed in trades connected with London's docks in the early nineteenth century, while the construction industry drew similarly on a vast pool of skilled and unskilled labour. 'London's manufacturing', Schwarz has emphasised, 'catered largely for the local market, which, although very large, was not a mass market in the modern sense'.[6]

London's highly stratified and localised economic structure had the effect of driving some trades out of the city altogether into surrounding areas or even further afield. 'The Metamorphosis of the Port of London' was one example of this effect.[7] In 1700, some 75–80 per cent of all England's overseas trade was handled by the Port of London, and this trade continued to grow through the eighteenth century though London's relative share declined. The Port, however, became increasingly unable to cope and unloading berths moved downstream from the Pool to Limehouse and Millwall. The resulting problems of theft, delay and congestion, with 3,500 craft ferrying goods from these 'sufferance wharfs' to the legal quays, emphasised that London was being by-passed technologically by other ports that could provide secure dock systems. Despite the opposition of the City Corporation, Parliament set up a committee in 1795 to investigate the best means of providing the necessary accommodation, and merchant monopolies subsequently built new docks and warehouses under special Acts of Parliament downstream from the old quays on both sides of the Thames.[8] This 'export' of London functions in an attempt to avoid restrictions and seek out more favourable locations occurred not only in dangerous and noxious trades but also in established trades such as shoemaking and framework knitting: these latter were transferred to Midland towns whilst continuing to serve the London market.[9] By 1820, London seemed poised on the verge of 'a new balanced completeness' but at the same time it required the input of goods

[5] P. Mathias, *The Transformation of England: Essays in the Economic and Social History of England in the Eighteenth Century* (1979), chaps. 11–13. W. L. Goodman, 'Christopher Gabriel, his Book', *Furniture History*, 17 (1981).
[6] L. D. Schwarz, 'Social Class and Social Geography: The Middle Classes in London at the End of the Eighteenth Century', *Social History*, 7 (1982), pp. 167–85.
[7] R. C. Jarvis, 'The Metamorphosis of the Port of London', *London Journal*, 3 (1977).
[8] Corfield, *Impact of English Towns*, p. 71.
[9] P. G. Hall, 'The East London Footwear Industry: An Industrial Quarter in Decline', *East London Papers*, 5 (1962).

and services at an ever-increasing scale to maintain its growth and equilibrium.

The impact of London on the economy as a whole and on local employment markets has been discussed by historians over many decades, yet there is still clearly a great deal to be explored. In many respects, London's commercial and trading links were a force for integration, both at the global scale, and no less at the national scale. As an entrepôt for the resale of colonial goods for home and European consumption, London became a clearing house for the produce of the East and West Indies. Spectral analysis has revealed the integration of London's credit and banking systems with those of Amsterdam, and, indeed, London eventually eclipsed the Dutch capital as Europe's premier money and investment market. At home, a model of London's economic importance 'as a potent engine working towards change in England' has been postulated by Wrigley, while Braudel has used eighteenth-century London as an example of *moyenne durée* in historic time, i.e. a phase of some 50 to 100 years with a distinctive and identifying feature. In this case, the distinguishing feature was the reign of London and its money market, by which unity was created in the British market through 'flux et reflux de merchandises vers et partir de Londres, enorme coeur exigeant qui rythme tout, bouleverse et apaise tout'.[10]

With its population rising from 575,000 in 1700 to 900,000 in 1801, there is no doubt that London required vast supplies of daily necessities, especially food, water and fuel. Attempts to specify the effects of this demand have been made by Fisher and by Wrigley – notably, a rapid spread of market gardening, especially in Surrey, Kent and other suitable areas near to London, increasing local crop specialisation, as, for instance, the conversion of Middlesex to monoculture of hay during the eighteenth century, and the involvement of wholesalers either directly in food production, or indirectly through investment of capital to improve production methods.[11] Wrigley estimates that the resulting annual rise in national agricultural productivity during the period 1650–1750 was of the order of 10 per cent, though

[10]   E. A. Wrigley, 'A Simple Model of London's Importance in Changing English Society and Economy 1650–1750', *Past & Present*, 37 (1967), pp. 44–70. F. Braudel, *Civilisation matérielle, économie et capitalisme, XVe–XVIIIe siècle* (Paris, 1979), p. 465.

[11]   Wrigley, 'A Simple Model of London's Importance'. F. J. Fisher, 'London as an Engine of Growth', in J. S. Bromley and E. H. Kossman, eds., *Britain and the Netherlands* (The Hague, 1971). F. M. L. Thompson, *Hampstead: Building a Borough 1650–1964* (1978). Mathias, *Transformation of England*, chap. 13.

this cannot be attributed solely to London.[12] London's indirect effect, however, must have been significant since its distant consumption market stimulated local secondary and tertiary employment, which in turn created its own demand for food. 'Drovers, carters, badgers, brokers, cattle dealers, corn chandlers, hostlers, innkeepers and the like grew more and more numerous as larger and larger fractions of the year's flocks and crops were consumed at a distance from the areas in which they were produced.'[13]

Nevertheless, the London market for goods was a volatile one, subject to wide seasonal fluctuations following the ebb and flow of society and 'the Season'. Such fluctuations produced adolescent boys in London slums whose growth was so stunted by childhood deprivation that it scarcely matched that of West Indian slaves.[14] Moreover, in the south-east outside London and its immediate environs, Harvey has shown the prevalence of low incomes, and Snell has suggested that there was 'a marked collapse of demand' after 1770 because of a decline in rural family incomes in the Home Counties due to agricultural responses to the London market. Evidence based on the Provisions' Accounts of Kent Poor and Workhouses suggests a rise of 120 per cent in agricultural labourers' living costs between 1790 and 1812.[15] Falling purchasing power led industry to seek out alternative markets in the north and overseas. London itself indirectly assisted this adjustment through its insurance and banking services ensuring 'a sort of natural balance' via the circulation of capital between agriculture, trade and the developing manufacturers of the Midlands and north. Overall, one must agree that the nature and location of 'home demand' 'remains an elusively vague concept' and therefore neat conclusions about London's role are likely to prove premature.[16]

While concluding that 'it is therefore no part of this argument that the growth of London in the century before 1750 was the sole engine of change in the country', Wrigley has argued that demographically,

[12] Wrigley, 'A Simple Model of London's Importance'.

[13] *Ibid.*, p. 229. P. E. Jones, *The Butchers of London* (1976).

[14] R. Floud and K. W. Wachter, 'Poverty and Physical Stature: Evidence on the Standard of Living of London Boys, 1770–1870, *Social Science Journal*, 4 (1982).

[15] A. D. Harvey, 'The Regional Distribution of Incomes in England and Wales, 1803', *Local Historian*, 13 (1979). Snell, 'Agricultural Seasonal Unemployment'.

[16] P. G. M. Dickson, *The Financial Revolution in England: The Story of the Development of Public Credit 1688–1756* (1967). S. R. Cope, 'Bird, Savage and Bird of London, Merchants and Bankers, 1782–1803', *Guildhall Studies in London History*, 4 (1982). On the nature of 'home demand', see N. McKendrick, in N. McKendrick, J. Brewer and J. H. Plumb, *The Birth of a Consumer Society: The Commercialisation of Eighteenth-Century England* (1982).

at least, London's expansion was crucial in engendering 'the magic "take-off" '. He argues that the changes which took place in the agricultural sector, and the failure of the population to increase, 'are closely intertwined with the growth of London, but *not with each other*' (my italics). Without London's growth and the demand it created, 'the absence or slightness of population growth overall . . . might well have inhibited agricultural change'. Wrigley notes that in London the crude death rate was substantially higher than the crude birth rate for most of the eighteenth century, yet the proportion of England's total population living in the capital rose from about 7 per cent in 1650 to about 11 per cent in 1750. Wrigley estimates that net immigration into London in the mid-eighteenth century must have been about 8,000 per annum, representing the natural increase of 2.5 million out of England's total population (outside the capital) of only 5 million. Furthermore, the demographic pull of London appears to have become more concentrated on the extra-metropolitan parts of the Home Counties and the Midlands where a surplus of births over deaths was maintained, while the rest of the country barely held its own in this respect.[17] In the south-east, Snell suggests, women's employment opportunities declined because of men's dominance in arable cultivation: they were drawn instead into domestic service and prostitution in London, a state he describes as 'disguised underemployment' carrying high moral risks even for the 'better sort' of servant girl.[18] Migration to London, therefore, seems to have become more localised though Welsh, Scottish and Irish migrants still came in varying numbers:[19] Wrigley concludes that fully one sixth of the adult population of England must have spent at least part of their lives in the city. More recently, Wareing has argued that the significance of migration to London needs to be re-examined. Drawing on somewhat variable apprenticeship evidence, he argues that the declining distances travelled by apprentices by 1750 reflects a long-term decline in London's function as a training centre. Furthermore, he shows that London was not the ultimate destination for many transients, since it represented for some only a first step towards emigration

[17] Wrigley, 'A Simple Model of London's Importance'. See also A. Redford, *Labour Migration in England, 1800–1850*, 2nd edn (Manchester, 1964), pp. 184–5.
[18] Snell, 'Agricultural Seasonal Unemployment', p. 420. J. R. Gillis, 'Servants, Sexual Relations, and the Risks of Illegitimacy in London, 1801–1900', *Feminist Studies*, 5 (1979).
[19] E. Jones, 'The Welsh in London in the Seventeenth and Eighteenth Centuries', *Welsh History Review*, 10 (1981), pp. 461–79.

to America.[20] One must conclude that in terms of migration patterns and experiences, employment generation or consumer demand, many aspects of London's impact remain elusive, despite historians' recent attempts to address such questions specifically.

The occupational structure of London and the surrounding areas has been a particularly neglected subject partly due to the lack of concise sources. Though parish registers begin to record occupations from the early eighteenth century onwards, the time and effort involved in using these sources to establish employment changes has prevented their systematic exploitation. Indeed, none of London's parishes is represented in the 404 investigated by the Cambridge Group. Schwarz based his study of London's middle class on the 1798 returns of the commissioners for assessed taxes, but the connections between house tax, income and occupation are at best impressionistic, with the exception of shopkeepers. Snell has used evidence from rural settlements to identify some causes of unemployment in the south-east during the eighteenth and early nineteenth centuries, but he recognises that an understanding of the absolute or relative size of the workforce or its constituent parts remains 'beyond the reach of historians'. Even if the picture could be established, the problem of interpretation would remain. Of central importance for historians of London, is the question of how far the changes identified can be attributed to the capital itself. Corfield treats London both as 'exemplar' and 'exception' in her study of the impact of English towns, but this distinction fails to recognise the significance of the disparate nature of towns at *every level*. We are still, therefore, unable to determine the nature of changes in the economic and employment structure of London and the south-east, still less to assess the relative impact of London compared with the spectrum of other towns.

Though systematic understanding is not within our grasp, we cannot doubt that the sheer presence of London dominated the British, European and world scene of 1801. No other capital city could match it for population size, physical extent or economic complexity. Though its share of the national population was no longer increasing at its previous rate, there was no doubting London's continued immense attraction for national and international produce of every kind.

---

[20]   J. Wareing, 'Changes in the Geographical Distribution of the Recruitment of Apprentices to the London Companies 1486–1750', *Journal of Historical Geography*, 6 (1980). J. Wareing, 'Migration to London and Transatlantic Emigration of Indentured Servants, 1683–1775', *Journal of Historical Geography*, 7 (1981).

Paradoxically, however, this huge demand operated partly as a force for market integration and partly for differentiation. It promoted growth in some sectors and decay in others at every scale from London's own core to the surrounding region and beyond. The concept of London as 'an engine' of social and economic change has been modified by the recognition that its impact was differential, even negative, and that in certain respects London acted as a divisive force. While operating overall as a promoter of economic growth, London's local and regional impact was uneven. Its influence on standards of living varied widely – City moguls and suburban farmers and landowners flourished, while some agricultural workers and slum-dwellers suffered severely from shifts in London's demand for goods and services. London's national and international pre-eminence in finance and commerce was being built at considerable cost for certain segments of its own population and that of surrounding counties.

London life

London's national and international role gave a distinctive character to its social structure. In particular, London exhibited a marked concentration of aristocratic and mercantile wealth, increasingly complex gradations among 'the middling sort', and a variety of occupational experiences differentiating 'the working trades'. Rudé estimates that during the eighteenth century London's social pyramid was topped by some 180–300 noble families ranging from 'the ordinary aristocrat' with an estimated annual income of £8,000 to the 'great landed magnates' whose agricultural income alone might reach several times that amount. Beneath these were some several thousand 'gentle families' deriving their wealth from sources similar to the aristocracy – land, trade and inheritance. The income of the City's mercantile and financial bourgeoisie, however, was largely derived from overseas trade and banking, and insurance records have been used to demonstrate that these activities were dominated by a handful of merchants.[21] The conventional view that these City moguls, whose wealth outstripped many aristocratic families, themselves sought landed status has recently been challenged. Rogers has argued that by 1760 London Aldermen had gone beyond this – not merely gracefully welding

---

[21]   Rudé, *Hanoverian London*. L. D. Schwarz and L. J. Jones, 'Wealth, Occupations and Insurance in the Late Eighteenth Century: The Policy Registers of the Sun Fire Office', *Economic History Review*, 2nd ser., 36 (1983), pp. 365–73.

themselves to the 'world of gentility' through marriage, but in the process replacing aristocratic values with a bourgeois and plutocratic ethos. Andrew has challenged this interpretation, arguing that aristocratic exclusiveness in the marriage market remained. Both agree, however, that the tendency for intermarriage between merchants, financiers and gentry had increased by 1800 as polite society became more 'socially ambiguous' and open to all with the necessary credentials.[22]

In contrast to the merchants with overseas interests, London's home traders appear to have been highly stratified. At one extreme, the cheese trade was apparently dominated by a ring of twenty-five merchants, who maintained their position partly through monopoly provision of transport and partly through control of local (especially Cheshire) producers. Bakers, because of the relative costs of their operation were uniformly 'middling', while carpenters and builders operated at various scales, having some rich, large-scale contractors, although, overall, a generally low level of wealth prevailed.[23] The multiplicity of London manufactures and crafts has already been discussed, and further light has been shed on the very varied experiences of shipwrights, coopers, shoemakers, toolmakers and journeymen to supplement Rudé's still valuable generalisations about the character of this 'other' London.[24]

London's physical fabric reflected its diverse social and economic structure, especially in terms of land use and population density. The City of London itself was increasingly given over to offices, warehouses and shops and the City gates were removed after 1760 to prevent hindrance to commercial traffic. Rising ground rents associated with commercial redevelopment encouraged an exodus which affected almost all sections of the population – only tradesmen and the poorest remained concentrated in the overcrowded 'rookeries' of East Smithfield and Moorfields, while others relocated in St Giles,

[22] N. Rogers, 'Money, Land and Lineage: The Big Bourgeoisie of Hanoverian London', *Social History*, 4 (1979). D. T. Andrew, 'Aldermen and Big Bourgeoisie of London Reconsidered', *Social History*, 6 (1981).

[23] W. M. Stern, 'Where, Oh Where, Are the Cheesemongers of London?', *London Journal*, 5 (1979). J. M. Imray, 'The Mercers' Company and East London, 1750–1850', *East London Papers*, 9 (1966). Schwarz and Jones, 'Wealth, Occupations and Insurance'. Jones, *The Butchers of London*.

[24] Prothero, *Artisans and Politics*. P. Hudson and L. Hunter, 'The Autobiography of William Hart, Cooper, 1796–1857: A Respectable Artisan in the Industrial Revolution', *London Journal*, 7 (1981). J. Mansfield, 'John Brown, a Shoemaker in Place's London', *History Workshop Journal*, 8 (1979), pp. 129–36. Goodman, 'Christopher Gabriel'. S. Shipley, 'London Journeymen 1810–30', *Bulletin of the Society for the Study of Labour History*, 36 (1978).

a parish located west of the City and by 1801 the most densely occupied registration district.[25] Though a tendency to social segregation was clear by 1800, it had only occurred to a limited degree. Schwarz has shown that among the 'middling sort' who formed some 25 per cent of London's population, the richest were concentrated in three Westminster parishes, and in eighteen wards within-the-walls, while the poorer sections of the middle class were concentrated to the south and east of the City, especially around the Tower. Yet throughout London, taxpayers *at all levels* lived near to those not paying taxes at all, and nowhere did the very wealthy form more than a half of the population of a parish, usually less. This distribution, Schwarz suggests, reflected the wide spread of manufacturing, small-scale artisan industry and shopkeeping in London, as well as the demand for seasonal, labour-intensive services (and therefore slums) from the middle-class enclaves of squares and avenues.[26]

Grytzell's detailed account of changes in population numbers and densities at district and sub-district level for the century after 1801 helps to pin-point change, showing, for example, that the decline in the City population began in that portion 'within-the-Walls', while the sharpest declines were in Shadwell – 10 per cent between 1801 and 1811, and 4 per cent between 1811 and 1821. He cites Spate's explanation for the latter, that clearances for dock-building were responsible. In general, Grytzell shows that areas immediately surrounding the City increased in population size and density, and that by 1821 the trend for densities to increase over the whole of the census London division was clearly established, with the fastest-growing areas lying at the periphery in Kensington, Poplar and Bromley. Grytzell, however, offers no general explanations of his own, relying on Spate and the census reports which offer somewhat eclectic explanations for local population variations in terms of generous poor law provisions (Clerkenwell), better census returns (Saffron Hill), demolitions (St James) and prison- and asylum-building (St John's and Greenwich). There is as yet no study which incorporates such local detail into a general framework for explaining demographic changes in London.

The objectives and impact of 'improvement' is a subject which has been widely discussed in terms of its economic and social significance. There is no doubt that dock-building, the cutting of Parliament Street,

[25] K. Grytzell, *Population Changes in London, 1801–1901* (Lund, 1969).
[26] Schwarz, 'Social Class and Social Geography'.

the opening of second and third Thames bridges at Westminster (1750) and Blackfriars (1769), the creation of London's first by-pass along the New Road from Paddington to Islington (1756) and the construction of the Regents' Canal linking Paddington with the docks (1811) were intended in part simply to improve communications within London, and between London and the rest of the country. Dyos, however, has argued that these and other improvements were not merely attempts to remove barriers to commerce, but were empirical solutions that enabled landowners to meet the increased demand for housing which the rapidly expanding suburbs could only partly accommodate, and to further enhance property values by clearing some slums, while containing those that remained in separate, demarcated areas.[27] Certainly, the great landlords of London's West End, not least the crown under John Nash's guidance, responded by creating 'courtly suburbs' to cater for the relocation of merchant residences. The town villages that were growing up a few miles outside the built-up area at Hampstead, Chelsea, Greenwich, Camberwell, Clapham, Dulwich, Twickenham and Wandsworth have been shown to be residential or semi-residential in nature rather than commuter suburbs before 1820.[28] Their individual characteristics, and the social groups attracted to them, were markedly different, with both local topography and the structure of the property market helping to determine relative degrees of exclusiveness. The story of London development and improvement strongly suggests that the response of individual proprietors is crucial in understanding its pace and character. The Middlesex Register of Deeds records in daunting detail every individual transaction in property from 1710, but in sum it is also useful for charting London's building cycle.[29] John Gwynne (1766) and John Nash (1812) both proposed dramatic and comprehensive schemes to dignify London's individualistic and non-authoritarian expansion, but the former failed and the latter was much modified in the face of those same independent forces. Dyos's concern with the interaction between process and place has been most fully explored in relation to London's physical development in the eighteenth and early

---

[27] H. J. Dyos, 'The Objects of Street Improvement in Regency and Early Victorian London', *International Review of Social History*, 2 (1957).

[28] M. H. Port, 'Metropolitan Improvements: From Grosvenor Square to Admiralty Arch', *London Journal*, 7 (1981). John Summerson, *The Life and Works of John Nash, Architect* (1981), chap. 12. Thompson, *Hampstead*, pp. 54–7.

[29] F. H. W. Sheppard, V. Belcher and P. Cottrell, 'The Middlesex and Yorkshire Deeds Registries and the Study of Building Fluctuations', *London Journal*, 5 (1979), pp. 176–217.

nineteenth centuries, but the operation of land and housing markets and their influence on individual proprietors and their schemes is not yet properly understood.[30]

It is clear that the relationship between London's built form and economic and social change should not be regarded as a one-way process. The interrelation between them has been suggested in studies of four quite different structures – inns which sprang up, architecturally distinct and commanding, on London's thoroughfares, clubs and coffee-houses, public buildings associated with science, from Somerset House to the Mechanics' Institutes, and formal parks and theatres in London's West End.[31] Each of these building types may be represented as a reaction to economic forces, but each played also some specific and positive role in promoting or easing social and economic change. Inns served as informal labour exchanges for new immigrants; clubs and coffee-houses as well as public houses engendered the newspaper and served as the focus of political and educational activity for various groups including the journeymen's friendly societies; scientific meeting houses were places where 'groups being continually redefined as marginal in a period of staggering economic and social change' could legitimise their claims to social status, and parks and pleasure gardens, exclusive at first, ultimately came to act as 'a unifying social influence', a common meeting ground for London's aristocratic and 'carriage-folk' thereby further eroding aristocratic exclusiveness and promoting the 'new values' of London's commercial middle class.[32]

The role of land-use changes and public building in furthering 'social control' of the working classes is a preoccupation of historians of the Victorian rather than the Georgian period. Nevertheless, as well as the early street improvements objects as varied as prisons, hospitals, turnpikes, docks and schools have been cited as instruments whereby the unruly, not to say criminal, tendencies of the lower classes might be curbed. This is scarcely a major theme, however, and Sheenan, in fact, shows how solace as well as punishment could be achieved

---

[30] D. J. Olsen, *Town Planning in London in the Eighteenth and Nineteenth Centuries* (1964).
[31] J. A. Chartres, 'The Capital's Provincial Eyes: London's Inns in the Early Eighteenth Century', *London Journal*, 3 (1977). A. Lejeune, *The Gentlemen's Clubs of London* (1979). B. Lillywhite, *London Coffee Houses* (1963). McKendrick, Brewer and Plumb, *Birth of a Consumer Society*. A. Osler, 'The London University of 1742', *London Journal*, 6 (1980). I. Inkster, 'Science and Society in the Metropolis: A Preliminary Examination of the Social and Institutional Context of the Askesian Society of London, 1796–1807', *Annals of Science*, 34 (1977).
[32] G. Rudé, *Paris and London in the Eighteenth Century* (1952).

in newly rebuilt Newgate, while Tobias argues that though both secure docks and turnpikes led initially to a decline in crime, criminals subsequently changed their methods to meet the new conditions, becoming less personally and physically violent, but more organised and more concerned with the opportunities offered by unoccupied shops and warehouses, and unprotected houses.[33] The nature of London's lawlessness and the criminality associated with the Gin Age (1720–51) was apparently transformed by social and economic change, and by the establishment of agencies such as Henry Fielding's Bow Street runners, and the Horse Patrole. Despite the emergence of the concept of a 'criminal class' in London, the evidence suggests a relatively low rate of per capita crime in both the metropolis and the Home Counties.[34]

Questions of law and order in the broader sense have been a growing concern of historians in recent years. The social and political significance of criminal activity has been of particular interest.[35] Elton, however, has warned of the danger of using preconceived modern categories which would have been meaningless to contemporaries and which can result in misleading and distorted interpretations of particular criminal activities. He emphasises that the subject matter of crime must be defined, and contemporary distinctions between different types of crime established, *before* modern analytical categories are introduced. Historians against whom such criticisms are directed, however, maintain that this kind of ground-clearing operation already features in recent research. Cockburn, and Brewer and Styles, for example, have examined the nature of law, law enforcement and law breaking and have underlined the essentially political nature of law in the seventeenth and eighteenth centuries, as well as the legal nature of politics.[36]

---

[33] C. W. Chalklin, 'The Reconstruction of London's Prisons, 1770–1799: An Aspect of the Growth of Georgian London', *London Journal*, 9 (1983), pp. 21–32. W. J. Sheenan, 'Finding Solace in Eighteenth-Century Newgate', in J. S. Cockburn, ed., *Crime in England 1550–1800* (1977). J. S. Taylor, 'Philanthropy and Empire: Jonas Hanway and the Infant Poor of London', *Eighteenth Century Studies*, 12 (1979). P. McCann, 'Popular Education, Socialization and Social Control: Spitalfields 1812–24', in P. McCann, *Popular Education and Socialization in the Nineteenth Century* (1977). J. J. Tobias, *Crime and Industrial Society in the Nineteenth Century* (1967).

[34] J. M. Beattie, 'Crime and the Courts in Surrey 1736–53', in Cockburn, ed., *Crime in England*, pp. 155–86.

[35] N. Rogers, 'Popular Protest in Early Hanoverian London', *Past & Present*, 74 (1978).

[36] J. Brewer and J. Styles, *An Ungovernable People: The English and their Law in the Seventeenth and Eighteenth Centuries* (1980). G. R. Elton, 'Crime and the Historian', in Cockburn, ed., *Crime in England*.

The close interrelation between political and legal systems had important implications both for the exercise of authority by the state, and for the tenor of opposition. For its part, the state employed the courts as the chief means of exercising authority and enforcing regulations. Conversely, it was acceptance of, and regard for, 'the rule of law' at least as an *idea*, which prevented individual grievances from becoming generalised into a critique of authority or the law. This is not to say that some 'consensual view' prevailed. Conflict could and did occur where participants were unmistakably motivated by political aims, as in the London food riots and Wilkite agitations of the mid-eighteenth century. Such protests, however, could be accepted as an attempt to provoke a remedial response and not as a challenge to authority *per se*.[37]

The essentially legal nature of politics at this time should caution against simplistic attempts to associate specific occupational groups with particular forms of political activity, not least in London where the legal and social structure was so complex. Schwarz has pointed to the socially and politically ambiguous position of London's very numerous small employers and shopkeepers: potential social leaders in the poorer parts of London, but of inferior status elsewhere; wooed by the London Corresponding Society in the 1790s, but emerging as the defenders of 'law and order' by 1848. Their social and political characteristics, Schwarz suggests, must be analysed in the context of their everyday experiences, and not assumed from their occupational labels.[38] The political role of these 'middling sorts of people' has been emphasised, and Prothero has concluded that 'instead of ... treating "the artisans" collectively, we must analyse the differing experiences of some of the trades. Occupational differentiation is essential.' Prothero's study of John Gast, the London shipwrights and their participation in radical 'supra-trade activity' in the early nineteenth century is a richly detailed example of the cultural, social and political worlds of one group of 'skilled artisans'.[39]

The nature and scale of political agitation in London between 1750 and 1820 has led many observers to think that London's 'repertoire of contention' came close to revolution. They point to the frequency of industrial disputes, the size of demonstrations, the Gordon Riots

---

[37] N. Rogers, 'Popular Disaffection in London during the Forty-Five', *London Journal*, 1 (1975). J. Stevenson, ed., *London in the Age of Reform* (1977).
[38] Schwarz, 'Social Class and Social Geography'.
[39] Prothero, *Artisans and Politics*, p. 6.

(1780), the high degree of political organisation displayed by the London Corresponding Society and the insurrection of 1820 planned by the Cato Street conspirators. The problem, however, is to account for the failure of London's 'revolutionary moment' to materialise. Stevenson takes as his starting point the 'constitutional' nature of London political agitation, and emphasises that the socio-economic demands of the groups involved were harnessed by Wilkes to the cause of parliamentary reform. In an interim report on a long-term study of the changing spatial pattern of 'contentious gatherings' in London and the Home Counties, Tilly and Schweitzer have suggested that the riots and demonstrations typical of the 1760s and 1770s came to be replaced over the next fifty years by scheduled meetings and symbolic public assemblies where large numbers of workers travelled long distances to make orderly, but emotionally powerful, forays into the alien, middle-class territory of London's West End. Hone has questioned the revolutionary commitment of radical leaders, emphasising instead their preference for 'keeping their political options open' and their involvement in a wide range of activities – philanthropic, scientific and educational – in the pursuit of social change.[40]

While Stevenson, Tilly and Schweitzer and Hone have argued that London's revolutionary moment was transformed by political leadership or structural change, others have cast doubt on its very existence. Dobson has underlined the essential continuity of pre- and post-industrial labour relations, especially in the high proportion of labour disputes which occurred in London. Emsley has discussed the possibility that the government 'concocted' evidence of an insurrection for its own ends in the winter of 1792 in order to create a loyalist reaction against the popular turbulence of the time. Similarly, the reliability of evidence about events leading up to the raid on the Cato Street stable has been questioned since much of it derives from government sources based on spies' reports.[41] It is, therefore, widely accepted that the character of London politics and political consciousness cannot be explained simply in terms of economic and industrial

[40]   T. M. Parsinnen, 'The Revolutionary Party in London', *Bulletin of the Institute of Historical Research*, 45 (1972). J. Stevenson, 'Disturbances and Public Order in London 1790–1821' (unpublished DPhil. thesis, Oxford University, 1973). C. Tilly and R. A. Schweitzer, 'How London and its Conflicts Changed Shape 1758–1834', *Historical Methods*, 15 (1982). J. A. Hone, *For the Cause of Truth: Radicalism in London 1796–1821* (Oxford, 1982).

[41]   C. R. Dobson, *Masters and Journeymen: A Pre-History of Industrial Relations 1717–1800* (1980). C. Emsley, 'The London "Insurrection" of December 1792: Fact, Fiction or Fantasy?', *Journal of British Studies*, 17 (1978). Hone, *For the Cause of Truth*.

change – the varied experiences between and within social groups, the influence of tradition and social ideals, and the complex interrelation between London and national affairs all have to be taken into account. Throughout the period 1750–1820, several political centres are identifiable in London and this factor tended to limit London's role in radical movements. Initially, the City, governed by its three courts, had the central role, providing 'continuous opposition' to the government of the day most particularly during the Wilkite agitation of the 1760s and the 1770s. After 1790, however, the level and character of City agitation changed, and though radical activity continued, relations with the government became more conciliatory.[42] Opposition to income tax, the suspension of Habeas Corpus and the Six Acts came not so much from the City as from Westminster. Indeed, attempts were made to extend co-operation between radicals across the metropolis as a whole, and to develop a political body uniting not only the twin cities but also Southwark, Middlesex, Surrey, Essex and Kent. Despite these hopes of a metropolitan radical movement, the focus of political attention began to shift to the provinces after 1815. Though the retreat of London radicalism should not be overemphasised, London failed to maintain its previously high level of political involvement and leadership. Stevenson has argued that this was not due to structural factors such as London's lack of a manufacturing base, nor to a lack of interest there in the dominant issue of parliamentary reform, but to the city's sheer size and multiple specialised hierarchies which made political mobilisation on any particular issue very difficult to achieve.[43] Paradoxically, the diversity of London life not only created the preconditions for disorder and disintegration, but also at the same time prevented the city's inherent instability from manifesting itself in metropolitan and national politics.

The period between 1750–1820 was one of great change for London and the Home Counties, which was as enigmatic and difficult for contemporaries to understand as it has been for modern social historians. London's complexities and paradoxes confounded the language of eighteenth-century observers as well as twentieth-century economists and sociologists. Social historians have come to recognise the need

---

[42] J. R. Dinwiddy, '"The Patriotic Linen-Draper"': Robert Waithman and the Revival of Radicalism in the City of London, 1795–1818', *Bulletin of the Institute of Historical Research*, 46 (1973), pp. 72–94.

[43] Stevenson, 'Disturbances and Public Order'. Hone, *For the Cause of Truth*.

to understand the contemporary meanings attached to occupational groups ('artisans', 'journeymen', 'mechanics') and to political and criminal activity before adopting analytical frameworks borrowed from modern economic and social theorists. Though major changes were underway, not all of them appear to have worked in the direction theory suggests. Demographically and educationally, and even politically, London's influence seemed to have become more localised by 1820. London's transformation was incomplete: the influence of its history and traditions continued to mark its character, and the opportunity of transforming British society was passing from London and its radicals to the industrially based provincial cities.

II METROPOLITAN MIST: LONDON AND ITS PROVINCIAL RIVALS 1820–1870

> Hell is a city much like London –
> A populous and smoky city
>
> P. B. Shelley, *Peter Bell the Third*, Part 3, 'Hell'

It was London's 'particular' qualities which caught the imagination of mid-nineteenth-century writers. To Dickens, Shelley, Disraeli and Tennyson, as well as to the lesser known Gerald Massey and James Thomson, London was a city like no other – at least, not this side of Heaven or Hell. Its smokiness provided a powerful image of the city's ability to swallow up countless multitudes in its mysterious depths – guaranteeing anonymity. London, Bagehot said, was like a newspaper: everything was there, and nothing was connected to anything else. Nevertheless, London's repellent strangeness and formlessness could not extinguish the possibility that a poetic, surrealist beauty might yet emerge from the city. Such a vision may perhaps be explained by the survival of many of London's pre-industrial qualities and attributes, and by its incomplete transformation into an archetypal industrial city. The village-like character of many of its residential areas (whether humble or grand), the persistence of old physical and institutional forms alongside the new, and its resemblance to great and luxurious cities of the past – all these sustained intimations of humanity and splendour despite the poverty, disease and filth that hung about the city. The period 1820–70 saw many distinctive changes in the life of London yet their impact was mediated both by visions of the future, and by shadows of the past.

London and industrialisation

London's share in the unprecedented, bizarre and momentous changes associated with the industrial revolution has been variously interpreted. Sheppard has portrayed London as a city in the industrial revolution, but not of it – its hub, but not its driving force.[44] Certainly, the overwhelming growth of London cannot be denied: decade after decade its population expanded at a constant rate between 16 and 21 per cent: by 1877, it had reached the enormous size of 3.25 million people. Yet London's position in the urban hierarchy was being challenged by the burgeoning growth of a dozen or more provincial cities in the Midlands and the north, each with a population of more than 100,000 in 1871. The growth of these 'shock cities' suggested that the centre of national economic life had shifted, leaving London 'almost totally isolated' in the still predominantly agricultural south. This provincial approach to explanations of Britain's economic growth has been challenged. The exploitation of the northern provinces, Dyos argued, occurred 'not as an abatement of the centripetal forces which were concentrating the population and economic power on London, but primarily as a redeployment of provincial resources, some of them having been, as it were, processed in London *en route*'.[45] On this interpretation, London played an essential part as one of the 'world cities', functioning as a primary element in a national and international control mechanism which fostered both industrial and urban growth. London was, at one and the same time, central yet peripheral, economically secondary yet socially dominant, culturally inspirational yet parasitic. For contemporaries, the duality of London's role found expression in dislike, suspicion and hostility. Their desire to keep London in its place, and to nurture the new-grown industrial centres is reflected in the fact that the term 'provinces' became established as a collective and favourable expression long before 'metropolis' shed its unacceptably pompous overtones.

In the half-century between 1820 and 1870, London indeed appeared overshadowed by these provincial towns – economically, politically and administratively. Nonetheless, London's aggrandisement continued and its isolation from the mainstream of the industrial revolution ensured that its development remained unique, 'a formation for which

---

[44] F. H. W. Sheppard, *London 1808–1870: The Infernal Wen* (1971), pp. xvii–xix.

[45] H. J. Dyos, 'Greater and Greater London: Notes on the Metropolis and the Provinces in the Nineteenth and Twentieth Centuries', in J. S. Bromley and E. H. Kossman, eds., *Britain and the Netherlands* (The Hague, 1971).

no name exists'.[46] This section examines the significance of London's apparent isolation in terms of its economy, its physical development, its social structure and its political life.

London's economic growth – a provincial or metropolitan phenomenon?

Despite the continued absence of 'a full-scale economic history of Victorian London' lamented by Dyos in 1971, the main elements are quite clear, namely a significant though unobtrusive manufacturing base, with consumer-oriented enterprises largely organised in small specialist workshops, and an increasingly wide-ranging service sector, with specialist financial and banking activities centred on the City. London industry and London finance served not only metropolitan markets, but also regional and national markets. Indeed, it has been argued that the international market for its goods and services out-stripped domestic ones, no matter what level is used for comparison. Certainly, the growing domination of London in the international money markets led to the City's relative decline in the home market. Yet it must be emphasised that such a decline *was* only relative, and London dominance of the domestic securities market was clearly established after 1850. Increasingly extensive public involvement in investment, therefore, came to be channelled through London despite the establishment of exchanges in the provinces.[47] The power and size of London's financial institutions derived partly from increased provincial wealth, but also from enterprises carried on in London itself, and throughout the world. In return, London acted as an essential intermediary in managing supply and demand for investment from industrialists and entrepreneurs in Britain, Europe and the Empire, especially after 1850. Investment both at home and abroad tended to be in infrastructure, notably railways, rather than in direct industrial capital. Nevertheless, the market proved precarious, and the speculative bubble of the 1860s which culminated in the collapse of Overend and Gurney was largely due to over-extensive railway investment in and around London itself. Such an analysis suggests that London should not be thought of as an 'independent variable' in the growth of the new industrial economy, but neither should the rise of the industrial north be seen as 'some kind of clandestine

[46] Quoted in *ibid.*, p. 54.
[47] R. C. Michie, 'The London Stock Exchange and the British Securities Market 1850–1914', *Economic History Review*, 2nd ser., 38 (1985), pp. 61–82.

extramural activity of London'.[48] London's specific involvement lay in providing specialist financial services to secure investment capital and insurance protection necessary to support the industrial infrastructure. Its influence was not wholly benign – the vulnerability of the system was demonstrated by the periodic crises of 1825, 1836–9 and 1857, and the influence of London made itself felt in cultural as well as financial terms through the spread of associated communications – not only the railway, but also the mail, press and electric telegraph.

Historians' efforts to determine London's role in the 'industrial revolution' have tended to proceed on the assumption that manufacturing provided the key element in Britain's economic growth in the nineteenth century. Recently, however, this assumption has been challenged in ways which throw a very different light on London and the national economy at this time. Attempts have been made to quantify changes in Britain's economic structure at a regional rather than a national level, with the metropolitan region receiving particular attention. Both Rubinstein's study of the distribution of wealth and Lee's analysis of types of regional development have shown the value of such attempts at quantification, whether they are conducted at the basic level of careful counting, or at the more sophisticated level of factor analysis.[49] In their different ways, both Rubinstein and Lee show that traditional generalisations concerning the rise of industry, and of industrial wealth, do not survive quantitative analysis. They both underline the importance of the service sector and of consumer-oriented industry as an economic force in Victorian Britain – generating large personal fortunes, and at the same time forging a new and highly successful economic sector. This large, highly integrated, homogeneous market initially comprised London and Westminster, but expanded rapidly into neighbouring, contiguous counties. Lee, indeed, goes so far as to conclude 'we should interpret Victorian Britain in terms of the South-East being the most advanced region in the British economy, and making a commensurate contribution to the development of that national economy'. What that 'commensurate contribution' was has yet to be determined. Clearly, however, London lacked those activities traditionally regarded as the 'driving forces' of Victorian expansion – mining, heavy industry, large-scale

[48] Dyos, 'Greater and Greater London', p. 47.
[49] W. D. Rubinstein, 'Wealth, Elites and the Class Structure of Modern Britain', *Past & Present*, 76 (1977). C. H. Lee, 'Regional Growth and Structural Change in Victorian Britain', *Economic History Review*, 2nd ser., 34 (1981), pp. 438–52.

textile manufacturing. Indeed, some textile factories which had existed in London in the early nineteenth century were exported to outlying towns such as Colchester: the decline of these silk and woollen weaving firms continued in their new locations, however, despite the lower local wages.[50] Heavy industry along the Thames also tended to move out – larger chemical industries sought cheaper land and fewer restrictions and migrated across the Lee valley to West Ham after 1850. In Stratford, however, smaller chemical firms formed a 'quarter' for themselves where they developed that interdependence and proximity most usually associated with London's clothing, furniture and instrumentmakers.

The London economy was increasingly based on high-technology, consumer-oriented industry and an associated service sector, relying above all on its own large, densely populated and relatively wealthy market. This great metropolitan market was essentially divided into two, both physically and socially. The clothing trades illustrate this division – there was the West End centre, north of Piccadilly and east of Regent Street, specialising in the highest grade bespoke tailoring and 'Court Dressmaking', well placed to serve the highly personal demands of its fashionable clientele. Quite separate, was the clothing industry of the East End, where 'Petticoat Lane' developed as the centre for cheap ready-made clothes about 1850. Nevertheless, no factory system emerged, rather the productive process disintegrated into small 'sweated' shops equipped with cheap technical innovations such as the sewing machine and the band saw. Furnituremaking showed a very similar kind of spatial and organisational structure, as did printing and the highly skilled crafts involved in the manufacture of watches, clocks and scientific instruments. All these trades needed to be near their market, which because of its size and complexity, tended to support a system of specialised but highly interdependent workshops. The 1851 census documented the extraordinary range of London's occupations, and by 1861, three-fifths of all employment in the City was provided by small-scale industry and the service sector.

The mid-nineteenth-century metropolitan economy was centred on the Cities of London and Westminster and the county of Middlesex, and was characterised by a highly integrated group of consumer goods

---

[50] A. F. J. Brown, 'Colchester 1815–1914', *Essex Record Office Publications*, 74 (1980).

and service industries: this economic sector was expanding more quickly than the industrial sectors which have traditionally been regarded as the major growth generators. Over a half of all new jobs in Britain between 1841 and 1911 were created in service employment, and a high proportion of these jobs were located in the south-east, initially in London and Middlesex. The Home Counties were not fully incorporated into the metropolitan economy by 1870, and Lee's factor analysis of the 1851 and 1861 census shows the outer counties falling into three separate groups with common features distinguishing them both from each other and from London itself. Similar growth profiles distinguished first, Kent, Surrey and Hampshire, secondly, Sussex, Berkshire and Oxford and finally, Buckinghamshire, Bedfordshire and Hertfordshire. Each of these counties, however, moved to adopt the structural pattern of the London economy, as the century progressed. An important element in Lee's argument is that these structural changes were internally generated – the product of a large affluent society 'enjoying conspicuous consumption and giving employment to a wide range of labour intensive services – from domestic service at one extreme to traditional professions like medicine, law and education at the other'. Lee emphasises the self-generating character of London's growth and calls into question the common assumption that service employment was primarily a by-product of manufacturing (i.e. provincial) growth. Rather, he asserts, service employment arose chiefly from certain types of consumer-oriented manufacturing – paper, printing and publishing, timber and furniture, clothing, chemicals and 'high-tech' instrument and electrical engineering industries – all of which were particularly associated with nineteenth-century London and the surrounding counties. In other words, the London region was on the way to becoming 'the world's first large-scale consumer society', not in any vital respect dependent on provincial manufacturing, but independent and self-sustaining. Such an analysis goes much further than Barker or Dyos, and does not merely alter the provincial perspective on London's economic growth and role, but virtually removes it altogether. London's economic achievements in the mid-nineteenth century were not derived from, nor even interdependent with provincial manufacturing towns: it was neither parasitic nor ambiotic – it was separate, self-generating and highly successful.[51]

[51] Lee, 'Regional Growth', pp. 450, 452.

London – the infernal wen

It is important to set this analysis of an integrated, dynamic and high-technology London economy in the contemporary physical and social context. Cobbett's unbridled fury against the swelling growth of London as he rode through Surrey and Sussex was portentous, but in 1822 the transformation of the Home Counties into metropolitan suburbia was certainly incomplete, and remained so as late as 1870. Even in Middlesex in 1882, a Wealdstone vicar complained that he 'might just as well be in a remote part of Yorkshire' for all the difference London made. Though Lee's statistical analysis of occupations shows Middlesex firmly tied to the structure of a metropolitan economy, actual circumstances suggested distance, separation and rusticity in many areas.[52] While the system of turnpikes provided passable routes towards London, many lanes of sticky mud or rutted hard-baked clay persisted far into the century. The neglect of local parish roads might indeed be linked to the creation of the turnpikes which starved other routes of investment and attention. Surrey, for example, came to be traversed by a new system of direct trunk roads between London and the coast, and also by a close network of cross-country connections. At the same time, many of the old pathways which followed natural contours and cut circuitous routes became derelict. Much of the Surrey Weald remained inaccessible at mid-century, the land uncultivated, beyond the reach of the metropolitan market for food.[53]

Where communications were good, whether at the fringe of London's built-up area, or at nodal points in the transport system, the impact of 'London-out-of-town' was strongly felt. Until 1870, roads, rather than railways, were the major carriers of people and goods. Nevertheless, though transport was a necessary cause of suburbanisation, it was not a sufficient one – also important was the availability of land, credit and investment in infrastructure. The physical spread of London, therefore, proceeded along a very irregular path both in time and space, diverted now by landownership patterns, now by the general financial situation. In the building boom which followed the end of the French Wars in 1815, areas to the west and south of London saw the most rapid growth. The fashionable estates of Tyburnia and Belgravia in Paddington were begun in the 1820s, while south of the Thames the three new bridges at Vauxhall, Waterloo

---

[52] M. Robbins, 'Transport and Suburban Development in Middlesex down to 1914', *Transactions of London and Middlesex Archaeological Society*, 29 (1978), pp. 129–36.
[53] P. Brandon, *A History of Surrey* (1977), pp. 71–6.

and Southwark and their associated turnpikes opened up hitherto isolated areas. In the 1820s, the population of both Lambeth and Camberwell increased by over 50 per cent, and it was through rows of their terrace houses that Cobbett rode on his way to Croydon, itself the fastest-growing outpost of the 'Great Wen'. Cobbett railed against these 'horrible and ridiculous' rows surpassed in ugliness only by the more distant 'hideous villas' of 'Jews and jobbers' – bankers, stockbrokers and distillers – clustered around newly enclosed Surrey commons. Even worse to Cobbett, was the jobbers' practice of buying up old Surrey farmhouses and furnishing them in new-fangled styles with parlours, fine tableware set on mahogany tables and with 'carpet and bell-push too'. As the new owners 'skip backwards and forwards' on coaches along the turnpikes, they transformed the physical and social fabric of the places they touched, sometimes deliberately, often unconsciously. Not until the 1860s did a concern for traditional building styles, and for the preservation of commons, emerge to modify these alien metropolitan advances.[54]

London's influence could reach even as far as small towns on the coastal fringe of the south-east. Local studies of Colchester and Ramsgate have shown how generalisations at county level about the extent of metropolitan influence may conceal much variation – in rural Middlesex and Surrey the 'metropolitan effect' was often weak, while in some urban coastal centres in Essex and Kent it was clearly strong.[55] The attraction of Colchester for some of London's consumer industries has already been mentioned – successive textile, tailoring and shoemaking firms took advantage of its cheap, readily available labour force and established branches in the town between 1815 and 1870, putting out work from their London showrooms. The coming of the London–Chelmsford–Colchester railway in 1843 expanded the consumer market for these firms beyond London to a wider area of southeast England. Indeed, in 1857 Colchester's shoemakers claimed that they had become the Great Eastern Railway's chief commercial customer in the town. Commercial links also lay behind some important political interplay between London and Colchester. Colchester 'outvoters' formed a cohesive group in the 1820s. Liberal in sympathy, these Colchester-born artisans, commercial and professional men met

[54]   W. Cobbett, *Rural Rides* (1930 edn), quoted in Sheppard, *Infernal Wen*.
[55]   Brown, 'Colchester 1815–1914'. R. S. Holmes, 'Continuity and Change in a Mid-Victorian Resort: Ramsgate 1851–1871' (unpublished DPhil. thesis, University of Kent, 1977).

in certain London inns and espoused the cause of parliamentary reform. Led by Colchester's Liberal MP, D.W. Harvey, whom they had themselves helped to elect, these Colchester out-voters came home to vote 'for the extinction of their own political franchise', and were duly disenfranchised by the Reform Bill.[56] The coming of the railway made London available to a wide section of Colchester's residents, especially for enjoyment and for social activities. Cheap excursions at Bank Holidays were popular, and special attractions like the Great Exhibition, conferences and political rallies such as the People's Welcome to Garibaldi attracted thousands of Colcestrians to the capital. For them, London was not remote, but an immediate and direct experience.

While Colchester's relation with London was primarily commercial, Ramsgate valued a certain social 'tone' which reflected a more intimate relationship with some of the wealthier members of London society. Here Londoners established not branch factories, but residential enclaves, thereby heightening residential segregation within the town. The size of Ramsgate – 11,000 population in 1851 and 14,000 in 1871 – has made possible a study of the town's structure without the need for sampling: using a combination of census and rate book data, Holmes has compared social and economic variables between neighbouring households, streets and areas. Rejecting factor analysis as 'inappropriate and misleading', Holmes has concentrated on an analysis of 'key' variables, in particular, tenurial status, residential mobility and rateable values. He draws attention to one striking dichotomy – the town's stability in terms of overall structure, and its fluidity in terms of individual movements. A major factor in this situation was undoubtedly the influence of wealthy London families who sought ever more exclusive locations, but who, once satisfied, seldom moved, thereby creating a stable growth pole of high-status households, where they welcomed London lodgers and visitors with the help of their London-born servants. Such a well-entrenched, high-status component in Ramsgate's social and economic structure made for overall stability in the town's spatial and societal character, and ensured a growing London influence on household structure, residential patterns and internal mobility.

The impact of London on the inner ring of Home Counties and

---

[56] Harvey is said to 'have made history by inspiring fifty wives of London voters to form a group to raise funds for him and to assist in other ways, the earliest known case of women participating in Colchester politics', *ibid.*, p. 79.

on those beyond in the mid-nineteenth century was clearly not simply a matter of geographic propinquity, but was related to many other factors not least the circumstances prevailing in the 'receiving' locality, and the type of involvement sought by Londoners on the move. It is the diversity of London's impact and the resilience of local ways in life that is most striking: Cobbett's view of the unremitting, undifferentiated absorption of neighbouring areas by relentlessly expanding and multiplying suburbs is polemical rather than factual. At the same time, however, recent statistical generalisations at county level suggest a greater degree of economic integration than was apparent to many at the time.

Demographic transition

In many respects 1871 represents a demographic watershed for London and its neighbouring counties, for by that date the area was beginning to show a buoyant and self-generating growth in terms of population, as much as in economic activity. The 1871 census was the last one to record population increases in the inner area that was to become the Administrative County of London although overall, London and the Home Counties were growing rapidly and remained the largest national focus for migrants. The proportion of migrants in London's population was falling, however, as the birth rate rose above the national average between 1865–1870 and the death rate began to fall.

Assessments of London's demographic structure from 1840 onwards rest on what Wrigley has called the 'delusive clarity and apparent authority' of official statistics – primarily the census (where the names of household members were recorded from 1841) and the records of the Registrar General of Births and Deaths (from 1836).[57] Embarrassing as these sources are in their sheer bulk, historians have been devising techniques for classifying and marshalling these sets of data, and for developing appropriate explanatory frameworks. A serious problem for London historians is that many of the techniques that have been developed for census analysis – for example, sampling, and family or household reconstruction – are very difficult to apply in such a large and heterogeneous city. The census permits London historians to identify general demographic trends and characteristics,

[57] E. A. Wrigley, 'Baptism Coverage in Early Nineteenth Century England', *Population Studies*, 29 (1975), pp. 229–316.

but these merely 'set the stage' for an exploration of the circumstances surrounding the population changes. This kind of explanation has proved very difficult, and very few attempts have been made to explore the process of demographic change in relation to particular areas or occupational groups.[58]

The value and limitations of the new demographic techniques can be illustrated by Friedlander's study of inter-censal migration flows between the counties of south-east England.[59] Friedlander shows the changing pattern of origin and destination of London migrants from 1851 to 1951. In the 1840s, London and Middlesex gained population at the expense of the adjacent counties of Essex, Surrey and Kent. Though there were some early signs of population dispersal from London to Middlesex, the dominant feature was one of massive population concentration in the centre. Most migrants to London, however, travelled only short distances even after the construction of railways. Important migration flows are established by Friedlander, yet his explicit assumptions clearly show that here too there is a 'deceptive clarity'. In constructing his analytical framework, Friedlander adopts the following conventions.

1. A person who moves and then dies in the inter-censal period is deemed only to die, and to do so in his locality at the former census.
2. A person moving from K to L, and then L to M in an inter-censal period is deemed to have moved only from K to M.
3. If a native of any county moves from K to L and another native of the same county moves from L to K, no movement is assumed.

This 'smoothing' of the data distorts the subsequent analysis to an unknown extent: these unknowns are compounded by the fact that the census itself records no intervening moves within decades, thus limiting the completeness of the raw data itself. Such analysis can

[58] Census studies show 'a marked concentration on localities in Lancashire, Yorkshire and the East Midlands' according to C. G. Pearce and D. R. Mills, *Census Enumerators' Books: An Annotated Bibliography of Published Work Based Substantially on the Nineteenth Century Census Enumerators' Books* (Milton Keynes, 1982), p. vi. The Home Counties in particular have received little attention. They are (a) *Essex*: Colchester (L. Davidoff), Elmdon (J. Robin) and Little Beddow (S. V. Rowley); (b) *Kent*: Margate (L. Davidoff), Preston-next-Faversham (K. Duffy), Ramsgate (R. Holmes), Sheergate (N. Buck); and (c) *Middlesex*: Ealing (D. Thompson). The *Inner London Suburbs* feature in several publications, they are: Bethnal Green (B. Coleman), Camberwell (H. J. Dyos), Highbury (T. Hinchcliffe), Hoxton (B. Knott), Kensington (P. Malcolmson), North Lambeth (H. C. Binford), and five inner parishes (L. Lees).

[59] D. Friedlander, 'London's Urban Transition, 1851–1951', *Urban Studies*, 2 (1974), pp. 127–41.

throw no light on the questions raised by Holmes in his study of Ramsgate about the strength of 'counter-currents' between the seaside town and London, nor about the extent of direct moves via London into Ramsgate – a phenomenon suggested by data on the birthplace of youngest children.[60]

Within these limitations, Friedlander's decennial county level analysis shows the interconnections between immigration flows into and within London and the surrounding counties. Sub-division below county level is not attempted but, nevertheless, Friedlander presents a series of snapshots of the aerial variation of migration flows and confirms the absorption of surrounding counties like Surrey and Middlesex into the London migration zone. By 1871, the expanding area of attraction for London migrants had reached Dorset, Somerset and Devon, while the preferred reception areas had begun to shift from London and Middlesex to adjacent counties.

While long-distance migration to London from English counties was growing by 1871, that from Ireland was falling: the 1840s had seen a tremendous Irish exodus following successive failures of the potato harvest. In the decade 1841–51, out of an estimated total of 330,000 new migrants arriving in London, 46,000 were 'exiles of Erin'.[61] By 1851, there were some 109,000 Irish living in London, no less than 4.6 per cent of the metropolitan population. From that peak, the Irish proportion declined, and the numbers arriving fell to 14,000 in the 1850s, with a slight rise to 19,000 in the 1860s. Such figures exclude English-born children, so the total number of Irish residents might well have been 50 per cent higher, as Lynn Lees has suggested.[62] In many ways, the Irish seem to have reversed the common patterns of migration in England. Whereas English urban migrants most frequently moved short distances, proving themselves in smaller and less complicated towns before moving on to the larger centres, the Irish leapt straight to London. Though poorly suited to the capital by skills, contacts and experience, the Irish urban scene offered the rural migrants no easier alternatives. Pitched into London's casual labour market, the Irish formed close communities in the 'rookeries'

---

[60]   Holmes, 'Continuity and Change: Ramsgate 1851–1871', p. 201. Holmes found that the youngest child of migrants to Ramsgate was three times as likely to be London-born as the head of the household, and suggests that this might be due to indirect moves via London.

[61]   H. A. Shannnon, 'Migration and the Growth of London 1841–91', *Economic History Review*, 2nd ser., 5 (1955), p. 81.

[62]   L. H. Lees, 'Social Change and Social Stability among the London Irish, 1830–1870' (unpublished PhD thesis, Harvard, 1969).

of the central districts – the notorious St Giles area of Holborn, the Seven Dials and the riverside parish of St Olave's, east of London Bridge. Some Irish enclaves also formed in suburban areas such as North Kensington and North Camberwell where there were local shortages for unskilled labour, especially in building. Their isolation was not, however, total: recent research based on 1851 and 1861 census data has shown how Irish settlers came to adopt similar fertility patterns to Londoners in general – marrying younger, but nevertheless having fewer children than their countrymen in rural Ireland.[63]

Employment and unemployment

A particular value of the Irish studies is that they provide a 'tracer' flowing along well-marked channels which show by their surges and diversions the areas of flux and stability in London's social and economic structure. In particular, concentrations of Irish settlement act as pointers, drawing attention to the basic structure of the London labour market, with its high level of unemployment and casual labour. Wherever the Irish settled, their presence indicated a market for unskilled, itinerant workers, bordering always on destitution and crime. The docks, the markets, the brickfields and the West End streets offered employment of this kind to 'everyone (for the work needs no training) who wants a loaf, and who is willing to work for it'.[64] Employment in the capital was sporadic and fiercely competitive – the 1851 census showed almost half London's population to be without formal employment. Closed to all except the most persistent and fortunate, were the employment networks for craftsmen and professionals, each with their own codes and rules of entry: new migrants 'knowing no-one, nor being known to any' were particularly excluded.[65]

Each employment group developed very specific mechanisms and pathways for new recruits. For women, the main pathways led to domestic service and to prostitution: indeed, the two virtually amounted to the same thing in some wealthier households.[66] The 1861 census recorded a quarter of a million domestic servants in

---

[63] L. H. Lees and J. Modell, 'The Irish Countryman Urbanized: A Comparative Perspective on the Famine Migration', *Journal of Urban History*, 3 (1977).

[64] Henry Mayhew and John Binney, *The Criminal Prisons of London and the Scenes of Prison Life* (1862), quoted in Sheppard, *Infernal Wen*, p. 364.

[65] William Lovett, *The Life and Struggles of William Lovett in his Pursuit of Bread, Knowledge and Freedom* (1876), quoted in Sheppard, *Infernal Wen*, p. 3.

[66] See above p. 478.

London, of whom five-sixths were women, many of them recent migrants. In all, one in every six London women were employed in domestic service: of those in paid employment, the proportion was nearer two-thirds. The vast majority of other London jobs were strictly male preserves, with the exception of the clothing trade. One large group of women used the home itself to increase family incomes by taking in lodgers, especially the clerks and shop assistants who sought accommodation in districts like Kensington and Camberwell.[67]

Many skilled and semi-skilled workers sought to establish and maintain London-wide conditions of employment and wage rates, but the size and diversity of the labour market led instead to a good deal of localisation. Nevertheless, as Hobsbawm has pointed out, there is great significance for the historian in the development of the *idea* of a single, all-London district for wages and conditions, a concept which never developed in any of the other conurbations.[68] Trade-union London did not coincide with administrative boundaries – the Metropolitan Police District, the Metropolitan Board of Works, or the London Postal District – but was usually represented as a circle of given radius from Charing Cross: the radius was expanded as the century progressed, eventually outstripping for some trades even the newly created administrative and political boundaries. By 1855, the London compositors were claiming an area of 15 miles from Charing Cross, plus some isolated places further afield: in 1877 the bricklayers were using a 12-mile radius. Again, incorporation in the metropolitan wage structure was not defined by the built-up area, nor by geographical propinquity: absorption reflected economic reality that was not spatially defined, but was determined by patterns of interaction. The tailors, for example, were content to enforce wage rates over a very small district (reflecting their concentration in central London and their weak, female, sweated labour force); printers on the other hand sought to establish a much wider district (reflecting the decentralisation of their trade). Where demand for labour was strong, as it was for carpenters, trades used their bargaining power to widen the area of standard wages, and these groups reached Ealing in the west, Wood Green in the north, and Greenwich and Forest Hill in the south. Even among some unskilled, unorganised occupations such as

---

[67] L. Davidoff, 'Separation of Home and Work?', in S. Burman, ed., *Fit Work for Women* (1979), pp. 64–97.
[68] E. J. Hobsbawm, 'The Nineteenth Century London Labour Market', in R. Glass, ed., *London: Aspects of Change* (1964), pp. 3–28.

building, a metropolitan level of wages and conditions came to be accepted by men and employers alike.

Up to the 1870s, however, when cheap and widespread public transport was introduced, local sub-divisions persisted in the labour market. For most unskilled workers, 'all that lay beyond a tiny circle of personal acquaintance or walking distance was darkness'.[69] Lovett describes the 'footsore and hungry' walking about that he and three fellow-Cornishmen were engaged in day after day during their search for work. More settled searchers, whether skilled or unskilled, depended largely on hearsay and personal tips, so that from the individual worker's point of view the metropolitan ideal faded before the reality of a much more localised pattern of employment. Even the unions recognised a sub-division into districts, often coinciding with branch boundaries, and reflecting above all a tripartite division into north and west, north and east, and south regions. The boundaries between these districts were marked by the Thames, and by the wide wedge of business districts (the City and Holborn), open spaces and high-class residential areas (Highgate and Hampstead) running out from the centre to the north.

Each of these districts differed in ideological and political character, and represented very real divisions between London's working-class areas. The south had a particularly strong radical character, having the largest concentration of trade unionists and activists in the metropolis. Western working-class London, on the other hand, was 'merely a geographical category' and even east London was 'little more than a trade unionist desert, an amorphous zone of weak and fluctuating organisation united only by its general poverty'.[70] Despite the desire for metropolitan wage rates, the reality was of localised and capricious variations which sometimes bordered on total incoherence.

One cannot therefore visualise London as a high plateau of wage rates, exercising some general influence over the situation in neighbouring counties. What that situation was remains unclear, but Hobsbawm's general outline is still worth considering especially now that some local accounts of wage rates have also become available. Kent seems to have had closer links with the London labour market than any of the other Home Counties. Nevertheless, the influence was by no means all one way: the extent of rural unemployment and

---

[69] *Ibid.*, p. 8. [70] *Ibid.*, pp. 12–13.

underemployment in Kent, amounting to penury for some third of the labour force produced not only the 'Swing' riots of the 1830s, but also relatively *lower* wage rates in south-east London at the point of entry for Kentish migrants.[71] North and westwards from London, the metropolitan effect was less marked. Most striking perhaps are the tentacles which linked London with remoter parts of the country, especially where sea links were strong. In 1853, Colchester's building workers, for example, secured an increase of 4–6d. a day to bring their wages a little nearer London rates. Other data, admittedly fragmentary, suggest a pattern of influence through a series of jumps to major centres around the coast of the north, south and east, and even as far afield as Bristol and South Wales.

Places and classes

The primary focus of this section has been the significance of London in the life of the region and of the nation as a whole. This emphasis is justifiable given the overall concern of the volume for the interaction of localities, regions and national life. It also reflects the fact that the enigma of London's wider influence has recently been evaluated in some particularly innovative research. In the period to be considered next, however, the half-century after 1870, the focus has to change. London's own domestic problems were to force themselves forward as *the* national issues of the moment. In the 1880s and 1890s problems of unemployment, poverty, housing and law and order were to be viewed through the prism of the London experience. Nevertheless, the policies devised to meet these metropolitan problems were to be applied through national legislation to the whole of the country.

In many ways, the feature of London life which distinguishes the pre-1870 period from the one that followed is the nature of the relationship within and between the social classes, particularly that of the middle and the working classes. With the burgeoning of London's own service sector, the metropolis came to display 'an aggregate of persons of middle rank collected in one spot ... The like of which exists in no other spot on earth.' In consequence, the fabric of

---

[71]   T. L. Richardson, 'The Agricultural Labourers' Standard of Living in Kent, 1790–1840', in D. J. Oddy and D. S. Miller, *The Making of the Modern British Diet* (1976), pp. 103–16.

London's inner areas was physically and architecturally transformed. The railways above all played this dual role – dispersing the middle classes to their allotted addresses, each with its own 'distinctive sound' and concentrating the working classes in the ever-more compacted centre.[72] The building and operation of transport services, department stores, parks and pleasure gardens, museums and galleries pushed the working classes 'further down and down' and held them there by the demand for casual and seasonal labour that was generated.[73] For the time being, however, the situation and its implications were hidden. Masterman employed the powerful image of the railway viaducts to convey the ease with which the middle classes rose above the nether world of the slums in reaching their jobs and pleasures in the heart of the metropolis.[74] As the earlier passion for exact knowledge of the circumstances of the urban poor faded and the journalism of Mayhew replaced the social analysis of Disraeli, the relationship between the classes became one of separation and ignorance. Regarded as a public spectacle by some and as an object of charity by a few, London's slum communities remained untouched by the middle class and developed their own distinctiveness and value systems. Even the early Victorian obsession with urban disorder waned, as the formation of the Metropolitan Police provided the means for achieving social stability through a 'considerable degree of bureaucratic intervention in daily life'.[75]

The middle classes turned in on themselves to explore and come to terms with their own internal problems of social cohesion and differentiation. As the gap between slum-dwellers and the rest of society widened, more and more steps appeared in the social ladder at the higher levels, and the gaps between the steps occurred at smaller intervals. Social and geographical mobility created the need for the 'paraphernalia of gentility' to define propriety, decorum and proper behaviour for each status group. This need found social expression in intricate rituals of etiquette, and physical expression in the varied location and form of suburbs, and the façade and ornamentation of

---

[72] H. McLeod, *Class and Religion in the Mid-Victorian City* (1974), p. 2.
[73] H. J. Dyos, 'The Slums of Victorian London', *Victorian Studies*, 11 (1968) (reprinted in D. Cannadine and D. Reeder, eds., *Exploring the Urban Past* (Cambridge, 1982), p. 149).
[74] *Ibid.*, p. 142.
[75] H. Cunningham, 'The Metropolitan Fairs: A Case Study in the Social Control of Leisure', in A. P. Donajgrodzki, ed., *Social Control in Nineteenth Century Britain* (1977).

houses.[76] By negotiating their way through the labyrinth of rules governing social acceptance or rejection, newcomers sought to establish their place in London 'society'.

The calling-card system protected the sanctity of the home as the heart of middle-class private and social life. Opportunities for amusements, however, increasingly took the middle class out of doors, into the 'relatively unstructured area in life-space', giving rise to renewed anxieties about status boundaries which were easily breached in these pleasurable but unprotected leisure arenas.[77]

The physical and social separation of London's middle and working classes, and the size and differentiation of both groups had a profound impact on London political life around mid-century: particularly significant was the cardinal distinction between the skilled and unskilled sections of the working class. London's political organisation and will were undermined by these gulfs and gradations despite the involvement in the promotion of new ideas and in political agitation. In the aftermath of the 1832 Reform Bill, Robert Owen formed the Grand National Consolidated Trades Union in London, only to see it rapidly collapse. London leadership was noticeably absent from the Chartist movement. The alienation and rifts between London's middle- and working-class political leaders culminated in lock-outs in the engineering and building industries. London middle-class reformers like Lovett found themselves overtaken by the more radical and violent political leaders, while London's labour leaders concentrated on building up their own authority through amalgamation and absorption of smaller unions. The 1860s saw the foundation of both the London Trades Council and the International Working Men's Association, both of which were used as instruments of political pressure at national and international level. London's role was as a source of ideas, rather than as a centre of action.

The promotion of radical ideas *in* London did not, however, result in the development of radical views *about* London – its diversity hampered the development of a metropolitan political consciousness, and gave rise to a disjuncture between administrative and political

[76] L. Davidoff, *The Best Circles: Society, Etiquette and the Season* (1973). T. Hinchcliffe, 'Highbury New Park: A Nineteenth Century Middle-Class Suburb', *London Journal*, 7 (1981). H. J. Dyos and D. A. Reeder, 'Slums and Suburbs', in H. J. Dyos and M. Wolff, eds., *The Victorian City*, vol. 1: *Images and Realities* (1973). S. Muthesius, *The English Terraced House* (1982).

[77] P. Bailey, '''A Mingled Mass of Perfectly Legitimate Pleasures'': The Victorian Middle Class and the Problem of Leisure', *Victorian Studies*, 21 (1977).

London. For certain practical purposes, it is true, London came to be treated as a whole after 1820. Sewerage, police, casual wards for vagrants, asylums and provision for the sick poor – all these were considered appropriate for unified treatment across the metropolis. Yet as late as 1855, *The Times* judged that London was 'rent into an affinity of divisions, districts and areas . . . Within the metropolitan limits, the local administration is carried on by no fewer than 300 different bodies deriving powers from about 250 different local Acts.'[78] London had failed to pass through the municipal revolution of 1835, and although Chadwick's 1847 report on the Health of the Metropolis led to the immediate setting up of the Metropolitan Commission of Sewers, yet discredit quickly followed after the mishandling of the 1848 cholera epidemic. Even when the Metropolitan Board of Works was set up in 1855, Chadwick complained that Parliament had ignored 'The experience of evils arising from the want of unity in the metropolis.'[79] Instead, the Metropolitan Management Act was said to represent the 'definitive triumph of the vestry movement'.[80] Nevertheless, the glorification of London's local leaders was incomplete – at least outside the City and its Corporation, vestrymen could not claim political parity with provincial towns. Furthermore, as the Metropolitan Board of Works steadily expanded its activities, the multi-faceted functional unit of the metropolis was underlined. A focus for metropolitan consciousness was being created, stimulating visions and images of a future London which seemed both poetic and practical.

III 'THE NEW URBAN REGION': LONDON AND THE HOME COUNTIES 1870–1918

> Forget six counties overhung with smoke,
> Forget the snorting steam and piston stroke,
> Forget the spreading of the hideous town;
> Think rather of the pack-horse on the down,
> And dream of London, small, and white and clean,
> The clear Thames bordered by its gardens green.
>
> William Morris, *The Wanderer*

The end of the nineteenth century clearly represented a turning point in London's development – by 1891, it had grown to be the largest

[78] *The Times*, 20 March 1855.
[79] E. Chadwick, 'London Centralised', *Contemporary Review*, 45 (1884), p. 794.
[80] S. E. Finer, *The Life and Times of Sir Edwin Chadwick* (1952), p. 484.

city the world had ever known. With a population of more than 5.5 million, London was five times more populous than either of its provincial rivals, Liverpool and Manchester, absorbing some 20 per cent of the population of England and Wales. After 1891, however, the population of London's central districts began to fall, and even the congested districts of the East End barely retained their numbers. By contrast, growth in the adjoining counties was dramatic. As the new century opened, Essex (36.3 per cent), Surrey (20.5 per cent) and Kent (16.8 per cent) had the fastest growth rates in the country.[81] The boundaries of London, even in simple, physical terms had become obscure; moreover, massive complex movements in goods and services, and increased personal mobility, challenged the nascent, fragile sense of metropolitan wholeness and unity. The City of London displayed these paradoxes most dramatically – in 1871, 750,000 clients a day poured into the commercial heart of London, served by 12 railway stations and 170,000 employees, but fewer than 75,000 residents.[82] The scale and intricate interdependence of the expanding metropolis reawakened public concern and unease and the fifty years between 1870 and 1920 saw repeated and continually shifting attempts to comprehend the phenomena that was London. The task was not only to assemble the facts, but also to order and interpret them – a task which required new concepts and terminologies to describe what it was that was happening to this 'Greater London', itself a term invented for statistical purposes in the 1881 census.[83]

The London phenomenon

A few simple protagonists of London could still be found. On an intellectual plane, its diversity still provided a dazzling and unending spectacle – 'a perennial Nijins Novgorod bazaar, a permanent world's fair'.[84] Such admiration derived from London's role as a world city, the commercial and cultural hub of a vast, expanding and unrivalled overseas Empire. London, Dyos has written, was 'The Babylon' of

---

[81] S. J. Low, 'The Rise of the Suburbs', *Contemporary Review*, 60 (1891), p. 546.
[82] M. Drake, 'The Census 1801–1901', in E. A. Wrigley, *Nineteenth-Century Society: Essays in the Use of Quantitative Methods for the Study of Social Data* (Cambridge, 1972), p. 19.
[83] Dyos, 'Greater and Greater London', p. 46.
[84] Quoted in A. Lees, 'The Metropolis and the Intellectual', in A. Sutcliffe, ed., *Metropolis 1890–1940* (1984), p. 88.

the Victorians, displaying a range of both ordinary and extraordinary events that were at once wonderful and terrible. Accounts of London's pleasures readily shaded into catalogues of London's sins, calling up visions of incipient disaster. Jefferies offered one such apocalyptic vision in *After London: Or Wild England* (1885). Submerged in its own filth as a result of some unexplained catastrophe, the ruins of London had become a swamp 'which no man dare enter, since death would be his inevitable fate'.[85] Those who survived the deluge are portrayed not as noble savages in their new, primitive habitat, but as corrupt enslavers. One man, Felix, keeps alive the hope of a new civilisation and a new nobility, as he sails the polluted waters alone. Other writers, while sharing Jefferies's fear of disaster, offered a greater hope of redemption through reconstruction, both physical and moral. All were seeking to grasp and express the totality of the modern city, exemplified in London. H. G. Wells put his faith in the power of science to transform urban life into a glass-domed city supported by and wholly dependent on new technologies in building and energy supply.[86] To Ebenezer Howard and William Morris, however, the new technologies, especially in transport, seemed to offer a different kind of transformation – for them, the hope of decentralising and breaking up large cities, especially London, found expression in Garden City ideas which were first elaborated in the 1890s. By such reformation, London might yet emerge 'small, and white and clean'. Through reconstruction, the new London would embody a new 'Social City' based on social co-operation and social cohesion.

In the first decades of the twentieth century, these ideas were elaborated and developed by town planners whose sights remained set above all on London and its problems. Arthur Crow's 'cities of health', George Pepler and Raymond Unwin's 'green girdle' and C. B. Purdom's 'new towns' all focussed on London – their underlying message being that the giant and sprawling city must and should be structured and controlled, its social and economic processes directed and manipulated, so that disaster could be averted. The irony is that the process of London's growth continually outran the concepts and structures evolved to manage it.

---

[85] E. Thomas, *Richard Jefferies* (1977), p. 234.
[86] H. G. Wells, *When the Sleeper Wakes* (1899), revised as *The Sleeper Wakes* (1910).

The 'residuum', revolution and reform

In the 1880s and 1890s, the introduction of new means of communication and electric power enabled London to begin shedding its population and industry, yet concern was increasingly focussed on the problems of the centre – overcrowding and congestion, 'the raw facts of poverty, poor housing and social malaise'.[87] Despite the growth of suburban low-density, single-family dwellings, the urgent debates about London living and working conditions obsessively revolved around the sub-standard and overcrowded homes of the centre and the East End.

Against a background of increasing social turmoil and fears of political upheaval and actual revolution, two very different approaches to London's problems were proposed in the closing decades of the nineteenth century. There was, on the one hand, an international solution and, on the other, a local solution – notable by its absence was any solution which acknowledged the regional interdependence of London with the Home Counties.

As an intellectual centre, London harboured many Communist and anarchist theorists. Many of them found actual and spiritual homes in the East End, thereby cementing in many minds the association between poverty and revolution. London's casual workers, suffering miserably from the effects of declining profits and rising unemployment between 1883 and 1887, seemed about to fall under the sway of socialist orators like Burns and Mann: even Engels himself felt that the great Dock Strike of 1889 heralded the creation of a truly revolutionary workers' party in the East End. 'How glad I am to have lived to see this day', he wrote.[88] Masterman later recalled that in the 1880s, the future that all had foretold was one of class war. Nevertheless, fears of insurrection faded rapidly once the depression lifted and London failed to lead the 'social revolution' as Hyndman had predicted. The Dock Strike offered at best a pyrrhic victory to those who supported it, as employers weeded out the unfit, while expanding and securing the work available for 'fitter' labourers.

Socialism maintained some of its appeal only in the outlying, more industrial districts of Bow, West Ham and Woolwich, and the radical

---

[87]   P. Hall, 'Metropolis 1890–1940: Challenge and Response', in Sutcliffe, ed., *Metropolis*, p. 19.

[88]   Letter from Engels to Bernstein, 22 August 1889, quoted in G. Stedman Jones, *Outcast London: A Study in the Relationship between Classes in Victorian Society* (1976 edn), p. 346.

initiative passed to the now sober, co-operative and nonconformist provinces. Neither the SDF nor its successor the BSP ever possessed more than 3,000 members out of London's population of 5.5 million. The solution offered by international Communism made no lasting impression on the London labour movement nor any, by default, on the wider British scene.

In contrast to the broad horizons of revolutionary socialists, reformers as diverse as Charles Booth, Octavia Hill and the early eugenists sought to treat London as a localised, self-contained unit, to which independent remedies could be applied. Undismayed by his findings that in most of inner London 40 per cent of families were in poverty, Booth argued that removing the lowest socio-economic groups to labour colonies beyond the built-up area would enable the self-regulating London economy to recover its equilibrium and restore adequate wages and employment levels to all those who remained behind.[89] Booth's proposition is a clear example of a solution which took no account of London's interdependence at the regional scale, still less at the national and international scale. Fundamentally similar in this respect were the eugenists' plans for enforced detention of the 'feeble minded' and the pauper, and for controlled reproduction of London's genetically 'unfit'.[90] At a distinctly smaller but certainly more humane level, Octavia Hill directed the efforts of her women house property managers towards training the London poor: by their regular visiting and discipline, housing managers were to raise standards of housekeeping and behaviour so as to fit slum-dwellers for living in London's congested centre.

Despite widespread fears that London's poverty, unemployment and overcrowding might lead to revolution, the economic and imperial bases of these problems were ignored and they came to be presented as local, environmental, social issues. The solutions envisaged were primarily physical, parochial and personal and centred above all on remedying the domestic conditions which prevailed in London slums. The Home Counties were not regarded as part of the problem, nor were they seen as the unit within which a solution should be sought. Even to Booth, the Home Counties appeared simply as an

[89] E. P. Hennock, 'Poverty and Social Theory in England: The Experience of the 1880s', *Social History*, 1 (1976), pp. 67–92.

[90] P. M. H. Mazumdar, 'The Eugenists and the Residuum: The Problem of the Urban Poor', *Bulletin of the History of Medicine*, 54 (1980), pp. 204–15.

undeveloped hinterland which could provide the physical separation necessary for the dispersion and isolation of 'unfits'.

Metropolitan management

The events of the 1880s and the reformulation of the London problem which ensued placed the question of metropolitan management in a new context. In the aftermath of the Dock Strike, the capital no longer seemed at risk from destruction by an overwhelming catastrophe. Such fears could be dismissed as 'a fantastic myth'. The vast and uncontrollable mass of London's East End was now seen as a highly differentiated group, with large numbers of respectable working-class people quite separate from the feckless, hopeless remnant of the 'residuum'. This unfit rump was no longer perceived as a political threat: they could be regarded as an urgent but limited social problem – 'a nuisance to administrators rather than a threat to civilization'.[91] Revolutionary demands had been turned aside, and recognition could be extended to the legitimate grievances of London's respectable working class. In this new, more relaxed atmosphere, the role of the state needed to be redefined, and the functions of local and central government evaluated afresh.

Now that London had been made safe from revolution, the national government's dislike of giving the capital its own elected authority diminished. The reform of London government along the lines already applied to provincial cities was no longer unthinkable – positive action in Parliament, however, required the politicians to give priority to the issue. The growing recognition of the need for a central authority in London could be jeopardised at national level by calculations of party advantage, and at local level by powerful interests in the City and the vestries. Nevertheless, the unity of London for practical purposes which had been exemplified by the Metropolitan Board of Works and the London School Board became a central tenet of London radicals, as well as of some key professions such as public health officials, statisticians and engineers.

Major obstacles to the reform of London government nevertheless remained. Both parochial and national authorities feared that they would have to cede power before a central London authority could be established. Dismantling not only the power of the City Corporation, but also possibly government control of the Metropolitan Police

---

[91] Stedman Jones, *Outcast London*, p. 320.

were particularly contentious issues. It was the intense debates about housing and the casual poor in the late 1880s which renewed pressure on the cabinet, and ultimately overcame ministers' reluctance to confront the resurgence of London localism which had defeated the London Municipal Bill of 1884. A directly elected London County Council was finally created in 1888, almost as an afterthought in a general reform of English local government.

Boundary changes after the Third Reform Bill offered the prospect of London as a Tory stronghold, yet victory in the 1889 LCC elections went to the Progressives. Lord Salisbury remained sanguine, confident that London's basic conservatism would assert itself: 'I rather look to the new London County Council to play the drunken helot for our benefit. Such a body at the outset must make some portentous blunders: and I am not sorry that, as luck will have it, they will be carried to the account of the Radicals.'[92]

Although the issue of London government had become a party question, discussion did not polarise along party lines. Though Conservative politicians most often favoured localism and the decentralisation of power in London government, and Liberals supported a central authority for the metropolis, yet the parties were themselves divided. Political allies found themselves taking up opposing positions on the issue, depending on their different vantage points as vestrymen, provincial MPs or London MPs.

The LCC itself was established as an additional arena for party conflict from the first elections: within a few years, the mechanisms for party control over its business had been established. The radical platform adopted by the Progressives did, as Salisbury had predicted, engender organised opposition especially from London's property interests. The London Municipal Society was formed in 1894 to oppose the 'spendthrifts' of County Hall, and to revive pressure for the decentralisation of power from the LCC to new metropolitan borough councils. Some Progressives welcomed this in principle, but baulked at the links being drawn between the establishment of borough councils, and the preservation of the City Corporation. Criticism of the LCC mounted, not only because its policies were radical in tone, but also because its size prevented it from dealing adequately with London's problems.

Efficient management of the metropolis, Lord Salisbury argued,

---

[92] R. Taylor, *Lord Salisbury* (1975), p. 126.

required an 'aggregate of municipalities' to be established within London: such a structure would remedy the overconcentration of power in the LCC, and recognise the status and wealth of many of London's individual districts. Some Liberal MPs were persuaded of the need to increase the efficiency and representativeness of London government by devolving power to metropolitan borough councils and they supported the principle of the London Government Bill which established them in 1899. London Liberals, however, bitterly attacked the Bill with its 'conglomerate of sham municipalities', fearing for the 'unity, simplicity and equality of treatment which are the cardinal principles of the reformation of London'.[93]

In practice, the new structure did not diminish the power of the LCC. Indeed, it could be argued that the LCC's broader vision was strengthened. With the metropolitan borough councils offering a focus for parochial pride, the LCC could more easily insulate itself from local interests, projecting and developing a London-wide base as a framework for policy and decision-making. The LCC could avoid the pressures of 'ward politics', encouraging its members to regard themselves as representative of the County of London, no matter which area had elected them. This broad approach was a hallmark of many of the LCC's activities in the early twentieth century, most notably in education and housing.

Slums and housing policy

In the 1880s and 1890s, London's housing problems had emerged as *the* most important social and political issue for government. The persistence of London's slums, their poverty, their extent – above all, their location at the 'Heart of the Empire' seemed to threaten the stability of metropolis, nation and colonies alike. To acknowledge that neither London's magnitude nor London's slums could be matched by any other great city was to confront the real paradox of Britain's imperial status and power.

The centre of imperialism, as Lord Rosebery is never tired of reiterating, rests in London. With the perpetual lowering of the Imperial Race in the great cities of the kingdom through overcrowding in room and area, no

---

[93]   Quoted in K. Young and P.L. Garside, *Metropolitan London: Politics and Urban Change 1837–1981* (1982), p. 101.

amount of hectic, feverish activity on the confines of the Empire will be able to arrest the inevitable decline.[94]

The severity of London's problems had been exposed, not least by the Royal Commission on the Housing of the Working Classes (1884–5) – the remedies required, however, had still to be identified. The making of policies and programmes required the development of concepts to formulate and define the nature of the housing problem in London. The matter was also dependent on economic circumstances and political will. Most significant of all was to be the interaction of London's 'principalities and powers' – not only conflict between the various political arenas, but also within them, as differences widened and deepened. As the LCC began to formulate a broadly based and London-wide approach to metropolitan problems, it was matched by opposition in kind. The language of debate was derived not from economic or personal interest, but from political principle. This high level of politicisation was a distinguishing feature of London administration, affecting the initiation, implementation and outcome of policy in a direct but often complex manner.

The first step along this road was a semantic shift in the term 'slum' which had a profound effect on the remedies proposed. This shift occurred between the Cross Act of 1875, and the Housing Act of 1890. The Cross Act was distinguished by its emphasis on the physical and social isolation of slums, those 'plague spots where all these evils flourish and whence they spread are mapped out . . . as clearly as the mountains of the moon are, by the aid of scientific discovery'.[95] This typification set the slum apart from the normal workings of London society, removing such places from any general, economic framework, and presenting them as insanitary and immoral 'pockets' clearly demarcated in extent, and distinguished by their grim bleakness from the 'normal' world outside. Such a formulation suggested remedies which would erase these alien phenomena and normalise them through rebuilding with sanitary dwellings. The problem and the remedy was thus physical and finite. Both Booth's London survey and the Royal Commission of 1884–5, however, undermined the clarity of this approach. Above all, these investigations helped to break down the way in which the slums had been separated off from the rest of society. Their findings showed overcrowding and poor housing to be a general problem which affected a wide spectrum of the working

[94] C. F. G. Masterman, ed., *The Heart of Empire* (1901).
[95] R. Cross, *Homes of the London Poor in the Nineteenth Century* (1882), p. 231.

class, and whole areas of inner London. The solution that was required came to be seen as something different from isolated slum clearance schemes. 'What is wanted is more – much more – home accommodation.'[96] In effect, this meant harnessing and promoting the general development processes at work in London, and especially the growth of the suburbs. Housing policy thus became linked to issues of regional development, and in particular the provision of transport. By 1900, an American expert on municipal government, Albert Shaw, was noting that London's governors were investing much more in surface and underground transport to decant population than in health and housing directly.[97] Indeed, slum clearance and rehousing schemes of the Cross type were now themselves being depicted as an interference in the natural development of London.[98]

Though the diagnosis and the remedy for London's housing problems had changed, the various agencies involved in the implementation of policy were confronted with extremely difficult economic and political realities. The very scale and intensity of the London housing problem, high land prices and rising residential rents all affected the ability of local authorities to respond. Though London property prices slumped at the end of the nineteenth century, they remained higher than comparable prices elsewhere, and rents remained high throughout. It has been estimated that in 1901, a built-up acre in the City of London rented on an average for about four thousand times as much as an acre of farmland. In 1905, a plot of land near the Bank of England was sold for the equivalent of £3.25 million an acre, 'about one-tenth of the bullion in the vaults'.[99] House rents remained stable at high levels, with particularly steep increases in the expanding north-west suburbs, and in the East End – rents in West Ham rose by 15 per cent, and in Stepney by 25 per cent over the period 1890 to 1912. Residential redevelopment in the central area could scarcely be contemplated except in special circumstances, and even the suburban solution was put in jeopardy as potential sites

[96]   RC on Alien Immigration, PP 1903, IX, evidence of Sanitary Officer for Bethnal Green, q. 6719. This shift in attitudes to slums clearly follows shifts in attitude towards the poor, see above, pp. 510–11.

[97]   Quoted in P. J. Waller, Town, City and Nation, England 1850–1914 (Oxford, 1983), p. 30.

[98]   The change from inner area clearance to suburban estate-building is clearly indicated by maps locating LCC housing sites in Young and Garside, Metropolitan London, Figures 6.3 and 6.4, pp. 164–5.

[99]   A. Offer, Property and Politics 1870–1914: Landownership, Law, Ideology and Urban Development in England (Cambridge, 1981), p. 255.

receded further and further from the centre. 'Yesterday', one commentator wrote in 1901, '[the solution] lay in West Ham, in Streatham, Hackney and Tottenham: today it lies in East Ham, in Croydon and in Harrow: tomorrow it will be the belt of country lying beyond.'[100]

Economic variables, however, should not be seen as exercising a wholly independent effect on housing policy – the work of Offer and Englander has shown that there was a political dimension at work which operated most directly on property values through the instrument of the rates.[101] The first decade of the twentieth century saw overcrowding once more on the increase in London despite the collapse in the residential property market and the abundance of empty property. Offer has argued that this situation was not the result of market economics alone, but is to be explained by reference to political struggles. The element that gained most from politics, it seems, was that of rising rates. Offer has estimated that increases in this local taxation could account for about one quarter of the decline of property values in London. The impact of this, however, was magnified in investors' minds by national Conservative propaganda after 1905, and more immediately by the mobilisation of ratepayers into municipal, and especially London, politics by bodies such as the Property Owners' Protection Association. Furthermore, the introduction of land value taxes in Lloyd George's 'People's Budget' of 1909 only increased the financial insecurity and political awareness of investors in housing.[102]

The effect on London politics was dramatic. From the early 1900s, metropolitan conservatism began to construct a new populist platform under the banner of a 'non-political' 'Municipal Reform Society'. The rallying cry of the movement, based in rejuvenated ratepayers' associations was opposition to 'municipal socialism' and civic expenditure. The campaign fell on willing ears – London's shopkeepers, clerks and professionals were being severely affected by the combination of economic stagnation and rising rates. Against the tide of national politics, the ratepayer revolt brought defeat to Progressives at the metropolitan borough elections in 1906, and at the LCC elections in 1907. After these Conservative victories, both LCC rates and municipal debt levelled off.

---

[100] F. W. Lawrence, 'The Housing Problem', in Masterman, *Heart of Empire*.
[101] D. Englander, 'Landlord and Tenant in Urban Britain: The Politics of Housing Reform 1838–1924' (unpublished PhD thesis, University of Warwick, 1979).
[102] Offer, *Property and Politics*, pp. 308–11.

This interplay between concepts, economics and politics prevented any unilinear development towards municipal housing provision in London. While Progressives were forced to take account of market pressures and of the activities of other agencies, Municipal Reformers remained receptive to arguments about the need for housing reform in the interests of the Nation, the Race and the Empire.[103] For the Progressives on the LCC, the dilemma hinged on their commitment to build in the poorest parts of east and south-east London, while at the same time they required high-quality construction, economic rents and responsible tenants. This led them eventually to prefer lower-cost suburban sites, and socially superior tenants. Many of the early LCC estates built on central sites resulted not from direct policy, but were the result of other public construction such as the Rotherhithe and Blackwall tunnels, and East End Board Schools. After Municipal Reformers gained power in 1907, the emphasis on public housing diminished: the slum clearance programme was wound down and the Works Department was abolished. Some building continued on suburban estates at Old Oak and Totterdown Fields, but undeveloped parts of Norbury and White Hart Lane were sold.

Overall, the housing policy of the LCC reflects the outcome of political conflicts at both central and local level centring on the issue of rates: overlaying this was an unresolved tension between a commitment to some public housing provision, and building and management strategies which were enmeshed in the economics of the private sector. The LCC was free from the direct influence of slum landlords who had dominated the vestries, but its members could not ignore the changing character of investors in house property which its own interventionist policies had brought about. Moreover, though the LCC consciously projected a London vision, it remained constrained by market forces and by the Balkanisation of powers and spheres of influence, some of which again were of its own making.

Metropolitan man

The LCC's early struggles to determine what London might be were matched by the efforts of social commentators to establish what London *was* – in particular, to define the character and personality

---

[103]   S. Lawrence, 'The Politics of Housing: Ratepayers and Municipal Reformers in Hackney 1880–1914' (paper presented to Urban History Group Conference, April 1986).

of Londoners, and to discover the characteristics of the new 'metro-politan man'. Many reporters were simply overwhelmed by the sheer range of characters they encountered, not least those who sought to identify some standard metropolitan type. For historians, these attempts to document London's people are a significant event since they reflect renewed interest in London's character, and in its potential significance as a social force, capable of moulding attitudes and values over an ever-widening area.

Henry Mayhew and Charles Booth were the most indefatigable of London's explorers. Mayhew, in particular, demonstrated in his 'cyclopaedia' an endless curiosity about London labour, and especially its street-folk, 'comprising street sellers, street buyers, street finders, street performers, street artisans [and] street labourers'.[104] Limited though its scope was, Mayhew was rightly proud of his work 'as being the first commission of inquiry into the state of the people, undertaken by a private individual.' Booth, by contrast, sought a wider canvas and a more analytical approach.[105] Booth included statis-tics of poverty, and classifications and descriptions of streets, trades, institutions and groups, such as model dwellings, common lodging-houses and homeless men. Though in the beginning Booth claimed that 'I had no preconceived ideas, no theory to work up to, no pet scheme into agreement with which the facts collected were to be twisted or to which they would have to be squared', yet 'At the same time the consideration and hope of remedy have never been out of my mind.' For seventeen years Booth's 'spirit of enquiry' was abroad in London. Overwhelmed by his own appetite for facts, Booth con-fessed that 'I have at times doubted whether the prolongation of this work has had any other basis than an inability on my part to come to a conclusion.' Nevertheless, later commentators have detected a conceptual framework underpinning Booth's gargantuan diet of observations which enabled him to present his optimistic view of Lon-don poverty, and his simple remedy for its eradication.[106]

Alongside the mammoth investigations of Booth and Mayhew, other individual revelations of life in London's workhouses and rookeries caused a sensation at the time as 'the holes and corners' of London society were revealed. Their horrors were compared with those of

---

[104]   H. Mayhew, *London Labour and the London Poor*, 4 vols. (1861–2).
[105]   C. Booth, ed., *Life and Labour of the People in London*, 1st ser., *Poverty*, 4 vols. (1889–91).
[106]   See above, pp. 511–12.

'distant tribes' and 'the middle passage of some slave ship', while alongside and interdependent with them lay the 'unrestricted luxury and worse than useless extravagance that characterise the wealthy neighbouring districts'.[107] Stories and novels also provided outstanding social reportage in the form of fiction. Arthur Morrison's portrayal of East End life was violent and pessimistic – even the LCCs Boundary Street clearance scheme could not clear away the foulness of an area like the Jago. In the preface to the third edition of *A Child of the Jago*, Morrison wrote: 'The Jago as mere bricks and mortar is gone. But the Jago in flesh and blood still lives, and is crowding into neighbourhoods already densely populated.'[108] To George Gissing, the flesh and blood of metropolitan man was unremittingly drab and desolate – not only the slum-dweller, but the better paid also.

To walk about a neighbourhood such as this [the Wilton Square district of Islington] is the dreariest exercise to which a man can betake himself: the heart is crushed by uniformity of decent squalor; one remembers that each of the dead-faced houses, often each separate blind window represents a 'home', and the associations of the word whisper blank despair.[109]

Metropolitan life represented to Gissing the defeat of humanity, a dreadful, damned and nightmare experience 'beyond the outmost limits of dread'.

Walter Besant portrayed London life outside the City and the West End as a travesty of urban civilisation.[110] Whatever identity emerged from this vacuity, it appeared even to the most optimistic as merely 'something more than confusion of casual accidents'.[111] More mobile Londoners sought individual identity in the anonymity of suburban family life. Here the main focus of public activity was the self-effacing arena of church or chapel. In London's inner areas, however, workers other than Jews did not look to the church for spiritual refreshment. Many of them found that in the narrow confines of their houses and yards. Booth drew attention to the 'small rough roofed erections interspersed with little glass houses' at the backs of the cramped houses. 'These', he wrote, 'represent hobbies, pursuits of leisure

---

[107]   A. Sherwell, *Life in West London: A Study and a Contrast* (1897).
[108]   A. Morrison, *A Child of the Jago*, 3rd edn (1897). Also, *idem, The Hole in the Wall* (1902), and *idem, Tales of Mean Streets* (1906).
[109]   Quoted in Waller, *Town, City and Nation*, p. 43.
[110]   W. Besant, *South London* (1899), and *idem, East London* (1901).
[111]   Quoted in A. Briggs, *Victorian Cities* (Harmondsworth, 1968), pp. 348–9.

hours – plants, flowers, fowls, pigeons, and there is room to sit out, when the weather is fine enough, with friend and pipe.'[112] The LCC and the metropolitan borough councils sought to expand the recreational room available to Londoners by providing parks and open spaces. The LCC alone controlled 113 parks, gardens and open spaces by 1910, representing £2m of capital expenditure, £130,000 annual maintenance and direct employment for 1,000 workers.

By 1914, such parks played their part in working-class leisure along with music halls, dance halls, cinemas, football and dog racing. Whether these more formalised types of leisure provision should be regarded as an attempt at 'social control' is open to question. F. M. L. Thompson has drawn attention to the distinction between 'socialisation' where a group socialises its members by imbuing them with *its own* mores, and 'social control' where the process takes place on an *inter-class* basis.[113] Whatever intentions there may have been, Stedman Jones has concluded that 'By the Edwardian period, it had become inescapably clear that middle class evangelism had failed to create a working class in its own image. The great majority of London workers were not Christian, provident, chaste or temperate.'[114]

A new urban region

The rapid expansion of London suburbs up to 1914 overtook not only the recently drawn administrative boundaries, but even the language available to describe the process. New terms had once more to be forged to label the phenomenon that London had become. It was Geddes who offered a new, sociological dimension to metropolitan analysis, and who coined the term 'conurbation' to articulate such growth at the regional scale.[115]

London's new Edwardian suburbs were predominantly residential in character, with few industrial establishments, as befitted their status as dwelling-places for London's more senior clerks and executives. Working-class suburbanisation had fallen away, the victim of rising unemployment and stagnation in the standard of living. In the decade before the First World War, moving to the suburbs became the

[112] Quoted in Waller, *Town, City and Nation*, p. 51.
[113] F. M. L. Thompson, 'Social Control in Victorian Britain', *Economic History Review*, 2nd ser., 34 (1981), pp. 189–208.
[114] G. Stedman Jones, 'Working-Class Culture and Working-Class Politics in London, 1870–1900: Notes on the Remaking of a Working Class', *Journal of Social History*, 7 (1974), p. 471.
[115] G. Cherry, *The Evolution of British Town Planning* (1974), p. 52.

preserve of social groups of the rank of clerk and above.[116] Their aspirations found a response in the ideals of the Garden City movement. As its reduced housing programme moved outwards physically and upwards socially, the LCC also adopted Garden City forms in its suburban estates. The Old Oak estate reflected this mode in the picturesque style of its houses, with their steeply pitched roofs and gables, and in the layout, with its setbacks and 'village' greens. At Letchworth Garden City (1903) and at Hampstead Garden Suburb (1906) private capital underpinned attempts to carry out Garden City ideals, though at Hampstead the new suburb remained closely tied to London labour and consumer markets.

As the middle-class suburbs around London grew, so did commuting and traffic congestion. The problems of London transport prompted new questions about the form, function and co-ordination of the Home Counties in relation to London.[117]

Some planners sought solutions derived from the American City Beautiful movement, advocating 'radial motorways' and parkway ringroads to organise and deliver a road system for London.[118] In 1903, the Royal Commission on London Traffic was set up 'to enquire into the means of locomotion and transport in London'. While recognising the appeal of suburban ringroads, the Commission favoured tackling London's problem at the centre – partly by restricting parking but chiefly by constructing two cross-London double-deck avenues intersecting near the British Museum.[119] Such a drastic scheme can only be explained by the very real fears that London might 'suffocate' if traffic was not dealt with. Nevertheless, the Board of Trade's London Traffic Branch which succeeded the Royal Commission in 1907 put its faith in suburban by-passes – a solution which restored the question of the London 'region' to the political agenda.

The Royal Commission had found that London traffic suffered fundamentally from a want of co-ordination and planning and recommended a London Traffic Board, but the suggestion was not implemented. Although the tramways, railways and bus services were being brought under single ownership by Albert Stanley's Underground group, the mainline railways remained outside its control.

---

[116]   P. L. Garside, 'West End, East End: London 1890–1940', in Sutcliffe, ed., *Metropolis*, p. 238.
[117]   P. L. Garside, 'London 1919–1950: Metropolitan Development and Planning', *Planning History Bulletin*, 6 (1984).
[118]   H. W. Wilson, 'Will London be Suffocated?', *National Review*, 37 (1902), pp. 598–609.
[119]   Garside, 'West End, East End', p. 238.

Moreover, responsibility for roads remained divided between the local authorities of London and the Home Counties who bridled at relinquishing authority to any central body. The question was dealt with at a series of conferences – the Greater London Arterial Roads Conferences 1913–16 – which split London into seven sections with the constituent local authorities working under a central government department – the Local Government Board. This solution displayed many of the features which were to typify solutions to London's regional problems – the *ad hoc* single-purpose body, the avoidance of local authority reform, a reliance on private enterprise, the shelving of the problems of central London, and a concentration on managing growth at the periphery.

Improving transport links with the suburbs, it was acknowledged, would inevitably generate further suburban development. Charles Booth had assumed that one effect of this would be an increase in 'local life' so that there would be no need to fear that 'better and more rapid communication would ... increase centralisation'.[120] H. G. Wells, however, maintained that this process of 'delocalisation' was irreversibly underway in London, brought about by improvements in communication: 'every tramway, every twopenny tube, every improvement in your omnibus services, in your telephone services, in your organisation of credit increases the proportion of your delocalised class, and sucks the ebbing blood from your old communities into the veins of the new'.[121] The answer to this delocalisation, Wells argued, was new 'mammoth municipalities' delimited by the natural watersheds of economic activity and movement. In London, he envisaged an area much larger than the Administrative County, including within it 'The whole system of what I might call the London-centred population.'

Wells's proposals found favour with the Fabians and LCC Progressives but were opposed in Conservative circles as 'centralisation gone mad'. Suburban authorities, whatever their political persuasion, opposed the idea of 'annexation'. The onset of war, however, brought LCC Progressives and Municipal Reformers into agreement on the need to consolidate government in the London region. Building on the new 'scientific understanding' of geographers, sociologists and

[120]   C. Booth, *Improved Means of Locomotion as a First Step towards the Cure of the Housing Difficulties of London* (1901).
[121]   H. G. Wells, 'The Question of Scientific Administrative Areas', published as an appendix to *Mankind in the Making* (1903).

political scientists, the politicians hoped peace would bring 'a new era in London government' based on a recognition of the complex and nebulous structure that London now possessed. In 1919, the LCC called on the government to institute an enquiry to determine

The particular services which should be brought under a single administration throughout Greater London; the area of Greater London which should be unified in respect of the administration of those services; the authority to which should be entrusted the administration of those services; and the relation of that authority to other local committees in the area.[122]

The clear message was that London could no longer be regarded as coterminous with its built-up area – rather it had to be recognised that 'in a manner, all south-east England is a single urban community, for steam and electricity are changing our geographical conceptions'.[123]

In 1919, the prophets of the new age could delineate the London region with their innovative statistical and graphical techniques. In many respects, the truth of the image they drew could not be denied. The commercial pull of London for work, for services and for leisure was unmistakable. Suburbanisation seemed to feed on itself moulding rural immigrants from the depressed and conservative Home Counties and the ex-urbanites into one huge consumer market. One section of London, however, still stood apart – the casual poor of London's East End. As rents and prices rose after 1900, as wages stagnated and unemployment featured prominently in their lives, these Londoners remained stranded 'between a small workshop system that refused to die and a system of factory production which had scarcely begun to develop'.[124] They were still recognisable and stigmatised as 'unfit', 'loafers', 'unemployables' and 'degenerates'. The anxieties generated by London's casual labourers remained widely shared by politicians across the political spectrum – verminous and foul-smelling, their memory lingered powerfully and long wherever they were encountered, even as far afield as the hopfields of Kent.[125] Their problems, and the problem they presented, however, temporarily evaporated with the First World War as all surplus labour was absorbed by the needs of war. Despite the immediate postwar crisis, attention switched elsewhere as the world depression of the 1930s undermined

---

122   LCC, Minutes of Proceedings, 28 October 1919.
123   H. J. Mackinder, *Britain and the British Seas* (Oxford, 1907), p. 258.
124   Stedman Jones, 'Working-Class Culture', p. 489.
125   T. C. Barker and J. Whyman, *Life in Kent before 1914*, SSRC Final Report, HR 2830 (1977), pp. 51–4.

the staple industries of the provincial cities leaving a million unemployed. The nature of Britain's regional problem came to be fundamentally redefined – London was no longer at its centre, but represented an enclave of success and prosperity aloof from but nevertheless perhaps responsible for the painful decay of the provinces.

IV THE 'WALL-LESS WORLD' OF LONDON 1918–50

> No place is safe: no place at peace. There is no place where a woman
> and her daughter can hide and be at peace. The war comes through
> the air, bombs drop in the night. Quiet people go out in the morning
> and see air-fleets passing overhead – dripping death – dripping death.
>   H. G. Wells, *War in the Air* (1908)

The decades spanning the two world wars heightened the need to analyse the 'wall-less world' that London had become and to evaluate its actual and symbolic significance. Reports of enquiries, investigations and analyses appeared regularly as the effort to comprehend, assess and manage the capital continued. To some, like Lewis Mumford, it seemed that the familiar metropolitan problems of overgrowth and disintegration were simply intensifying. 'The Parasitopolis of the late nineteenth century has already become the spectral Necropolis of the mid-twentieth century', Mumford wrote.[126] By 1939, it was being said that London was no longer simply a problem 'sui generis', but had become a threat to national life as a whole. In the 1920s, the problems of metropolitan expansion were identified as internal congestion and co-ordination but in the 1930s opinion shifted. Within the capital, London's Labour politicians raised the issues of equity and the distribution of resources. At the same time, national politicians and experts were presenting those same issues as a problem of London's relationship with the provinces. From the national perspective, London's overgrowth and the depression suffered in the regions were but two aspects of the same problem. By 1939, the London question had become a national, intra-regional issue as the inexorable 'drift to the south-east' continued.

The urgency of the problem was increased as London's continued physical expansion and its growing economic importance appeared vulnerable as never before. The experience of total war bequeathed new social tensions and forebodings of unprecedented horror still

---

[126] L. Mumford, 'The Plan for London', in *City Development: Studies in Disintegration and Renewal* (1947), p. 184.

to come from aerial bombardment. The metropolis had long seemed dangerous; in 1919 and even more in 1939, it seemed simply disastrous.

Despite the wealth of contemporary material and comment, the history of interwar and wartime London is nevertheless largely unwritten. Housing and politics are the major exceptions to this. For the most part, while contemporary accounts provide a wealth of detail on London's physical, economic and social fabric, we lack the necessary synthesis. Much of the secondary data such as the census remain unexplored. There are no analyses of London's overall structure, and only a very few intensive studies of the quality of metropolitan life. This final section, therefore, is inevitably more impressionistic and speculative than those that have gone before. The major themes are the nature of metropolitan growth and politics and their impact on environmental management, especially in terms of housing and planning policy.

The Armistice, peace and urban order

The Armistice of November 1918 brought relief from hostilities abroad and from Zeppelins over London, but at the same time it brought the threat of bitter conflict at home. Evidence from cabinet papers strongly suggests a growing fear of insurrection as the troops returned. Their discipline and training acquired for war, it was feared, would prove dangerous assets in a disaffected working class with the example of recent Bolshevik uprisings in European capitals and in Russia before them. The prospect of civil unrest, especially in London, had again become a real and alarming possibility. Lloyd George's 'Homes for Heroes' campaign was tactically instigated as a means of defusing potential revolution through the promise of a massive housing programme whose every aspect was imbued with the social and architectural values of order, balance and harmony.[127]

This vision of social harmony was especially difficult to achieve in London. Rustic housing estates planned on Garden City lines and separated from existing built-up areas were the ideal, but problems arose because of London's existing size (the 1921 census recorded a population of 7.5 million for Greater London) and because of its

---

[127]   M. Swenarton, *Homes Fit for Heroes: The Politics and Architecture of Early State Housing in Britain* (1981).

fragmented governmental structure. H. de R. Walker, Progressive Chairman of the LCC's Housing of the Working Classes Committee lamented this fragmentation and expressed apprehension that chaos might ensue in any attempt to mount an ambitious housing programme in the region. 'I may add', he continued enviously, 'that such a problem would not arise in those of the great provincial cities which, having extended their borders, have the whole matter within their survey, and are able to solve it within the limits of their own municipal area.'[128] The urgency of the immediate situation meant that efforts to reform London government had to be shelved and policy-making in London became increasingly dependent on bargainings, compromises, action and counteraction between the parties concerned at national, regional and local level. The effect was to attenuate the links between London's problems and the objectives and outcomes of policy.

The postwar debate about London's housing, the 'Greater London Housing Campaign' and the reform of local government revolved around the future of the LCC. In 1919, Progressive and Municipal Reform leaders at County Hall and the Minister of Health all seemed to agree that London government should be reviewed, and that in the meantime the LCC should 'take the lead' in meeting housing needs throughout the Conurbation. The reaction of the outer areas was, however, both hostile and well organised. Suburban fears of invasion and annexation provoked powerful resistance to the LCC – a 'wolf on the prowl' stalking defenceless rural 'chickens' to provide sites for vast working-class housing estates. In 1920, the Ministry of Health's Committee on Unhealthy Areas had called for London government to be unified, but by 1923 a Royal Commission on London Government opposed any change, recognising that any attempt to extend the authority of the LCC would provoke such extensive opposition as to render proposals futile. Municipal Reformers also reverted to opposition – their misgivings were partly based on the grounds of efficiency, but to a great extent they feared the threat that a Greater London authority would pose to national government because of its scale, and because such aggrandisement represented 'a part of the plan for the establishment of Socialism'. Few supporters of a Greater London authority remained, and throughout the interwar period the

---

[128] Quoted in Young and Garside, *Metropolitan London*, p. 148.

LCC faced a defensive alliance of suburban authorities and a 'delicate, diplomatic situation' in dealing with them.[129]

The 'Homes for Heroes' campaign nevertheless placed a major housing responsibility on the LCC, and the President of the Local Government Board, Hayes Fisher, specifically enjoined the LCC to give 'a certain amount of leading light and guidance' over the whole metropolitan area. Suburban opposition, however, shaped the LCC's activities, confining its estates to areas of low social status and compliant local councils mainly to the south and east of London. The scale of LCC housing operations where conditions proved favourable only served to strengthen opposition elsewhere. The visual and social impact of Becontree, set down in the Essex marshes, could only reinforce the misgivings of suburban authorities. Absolute resistance seemed the only viable strategy. Where chinks appeared in suburban defences, the LCC poured through, building more than 17,000 houses in the Home Counties between 1919 and 1929, 13,000 of them at Becontree.

Social polarisation and the 'unhealthy areas'

It was quickly apparent at the time, and has generally been agreed since, that the suburban estates created in the 1920s did little to meet the general needs of London's slum-dwellers and still less to solve the problem of the 'residuum'. The 1921 census showed that the collapse of the private housing market was trapping a wide social range of newly formed households in London's inner areas. Major Harry Barnes, a leading Labour member of the LCC wrote in 1925 that 'Overcrowding in London is developing a new and sinister aspect . . . It is spreading and rapidly making inner London into one vast slum. Hardworking, self-respecting people . . . are now living in hidden dens that are not fit to house the most degraded of human beings.'[130] It was these newly and 'unjustifiably' overcrowded people that the 'Homes for Heroes' campaign aimed to help – establishing a new definition of the deserving and the undeserving which could command immediate and wide support. The problem of the old-established slums was consciously and deliberately shelved by civil servants

[129]   Ibid., 126–39.
[130]   Major H. Barnes, 'The Slum Problem', Journal of the Town Planning Institute, 13 (1926–7), p. 148.

and ministers who recognised the extent of 'unhealthy areas' but could see no means of confronting them publicly.[131]

The radical proposals of the Unhealthy Areas Committee for a regional government with wide planning powers for London derived from its original brief 'to explore further some of the very difficult questions relating to slum areas' in the capital. The scale and costliness of the replanning and the development proposed alarmed Ministry of Health officials: even though the Ministry acknowledged that conditions in London slums were 'atrocious' they were unwilling to investigate or discuss this publicly because of the effect on public expectations. The true extent of the 'lamentable conditions' that existed had to remain hidden, slum clearance schemes were deliberately allowed to 'proceed slowly' through Whitehall, and official policy rested on limited, token activity – 'patch repairs' of unfit houses, and management of the worst property on Octavia Hill lines to secure 'as little deterioration as possible'. It was, at best, a cosmetic holding operation, a gesture that something was being done. During the 1920s, the calls of eugenists that public health required the controlled breeding of people living in slums was heard with renewed insistence as conditions there worsened and the policy vacuum persisted.

In the late 1920s, it could no longer be denied that some new ground had to be defined on which to base future housing policy. Political and social misgivings about the wisdom of the LCC's suburban estate-building programme and the consequent neglect of the slums were reinforced by the consequences of a private sector house-building revival, only briefly interrupted by the 1929–31 slump. Competition for scarce sites in outer London intensified and the opposition of suburban local authorities to the LCC increased. The housing record of the Municipal Reform party became a prominent election issue. By the end of 1933, only 118 dwellings had been completed out of a target of 2,000. Herbert Morrison's Labour members on the LCC committed themselves to replacing this 'as and when' housing policy with 'plan and drive', ending the slums with 'a vigorous rehousing drive'.[132] The emphasis changed from suburban cottage estates to building dwellings in or near the centre of London. The huge dormitory cottage estates were condemned as 'depressingly uniform', and 'of no practical use to most families living in slum houses or in overcrowded

---

[131]   P. L. Garside, '"Unhealthy Areas": Town Planning and the Slums', *Planning Perspectives*, 2 (1987).
[132]   H. Morrison, 'Plans for London', *Geographical Magazine*, 8 (1938), p. 83.

conditions'.[133] After Labour's victory in the LCC elections of 1934, policy shifted towards clearance and redevelopment in 'unhealthy areas' and the pace of building quickened considerably. Nevertheless, if sites close to the periphery of London became available attempts continued to be made to secure them. Despite the change of emphasis, an opportunistic housing policy continued to be pursued. In Essex, a further 1,000 acres at Fairlop Plain was acquired by the LCC in 1935 despite the opposition of Ilford Council. Within the Administrative County itself, four boroughs received half of the LCC's entire building programme in the late 1930s – Camberwell, Lewisham, Wandsworth and Lambeth, whilst in others the LCC was totally excluded. The correlation of housing stress with LCC house-building in London was poor, and the location of flats was determined not by housing need, but by the political complexion of the local borough council and the availability of sites. Morrison and the London Labour party accepted this containment as the price of low-profile politics and minimum cost policies designed to restore above all Labour's fitness to govern after the débâcle of 1931. In the process, the face of large parts of London was transformed by ranks of five-storey high-density flats. Greenwood commented that 'London has indeed succumbed to the "flat" method of accommodation to a greater degree than any other part of the country.'[134]

Less sanguine in his attitude was Frederic Osborn, one of the original and most vociferous advocates of Garden Cities. Osborn derided the options open to Londoners of a centrally located tenement or a suburban house and garden. 'Thus the Londoner has to choose between being a rat in a drain or a squirrel in a cage', he raged. Neither decentralisation into Garden Cities, nor large-scale redevelopment of London's congested areas could find much support among policy-makers before the end of the 1930s. The need to promote economic growth and enterprise and the pursuit of self-interest by politicians, property owners and speculators alike stifled attempts to legislate for a broader approach.[135] Such limitations enabled backwaters such as Campbell Bunk in North Islington to survive, stigmatising thousands of London's 'lumpenproletariat' simply by virtue of their address, while providing them with the necessary arena for the 'whirlwind of motion'

---

[133]   London Labour party, *A Housing Policy for London* (1934).
[134]   Introduction to H. Bingham Ashworth, *Flats: Design and Equipment* (1936).
[135]   Garside, '"Unhealthy Areas"', and P. L. Garside, 'Town Planning in London 1930–1961: A Study of Pressures, Interests and Influences Affecting the Formation of Policy' (unpublished PhD thesis, University of London, 1979).

that was the life of the casually self-employed. In such places, 'the very poor helped the very poor within the constrained limits of their poverty' but support vied with competition and at times the people of Campbell Bunk fought among themselves for the little that was available in a 'dog-eat-dog' affair. The separateness of enclaves like Campbell Bunk was ensured by their very life style – the fights, the slang, the gang activities. Campbell Bunk is a vivid example of a sub-cultural zone that remained unassimilated into London life until after 1950. The contrast with the new working-class 'norm' of tenement blocks was strong, but that with the newly built suburbs was extreme. In their healthiness, orderliness and quietness, the suburbs presented a wholly different scene, where life centred on home and family, and interests revolved around 'cricket and football results, book-talk, love-making, croquet and tennis parties for young men and women'.[136] The realities of life in London slums must indeed have seemed remote and beyond imagining. As Lord Moyne commented in 1934, 'Many interests were combining to cause the well-to-do and the poor to live apart in separate territories.'[137]

Semi-detached London

To a considerable extent, the social polarisation of London, the rise of Labour to power, and the LCC's retreat from out-county estates, all derived from the same set of circumstances – the resurgence of London's growth and the continued exodus of people from the County of London. While the inner London population continued to decline, the surrounding areas grew by more than a million between 1921 and 1931. As Chamberlain graphically pointed out in 1927, 'a city the size of Manchester has been added to London since the War'.[138] Migration from areas as far away as Northumberland and Glamorgan made a significant contribution to London's suburban growth, accounting for two-fifths of the total population increase – the rest being supplied by natural growth of the existing population.[139] The major contibutor to suburban expansion was the private builder who

[136] J. White, 'Campbell Bunk: A Lumpen Community in London between the Wars', *History Workshop Journal*, 8 (1979), pp. 2–42.
[137] *The Times*, 23 March 1934.
[138] Young and Garside, *Metropolitan London*, pp. 200–1.
[139] D. Friedlander and R. J. Roshier, 'A Study of Internal Migration in England and Wales: Part I', *Population Studies*, 19 (1965–6), p. 264.

contributed 80 per cent of all the houses built in the Conurbation between the wars. The connections between suburban living, owner-occupation and rising social status were being forged and reinforced in the Home Counties especially in the area between the Administrative County and the Conurbation boundaries.

Nevertheless, many of the outer districts in the Conurbation were only loosely tied to London as a whole and many remained 'beyond the daily sphere of influence' of the metropolis. Places such as Orpington, Bexley, Chislehurst and Sidcup in Kent, Benstead, Epsom and Esher in Surrey, and others in Hertfordshire, Middlesex and Essex saw less than 15 per cent of their occupied 'night population' taking the morning train to London. Generally, journeys to work throughout the Conurbation were local, within the immediate or neighbouring districts from the home. Only the centre of London exercised any long-distance attraction for employment – one third of its workers journeyed from homes beyond the County, though only one sixth came from the outer fringes of the Conurbation.[140] Almost all of these com- muters were male. Many suburban areas were largely self-contained economically, especially where unskilled or semi-skilled jobs offered employment for a resident working-class population. Between 1932 and 1936, almost half of all new factories employing more than twenty-three persons which opened in Greater London were located in the outer suburbs. The western approaches of the A40 to the Midlands, and the Upper Lea valley suburbs of Enfield and Edmonton were particularly favoured, and the modern functional architecture of the new factories of Hoover and Firestone in Hounslow symbolised the new industrial order.

Even middle-class suburbs were coming to offer an increasing range of employment, more especially for men, though less so for women. The expansion of shops, transport, education and other services provided varied and relatively secure, if not always highly paid, employment. The suburbs provided their own rich recreational mix of clubs and societies, cinemas and music halls, and the roads were a haven for the motorist and cyclist. Many hands were needed to cater for these eclectic leisure outlets. For many, London remained simply 'the smoke' to be visited, if at all, only for ceremonial occasions and specialist services. Developers might resort to 'hard-sell' techniques to

---

[140]   J. H. Westergaard, 'The Structure of Greater London', in Ruth Glass, ed., *London: Aspects of Change* (1964), p. 105.

capture individual buyers, but the general appeal of suburban life was unmistakable by the 1930s.[141]

The apparently endless flood of London's suburbs in the interwar period raised continually and insistently the dual problem of comprehension and appropriate action. It seemed impossible for Londoners any longer to have a distinct image of the metropolis in its entirety. Even the efforts of cartographers which had enabled nineteenth-century residents and visitors to map the city no longer provided a usable guide. London came to be represented not by its actual shape, but by a series of abstract diagrams, each a specialised representation of London for some specific or particular purpose. The most striking example of the change is the realignment of London's underground system by Frank Pick. Abandoning links with the real world above, Pick's 'tube map' recast the Underground into a rationalised but unrealistic diagram of suburban and subterranean lines.[142] A whole range of such 'urban experts' came to the fore in the 1930s, each presenting their own stylised version of London. Traffic engineers and town planners were at the centre of this kind of activity as they sought to devise ways of bringing order from disorder, and control from chaos. By superimposing a simplified plan onto the uncoordinated and anarchic mixture of London life, the medium came to be identified with the message – the process of plan-making and the achievement of ordered urban management were presented as essentially the same thing.

The claim of planners to know London in a new and authoritative way did not, however, carry the day until the very end of the 1930s. The demise of the Greater London Regional Planning Committee, the 'butchering' of the 1932 Town and Country Planning Act, the narrow compass of the LCC's town planning schemes, and the piecemeal implementation of the London Green Belt all illustrate the prevailing power of the status quo – not only in terms of economic and industrial interests, but also in terms of existing political and administrative structures and prevailing political norms. Above all, the 'bureaucratic machine politics' of Herbert Morrison's London Labour party reinforced rather than challenged those norms and structures in planning, as in housing.[143]

---

[141] A. A. Jackson, *Semi-Detached London: Suburban Development, Life and Transport, 1900–39* (1973).

[142] Garside, 'West End, East End', p. 252.

[143] G. W. Jones and B. Donoughue, *Herbert Morrison: Portrait of a Politician* (1973).

Neither central London nor the London region was recast in the 1930s. The desire to deal with London's growth in a comprehensive manner, and at a scale dictated by 'natural' boundaries faltered largely because of the constitutional and political questions that were inevitably raised. As the Second World War approached, it was the reality of London rather than any planner's scheme that demanded a response. In a series of articles published in 1938 and 1939, *The Economist* and the *Spectator* asked 'Can We Scrap London?' and 'Why London?'. Llewellyn Smith had concluded his nine-volume *Survey of London Life and Labour* with an affirmation of hope in London's vitality despite the dire poverty of half a million of its people. Clough Williams-Ellis recognised that the fashion was 'to deplore the size of London', but the editor of *The Economist* concluded that in economic terms the continued growth of London had been a clear gain for the nation.[144] Not even the Royal Commission on the Distribution of the Industrial Population appointed in 1937 could deny the economic contribution of London, whatever its wider social effects.

War and the re-evaluation of London

War, it seemed, was the one factor that could shift the balance of opinion. When he announced the appointment of the Barlow Commission, Ernest Brown, Minister of Labour, had referred specifically to strategic considerations. 'The extension of industry in Greater London', he said, 'gives rise to grave problems, not merely of industry, but of health , communications, and vulnerability from the air.' Many people shared Bertrand Russell's view that 'an avalanche of terror' would follow an outbreak of war as London was 'levelled to the ground'.[145] For 'the clean sheet' that London would then present, a choice of plans was at hand – there might be the Garden City model of total dispersal, or Garden Suburbs around a central city, or the economic/functional model set out by the MARS group, or the arterial/architectural mode of Bressey and the Royal Academy.[146] When war finally came, the 'Blitz' brought fearsome, but far from total, devastation to London. Neither the physical fabric nor the institutional framework was swept away. Despite the swift preparation of the

---

[144]   C. Williams-Ellis, 'Can We Scrap London?', *Spectator*, 11 November 1938; *idem*, 'Why London?', *The Economist*, 18 February 1939.
[145]   B. Russell, *Which Way to Peace?* (1936), p.37.
[146]   D. Foley, *Controlling London's Growth: Planning the Great Wen 1940–1960* (London and Los Angeles, 1963), pp. 46–50.

County of London and Greater London Plans – those pinnacles of diagrammatic blueprint planning – the reality continued to be that of *ad hoc*, incremental adjustment. The emphasis shifted from physical reconstruction to economic revival and Sir Gwilym Gibbon, retired Director of the Local Government Division of the Ministry of Health was quick to urge all concerned that reconstruction must take the form of 'filling in gaps, some big, some small, not of providing a whole plate'. 'Resourceful opportunism' had been, and was to remain, the mainstay of redevelopment in London.[147]

As the war drew to a close, the belief that 'London must and shall remain London' gained ground.[148] Lord Latham, Labour leader of the LCC declared, 'London is London. It is immense, maybe too immense, but it is here, a living, vital human fact, and any unreasonable attempt forcibly to reduce it could do incalculable harm socially and economically.' War had in fact demonstrated not the monstrous folly of London, but rather its strength and resilience.[149] London's pride in its ability to solve its own problems, fostered by Morrison in the 1930s, had been reinforced. The power of London's institutions to resist, ignore or modify the views of experts was secured. The realisation of Abercrombie's postwar vision for London depended on government intervention in the structure of landownership and market values, in the extension of planning powers and in the institutions of local, regional and national government. The postwar distortion of the dream was inevitable because these matters proved too contentious and difficult to resolve, existing economic and political structures remained unaltered, and London's entrenched principalities and powers reasserted their influence. Most important, Morrison's London Labour party continued to dominate the postwar political scene, advised by a virtually unchanged group of LCC officials.

Postwar reconstruction

In the postwar decade, the government's priorities were to revive the British economy in a world undergoing fundamental trading realignments, and to create a comprehensive welfare state. At the end of the First World War, by contrast, any such economic and social objectives had been subsumed in the physical programme of the

147   Young and Garside, *Metropolitan London*, pp. 231–2.
148   W. H. Ansell, 'The London of the Future', *Journal of the Royal Society of Arts*, 18 April 1941, p. 317.
149   Young and Garside, *Metropolitan London*, pp. 232–4.

'Homes for Heroes' campaign. In 1945, housing and town planning was only one element in the new Labour government's broad social programme, and in many respects physical reconstruction was regarded as a subsidiary aim. London's central economic importance ensured its continued dominance and expansion whatever misgivings from a physical and aesthetic viewpoint there might be.

With so many social boundaries being redrawn, compromise on physical objectives seemed both reasonable and practical. Excessive insistence on ideal schemes such as the Greater London Plan was seen as counter-productive since it would 'paralyse the collaboration between central and local authorities, and private interests on which postwar development would depend'. *The Economist* took up the theme that 'Houses will have to be erected at once when the war is over, and as they cannot be put where they ought to go, they will go where they can.'[150] The general conclusion was that 'only by a cold assessment of the realities can the best possible results be achieved'. A retreat from the idealism of the wartime plans for London was welcomed, not only by politicians and officials of the LCC, but also by those in the Home Counties and especially in Middlesex. There was general agreement that 'the planners have very properly had their vision', but that actual reconstruction would proceed on less ambitious lines.[151] John Hare, one of the leading Conservatives on the LCC, summed up the situation:

The LCC had paid lip-service to Abercrombie, but its actions had belied that lip-service ... Instead, there has been a policy of grabbing land wherever it can be found, irrespective of the interests of its neighbours and of the Green Belt, and irrespective even of the health and interests of those people who are in fact going to be rehoused in those sites.[152]

Not surprisingly, therefore, postwar London took on the form familiar from the interwar years, with a well-defined centre, the inner suburbs contained within a roughly circular Green Belt, but with rapid economic growth on the fringes only partly organised into specific centres.

The re-establishment of old patterns, and especially the LCC's 'land-grab' tactics, briefly revived calls for the reform of London government. Yet again, however, the time did not appear propitious – like planning, reform of local government took second place to the government's social and welfare programmes. Lewis Silkin, ex-chairman of

[150]   *Ibid.*, p. 249.
[151]   Garside, 'Town Planning in London', pp. 289–90, 318–19.
[152]   *House of Commons Debates*, 5th ser., vol. 427, 21 October 1946, col. 1375.

the LCC's Town Planning Committee, and the Labour government's Minister of Town and Country Planning wrestled with the interconnected problems of government, employment and redevelopment that London presented in 1945.[153] Desperate to avoid a further round of LCC overspill estates, Silkin severed the Gordian knot by foisting a 'brazen start' to the New Town programme on an unwilling and unenthusiastic cabinet. In Labour circles, the New Town ideal was far from being accepted as 'a matter of conventional wisdom'.[154] Silkin, backed by the Reith Committee report that he himself had instigated, was able to win his colleagues over for two main reasons. First, because the programme enabled them to postpone the more contentious issues of compensation and betterment that were bedevilling the drafting of a new Planning Bill, and secondly, because the establishment of New Town Corporations gave the government a direct tool to promote decentralisation independent of London's existing local authorities.

By the end of 1949, eight New Towns had been designated around London. The very existence of the programme enabled Silkin to achieve his aim of containing the LCC housing machine and insulating the Green Belt from its 'largest developer'. In 1950, Aneurin Bevan, the Minister of Health announced that he would not approve any further acquisitions of housing sites by the LCC outside the County area. Furthermore, the creation of the New Town Development Corporations kept the reform of London government on the ministerial shelf, since they provided the means for handling overspill and decentralisation without interference with the existing structure of government in the south-east.

London in the mid-twentieth century

The mid-twentieth century saw London poised on the brink of a new age, but still anxious to reaffirm its links with the past. The 1951 Festival of Britain was the physical manifestation of a London poised between old and new. Designed partly to celebrate the hundreth anniversary of the Great Exhibition, it was also an affirmation of faith in the future. Symbolically, the site for the Festival had been reclaimed from the Thames alongside County Hall, and the familiar landmark of a shot tower had been destroyed to make way for the futuristic

---

[153]   P. L. Garside, 'Shaping London's Future: The Role of the New Towns', in Von Karl Schwarz, ed., *Die Zukunft der Metropolen* (Berlin, 1984), pp. 184–9.
[154]   Cherry, *Evolution of British Town Planning*, p. 140.

architecture of the Royal Festival Hall, and for the fragile and delicate frame of the 'Skylon'. Significantly, the Festival bore the hallmarks of Herbert Morrison – both the South Bank site and the LCC showpiece estate in Poplar's Lansbury neighbourhood had formed part of his prewar priorities for redevelopment. Redressing the balance between south and north, and between east and west in London, Morrison's aim was to remove the stigma that was still attached to those areas, and to render them at last 'a mere geographical expression'.

Nevertheless, in 1951, many new divisions were emerging superimposed on many of the old distinctions. Different parts of the Conurbation displayed distinct identities. An analysis of the 1951 census revealed a clear pattern of 'natural areas' – the centre itself, the inner working-class areas, a group of middle and outer zones of relatively low social status, a homogeneous area of intermediate status south of the Thames, a western enclave of very mixed social character where high-class residential streets in Kensington, Chelsea and Hampstead mingled with poor lodging-houses, and an outer suburban ring with relatively uniform high social status. Since 1921, central London, the East End and the south dockside boroughs had lost half of their population, yet the expansion of the Conurbation continued, with population growth now concentrated in districts 30–40 miles from the centre. While the central area provided 29 per cent of jobs in the Conurbation, other subsidiary employment centres continued to expand, especially in Middlesex. Most long-distance commuting still focussed on central London, which provided 'The common link without which Greater London would be rather like a conglomeration of independent towns and villages'.[155] The picture was still one of interdependence, but metropolitan integration seemed as far away as ever. Superimposed on the old cleavages was a web of newer divisions, which were as yet hardly recognised.

CONCLUSIONS

Despite nineteenth-century threats of revolution, despite the political upheavals and economic depression of the 1930s, despite the traumas of two world wars, the most striking feature of London in 1950 was its continuity. The dynamism of the consumer economy based on London and the Home Counties had absorbed these crises and had emerged with the momentum of metropolitan growth barely affected.

[155] Westergaard, 'Structure of Greater London', p. 109.

Poised between old and new, the 1950s were to bring challenges for London which demanded change. The return of a Conservative government in 1951 brought an even more determined attempt to confine the LCC to inner London housing, ending its efforts to open up 'millionaires' rows' in Roehampton and Dulwich with tower blocks of flats, albeit clothed in dramatic architectural forms.[156] Worsening traffic congestion forced the LCC to formulate a roads programme, requiring politicians and officials alike to reach out to metropolitan borough councils that had hitherto lain outside the LCC's sphere of operations. The continuing neglect of housing conditions in the 'twilight zones' of Kensington and Paddington was about to be thrust into the public eye by the concentration there of West Indian immigrants. As the structure of London became increasingly fragmented, the varied elements sought to assert their individual identity and significance. The LCC political machine that had survived by absorbing and defusing potentially radical demands was weakening: the gulfs between inner and outer London were widening socially, racially and economically. London was coming to display the features of political disintegration, social polarisation and economic upheaval typical of a post-industrial metropolis.

In 1800, London had been one of the world's great cities dominating long-distance trade and commerce and with an apparently inbuilt ability to combine turbulence with fundamental orderliness. By the late nineteenth century, London and the Home Counties were being forged into the world's first dynamic consumer economy which neither national nor local politicians were able to challenge or modify for long. By 1950, however, the tensions, conflicts and disparities within the metropolitan region were coming to the fore – London was beginning to be absorbed into a new global economy that it no longer dominated politically or commercially. Neither the economic, social or political structures that had served London for so long were to survive intact.

---

[156] P. L. Garside, 'Intergovernmental Relations and Housing Policy in London 1919–1970, with Special Reference to the Density and Location of Council Housing', *London Journal*, 9 (1983).

Bibliographies

Place of publication is London, unless otherwise stated.

1 TOWN AND CITY

Anderson, Michael, *Family Structure in Nineteenth-Century Lancashire* (Cambridge, 1971)

Andrews, C. Bruyn, ed., *The Torrington Diaries* (1954 edn)

Beckett, J. V., *The Aristocracy in England, 1660–1914* (Oxford, 1986)

Beresford, M. W., 'The Back-to-Back House in Leeds, 1787–1937', in S. D. Chapman, ed., *The History of Working-Class Housing* (Newton Abbot, 1971)

Booth, Charles, ed., *Life and Labour of the People in London*, 1st ser., 4 vols. (1889–91); 3rd ser., 7 vols. (1902–3)

Borsay, Peter, ' ''All the Town's a Stage'': Urban Ritual and Ceremony, 1660–1800', in Peter Clark, ed., *The Transformation of English Provincial Towns, 1600–1800* (1984)

Briggs, Asa, *Victorian Cities* (1963)

Brown, J., 'Charles Booth and Labour Colonies, 1889–1905', *Economic History Review*, 2nd ser., 21 (1968)

Cannadine, David, *Lords and Landlords: The Aristocracy and the Towns 1774–1967* (Leicester, 1980)

'Introduction', in David Cannadine, ed., *Patricians, Power, and Politics in Nineteenth-Century Towns* (Leicester, 1982)

Carr, M. C.,' The Development and Character of a Metropolitan Suburb: Bexley, Kent', in F. M. L. Thompson, ed., *The Rise of Suburbia* (Leicester, 1982)

Chadwick, Edwin, *Report on the Sanitary Condition of the Labouring Population of Great Britain* (1842)

Chalklin, C. W., *The Provincial Towns of Georgian England* (1974)

'Capital Expenditure on Building for Cultural Purposes in Provincial England, 1730–1830', *Business History*, 22 (1980)

Chapman, S. D., 'Working-Class Housing in Nottingham', in S. D. Chapman, ed., *The History of Working-Class Housing* (Newton Abbot 1971)

Cherry, Gordon, ed., *Pioneers in British Planning* (1981)

Clapham, J. H., *An Economic History of Modern Britain: The Early Railway Age, 1820–50* (Cambridge, 1950 edn)

Clark, Peter, ed., *The Transformation of English Provincial Towns, 1600–1800* (1984)

Coppock, J. T., 'Dormitory Settlements around London', in J. T. Coppock and H. C. Prince, eds., *Greater London* (1964)

Corfield, P. J., *The Impact of English Towns, 1700–1800* (Oxford, 1982)

Crossick, Geoffrey, 'The Emergence of the Lower Middle Class in Britain: A Discussion', in Geoffrey Crossick, ed., *The Lower Middle Class in Britain, 1870–1914* (1977)

   'Urban Society and the Petty Bourgeoisie in Nineteenth-Century Britain', in Derek Fraser and Anthony Sutcliffe, eds., *The Pursuit of Urban History* (1983)

   ed., *The Lower Middle Class in Britain, 1870–1914* (1977)

Daunton, M. J., *Coal Metropolis: Cardiff, 1870–1914* (Leicester, 1977)

Davidoff, Leonore, *The Best Circles: Society, Etiquette and the Season* (1973)

Davidoff, Leonore, and Hall, Catherine, *Family Fortunes: Men and Women of the English Middle Class, 1780–1850* (1987)

Deane, P., and Cole, W. A., *British Economic Growth 1688–1959*, 2nd edn (Cambridge, 1967)

Dennis, Richard, *English Industrial Cities of the Nineteenth Century* (Cambridge, 1984)

Dix, Gerald, 'Patrick Abercrombie', in Gordon Cherry, ed., *Pioneers in British Planning* (1981)

Dyos, H. J., ed., *The Study of Urban History* (1968)

Dyos, H. J., and Wolff, Michael, eds., *The Victorian City*, vol. 1: *Images and Realities* (1978 edn)

Engels, F., *The Condition of the Working Class in England* (Panther edn, 1969)

Englander, David, *Landlord and Tenant in Urban Britain, 1838–1918* (Oxford 1983)

Faucher, L., *Manchester in 1844* (1844)

Feinstein, C. H., *Statistical Tables of National Income, Expenditure, and Output of the U.K. 1855–1965* (Cambridge, 1976)

Foster, John, *Class Struggle and the Industrial Revolution* (1974)

Fraser, Derek, *Urban Politics in Victorian England* (Leicester, 1976)

   Power and Authority in the Victorian City (1979)

   ed., *A History of Modern Leeds* (Manchester, 1980)

Fraser, Derek, and Sutcliffe, Anthony, eds., *The Pursuit of Urban History* (1983)

Girouard, M., *The Victorian Country House* (1979)

Gordon, George., ed., *Regional Cities in the U.K. 1890–1980* (1986)

Harris, J. R., 'The Employment of Steam Power in the Eighteenth Century', *History*, 52 (1967)

Hennock, E. P., 'The Social Composition of Borough Councils in Two Large Cities, 1835–1914', in H. J. Dyos, ed., *The Study of Urban History* (1968)

   Fit and Proper Persons: Ideal and Reality in Nineteenth-Century Urban Government (1973)

Hobsbawm, E. J., *The Age of Capital, 1848–75* (1975)

Howell, David W., *Patriarchs and Parasites: The Gentry of South-West Wales in the Eighteenth Century* (Cardiff, 1986)

Jackson, A. A., *Semi-Detached London: Suburban Development, Life and Transport, 1900–39* (1973)

Kellett, J. R., *The Impact of Railways on Victorian Cities* (1969)

Law, C. M., 'The Growth of Urban Population in England and Wales, 1801–1911', *Transactions of the Institute of British Geographers*, 41 (1967)

Lees, Andrew, *Cities Perceived: Urban Society in European and American Thought, 1820–1940* (Manchester, 1985)

Lees, Lynn Holles, *Exiles of Erin: Irish Migrants in Victorian London* (Manchester, 1979)

McLeod, Hugh, 'White Collar Values and the Role of Religion', in Geoffrey Crossick, ed., *The Lower Middle Class in Britain, 1870–1914* (1977)

Meacham, Standish, *A Life Apart: The English Working Class, 1890–1914* (1977)

Meadowcraft, Michael, 'The Years of Political Transition, 1914–39', in Derek Fraser, ed., *A History of Modern Leeds* (Manchester, 1980)

Mellor, H. E., *Leisure and the Changing City, 1870–1914* (1976)

Mitchell, B. R., and Deane, P., *Abstract of British Historical Statistics* (Cambridge, 1962)

Mitchell, B. R., and Jones, H. G., *Second Abstract of British Historical Statistics* (Cambridge 1971)

Morris, R. J., 'Middle-Class Culture, 1700–1914', in Derek Fraser, ed., *A History of Modern Leeds* (Manchester, 1980)

Musson, A. E., 'Industrial Motive Power in the United Kingdom, 1800–70', *Economic History Review*, 2nd ser., 29 (1976)

Muthesius, Stefan, *The English Terraced House* (1982)

Newman, Gerald, *The Rise of English Nationalism, 1740–1830* (1987)

Newton, R., 'Society and Politics in Exeter, 1837–1914', in H. J. Dyos, ed., *The Study of Urban History* (1968)

Offer, Avner, *Property and Politics 1870–1914: Landownership, Law, Ideology and Urban Development in England* (Cambridge, 1981)

Olney, R. J., *Rural Society and County Government in Nineteenth-Century Lincolnshire* (Lincoln, 1979)

Olsen, Donald J., 'House upon House', in H. J. Dyos and Michael Wolff, eds., *The Victorian City*, vol. 1: *Images and Realities* (1978 edn)

The City as a Work of Art: London, Paris, Vienna (1986)

Pahl, R. E., *Urbs in Rure* (1965)

Perkin, H. J., *The Origins of Modern English Society, 1780–1880* (1969)

Pimlott, J. A. R., *The Englishman's Holiday* (Hassocks, Sussex, 1976 edn)

Ravetz, Alison, *The Government of Space* (1986)

Rawcliffe, J. M., 'Bromley: Kentish Market Town to London Suburb, 1841–81', in F. M. L. Thompson, ed., *The Rise of Suburbia* (Leicester, 1982)

Redford, A., *Labour Migration in England, 1800–50*, 2nd edn (Manchester, 1964)

Roberts, Richard, 'Leasehold Estates and Municipal Enterprise: Landowners, Local Government, and the Development of Bournemouth, *c.* 1850 to 1914', in David Cannadine, ed., *Patricians, Power, and Politics in Nineteenth-Century Towns* (Leicester, 1982)

'The Corporation as Impresario: The Municipal Provision of Entertainment in Victorian and Edwardian Bournemouth', in John K. Walton and James Walvin, eds., *Leisure in Britain, 1780–1939* (Manchester, 1983)

Roberts, Robert, *The Classic Slum* (Manchester, 1971)

Robson, B. T., *Urban Growth: An Approach* (1973)

'Coming Full Circle: London versus the Rest, 1890–1980', in George Gordon, ed., *Regional Cities in the U.K. 1890–1980* (1986)

Rogers, N., 'Money, Land and Lineage: The Big Bourgeoisie of Hanoverian London', *Social History*, 4 (1979)

Rubinstein, W. D., *Men of Property: The Very Wealthy in Britain since the Industrial Revolution* (1981)

Simpson, M. A., and Lloyd, T. H., eds., *Middle-Class Housing in Britain* (Newton Abbot, 1977)

Spring, D., 'English Landowners and Nineteenth-Century Industrialism', in

544   *Bibliographies*

J. T. Ward and R. G. Wilson, eds., *Land and Industry* (Newton Abbot, 1971)

Stedman Jones, G., *Outcast London: A Study in the Relationship between Classes in Victorian Society* (Oxford, 1971)

Stevenson, John, *British Society, 1914–45* (1984)

Stone, Lawrence, and Stone, Jeanne C. Fawtier, *An Open Elite? England, 1540–1880* (Oxford, 1984)

Summerson, John, *Georgian London* (1945)

Sutcliffe, Anthony, 'The "Midland Metropolis"': Birmingham, 1890–1980', in George Gordon, ed., *Regional Cities in the U.K. 1890–1980* (1986)

Swenarton, Mark, *Homes Fit for Heroes: The Politics and Architecture of Early State Housing in Britain* (1981)

Swenarton, Mark, and Taylor, Sandra, 'The Scale and Nature of the Growth of Owner-Occupation in Britain between the Wars', *Economic History Review*, 2nd ser., 38 (1985)

Taylor, A. J. P., *English History, 1914–1945* (Oxford, 1965)

Thane, Pat, *Foundations of the Welfare State* (1982)

Thompson, F. M. L., 'Towns, Industry, and the Victorian Landscape', in S. R. J. Woodell, ed., *The English Landscape* (Oxford, 1985)

 ed., *The Rise of Suburbia* (Leicester, 1982)

Treen, C., 'The Process of Suburban Development in North Leeds, 1870–1914', in F. M. L. Thompson, ed., *The Rise of Suburbia* (Leicester, 1982)

Waller, P. J., *Democracy and Sectarianism: A Political and Social History of Liverpool, 1868–1939* (Liverpool, 1981)

 Town, City and Nation: England, 1850–1914 (Oxford, 1983)

Walton, John K., *The English Seaside Resort: A Social History, 1750–1914* (Leicester, 1983)

Walton, John K., and Walvin, James, eds., *Leisure in Britain, 1780–1939* (Manchester, 1983)

Ward, J. T., and Wilson, R. G., eds., *Land and Industry* (Newton Abbot, 1971)

Weber, A. F., *The Growth of Cities in the Nineteenth Century* (1899; reprinted 1967)

Wiener, Martin J., *English Culture and the Decline of the Industrial Spirit, 1850–1980* (Cambridge, 1981)

Wilson, C., *England's Apprenticeship, 1603–1763* (1965)

Wilson, R. G., *Gentlemen Merchants: The Merchant Community in Leeds, 1700–1830* (Manchester, 1971)

Wohl, Anthony S., *Endangered Lives: Public Health in Victorian Britain* (1983)

Young, Michael and Willmott, Peter, *Family and Kinship in East London* (1957)

•

2 THE COUNTRYSIDE

Abrams, M. A., 'A Contribution to the Study of Occupational and Residential Mobility in the Cotswolds, 1921–31', *Journal and Proceedings of the Agricultural Economics Society*, 2 (1932)

Agar, N., *The Bedfordshire Farm Worker in the Nineteenth Century* (Bedfordshire Historical Record Society, 60, 1981)

Ambrose, P., *The Quiet Revolution: Social Change in a Sussex Village, 1871–1971* (1974)

Anderson, M., 'Marriage Patterns in Victorian Britain: An Analysis Based on Registration District Data for England and Wales', *Journal of Family History* 1 (1976)

Armstrong, W. A., 'La Population de l'Angleterre et du Pays de Galles, 1789–1815', *Annales de Demographie Historique*, 1 (1965)

'The Flight from the Land', in G. E. Mingay, ed., *The Victorian Countryside*, vol. 1 (1981)

'The Workfolk', in G. E. Mingay, ed., *The Victorian Countryside*, vol. 2 (1981)

Aronson, H., *The Land and the Labourer* (1914)

Ashby, A. W., and Evans, I. L., *The Agriculture of Wales and Monmouthshire* (Cardiff, 1944)

Ashby, A. W., and Smith, J. H. 'Agricultural Labour in Wales under Statutory Regulation of Wages, 1924–37', *Welsh Journal of Agriculture*, 14 (1938)

Ashby, M. K., 'Recent Rural Changes as they Affect the Younger Generation', *Journal and Proceedings of the Agricultural Economics Society*, 2 (1933)

Joseph Ashby of Tysoe, 1859–1919 (Cambridge, 1961)

Astor, Viscount, and Rowntree, B. S., *British Agriculture* (1938)

Bagwell, P. S., 'The Decline of Rural Isolation', in G. E. Mingay, ed., *The Victorian Countryside*, vol. 1 (1981)

Barnett, D. C., 'Allotments and the Problem of Rural Poverty', in E. L. Jones and G. E. Mingay, eds., *Land, Labour and Population in the Industrial Revolution* (1967)

Baugh, D. A., 'The Cost of Poor Relief in South-East England, 1790–1834', *Economic History Review*, 2nd ser., 28 (1975)

Bell, C., and Newby, H., *Community Studies* (1971)

Bennett, E. N., *Problems of Village Life* (n.d. 1913?)

Benusan, S. L., *Latterday Rural England* (1927)

Beresford, J., ed., *The Diary of a Country Parson*, 5 vols. (Oxford, 1924–31)

Blythe, R., *Akenfield* (Harmondsworth, 1972)

Bosanquet, B. S., 'Quality of the Rural Population', *Eugenics Review*, 42 (1950)

Bracey, H. E., 'Rural Planning: An Index of Social Provision', *Journal and Proceedings of the Agricultural Economics Society*, 9 (1951)

Bushaway, B., *By Rite: Custom, Ceremony and Community in England, 1700–1880* (1982)

Bythell, D., *The Sweated Trades: Outwork in Nineteenth Century Britain* (1978)

Caird, J., *English Agriculture in 1850–51*, 2nd edn (1968)

Cairncross, A. K., *Home and Foreign Investment, 1870–1913* (Cambridge, 1953)

Chalklin, C. W., 'Country Towns', in G. E. Mingay, ed., *The Victorian Countryside*, vol. 2 (1981)

Chambers, J. D., *The Vale of Trent, 1670–1800 (Economic History Review*, Supplement No. 3, 1957)

Nottinghamshire in the Eighteenth Century, 2nd edn (1966)

Chambers, J. D., and Mingay, G. E., *The Agricultural Revolution, 1750–1880* (1966)

Charlesworth, A., *An Atlas of Rural Protest in Britain, 1548–1900* (1983)

Chartres, J. A., and Turnbull, G. L., 'Country Craftsmen', in G. E. Mingay, ed., *The Victorian Countryside*, vol. 1 (1981)

Cirket, A. F., 'The 1830 Riots in Bedfordshire', in *Bedfordshire Historical Record Society*, 57 (1978)

Cresswell, G., *Norfolk and its Squires, Clergy, Farmers and Labourers* (1875)

Crosby, T. L., *English Farmers and the Politics of Protection, 1815–52* (Hassocks, Sussex, 1977)

Currie, R., Gilbert, A., and Horsley, L., *Churches and Churchgoers: Patterns of Church Growth in the British Isles since 1700* (Oxford, 1977)

Davies, C. S., *The Agricultural History of Cheshire, 1750–1850* (Manchester, 1960)

Davies, D., *The Case of the Labourers in Husbandry Stated and Considered* (1795)

Davies, E., 'The Small Landowner, 1780–1832, in the Light of the Land Tax Assessments', *Economic History Review*, 1 (1927)

Davies, M. F., *Life in an English Country Village: An Economic and Historical Survey of the Parish of Corsley in Wiltshire* (1909)

Deane, P., and Cole, W. A., *British Economic Growth 1688–1959* (Cambridge, 1962)

Dewey, P. E., 'Agricultural Labour Supply in England and Wales during the First World War', *Economic History Review*, 2nd ser., 28 (1975)

Digby, A., *Pauper Palaces* (1978)

Dunbabin, J. P. D., 'The Revolt of the Field: The Agricultural Labourers' Movement in the 1870s', *Past & Present*, 26 (1963)

 'The Incidence and Organisation of Agricultural Trades Unionism in the 1870s', *Agricultural History Review*, 16 (1968)

Eden, F. M., *The State of the Poor*, 3 vols. (1797)

Edsall, N. C., *The Anti-Poor Law Movement, 1834–44* (Manchester, 1971)

Erickson, C., *Emigration from Europe, 1815–1914* (1976)

Ernle, Lord, *English Farming, Past and Present*, 5th edn (1936)

Evans, G. E., *Where Beards Wag All* (1970)

Everitt, A. M., 'Farm Labourers', in J. Thirsk, ed., *The Agrarian History of England and Wales*, vol. 4: *1500–1640* (Cambridge, 1967)

 ed., *Perspectives in English Urban History* (1973)

Fairfax-Blakeborough, J., *Sykes of Sledmere* (1929)

Fitton, R. S., and Wadsworth, A. P., *The Strutts and the Arkwrights* (Manchester, 1958)

Fitzrandolph, H. E., and Hay, M. D., *The Rural Industries of England and Wales*, 4 vols. (Oxford, 1926–7)

Fletcher, T. W., 'The Great Depression of English Agriculture, 1873–96', *Economic History Review*, 2nd ser., 13 (1961)

Flinn, M. W., 'Trends in Real Wages, 1750–1850', *Economic History Review*, 2nd ser., 27 (1974)

Foster, J., *Class Struggle and the Industrial Revolution* (1974)

Gash, N., 'Rural Unemployment, 1815–34', *Economic History Review*, 6 (1935)

Glyde, J., *Suffolk in the Nineteenth Century* (1856)

 Autobiography of a Suffolk Farm Labourer (East Suffolk Record Office, q. S9)

Gosden, P. H. J. H., *The Friendly Societies in England, 1815–75* (Manchester, 1961)

Graham, P. A., *The Rural Exodus* (1892)

Green, F. E., *History of the English Agricultural Labourer, 1870–1920* (1920)

Gretton, M. S., *A Corner of the Cotswolds through the Nineteenth Century* (1914)

Groves, R., *Sharpen the Sickle: The History of the Farm Workers' Union*, 2nd edn (1981)

Haggard, H. R., *Rural England*, 2nd edn, 2 vols. (1906)

Hall, A. D., *A Pilgrimage of British Farming, 1910–12* (1912)

Hammond, J. L., and B., *The Village Labourer*, new edn (1978)

Hardy, T., *Tess of the d'Urbervilles*, new edn (1974)

Hasbach, W., *A History of the English Agricultural Labourer* (1894; Eng. edn 1908)

 Havinden, M. A., *Estate Villages* (1966)

 'The South-West: A Case of Rural De-Industrialisation?', in M. Palmer, ed., *The Onset of Industrialisation* (Nottingham University, Department of Adult Education, 1976)

Hobsbawm, E. J., and Rudé, G., *Captain Swing* (1969)

Hobson, J. W., and Henry, H., *The Rural Market: A Compilation of Facts Related to the Agricultural Industry and Rural Standards of Living and Rural Purchasing Habits* (1948)

Holdenby, C., *Folk of the Furrow* (1913)

Holderness, B. A., 'Personal Mobility in Some Rural Parishes of Yorkshire, 1777–1812', *Yorkshire Archaeological Journal*, 42 (1971)

'The Victorian Farmer', in G. E. Mingay, ed., *The Victorian Countryside*, vol. 1 (1981)

Horn, P., *Joseph Arch* (Kineton, Warwicks., 1971)

Labouring Life in the Victorian Countryside (Dublin, 1976)

The Rural World, 1780–1850 (1980)

'Women's Cottage Industries', in G. E. Mingay, ed., *The Victorian Countryside*, vol. 1 (1981)

Howkins, A., *Poor Labouring Men: Rural Radicalism in Norfolk 1870–1923* (1985)

Hunt, E. H., *Regional Wage Variations in Britain, 1850–1914* (Oxford, 1973)

Huzel, J. B., 'The Demographic Impact of the Old Poor Law: More Reflexions on Malthus', *Economic History Review*, 2nd ser., 33 (1980)

'The Labourer and the Poor Law', in G. E. Mingay, ed., *The Agrarian History of England and Wales*, vol. 6: *1750–1850* (Cambridge, 1989)

Inglis, K. S., 'Patterns of Religious Worship in 1851', *Journal of Ecclesiastical History*, 11 (1960)

Innes, J. W., 'Class Birth Rates in England and Wales, 1921–31', *Milbank Memorial Fund Quarterly*, 19 (1941)

Irons, W., 'Agriculture in Warwickshire', *Journal of the Royal Agricultural Society*, 91 (1930)

Itzkowitz, D. C., *Peculiar Privilege: A Social History of English Foxhunting, 1753–1885* (Hassocks, Sussex, 1977)

Jefferies, R., *Hodge and his Masters*, new edn (1979)

Jessopp, A., *Arcady: For Better for Worse* (1887)

Jones, D., 'Thomas Campbell Foster and the Rural Labourer: Incendiarism in East Anglia in the 1840s', *Social History*, 1 (1976)

Jones, E. L., 'The Agricultural Labour Market in England, 1793–1872', *Economic History Review*, 2nd ser., 17 (1964)

Agriculture and Economic Growth in England, 1650–1850 (1967)

The Development of English Agriculture, 1815–73 (1968)

Jones, R. E., 'Infant Mortality in Rural North Shropshire, 1561–1810', *Population Studies*, 30 (1976)

Julian, J., *A Dictionary of Hymnology* (1907)

Kenyon, G. H., 'Petworth Town and Trades, 1610–1760', *Sussex Archaeological Collections*, 95 (1958)

Kerridge, E., Review of G. E. Mingay, ed., *The Victorian Countryside*, in *Economic History Review*, 2nd ser., 35 (1982)

Kussmaul, A., *Servants in Husbandry in Early Modern England* (Cambridge, 1981)

Landsberger, H. A., ed., *Rural Protest: Peasant Movements and Social Change* (1974)

Levine, D., *Family Formation in an Age of Nascent Capitalism* (1977)

Lindert, P. H., and Williamson, J. G., 'English Workers' Living Standards during the Industrial Revolution: A New Look', *Economic History Review*,

2nd ser., 36 (1983)

Long, W. H., and Carson, S. H., 'Farmers and Motor Cars', *The Farm Economist* 1 (1935)

Longmate, N., *How We Lived Then* (1971)

Longstaff, G. B., 'Rural Depopulation', *Journal of the Royal Statistical Society* 56 (1893)

McClatchey, D., *Oxfordshire Clergy, 1777–1869* (Oxford, 1960)

MacDonald, S., 'Agricultural Response to a Changing Market during the Napoleonic Wars', *Economic History Review*, 2nd ser., 33 (1980)

Mann, H. H., 'Life in an Agricultural Village in England', *Sociological Papers*, 1 (1905)

Marshall, J. D., 'The Lancashire Rural Labourer in the Early Nineteenth Century', *Transactions of the Lancashire and Cheshire Antiquarian Society*, 71 (1961)

'Nottinghamshire Labourers in the Early Nineteenth Century', *Transactions of the Thoroton Society*, 64 (1961)

The Old Poor Law, 1795–1834 (1968)

Martins, S. W., *A Great Estate at Work* (Cambridge, 1980)

Mejer, E., *Agricultural Labour in England and Wales*, Part II, *Farm Workers' Earnings, 1917–51* (Nottingham University, Department of Agricultural Economics, 1951)

Mills, D., 'The Quality of Life in Melbourne, Cambs., in the Period 1800–50', *International Review of Social History*, 23 (1978)

Mingay, G. E., 'The Size of Farms in the Eighteenth Century', *Economic History Review*, 2nd ser., 14 (1962)

English Landed Society in the Eighteenth Century (1963)

Enclosure and the Small Farmer in the Age of the Industrial Revolution (1968)

Rural Life in Victorian England (1977)

ed., *The Victorian Countryside*, 2 vols. (1981)

ed., *The Agrarian History of England and Wales*, vol. 6: *1750–1850* (Cambridge, 1989)

Ministry of Agriculture, Fisheries and Food, *Report of Proceedings under the Agricultural Wages (Regulation) Act, 1924, for the Two Years Ending 1931* (1931)

Studies in Urban Household Diets, 1944–9. Second Report of the National Food Survey Committee (1956)

A Century of Agricultural Statistics. Great Britain, 1866–1966 (1968)

Ministry of Health, *Rural Housing. Third Report of the Rural Housing Sub-Committee of the Central Housing Advisory Committee* (1944)

Mitchell, B. R., and Deane, P., *Abstract of British Historical Statistics* (Cambridge, 1962)

Moore, D. C., 'The Gentry', in G. E. Mingay, ed., *The Victorian Countryside*, vol. 2 (1981)

Morris, R. J., *Class and Class Consciousness in the Industrial Revolution* (1979)

Munsche, P. B., *Gentlemen and Poachers: The English Game Laws 1671–1831* (Cambridge, 1981)

Murray, K. A. H., *Agriculture: History of the Second World War, Civil Series* (1955)

Newby, H., *The Deferential Worker* (1977)

Green and Pleasant Land? Social Change in Rural England (Harmondsworth, 1980)

Obelkevich, J., *Religion and Rural Society: South Lindsey, 1825–75* (Oxford, 1976)

O'Leary, J. G., ed., *The Autobiography of Joseph Arch* (1966)

Orwin, C. S., *Problems of the Countryside* (Cambridge, 1945)

Orwin, C. S., and Whetham, E. H., *History of British Agriculture, 1846–1914* (1964)

Pahl, R. E., *Urbs in Rure* (1965)

Peacock, A. J., *Bread or Blood: The Agrarian Riots in East Anglia, 1816* (1965)

Peake, H., *The English Village: The Origin and Decay of its Community* (1922)

Pedley, W. H., *Labour on the Land* (1942)

Perkin, H. J., *The Origins of Modern English Society, 1780–1880* (1969)

Phythian-Adams, C., 'Rural Culture', in G. E. Mingay, ed., *The Victorian Countryside*, vol. 2 (1981)

Poynter, J. R., *Society and Pauperism: English Ideas on Poor Relief, 1795–1834* (1969)

Razzell, P. E., and Wainwright, R. J. W., eds., *The Victorian Working Class: Selections from the Morning Chronicle* (1973)

Redford, A., *Labour Migration in England, 1800–50*, 2nd edn (Manchester, 1964)

Reeves, M., *Sheep Bell and Ploughshare* (1980)

'Reminiscences of Frederick Swaffield, 1895–1924' (Dorset Record Office, D459/1)

Rew, R. H., *An Agricultural Faggott* (1913)

Roberts, S. C., ed., *A Frenchman in England, 1784: Being the 'Mélanges sur l'Angleterre' of François de la Rochefoucauld* (Cambridge, 1933)

Robertson-Scott, J. W., *England's Green and Pleasant Land* (1925)

Robin, J., *Elmdon: Continuity and Change in a North-West Essex Village, 1861–1964* (Cambridge, 1980)

Rowntree, B. S., and Kendall, M., *How the Labourer Lives: A Study of the Rural Labour Problem* (1913)

Rudé, G., *The Crowd in History, 1730–1848* (1964)

Ruggles, T., 'On the Police and Situation of the Poor', *Annals of Agriculture*, 16 (1791)

Rule, J., 'Social Crime in the Rural South in the Eighteenth and Early Nineteenth Centuries', *Southern History*, 1 (1979)

Russell, R. C., *The Revolt of the Field in Lincolnshire* (Lincoln, 1956)

Savage, W. G., *Rural Housing* (1915)

Saville, J., *Rural Depopulation in England and Wales, 1851–1951* (1957)

Sellman, R. R., *Devon Village Schools in the Nineteenth Century* (Newton Abbot, 1967)

Snell, K. D. M., 'Agricultural Seasonal Employment, the Standard of Living, and Women's Work in the South and East, 1690–1860', *Economic History Review*, 2nd ser., 34 (1981)

Annals of the Labouring Poor: Social Change and Agrarian England 1660–1900 (Cambridge, 1985)

Spenceley, G. F. R., 'The English Pillow-Lace Industry, 1840-80: A Rural Industry in Competition with Machinery', *Business History*, 19 (1977)

Springall, L. M., *Labouring Life in Norfolk Villages, 1834–1914* (1936)

Stevens' Directory of Canterbury and Neighbourhood (1889)

Sturt, G., *The Memoirs of a Surrey Labourer* (1907)

Lucy Bettesworth (1913)

William Smith, Potter and Farmer (1919)

Change in the Village (Readers Library edn, 1920)

The Wheelwright's Shop (Cambridge, 1923)

Taylor, F. D. W., 'United Kingdom: Numbers in Agriculture', *The Farm*

Economist, 8 (1955)

Thomas, F. G., *The Changing Village* (1939)

Thomas, J., *The Rise of the Staffordshire Potteries* (Bath, 1971)

Thompson, E. P., 'Eighteenth-Century English Society: Class Struggle without Class?', *Social History*, 3 (1978)

Thompson, F., *Lark Rise to Candleford* (1954 edn)

Thompson, F. M. L., *English Landed Society in the Nineteenth Century* (1963)
'Landowners and the Rural Community', in G. E. Mingay, ed., *The Victorian Countryside*, vol. 2 (1981)

Thresh, J. C., *The Housing of the Agricultural Labourer, with Special Reference to Essex* (Chelmsford, 1919)

Tillott, P. M., ed., *Victoria County History: City of York* (1961)

Turner, M. E., *English Parliamentary Enclosure* (Folkestone, 1980)
'Sitting on the Fence of Parliamentary Enclosure: A Regressive Social Tax with Problematic Efficiency Gains', in *Agricultural History*, Papers Presented to the Economic History Conference (Canterbury, 1983)

Unwin, G., *Samuel Oldknow and the Arkwrights* (Manchester, 1924)

Ward, J. T., 'Changes in the Sale Value of Farm Real Estate in England and Wales', *The Farm Economist*, 7 (1953)

Ward, W. R., *Religion and Society in England, 1790–1850* (1972)

Welton, T., 'On the Distribution of Population in England and Wales, 1801–91', *Journal of the Royal Statistical Society*, 63 (1900)

Whetham, E. H., *The Agrarian History of England and Wales*, vol. 8: *1914–39* (Cambridge, 1978)

Williams, R., *The Country and the City* (1973)

Winstanley, M., *Life in Kent at the Turn of the Century* (Folkestone, 1978)
'Voices from the Past: Rural Kent at the Close of an Era', in G. E. Mingay, ed., *The Victorian Countryside*, vol. 2 (1981)

Woodruff, D., 'Expansion and Emigration', in G. M. Young, ed., *Early Victorian England*, vol. 2 (Oxford, 1934)

Wordie, J. R., 'Social Change on the Leveson-Gower Estates, 1714–1832', *Economic History Review*, 2nd ser., 27 (1974)

Wrigley, E. A., and Schofield, R. S., *The Population History of England, 1541–1871: A Reconstruction* (1981)

Yelling, J. A., *Common Field and Enclosure in England, 1450–1850* (1977)

Young, A., *General Report on Enclosures, 1808* (reprint, New York,1971)
'Gleanings in an Excursion to Lewes Fair', *Annals of Agriculture*, 27 (1792)

3 SCOTLAND

Adam, R. J., ed., *Papers on Sutherland Estate Management*, Scottish History Society, 2 vols. (Edinburgh, 1972)

Adams, I. H., *The Making of Urban Scotland* (1978)

Aiton, W., *General View of the Agriculture of the County of Ayr* (Glasgow, 1811)

Alison, W. P., *Observations on the Management of the Poor in Scotland* (Edinburgh, 1840)

Allan, C. M., 'The Genesis of British Urban Redevelopment with Special Reference to Glasgow', *Economic History Review*, 2nd ser., 18 (1965)

Anderson, R. D., *Education and Opportunity in Victorian Scotland* (Oxford, 1983)

Arnot, R. P., *A History of the Scottish Miners* (1955)

Aspinall, A., *The Early English Trade Unions* (1949)

Aspinwall, Bernard, *Portable Utopia: Glasgow and the United States, 1870–1920* (Aberdeen, 1984)

Baedeker, K., *Great Britain: Handbook for Travellers*, 9th edn (1937)

Baird, R., 'Housing', in A. J. Cairncross, ed., *The Scottish Economy* (Cambridge, 1954)

Barron, D. G., ed., *The Court Book of the Barony of Urie*, Scottish History Society, 12 (Edinburgh, 1892)

Best, G., 'The Scottish Victorian City', *Victorian Studies*, 11 (1968)

Bewley, Christina, *Muir of Huntershill* (Oxford, 1981)

Boyd, K., *Scottish Church Attitudes to Sex, Marriage and the Family 1850–1914* (Edinburgh, 1980)

Bradley, A. G., *When Squires and Farmers Thrived* (1927)

Brady, F., and Pottle, R. A., eds., *Boswell in Search of a Wife, 1766–1769* (1957)

Brennan, T., *Reshaping a City* (Glasgow, 1959)

Brewster, P., *The Seven Chartist and Military Discourses Libelled by the Marquis of Abercorn* (Paisley, 1843)

Brotherston, J. H. F., *Observations on the Early Public Health Movement in Scotland* (1952)

Brown. R., *The History of Paisley* (Paisley, 1886)

Brown, Stewart J., *Thomas Chalmers* (Oxford, 1982)

Bumsted, J. M., *The People's Clearance 1770–1815* (Edinburgh, 1892)

Butt, J., 'Working Class Housing in Glasgow, 1851–1914', in S. D. Chapman, ed., *The History of Working-Class Housing* (Newton Abbot, 1971)

Buxton, N. K., 'Economic Growth in Scotland between the Wars: The Role of Production, Structure and Rationalization', *Economic History Review*, 2nd ser., 33 (1980)

Cage, R. A., *The Scottish Poor Law 1745–1845* (Edinburgh, 1981)

Cage, R. A., and Checkland, O., 'Thomas Chalmers and Urban Poverty: The St John's Parish Experiment in Glasgow, 1819–1837', *Philosophical Journal*, 13 (1976)

Cameron, R., *Banking in the Early Stages of Industrialisation* (Oxford, 1967)

Campbell, Alan B., *The Lanarkshire Miners: A Social History of their Trade Unions 1775–1974* (Edinburgh, 1979)

Campbell, A. D., 'Income', in A. J. Cairncross, ed., *The Scottish Economy* (Cambridge, 1954)

'Changes in Scottish Incomes, 1924–1949', *Economic Journal*, 65 (1955)

Campbell, R. H., *Scotland since 1707: The Rise of an Industrial Society* (Oxford, 1965)

The Rise and Fall of Scottish Industry, 1707–1939 (Edinburgh, 1980)

Carter, Ian R., *Farm Life in North East Scotland, 1840–1914* (Edinburgh, 1973)

Chadwick, E., *Report on the Sanitary Condition of the Labouring Population of Great Britain* (1842; reprinted, M. W. Flinn, ed., Edinburgh, 1965)

Checkland, O., *Philanthropy in Victorian Scotland* (Edinburgh, 1980)

Checkland, S. G., *The Rise of Industrial Society in England* (1964)

The Upas Tree (Glasgow, 1977)

Clark, Ian D. L., 'From Protests to Reaction: The Moderate Regime in the Church of Scotland 1752–1805', in N. T. Phillipson and Rosalind Mitchison, eds., *Scotland in the Age of Improvement* (Edinburgh 1970)

Cockburn, H., *Memorials of his Time* (Edinburgh, 1909)

Collier, A., *The Crofting Problem* (Cambridge, 1953)

Cowan, R., *Statistics of Fever in Glasgow* (Glasgow, 1838)

Craig, D., *Scottish Literature and the Scottish People* (1961)

Cramond, R. D., *Housing Policy in Scotland, 1919–64* (Edinburgh, 1966)

Crowley, D. W., 'The "Crofters' Party", 1885–1892', *Scottish Historical Review*, 35 (1956)

Cullen, L. M., and Smout, T. C., eds., *Comparative Aspects of Irish and Scottish Economic and Social History, 1600–1900* (Edinburgh, 1977)

Damer, S., 'State, Class and Housing: Glasgow, 1885–1919', in J. Melling, ed., *Housing, Social Policy and the State* (1980)

Darling, F. F., *West Highland Survey: An Essay in Human Ecology* (1955)

Davie, G. E., *The Democratic Intellect* (Edinburgh, 1961)

Day, J. P., *Public Administration in the Highlands and Islands of Scotland* (1918)

Devine, T. M., 'Social Stability and Agrarian Change in the Eastern Lowlands of Scotland, 1810–1840', *Social History*, 3 (1978)

   'Temporary Migration and the Scottish Highlands in the Nineteenth Century', *Economic History Review*, 2nd ser., 32 (1979)

Dewey, C., 'Celtic Agrarian Legislation and the Celtic Revival: Historical Implications of Gladstone's Irish and Scottish Land Acts, 1870–1886', *Past & Present*, 64 (1974)

Dodgshon, R. A., *Land and Society in Early Scotland* (Oxford, 1981)

   'Agricultural Change and its Social Consequences in the Southern Uplands of Scotland, 1600–1780', in T. M. Devine and David Dickson, eds., *Ireland and Scotland 1600–1830* (Edinburgh, 1983)

Donachie, Ian, 'Scottish Criminals and Transportations to Australia, 1786–1852', *Scottish Economic and Social History*, 4 (1984)

Drummond, A. J., and Bulloch, J., *The Scottish Church, 1688–1843* (Edinburgh, 1973)

   The Church in Victorian Scotland, 1843–1874 (Edinburgh, 1975)

Dunlop, John, *Artificial and Compulsory Drinking Usages in North Britain* (Greenock, 1836)

DurKacz, V. E., *The Decline of the Celtic Languages* (Edinburgh, 1983).

Edwards, O. D., and Ransome, B., eds., *James Connolly, Selected Political Writings* (1973)

Erskine, S., ed., *The Earl of Mar's Legacies to Scotland*, Scottish History Society, 26 (Edinburgh, 1896)

Fenton, A., *Scottish Country Life* (Edinburgh, 1976)

Ferguson, T., *The Dawn of Scottish Social Welfare* (Edinburgh, 1948)

   Scottish Social Welfare, 1864–1914 (Edinburgh , 1958)

Ferguson, W., *Scotland, 1689 to the Present* (Edinburgh, 1968)

Flinn, M. W., ed., *Scottish Population History from the 17th Century to the 1930s* (Cambridge, 1977)

Fraser, David, ed., *The Christian Watt Papers* (Edinburgh, 1983)

Fraser Darling, F., ed., *West Highland Survey* (Oxford, 1955)

Fullarton, W., *General View of the Agriculture of the County of Ayr . . .* (Edinburgh, 1793)

Gourvish, T. R., 'The Cost of Living in Glasgow in the Early Nineteenth Century', *Economic History Review*, 2nd ser., 25 (1972)

Gray, Malcolm, *The Highland Economy, 1750–1850* (Oxford, 1955)

   'Scottish Emigration: The Social Impact of Agrarian Change in the Rural Lowlands, 1775–1875', *Perspectives in American History*, 8 (1973)

Gray, R. Q., *The Labour Aristocracy in Victorian Edinburgh* (Oxford, 1976)

Hamilton, H., *An Economic History of Scotland in the Eighteenth Century* (Oxford, 1963)

   The Healers: A History of Medicine in Scotland (Edinburgh, 1981)

Handley, J. E., *The Irish in Modern Scotland* (Cork, 1947)
  The Navvy in Scotland (Cork, 1970)
Hanham, H. J., *The Scottish Political Tradition* (Edinburgh, 1964)
  Scottish Nationalism (1969)
  'The Problem of Highland Discontent, 1880–1885', *Transactions of the Royal Historical Society*, 4th ser., 19 (1969)
Harvie, C., *Scotland and Nationalism* (1977)
  No Gods and Precious Few Heroes, Scotland 1914-1980 (Edinburgh, 1981)
Highet, J., 'The Churches', in A. J. Cairncross, ed., *The Scottish Economy* (Cambridge, 1954)
Hinton, James, *The First Shop Stewards' Movement* (1973)
Houston, R., 'The Literacy Myth? Illiteracy in Scotland, 1630–1760', *Past & Present*, 96 (1982)
Hunt, E. H., *Regional Wage Variations in Britain, 1850–1914* (Oxford, 1973)
Hunter, J., *The Making of the Crofting Community* (Edinburgh, 1976)
Hutchison, I. G. C., *A Political History of Scotland, 1832–1924: Parties, Elections and Issues* (Edinburgh, 1985)
Johnston, T., *Memories* (1952)
Journal of Henry Cockburn, 1831–1854, vol. 2 (Edinburgh, 1874)
Keating, M., and Bleiman, D., *Labour and Scottish Nationalism* (1979)
Kellas, J. G., *Modern Scotland* (1968)
  The Scottish Political System (Cambridge, 1973)
Kellett, J. R., *The Impact of Railways on Victorian Cities* (1969)
Kendall, Walter, *The Revolutionary Movement in Britain 1900–21* (1969)
Kerr, J., *Memories Grave and Gay* (Edinburgh, 1903)
Kinloch, J., and Butt, J., *History of the Scottish Co-Operative Wholesale Society Limited* (Glasgow, 1981)
Knox, W., ed., *Scottish Labour Leaders, 1918–39: A Biographical Dictionary* (Edinburgh, 1984)
Labour in Europe and America (Government Printing Office, Washington, DC, 1876)
Lee, C. H., *British Regional Employment Statistics 1841–1971* (Cambridge, 1979)
Lenman, B., *An Economic History of Modern Scotland* (1977)
Levitt, I., 'The Scottish Poor Law and Unemployment, 1890–1929', in T. C. Smout, ed., *The Search for Wealth and Stability: Essays in Economic and Social History Presented to M. W. Flinn* (1979)
Levitt, I., and Smout, T. C., *The State of the Scottish Working Class in 1843* (Edinburgh, 1979)
Lindsay, I. G., and Cosh, Mary, *Inveraray and the Dukes of Argyll* (Edinburgh, 1973)
Lindsay, P., *The Interest of Scotland Considered* (Edinburgh, 1733)
Logue, K., *Popular Disturbances in Scotland 1780-1815* (Edinburgh, 1979)
Lond, R. E.C., *Fortnightly Review* (Jan. 1903)
Lythe, S. G. E., and Butt, J., *An Economic History of Scotland, 1100–1939* (Glasgow, 1975)
McAllister, G., *James Maxton, the Portrait of a Rebel* (1935)
McCrone, Gavin, *Regional Policy in Britain* (1969)
Macintyre, S., *Little Moscows: Communism and Working-Class Militancy in Inter-War Britain* (1980)
Mackenzie, O. H., *A Hundred Years in the Highlands* (1921)
MacLaren, A. A., 'Presbyterianism and the Working Class in a

Mid-Nineteenth Century City', *Scottish Historical Review*, 46 (1967)

Religion and Social Class: The Disruption Years in Aberdeen (1974)

ed., *Social Class in Scotland* (1976)

McLean, I., 'Popular Protest and Public Order, Red Clydeside 1915–1919', in R. Quinault and J. Stevenson, eds., *Popular Protest and Public Order* (1974)

Keir Hardie (New York, 1975)

McPherson, A., 'An Angle on the Geist: Persistence and Change in the Scottish Educational Tradition', in W. M. Humes and H. M. Paterson, eds., *Scottish Culture and Scottish Education, 1800–1980* (Edinburgh, 1983)

McRoberts, D., ed., *Modern Scottish Catholicism, 1878-1978* (Glasgow, 1979)

McShane, Harry and Smith, Joan, *No Mean Fighter* (1978)

Marshall, Rosalind, *The Days of Duchess Anne*, (1973)

Marwick, W. H., *A Short History of Labour in Scotland* (Edinburgh, 1967)

Matheson, P., 'Scottish War Sermons', *Records of the Scottish Church History Society*, 17 (1972)

Mathieson, W. L., *Church and Reform in Scotland* (Glasgow, 1911)

Meikle, H. W., *Scotland and the French Revolution* (Glasgow, 1912)

Melling, J., 'Clydeside Housing and the Evolution of State Rent Control 1900–1939', in J. Melling, ed., *Housing, Social Policy and the State* (1980)

'Scottish Industrialists and the Changing Character of Class Relations in the Clyde Region, *c.*1880–1918', in T. Dickson, ed., *Capital and Class in Scotland* (Edinburgh, 1982)

Middlemas, R. K., *The Clydesiders* (1965)

Milton, N., *John Maclean* (1973)

Minutes of Evidence Taken before Glasgow Municipal Commission on the Housing of the Poor (Glasgow, 1904)

Mitchison, Rosalind, 'The Government and the Highlands, 1707-1745', in N. T. Phillipson and Rosalind Mitchison, eds., *Scotland in the Age of Improvement* (Edinburgh, 1970)

'The Making of the Old Scottish Poor Law', *Past & Present*, 63 (1974)

'Patriotism and National Identity in Eighteenth Century Scotland', in T. W. Moody, ed., *Nationality and the Pursuit of National Independence* (Belfast, 1978)

'The Creation of the Disablement Rule in the Scottish Poor Law', in T. C. Smout, ed., *The Search for Wealth and Stability: Essays in Economic and Social History Presented to M. W. Flinn* (1979)

'Death in Tranent', *Transactions of the East Lothian Antiquarian and Field Naturalist Society*, 16 (1979)

Morgan, K. O., *Keir Hardie, Radical and Socialist* (1975)

Morgan, V., 'Agricultural Wage Rates in Late-Eighteenth Century Scotland', *Economic History Review*, 2nd ser., 29 (1971)

Morris, R. J., *Cholera 1832* (1976)

Muir, Edwin, *Scottish Journey*, ed. T. C. Smout (Edinburgh, 1979)

Murray, N., *The Scottish Hand Loom Weavers 1790–1850: A Social History* (Edinburgh, 1971)

Murray, W. H., *The Islands of Western Scotland* (1973)

Nairn, T., *The Break-Up of Britain*, 2nd edn (London, 1981)

Neill, A. S., *A Dominie's Log* (1915)

Nicholson, N., *Lord of the Isles: Lord Leverhulme in the Hebrides* (1960)

Niven, D., *The Development of Housing in Scotland* (1979)

Orwin, C. S., and Whetham, E. H., *History of British Agriculture, 1846-1914* (1971)

Osborne, G. S., *Scottish and English Schools: A Comparative Survey of the Past Fifty Years* (Pittsburg, 1966)

Paterson, A., 'The Poor Law in Nineteenth-Century Scotland', in D. Fraser, ed., *The New Poor Law in the Nineteenth Century* (1976)

Paton, D. N., Dunlop, J. C., and Inglis, E. M., *A Study of the Diet of the Labouring Classes in Edinburgh* (Edinburgh, 1900)

Paton, H., ed., *The Session Book of Rothesay 1658-1750* (privately published, 1931)

Pennant, T., *Tour in Scotland and Voyages to the Hebrides, 1772* (1790)

Price, S. F., 'Rivetters' Earnings in Clyde Shipbuilding 1889-1913', *Scottish Economic and Social History*, 1 (1981)

Pryde, G. S., *Central and Local Government in Scotland since 1707* (Historical Association Pamphlet No. 45, 1960)

Reid, F., *Keir Hardie, the Making of a Socialist* (1975)

Report to the Board of Supervision by Sir John McNeill, GCB, on the Western Highlands and Islands (Edinburgh, 1851)

Report on the State of the Poor in Berwickshire (Edinburgh, 1841)

Richards, E., 'Patterns of Highland Discontent', in R. Quinault and J. Stevenson, eds., *Popular Protest and Public Order* (1974)

A History of the Highland Clearances: Agrarian Transformation and the Evictions, 1746-1886 (1982)

Roach, W. M., 'Alexander Richmond and the Radical Reform Movement in Glasgow in 1816-7', *Scottish Historical Review*, 51 (1972)

Robertson, D. J., 'Population Growth and Movement' and 'Wages', in A. J. Cairncross, ed., *The Scottish Economy* (Cambridge, 1954)

Robertson, G., *Rural Recollections* (Irvine, 1829)

Rubinstein, W. D., 'The Victorian Middle Classes: Wealth, Occupation and Geography', *Economic History Review*, 2nd ser., 30 (1977)

Saul, S. B., 'The Shortcomings of Scottish Industry', *Scottish Economic and Social History*, 1 (1982)

Saunders, L. J., *Scottish Democracy, 1815-1840* (Edinburgh, 1950)

Scotland, J., *The History of Scottish Education*, 2 vols. (1969)

Scott, J., and Hughes, M., *The Anatomy of Scottish Capital* (1980)

Shaw, J. S., *The Management of Scottish Society 1707-1764* (Edinburgh, 1983)

Sher, Richard B., 'Moderates, Managers and Popular Politics in Mid-Eighteenth Century Edinburgh: The Drysdale Bustle of the 1760s', in J. Dwyer, Roger A. Mason and Alexander Murdoch, eds., *New Perspectives on the Politics and Culture of Early Modern Scotland* (Edinburgh, 1982)

Slaven, A., *The Development of the West of Scotland, 1750-1960* (1975)

Smith, A., *The Third Statistical Account of Scotland: The County of Fife* (Edinburgh 1952)

Smout, T. C., *A History of the Scottish People, 1560-1830* (1969)

'The Landowner and the Planned Village in Scotland, 1730-1830', in N. T. Phillipson and Rosalind Mitchison, eds., *Scotland in the Age of Improvement* (Edinburgh, 1970)

'The Strange Intervention of Edward Twistleton: Paisley in Depression, 1841-3', in T. C. Smout, ed., *The Search for Wealth and Stability: Essays in Economic and Social History Presented to M. W. Flinn* (1979)

'U.S. Consular Reports: A Source for Scottish Economic Historians', *Scottish Historical Review*, 58 (1979)

'American Consular Reports on Scotland', Business History , 33 (1981)

'Scottish Marriage, Regular and Irregular, 1500–1940', in R. B. Outhwaite, ed., *Marriage and Society: Studies in the Social History of Marriage* (1981)

'Born again at Cambuslang: New Evidence on Popular Religion and Literacy in Eighteenth Century Scotland', *Past & Present*, 97 (1982)

Solow, Lee, 'An Index of the Poor and Rich in Scotland, 1861–1961', *Scottish Journal of Political Economy*, 18 (1971)

Sprott, Gavin, 'A Weel Plou'd Rig: The Era of the Working Horse on the Farms of the East Coast of Scotland', in B. Kay, ed., *Odyssey* (Edinburgh, 1980)

Symon, J. A., *Scottish Farming Past and Present* (Edinburgh, 1959)

Tannahill, R., *Poems and Songs, Chiefly in the Scottish Dialect* (1815)

Thom, W., *Rhymes and Recollections of a Hand Loom Weaver* (1843)

Thomson, G. M., *Scotland, that Distressed Area* (Edinburgh, 1935)

Timperley, L., 'The Pattern of Landholding in Eighteenth Century Scotland', in M. L. Parry and T. R. Slater, eds., *The Making of the Scottish Countryside* (1980)

Townshend, Joseph, *A Dissertation on the Poor Laws*, 2nd edn (1787), Section XIII

Transactions of the Highland and Agricultural Society of Scotland, new ser., 11 (1837)

Tuckett, A., *The Scottish Carter* (1967)

Vincent, J. R., *The Formation of the Liberal Party, 1857–68* (1966)

Watt, Robert, *An Inquiry into the Relative Mortality of Children in Glasgow* (Glasgow, 1813)

Webb, B., *Diaries 1924–32* (1956)

Whetstone, Ann E., *Scottish County Government in the Eighteenth and Nineteenth Centuries* (Edinburgh, 1981)

Whyte, I. D., *Agriculture and Society in Seventeenth Century Scotland* (Edinburgh, 1979)

Wilson, A., *The Chartist Movement in Scotland* (Manchester, 1970)

Wilson, G. B., *Alcohol and the Nation* (1940)

Withers, C. W. J., *Gaelic in Scotland, 1698–1981: The Geographical History of a Language* (Edinburgh, 1984)

Young, J. D., *The Rousing of the Scottish Working Class* (1979)

Youngson, A. J., *After the Forty Five* (Edinburgh, 1973)

4 WALES

Anthony-Jones, W. J., 'The Tourist Industry in Wales', *Welsh Anvil*, 3–4 (1951–2)

Ashby, A. W., 'The Agricultural Depression in Wales', *Welsh Outlook*, 16 (1929)

'Some Characteristics of Welsh Farming', *Welsh Outlook*, 20 (1933)

'The Peasant Agriculture of Wales', *Welsh Review*, 3 (1944)

Ashby, A. W., and Evans, I. L., *The Agriculture of Wales and Monmouthshire* (Cardiff, 1944)

Ashby, A. W. and Jones, J. M., 'The Social Origin of Welsh Farmers', *Welsh Journal of Agriculture*, 2 (1926)

Atkinson, M., and Baber, C., *The Rise and Decline of the South Wales Iron Industry, 1760–1880* (Cardiff, 1987)

Baber, C., 'The Subsidiary Industries of Glamorgan, 1760–1914', in A. H.

John and Glanmor Williams, eds., *Glamorgan County History*, vol. 5: *Industrial Glamorgan* (Cardiff, 1980)

'Canals and the Economic Development of South Wales', in C. Baber and L. J. Williams, eds., *Modern South Wales: Essays in Economic History* (Cardiff, 1986)

Baber, C., and Thomas, D., 'The Glamorgan Economy, 1914–1945', in A. H. John and Glanmor Williams, eds., *Glamorgan County History*, vol. 5: *Industrial Glamorgan* (Cardiff, 1980)

Baber, C., and Williams, L. J., eds., *Modern South Wales: Essays in Economic History* (Cardiff, 1986)

Baines, D., *Migration in a Mature Economy: Emigration and Internal Migration in England and Wales, 1861–1900* (Cambridge, 1985)

Bowen, E. G., 'The Heartland', in E. G. Bowen, ed., *Wales: A Physical, Historical and Regional Geography* (1957)

Boyns, T., Thomas, D., and Baber, C., 'The Iron, Steel and Tinplate Industries, 1750–1914', in A. H. John and Glanmor Williams, eds., *Glamorgan County History*, vol. 5: *Industrial Glamorgan* (Cardiff, 1980)

Brennan, T., Cooney, E. W., and Pollins, H., eds., *Social Change in South-West Wales* (1954)

Carter, H., *The Towns of Wales* (Cardiff, 1966)

'The Growth and Decline of Welsh Towns', in D. Moore, ed., *Wales in the Eighteenth Century* (Swansea, 1976)

Ceredig Davies, J., *Welsh Folk Lore* (Aberystwyth, 1911)

Chappell, Edgar, 'The Development of Rural Industries', *Welsh Outlook*, 10 (1923)

Checkland, S. G., *The Rise of Industrial Society in England, 1815–85* (1964)

Colyer, R. J., 'The Gentry and the County in Nineteenth-Century Cardiganshire', *Welsh History Review*, 10 (1980–1)

Coupland, R., *Welsh and Scottish Nationalism* (1954)

Daunton, M. J., *Coal Metropolis: Cardiff, 1870–1914* (Leicester, 1977)

Davies, D. H., *The Welsh Nationalist Party, 1925–45* (Cardiff, 1983)

Davies, E., and Rees, A. D., eds., *Welsh Rural Communities* (Cardiff, 1950)

Davies, E. T., *Religion in the Industrial Revolution in South Wales* (Cardiff, 1965)
Religion and Society in the Nineteenth Century (Llandybie, 1981)

Davies, G., 'The Agricultural Labourer in Wales', in Anon., *Social Problems in Wales* (1913)

Davies, G., 'Community and Social Structure in Bethesda, 1840–70', *Carnarvonshire Historical Society Transactions*, 41 (1980)

Davies, J., 'The End of the Great Estates and the Rise of Freehold Farming in Wales', *Welsh History Review*, 7 (1974)

Davies, R. C., 'The Present Condition of the Welsh Nation', *Red Dragon*, 4 (1883)

Dodd, A. H., *The Industrial Revolution in North Wales* (Cardiff, 1933)

Douglas, R., *Land, People and Politics* (1976)

Dunbabin, J. P. D., *Rural Discontent in Nineteenth-Century Britain* (1974)

Edmunds, E. L., ed., *I Was There: The Memoirs of H. S. Tremenheere* (Windsor, 1965)

Edwards, H. W., *The Good Patch* (1938)

Edwards, Wil Jon, *From the Valley I Came* (1956)

England, J. W., 'The Inheritance', in G. Humphrys, *Industrial Britain, South Wales* (Newton Abbot, 1972)

Evans, E. D., *A History of Wales, 1660–1815* (Cardiff, 1976)

Evans, E. W., *Mabon* (Cardiff, 1959)
  The Miners of South Wales (Cardiff, 1961)
Evans, F., 'The Problem of the Rural School', *Welsh Outlook*, 15 (1928)
Evans, N., 'The South Wales Race Riots of 1919', *Llafur*, 3 (1980)
  'The Welsh Victorian City: The Middle Class and Civic and National Consciousness in Cardiff', *Welsh History Review*, 12 (1985)
Francis, H., 'South Wales', in J. Skelley, ed., *The General Strike* (1976)
Francis, H., and Smith, D., *The Fed* (1980)
Griffith, Wyn, 'What is the Welsh Way of Life?', *Welsh Outlook*, 52 (1965)
Griffiths, Jim, *Pages from Memory* (1969)
Gwyther, C. E., *The Valley Shall Be Exalted* (1949)
Gwyther, C., 'Sidelights on Religion and Politics in the Rhondda Valley, 1906–26', *Llafur*, 3 (1980)
Heath, R., 'The Rural Revolution', *Contemporary Review*, 67 (1895)
Hobsbawm, E. J., *Industry and Empire* (1968)
Holloway, F., 'The Inter-War Depression in the Wrexham Coalfield', *Denbighshire Historical Society Transactions*, 27 (1978)
Hopkin, D., 'The Llanelli Riots, 1911', *Welsh History Review*, 11 (1983)
Hopkins, K. S., ed., *Rhondda Past and Future* (Rhondda Borough Council, 1975)
Howell, D. W., *Land and People in Nineteenth-Century Wales* (1978)
  Patriarchs and Parasites: The Gentry of South-West Wales in the Eighteenth Century (Cardiff, 1986)
Howse, W. H., *Radnorshire* (Hereford, 1949)
Hutt, A., *The Condition of the Working Class in Britain: South Wales* (1933)
Jenkins, D., 'The Part Played by Craftsmen in the Religious History of Modern Wales', *Welsh Anvil*, 5–6 (1953–4)
  The Agricultural Community of South-West Wales at the Turn of the Twentieth Century (Cardiff, 1971)
  'Rural Society Inside Out', in D. Smith, ed., *A People and a Proletariat* (1980)
Jenkins, J. G., 'Rural Industry in Cardiganshire', *Ceredigion*, 6 (1968–71)
  Welsh Crafts and Craftsmen (Llandysul, 1975)
  Maritime Heritage: The Ships and Seamen of Southern Ceredigion (Llandysul, 1982)
Jennings, H., *Brynmawr* (1934)
John, A. H., *The Industrial Development of South Wales* (Cardiff, 1950)
John, A. H., and Williams, Glanmor, eds., *Glamorgan County History*, vol. 5: *Industrial Glamorgan* (Cardiff, 1980)
John, A. V., 'The Chartist Endurance', *Morgannwg*, 15 (1971)
Jones, B., 'The Present Agricultural Position', *Welsh Outlook*, 10 (1923)
Jones, C. B., 'Some Welsh Rural Problems', *Welsh Outlook*, 17 (1930)
Jones, D. J. V., *Before Rebecca* (1973)
  'Crime, Protest and Community in Nineteenth-Century Wales', *Llafur* 1 (1974)
  'The Second Rebecca Riots', *Llafur*, 2 (1976)
  The Last Rising (Oxford, 1984)
  'The Welsh and Crime, 1801–1891', in C. Emsley and J. Walvin, eds., *Artisans, Peasants and Proletarians* (1985)
Jones, G. E., *Controls and Conflict in Welsh Secondary Education, 1889–1944* (Cardiff, 1982)
Jones, I. G., 'The South Wales Collier in Mid-Nineteenth Century', in *Victorian South Wales Architecture, Industry and Society* (Victorian Society, 7th

Conference Report, 1969)
'The Valleys: The Making of a Community', in P. H. Ballard and E. Jones, eds., *The Valleys Call* (Ferndale, 1975)
Health, Wealth and Politics in Victorian Wales (Swansea, 1979)
Explorations and Explanations (Llandysul, 1981)
Jones, I. W., *Llandudno* (Cardiff, 1975)
Jones, J. M., 'Agricultural Co-Operation in Wales, 1902–26', *Welsh Outlook*, 15 (1928)
Jones, Merfyn, 'Class and Society in Nineteenth-Century Gwynedd', in D. Smith, ed., *A People and a Proletariat* (1980)
Jones, P. N., *Colliery Settlement in the South Wales Coalfield, 1850–1926* (Hull, 1969)
Jones, R. M., 'A Note on 1926 in North Wales', *Llafur*, 2 (1977)
The North Wales Quarrymen, 1874–1922 (Cardiff, 1982)
Jones, T., *Rhymney Memories* (Newtown, 1938)
Jones, Thomas., *Welsh Broth* (1952)
Jones-Parry, S. H., 'Crime in Wales', *Red Dragon*, 4 (1883)
Khleif, Bud B., *Language, Ethnicity and Education in Wales* (The Hague, 1980)
Lambert, W., 'Some Working-Class Attitudes towards Organised Religion in Nineteenth-Century Wales', *Llafur*, 2 (1976)
Lewis, E. D., *The Rhondda Valleys* (1959)
Lewis, W. J., *Lead Mining in Wales* (Cardiff, 1967)
Lile, B., and Farmer, D., 'The Early Development of Association Football in South Wales, 1890–1906', *Transactions of the Honourable Society of Cymmrodorion* (1984)
Lush, A., *The Young Adult in South Wales* (Cardiff, 1941)
McCay, T., 'Edward Hughes, 1856–1925, North Wales' Miners' Agent', *Llafur*, 2 (1979)
Madgwick, P. J., *The Politics of Rural Wales* (1972)
Martin, A., 'Agriculture', in B. Thomas, ed., *The Welsh Economy* (Cardiff, 1961)
Matthews, E., 'Anglesey Union of Village Halls and Societies', *Welsh Outlook*, 10 (1923)
Minchinton, W. E., *The British Tinplate Industry: A History* (Oxford, 1957)
ed., *Industrial South Wales, 1750–1914* (1969)
Moore, D., ed., *Barry: The Centenary Book*, 2nd edn (Barry, 1985)
Morgan, Jane, 'Denbighshire's *Annus Mirabilis* : The County and Borough Elections of 1868', *Welsh History Review*, 7 (1974)
Morgan, K. O., *Wales in British Politics*, 2nd edn (Cardiff, 1970)
'From Cymru Fydd to Crowther', in B. Jones, ed., *The Anatomy of Wales* (Cardiff, 1972)
Rebirth of a Nation, Wales 1880–1980 (Oxford and Cardiff, 1981)
'The Welsh in English Politics', in R. R. Davies, R. A. Griffiths, I. G. Jones and K. O. Morgan, eds., *Welsh Society and Nationhood* (Cardiff, 1984)
Morgan, L., 'The Future of Welsh Nonconformity', *Welsh Outlook*, 18 (1931)
Morgan, P., *The Eighteenth-Century Renaissance* (Llandybie, 1981)
Morgan, P., and Thomas, D., *Wales: The Shaping of a Nation* (Newton Abbot, 1984)
Morgan, T. J., 'Peasant Culture in the Swansea Valley', in S. Williams, ed., *Glamorgan Historian*, vol. 9 (Cowbridge, 1973)
Morris, J., and Williams, L. J., *The South Wales Coal Industry, 1841–1875* (Cardiff, 1958)
Owen, T. M., *Welsh Folk Customs*, new edn (Llandysul, 1987)

Parry, Thomas, 'The Welsh Renaissance of the Twentieth Century', in A. J. Roderick, ed., *Wales through the Ages*, vol. 2 (Llandybie, 1960)

Parry-Jones, D., *My Own Folk* (Llandysul, 1972)

Peate, I., 'Society in Wales', in B. Jones, ed., *The Anatomy of Wales* (Cardiff, 1972)

Peate, I. C., 'Welsh Rural Crafts', *Welsh Outlook*, 16 (1929)

Perrie Williams, G., *Welsh Education in Sunlight and Shadow* (1916)

Philip, A. B., *The Welsh Question: Nationalism in Welsh Politics, 1945–1970* (Cardiff, 1975)

Phillips, T., *Wales* (1849)

Pierce, G. O., 'University College Cardiff 1883–1893', *Transactions of the Honourable Society of Cymmrodorion* (1984)

Pretty, D. A., *Two Centuries of Anglesey Schools* (Llangefni, 1977)

Price, C., 'Portable Theatres in Wales 1843–1914', *National Library of Wales Journal*, 9 (1955–6)

The Professional Theatre in Wales (Swansea, 1984)

Price, M. R. C., *Industrial Saundersfoot* (Llandysul, 1982)

Razell, P. E., and Wainwright, R. J. W., eds., *The Victorian Working Class: Selections from the Morning Chronicle* (1973)

Rees, A. D., *Life in a Welsh Countryside* (Cardiff, 1950)

Rees, D. B., *Chapels in the Valley* (Wirral, 1975)

Rees, J. L., and Nicholas, N., 'The Policy of the Colliers', *Welsh Outlook*, 2 (1915)

Richards, B., *History of the Llynfi Valley* (Cowbridge, 1982)

Roberts, R. O., 'The Smelting of Non-Ferrous Metals since 1750', in A. H. John and Glanmor Williams, eds., *Glamorgan County History*, vol. 5: *Industrial Glamorgan* (Cardiff, 1980)

Roberts, W. G., 'Nonconformity: A Force in Welsh National Life', *Young Wales*, 9 (1903)

Rocyn-Jones, D., 'Public Health in Wales', *Welsh Review*, 1 (1939)

Rogers, E., 'The History of Trade Unionism in the Coal Mining Industry of North Wales to 1914', *Denbighshire Historical Society Transactions*, 15 (1966)

Smith, D., 'Tonypandy 1910: Definitions of Community', *Past & Present*, 87 (1980)

Wales! Wales? (1984)

ed., *A People and a Proletariat* (1980)

Southall, J. E., *Bi-Lingual Teaching in Welsh Elementary Schools* (Newport, 1888)

Wales and her Language, 2nd edn (1893)

Stead, P., 'Working-Class Leadership in South Wales, 1900–20', *Welsh History Review*, 6 (1973)

'Schools and Society in Glamorgan before 1914', *Morgannwg*, 19 (1975)

Coleg Harlech (Cardiff, 1977)

'The Swansea of Dylan Thomas', in *A Memorable Year 1977–8*, (Dylan Thomas Society Wales Branch, 1978)

'Establishing a Heartland – The Labour Party in Wales', in K. D. Brown, ed., *The First Labour Party 1906–1914* (1985)

'The Town that had Come of Age, 1918–39', in D. Moore, ed., *Barry: The Centenary Book*, 2nd edn (Barry, 1985)

Thomas, B., 'Organisation of Religion in Wales', *Welsh Outlook*, 16 (1929)

Thomas, B., 'The Influx of Labour into London and the South-East, 1920–1936', *Economica*, 4 (1937)

'The Influx of Labour into the Midlands, 1920–37', *Economica*, 5 (1937)

'Wales and the Atlantic Economy', in B. Thomas, ed., *The Welsh Economy* (Cardiff, 1961)

'Post-War Expansion', in B. Thomas, ed., *The Welsh Economy* (Cardiff, 1961)

'The Industrial Revolution and the Welsh Language', in C. Baber and L. J. Williams, eds., *Modern South Wales: Essays in Economic History* (Cardiff, 1986)

Thomas, D. A., 'War and the Economy: The South Wales Experience', in C. Baber and L. J. Williams, eds., *Modern South Wales: Essays in Economic History* (Cardiff, 1986)

Thomas, J. G., 'Population Trends in Wales', *Welsh Anvil*, 3–4 (1951–2)

Tomley, J. E., 'The Inquiry into the Anti-Tuberculosis Service in Wales and Monmouthshire', *Welsh Review*, 1 (1939)

Vincent, J. E., *The Land Question in North Wales* (1896)

Williams, A. B., 'Courtship and Marriage in the Nineteenth Century', *Montgomeryshire Collections*, 51 (1949)

Williams, A. H., *Public Health in Mid-Victorian Wales* (Cardiff, 1983)

Williams, D., *Modern Wales* (1950)

The Rebecca Riots (Cardiff, 1955)

Williams, G., 'On Class and Status Groups in Welsh Rural Society', in G. Williams, ed., *Crisis of Economy and Ideology* (Sociology of Wales Studies Group, 1983)

Williams, Glanmor, *Religion, Language and Nationality in Wales* (Cardiff, 1979)

Williams, G. A., 'The Emergence of a Working Class Movement', in A. J. Roderick, ed., *Wales through the Ages*, vol. 2 (Llandybie, 1960)

The Merthyr Rising (1978)

'Locating a Welsh Working Class', in D. Smith, ed., *A People and a Proletariat* (1980)

When Was Wales? (1985)

Williams, L. J., 'The New Unionism in South Wales', *Welsh History Review*, 1 (1963)

'The Strike of 1898', *Morgannwg*, 9 (1965)

'The Road to Tonypandy', *Llafur*, 1 (1973)

'The Coalowners', in D. Smith, ed., *A People and a Proletariat* (1980)

'The Coal Industry, 1750–1914', in A. H. John and Glanmor Williams, eds., *Glamorgan County History*, vol. 5: *Industrial Glamorgan* (Cardiff, 1980)

Williams, L. J., and Boyns, T., 'Occupations in Wales, 1851–1971', *Bulletin of Economic Research*, 29 (1977)

Williams, T. N., 'The Sunday School: Its Failure and Future', *Welsh Outlook*, 17 (1930)

Williams-Davies, J., 'Merchedd y Gerddi: A Seasonal Migration of Female Labour from Rural Wales', *Folk Life*, 15 (1977)

Wynne Evans, L., *Education in Industrial Wales, 1700–1900* (Cardiff, 1971)

5 THE NORTH-WEST

Addy, J., 'Bishop Porteous' Visitation of the Diocese of Chester, 1778', *Northern History*, 13 (1977)

Ainsworth, A., 'Religion in the Working-Class Community and the Evolution of Socialism in Late Nineteenth-Century Lancashire: A Case of Working-Class Consciousness', *Histoire Sociale*, 20 (1977)

Anderson, G., *Victorian Clerks* (Manchester, 1976)

Anderson, M., *Family Structure in Nineteenth-Century Lancashire* (Cambridge, 1971)

'Sociological History and the Working-Class Family: Smelser Revisited', *Social History*, 3 (1976)

Ashmore, O., *The Industrial Archaeology of Lancashire* (Newton Abbot, 1969)

Ashton, T. S., *An Eighteenth-Century Industrialist: Peter Stubs of Warrington* (Manchester, 1939)

Aspinall, P. J., and Hudson, D., *Ellesmere Port: The Making of an Industrial Borough* (Neston, 1962)

Bailey, P., *Leisure and Class in Victorian England* (1978)

Barker, T. C., *The Glassmakers* (1977)

Barker, T. C., and Harris, J. R., *A Merseyside Town in the Industrial Revolution* (Liverpool, 1954)

Belchem, J., 'English Working-Class Radicalism and the Irish 1815–50', *North-West Labour History Society Bulletin*, 8 (1982–3)

Board of Trade, *An Industrial Survey of the Lancashire Area* (1932)

Bohstedt, J., *Riots and Community Politics in England and Wales 1790–1810* (1983)

Booth, A., 'Food-Riots in the North-West of England, 1790-1801', *Past & Present*, 77 (1977)

Bowker, B., *Lancashire under the Hammer* (1928)

Boyson, R., 'The New Poor Law in North-East Lancashire, 1834–71', *Lancashire and Cheshire Antiquarian Society*, 70 (1960)

The Ashworth Cotton Enterprise: The Rise and Fall of a Family Firm, 1818–80 (Oxford, 1970)

Bristow, B., 'An Artisan Elite Residential District in Preston, 1851', *Manchester Geographer*, N.S., 3 (1982)

Burgess, K., *The Origins of British Industrial Relations* (1975)

Burr-Litchfield, R., 'The Family and the Mill', in A. Wohl, ed., *The Victorian Family* (1978)

Bythell, D., *The Hand-Loom Weavers* (Cambridge, 1969)

Calhoun, C., *The Question of Class Struggle* (Oxford, 1982)

Challinor, R., and Ripley, B., *The Miners' Association: A Trade Union in the Age of the Chartists* (1968)

Chaloner, W. H., *The Social and Economic Development of Crewe* (Manchester, 1950)

Chapman, S. D., 'Fixed Capital Formation in the British Cotton Manufacturing Industry', in J. P. P. Higgins and S. Pollard, eds., *Aspects of Capital Formation in Great Britain 1750–1850* (1971)

'Financial Restraints on the Growth of Firms in the Cotton Industry, 1790–1850', *Economic History Review*, 2nd ser., 32 (1979)

Chorley, K., *Manchester Made Them* (1950)

Clarke, A., *The Effects of the Factory System* (1899)

Clarke, P. F., *Lancashire and the New Liberalism* (Cambridge, 1971)

Cruickshank, M., 'The Anglican Revival and Education: A Study of School Expansion in the Cotton Manufacturing Areas of North-West England, 1840–50', *Northern History*, 15 (1979)

Children and Industry (Manchester, 1981)

Danson, J. T., and Welton, T. A., 'On the Population of Lancashire and Cheshire and its Local Distribution during the Fifty Years 1801–51', *Transactions of the Historic Society of Lancashire and Cheshire*, 11 (1858–9)

Davies, C. S., *The Agricultural History of Cheshire, 1750–1850* (Manchester, 1960)

Davies, R. S. W., 'The Liverpool Labour Party and the Liverpool Working Class, 1900–39', *North-West Labour History Society Bulletin*, 6 (1979–80)

Dick, M., 'The Myth of the Working-Class Sunday School', *History of Education*, 9 (1980)

Didsbury, B., 'Cheshire Saltworkers', in R. Samuel, ed., *Miners, Quarrymen and Saltworkers* (1977)

Dutton, H. I., and King, J. E., *Ten Per Cent and No Surrender* (Cambridge, 1981)
  'The Limits of Paternalism: The Cotton Tyrants of North Lancashire, 1836–54', *Social History*, 7 (1982)

Edsall, M. C., *The Anti-Poor Law Movement, 1834–44* (Manchester, 1971)

Edwards, M. M., *The Growth of the British Cotton Trade 1780–1815* (Manchester, 1967)

Elbourne, R., *Music and Tradition in Early Industrial Lancashire 1780–1840* (Woodbridge, 1980)

Engels, F., *The Condition of the Working Class in England* (Panther edn, 1969)

Farnie, D. A., *The Lancashire Cotton Industry and the World Market 1815–96* (1979)
  The Manchester Ship Canal and the Rise of the Port of Manchester (Manchester, 1980)

Foster, J., *Class Struggle and the Industrial Revolution* (1974)

Fowler, A., 'Lancashire and the New Liberalism: A Review', *North-West Labour History Society Bulletin*, 4 (1977)

Fraser, D., *Urban Politics in Victorian England* (Leicester, 1976)

Freeman, T. W., Rodgers, H. B., and Kinvig, R. H., *Lancashire, Cheshire and the Isle of Man* (1966)

Gadian, D. S., 'Class Consciousness in Oldham and Other North-West Industrial Towns', *Historical Journal*, 21 (1978)

Garrard, J., *Leadership and Power in Victorian Industrial Towns 1830–80* (Manchester, 1983)

Gatrell, V. A. C., 'Labour, Power and the Size of Firms in Lancashire Cotton in the Second Quarter of the Nineteenth Century', *Economic History Review*, 2nd ser., 30 (1977)
  'Incorporation and the Pursuit of Liberal Hegemony in Manchester 1790–1839', in D. Fraser, ed., *Municipal Reform and the Industrial City* (Leicester, 1982)

Gibson, R., *Cotton Textile Wages in the United States and Great Britain: A Comparison of Trends, 1860–1945* (New York, 1948)

Hewitt, M., *Wives and Mothers in Victorian Industry* (1958)

Hikins, H., ed., *Building the Union* (Liverpool, 1973)

Hills, R., *Power in the Industrial Revolution* (Manchester, 1970)

Hindle, G. B., *Provision for the Relief of the Poor in Manchester, 1754–1826* (Manchester, 1975)

Hopwood, E., *The Lancashire Weavers' Story* (Manchester, 1969)

Hunt, K., 'Women and the Social Democratic Federation: Some Notes on Lancashire', *North-West Labour History Society Bulletin*, 7 (1980–1)

Hutchins, B. L., and Harrison, A., *A History of Factory Legislation*, 2nd edn (1911)

Hyde, F. E., *Liverpool and the Mersey* (Newton Abbot, 1971)

Jenkins, M., *The General Strike of 1842* (1980)

Jewkes, J., and Gray, F. M., *Wages and Labour in the Lancashire Cotton Industry* (Manchester, 1935)

John, A. V., *By the Sweat of their Brow: Women Workers at Victorian Coalmines* (1980)

Jones, D. Caradog, *The Social Survey of Merseyside*, 3 vols. (Liverpool, 1934)

Joyce, P., *Work, Society and Politics* (Brighton, 1980)

Kay, J. P., *The Moral and Physical Condition of the Working Classes Employed in the Cotton Manufacture of Manchester* (1832)

Kirby, R. G., and Musson, A. E., *The Voice of the People: John Doherty, 1798–1854* (Manchester, 1975)

Kirk, N., 'Ethnicity and Popular Toryism, 1850–70', in K. Lunn, ed., *Hosts, Immigrants and Minorities* (Folkestone, 1980)

Lancashire Industrial Development Association, *Industrial Reports* (1948–56)

Langton, J., *Geographical Change and Industrial Revolution: Coalmining in South-West Lancashire, 1590–1799* (Cambridge, 1979)

Laqueur, T. W., *Religion and Respectability: Sunday Schools and Working-Class Culture, 1780–1850* (1976)

Lazonick, W., 'Industrial Relations and Technical Change: The Case of the Self-Acting Mule', *Cambridge Journal of Economics*, 3 (1979)

'Factor Costs and the Diffusion of Ring Spinning in Britain prior to World War I', *Quarterly Journal of Economics*, 96 (1981)

Lee, J. M., *Social Leaders and Public Persons* (1963)

Liddington, J., and Norris, J., *One Hand Tied Behind Us* (1978)

Liddle, J. G., 'Estate Management and Land Reform Politics: The Hesketh and Scarisbrick Families and the Making of Southport, 1842–1914', in D. Cannadine, ed., *Patricians, Power and Politics in Nineteenth-Century Towns* (Leicester, 1982)

Lloyd-Jones, R., and Le Roux, A. A., 'The Size of Firms in the Cotton Industry: Manchester, 1815–41', *Economic History Review*, 2nd ser., 33 (1980)

Lowe, J. C., 'The Tory Triumph of 1868 in Blackburn and in Lancashire', *Historical Journal*, 16 (1973)

McCord, N., *The Anti-Corn Law League* (1958, reprinted 1968)

McKenzie, J., 'The Composition and Nutritional Value of Diets in Manchester and Dukinfield', *Lancashire and Cheshire Antiquarian Society*, 72 (1962)

Marriner, S., *The Economic and Social Development of Merseyside* (1982)

Marshall, J. D., 'The Lancashire Rural Labourer in the Early Nineteenth Century', *Transactions of the Lancashire and Cheshire Antiquarian Society*, 71 (1961)

Furness and the Industrial Revolution (Barrow, 1958; reprinted Beckermet, 1981)

ed., *The History of Lancashire County Council* (1977)

Mather, F. C., *After the Canal Duke* (Oxford, 1970)

Midwinter, E. C., *Social Administration in Lancashire, 1830–60* (Manchester, 1969)

Mitchell, H., *The Hard Way Up* (1968)

Musson, A. E., *Enterprise in Soap and Chemicals* (Manchester, 1965)

'Class Struggle and the Labour Aristocracy, 1830–60', and reply by J. Foster, *Social History*, 3 (1976)

Mutch, A., 'Lancashire's "Revolt of the Field"', *North-West Labour History Society Bulletin*, 8 (1982–3)

Poole, R., *Popular Leisure and the Music-Hall in Nineteenth-Century Bolton* (Lancaster, 1982)

'Oldham Wakes', in J. K. Walton and J. Walvin, eds., *Leisure in Britain, 1780–1939* (Manchester, 1983)

Pooley, C. G., 'The Residential Segregation of Migrant Communities in Mid-Victorian Liverpool', *Institute of British Geographers*, N.S., 2 (1977)

Porteous, J. D., *Canal Ports* (1977)

Read, D., 'Chartism in Manchester', in A. Briggs, ed., *Chartist Studies* (1959)

Roberts, E., 'Working-Class Standards of Living in Three Lancashire Towns, 1890–1914', *International Review of Social History*, 27 (1982)

Roberts, R., *The Classic Slum* (Manchester, 1971)

  A Ragged Schooling (Manchester, 1976)

Sandberg, L. C., *Lancashire in Decline* (Columbus, Ohio, 1974)

Sanderson, M., 'Education and the Factory in Industrial Lancashire, 1780–1840', *Economic History Review*, 2nd ser., 20 (1967)

Shallice, A., 'Liverpool Labourism and Irish Nationalism in the 1920s and 1930s', *North-West Labour History Society Bulletin*, 8 (1982–3)

Smelser, N. J., *Social Change in the Industrial Revolution* (1959)

Stedman Jones, G., 'The Language of Chartism', in J. Epstein and D. Thompson, eds., *The Chartist Experience: Studies in Working-Class Radicalism and Culture 1830–1860* (1982)

Stephens, W. B., *Adult Education and Society in an Industrial Town: Warrington, 1800–1900* (Exeter, 1980)

Sykes, R., 'Working-Class Consciousness in Oldham, 1830–42', *Historical Journal*, 23 (1980)

  'Early Chartism and Trade Unionism in South-East Lancashire', in J. Epstein and D. Thompson, eds., *The Chartist Experience* (1982)

Timmins, G., *Hand-Loom Weavers' Cottages in Central Lancashire* (Lancaster, 1977)

Turner, H. A., *Trade Union Growth, Structure and Policy* (1962)

Tylecote, M., *The Merchants' Institutes of Lancashire and Yorkshire before 1851* (Manchester, 1957)

Tyson, R. E., 'The Cotton Industry', in D. H. Aldcroft, ed., *The Development of British Industry and Foreign Competition 1875–1914* (1968)

Vigier, F., *Change and Apathy: Liverpool and Manchester during the Industrial Revolution* (1970)

Vincent, J. R., *The Formation of the Liberal Party, 1857–68* (1966)

  'The Effect of the Second Reform Act in Lancashire', *Historical Journal*, 11 (1968)

Wadsworth, A. P., and Mann, J. de L., *The Cotton Trade and Industrial Lancashire, 1600–1780* (1931)

Waller, P. J., *Democracy and Sectarianism: A Political and Social History of Liverpool, 1868–1939* (Liverpool, 1981)

Walton, J. K., *The Blackpool Landlady: A Social History* (Manchester, 1978)

  'Lunacy in the Industrial Revolution: A Study of Asylum Admissions in Lancashire, 1848–50', *Journal of Social History*, 13 (1979–80)

  'The Demand for Working-Class Seaside Holidays in Victorian England', *Economic History Review*, 2nd ser., 34 (1981)

Walton, J. K., and Poole, R., 'The Lancashire Wakes in the Nineteenth Century', in R. D. Storch, ed., *Popular Culture and Custom in Nineteenth-Century England* (1982)

Ward, J. T., *The Factory Movement 1830–55* (1962)

Warren, K., *Chemical Foundations* (Oxford, 1980)

White, B. D., *A History of the Corporation of Liverpool* (Liverpool, 1951)

White, J., 'A Panegyric on Edwardian Progressivism', *Journal of British Studies*, 16 (1976–7)

White, J. L., *The Limits of Trade Union Militancy* (1978)

6 THE NORTH-EAST

Armstrong, H. E., 'Sketch of the Sanitary History of Newcastle-upon-Tyne', *Transactions of the Sanitary Institute of Great Britain*, 4 (1883)

Atkinson, F., *Life and Tradition in Northumberland and Durham* (1977)

Briggs, A., *Victorian Cities* (1963)

Chadwick, E., 'Address on Health', *Transactions of the National Association for the Promotion of Social Science*, Aberdeen Meeting 1877 (1878)

Chaplin, S., *The Thin Seam* (1950)

Colls, R., *The Collier's Rent: Song and Culture in the Industrial Village* (1977)

Daysh, G. H., *et al.*, 'Inter-War Unemployment in West Durham 1929–39', in M. Bulmer, ed., *Mining and Social Change: Durham County in the Twentieth Century* (1978)

Deane, P., and Cole, W. A., *British Economic Growth 1688-1959*, 2nd edn (Cambridge, 1967)

Dewsnup, E. R., *The Housing Problem in England* (Manchester, 1907)

Goodfellow, D. M., *Tyneside: The Social Facts* (Newcastle upon Tyne, 1940)

Hadfield, J., *Health in the Industrial North-East* (n.d.)

House, J. W., *North-Eastern England: Population Movements and the Landscape since the Early Nineteenth Century* (King's College, Newcastle upon Tyne, Department of Geography, research series 1, 1954)

Hunt, E. H., *Regional Wage Variations in Britain, 1850-1914* (Oxford, 1973)

Lawson, J., *A Man's Life* (1932)

McCord, N., *North East England: The Region's Development 1760–1960* (1979)

McCord, N., and Rowe, D. J., 'Industrialisation and Urban Growth in North-East England', *International Review of Social History*, 22 (1977)

Macdonald, S., 'The Role of the Individual in Agricultural Change: The Example of George Culley of Fenton, Northumberland', in H. S. A. Fox and R. A. Butlin, eds., *Change in the Countryside* (1979)

Mess, H. A., *Industrial Tyneside* (1928)

Ministry of Health, *Report on the Overcrowding Survey in England and Wales* (1936)

Moore, R. S., *Pitmen, Preachers and Politics: The Effects of Methodism in a Durham Mining Community* (Cambridge, 1974)

Muthesius, S., *The English Terraced House* (1982)

Pickering, W. S. F., ed., *A Social History of the Diocese of Newcastle* (1981)

Pilgrim Trust, *Men Without Work* (Cambridge, 1938)

Reid, D. B., *Report on the State of Newcastle upon Tyne and Other Towns* (1845)

Rowe, D. J., 'The Culleys, Northumberland Farmers 1767–1813', *Agricultural History Review*, 19 (1971)

   'The Economy of the North-East in the Nineteenth Century: A Survey with a Bibliography of Works Published since 1945', *Northern History*, 6 (1971)

   'Occupations in Northumberland and Durham 1851–1911', *Northern History*, 8 (1973)

   'Population of Nineteenth Century Tyneside', in N. McCord, ed., *Essays in Tyneside Labour History* (Newcastle upon Tyne, 1977)

Smith, J., 'Public Health on Tyneside 1850–80', in N. McCord, ed., *Essays in Tyneside Labour History* (Newcastle upon Tyne, 1977)

Taylor, G., and Ayres, N., *Born and Bred Unequal* (1969)

Williamson,W., *Class, Culture and Community: A Biographical Study of Social Change in Mining* (1982)

7 LONDON AND THE HOME COUNTIES

Alexander, S., 'Women's Work in Nineteenth Century London: A Study of the Years 1820-1850', in J. Mitchell and A. Oakley, eds., *Rights and Wrongs of Women* (1976)

Andrew, D. T., 'Aldermen and Big Bourgeoisie of London Reconsidered', *Social History*, 6 (1981)

Ansell, W. H., 'The London of the Future', *Journal of the Royal Society of Arts* (1941)

Ashplant, T. G., 'London Working Men's Clubs 1875-1914', in E. Yeo and S. Yeo, eds., *Popular Culture and Class Conflict, 1590-1914: Explorations in the History of Labour and Leisure* (Brighton, 1981)

Atkins, P. J., 'London's Intra-Urban Milk Supply *c.* 1790-1914', *Institute of British Geographers Transactions*, 11 (1977)

Baer, M. B., 'Social Structure, Voting Behaviour and Political Change in Victorian London', *Albion*, 9 (1977)

Bailey, P., '"A Mingled Mass of Perfectly Legitimate Pleasures": The Victorian Middle Class and the Problem of Leisure', *Victorian Studies*, 21 (1977)

Bailey, V., 'The Metropolitan Police, the Home Office and the Threat of Outcast London', in V. Bailey, ed., *Policing and Punishment in Nineteenth-Century Britain* (1981)

Barker, T. C., and Robbins, M., *A History of London Transport* (1963)

Barker, T. C., and Whyman, J., *Life in Kent before 1914* (1977)

Barnes, H., 'The Slum Problem', *Journal of the Town Planning Institute*, 13 (1926-7)

Beattie, J. M., 'Crime and the Courts in Surrey 1736-53', in J. S.Cockburn, ed., *Crime in England, 1550-1800* (1977)

Besant, W., *South London* (1899)
East London (1901)

Binford, H. C., 'Land Tenure, Social Structure and Railway Impact in North Lambeth 1830-1861', *Journal of Transport History*, 2 (1974)

Bingham Ashworth, H., *Flats: Design and Equipment* (1936)

Booth, C., *Improved Means of Locomotion as a First Step towards the Cure of the Housing Difficulties of London* (1901)
ed., *Life and Labour of the People in London*, 1st ser., 4 vols. (1889-91)

Brandon, P., *A History of Surrey* (1977)

Branson, N., *Popularism 1919-1925: George Lansbury and the Councillors' Revolt* (1979)

Braudel, F., *Civilisation matérielle, économie et capitalisme XVe–XVIIIe siècle* (Paris, 1979)

Brewer, J., and Styles, J., *An Ungovernable People: The English and their Law in the Seventeenth and Eighteenth Centuries* (1980)

Briggs, A., *Victorian Cities* (Harmondsworth, 1968)

Brown, A. F. J., 'Colchester 1815-1914', *Essex Record Office Publications*, 74 (1980)

Bush, J., 'East London Jews and the First World War', *London Journal*, 6 (1980)

Chadwick, E., 'London Centralised', *Contemporary Review*, 45 (1884)

Chalklin, C. W., 'The Reconstruction of London's Prisons, 1770–1799: An Aspect of the Growth of Georgian London', *London Journal*, 9 (1983)

Chapman, I., 'Living Conditions in Nineteenth-Century London', *Bloomsbury Geographer*, 11 (1983)

Chartres, J. A., 'The Capital's Provincial Eyes: London's Inns in the Early Eighteenth Century', *London Journal*, 3 (1977)

Cherry, G., *The Evolution of British Town Planning* (1974)

Cooney, E. W., 'The Origins of the Victorian Master Builders', *Economic History Review*, 2nd ser., 8 (1955–6)

Cope, S. R., 'Bird, Savage and Bird of London, Merchants and Bankers, 1782–1803', *Guildhall Studies in London History*, 4 (1982)

Corfield, P. J., *The Impact of English Towns, 1700–1800* (Oxford, 1982)

Cox, J., *The English Churches in a Secular Society: Lambeth 1870–1930* (New York and Oxford, 1982)

Cox, R. C. W., 'The Old Centre of Croyden: Victorian Decay and Redevelopment', in A. Everitt, ed., *Perspectives in English Urban History* (1973)

Cross, R., *Homes of the London Poor in the Nineteenth Century* (1882)

Crossick, G., 'The Labour Aristocracy and its Values: A Study of Mid-Victorian Kentish London', *Victorian Studies*, 19 (1976)

Cullen, M., 'Charles Booths's Poverty Survey: Some New Approaches', in T. C. Smout, ed., *The Search for Wealth and Stability: Essays in Economic and Social History Presented to M. W. Flinn* (1979)

Cunningham, H., 'The Metropolitan Fairs: A Case Study in the Social Control of Leisure', in A. P. Donajgrodzki, ed., *Social Control in Nineteenth Century Britain* (1977)

Davidoff, L., *The Best Circles: Society, Etiquette and the Season* (1973)
　'Separation of Home and Work?', in S. Burman, ed., *Fit Work for Women* (1979)

Davies, W. K. D., 'Charles Booth and the Measurement of Urban Social Character', *Area*, 10 (1978)

Dickson, P. G. M., *'The Financial Revolution in England: The Story of the Development of Public Credit 1688–1756* (1967)

Dinwiddy, J. R., '"The Patriotic Linen-Draper": Robert Waithman and the Revival of Radicalism in the City of London, 1795–1818', *Bulletin of the Institute of Historical Research*, 46 (1973)

Dobson, C. R., *Masters and Journeymen: A Pre-History of Industrial Relations 1717–1800* (1980)

Drake, M., 'The Census 1801–1901', in E. A. Wrigley, *Nineteenth-Century Society: Essays in the Use of Quantitative Methods for the Study of Social Data* (Cambridge, 1972)

Dyos, H. J., 'Workmen's Fares in South London, 1860–1914', *Journal of Transport History* 1 (1953)
　'The Objects of Street Improvement in Regency and Early Victorian London', *International Review of Social History*, 2 (1957)
　Victorian Suburbs: A Study of the Growth of Camberwell (Leicester, 1961)
　'The Slums of Victorian London', *Victorian Studies*, 11 (1968)
　'The Speculative Builders and Developers of Victorian London', *Victorian Studies*, 11, Supplement (1968)
　'Greater and Greater London: Notes on the Metropolis and the Provinces in the Nineteenth and Twentieth Centuries', in J. S. Bromley and E. H. Kossman, eds., *Britain and the Netherlands* (The Hague, 1971)

'Some Social Costs of Railway-Building in London', in D. Cannadine and D. Reeder, *Exploring the Urban Past* (Cambridge, 1982)

Dyos, H. J. and Reeder, D. A., 'Slums and Suburbs', in H. J. Dyos and M. Wolff, eds., *The Victorian City*, vol. 1: *Images and Realities* (1973)

Elton, G. R., 'Crime and the Historian', in J. S. Cockburn, ed., *Crime in England 1550–1800* (1977)

Emsley, C., 'The London "Insurrection" of December 1792: Fact, Fiction or Fantasy?', *Journal of British Studies*, 17 (1978)

Englander, David, *Landlord and Tenant in Urban Britain, 1838–1918* (Oxford, 1983)

Fido, J., 'The Charity Organisation Society and Social Casework in London 1869–1900', in A. P. Donajgrodzki, ed., *Social Control in Nineteenth Century Britain* (1977)

Finer, S. E., *The Life and Times of Sir Edwin Chadwick* (1952)

Fisher, F. J., 'London as an Engine of Growth', in J. S. Bromley and E. H. Kossman, eds., *Britain and the Netherlands* (The Hague, 1971)

Floud, R., and Wachter, K. W., 'Poverty and Physical Stature: Evidence on the Standard of Living of London Boys, 1770-1870', *Social Science Journal*, 4 (1982)

Foley, D., *Controlling London's Growth: Planning the Great Wen 1940–1960* (London and Los Angeles, 1963)

Forbes, T. R., 'Weaver and Cordwainer: Occupations in the Parish of St Giles, London, in 1654-93 and 1729-43', *Guildhall Studies in London History*, 4 (1980)

Friedlander, D., 'London's Urban Transition, 1851-1951', *Urban Studies*, 2 (1974)

Friedlander, D., and Roshier, R. J., 'A Study of Internal Migration in England and Wales: Part I', *Population Studies*, 19 (1965-6)

Garside, P. L., 'Intergovernmental Relations and Housing Policy in London 1919-1970, with Special Reference to the Density and Location of Council Housing', *London Journal*, 9 (1983)
'Shaping London's Future: The Role of the New Towns', in Von Karl Schwarz, ed., *Die Zukunft der Metropolen* (Berlin, 1984)
'London 1919-1950: Metropolitan Development and Planning', *Planning History Bulletin*, 6 (1984)
'West End, East End: London 1890-1940', in A. Sutcliffe, ed., *Metropolis 1890-1940* (1984)
'"Unhealthy Areas": Town Planning and the Slums', *Planning Perspectives*, 2 (1987)

Gillis, J. R., 'Servants, Sexual Relations, and the Risks of Illegitimacy in London, 1801-1900', *Feminist Studies*, 5 (1979)

Goodman, W. L., 'Christopher Gabriel, his Book', *Furniture History*, 17 (1981)

Goodway, D., *London Chartism, 1838-1848* (Cambridge, 1982)

Green, D. R., 'Street Trading in London: A Case Study of Casual Labour 1830-1860', in J. H. Johnson and C. G. Pooley, *The Structure of Nineteenth-Century Cities* (1982)

Grytzell, K., *Population Changes in London, 1801-1901* (Lund, 1969)

Hall, P., 'Metropolis 1890-1940: Challenge and Response', in A. Sutcliffe, ed., *Metropolis 1890-1940* (1984)

Hall, P. G., 'The East London Footwear Industry: An Industrial Quarter in Decline', *East London Papers*, 5 (1962)
The Industries of London since 1861 (1962)

Hamley, W., 'The Expansion of Victorian and Edwardian Colchester', *Essex Journal*, 14 (1979)

Harvey, A. D., 'The Regional Distribution of Incomes in England and Wales, 1803', *Local Historian*, 13 (1979)

Hennock, E. P., 'Poverty and Social Theory in England: The Experience of the 1880s', *Social History*, 1 (1976)

Hinchcliffe, T., 'Highbury New Park: A Nineteenth Century Middle-Class Suburb', *London Journal*, 7 (1981)

Hirst, J. D., 'A Failure "Without Parallel": The School Medical Service and the LCC 1907–1912', *Medical History*, 25 (1981)

Hobsbawm, E. J., 'The Nineteenth Century London Labour Market', in R. Glass, ed., *London: Aspects of Change* (1964)

Hone, J. A., *For the Cause of Truth: Radicalism in London 1796–1821* (Oxford, 1982)

Howe, J. M., 'Occupations in Bermondsey 1701–3', *Genealogists' Magazine*, 20 (1982)

Hoyle, S. R., 'The First Battle for London: The Royal Commission on Metropolitan Termini 1846', *London Journal*, 8 (1982)

Hudson, P., and Hunter, L., 'The Autobiography of William Hart, Cooper, 1776–1857: A Respectable Artisan in the Industrial Revolution', *London Journal*, 7 (1981)

Husbands, C. T., 'East End Racism, 1900–80', *London Journal*, 8 (1982)

Imray, J. M., 'The Mercers' Company and East London, 1750–1850', *East London Papers*, 9 (1966)

Inkster, I., 'Science and Society in the Metropolis: A Preliminary Examination of the Social and Institutional Context of the Askesian Society of London, 1796–1807', *Annals of Science*, 34 (1977)

Inkster, I., and Morrell, J., eds., *Metropolis and Province in British Culture, 1780–1850* (1983)

Jackson, A. A., *Semi-Detached London: Suburban Development, Life and Transport, 1900–1939* (1973)

London's Local Railways (Newton Abbot, 1978)

Jarvis, R. C., 'The Metamorphosis of the Port of London', *London Journal*, 3 (1977)

Johnson, J. H., 'The Suburban Expansion of Housing in London 1918–1939', in J. T. Coppock and H. C. Prince, eds., *Greater London* (1964)

Jones, E., 'The Welsh in London in the Seventeenth and Eighteenth Centuries', *Welsh History Review*, 10 (1981)

Jones, G. W., 'How Herbert Morrison Governed London 1934–1940', *Local Government Studies*, 5 (1973)

Jones, G. W., and Donoughue, B., *Herbert Morrison: Portrait of a Politician* (1973)

Jones, J. W., 'The London Busmen's Rank-and-File Movement of the 1930s', *Bulletin of the Society for the Study of Labour History*, 38 (1979)

Jones., P. E., *The Butchers of London* (1976)

Judd, M., '"The Oddest Combination of Town and Country": Popular Culture and the London Fairs, 1800–1860', in J. K. Walton and J. Walvin, eds., *Leisure in Britain, 1780–1939* (Manchester, 1983)

Korr, C. P., 'West Ham United Football Club and the Beginnings of Professional Football in East London 1895–1914', *Journal of Contemporary History*, 13 (1979)

Large, D., 'London in the Year of Revolutions, 1848', in J. Stevenson, ed.,

London in the Age of Reform (1977)

Law, C. M., *British Regional Development since World War I* (Newton Abbot, 1980)

Lawrence, F. W., 'The Housing Problem', in C. F. G. Masterman, ed., *Heart of Empire* (1901)

Lawton, R., 'Regional Population Trends in England and Wales 1750–1971', in P. Rees and J. Hobcraft, eds., *Regional Demographic Development* (1979)

Lee, C. H., 'Regional Growth and Structural Change in Victorian Britain', *Economic History Review*, 2nd ser., 34 (1981)

Lees, A., 'The Metropolis and the Intellectual', in A. Sutcliffe, ed., *Metropolis 1890–1940* (1984)

Lees, L. H., *Exiles of Erin: Irish Migrants in Victorian London* (Manchester, 1979)

Lees, L. H., and Modell, J., 'The Irish Countryman Urbanized: A Comparative Perspective on the Famine Migration', *Journal of Urban History*, 3 (1977)

Lejeune, A., *The Gentlemen's Clubs of London* (1979)

Lillywhite, B., *London Coffee Houses* (1963)

London Labour party, *A Housing Policy for London* (1934)

Lovell, J., 'The Irish and the London Dockers', *Bulletin Society Study of Labour History*, 35 (1977)

Lovett, William, *The Life and Struggles of William Lovett in his Pursuit of Bread, Knowledge and Freedom* (1876)

Low, S. J., 'The Rise of the Suburbs', *Contemporary Review*, 60 (1891)

Luckin, W., 'The Final Catastrophe: Cholera in London 1866', *Medical History*, 21 (1977)

McCann, P., 'Popular Education, Socialization and Social Control: Spitalfields 1812–24', in P. McCann, *Popular Education and Socialization in the Nineteenth Century* (1977)

McKendrick, N., Brewer, J., and Plumb, J. H., *The Birth of a Consumer Society: The Commercialisation of Eighteenth-Century England* (1982)

Mackinder, H. J., *Britain and the British Seas* (Oxford, 1907)

McLeod, H., *Class and Religion in the Mid-Victorian City* (1974)

Malcolmson, P. E., 'Getting a Living in the Slums of Victorian London', *London Journal*, 1 (1975)

Mansfield, J., 'John Brown, a Shoemaker in Place's London', *History Workshop Journal*, 8 (1979)

Masterman, C. F. G., ed., *The Heart of Empire* (1901)

Mathias, P., *The Transformation of England: Essays in the Economic and Social History of England in the Eighteenth Century* (1979)

Mayhew, H., *London Labour and the London Poor*, 4 vols. (1861–2)

Mayhew, Henry, and Binney, John, *The Criminal Prisons of London and the Scenes of Prison Life* (1862)

Mazumdar, P. M. H., 'The Eugenists and the Residuum: The Problem of the Urban Poor', *Bulletin of the History of Medicine*, 54 (1980)

Michie, R. C., 'The London Stock Exchange and the British Securities Market 1850–1914', *Economic History Review*, 2nd ser., 38 (1985), pp. 61–82

Miller, W., 'Police Authority in London and New York City, 1830–1870', *Journal of Social History*, 8 (1975)

Morrison, A., *A Child of the Jago*, 3rd edn (1897)

Tales of Mean Streets (1906)

Morrison, H., 'Plans for London', *Geographical Magazine*, 8 (1938)

Mumford, L., 'The Plan for London', in *City Development: Studies in Disintegration and Renewal* (1947)

Muthesius, S., *The English Terraced House* (1982)

Offer, A., *Property and Politics 1870–1914: Landownership, Law, Ideology and Urban Development in England* (Cambridge, 1981)

Oliver, H., *The International Anarchist Movement in Late Victorian England* (1983)

Olsen, D. J., *Town Planning in London in the Eighteenth and Nineteenth Centuries* (1964)

The Growth of Victorian London (1976)

Osler, A., 'The London University of 1742', *London Journal*, 6 (1980)

Parsinnen, T. M., 'The Revolutionary Party in London', *Bulletin of the Institute of Historical Research*, 45 (1972)

Pearce, C. G., and Mills, D. R., *Census Enumerators' Books: An Annotated Bibliography of Published Work Based Substantially on the Nineteenth Century Census Enumerators' Books* (Milton Keynes, 1982)

Pepper, S., 'Ossulston Street: Early LCC Experiments in High-Rise Housing 1925–29', *London Journal*, 7 (1981)

Port, M. H., 'Metropolitan Improvements: From Grosvenor Square to Admiralty Arch', *London Journal*, 7 (1981)

Prothero, I. T., 'London Chartism and the Trades', *Economic History Review*, 24 (1971)

'London Trade Unionism in the 1830s–40s', *Bulletin Society Study of Labour History*, 36 (1978)

Artisans and Politics in Early Nineteenth-Century London (Folkestone, 1979)

Redford, A., *Labour Migration in England, 1800–50*, 2nd edn (Manchester, 1964)

Reeder, D. A., 'A Theatre of Suburbs: Some Patterns of Development in West London, 1801–1911', in H. J. Dyos, ed., *The Study of Urban History* (1968)

Richardson, T. L., 'The Agricultural Labourers' Standard of Living in Kent, 1790–1840', in D. J. Oddy and D. S. Miller, *The Making of the Modern British Diet* (1976), pp. 103–16

Robbins, M., 'Transport and Suburban Development in Middlesex down to 1914', *Transactions of London and Middlesex Archaeological Society*, 29 (1978)

Roebuck, J., *Urban Development in 19th Century London: Lambeth, Battersea and Wandsworth 1838–88* (Chichester, 1979)

Rogers, N., 'Popular Disaffection in London during the Forty-Five', *London Journal*, 1 (1975)

'Popular Protest in Early Hanoverian London', *Past & Present*, 74 (1978)

'Money, Land and Lineage: The Big Bourgeoisie of Hanoverian London', *Social History*, 4 (1979)

Ross, E., 'Survival Networks: Women's Neighbourhood Sharing in London before World War One', *History Workshop Journal*, 15 (1983)

Rowe, D. J., ed., *London Radicalism, 1830–1843* (1970)

Rubinstein, D., *School Attendance in London 1870–1904: A Social History* (1969)

Rubinstein, W. D., 'Wealth, Elites and the Class Structure of Modern Britain', *Past & Present*, 76 (1977)

'The Victorian Middle Classes: Wealth, Occupation and Geography', *Economic History Review*, 2nd ser., 30 (1979)

Rudé, G., *Paris and London in the Eighteenth Century* (1952)

Hanoverian London 1714–1808 (1971)

Russell, B., *Which Way to Peace?* (1936)

Ryan, P.A., ' "Poplarism" 1894–1930', in P. Thane, ed., *The Origins of British Social Policy* (1978)

'Politics and Relief: East London Unions in the Late Nineteenth and Early

Twentieth Centuries', in M. E. Rose, ed., *The Poor and the City: The English Poor Law in its Urban Context 1834–1914* (Leicester, 1985)

Samuel, R., 'The London Labour Movement', *Bulletin Society Study of Labour History*, 36 (1978)

Schwarz, L. D., 'Social Class and Social Geography: The Middle Classes in London at the End of the Eighteenth Century', *Social History*, 7 (1982)

'The Standard of Living in the Long Run: London, 1700–1860', *Economic History Review*, 2nd ser., 38 (1985)

Schwarz, L. D., and Jones, L. J., 'Wealth, Occupations and Insurance in the Late Eighteenth Century: The Policy Registers of the Sun Fire Office', *Economic History Review*, 2nd ser., 36 (1983)

Shannon, H. A., 'Migration and the Growth of London 1841–91', *Economic History Review*, 2nd ser., 5 (1955)

Sheenan, W. J., 'Finding Solace in Eighteenth-Century Newgate', in J. S. Cockburn, ed., *Crime in England 1550–1800* (1977)

Sheppard, F. H. W., *London 1808–1870: The Infernal Wen* (1971)

Sheppard, F. H. W., Belcher, V., and Cottrell, P., 'The Middlesex and York-shire Deeds Registries and the Study of Building Fluctuations', *London Journal*, 5 (1979)

Sherwell, A., *Life in West London: A Study and a Contrast* (1897)

Shipley, S., 'London Journeymen 1810–30', *Bulletin of the Society for the Study of Labour History*, 36 (1978)

Snell, K. D. M., 'Agricultural Seasonal Unemployment, the Standard of Living, and Women's Work in the South and East, 1690–1860', *Economic History Review*, 2nd ser., 34 (1981)

Stedman Jones, G., 'Working-Class Culture and Working-Class Politics in London, 1870–1900: Notes on the Remaking of a Working Class', *Journal of Social History*, 7 (1974)

Outcast London: A Study in the Relationship between Classes in Victorian Society (1976 edn)

Stern, W. M., 'Where, Oh Where, Are the Cheesemongers of London?', *London Journal*, 5 (1979)

Stevenson, J., 'The B.U.F., the Metropolitan Police and Public Order', in K. Lunn and R. Thurlow, eds., *British Fascism: Essays on the Radical Right in Inter-War Britain* (1980)

ed., *London in the Age of Reform* (1977)

Summerson, J., *The London Building World of the 1860s* (1973)

The Life and Works of John Nash, Architect (1981)

Swenarton, M., *Homes Fit for Heroes: The Politics and Architecture of Early State Housing in Britain* (1981)

Taylor, B., '''The Men Are as Bad as their Masters . . .'': Socialism, Feminism, and Sexual Antagonism in the London Tailoring Trade in the 1830s', in J. Newton, M. Ryan, and J. Walkowitz, eds., *Sex and Class in Women's History* (1983)

Taylor, J. S., 'Philanthropy and Empire: Jonas Hanway and the Infant Poor of London', *Eighteenth Century Studies*, 12 (1979)

Taylor, R., *Lord Salisbury* (1975)

Thomas, E., *Richard Jefferies* (1977)

Thompson, F. M. L., *Hampstead: Building a Borough 1650–1964* (1978)

'Social Control in Victorian Britain', *Economic History Review*, 2nd ser., 34 (1981)

ed., *The Rise of Suburbia* (Leicester 1982)

Thompson, P., *The Struggle for London 1885–1914* (1967)

Tilly, C., and Schweitzer, R. A., 'How London and its Conflicts Changed Shape 1758–1834', *Historical Methods*, 15 (1982)

Tobias, J. J., *Crime and Industrial Society in the Nineteenth Century* (1967)

Waller, P. J., *Town , City and Nation: England 1850–1914* (Oxford, 1983)

Walton, J. K., 'The Demand for Working-Class Seaside Holidays in Victorian London', *Economic History Review*, 2nd ser., 34 (1981)

Wareing, J., 'Changes in the Geographical Distribution of the Recruitment of Apprentices to the London Companies 1486–1750', *Journal of Historical Geography*, 6 (1980)

'Migration to London and Transatlantic Emigration of Indentured Servants, 1683–1775', *Journal of Historical Geography*, 7 (1981)

Wells, H. G., 'The Question of Scientific Administrative Areas', *Mankind in the Making*, appendix (1903)

When the Sleeper Wakes (1899), revised as *The Sleeper Wakes* (1910)

Westergaard, J. H., 'The Structure of Greater London', in Ruth Glass, ed., *London: Aspects of Change* (1964)

White, J., 'Campbell Bunk: A Lumpen Community in London between the Wars', *History Workshop Journal*, 8 (1979)

Rothschild Buildings: Life in an East End Tenement Block, 1887–1920 (1980)

'Police and People in London in the 1930s', *Oral History*, 11 (1983)

Whyman, J., 'Visitors to Margate in the 1841 Census Returns', *Local Population Studies*, 8 (1972)

Wilson, H. W., 'Will London be Suffocated?', *National Review*, 37 (1902)

Winstanley, M., *Life in Kent at the Turn of the Century* (Folkestone, 1978)

Wohl, A. S., 'The Housing of the Working Classes in London, 1815–1914', in S. D. Chapman, ed., *The History of Working-Class Housing* (Newton Abbot, 1971)

The Eternal Slum: Housing and Social Policy in Victorian London (1977)

Wrigley, E. A., 'A Simple Model of London's Importance in Changing English Society and Economy 1650–1750', *Past & Present*, 37 (1967)

'Baptism Coverage in Early Nineteenth Century England', *Population Studies*, 29 (1975)

Yelling, J. A., 'The Selection of Sites for Slum Clearance in London 1875–1888', *Journal of Historical Geography*, 7 (1981)

'LCC Slum Clearance Policies 1889–1907', *Institute of British Geographers Transactions*, 7 (1982)

Young, K., 'The Politics of London Government 1880–1899', *Public Administration*, 51 (1973)

'The Conservative Strategy for London 1855–1975', *London Journal*, 1 (1975)

Young, K., and Garside, P. L., *Metropolitan London: Politics and Urban Change 1837–1981* (1982)

Index